Nelson's Junior English Dictionary

Compiled by
F. R. WITTY
M.Ed., B.Sc.

NELSON

THOMAS NELSON AND SONS LTD
36 Park Street London W1Y 4DE
P.O. Box 18123 Nairobi Kenya

THOMAS NELSON (AUSTRALIA) LTD
597 Little Collins Street Melbourne 3000

THOMAS NELSON AND SONS (CANADA) LTD
81 Curlew Drive Don Mills Ontario

THOMAS NELSON (NIGERIA) LTD
P.O. Box 336 Apapa Lagos

Revised edition 1970
Sixth impression 1973

0 17 424309 X

Printed in Great Britain
by Richard Clay (The Chaucer Press), Ltd, Bungay, Suffolk

FOREWORD

This shorter school dictionary, containing some 13,000 words and phrases, is intended to meet the needs of schoolchildren who require not only a reference book of word meanings but also a useful and instructive guide to word usage.

It is new and up to date, containing such words as **astronaut, satellite, jet,** etc., and also many double-barrelled words which are often omitted from school dictionaries, such as **air-hostess, immersion heater, tape-recorder,** and similar terms.

It is designed to help pupils with their lessons and includes parts of speech, spelling, grammar, and the pronunciation of unusual words, as well as meanings of hundreds of idioms, proverbs, and phrases. Many terms in geography, science, and mathematics are given.

Confusions in spelling and meaning are signposted with special notes. The reader is warned not to confuse **affect** with **effect, stationary** with **stationery, licence** and **license, practice** and **practise, passed** and **past, its** and **it's;** and to distinguish between **lay** and **lie, hanged** and **hung.**

In a surprising number of small school dictionaries very easy common words are omitted to save space—such words as **bring, pay, make, who, dog, go,** and **have.** In this dictionary those are included. The child can find whether the past of **pay** is **payed** or **paid,** or whether the past tense of **swing** is **swang** or **swung.** These easy well-worn words are full of catches for the unwary. They are words which must be included.

An outstanding feature of the dictionary is the large number of idioms, proverbs, phrases, and compound words that have been included. Look up such words as **bring, day, do,** and **hand,** and see how many idioms there are.

These several unusual features of the dictionary should provide a rich reward to the child who will use the dictionary constantly and make it his friend.

How to use this book

Guide words The words in this dictionary are in alphabetical order. At the top of each page are two *guide words.* These name the first and last word on each page and help you to find quickly the word you want.

Meanings The dictionary tells you what each word means. But often a word has more than one meaning. The different meanings are numbered, and you must find the meaning which best fits the sentence in which the word occurs. For example—   **grit** *n.* 1. a particle of sand. 2. courage, pluck.

Identical spellings Words which are spelt the same but have very different meanings have separate entries and are numbered in a different way to tell you that there is more than one entry. For example—

> **port** (1) *n*. a harbour, or town with a harbour.
> **port** (2) *n*. the left side of a ship as one faces the front or bow.
> **port** (3) *n*. a red wine.

Pronunciation Inside the cover of this book is a table of the phonetic pronunciation for difficult words. These words are in brackets, re-spelt, and with syllables divided by full stops. The emphasized syllable is followed by a stress mark; thus *architect* is shown as ark'i.tect.

Slang Words that are not used in good speech may be labelled "slang" or, if they are nearly slang, may be labelled "loosely".

Cross-references Sometimes a word is more fully explained under another heading. In that case you will find a note telling you where to look. For example—

> **invasion** see **invade**.

Parts of Speech

After each word its part of speech is given, that is to say whether it is a noun, adjective, verb, and so on. On the endpapers of the book there is a table of the list of abbreviations used.

A **noun** is the name of something. A **proper noun** is the name of a person or place; *Mary* and *Liverpool* are proper nouns. A **common noun** is the general name of a person or thing, such as *boy*, *ink*, or *elephant*.

A **pronoun** is a word which stands in place of a noun, e.g. *she*, *who*, *it*.

An **adjective** is a word which refers to a noun or pronoun and tells more about it, as *red*, *bad*, *weak*, *this*.

A **verb** is the active or "doing" word in a sentence, as *speak*, *climbed*, *writes*. *To speak*, *to climb*, and *to write* are the **infinitives** of the same verbs. The tense of a verb tells you when it happened. *He climbed* happened in the past and is called the **past tense**. Usually the past tense is made by adding *-ed*, but some verbs have special spellings, and you will find this in brackets in black type at the end of the definition of a verb in this dictionary. In the same way, if the **present participle** is not made by adding *-ing* you will find that too. Sometimes a verb consists of two words, e.g. *has finished*; the extra word is called an **auxiliary verb**. The second word is called the **past participle**, which is usually the same as the past tense (*-ed* added) but if it is spelt differently it is given at the end of the list. So, under **go**, you will find (**going, went, gone**); *going* is the present participle, *went* is the past tense, and *gone* is the past participle.

An **adverb** is a word which refers to a verb and tells more about it, as *quickly*, *better*, *early*.

A **preposition** is a word which shows the relation between two nouns or pronouns, as *on*, *up*, *after*.

A **conjunction** is a word used for joining words or sentences, as *and*, *but*, *while*.

An **exclamation** or **interjection** shows sudden excitement, as *Oh! No!*

A

A, a *n.* the first letter of our alphabet.

a, an *adj.* and *indefinite article* one, any.

abandon *v.* to go away and give up something, as *to abandon a sinking ship* or *to abandon a game because it is raining*. *n.* **abandonment**.

abbess *n.* a woman who is head of a convent (*masc.* **abbot**).

abbey *n.* 1. a building in which monks or nuns live. 2. a great church.

abbot *n.* a man who is head of an abbey.

abdicate *v.* to give up a throne, as *the king said he would abdicate*.

abdication *n.* the giving up of a throne.

abdomen (*pron.* ab.doh'men) *n.* the part of the body below the chest in which food is digested.

abide *v.* to stay.

  abide by to stand by, to remain true to, as *let us abide by the rules*.

ability *n.* cleverness, skill (*pl.* **abilities**).

abject *adj.* miserable, worthless, wretched.

able *adj.* 1. having the power to do something, as *Fred is able to swim*. 2. clever, as *Mary is very able at cooking*. *adv.* **ably**.

abnormal *adj.* unusual, as *this heavy fall of snow is abnormal*. *adv.* **abnormally**. *n.* **abnormality**.

abolish *v.* to do away with, as *the government decided to abolish the tax*.

abolition *n.* doing away with, as *the abolition of slavery*.

abominable *adj.* hateful, as *an abominable crime*. *adv.* **abominably** very badly, as *Sam behaved abominably*.

aborigines (*pron.* ab.o.rij'i.neez) *n. pl.* the first native people of a country, as *the aborigines of Australia*.

about *prep.* 1. concerning, as *we heard about it*. 2. nearly, as *it is about ready*. *adv.* **about** around, as *they turned the ship about*.

above *prep.* higher than, as *Tom is above Eric in class*.

abreast *adv.* side by side, as *they rode two abreast*.

abroad *adv.* in (or to) a foreign land, as *he lived abroad* or *we went abroad to France*.

abrupt *adj.* 1. sudden, sharp, as *the path made an abrupt turn to the left*; or *an abrupt end to a speech*. 2. rude, sharp-tempered, as *an abrupt answer*. *adv.* **abruptly**.

absence *n.* not being present, as *an absence of noise*.

absent *adj.* not there, as *two boys were absent*. *adj.* **absent-minded** forgetful.

absolute *adj.* complete, as *absolute quiet*. *adv.* **absolutely** completely, as *he is absolutely wrong*.

absorb *v.* 1. to soak up, as *blotting paper will absorb ink*. 2. to interest very much, as *I am sure your hobby will absorb you* (note: **absorbent** means able to soak up liquid. **absorbing** means very interesting).

abstain *v.* to keep away from doing something, as *to abstain from smoking*.

abstract *v.* to take secretly, as *to abstract money from a purse*. *adj.* **abstract** only in your mind, not something you can see or touch, as *coldness, courage, love, are all abstract things*. The opposite of **abstract** is **concrete**.

absurd *adj.* silly, foolish. *n.* **absurdity**.

abundance *n.* plenty, a great quantity.

abundant *adj.* plentiful.

abuse (*pron.* a.byooz') *v.* 1. to use wrongly, as *to abuse your strength by bullying*. 2. to be rude to (someone). *n.* **abuse** (a.byoos') wrong use of something. 2. bad language. *adj.* **abusive** rude.

academy *n.* a high school, a college.

accelerate (*pron.* ak.sel'e.rayt) *v.* to make an engine, or something, go more quickly. *n.* **acceleration** ability to go more quickly, as *this car has powerful acceleration*.

accelerator (*pron.* ak.sel'e.ray.tor) *n.* a pedal on a car which is pressed to make it go more quickly.

accent *n.* 1. a stronger tone given to part of a word, or to a note of music, to make it stand out. 2. the way a person speaks, as *Mr Smith speaks with a Yorkshire accent*.

accept *v.* 1. to take what is offered, as *to

accept *a present.* 2. to agree to, as *to accept a decision. adj.* **acceptable** taken with pleasure. *n.* **acceptance** taking what is offered.

access *n.* a way into, an approach, as *only monitors are allowed access to the stationery cupboard.*

accessible *adj.* within reach. *n.* **accessibility** being easy to reach.

accession *n.* coming to a throne, as *the king's accession took place in July.*

accessory *n.* 1. an extra part or tool. 2. someone who helps, especially to carry out a crime.

accident *n.* 1. an unexpected happening, as *I met my friend by accident.* 2. a mishap, as *Eileen was hurt in the accident. adv.* **accidentally** by chance, as *Dick accidentally knocked me.*

acclaim *v.* to welcome with cheering.

accommodate *v.* to have (or make) room for, as *he asked if the landlord of the inn could accommodate him. n.* **accommodation** room.

accompaniment *n.* 1. something that goes on at the same time, as *we walked along to the accompaniment of thunder.* 2. a background to singing, as *Susan sang to a piano accompaniment.*

accompany *v.* 1. to go along with, as *will you accompany me down the road?* 2. to play music while someone sings, as *Mr Brown will accompany Susan on the piano* (**accompanies, accompanying, accompanied**).

accomplice *n.* a person who helps in a crime.

accomplish *v.* to bring to a finish, as *Jack said he would accomplish the task by evening.*

accomplished *adj.* 1. clever, as *an accomplished player.* 2. finished, as *the job is accomplished.*

accord *v.* to agree, as *Bill's story of the accident accords with Carole's. n.* **accord** 1. agreement. 2. friendship.

according to as told by, as *according to Robert they were late.*

of his own accord by himself, without being asked.

accordion *n.* a musical wind instrument with bellows, and keys like those of a piano.

accordingly *adv.* therefore.

account *n.* 1. a bill for money. 2. a statement showing how money has been received and spent. 3. a description, as *the Daily News gave a good account of the match.*

on account of because.

to account for to explain.

to take into account to allow for.

accountant *n.* a man who examines business accounts.

accumulate *v.* to gather, to pile up, as *the wind is causing snow to accumulate near the door. n.* **accumulation** a pile, a heap, a collection.

accumulator *n.* a battery for storing electricity.

accuracy *n.* exactness, correctness.

accurate *adj.* free from mistakes. *adv.* **accurately** exactly, as *Jim measured the line accurately.*

accuse *v.* to blame, to tell someone he has done wrong. *n.* **accusation** laying blame on someone.

ace *n.* a playing-card with one spot.

ache *n.* a continuous pain, as *a toothache. v.* **ache** to give pain.

achieve *v.* to succeed in getting something after trying hard, as *John achieved his ambition to be in the school team. n.* **achievement** success after trying hard.

acid *n.* a sharp, sour-tasting liquid which eats away metals. *adj.* **acid** sharp, sour-tasting.

acknowledge *v.* 1. to admit that something is true, as *Sheila had to acknowledge that she was wrong.* 2. to say that you have received something, as *to acknowledge an invitation. n.* **acknowledgement** or **acknowledgment**.

acorn *n.* the fruit of the oak tree.

acquaint *v.* to inform, to tell someone, as *I will acquaint you with our plans.*

to be acquainted with to know slightly.

acquaintance *n.* someone you know slightly, as *I do not know her well, she is only an acquaintance.*

acquire *v.* to obtain something by your own efforts, to gain, as *Margaret acquired a great reputation as a singer.*

acquit *v.* to say that a person is innocent, as *the jury say the prisoner is not* *guilty and acquit him* (**acquitting, acquitted**).

acre *n.* the size of a piece of land equal to 4840 square yards (4047 m²). *n.* **acreage** (*pron.* ak'ker.ayj) the number of acres in a piece of land.

acrobat *n.* a person who can do daring leaps and jumps with a trapeze or other apparatus.

across *adv.* from one side to the other, as *Malcolm walked across the road. prep.* on the other side, as *the house across the river.*

act *v.* 1. to do something, as *this is a time of danger, act now!* 2. to pretend, as *do not act as if you were ill.* 3. to take part in a stage-play. *n.* **act** 1. a deed. 2. a part of a stage play. 3. a law made by Parliament.

acting *n.* the performing of stage-plays, or of a part in a play.

action, *n.* 1. a deed. 2. movement, as *the action of a clock.* 3. a battle, as *the soldiers went into action.*

active *adj.* lively, quick-moving. *n.* **activity** movement, bustle.

actor (*fem.* **actress**) *n.* a player on stage, film, or radio.

actual *adj.* real, not imaginary. *adv.* **actually** really, as *it actually happened.*

acute *adj.* 1. sharp, pointed. 2. severe, keen, as *an acute pain.*

adapt *v.* to alter something for use in another way, as *to adapt a box to serve as a table.*

adaptable *adj.* 1. easily altered to suit another purpose. 2. (of a person) easily fitting in with other people or conditions.

add *v.* 1. to join one thing to another, as *to add sugar to tea.* 2. to find the total of a list of numbers.

adder *n.* a poisonous snake found in Britain.

addition *n.* 1. joining one thing to another. 2. finding the total of a list of numbers.
in addition besides, also.

additional *adj.* extra.

address *n.* 1. the house, street, and town where a person lives. 2. a speech, as *the mayor gave a short address. v.* **address** 1. to write on the cover of a letter or parcel where it is to go. 2. to give a speech to an audience.

adequate *adj.* enough, sufficient.

adhere *v.* to stick to, to hold on to.

adhesive *n.* a substance, such as paste or gum, used to stick things together. *adj.* **adhesive** sticky.

adjacent (*pron.* a.jay'sent) *adj.* lying close to, neighbouring.

adjective *n.* a word which describes a noun or pronoun. In the sentence *the red house stands next to the small one,* the words 'red' and 'small' are adjectives.

adjust *v.* to alter something to make it better. *adj.* **adjustable.** *n.* **adjustment** an alteration.

administer *v.* 1. to manage affairs. 2. to give out medicine, justice, punishment, etc. *n.* **administration.**

admirable *adj.* excellent, worth high praise.

admiral *n.* an officer who commands a fleet.

admiration *n.* thinking highly of some-one or something.

admire *v.* 1. to think highly of. 2. to look at with pleasure and respect.

admission *n.* 1. entering, or letting people enter, as *admission to the show is only on week-days.* 2. the cost of admission, as *admission is six pence.* 3. a confession, as *Sylvia made an admission that she broke the cups.*

admit *v.* 1. to let in, as *we do not admit dogs.* 2. to confess, as *Roy had to admit that he was wrong* (**admitting, admitted**). *n.* **admittance** entry, going in.

adopt *v.* to care for someone else's child, dog, etc. as your own, as *to adopt a child into your family* or *to adopt a new idea. n.* **adoption** taking over as your own.

adorable *adj.* lovable.

adrift *adj.* broken loose, floating with the wind and tide, as *the boat has gone adrift.*

adult *n.* a grown-up person or creature.

advance *v.* 1. to go forward, as *the troops will advance.* 2. to put forward, as *to advance your opinion. n.* **advancement** progress. **in advance** beforehand, as *to send luggage in advance.*

advantage *n.* a benefit, something that puts you ahead of others, as *it is an advantage to be able to swim.*

to take advantage of to benefit by, as *Colin decided to take advantage of the warm weather to have a swim.*

adventure *n.* a daring and exciting experience. *adj.* **adventurous** exciting and risky, as *an adventurous journey through a jungle.*

adverb *n.* a word which tells you how, when, or where an action takes place. In *he ran away, she sang well, they went early,* 'away', 'well', and 'early' are adverbs.

adverse *adj.* unfavourable, against you, as *the boat sailed out in adverse weather.*

adversity *n.* misfortune (*pl.* **adversities**).

advertise *v.* to make something widely known by posters, notices in the newspaper, etc. *n.* **advertisement** (*pron.* ad.vert'is.ment) a notice in a newspaper, magazine, etc., usually of goods for sale.

advice *n.* helpful suggestions, as *Charles was given advice on how to feed his dog* (note: *advice* and **advise** are spelt differently).

advisable *adj.* sensible, as *it is advisable to look both ways before crossing the road.*

advise *v.* to offer helpful suggestions (note: *advise* and **advice** are spelt differently).

aerial *n.* a wire or rod to send out, or receive, radio or television broadcasts.

aerodrome *n.* 1. a place where aeroplanes are kept. 2. an airport.

aeroplane *n.* a flying machine with wings.

affair *n.* a happening, an event, as *the school concert was a very successful affair.*

not your affair no concern of yours.

affect *v.* 1. to cause a change, as *the bad weather will affect our plans.* 2. to touch your feelings, as *his sad story affected me* (note: do not confuse *affect* with **effect**, which is the result of the change).

affection *n.* fondness. *adj.* **affectionate** loving.

afford *v.* 1. to spare money, as *I cannot afford to buy it.* 2. to spare time or trouble, as *I cannot afford the time to visit John.*

afloat *adv.* floating, as *they got the ship afloat.*

afraid *adv.* frightened, fearful.

aft *adv.* to the back part of a ship, as *the Captain went aft.*

after *prep.* later than, following, as *June comes after May.*

afternoon *n.* the time between midday and evening.

afterwards *adv.* later.

again *adv.* 1. once more, as *do it again.* 2. in return, as *Mary gave Joan the ball back again.*

against *prep.* 1. opposite to, as *we raced against the wind.* 2. facing, as *the soldiers lined up against the enemy.* 3. touching, as *she leaned against the table.*

age *n.* 1. how long a person has lived, or a thing has lasted. 2. a period in history, as *the Bronze age.* *v.* **age** to grow old. *adjs.* **aged** old; **ageless** never seeming to grow old.

of age becoming twenty-one years old, as *Henry will be of age next month.*

agency *n.* a firm which does business for other firms, as *a travel agency sells tickets for railways, airlines, and shipping companies.*

agent *n.* 1. someone who does business for a firm. 2. someone who acts on behalf of someone else.

aggressive *adj.* quarrelsome, bullying, attacking.

aggression *n.* an attack, starting a quarrel.

aghast *adj.* amazed and horrified.

agile *adj.* nimble, very active. *n.* **agility**.

agitate *v.* to shake, to quiver, to disturb. *adj.* **agitated** disturbed. *n.* **agitation**.

ago *adj.* gone, past, as *two years ago.*

agony *n.* intense pain, suffering. *adj.* **agonizing** very painful.

agree *v.* 1. to be of the same opinion, as *Joan and Hilary agreed not to go out.* 2. to say 'yes', as *Father will agree to the plan. n.* **agreement**.

agreeable *adj.* pleasant and friendly, as *what an agreeable nature Mavis has.*

agriculture *n.* farming, growing crops on the land. *adj.* **agricultural** connected with farming.

aground *adv.* held fast in mud or rocks in shallow water, as *the ship was driven aground.*

ahead *adv.* forward, in front, as *the two men went ahead of the party.*

aid *v.* to help. *n.* **aid** help, assistance.

ailment *n.* illness.

aim (at) *v.* 1. to point a gun or some other weapon at a target. 2. to try to do something, as *Ian aimed at being Captain of the school team. n.* **aim** 1. a target. 2. an ambition.

air *n.* 1. the atmosphere around us which we breathe in. 2. a tune, as *'The Londonderry Air' is a pleasant tune.* 3. appearance, as *he has a proud air. v.* **air** 1. to hang out in the air, as *to air clothes.* 2. to say what you think, as *Mary likes to air her opinions about school.*

on the air on radio or television.

aircraft *n.* any kind of flying machine.

aircraft-carrier *n.* a warship built to carry aeroplanes.

airfield *n.* a place where aeroplanes land and take off.

air-gun *n.* a gun which shoots pellets and darts by compressed air.

air-hostess *n.* a woman who looks after passengers on an aeroplane.

airline *n.* a company which owns and operates aeroplanes for passengers and mail.

airport *n.* a place where aeroplanes land and take off with passengers or mail.

air-raid *n.* an attack by aeroplanes on some place on the ground.

airy *adj.* 1. exposed to the air. 2. light as air.

aisle (*pron.* ile) *n.* a passage-way between the seats in a church, cinema, or theatre.

alarm *n.* 1. a warning of danger, as *we are on fire, sound the alarm!* 2. sudden fear, as *the rabbits fled in alarm.* 3. a warning bell, as a *fire-alarm* or an *alarm-clock. v.* **alarm** to frighten, to warn of danger.

alas a cry of sorrow, as *alas, I am weary.*

albatross *n.* a very large sea-bird found over southern seas.

album *n.* a book for holding stamps, cards, records, or photographs.

alcohol *n.* an intoxicating liquid found in wines, beer, and spirits.

alderman *n.* a senior member of a city, county, or borough council.

ale *n.* a kind of beer.

alert *adj.* watchful, ready to act. *n.* **alertness**.

algebra *n.* a kind of arithmetic in which letters are used as well as numbers.

alias (*pron.* ay'li.as) *n.* a false name, which someone uses instead of a real name (*pl.* **aliases**).

alibi *n.* the excuse that he was somewhere else at the time, made by someone accused of a crime.

alien (*pron.* ay'li.en) *n.* a foreigner. *n.* **alien** foreign.

alight *adj.* on fire, burning, as *the bonfire was well alight. v.* **alight** to dismount, to get down, as *do not alight from a moving bus.*

alike *adj.* similar, as *the twins are alike.*

alive *adj.* 1. living, as *this wasp is alive.* 2. alert, as *we are alive to the danger.*

all *n.* everyone, the whole.

after all when all is said and done.

all along the whole time.

all in the day's work all part of the job.

Allah *n.* the Mohammedan name for God.

allege *v.* to make a statement accusing someone, as *I heard Jim allege that Bob had his cap.*

allegiance *n.* loyalty, as *we owe allegiance to the Queen.*

alley *n.* a narrow passage (*pl.* **alleys**).

a blind alley a course of action which leads nowhere.

alliance *n.* a friendly union of people or nations.

allied *adj.* joined in friendship, united.

alligator *n.* a large reptile like a crocodile.

allow *v.* 1. to permit, to let. 2. to give money, as *I will allow you ten pence a week pocket money.* 3 to agree, as *I allow that you are taller than I am. n.* **allowance** 1. a grant of money. 2. provision.

to make allowances for to provide for.

alloy *n.* a mixture of metals, as *bronze is an alloy of copper and tin.*

allude (with **to**) *v.* to mention in a casual way, to refer to, as *the Mayor said he would allude to the new park in his speech. n.* **allusion**.

ally *n.* a person or country which fights on your side (*pl.* **allies**).

almanac *n.* a book giving the days, weeks, and months of the year.

almighty *adj.* all-powerful.

The Almighty God.

almond (*pron.* ah'mund) *n.* 1. a tree having pink blossom which bears nuts. 2. the nut of the tree.

almost *adv.* nearly, as *I was almost late.*

alms (*pron.* ahmz) *n. pl.* money or gifts for the poor.

alone *adv.* without others.

along *prep.* from one end to the other, as *they walked along the lane.*

alongside by the side of.

aloof *adv.* apart from others, as *the shy girl stood aloof from the other girls.*

aloud *adv.* loud enough to be heard.

alp *n.* 1. a mountain meadow. 2. a mountain. *adj.* **alpine** connected with alps.

alphabet *n.* the letters of a language, in order, as A B C ..., etc. *adj.* **alphabetical**.

already *adv.* before now, by this time.

also *adv.* too, besides, as *will you come also?*

altar *n.* the communion table in a church (note: do not confuse with **alter**).

alter *v.* to change. *n.* **alteration** a change (note: do not confuse with **altar**).

alternate (*pron.* awl'ter.nayt) *v.* to change first one way and then the other, as *days and nights alternate. adj.* **alternate** (*pron.* awl.ter'nayt) by turns, first one and then the other, as *you park on each side of the road on alternate days. adv.* **alternately** (*pron.* awl.ter'-nayt.li) by turns.

alternative *n.* a choice between two things, as *he had the alternative of using bus or train.*

although *conj.* even though, even if.

altitude *n.* height above sea level. *n. pl.* **altitudes** high places.

altogether *adv.* 1. as a whole, everyone together, as *let us sing altogether.*

aluminium *n.* a very light whitish metal which does not tarnish.

always *adv.* at all times, every time.

amateur (*pron.* am'a.tyer) *n.* someone who takes part in some activity for enjoyment and not for payment; not a professional, as *an amateur boxer.*

amaze *v.* to astonish, as *it will amaze me if you win. n.* **amazement** astonishment.

ambassador *n.* a man who represents his country in a foreign land, as *the British ambassador to Spain lives in Madrid.*

amber *n.* 1. a hard yellow gum. 2. a golden yellow colour, as *an amber traffic light.*

ambition *n.* a desire for some success or honour, as *Peter had an ambition to pass his examination.*

ambitious *adj.* full of desire to win an honour, or gain promotion.

amble *v.* to walk at a slow easy pace.

ambulance *n.* a van for carrying people who are ill or injured.

ambush *n.* a surprise attack on an enemy after lying in wait for him. *v.* **ambush** to pounce on an enemy from a hiding-place.

amen (*pron.* ay.men' or ah.men') *n.* a Hebrew word at the end of a prayer meaning 'so let it be'.

amend *v.* to alter something to make it better, as *to amend a law or a rule. n.* **amendment**.

amiable *adj.* friendly, kindly.

amid, amidst *preps.* in the middle of.

ammonia *n.* a strong-smelling gas that dissolves in water.

ammunition *n.* bullets, shells, etc., for guns.

among, amongst *preps.* in the middle of, between.

amount *n.* 1. a quantity. 2. the total sum, as *what is the amount I owe you?*

to amount to to add up to.

amphibian *n.* an animal able to live on land or in water. *adj.* **amphibious** 1. able to live on land or in water. 2. (of a vehicle) able to move on land or water, as *an amphibious car*.

ample *adj.* sufficient, enough.

amplifier *n.* an instrument to increase the volume of sound from a radio etc.

amplify *v.* to make larger or louder in volume, as *loud speakers helped to amplify the sound of the chairman's voice* (**amplifying, amplified**).

amply *adv.* fully, as *he was amply rewarded*.

amputate *v.* to cut off, as *to amputate an injured leg*. *n.* **amputation**.

amuse *v.* to entertain, to make someone smile. *n.* **amusement** entertainment, smiling.

anaesthetic (*pron.* an.es.thet'ik) *n.* a drug or gas which causes you not to feel pain.

anatomy *n.* a study of the structure of the bodies of living things.

ancestor *n.* someone from whom you are descended, a forefather. *n.* **ancestry**. *adj.* **ancestral** belonging to your ancestors, as *an ancestral home*.

anchor (*pron.* ang'ker) *n.* a heavy bar with hooks, to hold ships fast to the sea-bed.

to weigh anchor to lift the anchor, for a ship to move.

anchorage *n.* a place where a ship is anchored.

ancient *adj.* 1. belonging to times of long ago. 2. very old.

and *conj.* a joining word, linking together two words, phrases, or sentences.

anecdote *n.* a little story about some happening.

angel *n.* a messenger sent by God. *adj.* **angelic** (*pron.* an.jel'ik) like an angel.

anger *n.* rage, bad temper.

angle (1) *n.* a corner.

angle (2) *v.* to fish with rod and line. *n.* **angler**.

angry *adj.* full of anger, annoyed. *adv.* **angrily**.

anguish *n.* great pain, suffering, sorrow.

animal *n.* 1. any living creature that can move, as a bird, snake, insect, horse. 2. any mammal except man.

the animal kingdom all animals.

animate *v.* to give life to, to fill with energy.

ankle *n.* the joint between the foot and the leg.

anklet *n.* a bracelet on the ankle.

annihilate (*pron.* a.nī'hil.ayt) *v.* to destroy completely. *n.* **annihilation**.

anniversary *n.* a day celebrated each year, as *the anniversary of the opening of a church* (*pl.* **anniversaries**).

announce *v.* to make something known publicly. *n.* **announcement**. *n.* **announcer** someone who makes announcements, as *a radio announcer*.

annoy *v.* to worry or trouble someone (**annoys, annoying, annoyed**). *n.* **annoyance** irritation.

annual *adj.* happening each year, as *the school held its annual Prize Day*. *n.* **annual** 1. a book or magazine that comes out once a year, as 'The Girls' Own Annual'. 2. a plant that only lives one season, as *marigolds are annuals*. *adv.* **annually**.

anoint *v.* to pour oil on someone's head as part of a religious ceremony.

anonymous *adj.* sent without the sender's name being known, as *an anonymous letter* or *an anonymous gift*.

another *pronoun* and *adj.* 1. one more, as *she took one sweet and then another*. 2. different, as *he mistook me for another boy*.

answer *n.* 1. a reply to a question or a letter. 2. the result of a sum in arithmetic. 3. a way out of a difficulty, as *Clive found the answer to the problem of how to get into the locked shed*. *v.* **answer** to reply.

ant *n.* a small insect living in the ground.

antarctic *adj.* around the South Pole.

antelope *n.* a graceful animal like a deer.

anthem *n.* a song of praise, or a sacred song.

anthology *n.* a collection of poems or stories.

anti- *a prefix* meaning 'against', as **antiaircraft** used against aircraft; **antilitter drive** a campaign against litter.

anticipate *v.* 1. to expect, as *I anticipate a wet day*. 2. to look forward to, as *I anticipate going to the wedding with pleasure*. *n.* **anticipation**.

antics *n. pl.* comical tricks, as *a kitten's antics*

anticyclone *n.* winds blowing out from an area of high pressure, usually bringing fine weather. Opposite of **cyclone**.

antidote *n.* 1. a medicine which acts against poison. 2. a remedy for some ill or difficulty, as *a hobby is an antidote to boredom*.

antiquated *adj.* old-fashioned, out of date, as *an antiquated car*.

antique (*pron.* an.teek¹) very old, as *antique furniture*.

antiquity *n.* olden times, centuries ago.

antiseptic *n.* a medicine which kills germs and infection.

antler *n.* a branch of the horn of a stag or deer.

anvil *n.* an iron block on which a blacksmith hammers iron into shape.

anxiety *n.* fear of something that might or might not happen.

anxious *adj.* 1. concerned about something. 2. wanting something but afraid you might not get it, as *Doris was anxious to pass her test*.

any *adj.* and *pronoun.* 1. one of several, it does not matter which, as *any day will suit me*. 2. some, as *have you any sweets?* (**anybody, anyhow, anyone, anything, anyway, anywhere**).

apart *adv.* 1. separate, as *one tree stood apart from the others*. 2. (with **from**) leaving out, as *apart from the rain I enjoyed the walk*. 3. in pieces, as *Colin took the bicycle apart*.

apartment *n.* a few rooms in a house, set apart from the rest, in which a family lives.

ape *n.* a monkey without a tail, such as a chimpanzee or gorilla. *v.* **ape** to imitate in a silly way.

apologetic *adj.* full of regret.

apologize *v.* to say you are sorry.

apology *n.* saying that you are sorry, as *Dick made an apology for fighting* (*pl.* **apologies**).

Apostle, *n.* one of the twelve followers of Jesus.

apostrophe (*pron.* a.pos¹tro.fi) *n.* a sign (') used in such words as *can't, I'll, Tom's dog*.

appal *v.* to horrify, to shock, as *the dreadful accident appals me* (**appalling, appalled**).

apparatus *n.* the tools or equipment necessary for doing an experiment or piece of work.

apparel *n.* clothing, dress.

apparent *adj.* obvious, easy to see.

appeal *v.* 1. to ask earnestly, as *to appeal for money for a hospital* or *to appeal for help*. 2. to attract, to be interesting, as *tennis appeals to me*. *n.* **appeal** 1. a strong request. 2. an attraction, an interest.

appear *v.* 1. to come into sight, as *to appear from round a corner*. 2. to seem, as *David appears to be ill*. *n.* **appearance**.

appease *v.* to soothe, to satisfy, as *to appease an angry dog* or *to appease your hunger*. *n.* **appeasement,** soothing, satisfying.

appendix *n.* 1. a small section added to a book to give further information. 2. a small tube, closed at one end, attached to the large intestine in the abdomen, which sometimes gets inflamed and causes *appendicitis*.

appetite *n.* a wish for food.

appetizing *adj.* pleasant to eat.

applaud *v.* to cheer, to clap, to shout approval.

applause *n.* clapping, cheering.

apple *n.* a fruit.

in apple-pie order in perfect order.

to be the apple of someone's eye to be greatly loved by someone.

appliance *n.* a tool.

applicant *n.* someone who asks for something, as *an applicant for a job*.

application *n.* 1. a request. 2. putting one thing to another, as *the application of a bandage to a cut*.

apply *v.* 1. to ask for, as *I shall apply for the job*. 2. to put one thing to another, as *to apply ointment to a sore*. 3. (with **to**) to concern, as *does this apply to you?* (**applies, applying, applied**).

appoint *v.* 1. to choose someone for a job. 2. to decide on, as *he will appoint Monday as the day for the meeting*.

appointment *n.* 1. the choice of someone for a job. 2. a meeting arranged for a certain time and place, as *I must keep my appointment with the dentist*.

appreciate v. to value with pleasure, as *I appreciate your help.* n. **appreciation**.

appreciative adj. grateful.

apprentice n. a youth who is learning a craft or trade. n. **apprenticeship** the learning of a trade, as *Jim is serving his apprenticeship as a printer.*

approach v. to draw near to. n. **approach** 1. drawing near. 2. a way leading to a building, as *the approach to the house is paved.*

appropriate adj. suitable, as *he wore an appropriate suit for the funeral.* v. **appropriate** to seize, to take, as *to appropriate someone's seat.*

approval n. willing agreement, as *John joined the Scouts with his father's approval.*

approve v. to agree willingly, as *Mother approves of Betty visiting her sick friend.*

approximate adj. nearly correct, as *the approximate number of those in our class is thirty.*

apricot n. a fruit like a small peach.

April n. the fourth month of the year.

apron n. a cloth worn in front, to protect clothes.

apt adj. 1. inclined to, as *this pen is apt to scratch.* 2. quick at learning, as *an apt pupil.* 3. suitable, as *an apt reply to a question.*

aptitude n. ability to learn, as *Roger has an aptitude for music.*

aquarium n. a tank in which live fish and waterplants are kept.

aqueduct n. a bridge carrying water across a valley.

arable adj. fit for ploughing.

arable land ploughed land on which crops are grown.

arc n. part of a curve or circle.

arcade n. 1. a row of arches. 2. a covered walk.

arch n. the curved top of a doorway, window, bridge, or tunnel. adj. **arch** playful, mischievous, as *the puppy gave me an arch look.*

arch- *a prefix* meaning chief, as **archbishop, archduke.**

archer n. a man who uses a bow and arrows. n. **archery** the practice of using bows and arrows.

architect n. (*pron.* ark'i.tect) someone who designs buildings. n. **architecture** the art of designing buildings.

archway n. the passage under an arch.

arctic adj. around the North Pole.

arduous adj. difficult and tiring to do, as *Malcolm found digging very arduous.*

area n. 1. a flat surface of any shape. 2. the size of the surface, measured in square units, as *the area of the garden is 900 square metres.* 3. a space, a region, as *the area round the North Pole.* 4. a sunken space in front of the basement of a building.

arena n. a space where sports or shows are held, surrounded by raised seats.

argue v. to dispute, to give reasons for or against something. n. **argument** a dispute, a reason for or against something. adj. **argumentative** fond of arguing, quarrelsome.

arid adj. dry, waterless, as *an arid desert.*

arise v. to get up (**arising, arose, arisen**).

aristocracy (*pron.* ar.is.tok'ra.si) n. people of high rank, nobles.

aristocrat n. someone of high rank or noble birth. adj. **aristocratic.**

arithmetic n. reckoning with numbers.

ark n. 1. Noah's boat. 2. an oblong box used to contain the Covenant or Jewish scrolls.

arm n. 1. the part of your body between the shoulder and the hand. 2. anything like an arm as *the arm of a chair.* v. **arm** to provide with weapons.

armed to the teeth well supplied with weapons.

armada n. a fleet of warships, like the Spanish Armada of 1588.

armament n. 1. guns and ammunition. 2. an army or navy.

armour n. metal covering carried by warships, tanks, and soldiers in battle.

armoury n. a place where arms are kept.

arms n. pl. 1. weapons. 2. the badge of a person of high rank, or a city or borough, as *the arms of the city of London.*

a call to arms a call to take up arms and fight.

to lay down arms to surrender.

up in arms ready to fight.

army *n.* 1. a large body of soldiers. 2. a large number of living things moving like soldiers, as *an army of ants* (*pl.* **armies**).

aroma *n.* a pleasant smell, as *an aroma of coffee. adj.* **aromatic** having a sharp pleasant smell.

arose *past* of **arise**.

arouse *v.* to awaken, to excite, as *this discovery will arouse great interest.*

arrange *v.* 1. to put in order, as *to arrange flowers in a vase.* 2. to prepare, as *to arrange to meet someone. n.* **arrangement**.

arrears *n. pl.* debts, unpaid money. **in arrears** behindhand, as *to be in arrears with your work.*

arrest *v.* 1. to hold someone prisoner, as *the police will arrest the forger.* 2. to check, as *to paint a fence to arrest decay.*

arrival *n.* reaching a place, or coming to the end of a journey.

arrive *v.* to come to a place, or to the end of a journey.

arrogant *adj.* haughty, proud, conceited, treating others with contempt. *n.* **arrogance**.

arrow *n.* a thin, pointed stick with feathers at one end, shot from a bow.

arsenic *n.* a very poisonous powder.

art *n.* 1. the making and study of beautiful paintings, sculpture, music, etc. 2. skill, as *the art of making pottery.*

artery *n.* one of the tubes which carry blood from your heart to other parts of your body (*pl.* **arteries**). (note: **veins** carry blood *to* your heart.)

artful *adj.* cunning, crafty. *adv.* **artfully**.

article *n.* 1. a single thing. 2. a piece of writing in a newspaper or magazine. 3. in grammar, the words 'a,' 'an' and 'the' are called articles.

artificial *adj.* imitated, not real; manufactured, not natural, as *artifical pearls. adv.* **artificially**.

artillery *n.* 1. cannon, big guns. 2. the branch of the army which uses big guns.

artist *n.* 1. someone who makes a work of art. 2. someone who is very skilful. *adj.* **artistic**. *adv.* **artistically** done skilfully and with good taste.

as *adv.* equally, as *I can do it as well. conj.* **as** because, as *will you go as I am ill? pronoun* **as** that, which, as *we have the same kind of car as you have. prep.* **as** like, as *she went dressed as a fairy.*

asbestos *n.* a white wool-like fibre which will not burn.

ascend *v.* to climb upwards.

ascent *n.* 1. a slope up, as *a steep ascent in a road.* 2. a climb upwards, as *the men made an ascent of the mountain.*

ash *n.* 1. a tree. 2. the powder and cinders left by a fire (*pl.* **ashes**). *adj.* **ashen** very pale.

Ash Wednesday the first day of Lent.

ashamed *adj.* 1. sorry for having done wrong. 2. uneasy and embarrassed, as *John was ashamed to wear his old coat.*

ask *v.* 1. to put a question, to inquire. 2. to invite, as *to ask someone to tea.*

asleep *adv.* sleeping.

asphalt *n.* a mixture of tar and small chippings, used for paths and pavements.

aspirin *n.* a medicine for easing pain.

ass *n.* a donkey, a stupid person.

assault *n.* a fierce attack. *v.* **assault** to attack a person or a fort.

assemble *v.* to gather together, to call together. *n.* **assembly** a meeting, a collection.

assent *v.* to agree, to say 'yes'.

assert *v.* to state firmly, to declare. *n.* **assertion** a firm statement. *adj.* **assertive** self-confident and pushing, as *Brian's assertive manner offended many people.*

assess *v.* to judge the value of something, as *we did not assess the chances of Frank winning the race to be very good.*

asset *n.* something of value.

assist *v.* to help. *n.* **assistance** help. *n.* **assistant** someone who helps, as *a shop assistant.*

associate *v.* 1. to mix with, as *David does not associate much with other boys.* 2. to see a connection between, as *to associate green with fields. n.* **associate** a companion.

association *n.* a society, a group of people with the same interest, as *a motorists' association.*

assorted *adj.* of different kinds, as *assorted biscuits*. *n.* **assortment** a mixture of different kinds, as a *chocolate assortment*.

assume *v.* 1. to suppose, to take for granted, as *I assume he is in bed with his cold*. 2. to take over, as *the bosun will assume control of the boat*.

assurance *n.* 1. a promise, as *I have his assurance that he will pay*. 2. certainty, as *I know with assurance that I locked the door*.

assure *v.* 1. to promise. 2. to make sure.

asterisk *n.* a small star (*) used in printing.

astonish *v.* to surprise greatly, to amaze. *n.* **astonishment** amazement.

astound *v.* to amaze, to bewilder.

astrologer *n.* someone who tells the future from the stars. *n.* **astrology**.

astronaut *n.* traveller in space.

astronomer *n.* someone who studies the stars, planets, and other objects in the sky.

astronomy *n.* the scientific study of the stars.

astute *adj.* cunning, sharp.

asylum *n.* a refuge, a home for unfortunate people, especially for those mentally ill.

at *prep.* 1. in, near, close by. 2. busy in, as *Colin is hard at work*.

ate (*pron.* et) *past* of **eat**.

athlete *n.* someone who takes part in sports. *adj.* **athletic** strong, and active, good at games.

atlas *n.* a book of maps (*pl.* **atlases**).

atmosphere *n.* the air around the earth.

atom *n.* a tiny particle. *adj.* **atomic** connected with atoms. *n.* **atomic bomb** a very powerful bomb whose power comes from splitting atoms.

atrocious *adj.* cruel and wicked, very bad.

attach *v.* to fasten, to join. *n.* **attachment**.

to be attached to 1. to be joined to. 2. to be fond of, as *Judy is very attached to her dog*.

attack *v.* to set upon by force. *n.* **attack**.

attain *v.* to succeed in reaching, as *to attain the rank of Captain*. *n.* **attainment**.

attempt *v.* to try to do something. *n.* **attempt** an effort to do something.

attend *v.* 1. to be present at, as *to attend a wedding*. 2. to pay attention to, as *to attend to someone's words*. *n.* **attendance** 1. being present at. 2. the number present, as *the attendance at the concert was large*.

attendant *n.* a servant, a waiter. *adj.* **attendant** 1. waiting on another, as *an attendant nurse*. 2. going with, as *dirt with its attendant disease*.

attention *n.* care, consideration, as *we will give the matter every attention*.

to pay attention to to give careful thought to.

attentive *adj.* 1. listening or watching carefully. 2. polite, considerate.

attic *n.* a room under the roof of a house.

attitude *n.* 1. a position of the body. 2. a way of thinking, as *Gwen's attitude to the plan was one of dislike*.

attract *v.* 1. to draw towards, as *a magnet attracts iron*. 2. to interest, as *that man attracts me*.

attraction *n.* 1. drawing towards. 2. a cause of interest, as *the circus was a real attraction*.

attractive *adj.* 1. interesting, pleasing. 2. attracting, drawing closer.

auburn *adj.* reddish-brown.

auction *n.* a public sale in which goods go to the person who bids the most money. *v.* **auction** to sell by auction.

auctioneer *n.* a person who conducts sales by auction.

audacious *adj.* bold, daring, impudent.

audible *adj.* loud enough to be heard.

audience *n.* 1. a crowd of people listening to a speech, song, etc. 2. a reception by a person of high rank, as *the ambassador was granted an audience by the Queen*.

audition *n.* a hearing, a test given to someone who sings or performs.

auditorium *n.* a hall, especially the part of the hall in which the audience sits.

August *n.* the eighth month of the year.

aunt *n.* a sister of one's father or mother.

austere *adj.* 1. very simple and plain, as *an austere prison cell*. 2. strict, stern, as *monks live austere lives*.

author n. someone who writes books or articles. n. **authoress** a woman writer.

authoritative adj. with authority.

authority n. 1. power, command. 2. an expert, as my father is an authority on birds (pl. **authorities**).

authorize v. to give someone power or permission, as I authorize you to spend the money.

autobiography n. the life of a person written by himself (pl. **autobiographies**).

autograph n. a signature.

automatic adj. working as if by itself, as automatic traffic lights. n. **automatic** a revolver.

automobile n. a motor-car.

autumn n. the season after summer called, in the U.S.A., the fall. adj. **autumnal**.

available adj. here, ready to be used, as the bicycle is now available for you.

avalanche n. a mass of snow and ice falling down a mountain.

avenge v. to take revenge on someone. n. **avenger**.

avenue n. a road lined with trees.

average adj. 1. medium, ordinary, as Harry is of average height. 2. the medium or middle value, as the average of 3, 5, and 7, is 5.

aviary n. a place for keeping birds.

aviation n. flying in aircraft. n. **aviator** an airman.

avoid v. to keep away from, to shun. n. **avoidance**.

awake, awaken v. to rouse from sleep, to stir up (**awaking, awoke**, or **awaked**). adj. **awake** not asleep, as wide-awake.

award v. to give a prize. n. **award** a prize.

aware adj. knowing, conscious of, as I was aware of the danger. n. **awareness**.

away adv. 1. at a distance, far off, as he went away. 2. absent, as Brenda was away from school.

to do away with to get rid of.

to fire away to start a job with determination.

awe n. a mixture of fear and respect, as the criminal stood in awe of the judge. adj. **awe-inspiring** filling you with awe.

awful adj. dreadful, shocking. adv. **awfully**.

awkward adj. 1. clumsy, as he is an awkward skater. 2. inconvenient, as this is an awkward time to come. n. **awkwardness**.

awoke past of **awake**.

axe n. a tool for chopping trees and wood.

axis n. a line around which something turns, as the earth spins around its axis.

axle the rod on which a wheel turns.

aye adv. forever, always.

azure n. sky blue.

B

babble v. to chatter in a meaningless way.

baboon n. a large monkey with a dog-like face.

baby n. an infant (pl. **babies**). adj. **babyish**.

bachelor n. an unmarried man.

back n. 1. the opposite side to the front. 2. (in football) one of the two players who stands immediately in front of the goalkeeper. v. **back** to move backwards. adv. **back** in return, as I sent it back. adj. **back** overdue, as a back payment of money.

to back down to give way.

to back out to withdraw.

to put your back into to work hard at.

to take a back seat to be quiet and modest.

with one's back to the wall in a desperate condition.

backbone n. the spine.

background n. the scenery at the back of a picture.

backward adj. 1. to the back. 2. dull, as a backward pupil.

backwards adv. 1. back to front. 2. towards the back, as the van slid backwards.

backwoods n. pl. forest land away from towns.

bacon n. pig's meat, dried and salted.

bacteria n. pl. tiny living things only seen through a microscope, able to cause disease.

bad *adj.* evil, faulty, not good. *adj.* **bad-tempered** angry.
to go bad to decay.

badge *n.* a sign worn on the clothes, on a car, etc., showing that you belong to some group or association, as *a Scout's badge.*

badger *n.* a grey furry animal about two feet long.

baffle *v.* to bewilder, to puzzle. *adj.* **baffling**.

bag *n.* a sack of cloth, leather, or other soft material. *v.* **bag** 1. to bulge. 2. to put in a bag, as *to bag potatoes.* 3. to capture or kill, as *we hope to bag some rabbits* (**bagging, bagged**). *adj.* **baggy** bulging. *n.* **bagful** as much as a bag will hold.

baggage *n.* a traveller's luggage.

bagpipes *n. pl.* a wind instrument, with a leather bag and pipes, used especially in Scotland and Ireland.

bail *n.* 1. (in cricket) one of the two cross pieces on the wicket. 2. (in law) money paid to set a prisoner free, with the condition that he appears later in court for his trial. *v.* **bail** or **bale** to ladle water out of a boat.

bait *n.* food put on a hook to tempt a fish. *v.* **bait** to set a hook or a trap with food.

bake *v.* 1. to cook in an oven. 2. to dry and harden, as *to bake clay in the sun. n.* **baker** a man who makes bread.

bakery *n.* a place where bread is made (*pl.* **bakeries**).

baking powder *n.* a white powder used to make cakes light.

balance *n.* 1. a pair of scales (often *n. pl.* **balances**). 2. steadiness, as *Jack kept his balance when walking along the plank. v.* **balance** 1. to weigh in a balance. 2. to hold yourself steady, as *to balance on a plank.*

balcony *n.* 1. a gallery outside a window. 2. an upper floor in a cinema (*pl.* **balconies**).

bald *adj.* 1. without hair on the head. 2. plain, without frills, as *a bald account of what happened. n.* **baldness**.

bale *n.* 1. a package of goods or straw. 2. see **bail**.

ball *n.* 1. something round, as *a ball of wool* or *a cannon ball.* 2. a big dance.

ball bearing one of the small steel balls which make a bicycle wheel, etc., turn more smoothly.

ballad *n.* a song or poem that tells a story.

ballerina (*pron.* bal.e.ree¹na) *n.* a girl or woman who dances in a ballet.

ballet (*pron.* bal¹ay) *n.* 1. a performance of dancing in a theatre. 2. the company which performs the dance.

balloon *n.* a large bag filled with light gas.

ballot *n.* secret voting with marked papers. *v.* **ballot** to vote secretly.

bamboo *n.* a tropical reed, whose hollow jointed stem is called a *cane.*

ban *v.* to forbid, as *to ban smoking* (**banning, banned**). *n.* **ban** a statement that something is banned.

banana *n.* a long yellow-skinned fruit.

band *n.* 1. a narrow strip of material for binding. 2. a narrow strip, as *a band of paint.* 3. a group of people, as *a band of robbers.* 4. a group of musicians playing together. *v.* **band** to join together, to unite.

bandage *n.* a strip of cloth to bind wounds, or to blindfold someone.

bandit *n.* an outlaw or robber.

bang *n.* a heavy blow or a loud noise. *v.* **bang** to strike hard, to beat, to slam.

bangle *n.* a ring worn on the arm.

banish *v.* to drive someone out of the country. *n.* **banishment**.

bank *n.* 1. a mound of earth or snow. 2. the raised border of a river. 3. a mass of sand in the sea, *a sandbank.* 4. an office into which money is paid for safety. *v.* **bank** to deposit money in a bank. *n.* **banker** a man in charge of the work of a bank.

bank holiday a public holiday by law.

bankrupt *adj.* unable to pay one's debts. *n.* **bankruptcy**.

banner *n.* a large flag or cloth carried on a pole, or between two poles.

banns *n. pl.* notice of a coming marriage, read out in church.

banquet *n.* a large feast.

bantam *n.* a small kind of fowl.

baptism *n.* the ceremony of baptizing.

baptize *n.* to christen someone with a sprinkling of water.

bar *n.* 1. a stiff rod. 2. a stripe. 3 a bank of sand across the mouth of a river or harbour. 4. a place in court where prisoners stand. 5. a space in music which stands for a measure of time. *v.* **bar** to hinder, to shut out (**barring, barred**).

barb *n.* the sharp spike on a fish hook, pointing backwards. *n.* **barbed wire** fencing wire fitted with sharp spikes.

barbarian *n.* a rough uncivilized person. *adj.* **barbaric, barbarous** uncivilized. *n.* **barbarity** savage cruelty (*pl.* **barbarities**).

barber *n.* a man's hairdresser.

bard *n.* (in old times) a singer of songs, a minstrel.

bare *adj.* 1. uncovered, naked. 2. plain, simple, as *the bare truth*. 3. scanty, little, as *a bare mouthful*. *v.* **bare** to uncover (**baring, bared**). *adv.* **barely** scarcely, hardly, as *he had barely enough to live on*. *adv.* **bareback** without a saddle.

bargain *n.* 1. an agreement between two people. 2. something that is bought very cheaply. *v.* **bargain** to haggle over a price.

into the bargain also, as well.

to strike a bargain to come to terms about a deal.

barge *n.* a flat-bottomed boat.

bark *n.* 1. the covering of the branches and trunk of a tree. 2. the sharp cry of a dog or wolf. *v.* **bark** (of a dog) to make a sharp cry.

barley *n.* a grain used for food.

barn *n.* a building for storing hay or grain. *n.* **barn-owl** a large white owl.

barnacle *n.* a shell-fish that sticks to rocks and ships.

barometer *n.* an instrument which helps to tell changes in the weather, by measuring air-pressure.

baron *n.* a nobleman (*fem.* **baroness**). *adj.* **baronial** belonging to a baron, as *a baronial hall*.

barracks *n. pl.* buildings in which soldiers live.

barrel *n.* 1. a round tub made of wooden staves. 2. the metal tube of a gun or cannon.

barren *adj.* not able to bear fruit or crops.

barricade *n.* a barrier hastily made to hold back an enemy.

barrier *n.* a fence, wall, or obstacle.

barrister *n.* a lawyer who acts in higher courts.

barrow *n.* a small hand-cart.

barter *n.* to trade by exchanging goods instead of using money.

base *n.* the bottom part, the foundation. *adj.* **base** low, poor, as *base metal has little value*.

baseball *n.* a game, very popular in Canada and the U.S.A., played with bat and ball on a field with four bases.

basement *n.* a storey of a building below ground.

bashful *adj.* shy, timid. *n.* **bashfulness**.

basin *n.* 1. a round dish or bowl. 2. the land drained by a river.

basis *n.* the foundation, the main reason, as *the basis of my belief in John's guilt is that I saw him doing wrong*.

bask *v.* to lie in warmth or sunshine.

basket *n.* a carrier made of woven twigs or cane.

bat *n.* 1. a wooden club used in cricket, baseball, or rounders. 2. a winged mouse-like animal, which flies at night. *v.* **bat** to use a bat (**batting, batted**).

batch *n.* a collection of things all alike, as *a batch of loaves*.

bath *n.* 1. an all-over wash of your body. 2. a large container in which you bathe. *n.* **bathroom** a room with a bath in it.

bathe *v.* 1. to have a bath. 2. to soak in water. 3. to go swimming (**bathing, bathed**).

baton *n.* 1. a policeman's truncheon. 2. a short stick used by the conductor of an orchestra. 3. a Field-Marshal's staff of office.

battalion *n.* a large body of soldiers.

batter *n.* eggs, milk, and flour beaten together for cooking. *v.* **batter** to hit again and again, as *to batter down a door*.

battery *n.* a group, as *a battery of guns* or *a battery of electric cells* (*pl.* **batteries**).

battle *n.* 1. a fight between two armed forces. 2. any struggle, as *a battle against the wind*. *v.* **battle** to fight.

battlement *n.* a wall on top of a fort, with openings for shooting.

battleship *n.* the largest kind of warship with several big guns.

bawl *v.* to yell loudly.

bay *n.* 1. a broad, curved inlet of the sea. 2. the laurel tree. 3. the deep-toned bark of a hound. 4. a reddish-brown colour.

bazaar *n.* 1. an Eastern market. 2. a sale of goods from stalls.

be *v.* 1. to exist. 2. the verb whose present tense is **I am**, etc. and whose past tense is **I was**, etc. (**am, is, are, was, were, being, been**).

beach *n.* the sandy or pebbly shore of the sea.

beacon *n.* a warning fire or light.

bead *n.* 1. a small ball on a necklace. 2. a small drop, as *a bead of perspiration*.

beak *n.* a bird's bill.

beaker *n.* a deep drinking cup or glass.

beam *n.* 1. a long piece of timber or metal. 2. a ray of light. 3. the greatest width of a ship. *v.* **beam** 1. to shine. 2. to smile warmly.

bean *n.* a seed in a pod, used as a vegetable.

bear *v.* 1. to hold. 2. to put up with, to endure, as *I cannot bear to listen*. 3. to produce, as *this tree bears fruit* (**bearing, bore, borne**). *n.* **bear** a large furry animal.

to bear a hand to help.

to bear in mind to keep in mind.

beard *n.* the hair on a man's chin and face. *v.* **beard** 1. to take by the beard. 2. to face up to boldly.

bearings *n. pl.* direction, as *to lose your bearings in a fog*.

beast *n.* a four-footed animal, a brute. *n.* **beastliness** acting like a brute. *adj.* **beastly** very unpleasant.

beat *v.* 1. to keep striking. 2. to flap, as *a bird beats its wings*. 3. to defeat another person or team. 4. (in music) to mark time with a baton. (**beating, beat, beaten**). *n.* **beat** 1. a stroke. 2. a policeman's round.

to beat about the bush to talk round a subject instead of about the main point.

beauty *n.* loveliness. *adj.* **beautiful** lovely.

beaver *n.* a North American furry animal, living on land and in water.

became *past* of **become**.

because *conj.* for the reason that, since, as.

beckon *v.* to call someone to you by making a sign (**beckoning, beckoned**).

become *v.* 1. to come to be, to grow up to be, as *Ted wants to become a sailor*. 2. to suit, as *the dress becomes you* (**becoming, became, become**).

bed *n.* 1. something to sleep and rest on. 2. a garden plot, as *a flower bed*. 3. the channel of a river, as *the river bed*. 4. the bottom of the sea, *the sea bed*. *adj.* **bedridden** confined to bed.

bedroom *n.* a room to sleep in.

bedstead *n.* the iron or wooden framework of a bed.

bee *n.* a winged insect which makes honey and wax. *n.* **beehive** a house for bees. *n.* **beeswax** the wax made by bees to build their cells.

a bee in your bonnet a crazy fancy.

to make a beeline for to go straight towards.

beech *n.* a tree with grey bark and hard wood.

beef *n.* meat from cattle, used for food.

been *past participle* of the verb **to be**.

beer *n.* an alcoholic drink made from barley, malt, and hops.

beet *n.* a vegetable grown for its root. *n.* **beetroot** the large round root of the beet.

beetle *n.* an insect with hard, shining wing-cases.

before *prep.* 1. in front of, as *he stood before the house*. 2. earlier in time, as *I have seen this before*. 3. in case, as *tell me now before you forget*. 4. rather than, as *I would die before I would betray you*.

beg *v.* 1. to ask for food or money. 2. to ask earnestly for some favour, as *I beg you to let me go* (**begging, begged**).

beggar *n.* someone who lives by begging.

begin *v.* to start, to commence (**beginning, began, begun**).

beginner *n.* someone who starts to do something for the first time.

begun *past participle* of **begin**.

behalf *n.* defence, support, as *Paul spoke on John's behalf*.

behave *v.* 1. to act, as *this sewing-machine behaves in a very uneven way*. 2. to conduct yourself in an orderly and well-mannered way.

behaviour *n.* 1. manners, conduct. 2. how a thing acts.

behead *v.* to cut the head off.

behind *prep.* 1. after, at the back of. 2. late, as *Colin is behind with his work*.

behold *v.* to gaze upon (**beholding, beheld**).

being *n.* 1. existence. 2. a living person, as *no being lives on the moon*. *v.* **being** *present participle* of the verb **to be**.

belief *n.* 1. something that is thought to be true, an opinion. 2. a religious faith, as *the Christian belief*.

believe *v.* to think something is true, to hold an opinion. *n.* **believer**.

bell *n.* a hollow metal cup that makes a musical sound when struck.

bellow *v.* to roar, to shout angrily. *n.* **bellow** a deep roar.

bellows *n. pl.* an implement made of wood and leather for blowing air into a fire, or into the pipes of an organ.

belly *n.* the lower part of the trunk of a man or animal.

belong (with **to**) *v.* 1. to be the property of. 2. to be a member of, as *Joan belongs to the Brownies*.

belongings *n. pl.* possessions, property.

beloved *adj.* greatly loved. *n.* **beloved** someone dearly loved.

below *prep.* 1. under, as *below the ground*. 2. lower in place, or less in value than, as *the bicycle was sold below its price when new*.

belt *n.* 1. a strip of leather or cloth worn round the body. 2. a circular zone or area.

bench *n.* 1. a long seat or form. 2. a table at which carpenters or engineers work.

bend *v.* 1. to curve something, as *to bend a bow*. 2. to lean over, as *to bend over a table* (**bending, bent**). *n.* **bend** a curve.

beneath *prep.* 1. below, under. 2. unworthy of, as *it was beneath him to do wrong*.

benefit *n.* 1. an advantage or profit. *v.* **benefit** to gain an advantage (**benefiting, benefited**).

benevolent *adj.* kind, good-natured, generous.

bent *past* of **bend**.

bequeath *v.* to leave something in a will, as *Mr Brown decided to bequeath his money to his son*.

beret (*pron.* be'ray) *n.* a soft round woollen cap.

berry *n.* a small juicy fruit (*pl.* **berries**).

berth *n.* 1. a bunk in a ship or train, for sleeping in. 2. a place for a ship to lie at anchor.

to give a wide berth to to avoid.

beside *prep.* by the side of, as *the house beside the road*.

besides *adv.* also, in addition, as *I met several friends there, and there were others besides*.

besiege *v.* 1. to surround a fort with an armed force and attempt to capture it. 2. to crowd round, as *the boys began to besiege the winner*.

best (*superlative* of **good**) *adj.* the most valuable, the finest, as *this is the best bicycle*.

best man the man who looks after a bridegroom at a wedding.

to make the best of it to put up with some disadvantage.

bet *v.* to make a wager, and declare who will win in some event (**betting, betted**). *n.* **bet** a wager.

betray *v.* 1. to give someone away to an enemy. 2. to give a secret or some information away which should be kept to yourself (**betraying, betrayed**).

betrayal *n.* giving someone away to an enemy, or giving some secret or confidence away.

better (*comparative* of **good**) *adj.* more valuable, finer, as *this hat is better than that*.

better off in a better condition.

for better or worse whatever happens, whether good or bad.

between *prep.* 1. in the middle of two things, as *the house stands between the hills and the sea*. 2. belonging to two persons, as *they will share the money between them*.

beware v. to guard against, as *beware of the dog!*

bewilder v. to confuse, as *the fog bewilders me.* n. **bewilderment** confusion.

bewitch v. to put under a spell or charm.

beyond prep. 1. on the far side of, as *lands beyond the sea.* 2. out of reach of, as *he was beyond hearing my shout.* 3. past, too far gone for, as *the frozen bird was beyond help.*

Bible n. the book of the sacred writings of the Christian religion, containing the Old Testament and the New Testament.

bicycle n. a two-wheeled machine moved by pedals or a petrol engine.

bid v. 1. to command, as *I bid you go.* 2. to tell, as *I bid you farewell.* 3. to offer money at an auction, as *I will bid for that table* (**bidding, bade** pron. bad, **bidden**). n. **bid** an offer of money. n. **bidding**.

big adj. large, great (*comparative* **bigger**, *superlative* **biggest**).

bilge n. the bottom of a ship's hold. n. **bilge water** the water that collects in a ship's hold.

bill n. 1. an account of money to be paid. 2. a poster or small leaflet. 3. an Act of Parliament. 4. a bird's beak.

billiards n. a game played with small balls and a cue on a cloth-covered table.

billion n. (in Britain) one million millions. (in North America) one thousand millions.

billow n. a big wave. v. **billow** to bulge out.

billy-can n. a can for boiling water outdoors.

bin n. a large container for ashes, coal, corn, etc.

bind v. to tie up with rope, cord, etc. 2. to strengthen the hem of a dress with a thin strip of cloth. 3. to fasten pages together, with a cover, to make a book (**binding, bound**).

biography n. a person's life-story told by someone else (compare with **autobiography**). n. **biographer** a writer of someone's life-story.

biology n. the study of plant and animal life. n. **biologist** someone who studies biology.

birch n. a tall tree with silvery bark.

bird n. a two-legged animal with wings and feathers that lays eggs.

a bird in the hand is worth two in the bush something you have is worth more than something you expect.

bird's-eye view a general view of a place or problem.

birth n. 1. being born. 2. the beginning of anything.

birthday the date of someone's birth.

biscuit n. a crisp thin cake.

bishop n. a clergyman of high rank.

bison n. North American wild animal, a buffalo.

bit n. 1. a small piece. 2. a steel tool for drilling holes. 3. the metal part of a horse's bridle.

bite v. 1. to cut or seize with your teeth. 2. to cut into, as *the screw bites into the wood.* (**biting, bit, bitten**). n. **bite** 1. a cut made by teeth. 2. a mouthful, as *a bite of bread.*

to bite the dust to fall in combat.

bitter adj. 1. sharp and sour to the taste. 2. keen, as *a bitter wind.* 3. mournful, as *a bitter cry.* n. **bitterness** sharpness.

to the bitter end to the very end.

black adj. 1. the opposite of white, very dark. 2. sullen, as *a black look.* 3. gloomy, as *a black outlook.* v. **blacken** to make black.

blackmail v. to obtain money from someone by threatening to reveal a guilty secret.

blacksmith n. a man who shoes horses and repairs agricultural machinery.

blade n. 1. the cutting part of a knife, sword, etc. 2. a long, thin leaf, as *a blade of grass.* 3. the flat part of an oar.

blame v. to hold responsible, as *I blame you for the accident.* n. responsibility, as *Peter took the blame for the mistake.*

blank n. 1. an empty space. 2. anything not marked or written on. adj. **blank** 1. empty. 2. without understanding, as *there was a look of blank amazement on his face.*

blanket n. 1. a woollen bed-covering. 2. any soft covering, as *a blanket of fog covered the town.*

a wet blanket a gloomy person.

blast *n.* 1. a rush of air or steam. 2. an explosion. 3. a loud sound, as *the blast of bugles.*

blaze *v.* 1. to light up suddenly, to flare up. 2. to chip the bark of a tree in order to show the way, as *to blaze a trail.*

bleach *v.* to whiten by the sun or chemicals. *n.* **bleach** a chemical which whitens cloth.

bleak *adj.* cold and cheerless.

bled *past* of **bleed**.

bleed *v.* 1. to lose blood. 2. (of a tree) to lose sap (**bleeding, bled**).

blend *v.* to mix. *n.* **blend** a mixture.

bless 1. to wish happiness to, as *bless you!* 2. to ask God's favour on, as *the bishop will bless the new ship.* *n.* **blessing** 1. a good wish. 2. a cause of happiness, as *television is a blessing to old people. adj.* **blessed**.

blew *past* of **blow**.

blind *adj.* without sight. *n.* **blind** a covering for a window. *v.* **blind** 1. to deprive someone of sight. 2. to dazzle. *n.* **blindness**.

a blind alley 1. a path with no way out. 2. an occupation or activity which leads to no important result.

blindfold *v.* to bandage someone's eyes.

blink *v.* to open and shut the eyes suddenly.

bliss *n.* perfect happiness, joy.

blister *n.* a watery swelling on the skin.

blizzard *n.* a heavy snowstorm with wind.

block *n.* 1. a solid lump. 2. the wood on which criminals were beheaded. 3. a row of buildings. 4. an obstacle. *v.* **block** to stop the way.

blond *adj.* fair in colour (*fem.* **blonde**).

blood *n.* the red fluid in veins and arteries.

bloodcurdling *adj.* frightening.

bloodhound *n.* a very large dog used for tracking criminals.

bloodshed *n.* the spilling of blood.

bloodthirsty *adj.* eager for battle.

bloom *n.* 1. a flower. 2. a white coating on certain fruits. *v.* **bloom** to blossom, to flourish.

blossom *n.* the flower of a shrub or tree. *v.* **blossom** to flower.

blot *n.* a spot, a stain. *v.* **blot** 1. to smudge, to stain. 2. to dry with blotting-paper (**blotting, blotted**). *n.* **blotter** a paper or pad for blotting ink.

blouse *n.* a loose outer garment worn above the waist by girls and women.

blow *v.* 1. to move a current of air. 2. to puff, as *Father blows smoke from his pipe.* 3. to make a musical instrument or whistle sound (**blowing, blew, blown**). *n.* **blow** 1. a knock or stroke. 2. unexpected misfortune, as *it was a blow to hear of Mr Smith's death.*

to blow up to explode in pieces.

blubber *v.* to sob. *n.* **blubber** the fat of whales.

blue *n.* the colour of the sky.

once in a blue moon very rarely.

out of the blue unexpectedly.

bluebell *n.* a woodland flower.

bluff *n.* a high bank. *adj.* **bluff** open and outspoken. *v.* **bluff** to mislead or deceive.

blunder *n.* a stupid mistake. *v.* **blunder** 1. to make a clumsy mistake. 2. to move clumsily (into).

blunderbuss *n.* a shotgun with a wide muzzle, used many years ago.

blunt *adj.* 1. with a dull edge or point, as *a blunt knife.* 2. rough and outspoken, as *a blunt speaker. v.* **blunt** to make less sharp.

blur *v.* 1. to smudge, as *to blur your writing.* 2. to make indistinct, as *the rain blurs the view* (**blurring, blurred**). *n.* **blur** 1. a smudge. 2. a hazy impression.

blush *v.* to go red in the face through shame or shyness. *n.* **blush** a reddening of the face.

boar *n.* a male pig, a wild pig.

board *n.* 1. a wide, long, thin piece of wood. 2. a table. 3. a piece of wood on which to play a game, as *a draughts board* or *a darts board.* 4. a council, as *a board of school managers.* 5. providing food day by day, as *board and lodging. v.* 1. **board** to enter a ship or train. 2. to supply with food regularly for payment.

boarding school a school which provides board and lodging for its pupils.

boast v. to praise yourself, or speak proudly of your possessions.

boat n. a small open ship or vessel.

boatswain (*pron.* boh'sn) often spelt **bosun**. n. an under-officer in charge of a ship's boat.

bob v. to move quickly up and down (**bobbing, bobbed**). n. **bob** 1. a quick movement up and down. 2. a small weight at the end of a line. 3. a fishing-float at the end of a line.

bodily adj. 1. belonging to the body. 2. in one group, as *the men went bodily to the manager.*

body n. 1. the trunk or main part of a living creature. 2. the main part of anything. 3. a group of people (*pl.* **bodies**).

bodyguard n. a group of men protecting someone.

bog n. soft wet ground, a marsh. adj. **boggy** soft and muddy.

boil v. for a liquid to change to vapour, with bubbles. n. **boil** an inflamed swelling on the skin. n. **boiler** a tank in which steam is made.

boisterous adj. noisy and rough.

bold adj. 1. brave, confident. 2. clear and well-marked, as *the bold outline of the hills.* n. **boldness** courage, confidence.

bolt n. 1. a short metal rod threaded at one end for a nut. 2. a sliding bar for fastening a door. 3. a heavy arrow for a cross-bow. 4. a sudden dash away, as *the dog made a bolt for the gate.* v. **bolt** 1. to fasten with a bolt. 2. to eat food very quickly. 3. to dash away.

bomb n. a container filled with explosive, dropped from an aeroplane. n. **bomber** an aeroplane for carrying bombs.

bombard v. 1. to attack with shells or bombs. 2. to pelt, to throw at persistently, as *to bombard with stones* or *to bombard a speaker with questions.*

bond n. 1. a rope or chain which ties things together. 2. a written promise.

bone n. the hard substance of which a skeleton is made.

to have a bone to pick with someone to have a complaint to talk over with someone.

bonfire n. a large, open-air fire.

bonnet n. 1. a head-dress for girls or women. 2. part of a motor-car covering the engine.

bony adj. 1. made of bone. 2. full of bones. 3. lean and thin with bones sticking out.

book n. a number of sheets of paper bound together in a cover. v. **book** 1. to note down something in a book. 2. to reserve beforehand, as *to book seats in a cinema.*

bookcase n. a case with shelves for storing books.

bookworm n. 1. a tiny grub which lives in old books. 2. someone who is very fond of reading.

boom n. 1. a long pole at the bottom end of a sail. 2. a barrier of floating logs. 3. a deep roar, as *the boom of thunder.* v. **boom** to roar.

boomerang n. a curved wooden weapon that Australian natives use, and that always returns to the thrower when thrown into the air.

boot n. a leather or rubber covering for the foot and lower part of the leg.

the boot is on the other foot the advantage which someone expected proves to belong to someone else.

booty n. money and goods taken from an enemy by a victorious army.

border n. 1. the edge of anything. 2. the beds along the side of a lawn or path, as *a flower border.* 3. the frontier where two countries meet.

bore v. 1. to drill a hole into. 2. to weary by dull chatter or monotonous work. 3. the *past* of **bear** (**boring, bored**). n. **bore** 1. a hole made by drilling. 2. the inside size of a tube or a gun-barrel. 3. a tiresome person.

boredom n. weariness caused by dull and monotonous talk or work.

born brought into life.

borough n. a town which has received a charter giving it certain privileges.

borrow v. to obtain something with a promise to return it later.

bosom (*pron.* booz'um) n. the human breast. adj. **bosom** dear and very close, as *a bosom friend.*

bosun see **boatswain**.

botany *n*. the study of plants. *n*. **botanist** someone who studies plants.

both *adj*. two together, as *both men were there*.

bottle *n*. a narrow-mouthed container for liquids. *v*. **bottle** 1. to put into a bottle. 2. to store up, as *to bottle your anger*.

bottom *n*. the lowest part.

to get to the bottom of to solve (a mystery).

bough *n*. a large branch of a tree.

bought *past* of **buy**.

boulder *n*. a very large smooth stone.

bounce *v*. to jump about like a ball.

bound *v*. 1. *past* of **bind**. 2. to jump about, to leap. 3. to form a boundary, as *mountains bound the frontier*. *n*. **bound** a leap, a jump.

outward bound ready to go, or on the way outwards.

boundary *n*. a fixed limit, a border (*pl*. **boundaries**).

bouquet (*pron*. boo'kay) *n*. a bunch of flowers.

bout *n*. 1. a contest, a test of strength or skill. 2. a period or length of time spent in doing something, as *a bout of work*.

bow (1) (*pron*. like 'cow') *v*. to bend the head or body to show respect. *n*. **bow** the front part of a ship.

bow (2) (*pron*. boh) *n*. 1. bent wood or steel used for shooting arrows. 2. anything bent into an arch, as *a rainbow*. 3. a stick strung with horsehair for use with a violin. 4. a ribbon tied in loops. *adj*. **bow-legged** with legs bent outwards.

bowels *n. pl*. the digestive organs in the abdomen.

bowl *n*. 1. a basin for use in a kitchen. 2. a wooden ball used in the game of bowls. *v*. **bowl** to roll or pitch a ball in a game. *n*. **bowls** a game in which wooden balls are rolled along a grass plot. *n*. **bowling-green** a grass plot on which the game of bowls is played.

box *n*.1. a container with a lid. 2. an evergreen shrub. *v*. **box** to fight with gloves on your hands for sport. *n*. **boxer** someone who fights for sport, using padded gloves.

boy *n*. a male child. *n*. **boyhood** the time of being a boy.

Boy Scout a member of a world-wide organization for boys.

brace *n*. 1. a support. 2. a pair, as *a brace of rabbits*. 3. a carpenter's tool which holds a bit to drill holes. *v*. **brace** 1. to support. 2. to rouse yourself. *adj*. **bracing** rousing, as *bracing sea air*.

bracelet *n*. a ring or bangle worn on the wrist.

bracket *n*. 1. a support for a shelf. 2. a mark used in printing, as [ ] or ( ), to enclose words.

braid *n*. a narrow plaited band for trimming.

braille *n*. raised dots on paper for blind people to read by touch.

brain *n*. the grey matter in the skull. *n. pl*. **brains** intelligence. *adj*. **brainy** intelligent. *n*. **brain-wave** a good idea.

brake *v*. to use force to cause something to slow down. *n*. **brake** a system of levers for stopping a car or other vehicle.

bran *n*. the husk or outer cover of corn.

branch *n*. 1. the limb of a tree. 2. one of a group, as *a branch bank* or *a branch shop* (*pl*. **branches**). *v*. **branch** to divide into branches.

to branch out to strike out into new ground.

brand *n*. 1. a burning piece of wood. 2. a mark made by a hot iron on cattle. *v*. **brand** to mark with a brand. *adj*. **brand-new** quite new.

brandy *n*. an alcoholic spirit made from wine.

brass *n*. a yellow alloy of copper and zinc.

brave *adj*. 1. fearless, courageous. 2. splendid, as *the procession made a brave display*. *v*. **brave** to meet with courage, as *to brave someone's anger*. *n*. **bravery** courage.

brawl *n*. a noisy disturbance. *v*. **brawl** to quarrel and fight in a noisy way.

brawn *n*. 1. muscle, strength. 2. meat pressed and jellied. *adj*. **brawny** strong.

bray *v*. to make the cry of a donkey (**braying, brayed**). *n*. **bray** the sound a donkey makes.

brazen *adj*. 1. made of brass. 2. impudent.

breach *n*. a broken gap or opening, a break.

bread *n*. food made from flour and baked.

breadth *n*. width, or the side-to-side measurement.

break *v*. 1. to split into pieces, to destroy. 2. to soften, as *to break a fall*. 3. not to carry out, as *to break a promise*. 4. to set up afresh, as *to break a record*. 5. to interrupt, as *to break into someone's conversation* (**breaking, broke, broken**). *n*. **break** 1. a split, a gap. 2. an interruption.

break of day dawn.

to break down 1. to destroy. 2. to give way.

to break in to tame, as *to break in a wild horse*.

to break into to enter, to burgle.

to break loose to escape from captivity.

to break off to end suddenly.

to break out 1. to force a way out. 2. to spread, as *a rash breaks out on someone's body*.

breakage *n*. 1. breaking. 2. damage caused by breaking.

breakdown *n*. a failure, as *the breakdown of a car*.

breakfast *n*. the first meal of the day.

breast *n*. the front part of the body, between the neck and the stomach, the bosom.

breath (*pron*. breth) *n*. air which we breathe in and out.

under your breath very quietly.

breathe (*pron*. breeTH) *v*. 1. to draw air in and out of your lungs. 2. to blow softly, as *to breathe on a mirror*.

to breathe freely to feel free from danger.

breeches (*pron*. brich'iz) *n. pl.* short trousers fastened below the knee.

breed *v*. 1. to give birth to, or to rear, young ones. 2. to produce, as *dirt breeds disease* (**breeding, bred**). *adj.* **well-bred** well brought up.

breeze *n*. a gentle wind. *adj.* **breezy**.

brew *v*. 1. to make a drink by boiling. 2. to gather together, as *a storm brews*.

brewery *n*. a place where beer is made.

bribe *v*. to offer a gift to someone, hoping for a favour in return. *n*. **bribery** offering a bribe.

brick *n*. a block of clay burnt hard for building.

bricklayer *n*. a man who builds walls, etc., with bricks.

bridal *adj.* belonging to a bride.

bride *n*. a woman on her wedding day.

bridegroom *n*. a man on his wedding day.

bridesmaid *n*. an unmarried woman who attends a bride.

bridge *n*. 1. a passageway across a river or valley. 2. the captain's platform over a ship's deck. 3. a card game like whist.

bridle *n*. the part of a horse's harness which fits over its head.

brief *adj.* short.

in brief in a few words.

brigade *n*. 1. a unit of an army consisting of two or more regiments. 2. an organized body, as *the Boy's Brigade*.

brigand *n*. one of a gang of bandits.

bright *adj.* 1. shining. 2. clever, as *Pat is a bright girl*. *n*. **brightness**.

brilliance *n*. sparkle, dazzle.

brilliant *adj.* very bright, dazzling.

brim *n*. 1. the rim of a cup or bowl. 2. the edge of a hat. *adj.* **brimful** full to the brim.

bring *v*. to fetch, to bring towards you (**bringing, brought**).

to bring about to cause to happen, as *to bring about a change of plan*.

to bring off to carry out successfully, as *to bring off a business deal*.

to bring up to rear, to feed and clothe, as *to bring up a family*.

brink *n*. the edge of a cliff, river, or lake.

brisk *adj.* lively, very active.

bristle *n*. a short stiff hair. *v*. **bristle** to show defiance, as *the dog began to bristle with rage*.

brittle *adj.* easily broken, as *glass is brittle*.

broad *adj.* 1. wide. 2. vast, as *the broad plains*.

broad daylight in full daylight.

broad hint a plain suggestion.

broad-minded understanding and tolerant of the opinions and actions of others.

as broad as it is long the arguments for and against are equal.

broadcast v. 1. to spread news or a rumour. 2. to send out news or entertainment by radio.

broaden v. 1. to grow wider. 2. to make wider, as *travel broadens your mind*.

broadside n. the firing of guns from all along one side of a ship.

brogue n. a way of speaking, as *an Irish brogue*.

broke, broken past of **break**.

bronco n. a wild or half-tamed American horse (*pl.* **broncos**).

bronze n. an alloy of copper and tin.

brooch n. an ornamental clasp with a pin.

brood n. a number of young birds hatched at one sitting. v, **brood** to think over something in a sullen way. *adj.* **broody** 1. wanting to hatch eggs, as *a broody hen*. 2 sullen.

brook n. a small stream of water, a rivulet.

broom n. 1. a sweeping-brush with a long handle. 2. a yellow-flowered shrub.

broth n. a thin soup.

brother n. a man or boy who has the same father and mother as another person.

brotherhood n. a group of men in a society.

brother-in-law n. the brother of a husband or a wife, or a sister's husband (*pl.* **brothers-in-law**).

brought past of **bring**.

brow n. 1. the forehead. 2. the top of a hill.

brown n. the colour of cocoa, chocolate, or earth.

brownie n. 1. a good-natured elf. 2. a junior Girl Guide.

bruise n. a mark on the skin caused by a knock.

brush n. 1. bristles, hairs, or feathers, fastened to a handle, for sweeping or painting. v. **brush** 1. to clean or paint with a brush. 2. to touch lightly, as *to brush past someone*.

to brush up to learn again something that was half-forgotten, as *to brush up your arithmetic*.

brutal *adj.* like a wild beast, cruel.

brute n. a wild beast, a savage.

bubble n. 1. a little ball of air, steam, or gas, rising in a liquid. 2. a thin ball-shaped film of liquid, filled with air, as *a soap bubble*. v. **bubble** to rise in bubbles.

buccaneer n. a pirate.

buck n. 1. the male of certain animals, such as a deer or rabbit, the female being *the doe*. 2. a sudden leap upwards. v. **buck** to leap up.

to buck up 1. to be quick. 2. to cheer up.

bucket n. a metal or wooden container for water.

buckle n. a metal clasp to fasten a strap.

to buckle to to set to work briskly.

bud n. a young growth from a stem which may become a leaf or a flower. v. **bud** to sprout (**budding, budded**).

to nip in the bud to tackle a problem while it is still small.

Buddha n. the founder of the Buddhist religion in India.

budgerigar (*pron.* buj'e.ree.gar) n. (often called **budgie** for short) a small pet bird.

budget n. a plan or forecast of how money is to be spent in the future.

buffalo n. a wild ox, the American bison (*pl.* **buffaloes** or **buffalo**).

buffer n. a shock-absorber, such as that fitted to a railway carriage.

bug n. a small, flat, crawling insect.

bugle n. a short, brass, wind instrument.

build v. to make something, as a house or a nest, by putting materials together (**building, built**) n. **builder** a man who makes buildings.

building n. a brick or stone construction made by men.

built past of **build**.

bulb n. 1. a plant like an onion or tulip which develops roots and a stem. 2. the glass of an electric lamp.

bulge v. to swell out or curve outwards (**bulging, bulged**). n. **bulge** a swelling.

bulk n. 1. a large size, as *the bulk of this parcel makes it awkward to carry*. 2. the greater part, as *the bulk of the farmer's hay was cut*.

bull n. 1. the male of cattle and other large animals (*fem.* **cow**). 2. the centre spot of a target, often called *the bull's eye*.

like a bull in a china shop clumsy and awkward.

to take the bull by the horns to attack boldly.

bulldog *n.* a sturdy dog once used in fighting bulls.

bullet *n.* a small piece of metal fired from a rifle or revolver.

bully *n.* someone who tries to get his way over others by threats and blustering (*pl.* **bullies**). *v.* **bully** to menace and threaten (**bullying, bullied**).

bulrush *n.* a large water-rush.

bulwark *n.* 1. a defensive wall. 2. a ship's side above the deck.

bump *n.* 1. a dull, heavy thump. 2. a collision.

bumper *n.* 1. a metal bar to protect a car from bumps. 2. a glass or cup filled to the brim. *adj.* **bumper** very large, as *a bumper harvest*.

bun *n.* a small soft round cake.

bunch *n.* a cluster of things of the same kind, as *a bunch of grapes* or *a bunch of keys*.

bundle *n.* 1. a number of things tied together loosely. 2. a shapeless parcel.

bungalow *n.* a house of one storey.

bungle *v.* to fail to do something well, through clumsiness or lack of skill. *n.* **bungler**.

bunk *n.* a sleeping-berth in a railway-carriage or a ship's cabin.

buoy *n.* a floating anchored mark, used at sea.

buoyant *adj.* 1. able to float. 2. (of a person) of a light, cheerful nature.

burden *n.* a heavy load. *v.* **burden** to weigh down.

bureau (*pron.* byoo'roh) *n.* 1. a writing-table. 2. an office, as *a travel bureau*.

burglar *n.* someone who breaks into a house to steal. *n.* **burglary** house-breaking (*pl.* **burglaries**).

burial (*pron.* ber'i.al) *n.* 1. laying a body in a grave or in the sea. 2. hiding in the ground, as *the burial of a bone by a dog*.

buried *past* of **bury**.

burn *v.* 1. to destroy by fire or acid. 2. to scorch or heat, as *the sun burns my face*.

3. to be aroused, as *to burn with anger* (**burning, burned** or **burnt**).

burned, burnt *past* of **burn**.

burrow *n.* a hole in the ground made by an animal for shelter. *v.* **burrow** to make a passage in the ground.

burst *v.* 1. to blow up, to fly into pieces. 2. to show sudden feeling, as *he burst into tears* (**bursting, burst**). *n.* **burst** a sudden explosion.

bury *v.* 1. to place a dead body in the earth or sea. 2. to hide from sight (**he buries, burying, buried**). See **burial**.

bus *n.* a large motor-vehicle for paying passengers (*pl.* **buses**).

bush *n.* 1. a large shrub. 2. uncultivated land, as *the Australian bush*.

to beat about the bush to talk around a subject and not come to the point.

bushel *n.* a measure of corn and dry goods.

bushman *n.* a primitive black man.

bushranger *n.* an Australian robber of olden days.

business (*pron.* biz'nes) *n.* 1. trade, occupation, as *he has a grocer's business*. 2. duty, as *that is not your business*.

bust *n.* 1. a carving or mould of a person's head and shoulders. 2. the upper part of a person's body.

busy (*pron.* biz'i) *adj.* 1. very active, as *a busy town*. 2. fully occupied, as *I am too busy to see Mr Jones* (*comparative* **busier,** *superlative* **busiest**).

but *conj.* although, as *I will go but I do not want to*. *prep.* **but** except, as *all but John were there*.

butcher *n.* 1. a man who kills cattle for food. 2. a man who sells meat.

butler *n.* a man-servant in charge of the wines and silver plate in a house.

butter *n.* solid fat obtained by churning cream.

buttercup *n.* a yellow wild flower.

butterfingered *adj.* said of someone who misses a catch.

butterfly *n.* a brightly coloured insect which, unlike a moth, has club-shaped feelers and large, upstanding wings (*pl.* **butterflies**).

buttermilk *n.* the sour liquid left in a churn after butter is made.

button *n.* 1. a disk of bone, glass, etc., to be sewn on to clothes. 2. any small knob, as *the push-button of an electric bell*. *v.* **button** to fasten clothes with buttons.

buy *v.* to obtain something in exchange for money (**he buys, buying, bought**). *n.* **buyer**.

buzz *n.* the hum of a bee or fly.

by *prep.* 1. at the side of, as *the house by the big tree*. 2. showing the author or the cause, as *this book is by Charles Dickens*. 3. not later than, as *by next week*. 4. in or on, as *she went by bus*.

bye *n.* (in cricket) a run obtained without the batsman striking the ball, although neither a 'wide' nor a 'no-ball'.

C

cab *n.* 1. a carriage for hire. 2. the driver's shelter on a railway engine.

cabbage *n.* a round, green vegetable.

cabin *n.* 1. a hut. 2. a small room in a ship.

cabinet *n.* 1. a wooden case with drawers. 2. a committee of heads of government departments which advises the Prime Minister.

cable *n.* 1. a strong rope or chain. 2. a bundle of rubber-covered wires for carrying electricity. 3. a telegraph line under the sea. *v.* **cable** to send a message by cable.

caboose *n.* 1. a kitchen on a ship's deck. 2. a railway workers' van at the end of an American or Canadian freight train.

cackle *n.* the noise made by a hen or goose. *v.* **cackle** to cluck like a hen (**cackling**).

cactus *n.* a prickly desert plant (*pl.* **cacti**).

cadet *n.* a young man training to be an officer.

café (*pron.* ka'fay) *n.* a place for a light meal.

cafeteria *n.* a restaurant where customers serve themselves.

cage *n.* a box with bars to hold birds or animals. *v.* **cage** to imprison.

cake *n.* 1. a cooked mixture of flour, butter, and sugar. 2. a mixture of foods cooked in a flat lump, as *a fish-cake*. 3. a small lump, as *a cake of mud*.

calamity *n.* misfortune, disaster, as *a shipwreck is a calamity* (*pl.* **calamities**).

calculate *v.* 1. to reckon, using numbers. 2. to guess, as *Tom calculates he will soon be home* (**calculating**). *n.* **calculation** reckoning.

calendar *n.* a list of days, weeks, and months.

calf (*pron.* kahf) *n.* a young cow, elephant, whale, etc. (*pl.* **calves** *pron.* kahvz).

caliph (*pron.* kay'lif) *n.* an Eastern ruler.

call *v.* 1. to cry out, as *to call for help*. 2. to name, as *we call him Sandy*. 3. to summon, as *the king will call his advisers*. 4. to make a short visit, as *we will call at the grocer's*. 5. to telephone, as *let us call Mary from the phone-box*. *n.* **call** 1. a shout. 2. a summons. 3. a short visit. 4. a telephone message or conversation.

to call off to cancel.

to call out to summon, as *to call out the fire brigade*.

to call to mind to remember.

calm *adj.* 1. still, windless, as *a calm sea*. 2. quiet, unexcited, as *he kept calm after the accident*. *v.* **calm** to make quiet. *n.* **calmness** stillness, quietness.

to calm down 1. to become quiet. 2. to quieten.

came *past* of **come**.

camel *n.* an Eastern animal with one or two humps.

camera *n.* a kind of box with sensitive film for taking photographs.

camp *n.* 1. a group of tents or huts. 2. an army training centre. *v.* **camp** to live in tents.

campaign (*pron.* kam.payn') *n.* a series of operations by an army. *v.* **campaign** to take part in warfare.

can *v.* 1. to be able to, as *he can do it if he tries* (**could**). 2. to preserve food in tins (**canning, canned**). *n.* **can** a metal container. *adj.* **canned** sealed in a can.

canal *n.* a man-made waterway for ships or barges.

canary (*pron.* kan.ayr'i) *n.* a yellow songbird (*pl.* **canaries**).

cancel *v.* 1. to cross out, as *to cancel a postage-stamp by a date-mark*. 2. to do away with, to call off, as *Jim will cancel the order for a camera* (**cancelling, cancelled**). *n.* **cancellation** 1. crossing out. 2. doing away with.

candid *adj.* frank, sincere, honest, as *give me your candid opinion of this picture*.

candidate *n.* someone who applies for election to a post.

candle *n.* a stick of wax or tallow with a wick in it. *n.* **candlestick** a candle holder.

candy *n.* a sweet made of sugar.

cane *n.* a thin hollow stick from a raspberry, sugar, or bamboo plant. *v.* **cane** to strike with a cane (**caning, caned**).

canine *adj.* connected with dogs; dog-like.

canine teeth the two pointed teeth in each jaw.

canned *adj.* sealed in a can. See **can**.

cannibal *n.* a savage who eats people. *n.* **cannibalism**.

cannon *n.* a large gun which fires iron balls.

cannot (**can** and **not**) not able to.

canny *adj.* sly, cautious, thrifty.

canoe *n.* a very light boat driven by paddles.

canon *n.* a cathedral clergyman.

can't *v.* short for **cannot**.

canteen *n.* 1. a dining-room in a camp or factory. 2. a case of cutlery.

canter *n.* a gentle gallop.

canvas *n.* strong, coarse cloth used for tents or sails.

under canvas 1. living in tents. 2. (of a boat) under sail.

canyon *n.* a deep, narrow river valley.

cap *n.* 1. a soft hat with a peak worn by men and boys. 2. a lid, as *the cap of a bottle*. 3. a round piece of paper holding explosive for a toy pistol. *v.* **cap** to do better than someone else, as *Bob caps Sam's score at cricket by ten runs* (**capping, capped**).

a feather in your cap something to be proud of.

the cap fits him the remark applies to him.

capable (*pron.* kay'pa.bl) *adj.* able to do things, skilful, as *Mary is a capable cook*. *adv.* **capably** skilfully.

capacity (*pron.* ka.pas'i.ti) *n.* 1. amount of space, as *the capacity of a box*. 2. power to do things, as *he is a man of capacity*. 3. in the position of, as *to act in the capacity of captain*.

cape *n.* 1. a short cloak. 2. a head of land running into the sea, as *the Cape of Good Hope*.

capital *n.* 1. a chief city. 2. a large letter. 3. money put into a bank or business. *adj.* **capital** 1. chief. 2. excellent, as *it was capital fun*.

capitulate *v.* to surrender, to yield (**capitulating, capitulated**). *n.* **capitulation** surrender.

capsize *v.* to overturn, as *the boat will capsize in this rough sea* (**capsizing, capsized**).

capsule *n.* 1. a small container usually made of gelatine and containing medicine. 2. the cabin of a space-craft.

captain *n.* 1. a man in command of a ship. 2. an army officer in command of a company. 3. a leader of a group or sports team. *v.* **captain** to lead or command.

captive *n.* a prisoner. *n.* **captivity** imprisonment.

captor *n.* someone who takes a prisoner.

capture *v.* 1. to hold fast. 2. to make prisoner (**capturing, captured**).

car *n.* a vehicle or carriage on wheels.

caravan *n.* 1. a covered van to live in. 2. a band of travellers crossing a desert.

carbon *n.* the chemical in charred wood and soot.

carburettor (sometimes spelt **carburetter**) *n.* the part of an engine in which petrol and air meet to make an explosive mixture.

carcass (sometimes spelt **carcase**) *n.* the body of a dead animal.

card *n.* a piece of very stiff paper. *n. pl.* **cards** any game using playing-cards.

to lay your cards on the table to let people know your plans.

cardboard *n.* thick card used for making boxes.

cardinal *n.* one of the princes of the Roman Catholic Church. *adj.* **cardinal** of first importance.

care *n.* 1. worry, as *her face was full of care.* 2. attention, thought, as *his plans were made with care.* 3. caution, as *take care in crossing the road!* *v.* **care** to worry over something, as *David never cares!*

to care for to be fond of.

to take care to be watchful.

to take care of to look after.

career *n.* 1. a life's occupation, as *John will make the navy his career.* 2. a fast run, as *the hare fled in full career.* *v.* **career** to run at full speed.

carefree *adj.* without worries

careful *adj.* cautious. *adv.* **carefully.**

careless *adj.* thoughtless, without caution.

caress *v.* to stroke fondly.

caretaker *n.* someone in charge of a building.

cargo *n.* a ship's load (*pl.* **cargoes**).

caribou (*pron.* kar'i.boo) *n.* a North American reindeer (*pl.* **caribous** or **caribou**).

caricature *n.* a funny drawing or description of a person.

carnival *n.* merrymaking by a crowd of people.

carol *n.* a song of praise, a Christmas hymn. *v.* **carol** to sing carols (**carolling, carolled**).

carpenter *n.* a man who works with timber. *n.* **carpentry** working with timber.

carpet *n.* a thick fabric covering for floors or stairs. *v.* **carpet** to cover with a carpet.

carriage (*pron.* kar'ij) *n.* 1. a vehicle for carrying people. 2. a railway passenger car. 3. the way a person holds himself, as *Eileen has a very upright carriage.* 4. the cost of carrying goods, as *the parcel came carriage paid.*

carrier *n.* a person who carries goods, or a grid or basket on a bicycle for carrying things.

carrot *n.* a vegetable of which the long red root is eaten.

carry *v.* 1. to take something from one place to another. 2. to support, as *this beam can carry a heavy weight.* 3. to hold yourself, as *she carries herself with dignity.* 4. to reach across, as *his voice carries to the back of the hall* (**he carries, carrying, carried**).

carried away by full of enthusiasm for.

to carry on to continue.

to carry out to complete, as *to carry out a plan.*

cart *n.* a two-wheeled vehicle for heavy loads. *v.* **cart** to move goods by cart.

to put the cart before the horse to put things in the wrong order.

carton *n.* a cardboard box.

cartoon *n.* a funny drawing in a newspaper or magazine. *n.* **cartoonist** a drawer of cartoons.

cartridge *n.* a cardboard or metal tube holding explosive for use in a gun or rifle, without a bullet in *a blank cartridge*, and with a bullet in *a live cartridge.*

carve *v.* 1. to cut something into shape with a knife or chisel. 2. to cut meat into slices (**carving, carved**). *n.* **carving** sculpture in wood, ivory, etc.

case *n.* 1. a box, as *a case of jewellery*, or a glass-sided box for displaying goods in a shop, as *a show case.* 2. a problem, an event, as *Sherlock Holmes investigated a strange case.* 3. a trial in a court of law, as *the case of Brown versus Smith.* 4. a patient receiving medical aid, as *the doctor had many cases.*

in any case whatever happens.

in case if it should happen that, as *let us stay here in case he comes.*

cash *n.* money. *v.* **cash** to turn (a cheque, postal order, etc.) into money. *n.* **cashier** a person who takes charge of money.

cask *n.* a barrel for holding liquids.

casket *n.* 1. a small box for jewels. 2. (in **North America**) a coffin.

cast *v.* 1. to throw, as *to cast a fishing-line.* 2. to mould or shape, as *to cast iron.* 3. to give a part in a play, as *Tom was cast for the part of Hamlet.* 4. to search round for (**casting, cast**). *n.* **cast** 1. a throw. 2. a squint of the eye. 3. a moulding. 4. the performers of a play. 5. a colour tint. *n.* **casting** a moulding.

cast down sad.

castaway *n.* a shipwrecked person.

caste (*pron.* kast) *n.* a class of people in India.

castle *n.* 1. a fort. 2. a chess piece.

casual *adj.* 1. by chance, as *a casual meeting*. 2. easygoing, careless, as *Jean has a very casual manner*. 3. happening now and then, not continuous, as *Bill Brown obtained casual work as a labourer*. *adv.* **casually**.

casualty *n.* 1. an accident. 2. a sick or injured person (*pl.* **casualties**).

cat *n.* a small, furry domestic animal. *adj.* **catty** spiteful. *n.* **cat-call** a shrill cry.

to see which way the cat jumps to watch how things turn out before deciding.

catalogue (*pron.* kat'a.log) *n.* a list of articles, books, names, etc.

catapult *n.* 1. an elastic string on a forked stick, or a war-machine of olden days, for flinging stones. 2. a machine for hurling aeroplanes off the deck of a ship. *v.* **catapult** to fling.

catastrophe (*pron.* kat.as'trof.i) *n.* a disaster.

catch *v.* 1. to seize, to capture. 2. to be in time for, as *to catch a bus* (**catching, caught**). *n.* **catch** 1. a capture. 2. a fastening for a door or window. 3. a trick, as *there is a catch in the question*. **to catch up** to draw level with.

catchword *n.* a slogan, a password.

catechism (*pron.* kat'e.kiz.m) *n.* teaching by question and answer, especially in religion.

cater *v.* to supply, to provide. *n.* **caterer** a supplier, especially of foodstuffs.

caterpillar *n.* the grub, or larva, of a butterfly or moth.

caterpillar tractor a tractor moved by an endless belt round its wheels.

catgut *n.* elastic string made from part of a sheep's stomach.

cathedral *n.* a principal church in which is the throne of a bishop.

catholic *adj.* general, universal. *n.* **Catholic** a member of the Roman Catholic Church.

cattle *n. pl.* bulls, cows, oxen and their young.

caught *past* of **catch**.

cauliflower *n.* a kind of cabbage with a white flower-like centre.

cause *n.* something which leads to an effect, as *the sun is the cause of the ice melting*. 2. a reason, as *you have no cause to object*. *v.* **cause** to be responsible for something happening.

caution *n.* 1. care, alertness to danger. 2. a warning. *v.* **caution** to warn.

cautious *adj.* careful, mindful of danger.

cavalry *n.* horse-soldiers.

cave *n.* a hole in a rock or hillside.

to cave in to give way, to collapse.

cease *v.* to stop, to come to an end, as *talking must cease when the lesson begins* (**ceasing, ceased**). *adj.* **ceaseless** continuous.

ceiling *n.* 1. the upper lining of a room. 2. the greatest height an aeroplane can fly.

celebrate *v.* to go through a ceremony in honour of some special occasion, as *to celebrate a wedding* (**celebrating, celebrated**). *adj.* **celebrated** famous. *n.* **celebration**.

celebrity *n.* a famous person (*pl.* **celebrities**).

celery *n.* a vegetable with long white stalks.

cell *n.* 1. a small room in a prison or a monastery. 2. one of the spaces in a honeycomb. 3. part of an electric battery, an *electric cell*.

cellar *n.* an underground storeroom.

cello (*pron.* chel'oh) *n.* a stringed instrument larger than a violin, but not as large as a double bass (*pl.* **cellos**).

cellophane *n.* a transparent material used for wrapping.

celluloid *n.* a material used in films, combs, etc.

cement *n.* a substance used in making hard mortar and concrete.

cemetery *n.* a burial ground (*pl.* **cemeteries**).

census *n.* an official count of the people.

cent *n.* a hundredth part of a dollar.

centenary (*pron.* sen.tee'ner.i) *n.* a celebration of something that happened a hundred years ago (*pl.* **centenaries**)

centigrade *adj.* referring to a scale, used in certain thermometers, having a hundred degrees (the Celsius scale).

centimetre *n.* the hundredth part of a metre in the metric system of measurement.

centipede *n.* an insect with a great many legs.

central *adj.* at the centre.

central heating a method of heating a building by hot-water pipes from a boiler.

centre *n.* 1. the middle point of anything. 2. an important or special place.

centre-forward (in games) the player in the centre of the line of forwards.

centurion *n.* in Roman times, the commander of a hundred soldiers.

century *n.* 1. a hundred years. 2. (in cricket) a hundred runs (*pl.* **centuries**).

cereal *n.* a grain, such as wheat, used as food.

ceremonial *adj.* with pomp and dignity.

ceremony *n.* a solemn service as *a funeral service* or *a wedding ceremony* (*pl.* **ceremonies**).

certain *adj.* 1. sure, without doubt. 2. particular, as *a certain person.*

certificate *n.* a signed statement about something, as *a doctor's certificate.*

certify *v.* to sign a statement that something is true (**certifies, certifying, certified**).

chaff *n.* 1. husks of corn. 2. chopped hay or straw for cattle. 3. teasing. *v.* **chaff** to tease in a good-natured way.

chain *n.* 1. a series of rings or links joined together. 2. a unit of length equal to 22 yards (about 20 metres).

chain store one of a group of shops owned by one firm.

chair *n.* a movable seat with a back, for one.

chairman *n.* the person who takes charge of a meeting; the head of a committee.

chalet (*pron.* shal'ay) *n.* a Swiss summer hut or a similar holiday hut.

chalk *n.* limestone, a substance for writing on blackboards. *v.* **chalk** to mark with chalk.

challenge *v.* to invite someone to a contest. *n.* **challenge** 1. an invitation to a contest. 2. a sentry's cry of '*Who goes there?*'

chamber *n.* 1. a room. 2. a small hall where committees meet.

chamois (*pron.* sham'wa) *n.* a mountain antelope.

champion *n.* someone who is better than others at sport, a winner. *v.* **champion** to support someone and fight for him. *n.* **championship.**

chance *n.* luck, an unexpected event, as *to find something by chance. v.* **chance** to risk, as *I will chance it* (**chancing, chanced**).

to chance upon to find unexpectedly.

to stand a good chance to expect fairly confidently.

chancellor *n.* a minister of state.

Chancellor of the Exchequer the British Finance Minister.

change *v.* 1. to alter. 2. to exchange, as *to change places* (**changing, changed**) *n.* **change** 1. an alteration. 2. the money you receive back when you pay more than the cost of what you buy. 3. small coins. *adj.* **changeable** variable. *adj.* **changeless** unchanging.

to change your mind to alter a decision.

channel *n.* 1. the bed of a stream or river. 2. a narrow stretch of sea. 3. a groove or furrow.

chant *v.* 1. to sing solemn music. 2. to recite in a sing-song voice. *n.* **chant** a solemn song.

chaos (*pron.* kay'os) *n.* confusion, complete disorder. *adj.* **chaotic** in utter confusion.

chapel *n.* a small church.

chaplain *n.* a clergyman attached to a college, ship, regiment, etc.

chapter *n.* a part of a book or story.

char *v.* to scorch (**charring, charred**).

character *n.* 1. the nature of a person or thing which makes it stand out from others, as *Ruth has a lovable character.* 2. a reputation, as *Brian has a good character.* 3. a person in a story or play.

charade (*pron.* sha.rahd') *n.* a game of guessing a word after seeing little plays representing each syllable, and one representing the whole word.

charcoal *n.* black charred wood.

charge v. 1. to attack. 2. to ask a price for something. 3. to accuse someone, as I charge you with theft. 4. to put electricity into an electric cell or battery (**charging, charged**). n. **charge** 1. an attack. 2. a price. 3. blame. 4. explosive put in a gun or other firearm.
in charge of responsible for.
to take charge of to look after.

chariot n. a two-wheeled cart, drawn by horses, used in Roman times.

charioteer n. a chariot driver.

charitable adj. generous, kindly.

charity n. generous giving, kindliness.

charm n. 1. a magic sign or spell. 2. attractiveness, making people like you. v. **charm** to attract people to you.

charming adj. pleasing, attractive.

chart n. 1. a map used by sailors. 2. a table of facts and information. v. **chart** 1. to survey unknown seas. 2. to mark on a chart.

charter n. a legal document giving certain rights or privileges. v. **charter** to hire, as to charter a bus.

charwoman n. a woman cleaner.

chase v. to run or ride after (**chasing, chased**). n. **chase** a hunt.
wild goose chase a foolish run after something that cannot be reached.

chastise v. to punish, to beat, to reprove (**chastising, chastised**). n. **chastisement** punishment.

chat v. to talk in a free and easy way (**chatting, chatted**).

chauffeur (pron. shoh'fer) n. a man paid to drive a motor-car.

cheap adj. 1. low in price. 2. of poor value. n. **cheapness**.

cheat v. 1. to deceive or defraud someone. 2. to break the rules of a game in an underhand way, in order to win.

check v. 1. to stop or slow down, as to check a horse or check an advancing enemy. 2. to examine, as to check a money account. 3. (in the game of chess) to threaten a king. n. **check** 1. a halt or slowing-down. 2. an examination. 3. (in chess) a threat to a king. 4. a cloakroom ticket. 5. a restaurant bill. 6. (in North America) an order for money, a cheque.
to check up to examine.

checkmate n. the winning move in a game of chess.

cheek n. 1. the side of the face. 2. impudence.

cheer n. 1. a shout of joy. 2. high spirits, gaiety, as the party was full of good cheer. v. **cheer** 1. to shout encouragement and applause. 2. to comfort someone. adj. **cheery** happy.
to cheer up 1. to be happier. 2. to comfort.

cheese n. food made from curdled milk.

chef (pron. shef) n. a head cook.

chemical adj. concerning chemistry. n. **chemical** a substance used in chemistry.

chemist n. 1. a man who studies chemistry. 2. a man who sells medicines, a druggist.

chemistry n. the study of how substances act on one another to form new substances.

cheque n. a written order to a bank to pay money to someone (in North America a check).

chequers (in North America **checkers**) n. a game played with twelve pieces on each side of a chequer-board; draughts.

cherry n. 1. a tree with white or pink blossom. 2. the stony fruit of this tree.

chess n. a game played with sixteen pieces on each side of a board of sixty-four squares.

chest n. 1. a large strong box. 2. the upper part of the body between the neck and the stomach. n. **chest of drawers** a piece of furniture fitted with sliding drawers.
to get something off your chest to speak out about something that worries you.

chestnut n. 1. a tree with nuts in prickly husks. 2. a reddish-brown colour.

chew v. to bite food while turning it over and over in your mouth. n. **chewing-gum** gum from a South American tree, sweetened and flavoured.

chick, chicken n. a young bird or domestic fowl. adj. **chicken-hearted** cowardly.

chickadee n. a small North American bird.

chief n. the head, a leader (pl. **chiefs**). adj. **chief** the most important, or main, as wheat is one of the chief crops of Canada.

chieftain n. the head of a clan.

chilblain n. a painful swelling on a finger or toe due to the cold.

child n. a young boy or girl (pl. **children**).

chill n. 1. coldness. 2. a cold, with shivering. adj. **chilly** cold.

chime v. (of bells) to ring out.

chimney n. a passage for the escape of smoke from a fire (pl. **chimneys**).

chimpanzee n. an African ape.

chin n. part of the face below the mouth.

chip v. to break small pieces off something (**chipping, chipped**). n. **chip** 1. a piece chipped off. 2. a small slice of fried potato.

chipmuck or **chipmunk** n. a striped North American ground squirrel.

chirp n. the sharp squeak of some birds and insects.

chisel n. a steel tool for carving wood and stone. v. **chisel** to cut with a chisel (**chiselling, chiselled**).

chivalry (pron. shiv'al.ri) n. gentlemanly conduct as shown by knights of the Middle Ages. adj. **chivalrous**.

chocolate n. a sweet or drink made from cocoa.

choice n. 1. choosing something. 2. the thing chosen, as this book is my choice. adj. **choice** of excellent quality, as choice plums.

choir n. 1. a group of singers. 2. the part of a church in which the choir sings.

choke v. 1. to suffocate. 2. to block, as to choke a pipe with grease (**choking, choked**).

choose v. 1. to pick, as to choose an apple. 2. to do what you prefer, as I choose to stay here (**choosing, chose, chosen**).

chop v. to cut with sharp blows, as to chop firewood (**chopping, chopped**). n. **chop** 1. a sharp blow. 2. a small piece of meat with a bone.

chopsticks n. pl. two thin sticks used by the Chinese to carry food to the mouth.

choral (pron. kaw'ral) adj. concerning a choir.

chord (pron. kord) n. (in music) several notes played together to make a tuneful sound.

chorus n. 1. a group of people singing or reciting together. 2. a song, or part of a song, sung by everyone together.

chose, chosen past of **choose**.

christen v. to baptize someone in Christ's name.

christening n. the ceremony of baptizing a child.

Christian n. a follower of Jesus Christ, and a believer in the religion founded by him. n. **Christian name** your first name, given when you are christened.

Christianity n. the religion of Jesus Christ.

Christmas n. the yearly festival held each December 25th to honour the birth of Christ.

chromium n. a silvery metal which does not tarnish.

chronological adj. in order of time, as the dates of the battles are written in chronological order.

chrysalis (pron. kris'a.lis) n. the form which an insect takes when changing from a grub to the full-grown insect, like the brown cocoon of the butterfly.

chuckle n. a quiet laugh to yourself.

chunk n. a thick piece of anything.

church n. 1. a building used for worship. 2. all the members of a religious group, as the Church of England.

churchwarden n. 1. an officer of a church who helps in its organization. 2. a very long clay pipe.

churchyard n. a graveyard round a church.

churlish adj. surly, ill-mannered.

churn n. 1. a wooden tub in which cream is made into butter. 2. a large milk can. v. **churn** to make butter from cream.

chutney n. a pickle.

cider n. fermented apple-juice, for drinking.

cigar n. rolled tobacco leaves, for smoking.

cigarette n. a roll of shredded tobacco, wrapped in paper for smoking.

cinder *n.* a half-burned piece of coal or coke left from a fire.

cinema *n.* a building where films are shown to an audience.

circle *n.* 1. a ring. 2. a balcony in a theatre or cinema. *v.* **circle** to move round in a circle.

circuit (*pron.* sir'kit) *n.* 1. a journey round, as *the runners made a circuit of the sports arena.* 2. electrical wiring which makes current go a certain way.

circular *adj.* round, like a circle. *n.* **circular** a notice sent round to a number of people.

circulation *n.* 1. moving round. 2. the number of copies of a newspaper or magazine sold at each issue.

circumference *n.* the distance round, especially of a circle.

circumstance *n.* anything connected with an event, as *to consider every circumstance of a crime.*

in the circumstances taking everything into account.

circus *n.* a building or large tent for shows by clowns, acrobats, and animals (*pl.* **circuses**).

cistern *n.* a large tank used for storing water.

citizen *n.* 1. someone living in a city. 2. a member of a nation, as *he is a citizen of France. n.* **citizenship.**

city *n.* a large town having a cathedral (*pl.* **cities**).

civic *adj.* concerning a town or city.

civil *adj.* 1. concerning a town. 2. polite, as *he gave a civil answer to my question.* **Civil Service** the public services of a nation.

civil war war between people of the same country.

civilian *n.* an ordinary man who is not a soldier, sailor, or airman.

civility *n.* politeness.

civilize *v.* to educate and save from barbarism. *adj.* **civilized** cultured and refined. *n.* **civilization** all the civilized countries.

clad *past* of **clothe.**

claim *v.* to demand your right to something. *n.* **claim** a demand, a statement of your rights.

clam *n.* a shell-fish which is difficult to open.

clan *n.* a group of families under a chief.

clannish *adj.* closely united like the members of a clan.

clang *n.* a deep, ringing sound like metal when hit.

clank *n.* a sharp sound as when a heavy chain is rattled.

clap *v.* to applaud with your hands (**clapping, clapped**). *n.* **clap** 1. a hand-slap. 2. a loud sound, as *a clap of thunder.*

clash *n.* 1. a loud noise. 2. a disagreement, as *there was a clash of opinion between the players about the rules. v.* **clash** 1. to bang noisily. 2. to disagree.

clasp *n.* 1. a fastening, a brooch. 2. an embrace, a hug. *v.* **clasp** 1. to fasten. 2. to embrace.

class *n.* 1. a group of pupils or students taught together. 2. a grade in travelling by train or ship, as *we travelled first class.*

classic *n.* a book or work of art of the highest quality.

clatter *n.* to make sharp noisy sounds.

clause *n.* 1. a part of a sentence. 2. a paragraph or section of a document.

claw *n.* 1. the hooked nail of an animal or bird. 2. the pincer of a crab or lobster. *v.* **claw** to tear at.

clay *n.* a smooth heavy earth used for making bricks, pottery, etc. *adj.* **clayey.**

clean *adj.* 1. free from dirt, as *a clean frock.* 2. neat, as *Dick made a clean job of it.* 3. clear-cut, as *a clean edge. adv.* **clean** entirely, as *I had clean forgotten.*

cleanliness (*pron.* klen'li.nes) *n.* purity, freedom from dirt.

cleanse (*pron.* klenz) *v.* to clean.

clear *adj* bright, pure, distinct.

clear cut sharp.

clear-headed intelligent.

to clear up to clean out, to tidy.

clearness *n.* distinctness, brightness.

cleft *n.* a crack.

clench *v.* 1. to close tightly, as *to clench your teeth.* 2. to grasp firmly, as *to clench a stick.*

clergy *n. pl.* ministers of religion. *n.* **clergyman.**

clerical *adj.* concerning the clergy. 2. concerning office work, as *a clerical worker* (in an office).

clerk (*pron.* klark in Britain, and klurk in North America) *n.* 1. a worker in an office. 2. (in North America) an assistant in a shop or store.

clever *adj.* able, skilful. *n.* **cleverness**.

click *n.* a short sharp sound.

client *n.* a customer of a lawyer or businessman.

cliff *n.* a high steep rock or hillside.

climate *n.* the usual weather of a place. *adj.* **climatic** concerning weather, as *the climatic conditions were bad*.

climax *n.* the most interesting point, as *the climax of a story*.

climb *v.* to go up, to mount up, as *to climb a hill* or *the aeroplane climbs into the sky* (**climbing, climbed**).

to climb down to give way.

clinch *v.* 1. to fasten a nail by beating it down. 2. to settle a matter, as *to clinch a bargain*. 3. (in boxing) to hold an opponent.

cling *v.* to stick firmly (to) (**clinging, clung**).

clinic *n.* a building where medical treatment is given to out-patients.

clip *v.* 1. to trim with shears or scissors. 2. to fasten together, as *to clip loose papers* (**clipping, clipped**). *n.* **clip** 1. a trim. 2. a fastener, as *a hair-clip*.

clippers *n. pl.* shears, scissors.

cloak *n.* a sleeveless coat, a cape.

cloakroom *n.* a place for hanging hats and coats.

clock *n.* an instrument that shows the time.

anti-clockwise in the opposite direction to the movement of the hands of a clock.

clockwise in the same direction as a clock's hands.

clockwork *n.* a spring motor like a clock's.

clod *n.* a lump of earth.

clog *v.* to block up, as *to clog a drainpipe with grease* (**clogging, clogged**). *n.* **clog** a strong shoe with a wooden sole.

cloisters *n.* a covered walk in a college, convent, or cathedral.

close (1) (*pron.* klohs) *adj.* warm and stuffy, as *a close day*. *adv.* **close** 1. near, as *he came close to me*. 2. tightly, as *the mother held the baby close* (*comparative* **closer**, *superlative* **closest**).

close call or **close shave** a narrow escape.

close-fisted mean.

close (2) (*pron.* klohz) *v.* 1. to shut, as *to close a box*. 2. to end or come to an end, as *the day closes*. *n.* **close** the end.

clot *v.* to thicken and become stiff (**clotting, clotted**). *adj.* **clotted** very thick, as *clotted cream*. *n.* **clot** thickened fluid.

cloth *n.* woven material for clothes and covers.

clothe *v.* 1. to dress. 2. to cover, as *the valley was clothed in mist* (**clothing, clothed**).

clothes *n. pl.* dress, garments.

clothier *n.* someone who makes or sells clothes.

cloud *n.* 1. a mass of water vapour in the sky. 2. anything like a cloud, as a mass of smoke, insects, etc.

under a cloud in disgrace.

clover *n.* a meadow plant used as cattle-food.

clown *n.* a fool or jester, especially in a circus.

club *n.* 1. a short heavy stick, a cudgel. 2. a stick for striking a ball, as *a golf club*. 3. a group of people with the same hobby, as *a tennis club*. 4. one of the four suits of playing cards. *v.* **club** to beat with a club (**clubbing, clubbed**).

cluck *v.* to make a noise like a hen.

clue *n.* some small thing that helps to solve a mystery, like a finger-print or a footprint.

clump *n.* a group or cluster, as *a clump of trees*.

clumsy *adj.* 1. awkward in moving about. 2. badly made (*comparative* **clumsier**, *superlative* **clumsiest**) *n.* **clumsiness**.

clung *past* of **cling**.

clutch *v.* to brag, to seize hold. *n.* **clutch** 1. a snatch. 2. a cluster, as *a clutch of eggs*. 3. an arrangement in a motor car or automobile which lets the engine run

without moving the car (*pl.* **clutches**).
in someone's clutches in his power.

coach *n.* 1. a large four-wheeled carriage used in olden days. 2. a railway carriage. 3. a bus for tourists. 4. a sports trainer. *v.* **coach** to train.

coal *n.* a black mineral for burning.

coalfield *n.* an area rich in coal.

coal-mine an underground mine, for coal.

coarse *adj.* 1. rough, rude. 2. of poor quality. *n.* **coarseness** roughness.

coast *n.* the seashore. *v.* **coast** 1. to sail close by the shore. 2. to glide downhill on a machine.

the coast is clear the way is open, all is well.

coastguard *n.* a man who watches the coast for smugglers or wrecks, and who saves lives.

coat *n.* 1. a jacket or overcoat. 2. a covering, as *a coat of paint.*

coat of arms a badge on anything showing the owner and his rank.

coating *n.* a covering, a layer.

coax *v.* to persuade patiently with kind words.

cob *n.* 1. a large kind of hazel-nut. 2. a corncob or ear of maize. 3. a round loaf. 4. a pony. 5. a male swan (*fem.* **pen**).

cobbler *n.* a shoe-repairer.

cobweb *n.* a spider's web.

cock *n.* a male bird. *v.* **cock** to raise the hammer of a gun ready to fire it.

cock and bull story a tale hard to believe.

cockle *n.* a kind of shell-fish.

cockpit *n.* a place for the pilot in some aeroplanes.

cockroach *n.* a kind of beetle.

cocoa *n.* 1. a brown powder made from the seeds of the cacao or cocoa tree. 2. a hot drink made from the powder.

coconut *n.* 1. the large nut of the coco-palm. 2. the white kernel of the nut.

cocoon *n.* the silken case spun by some insect grubs, like the silkworm, in which they lie during the winter.

cod *n.* a sea-fish used for food (*pl.* **cod**).

code *n.* 1. a collection of rules, as *the highway code.* 2. a system of signs or

signals used for messages, as *the Morse code* or *a secret code.*

coffee *n.* 1. a brown powder made from the roasted seeds of the coffee plant. 2. a hot drink made from the powder.

coffin *n.* the wooden chest in which a dead body is buried.

cog *n.* a tooth on a gear wheel. *n.* **cogwheel** a gear-wheel.

coil *n.* wire, rope, or a pipe, wound in a spiral. *v.* **coil** to wind round.

coin *n.* a metal disk stamped, and used as money. *n.* **coinage** the various coins used by a country as money.

coincidence (*pron.* koh.in'si.dens) *n.* things happening by chance in the same way at the same time, as *it was a coincidence that I met Mrs Brown in the shop.*

coke *n.* the solid fuel left after gas and tar have been removed from coal at a gasworks.

cold *adj.* 1. without warmth, as *a cold wind.* 2. unfriendly, as *a cold look. n.* **cold** 1. lack of heat. 2. an illness of your head and chest.

to give the cold shoulder to to treat in an unfriendly way.

to throw cold water on to discourage.

cold-blooded *adj.* 1. deliberately cruel, as *a cold-blooded crime.* 2. having a body temperature the same as the surroundings, as *fish are cold-blooded.*

coldness *n* 1. lack of warmth. 2. unfriendliness.

collapse *v.* to break down, to fall to pieces.

collapsible *adj.* able to be broken into its parts or dismantled, as *a collapsible boat.*

collar *n.* something worn round the neck, as *a dog-collar. v.* **collar** (slang) to get hold of, to seize (**collaring, collared**).

collar-bone *n.* a bone above the shoulder-blade.

collect *v.* 1. to bring together, as *to collect strayed sheep.* 2. to meet, as *a number of dogs collect in the street.* 3. to gather together as a hobby, as *to collect stamps.*

to collect your thoughts to put your thoughts in order.

collection *n.* a group of things brought together.

collector *n.* someone who collects.

college *n.* 1. a school for higher learning. 2. a building which is part of a university.

collide *v.* 1. to clash, to dash together. 2. to meet and knock against someone.

collie *n.* a kind of sheepdog.

collier *n.* 1. a coal-miner. 2. a ship which carries coal.

colliery *n.* a coal-mine (*pl.* **collieries**).

collision *n.* a violent clash between persons or things.

colon *n.* a punctuation mark (:).

colonel (*pron.* ker'nel) *n.* an army officer who commands a regiment.

colonial *adj.* concerning a colony.

colonist *n.* a person who lives in a colony.

colonize *v.* to form a colony. 2. to settle persons in a colony. *n.* **colonization**.

colony *n.* 1. a group of people settling in a new land. 2. the settlement made by such people. 3. a group of people living among people of another nation, as *the Italian colony in London.* 4. a group of animals or plants of the same kind, living together, as *a colony of rats.*

colossal *adj.* huge, immense.

colour (in America spelled **color**) *n.* a hue, dye, tint, or paint. *v.* **colour** to dye, stain, or paint. *n. pl.* **the colours** the national flag, or a regimental standard. *adj.* **colour-blind** unable to tell one colour from another.

colourful *adj.* 1. full of colour. 2. bright, gay.

colouring *n.* 1. the way something is coloured. 2. a substance used to give colour.

colourless *adj.* 1. without colour. 2. dull, drab.

colt *n.* a young horse (*fem.* **filly**).

column *n.* 1. an upright pillar. 2. anything slender and upright, as *a column of figures, a column of newsprint,* or *a column of smoke.* 3. a body of soldiers in file.

comb *n.* 1. a strip of metal, celluloid, etc., fitted with teeth to smooth the hair or fix it in place. 2. a cock's crest. 3. a mass of wax cells made by bees in which they store honey. *v.* **comb** to dress hair with a comb.

combat *n.* a fight, a struggle. *v.* **combat** to fight, to struggle against (**combating, combated**).

combination *n.* a union or joining together.

combine (*pron.* kom.bīn') *v.* to join together, to unite.

combustion *n.* the process of burning.

come *v.* 1. to approach, to arrive. 2. to happen, as *come what may* (**coming, came, come**).

comedian *n.* a comic actor (*fem.* **comedienne**).

comedy *n.* a light amusing play (*pl.* **comedies**).

comet *n.* a starlike body in the sky with a long tail of light. Comets move round the sun like planets, but in the path of an ellipse.

comfort *n.* 1. anything that makes sorrow or trouble easier to bear. 2. ease and contentment. *v.* **comfort** 1. to ease someone's sorrow by kind words or actions. 2. to cheer someone.

comfortable *adj.* at ease, contented. *adj.* **comfortless** lacking comfort. *adv.* **comfortably**.

comic *adj.* funny, amusing, laughable. *n.* **comic** 1. a funny man. 2. an amusing paper.

comical *adj.* humorous, amusing. *adv.* **comically**.

coming (1) *present participle* of **come**.

coming (2) *adj.* approaching, future, as *a coming event.*

comma *n.* a punctuation mark (,).

command *n.* 1. an order. 2. authority over, as *the captain has command of the ship.* *v.* **command** 1. to order. 2. to have authority over. 3. to overlook, as *the watch-tower commands the valley.*

commander *n.* 1. a leader. 2. (in the navy) an officer between a lieutenant and a captain in rank. *n.* **commander-in-chief** the officer in command of a whole army or navy.

commandment *n.* 1. a command, a law. 2. one of the ten commandments of Moses in the Old Testament.

commence *v.* to begin (**commencing, commenced**).

commencement *n.* a beginning.

commendable *adj.* praise-worthy. *adv.* **commendably.**

comment (*pron.* kom'ent) *n.* a note or remark. *v.* **comment** to write a note or make a remark (about).

commentary (kom'ent.ari) *n.* a series of remarks or notes, as *the radio announcer gave a commentary on the match.*

commentator *n.* 1. a person who gives a commentary. 2. someone who describes or explains.

commerce *n.* trade, business, exchange of goods and money between countries.

commercial *adj.* concerning trade or business. *adv.* **commercially.**

commission *n.* 1. appointment as an officer, as *to receive a commission as an army officer.* 2. an errand or task given to someone to do. 3. money paid to a salesman in proportion to the amount of goods he sells, as *Mr Jones receives seven per cent commission on all he sells. v.* **commission** 1. to give a person authority to do something. 2. to make ready for use, as *to commission a ship.*

commissioner *n.* a government official with authority over a department or district.

commit *v.* 1. to do something, as *to commit a crime.* 2. to hand something over for safety, as *to commit a purse to someone's care.* 3. to carry out a solemn, deliberate, or difficult task, as *to commit a poem to memory* (**committing, committed**).

committee *n.* a group of people elected or appointed to carry out some special duties, as *a tennis club committee.*

commodity *n.* 1. something bought or sold. 2. any useful thing (*pl.* **commodities**).

commodore *n.* 1. a commander of a squadron of ships, ranking above a captain and below an admiral. 2. a high-ranking officer in the Royal Air Force. 3. the president of a yacht squadron.

common *adj.* 1. belonging to everyone, as *a common desire for happiness.* 2. frequent, usual, as *a common saying.* 3. public, as *the common law of the land.* 4. ordinary, as *common sense.* 5. low, vulgar, as *he is a common man. n.* **common** an area of public land, as *the village common. n. pl.* **commons** 1. ordinary people, as *the House of Commons,* the lower House of Parliament. 2. rations, as *they were on short commons.*

common noun a noun which refers to general things, as *table, town, pen.*

commonly *adv.* usually.

commonwealth *n.* a state in which the people govern themselves.

commotion *n.* confusion, a noisy disturbance.

communal *adj.* public, belonging to the people, as *communal land.*

communicate *v.* 1. to speak, write, or get in touch with, as *I will communicate with you while I am away.* 2. to connect with, as *this passage communicates with the kitchen.*

communication *n.* 1. speaking or writing to. 2. connection with. 3. a passage.

communion *n.* fellowship. *n.* **Communion** sharing in the wafer and wine of the Lord's Supper.

communism *n.* a belief that all property should be publicly owned, and the people should share equally all profits.

communist *n.* someone who believes in communism.

community *n.* 1. people of a district or town. 2. the general public, as *the whole community.* 3. a group of people living together, as *a community of nuns.* 4. a group of creatures living together, as *a community of ants* (**communities**).

compact (1) (*pron.* kom'pakt) *n.* 1. an agreement, a treaty. 2. a small case carried by ladies containing powder.

compact (2) (*pron.* kom.pakt') *adj.* compressed, packed tightly together. **compactness** compression.

companion *n.* 1. a friend. 2. a fellow-traveller on a journey. 3. one of a pair, as *the companion to a glove. n.* **companionship** friendship.

company *n.* 1. a gathering of people. 2. a group of soldiers led by a captain. 3. a ship's crew. 4. a firm, a group of people engaged in business. 5. companionship, as *I welcome your company* (*pl.* **companies**).

comparative *adj.* in part, as compared with something greater, as *this tree gives comparative shade* (but not complete shade). *n.* **comparative** (in grammar) applied to an adverb or adjective, means 'more' or 'to a greater degree', as *'quicker' is the comparative of 'quick'*. *adv.* **comparatively** partly, somewhat.

compare *v.* to set things side by side to see how far they are alike.
 beyond compare without an equal, very good.

comparison *n.* the comparing of things.
 by comparison, in comparison with as compared with.

compartment *n.* 1. a division, a section. 2. (in Britain) a division of a railway carriage.

compass *n.* 1. space or range, as *a voice of small compass*. 2. an instrument for finding the north. *n. pl.* **compasses** an instrument for drawing circles.

compassion *n.* pity, sympathy, mercy.

compel *v.* to force, to urge on by force (**compelling, compelled**).

compensate *v.* to pay for some loss or damage you have caused. 2. to make up for, as *Jack worked hard to compensate for time lost*.

compensation *n.* something to make up for loss, damage, trouble, etc.

compete *v.* to try to win in a competition against others (**competing, competed**).

competence *n.* ability.

competent *adj.* capable.

competition *n.* 1. a contest. 2. rivalry.

competitive *adj.* contesting, rivalling.

competitor *n.* a contestant, a rival.

compile *v.* to collect, to make up, as *to compile a list of names* (**compiling, compiled**). *n.* **compilation**.

complain *v.* 1. to find fault. 2. to speak or write about something you do not like.

complaint *n.* 1. finding fault. 2. an illness.

complete *adj.* whole, perfect, finished. *v.* **complete** to fulfil, to finish (**completing, completed**). *adv.* **com-**

pletely wholly. *n.* **completion** finishing.

complex *adj.* difficult, not simple, with many sides to it, as *a complex problem*.

complexion *n.* 1. the colour and appearance of your skin. 2. the appearance of a situation, as *this fact puts a new complexion on things*.

complexity *n.* difficulty, lack of simplicity, many-sidedness.

complicate *v.* to make difficult, to make confused (**complicating, complicated**). *adj.* **complicated** complex, difficult.

complication *n.* difficulty, complexity.

compliment *n.* pleasant words of praise or gentle flattery paid to someone. *v.* **compliment** to praise gracefully.

complimentary *adj.* 1. praising. 2. given free as a compliment, as *complimentary tickets*.

component *n.* one of the parts of which a thing is made, as *a component of a bicycle*.

compose *v.* 1. to build up or put together. 2. to create, as *to compose some music*. 3. to calm. (**composing, composed**). *adj.* **composed** calm, settled in mind. *n.* **composer** someone who creates music, etc.

composition *n.* 1. composing. 2. something made or created. 3. a piece of music or writing.

composure *n.* calmness.

compound *n.* 1. a union of several parts. 2. (in chemistry) a substance formed of two or more elements. 3. (in Africa) an enclosed group of houses. *v.* **compound** to unite substances.
 compound fracture a broken bone, with a flesh wound.

comprehend *v.* 1. to understand. 2. to include, as *the word 'people' comprehends both men and women*.

comprehension *n.* 1. understanding. 2. inclusion.

compress *v.* to make smaller by pressing or squeezing.

compromise (*pron.* kom'prom.ize) *n.* an agreement reached by both sides giving way. *v.* **compromise** to reach agreement by giving way (**compromising, compromised**).

compulsion *n.* force, the compelling of someone.

compulsory *adj.* compelled, forced, not voluntary.

computer *n.* a machine for working out complicated problems with figures.

comrade *n.* a close companion. *n.* **comradeship**.

concave *adj.* curved inwards, the opposite of *convex n.* **concavity**.

conceal *v.* to hide. *n.* **concealment**.

concede (*pron.* kon.seed') *v.* 1. to give up, to yield, as *to concede your point of view in an argument.* 2. to grant, as *to concede a privilege* (**conceding, conceded**).

conceit *n.* vanity, too much pride.

conceited *adj.* vain and too proud.

conceivable *adj.* imaginable, as *I know of no conceivable reason why he should do it.*

concentrate *v.* 1. to gather to one place, as *they concentrated by the town hall.* 2. to make a solution stronger by boiling off some of the liquid. 3. to fix the mind on one thing, as *concentrate on what I say!* (**concentrating, concentrated**). *n.* **concentration**.

concentrated *adj.* strengthened.

concern *n.* 1. an affair, as *that is not my concern.* 2. anxiety, as *Mother showed her concern.* 3. a business firm, as *a prosperous concern.* *v.* **concern** 1. to relate to, to affect, as *this letter concerns you.* 2. to make anxious, as *Sam's illness concerns me.* *prep.* **concerning** about.

concert *n.* 1. a musical entertainment. 2. agreement, as *they acted in concert.*

concession *n.* 1. an admission, as *a concession of failure.* 2. something granted or conceded, as *the concession of an honour to someone.*

conclude *v.* 1. to end, to bring to a close. 2. to form a careful opinion, as *I conclude that what you say is true* (**concluding, concluded**).

conclusion *n.* 1. an ending. 2. a careful opinion.

conclusive *adj.* 1. final. 2. convincing, as *conclusive evidence of a crime.*

concrete (1) *n.* a mixture of cement, small stones, sand, and water, used in building.

concrete (2) *adj.* real, not just an idea, as *a concrete suggestion.*

concussion *n.* 1. a violent shock. 2. a dazed feeling caused by a blow.

condemn *v.* 1. to blame. 2. to find guilty 3. to declare unfit for use, as *to condemn a box of bad eggs.* *n.* **condemnation**.

condensation *n.* 1. condensing. 2. water formed from vapour, as *condensation on a window.*

condense *v.* 1. to make thicker, as *to condense milk.* 2. to change from vapour to liquid, as *steam condenses to water* (**condensing, condensed**).

condescend *v.* 1. to behave as if granting a favour to someone of lower position, to stoop to do, as *the prim lady condescends to speak to the tramp.* *n.* **condescension**.

condition *n.* 1. the state a thing is in. 2. a requirement in a contract, as *I will lend you the book on the condition that you return it.*

conditional *adj.* depending on some condition, as *conditional surrender.*

conduct (1) (*pron.* kon'dukt) *n.* 1. behaviour. 2. management, as *his conduct of the plan was good.*

conduct (2) (*pron.* kon.dukt') *v.* 1. to lead. 2. to direct a band or orchestra.

conduction *n.* 1. leading or directing. 2. the passage of heat or electricity.

conductor *n.* 1. a man who directs an orchestra. 2. a man in charge of a bus, or (in North America) a railway train (*fem.* **conductress**). 3. a substance, such as a metal, which conveys heat or electricity well.

cone *n.* 1. a solid body with a circular base which rises up to a point. 2. the wooden scaly fruit of the pine, fir, etc. *adj.* **conical** cone-shaped.

confectioner *n.* someone who sells cakes and sweets of various kinds. *n.* **confectionery**.

confederate *n.* 1. an ally, a member of a league. 2. one who was on the side of the Confederates in the American Civil War.

confederation *n.* a union of states.

conference n. a meeting for consultation and discussion.

confess v. 1. to own up, to admit. 2. to admit sins to a priest. n. **confession.**

confetti n. pl. used as sing. tiny pieces of coloured paper thrown at weddings.

confide v. 1. to share a secret with, as Janet confided in her friend. 2. to trust, as to confide valuables to someone (**confiding, confided**).

confidence n. 1. trust. 2. a shared secret.

confident adj. 1. trusting. 2. very sure, bold.

confidential adj. 1. private, secret. 2. trusted with private matters, as a confidential clerk.

confine v. 1. to shut up, as to confine to jail. 2. to keep within limits, as confine your laughter till later. 3. to keep indoors, or in bed (**confining, confined**).

confirm v. 1. to make stronger, as that confirms what I think 2. to establish as true, as you confirm the report. adj. **confirmed** regular, as a confirmed invalid.

confirmation n. 1. making sure, or stronger. 2. the ceremony of being admitted to full membership of a church.

confiscate v. for someone in authority to take something and keep it (**confiscating, confiscated**). n. **confiscation.**

conflict (pron. kon'flikt) n. a fight, a battle. v. **conflict** (pron. kon.flikt') to oppose, to clash.

confront v. 1. to come face to face with. 2. to bring in front of.

confuse v. 1. to bewilder, to muddle. 2. to embarrass, as do not laugh at Eric, or you will confuse him (**confusing, confused**).

confusing adj. bewildering, muddled.

confusion n. 1. muddle, disorder. 2. embarrassment.

congratulate v. to compliment someone and show pleasure in his success or good fortune (**congratulating, congratulated**). n. **congratulation.**

congregation n. 1. a crowd. 2. a gathering of people in church.

congress n. an assembly of delegates.

Congress the chief assembly of the U.S.A.

conical see **cone.**

conifer n. a cone-bearing tree such as the yew, pine, or fir. adj. **coniferous.** See **deciduous.**

conjunction n. 1. a union. 2. (in grammar) a word such as and, but, because which connects phrases in a sentence.

conjure v. to practise magic, to do something as if by magic, as she conjured up a wonderful meal (**conjuring, conjured**). n. **conjuror.**

connect v. 1. to join together. 2. to think of as going together, as I always connect strawberries with cream. n. **connection.**

conquer v. 1. to overcome. 2. to defeat in battle.

conqueror n. a victor.

conquest n. 1. victory by force. 2. something conquered.

conscience n. an inner feeling of what is right or wrong.

conscientious adj. 1. careful, particular. 2. guided by conscience. adv. **conscientiously.**

conscious adj. awake and aware. adv. **consciously.** n. **consciousness.**

conscript (pron. kon.skript') v. to compel someone to enrol in the armed forces. n. **conscription.**

consecrate v. to declare sacred, as to consecrate a new church (**consecrating, consecrated**). n. **consecration.** adj. **consecrated** holy, sacred.

consecutive (pron. kon.sek'yoo.tiv) adj. in order, one after another, as 1, 2, 3, are consecutive numbers. adv. **consecutively.**

consent v. 1. to agree. 2. to give permission. n. **consent** 1. agreement. 2. permission.

with one consent by general agreement.

consequence n. what follows as a result, the effect.

consequent adj. following as a result, as heavy rains and consequent floods. adv. **consequently.**

conservative adj. 1. wanting to keep things unchanged. 2. cautious, moderate.

CONSERVE

CONSERVE

39

CONTENTS

conserve v. 1. to preserve, to keep from wasting. 2. to preserve fruit in sugar (**conserving, conserved**). n. **conserve** 1. fruit in sugar. 2. jam.

consider v. 1. to think over carefully. 2. to believe.

considerable adj. large, important, worth considering. adv. **considerably.**

considerate adj. kindly, thinking of the feelings of others.

consideration n. 1. careful thought. 2. thoughtfulness for others, as we should always show consideration for old people. 3. payment, as I will do it for a consideration.

consist v. to be made up of.

consistency n. 1. being consistent. 2. degree of thickness or stiffness, as the consistency of this paint is too thin. 3. steadiness, as Tom worked with great consistency.

consistent adj. firm, steady, unchanging.

consolation n. comfort in time of sorrow.

consolation prize n. a prize for nearly winning.

console (pron. kon.sōl') v. to comfort someone (**consoling, consoled**).

consonant n. any letter which is not one of the five vowels, a, e, i, o, u.

conspicuous adj. easily seen, arousing attention.

conspiracy n. banding together for some unlawful purpose, a plot (pl. **conspiracies**).

conspirator n. a plotter.

constable n. a policeman.

constabulary n. a police force.

constancy n. firmness, unchangeableness.

constant adj. unchanging, faithful.

constantly adv. always, for ever.

constellation n. a group of stars bearing a name, as the Great Bear is a constellation.

consternation n. dismay, terrified confusion.

constituency n. the voters of a district.

constituent n. 1. a part of anything. 2. a voter.

constitute v. to form, to make up, as this money constitutes all my wealth (**constituting, constituted**).

constitution n. 1. the make-up or composition of a thing. 2. bodily health, as a man of strong constitution. 3. the laws and customs by which a nation is governed. adj. **constitutional.**

construct v. to build, to put together. n. **construction** building.

constructive adj. helpful, as constructive advice.

consul n. an official representing his government in another country. n. **consulate** a consul's house.

consult v. 1. to ask advice of. 2. to look up for information, as to consult a dictionary.

consultation n. 1. seeking advice or information. 2. a meeting to talk over something.

consume v. to eat, to drink up, to use up, to destroy (**consuming, consumed**).

consumer n. a person who consumes or buys things made by others.

consumption n. using up.

contact n. 1. touching, meeting. 2. the touching of metals to pass an electric current. v. **contact** to touch. **to come into contact with, to make contact with** to touch.

contain v. 1. to hold, to include. 2. to hold back, as Billy contained his joy at winning.

container n. a box, tin, barrel, or other holder.

contaminate v. to defile or infect by touching, as rats contaminate food (**contaminating, contaminated**). n. **contamination.**

contemplate v. 1. to look at thoughtfully. 2. to think of doing, as Betty contemplates learning to play tennis.

contemporary n. belonging to the same time.

contempt n. scorn or disgust.

contemptible adj. mean.

contemptuous adj. scornful. adv. **contemptuously.**

content adj. pleased, satisfied. v. **content** to please.

contentment n. satisfaction, quiet happiness.

contents (pron. kon'tents) n. pl. what is in a container, as the contents of a bottle.

contest (*pron.* kon'test) *n.* a competition, a struggle. *v.* **contest** (*pron.* kon.test') to compete, to fight.

contestant *n.* a competitor, a fighter.

continent *n.* a very large mass of land, one of the five main continents. *adj.* **continental**.

the Continent Europe, apart from the British Isles.

continual *adj.* happening often. *n.* **continuation**.

continue *v.* 1. to keep on doing. 2. to go on again after a stop. 3. to remain, as *to continue at school* (**continuing, continued**).

continuous *adj.* without stopping, unbroken, as *the noise is continuous.*

contour *n.* 1. an outline. 2. a line on a map marking points of equal height.

contract (*pron.* kon.trakt') *v.* 1. to grow smaller. 2. to carry out work according to an agreement. *n.* **contract** (*pron.* kon'trakt) a business agreement.

contraction *n.* 1. growing smaller. 2. a shortening.

contractor *n.* an engineer, builder, or other businessman who carries out contracts.

contradict *v.* 1. to deny something. 2. to say the opposite. *n.* **contradiction**. *adj.* **contradictory**.

contrary (*pron.* kon'tra.ri) *adj.* opposite, completely different.

on the contrary not at all, the opposite is true.

contrast (*pron.* kon'trast) *n.* a difference between things, where one shows up the other, as *a contrast between light and dark*. *v.* **contrast** (*pron.* kon.trast') to compare things and see the difference.

contribute (*pron.* kon.trib'yoot) *v.* to pay a share, to help (**contributing, contributed**). *n.* **contribution**.

control *v.* 1. to check, as *to control a restive horse*. 2. to govern, to regulate, as *to control imports* (**controlling, controlled**). *n.* **control** 1. authority over. 2. a check.

self-control being able to govern your own desires.

controversial *adj.* arguable, disputable.

controversy (*pron.* kon'tro.ver.si) *n.* an argument, a dispute (*pl.* **controversies**).

conundrum *n.* a riddle, a puzzling question.

convalescent *adj.* recovering from an illness.

convection *n.* the passing of heat by warm currents of air or water.

convenience *n.* suitability, handiness, easiness in use.

convenient *adj.* suitable, trouble-saving, easy to use.

convent *n.* a building occupied by nuns.

conventional *adj.* usual, customary.

conversation *n.* talk, chat. *adj.* **conversational**.

converse (1) (*pron.* con.vers') *v.* to talk with someone, to chat (**conversing, conversed**).

converse (2) (*pron.* con'vers) *n.* the opposite, as *hard is the converse of soft.*

conversion *n.* 1. a change from one use to another. 2. a change from one religion to another, as *the conversion of heathens.*

convert (*pron.* kon.vert') *v.* 1. to change, as *to convert French money into British*. 2. to cause a change of opinion or belief, as *to convert heathens to Christianity.*

convex *adj.* curved outwards.

convey *v.* to carry from one place to another (**conveying, conveyed**).

conveyance *n.* 1. carrying from place to place. 2. a vehicle used for carrying.

convict (*pron.* kon.vikt') *v.* to find someone guilty of a crime. *n.* **convict** (*pron.* kon'vikt) a man sent to prison.

conviction *n.* 1. finding someone guilty. 2. a firm belief.

convince *v.* 1. to satisfy someone of the truth. 2. to persuade someone strongly (**convincing, convinced**).

convincing *adj.* persuasive, satisfying, as *Jack gave a convincing reason for being late.*

convoy *n.* a line of ships escorted by others for protection. *v.* **convoy** to escort others for protection (**convoying, convoyed**).

cook v. 1. to prepare food by heating. 2. to undergo cooking. 3. to tamper with accounts, etc. n. **cook** someone whose occupation is cooking. n. **cooker** a stove for cooking. n. **cookery** the art of cooking.
  to cook someone's goose to spoil someone's plans, or finish him off.

cookie n. a small flat round cake.

cool adj. 1. slightly cold. 2. calm, unexcited. 3. without warmth or joy, as a cool reception. v. **cool** 1. to make colder. 2. to calm down. n. **coolness**.
  to cool your heels to be kept waiting.

coolie n. a Chinese or Indian labourer.

coop n. a basket, box, shed, or cage for fowls or small animals. v. **coop** to shut up or imprison.

co-operate v. to work together for some special purpose. n. **co-operation**. adj. **co-operative**.

cope (with) v. to manage a difficult situation, to deal successfully with (**coping, coped**).

copper n. 1. a reddish metal used in electrical wiring. 2. a copper coin.

coppice or **copse** n. a wood of shrubs and small trees.

copy n. 1. an imitation. 2. one of a number of printed books or papers, as a copy of a magazine. v. **copy** to imitate, to make a similar thing (**copying, copied**).

copyright n. the sole right to publish a book, picture, etc.

coracle n. a small round Welsh or Irish rowing boat, of tarred canvas or skins on wickerwork.

coral n. the hard pink or white skeletons of tiny sea insects, forming reefs or islands in tropical seas. n. **coral-reef**.

cord n. 1. thick string. 2. a measure of firewood.

cordial adj. warm-hearted, friendly, as a cordial greeting. n. **cordial** a refreshing drink.

corduroy n. 1. a corded velvety material. 2. (in Canada) a road made of logs (pl. **corduroys**).

core n. the inner part or centre, as the core of an apple. v. **core** to take out the core.

cork n. 1. the bark of the cork-tree, found in South Europe and Africa. 2. a stopper or fishing-net float made of this.

corkscrew n. a spiral-shaped tool for removing corks from bottles.

corn (1) n. a hard tender growth on the foot.

corn (2) n. grain or seed of wheat, barley, oats, rye, or maize (Indian corn). n. **corn-cob** an ear of maize with its seeds.

corner n. 1. the place where two lines, walls, roads, etc., meet. 2. the buying up of a large supply of a material, to raise the price later, as a corner in wheat. v. **corner** 1. to drive someone into an awkward situation. 2. to buy up the supply of a material.
  to turn the corner to get past a difficulty, or to get past the most serious part of an illness.

cornet n. a kind of trumpet.

cornflour n. flour made from maize.

cornflower n. a tall plant with a blue flower.

coronation n. the crowning of a king or queen.

coroner n. an officer who holds an inquiry into the cause of sudden death.

coronet n. a small crown worn by nobles or ladies of high rank.

corporal n. a non-commissioned army officer, next in rank below a sergeant.

corporation n. 1. a group of persons with power to act together. 2. the whole of the councillors or representatives of a town or city.

corps (pron. kōr) n. 1. a body of troops. 2. a trained group, as a nursing corps (pl. **corps** pron. kōrs).

corpse (pron. korps) n. a dead human body.

corral n. 1. an enclosure for horses or cattle. 2. a circle of wagons making a protection for a camp.

correct adj. 1. true, accurate. 2. with good manners or standards, as correct behaviour or correct dress. v. **correct** 1. to put right, as correct your mistakes. 2. to scold or punish, as the teacher corrected John. n. **correction**.

correctness n. being correct or well-mannered, as I admired the correctness of Jim's behaviour.

correspond v. 1. to be equal to, as *a captain in the navy corresponds to a colonel in the army.* 2. to agree (with), as *your opinion corresponds with mine.* 3. to write and exchange letters, as *Joan corresponds with her friend Mary in Canada.* n. **correspondence.**

correspondent n. 1. a writer of letters. 2. someone who sends news to newspapers.

corridor n. a passage in a building or a train.

corroboree n. (in Australia) a festival held by aborigines.

corrode v. to rot or eat away gradually, as *acids corrode iron* (**corroding, corroded**).

corrosion n. the gradual eating away of metal or stone.

corrugated adj. wavy, in folds, as *a corrugated iron roof.*

corrupt v. to make rotten or evil, as *love of money corrupts men.* adj. **corrupt** spoiled, rotten. adj. **corruptible.** n. **corruption.**

corset (usually n. pl. **corsets**) n. a tight-fitting undergarment.

cosmetic n. a powder, cream, or paste for beautifying the skin.

cosmic adj. relating to the universe. **cosmic rays** powerful rays from outer space.

cost n. the price paid for something, in money, time, or labour. v. **cost** to be obtained at a price.

at all costs at any price.

cost price the price paid for a thing compared with the price at which it is later sold.

costly adj. expensive (*comparative* **costlier,** *superlative* **costliest**).

costume n. 1. dress, especially a woman's two-piece coat and skirt. 2. style of dress, as *the Swiss national costume.*

cosy adj. warm and snug (*comparative* **cosier,** *superlative* **cosiest**). n. **cosy** a cover for a teapot (*pl.* **cosies**).

cot n. a baby's bed or crib.

cottage n. a small house.

cotton n. 1. the long white hairs of the cotton plant. 2. thread or cloth made from these hairs.

cotton-wool n. loose cotton made into a pad.

couch n. a sofa or resting-place. v. **couch** to express in words, as *Mary couched her letter in polite phrases.*

cough v. to force air from the lungs with a sharp sound. n. **cough** the noise of coughing.

could *past* of **can.**

council n. 1. a committee or group of people called together to discuss something. 2. a group of people who look after the affairs of a city or town. n. **councillor** a member of a council.

counsel n. 1. advice. 2. a lawyer who conducts a law case. v. **counsel** to advise (**counselling, counselled**). n. **counsellor** an adviser.

counsel of perfection good advice, not easy to put into practice.

count (1) v. 1. to reckon up numbers. 2. to depend on, as *we count on your help.* 3. to consider, as *count yourself lucky.* n. **count** an adding up.

do not count your chickens before they are hatched do not reckon on things which are not certain.

out for the count unconscious, exhausted.

count (2) n. a nobleman, especially in some European countries (*fem.* **countess**).

counter (1) n. 1. a bench in a shop across which goods are sold. 2. a small token used in games.

counter (2) v. to oppose. adj. **counter** opposite, against, as *a counter argument.*

counter attack to attack back.

counteract v. to act against.

counter-attraction n. a rival attraction.

counterfeit v. to imitate something exactly in order to deceive, to forge.

counterfoil n. part of a cheque or postal order kept as a record.

counterpane n. a bedspread.

countess n. the wife of an earl or a count.

countless adj. many, more than can be counted.

country n. 1. a region of land, as *hilly country.* 2. a rural district away from cities. 3. one's native land. 4. the people of a nation, as *the whole country was aroused* (*pl.* **countries**). *n.* **countryside** a rural area.

county *n.* a division of a country ruled by a county council, a shire (*pl.* **counties**).

couple *n.* a pair, two. *v.* **couple** to join two things together (**coupling, coupled**).

coupling *n.* a connecting bar or link, joining two things together.

coupon *n.* a slip of paper entitling the holder to money or goods.

courage *n.* bravery, fearlessness. *adj.* **courageous**.

course *n.* 1. the path along which anything moves, as *the course of a ship on the sea*. 2. (in sport) the ground along which people or animals move, as *a race-course*. 3. a series of events or actions, as *a course of lessons*. 4. part of a meal, as *a four-course dinner*. 5. a layer of bricks, as *the top course of a wall*. *v.* **course** to hunt, to chase (**coursing, coursed**).

in due course at a later time.

of course naturally.

court *n.* 1. an enclosed space. 2. a royal palace. 3. a king's or queen's attendants at a palace. 4. the place where judges or magistrates hear cases. *v.* **court** 1. to make love to. 2. to try to win someone over. *n.* **courtship**.

courteous (*pron.* kur'tee.us) *adj.* polite, respectful.

courtesy (*pron.* kur'tes.i) *n.* politeness.

courtier *n.* a member of a royal court.

court-martial *n.* trial by a naval or military court (*pl.* **courts-martial**).

courtyard *n.* a space surrounded by buildings.

cousin *n.* the son or daughter of an uncle or aunt.

cove *n.* a small bay.

cover *v.* 1. to hide or protect. 2. to be over something, as *hairs cover my head*. 3. to provide for, as *the house is covered against fire by insurance*. 4. to point a weapon against someone. *n.* **cover** 1. shelter, protection. 2. a lid. *n.* **covering** something that provides cover.

to take cover to hide.

covet *v.* to want very much something that belongs to someone else. *adj.* **covetous**.

cow (1) *n.* 1. a female ox. 2. a female elephant or whale (*masc.* **bull**).

cow (2) *v.* to subdue or repress by fear.

coward *n.* someone with no courage, who runs away or shirks his duty through fear. *n.* **cowardice**.

cowboy *n.* a man who looks after cattle on a ranch.

coxswain (*pron.* cok'sn) *n.* a man who steers or has charge of a small boat.

coyote (*pron.* koy.ō'ti) *n.* a small wolf which lives in western North America.

crab *n.* 1. a shell-fish with a flat body and several legs. 2. a small sour apple. *adj.* **crabbed** or **crabby** (of a person) sour, bad-tempered.

to catch a crab (in rowing) to dig your oar too deeply into the water.

to walk crabwise to walk sideways.

crack *n.* 1. a sharp sound, as *the crack of a rifle*. 2. a split, as *a crack in a wall*. 3. a sudden blow, as *a crack on the head*. *v.* **crack** 1. to split open, as *to crack a nut*. 2. to partly split something, as *to crack a cup*. 3. to make (a joke). 4. (of the voice) to break.

to crack up to lose your strength.

cracker *n.* 1. a small firework, or a party novelty. 2. a hard biscuit.

crackle *v.* to make a sharp snapping noise, like burning wood (**crackling, crackled**).

cradle *n.* a baby's cot. *v.* **cradle** 1. to rock in a cradle. 2. to be the birthplace of something or someone (**cradling, cradled**).

craft *n.* 1. an art or skill, as *weaving is a craft*. 2. a trade, as *the craft of cabinet-making* (*pl.* **crafts**). 3. cunning. 4. a ship or aeroplane (*pl.* **craft**). *adj.* **crafty** cunning. *adv.* **craftily**. *n.* **craftiness**.

craftsman *n.* a skilled worker. *n.* **craftsmanship**.

crag *n.* a rugged rock. *adj.* **craggy**.

cram *v.* 1. to stuff, to pack in. 2. to study hard (**cramming, crammed**).

cramp *n.* 1. a painful tightening of a muscle. 2. a metal bar with bent ends to hold things tightly together. *v.* **cramp** 1. to fasten by a cramp. 2. to hinder.

crane *n.* 1. a wading bird with a long beak and legs. 2. a machine with a long arm for lifting heavy weights. *v.* **crane** to stretch your neck to see something.

crank *n.* 1. a long handle with a bend in it, for turning a machine. 2. a person with queer ideas.

crash *n.* the noise of something falling or breaking. *v.* **crash** to smash, to break into pieces.

crate *n.* a wooden packing-case.

crater *n.* 1. the mouth of a volcano. 2. a hole in the ground caused by a bomb or shell.

crave *v.* 1. to beg for. 2. to want something very much (**craving, craved**). *n.* **craving** longing.

crawl *v.* 1. to creep on hands and knees. 2. to move very slowly. *n.* **crawl** 1. creeping. 2. an overarm swimming stroke.

crayon *n.* a pencil of coloured chalk, clay, or wax. *v.* **crayon** to draw with crayons.

craze *n.* a passing fashion which arouses interest for a time.

crazy *adj.* silly, mad (*comparative* **crazier,** *superlative* **craziest**). *n.* **craziness.** *adv.* **crazily**.

creak *v.* to make a squeaking sound. *n.* **creak** a small, squeaking sound.

cream *n.* 1. the fat on the surface of milk. 2. anything similar, as *ice-cream* or *cold cream*. 3. the best part, as *she picked the cream of the fruit*. *v.* **cream** to skim the cream off milk. *adj.* **creamy** (*comparative* **creamier,** *superlative* **creamiest**). *n.* **creaminess**.

crease *n.* 1. a mark made by folding. 2. (in cricket) a line beyond which a bowler or batsman must not step. *v.* **crease** to put a wrinkle or crease into something by folding or pressing (**creasing, creased**).

create *v.* to make or bring into being (**creating, created**). *adj.* **creative**.

creation *n.* 1. creating. 2. the universe. 3. a specially designed dress.

the Creator God.

creature *n.* a living being.

credit *n.* 1. trust, belief, as *we can give credit to your story*. 2. honour, esteem, as *Richard is a boy of credit*. 3. a source of honour, as *Robert is a credit to his school*. 4. money in the bank, as *I have a large sum of money to my credit*. 5. time allowed for the payment of goods which are *bought on credit*. *v.* **credit** 1. to believe. 2. to pay money into an account.

creditable *adj.* 1. trustworthy. 2. bringing honour to someone.

creed *n.* a list or statement of religious beliefs.

creek *n.* a narrow inlet from the sea.

creep *v.* 1. to crawl on hands and knees. 2. to walk slowly and stealthily (**creeping, crept**). *n.* **creeper** a plant which grows over a fence or wall. *adj.* **creepy**.

cremate *v.* to burn a dead body. *n.* **cremation**.

crematorium *n.* a place for burning the dead.

crêpe (*pron.* krayp) *n.* a fabric or paper with a fine wrinkled surface.

crept *past* of **creep**.

crescendo (*pron.* kresh.en'doh) *adj.* and *adv.* (in music) increasing in loudness.

crescent (*pron.* kres'nt) *n.* 1. the shape of the new moon. 2. a row of houses in this shape.

cress *n.* a plant whose leaves are used in salads.

crest *n.* 1. a cock's comb. 2. an ornament on a helmet. 3. the highest point, as *the crest of a hill*. 4. a design over a coat of arms.

crestfallen *adj.* cast down, discouraged by defeat.

crevice *n.* a narrow crack in a rock or wall.

crew *n.* 1. the men who work in a ship or who row a boat. 2. a gang of men working together.

crib *n.* 1. a baby's bed. 2. a manger for cattle. 3. a schoolboy's book of answers. *v.* **crib** to cheat, to copy (**cribbing, cribbed**).

cricket (1) *n.* a summer game played by eleven players a side, with bats and ball and two sets of stumps. *n.* **cricketer**.

cricket (2) *n.* an insect like a grasshopper.

crime *n.* law-breaking of a serious kind.

criminal *n.* someone who has committed a crime. *adj.* **criminal** unlawful.

crimson *n.* a deep red colour.

cringe *v.* to shrink or cower in fear or embarrassment (**cringing, cringed**).

cripple *n.* a lame person. *v.* **cripple** to disable.

crisis (*pron.* krī'sis) *n.* a turning point or decisive moment in an illness, or at some other important time (*pl.* **crises** *pron.* krī'seez).

crisp *adj.* brittle and firm, fresh. *n.* **crisp** a fried slice of potato.

critic *n.* 1. an expert who judges books, films, or some work of art. 2. one who finds fault.

critical *adj.* 1. judging carefully. 2. fault-finding. 3. risky, as *a critical venture.* 4. important, as *a critical decision.*

criticism *n.* 1. judgement. 2. fault-finding.

criticize *v.* to judge, to find fault (**criticizing, criticized**).

croak *v.* to make a harsh, throaty noise. *n.* **croak** a harsh noise.

crockery *n.* cups, saucers, plates, and dishes.

crocodile *n.* a large reptile with a pointed snout, found in the rivers and lakes of some warm countries.

crocodile tears false tears.

crocus *n.* a small spring flower growing from a bulb.

croft *n.* a small farm and farm-house in Scotland. *n.* **crofter** a man who lives on a croft.

crook *n.* 1. a shepherd's hooked stick. 2. a swindler. 3. a curve, a bend.

crooked *adj.* 1. bent. 2. dishonest, of bad character.

croon *v.* to sing or hum a sentimental tune. *n.* **crooner.**

crop *v.* to cut short, to mow (**cropping, cropped**). *n.* **crop** 1. what is grown on the land, as *the wheat crop.* 2. a pouch in which a bird stores food before digesting it. 3. a huntsman's whip.

to come a cropper to have a fall.

to crop up to happen.

cross *n.* 1. a mark made by one line crossing another (X). 2. a post with a cross bar, used in Roman times for executing criminals. 3. the emblem of Christianity. 4. a medal in the shape of a cross, as *the Victoria Cross.* 5. a mixture of breeds in plants and animals. *v.* **cross** 1. to lay one thing across another, or for two things to lie across one another. 2. to go from one side to the other, as *to cross the road.* 3. (oneself) to make the sign of the cross. 4. to anger someone by interfering with his plans. 5. (in biology) to produce a mixed breed of animals or plants. *adj.* **cross** 1. cutting across, as *crossroads.* 2. angry, as *Mother is cross with me.*

to cross someone's path to interfere with someone's plans.

to cross one's mind to occur to one.

crossbred *adj.* produced by crossing two breeds.

cross-examine *v.* to question someone carefully to obtain evidence.

crossing *n.* a place where a road or railway line may be crossed.

crossroads *n.* the junction of two roads.

crouch *v.* to bend low.

crow (1) *n.* a fairly large black bird.

as the crow flies in a straight line.

crow (2) *v.* to make a shrill cry like a cock (**crowing, crew,** or **crowed**).

to crow over to boast about some success.

crowd *n.* a number of people or things closely packed together. *v.* **crowd** to press or pack together. *adj.* **crowded** packed close.

crown *n.* 1. the circular head-dress of a king, queen, or nobleman. 2. a wreath of victory worn on the head, as *a crown of laurel leaves.* 3. a British coin worth 25p, now rare. 4. the top of a hat, the head, or a hill. *v.* **crown** to put a crown on.

crucifix *n.* a figure of Christ on the cross.

the Crucifixion the death of Christ on the cross.

crucify *v.* to put to death on a cross (**crucifying, crucified**).

crude *adj.* 1. raw, not refined, as *crude oil.* 2. rough, as *a crude drawing. n.* **crudity.**

cruel *adj.* fond of seeing or causing pain, merciless. *adv.* **cruelly.**

cruelty *n.* 1. taking pleasure in causing pain. 2. a cruel deed.

cruet *n.* a set of pots for vinegar, mustard, etc.

cruise *v.* to sail to and fro. *n.* **cruise** a voyage for pleasure. *n.* **cruiser** a light warship.

crumb *n.* a tiny bit of bread or cake.

crumble *v.* 1. to break into small pieces. 2. to decay and fall into ruins (**crumbling, crumbled**).

crumple *v.* to crush untidily, to wrinkle (**crumpling, crumpled**).

crunch *v.* to grind noisily with the teeth or foot.

crusade *n.* 1. a war of the Middle Ages to gain the Holy Lands from the Turks. 2. any fight for a cause, as *a crusade against disease. n.* **crusader** someone taking part in a crusade.

crush *v.* 1. to squeeze together. 2. to damage or break by squeezing. 3. to defeat, as *to crush a revolt. n.* **crush** 1. a crowd. 2. a fruit drink. *adj.* **crushing** complete, decisive, as *a crushing defeat.*

crust *n.* a hard outer covering, as *piecrust. adj.* **crusty** 1. covered with crust. 2. bad-tempered.

crutch *n.* a supporting staff, fitting under the armpit, used by cripples (*pl.* **crutches**).

cry *v.* 1. to make a shrill call, to shout. 2. to shed tears (**cries, crying, cried**). *n.* **cry** 1. a shout. 2. a shedding of tears.

in full cry in full chase.

to cry down to make little of.

to cry off to withdraw from an agreement.

to cry over spilt milk to worry over something that has gone wrong and cannot be put right.

within cry of close to, near.

crystal *n.* 1. a glasslike mineral found in the earth. 2. a regular-shaped glasslike solid, formed in numbers when a solution is boiled down.

crystallize *v.* 1. to form crystals. 2. to become clear, as *his ideas crystallized* (**crystallizing, crystallized**).

cub *n.* the young of such animals as foxes, bears, wolves, and lions.

cube *n.* 1. (in geometry) a solid body having six equal square faces. 2. the result of multiplying a number by itself twice. *The cube of 3 is $3 \times 3 \times 3 = 27$. adj.* **cubic** 1. in the form of a cube. 2. measuring volumes, as *a cubic metre is equal to 10,000 cubic centimetres.*

cubicle *n.* a small separate compartment, as in a public baths or in a dormitory.

cuckoo *n.* a grey bird which calls 'cuckoo'.

cucumber *n.* a plant whose long green fruit is used in pickles or salads.

cud *n.* food which certain animals bring back from their stomach to chew again. Cows, sheep, and goats chew the cud.

cuddle *v.* to hug and fondle (**cuddling, cuddled**).

cue (1) *n.* 1. the last words of an actor's speech, which tell the next speaker to continue. 2. a hint.

cue (2) *n.* the long stick used in billiards.

cuff (1) *n.* a blow with the open hand.

cuff (2) *n.* the end of the sleeve near the wrist.

cul-de-sac *n.* a road closed at one end, a blind alley.

culprit *n.* an offender, someone at fault.

cultivate *v.* 1. to grow crops by preparing the ground. 2. to pay careful attention to, to foster, as *to cultivate someone's friendship.* 3. to improve, as *to cultivate one's mind* (**cultivating, cultivated**). *adj.* **cultivated** 1. (of the earth) prepared and tilled. 2. (of people) cultured and refined. *n.* **cultivation.**

culture *n.* 1. cultivation of crops. 2. careful training, as *voice culture.* 3. refinement or improvement of the mind. 4. civilization. *adj.* **cultured** educated, refined.

cunning *adj.* wily, sly, crafty. 2. skilful. *n.* **cunning** craftiness, skill.

cup *n.* 1. a small drinking-vessel with a handle. 2. something shaped like a cup, as *an egg-cup.* 3. a metal cup given as a prize, as *a sports cup. v.* **cup** to form the hands into a cup (**cupping, cupped**). *n.* **cupful** (*pl.* **cupfuls**).

there's many a slip twixt cup and lip a mishap can happen at the last minute.

cupboard *n.* a set of shelves with a door or doors in front.

curate *n.* a Church of England clergyman of lowest rank, who assists a vicar or rector.

curb *v.* to hold something back, to check. *n.* **curb** 1. a chain or strap attached to a bit for holding back a horse. 2. a pavement edge, or hearth fender (often spelled **kerb**).

curd *n.* sour thickened milk. *v.* **curdle** (of milk) to go sour and thick (**curdling, curdled**).

cure *v.* 1. to heal, to make well. 2. to preserve meat or skins by drying (**curing, cured**). *n.* **cure** a recovery from illness.

curfew *n.* 1. a bell rung as a signal for people to remain indoors, or (in feudal times) for lights and fires to be put out.

curio *n.* something rare and curious (*pl.* **curios**).

curiosity *n.* 1. inquisitiveness. 2. a strange rare thing.

curious *adj.* 1. (of a person or animal) inquisitive, wanting to know. 2. (of a thing) strange, unusual. *adv.* **curiously**.

curl *v.* to twist into loops or a spiral (**curling, curled**). *n.* **curl** a twisted lock of hair. *adj.* **curly** (*comparative* **curlier**, *superlative* **curliest**).

currant *n.* 1. a small black raisin. 2. a garden shrub with red, black, or white berries (note: do not confuse with **current**).

currawong *n.* a common Australian bird about the size of a crow.

currency *n.* money used in a country.

current *n.* a flow or stream of water, air, or electricity (note: do not confuse with **currant**). *adj.* **current** in general use, as *a current fashion*.

curry *n.* 1. a highly spiced sauce used in India. 2. rice or meat cooked with this sauce.

curse *n.* 1. a prayer for evil to fall on someone. 2. evil brought on someone, as *the curse of poverty*. *v.* **curse** 1. to swear. 2. to wish evil on someone. 3. to torment, as *they were cursed with flies* (**cursing, cursed**).

curt *adj.* short and rude, as *a curt reply*.

curtail *v.* to cut short, as *to curtail a holiday*. *n.* **curtailment** a cutting short.

curtain *n.* 1. a hanging cloth in front of a window or in front of a theatre stage. 2. anything that hides, as *a curtain of smoke*.

curtsy *n.* a bow that a lady makes. *v.* **curtsy** to bow (**curtsies, curtsying, curtsied**).

curve *n.* a smooth bend, an arch. *v.* **curve** to bend round in a smooth line (**curving, curved**). *n.* **curvature**.

cushion *n.* a bag filled with soft padding. *v.* **cushion** to soften a blow with protective material.

custard *n.* pudding made of eggs, sugar, and milk boiled together.

custody *n.* protection, imprisonment, as *the prisoner was held in custody*.

custom *n.* 1. a regular habit, as *it was his custom to have a walk each day*. 2. regular trade, as *the shopkeeper was glad to have my custom*.

customary *adj.* usual.

customer *n.* someone who buys.

customs *n. pl.* taxes on imported goods.

cut *v.* 1. to slash, divide, or carve with a sharp tool. 2. to divide a pack of cards in two. 3. to hurt someone with a word or remark. 4. to pretend not to see someone because you dislike him. 5. (slang) to miss a class or lecture (**cutting, cut**). *n.* **cut** 1. a slash. 2. a stroke in cricket or some other game. 3. a quick way, as *a short cut*.

to cut your coat according to your cloth not to spend more than you have got.

cutlass *n.* a short sword once used by sailors (*pl.* **cutlasses**).

cutlery *n. pl.* table knives and forks.

cycle *n.* 1. a bicycle. 2. a regular happening, as *the cycle of the seasons*. *v.* **cycle** to ride on a bicycle. *n.* **cyclist**. *n.* **cycling**.

cyclone *n.* a violent storm with winds blowing in towards a calm centre (see **anticyclone**).

cygnet *n.* a young swan.

cylinder (*pron.* sil'in.der) *n.* 1. an object shaped like a tube with circular ends. 2. the part of a petrol or gas engine where the gases are fired. *adj.* **cylindrical** in the shape of a cylinder.

cymbals (*pron.* sim'balz) *n. pl.* a pair of circular brass plates used in orchestras to make a clashing noise.

cynic (*pron.* sin'ik) *n.* a fault-finding person who throws doubts on the good works of others. *adj.* **cynical**. *n.* **cynicism**.

czar (sometimes spelled **tzar**) *n.* the title of the Russian emperors.

D

dab *v.* to pat with something soft (**dabbing, dabbed**). *n.* **dab** 1. a soft pad. 2. a small soft lump. 3. a fish.

dachshund (*pron.* daks'hoond) *n.* a long black or brown dog with short legs.

dad, daddy *ns.* father.

daddy-long-legs *n.* an insect with six very long legs, whose real name is *a crane fly.*

daffodil *n.* a tall yellow, spring flower which grows from a bulb.

dagger *n.* a short knife for stabbing.

at daggers drawn full of hate.

daily *adj.* and *adv.* every day. *n.* **daily** a daily newspaper (*pl.* **dailies**).

dainty *adj.* pretty, delicate and refined (*comparative* **daintier,** *superlative* **daintiest**). *n.* **dainty** a titbit.

dairy *n.* a place where milk, butter, and cheese are kept, or sold (*pl.* **dairies**). *n.* **dairy-maid**.

daisy *n.* a small white flower with a yellow centre.

dale *n.* a valley.

dam *n.* 1. a wall built to hold back water. 2. the water held back by the wall. 3. (of animals) a mother (*masc.* **sire**). *v.* **dam** to hold back water with a wall (**damming, dammed**).

damage *n.* injury, breakage, harm. *v.* **damage** to injure or harm (**damaging, damaged**). *n. pl.* **damages** money paid to someone to make up for injury or harm which has been caused.

dame *n.* a lady of rank, a title of respect.

damn *v.* 1. to curse. 2. to condemn, to doom.

damp *n.* 1. moisture. 2. (in coal mines) an explosive gas, *fire-damp*. *v.* **damp** or **dampen** to moisten. *n.* **dampness**.

dance *v.* 1. to move feet and body to music. 2. to leap with joy (**dancing, danced**). *n.* **dance** 1. a gathering of people moving to music. 2. a piece of music for dancing. *n.* **dancer**.

to lead someone a dance to keep someone busy in a tiring chase.

dandelion *n.* a common yellow flower with many petals.

danger *n.* risk, peril. *adj.* **dangerous** unsafe, risky. *adv.* **dangerously**.

dangle *v.* to swing to and fro, hanging loosely (**dangling, dangled**).

dappled *adj.* spotted.

dare *v.* 1. to be bold enough to take a risk. 2. to challenge, as *to dare someone to climb a tree* (**daring, dared**). *n.* **dare** a challenge. *adj.* **daring** bold, reckless.

dare-devil *n.* a reckless person.

dark *adj.* 1. without light. 2. black, or nearly black. 3. gloomy, secret, as *dark thoughts*. *n.* **darkness** absence of light.

a dark horse a person (or horse) about whom little is known.

keep it dark say nothing about it.

darkroom *n.* a room free from light, used in photography.

darling *n.* someone well loved.

darn *v.* to mend a hole in fabric with criss-cross stitches. *n.* **darning**.

dart *v.* to rush forward quickly. *n.* **dart** 1. a quick sudden movement. 2. a small arrow thrown by hand at a board, or blown from a bamboo pipe.

dash *v.* to rush. 2. to throw with force. 3. to destroy, as *his hopes were dashed*. *n.* **dash** 1. a rush, as *a dash for the bus*. 2. energy. 3. a stroke (—) used in writing or printing. *adj.* **dashing** spirited, showy.

to dash off 1. to rush off. 2. to write hurriedly.

date *n.* 1. the day, month, and year, of a certain event. 2. the year in history when something happened. 3. the fruit of the date-palm. 4. an appointment with someone. *v.* **date** 1. to give a date to, as *to date an antique chair.*

2. to seem old-fashioned, as *this old hat is beginning to date*.

out-of-date old-fashioned.

up-to-date modern, new.

daub *v.* 1. to smear. 2. to splash paint or mud on. **daub** 1. a smudge. 2. a poor painting.

daughter *n.* a female child.

daughter-in-law *n.* a son's wife (*pl.* **daughters-in-law**).

davenport or **devonport** *n.* (in North America) a large sofa.

Davy Jones *n.* a sailor's name for the devil.

Davy Jones's locker the sea bed, the grave of those drowned at sea.

Davy-lamp *n.* a miner's safety lamp, invented by Sir Humphrey Davy.

dawdle *v.* to waste time, to go slowly.

dawn *n.* sunrise, daybreak. *v.* **dawn** to grow light.

to dawn on to become clear (to), as *the answer dawned on him*.

day *n.* 1. the time between sunrise and sunset. 2. a period of 24 hours. 3. a period or age, as *in my day it was different*. 4. daylight, as *night and day*. *ns.* **daybreak** dawn; **daydream** a waking dream; **daytime** during daylight.

day in day out each day for a long time.

to call it a day to finish work.

daze *v.* to stun, to bewilder. *adj.* **dazed** bewildered.

dazzle *v.* to blind or confuse with a brilliant light, or with richness or cleverness (**dazzling, dazzled**). *adj.* **dazzling**.

deacon *n.* an assistant clergyman, or a church official who assists a minister (*fem.* **deaconess**).

dead *adj.* 1. no longer alive. 2. not active or lively. 3. no longer used, as *a dead language*. 4. (of a ball in a game) out of play. 5. complete, as *a dead loss*. 6. the *past participle* of **die**. *adv.* **dead** completely, as *you are dead wrong*. See **die**.

dead end a closed end, a road with no way through.

deaden *v.* to make less, as *to deaden a noise*.

dead-heat *n.* a finish of a race with two or more runners equal.

deadlock *n.* when neither of two sides will give way.

deadly *adj.* fatal, causing death, as *a deadly poison*.

deaf *adj.* unable to hear, or unwilling to hear. *n.* **deafness**.

deafen *v.* to make deaf (**deafening, deafened**).

deal *v.* 1. to do business with someone. 2. to share out playing cards (**dealing, dealt**, *pron.* delt). *n.* **deal** white pine wood. *n.* **dealer** 1. a trader. 2. the person who divides out playing cards.

a square deal a fair deal.

dean *n.* a cathedral clergyman who ranks between a bishop and a canon.

dear *adj.* 1. beloved. 2. costly. *n.* **dear** someone beloved. *adv.* **dearly**.

death *n.* being dead, the end of life. *adjs.* **deathless** everlasting, as *deathless fame*; **deathly** like death, as *deathly pale*.

debate *v.* to argue, to discuss (**debating, debated**). *n.* **debate** a discussion. *adj.* **debatable** doubtful, open to question.

debt *n.* something owed. *n.* **debtor** a person who owes money.

a bad debt a debt which is not likely to be paid.

in debt owing more than can be paid.

decade *n.* a period of ten years.

decapitate *v.* to cut off the head. *n.* **decapitation**.

decay *v.* to waste away, to rot. *adj.* **decayed** rotten.

deceased (*pron.* de.seest') *adj.* dead.

the deceased the dead person.

deceit (*pron.* de.seet') *n.* making someone believe what is not true. *adj.* **deceitful** misleading, lying.

deceive *v.* to mislead, to make someone believe what is not true (**deceiving, deceived**).

December *n.* the twelfth month.

decency *n.* good behaviour, a respectable way of living.

decent *adj.* respectable, well-behaved, suitable.

deception *n.* a fraud, a trick to mislead someone.

deceptive *adj.* not what it seems to be.

decide *v.* 1. to settle something, as *to decide an argument.* 2. to make up one's mind, as *to decide to buy something* (**deciding, decided**).

decided *adj.* 1. definite, as *the shed has a decided slant.* 2. with a firm purpose, as *Susan set out with a decided step.* *adv.* **decidedly** definitely.

deciduous *adj.* (of a tree) losing its leaves each year, not evergreen.

decimal *adj.* numbered in tens or tenths. *n.* **decimal** the point between the numbers in a *decimal fraction.*

decimal currency a money system in which the main unit has 100 parts.

decimal fraction a fraction whose denominator (bottom figure) is ten, a hundred, a thousand, etc., as *in the number 3·7 the ·7 is a decimal fraction equal to $\frac{7}{10}$.*

decipher (*pron.* de.sī'fer) *v.* to make out the meaning of a secret message, or of something badly written.

decision *n.* 1. something decided or settled, as *the council came to a decision to open a new library.* 2. firmness, as *he spoke with decision.* See **decide**.

decisive *adj.* 1. final, most important, as *a decisive battle which ends a war.* 2. determined, as *he is a man of decisive character.* *adv.* **decisively.**

deck *n.* 1. a floor on a ship or bus. 2. (in the U.S.A.) a pack of playing cards. *v.* **deck** to clothe, to decorate, as *Jean decked herself in her finest clothes.* *ns.* **deck-chair** a folding easy chair with a canvas seat; **deck-hand** a sailor who works on deck.

declaration *n.* an announcement.

declare *v.* 1. to announce, to state publicly. 2. (in cricket) to close an innings before all the side has played (**declaring, declared**).

decline *v.* 1. to go down, to sink, as *the sun declined.* 2. to refuse, as *Jack declined the gift.* 3. to grow weaker, as *the old man declined in health* (**declining, declined**).

decode *v.* to read the meaning of a code, to decipher (**decoding, decoded**).

decompose *v.* to rot, to break up into bits (**decomposing, decomposed**).

decorate *v.* 1. to make more beautiful. 2. to give a medal to, as *the soldier was decorated for bravery* (**decorating, decorated**). *ns.* **decoration** 1. making beautiful. 2. a medal given in honour; **decorator** someone who beautifies a house.

decrease *v.* to grow less (**decreasing, decreased**).

dedicate *v.* 1. to devote to a good cause, as *a nurse dedicates her life to the care of the sick.* 2. to inscribe a book to someone. 3. (in the U.S.A.) to open a new building with a ceremony (**dedicating, dedicated**). *n.* **dedication.**

deduce *v.* to reach the answer to a problem by reasoning, as *Sherlock Holmes deduced that the butler was guilty from the clues he left behind* (**deducing, deduced**). *n.* **deduction.**

deduct *v.* to take away, to subtract, as *the workman had insurance money deducted from his wages.*

deduction *n.* 1. taking away, subtraction. 2. finding the answer to a problem by reasoning.

deed *n.* 1. an action, as *a brave deed.* 2. a legal document.

deep *adj.* 1. reaching a long way down or back, as *deep water* or *a deep cave.* 2. heavy, as *deep sleep.* 3. dark, as *deep brown.* 4. absorbed, as *deep in thought.* 5. profound, extreme, as *deep gratitude.* *adv.* **deep** well down, as *it fell deep into the cleft.* *v.* **deepen** to make deeper.

deep-seated deep down, well in.

in deep water in difficulties.

the deep the sea.

to go off the deep end to become very angry.

deer *n.* a swift-running wild animal, whose male has horns or antlers (*pl.* **deer**).

deface *v.* to spoil the look of anything with marks or cuts (**defacing, defaced**).

default *n.* 1. failure to do a duty, or to pay a debt. 2. failure to appear, as *Jack won his game by default, as his opponent did not arrive.*

defeat *v.* to win a victory over, to overcome. *n.* **defeat** the loss of a game, race, or battle.

defect *n.* a fault, a blemish. *adj.* **defective**.

defence *n.* 1. a protection against attack. 2. active resistance to attack. 3. (in law) the case supporting the innocence of a person accused of a crime (spelt **defense** in the U.S.A.). *adjs.* **defensible** defendable; **defensive** helping defence.

defend *v.* to guard, to shield. *ns.* **defendant** (in a court of law) the accused person; **defender** a protector. *adj.* **defendable**.

defiance *n.* 1. a challenge to fight. 2. resistance, or disobedience. *adj.* **defiant**.

deficient *adj.* short of something, not having enough, as *the army was deficient in guns. n.* **deficiency** a shortage. *n.* **deficit** a shortage of money.

defile (*pron.* de.fil[1]) *v.* 1. to make dirty or impure. 2. to dishonour, as *to defile someone's good name. n.* **defilement**.

define *v.* 1. to explain very carefully. 2. to mark out a boundary, as *to define the limits of an estate with a fence.* (**defining, defined**).

definite *adj.* exact.

definition *n.* an exact description of the meaning of a word.

deflate *v.* 1. to let air or gas out, as *to deflate a balloon.* 2. to lower someone's pride. *n.* **deflation**.

deform *v.* to twist out of shape. *adj.* **deformed**. *n.* **deformity** disfigured part of body.

defraud *v.* to cheat, to swindle.

defy *v.* 1. to challenge. 2. to resist or disobey (**defies, defying, defied**). See **defiance**.

degrade *v.* 1. to put into a lower rank. 2. to remove some honour. 3. to spoil the character of (**degrading, degraded**). *n.* **degradation**.

degree *n.* 1. a space on a thermometer scale, to show how hot a thing is, as *a temperature of 60 degrees.* 2. (in geometry) a space on a scale for measuring angles, a 360th part of a circle, as *an an angle of 45 degrees.* 3. a unit in which the position of a line of longitude or of latitude is measured. 4. a small advance, as *he progressed by degrees.* 5. a university honour.

deign (*pron.* dayn) *v.* to decide in a haughty way, to condescend, as *the rich man deigned to smile at me.*

deity *n.* a god or goddess (*pl.* **deities**).

dejected *adj.* sad, discouraged, as *the loser was dejected. n.* **dejection**.

delay *v.* 1. to put off until later, as *Susan delayed posting the letter.* 2. to keep back, as *do not delay him, as he is in a hurry* (**delaying, delayed**). *n.* **delay** 1. putting off. 2. making late.

delegate *n.* someone sent to represent others at a conference. *v.* **delegate** 1. to send as a representative. 2. to hand over to a representative, as *the king delegated some of his power to the prince. n.* **delegation** a group of delegates.

delete *v.* to cross out, to rub out.

deliberate *v.* to think carefully about something. *adj.* **deliberate** carefully thought out. *adv.* **deliberately**. *n.* **deliberation**.

delicacy *n.* something dainty or delicate (*pl.* **delicacies**).

delicate *adj.* 1. dainty. 2. frail, poor in health.

delicious *adj.* delightful, pleasant to eat or to smell.

delight *n.* 1. great pleasure, joy. *v.* **delight** to give pleasure. *adj.* **delighted** pleased.

delinquent *n.* an offender. *n.* **delinquency**.

delirious *adj.* light-headed, feverish. *n.* **delirium**.

deliver *v.* 1. to hand over, as *to deliver newspapers.* 2. to set free, as *to deliver slaves from slavery.* 3. to rescue, as *to deliver someone from death.* 4. to give forth, as *to deliver a speech. ns.* **deliverance** freedom; **delivery** 1. handing over. 2. setting free, rescuing. 3. the way a speech is given, as *Tom gave a speech, and his delivery was good.* 4. the way a ball is bowled. 5. childbirth.

dell *n.* a small valley with trees.

delta *n.* a triangular piece of land at the mouth of a river (especially the River Nile), where the river breaks up into several outlets.

delusion *n.* a wrong belief, deception.

deluge *n.* a downpour, a flood.

demand *v.* 1. to ask firmly, expecting an answer, as *I demand to know where he is.* 2. to claim, as *he demanded his money. n.* **demand** 1. a forceful question. 2. a claim.

in demand greatly desired.

democracy *n.* 1. government by all the people. 2. a country governed in this way, as *Britain is a democracy* (*pl.* **democracies**).

democrat *n.* someone who believes in democracy. *adj.* **democratic**.

demolish *v.* to destroy. *n.* **demolition**.

demon *n.* a devil, an evil spirit.

demonstrate *v.* 1. to show how something works, as *the lady demonstrated the new washing machine.* 2. to prove by reasoning, as *he demonstrated the answer to the problem* (**demonstrating, demonstrated**). *n.* **demonstration** 1. showing how a thing works. 2. a proof. 3. a show of feeling. 4. a mass meeting or procession to show public feeling. *adj.* **demonstrative**. *n.* **demonstrator**.

demure *adj.* modest, shy, coy.

den *n.* 1. a pit or cave where a wild animal lives. 2. a small room.

denial *n.* 1. a statement that something is not true. 2. a refusal, especially a refusal of luxuries, as *self-denial.*

denomination *n.* the members of a particular kind of church, as *the Methodist, Baptist, and Roman Catholic denominations.*

denominator *n.* (in arithmetic) the lower number in a fraction. In the fraction $\frac{3}{8}$, the figure 8 is the denominator. See **numerator**.

denote *v.* to mean, to show, as *these black clouds denote a coming storm* (**denoting, denoted**).

denounce *v.* 1. to accuse someone, to show him up. 2. to lay bare, to show up, as *to denounce a fraud* (**denouncing, denounced**).

dense *adj.* 1. thick, tightly packed, as *a dense crowd.* 2. (slang) stupid.

density *n.* closeness, compactness.

dent *n.* a notch, a mark made by a blow. *adj.* **dented** notched, bent.

dental *adj.* concerning teeth or dentistry, as *a dental clinic.*

dentist *n.* someone who cares for your teeth.

dentistry *n.* the care of teeth.

deny *v.* 1. to say that something is not true, as *I deny that I have the money.* 2. to refuse someone something, as *to deny someone permission to smoke* (**denies, denying, denied**).

depart *v.* to go away. *n.* **departure**.

department *n.* 1. a separate part. 2. a branch of a business or shop, as *the clothing department.*

department store a large shop with many departments for different goods.

depend (used with **on**) *v.* 1. to rely on, as *I depend on you for help.* 2. to follow from, as *that depends on what you do.*

dependable *adj.* reliable.

dependant *n.* someone who relies on another for support, as *my mother is my only dependant.*

dependence *n.* trust, reliance.

dependent *adj.* relying on, as *I am dependent on your help.*

deposit *v.* 1. to lay down, as *he deposited his hat on a chair.* 2. to place in a bank, as *to deposit money. n.* **deposit** 1. a first instalment of money, with more to follow. 2. a powder which settles at the bottom of a liquid, as *a deposit of mud.*

depot (*pron.* dep'ō) *n.* 1. a storehouse. 2. transport headquarters. 3. army headquarters.

depraved *adj.* wicked. *n.* **depravity**.

depress *v.* 1. to press down. 2. to make sad. *n.* **depression**.

depressed *adj.* 1. poor and humble. 2. forced down. 3. sad, miserable.

deprive *v.* to take away from somebody, as *to deprive a man of his freedom* (**depriving, deprived**). *n.* **deprivation**.

depth *n.* 1. deepness, distance from top to bottom. 2. distance from back to front, as *the depth of a stage.*

out of your depth 1. in water too deep for you to stand in. 2. trying to do a task which is too hard.

deputy *n.* someone chosen to stand in place of another, as *while the football* *captain was ill, Smith acted as his deputy.*

derision *n.* scorn, mocking laughter. *adj.* **derisive**.

derrick *n.* 1. a crane. 2. a steel tower above an oil well, holding a drill.

descend *v.* 1. to go down or come down. 2. (with **on**) to invade or attack, as *a swarm of wasps descended on the jam.* **to be descended from** to have as an ancestor.

descendant *n.* a son, grandchild, or other person, born from certain ancestors.

descent *n.* a going down.

describe *v.* 1. to relate in words. 2. to draw, as *to describe a circle.*

description *n.* a tale, an account.

desert (1) (*pron.* de.zert¹) *v.* 1. to run away from) as *to desert from the army.* 2. to abandon, as *the mother deserted her child. n.* **deserter** a man who runs away from his duties. *n.* **desertion** running away, abandoning.

desert (2) (*pron.* de¹zert) *n.* dry sandy waste land (note: do not confuse the spelling with **dessert**). *adj.* **desert** barren, waste.

deserts (*pron.* de.zerts¹) *n. pl.* what you deserve, either a reward or punishment.

deserve *v.* to be worthy of, or to have earned, some reward, or punishment (**deserving, deserved**).

design *n.* 1. a drawing or plan. 2. a plot. *v.* **design** to draw or plan. **to have designs on** to plot to get hold of.

desirable *adj.* desired, wanted. *n.* **desirability**.

desire *v.* to wish for, to want (**desiring, desired**).

desk *n.* a small table for writing or reading.

desolate *adj.* 1. empty, deserted. 2. lonely, miserable. 3. laid waste. *n.* **desolation**.

despair *v.* to give up hope. *n.* **despair** 1. hopelessness. 2. what causes hopelessness, as *he was the despair of his teachers.*

despatch see **dispatch**.

desperate *adj.* 1. made reckless by despair. 2. with little hope of success, as *a desperate fight. adv.* **desperately.** *n.* **desperation**.

despicable *adj.* worthless, mean, vile.

despise *v.* to look down on with scorn and contempt (**despising, despised**).

despite *prep.* in spite of, as *I went despite the bad weather.*

despondent *adj.* sad, without hope. *n.* **despondency**.

dessert (*pron.* de.zert¹) *n.* fruit, nuts, or sweets served after dinner (note: do not confuse the spelling with **desert**).

destination *n.* 1. the place to which you are travelling on a journey. 2. the place to which you send a letter or parcel.

destined *adj.* intended by fate, fixed beforehand, as *he was destined to be great.*

destiny *n.* fate, that which happens no matter what you do (*pl.* **destinies**).

destitute *adj.* penniless, without a single possession. *n.* **destitution** utter poverty.

destroy *v.* 1. to break into pieces. 2. to ruin.

destroyer *n.* 1. a person who destroys. 2. a small warship.

destruction *n.* 1. breaking, destroying. 2. ruin.

destructive *adj.* causing destruction.

detach *v.* to disconnect, to undo.

detached *adj.* separate, on its own, as *a detached house.*

detachment *n.* 1. separateness. 2. a group of ships or soldiers.

detail (*pron.* dee¹tayl) *n.* a small bit, a tiny part. **in detail** (examined, told, or counted) bit by bit.

detain *v.* 1. to keep waiting, as *I shall not detain you more than a moment.* 2. to keep prisoner.

detect *v.* to find out, to discover. *adj.* **detectable** noticeable. *n.* **detection**.

detective *n.* a person who tries to solve crimes.

detention *n.* 1. keeping waiting. 2. holding a prisoner.

determination *n.* 1. resolving, deciding firmly. 2. a resolve, a decision.

determine v. 1. to decide, to make up one's mind, as *to determine to win*. 2. to fix, as *to determine the date of a holiday* (**determining, determined**). *adj.* **determined** with a firm purpose, decided.

detest v. to hate, to loathe. *adj.* **detestable** hateful. *n.* **detestation** hatred, loathing.

detonate v. to explode. *n.* **detonator** a chemical which when struck explodes the powder in a cartridge. *n.* **detonation** explosion.

detour (*pron.* dee'toor) *n.* a new and roundabout way, used when an old way is blocked, as *the party made a detour round the fallen rocks*.

devastate v. to destroy, to ruin (**devastating, devastated**).

develop v. 1. to grow larger or make larger, as *to develop a business*. 2. to change gradually into something more advanced, as *a child's mind develops*. 3. to bring out the picture in a photographic film. *n.* **developer** a chemical used in photography. *n.* **development** growth.

deviate (*pron.* dee'vi.ayt) v. to turn aside off the main path. *n.* **deviation**.

device *n.* a plan, an invention.

devil *n.* 1. an evil spirit, Satan. 2. a very wicked person. *n.* **devilry**.
between the devil and the deep blue sea caught between two evils.
devil-may-care reckless.

devise (*pron.* de.vīz') v. to invent, to plan (**devising, devised**).

devote v. to put aside, to give up to, as *he devoted his spare time to gardening* (**devoting, devoted**). *adj.* **devoted** given up to, very fond. *n.* **devotion**.

devour v. to eat greedily.

devout *adj.* 1. religious, holy, as *a devout nun*. 2. sincere, earnest, as *a devout wish*.

dew *n.* water-drops on the ground, formed at night by the cooling of the air.

diabolical *adj.* devilish, cruel.

diagnose v. to find out what is wrong with someone or something from the symptoms.

diagnosis *n.* an investigation into the cause of an illness (*pl.* **diagnoses**).

diagonal *n.* a line passing from corner to corner of a rectangle. *adv.* **diagonally**.

diagram *n.* a drawing or plan which shows how something works or is made up.

dial *n.* the face of a clock or any similar instrument such as a meter. v. **dial** to make a telephone call by moving the dial of an automatic telephone (**dialling, dialled**).

dialect *n.* the language of a particular district, as *the Yorkshire dialect*.

dialogue *n.* 1. conversation between people. 2. the words of a play.

diameter *n.* a straight line across a circle through the centre.

diamond *n.* 1. a glittering precious stone. 2. one of the four suits of playing cards. 3. the shape ◇.
a rough diamond a good-hearted person without manners.
diamond wedding a sixtieth wedding anniversary.

diaper *n.* (in North America) a baby's napkin.

diaphragm (*pron.* dī'a.fram) *n.* 1. a muscular skin between the chest and stomach. 2. any flexible sheet, as *the vibrating diaphragm of a telephone*. 3. in a camera, a metal plate which lets in more or less light.

diary *n.* a little book in which a person writes the events of the day (*pl.* **diaries**).

dice *n. pl.* used as *sing.* a small cube marked on each face with one to six dots, used in some games.

dictate v. 1. to say aloud something to be taken down in writing, as *to dictate a letter to a secretary*. 2. to command (**dictating, dictated**). *n.* **dictation**.

dictator *n.* a ruler with full power over others. *n.* **dictatorship**.

dictionary *n.* a book of words in alphabetical order, with the meaning of each word (*pl.* **dictionaries**).

die (1) v. 1. to stop living, to lose your life. 2. to wither and decay (**he dies, dying, died**).
to die down to pass away.
to die out to disappear completely.

die (2) *n.* a tool for cutting threads on screws (*pl.* **dies**).

the die is cast there is no turning back.

diesel engine *n.* an engine invented by a German named Diesel, burning oil to drive heavy vehicles.

diet *n.* 1. the kinds of food one eats. 2. a course of special food eaten for good health. *v.* **diet** to eat only special food.

differ *v.* 1. to be different, to be unlike. 2. to disagree, to quarrel.

difference *n.* 1. unlikeness. 2. disagreement.

diffused *adj.* scattered.

dig *v.* 1. to turn over the earth with a spade, claws, etc. 2. to poke playfully, as *he dug me in the ribs* (**digging, dug** or **digged**).

to dig up to bring up, to discover.

digest (*pron.* di.jest') *v.* 1. to absorb food in the stomach to give energy. 2. to think over carefully. *n.* **digest** (*pron.* di'jest) a short account of a long story.

digestion *n.* the absorbing of food.

digit (*pron.* dij'it) *n.* 1. a finger or a toe. 2. any of the figures one to nine.

dignified *adj.* grave and noble looking, stately.

dignify *v.* to give dignity to (**he dignifies, dignifying, dignified**).

dignity *n.* 1. being dignified. 2. a title granted to someone.

on one's dignity pompous or aloof.

dike also spelt **dyke** *n.* the banks of a ditch or a wall built for defence against floods.

dilemma (*pron.* dī.lem'a) *n.* a choice between two bad things.

on the horns of a dilemma having to choose between two evil things.

diligent (*pron.* dil'i.jent) *adj.* hard-working, steady. *n.* **diligence**.

dilute (*pron* dī.lyoot') *v.* to weaken with water or some other fluid, as *to dilute thick paint with turpentine* (**diluting, diluted**). *n* **dilution**.

dim *adj.* faint, not bright, hazy (*comparative* **dimmer,** *superlative* **dimmest**). *v.* **dim** to grow dim or make dim (**dimming, dimmed**). *n.* **dimmer** an electrical appliance for dimming stage lights or car headlights.

dime *n.* a North American silver coin equal to ten cents.

dimension *n.* measurement in any one direction, as length, breadth, or depth. *n. pl.* **dimensions** size, as *a building of big dimensions*.

diminish *v.* to make smaller, to grow less.

dimple *n.* a small hollow in the cheek or chin.

din *n.* a loud continuous noise. *v.* **din** to make a loud noise (**dinning, dinned**).

dine *v.* to eat a dinner, or give a dinner to (**dining, dined**). *n.* **diner** someone who dines. *n.* **dining-room** a room where meals are eaten.

dinghy (*pron.* ding'gi) *n.* a small boat (*pl.* **dinghies**).

dingo *n.* an Australian wild dog (*pl.* **dingoes**).

dingy (*pron.* din'ji) *adj.* dull, dirty-looking.

dinner *n.* the chief meal of the day.

dioxide *n.* a chemical containing oxygen.

dip *v.* 1. to put into a liquid for a short time. 2. (of a flag) to lower and raise again. 3. to slope down. 4. to read bits of, as *to dip into a book* (**dipping, dipped**). *n.* **dip** 1. a slope down. 2. a short bathe.

diploma (*pron.* di.plō'ma) *n.* a certificate given after completing a course of study.

diplomacy (*pron.* di.plō'ma.si) *n.* the art of keeping good relations between nations or people.

diplomat *n.* 1. a person busy in keeping good will between nations. 2. a tactful person. *adj.* **diplomatic** tactful.

direct *adj.* 1. straight, as *in a direct line*. 2. straightforward, as *a direct manner*. *v.* **direct** 1. to show someone the way. 2. to aim, as *to direct a gun*. *adv.* **directly** 1. soon. 2. in a direct way. *n.* **directness**.

direction *n.* 1. the point towards which someone or something moves. 2. an order.

director *n.* the manager of a business.

directory *n.* a list of names and addresses in alphabetical order (*pl.* **directories**).

dirk *n.* a short Scottish dagger.

dirt *n.* filth, mud. *n.* **dirtiness**. *adj.* **dirty** filthy (*comparative* **dirtier,** *superlative* **dirtiest**). *v.* **dirty** to make dirty (**dirtying, dirtied**).

dis- *a prefix* which means 'not', as 'displeased' means 'not pleased'.

disabled *adj.* 1. crippled. 2. useless.

disadvantage *n.* something unfavourable, a handicap.

disagree *v.* 1. to quarrel. 2. not to suit, as *this food disagrees with me. adj.* **disagreeable** unpleasant. *n.* **disagreement**.

disappear *v.* to pass out of sight. *n.* **disappearance**.

disappoint *v.* not to be what one hopes or expects. *n.* **disappointment**.

disarm *v.* 1. to take weapons off someone. 2. to lay down arms.

disarmament *n.* reducing a nation's armed forces.

disaster *n.* a great misfortune. *adj.* **disastrous**.

disbelieve *v.* to refuse to believe. *n.* **disbelief** lack of belief.

disc (also spelt **disk**) *n.* a round plate such as a gramophone record.

discard *v.* 1. to throw away as not wanted. 2. (in card games) to throw away a card of little value.

discharge *v.* 1. to unload, as *to discharge a cargo.* 2. to fire, as *to discharge a gun.* 3. to set free, as *to discharge a prisoner.* 4. to dismiss, as *to discharge a workman.* 5. to carry out, as *to discharge a duty. n.* **discharge** 1. an unloading. 2. a shot. 3. a setting free, or dismissal. 4. a carrying out of a task.

disciple *n.* someone who follows a great leader.

discipline *n.* 1. training in obedience. 2. self-control.

disclose *v.* to reveal, as *to disclose a secret* (**disclosing, disclosed**). *n.* **disclosure**.

discontent *n.* lack of satisfaction, unrest. ill-will. *n.* **discontentment**.

discount (*pron.* dis'kownt) *n.* money taken off a bill for prompt payment.

discourage *v.* 1. to take away hope, to cast down. 2. to try to stop something, as *to discourage carelessness on the*

roads (**discouraging, discouraged**). *n.* **discouragement**.

discourteous (*pron.* dis.kurt'e.us) *adj.* rude, impolite. *n.* **discourtesy**.

discover *v.* to find out, to learn something new. *n.* **discovery** 1. finding something new. 2. something new that is found out (*pl.* **discoveries**).

discredit *n.* disgrace.

discreet *v.* tactful, careful in what one says. See **discretion**.

discrepancy *n.* a difference, a lack of agreement, as *a discrepancy between money in hand, and money required for a purchase* (*pl.* **discrepancies**).

discretion *n.* 1. tact, being discreet. 2. freedom to do as one chooses, as *use your discretion whether to write or not.* See **discreet**.

discretion is the better part of valour even a brave man should be prudent.

discriminate *v.* 1. to see a difference between things. 2. to be unfair by favouring one person rather than another, as *the referee discriminated between the home team and the other. n.* **discrimination**.

discuss *v.* to talk over something fully. *n.* **discussion**.

disdain *n.* contempt, looking down on someone. *v.* **disdain** to look on with scorn. *adj.* **disdainful**.

disease *n.* illness, an ailment. *adj.* **diseased**.

disfigure *v.* to spoil the beauty of something or someone (**disfiguring, disfigured**). *n.* **disfigurement**.

disgrace *n.* shame, dishonour. *v.* **disgrace** to bring shame on (**disgracing, disgraced**). *adj.* **disgraceful**.

disgruntled *adj.* surly, discontented.

disguise *v.* to alter the appearance of someone, so that he cannot be recognized (**disguising, disguised**). *n.* **disguise** a change of appearance to avoid recognition.

disgust *n.* loathing, contempt. *adj.* **disgusting**.

dish *n.* 1. a plate on which food is served. 2. a particular kind of food, as *a meat dish.*

dishearten *v.* to discourage.

dishevelled (*pron.* di.shev'eld) *adj.* untidy, with ruffled hair.

dishonest *adj.* not honest.

disinfect *v.* to destroy germs. *n.* **disinfectant** a substance which destroys germs.

disk see **disc.**

dislike *v.* not to like, to hate (**disliking, disliked**).

dislocate *v.* to put out of joint, as *he dislocated a shoulder* (**dislocating, dislocated**).

disloyal *adj.* unfaithful. *n.* **disloyalty.**

dismal *adj.* dreary, gloomy. *adv.* **dismally.**

dismantle *v.* 1. to take to pieces, as *to dismantle a bicycle.* 2. to remove furnishings, etc., as *to dismantle a shop* (**dismantling, dismantled**).

dismay *v.* to dishearten, to cause fear. *n.* **dismay** fear, discouragement. *adj.* **dismayed** disheartened.

dismiss *v.* 1. to send away, as *to dismiss one's fears from mind.* 2. to discharge from employment, as *to dismiss an employee. n.* **dismissal.**

disobedient *adj.* refusing to obey. *n.* **disobedience.**

disobey *v.* not to obey.

disorder *n.* 1. confusion, untidiness. 2. an illness. *adj.* **disorderly.**

disorganized *adj.* confused, thrown into disorder.

dispatch or **despatch** *v.* 1. to send away quickly. 2. to finish. 3. to kill. *n.* **dispatch** 1. speed. 2. a message.

dispel *v.* to drive off, as *the good news dispelled his fears* (**dispelling, dispelled**).

dispense *v.* to distribute or deal out, as *to dispense justice, or medicine. n.* **dispensary** a hospital department where medicine is provided.

to dispense with to do without.

disperse *v.* to scatter in all directions (**dispersing, dispersed**). *n.* **dispersal** a scattering.

displace *v.* 1. to move out of position. 2. to take the place of, as *trains have displaced mail-coaches* (**displacing, displaced**).

display *n.* a show, an exhibition. *v.* **display** to make a show of, as *the peacock displays its feathers* (**displaying, displayed**).

displeased *adj.* annoyed, not pleased. *n.* **displeasure.**

disposal *n.* getting rid of.

dispose *v.* 1. to arrange, as *to dispose flowers.* 2. to get rid of, as *to dispose of some books.* 3. to be willing, as *he is disposed to be lenient* (**disposing, disposed**).

dispute *v.* to argue, to quarrel (**disputing, disputed**). *n.* **dispute** an argument.

disqualify *v.* to rule someone out of a competition, to debar (**disqualifies, disqualifying, disqualified**).

disreputable (*pron.* dis.rep'you.ta.bl) *adj.* not respectable, shabby.

dissatisfy *v.* to cause discontent, not to please (**dissatisfies, dissatisfying, dissatisfied**). *n.* **dissatisfaction** discontent, displeasure.

dissect *v.* to cut something into pieces in order to examine it, as *to dissect a dead frog in a biology lesson. n.* **dissection.**

dissolve *v.* 1. (of a solid substance) to disappear when stirred in a liquid, as *sugar dissolves in tea.* 2. to break up a meeting or a partnership.

distance *n.* 1. the space between two places. 2. a place far off, as *away in the distance.*

distant *adj.* 1. far off, as *a distant cry.* 2. cold, aloof, as *she greeted me with a distant manner.*

distemper *n.* 1. a kind of water-paint. 2. an illness of dogs.

distend *v.* to swell up. *n.* **distension.**

distil *v.* to purify a liquid by boiling, and then by cooling the vapour, change it back to a liquid (**distilling, distilled**). *n.* **distillation.**

distillery *n.* a place where whisky is distilled.

distinct *adj.* 1. different from others of the kind, as *the colour of her coat is a distinct shade of red.* 2. clear, definite, as *he heard a distinct sound.*

distinction *n.* 1. a difference between things, as *there is a clear distinction between these shades of pink.* 2. an honour, as *he won a distinction in the war.*

distinctive *adj.* different from others, as *she wore a distinctive hat.*

distinguish *v.* 1. to see a difference, as *to distinguish between olive-green and apple-green.* 2. to show a difference, as *his red hair distinguishes him from the others.* 3. to make out, as *I can just distinguish the rabbit in the shadow.* *adj.* **distinguished** important, as *a distinguished visitor.*

distort *v.* 1. to twist out of shape, as *he distorted his mouth.* 2. to twist words out of their real meaning, as *when he speaks he distorts the truth.* *n.* **distortion.**

distract *v.* to draw aside someone's attention, as *to distract a man from his work by talking.* *n.* **distraction.**

distress *v.* to cause pain or suffering. *n.* **distress** 1. grief, pain. 2. danger, misfortune, as *a flag of distress.* *adj.* **distressed** very uneasy, worried.

distribute (*pron.* dis.trib'yoot) *v.* to share, to give round (**distributing, distributed**). *n.* **distribution** a sharing out.

district *n.* part of a country, an area of land.

distrust *v.* to doubt, not to trust. *n.* **distrust** doubt, suspicion. *adj.* **distrustful.**

disturb *v.* to interrupt, to interfere with. *n.* **disturbance** interference, excitement.

disused *adj.* no longer used, as *a disused mine.*

ditch *n.* a trench for draining cut in the earth.

ditto *n.* the same as before, often written *do* or marked as ,, .

divan *n.* a sofa without back or ends.

dive *v.* 1. to plunge down through air or water, as *the seagulls dive for food.* 2. to disappear into a hiding-place, as *to dive for shelter in an air-raid* (**diving, dived**). *n.* **dive** 1. a downward plunge. 2. a low haunt. *n.* **diver** 1. a man who swims under water for pearls. 2. a man who goes under water in a diving-suit. 3. a water-bird.

diverse *adj.* varied, different, as *they hold diverse opinions.* *n.* **diversity** a variety.

diversion *n.* 1. a turning to one side, as *a traffic diversion.* 2. something distracting. 3. an amusement.

divert *v.* 1. to turn in another direction, as *to divert traffic while a road is being repaired.* 2. to entertain, to amuse, as *the clown diverted the crowd with his tricks.* See **diversion.**

divide *v.* 1. to cut up or share out, as *to divide a cake among four girls.* 2. (in arithmetic) to see how many times one number is contained in another (**dividing, divided**). See **division.**

dividend *n.* 1. (in arithmetic) the number which is to be divided by another number, as *when 6 is divided by 3 to give 2, the number 6 is the dividend.* 2. a share of the profits of a business, as in a co-operative society.

divine *adj.* holy, sacred. *n.* **divine** a priest. *adv.* **divinely.**

divinity *n.* 1. a god. 2. the study of the Scriptures.

divisible *adj.* (in arithmetic) able to be divided into equal parts, as *12 is divisible by 4.*

division *n.* 1. dividing into parts. 2. a part. 3. a partition in a room. 4. an army unit of several thousand men.

divisor *n.* (in arithmetic) the number which is divided into another number, as *12 divided by 4 equals 3, where the number 4 is the divisor.*

divorce *v.* 1. for a husband and wife to end a marriage legally. 2. to separate, as *your words are divorced from the truth* (**divorcing, divorced**).

divulge *v.* to tell (a secret), to reveal, as *Father divulged his plans for the holiday* (**divulging, divulged**).

dizzy *adj.* giddy, confused. *n.* **dizziness.**

do (*pron.* dōō) *v.* to perform, to carry out (**I do** *pron.* dōō, **thou doest** or **dost** *pron.* dust, **he does** *pron.* duz, **we do, you do, they do, doing, did, done**). **done for** finished.
to do away with to get rid of.
to do up to fasten.
up and doing active.

docile (*pron.* dō'sīl) *n.* easy to manage, obedient, as *a docile horse.* *n.* **docility.**

dock (1) *n.* a weed with broad leaves.

dock (2) *v.* to cut short, as *to dock a puppy's tail*.

dock (3) *n.* 1. a place where large ships are moored or repaired. 2. a place where the accused person stands in a courtroom. *v.* **dock** to moor a ship by a pier or jetty. *n.* **dockyard** a naval repair depot.

doctor *n.* 1. a person who attends to illnesses or injuries. 2. a person who holds a university's highest degree, as *a doctor of science*.

doctrine *n.* a belief that is taught.

document *n.* a form or official paper.

dodge *v.* to jump aside quickly to escape something, as *to dodge a car. n.* **dodge** a clever trick.

doe *n.* the female of the rabbit, hare, deer, and certain other animals.

dog *n.* 1. a well-known domestic animal. 2. the male of the species (*fem.* **bitch**), as *a dog-fox*. 3. a metal bracket or tool for holding, as a *fire-dog* or *a pair of dogs* (an adjustable spanner or wrench). *v.* **dog** to follow closely (**dogging, dogged**), as *to dog someone's footsteps*.

being a dog in a manger not letting others use what one cannot use oneself.

dog-tired very tired.

give a dog a bad name and hang him let someone gain a bad reputation and he will never lose it.

to go to the dogs to go to ruin.

dogmatic *adj.* stating opinions very strongly, as *Bob was very dogmatic in saying how his football team would win. adv.* **dogmatically**.

dog-watch *n.* a two-hour watch on ship, not the usual four-hour watch.

dole *n.* money or food shared out among people who are in need.

to dole out to share round.

doleful *adj.* gloomy, sad.

doll *n.* a child's toy baby. *n.* **dolly** a little doll.

dollar *n.* a silver coin of Canada, the U.S.A., Mexico, etc., equal to 100 cents.

dolphin *n.* a sea-animal like a porpoise.

dome *n.* a roof shaped like half a ball, seen on some buildings.

domestic *adj.* 1. concerning the home, as *a domestic servant works in a house*.

2. concerning the homeland, not a foreign country, as *domestic trade*. 3. (of animals) tame, not wild as *a dog is a domestic animal*.

domestic science a study of cookery and laundrywork and other housework.

domesticated *adj.* tamed, as *a domesticated animal*.

dominant *adj.* the chief, most powerful, as *the dominant member of a gang*.

dominate *v.* 1. to rule over, as *the bull dominated the herd*. 2. to tower over, as *the mountain dominates the town* (**dominating, dominated**). *n.* **domination**.

domineer *v.* to rule over like a tyrant.

dominion *n.* 1. rule. 2. a land over which a king or queen rules. 3. a self-governing member of the British Commonwealth of Nations, as *the Dominion of Canada*.

domino *n.* an oblong piece of wood or bone with dots for numbers, used in a game (*pl.* **dominoes**).

don *n.* 1. a Spanish nobleman. 2. a university tutor or fellow.

Don a Spanish title, like the English *Mr.*

donate *v.* to give (**donating, donated**). *n.* **donation** a gift.

done *past participle* of **do**.

donkey *n.* 1. an ass, a long-eared animal like a horse. 2. a stupid person (*pl.* **donkeys**).

for donkey's years for a very long time.

don't short for *do not*.

don't count your chickens before they are hatched do not rely on anything until it is certain.

don't put all your eggs in one basket do not put all your trust in one venture.

doom *n.* 1. death, ruin, as *the ship sailed to her doom and was wrecked*. 2. fate. 3. judgement.

doomsday *n.* the day of Judgement at the end of the world.

door *n.* a wooden structure which closes an entrance. *n.* **door-keeper** a man who attends at the main door of a building. *n.* **doorway** the entrance to which a door is fitted.

out of doors in the open air.

dormitory *n.* a large room with many beds (*pl.* **dormitories**).

dorp *n.* a South African village.

dose *n.* an amount of medicine to be taken at a time.

dot *n.* a small spot or point. *v.* **dot** to mark with dots (**dotting, dotted**).

on the dot exactly on time.

double *adj.* 1. twice as much. 2. two together, as *a double-decker bus.* 3. (of paper) folded in two sheets. *v.* **double** 1. to multiply by two. 2. to fold in two. 3. to turn sharply on one's footsteps, as *the detective doubled back.* 4. to take the place of someone, as *the actress doubled for the star who was ill.* (**doubling, doubled**). *n.* **double** 1. a person exactly like another. 2. (in tennis) two false serves one after the other. *n. pl.* **doubles** (in tennis) a game for four people.

at the double running.

double Dutch language which cannot be understood, gibberish.

to double-cross to betray.

doubloon *n.* a Spanish gold coin of old times.

doubt *n.* suspicion, uncertainty. *v.* **doubt** not to be sure, to be suspicious. *adj.* **doubtful** uncertain. *adj.* **doubtless** without doubt. *adv.* **doubtfully**.

dough *n.* a stiff paste of flour, yeast, and water from which bread is made.

doughnut *n.* sweetened dough fried in fat.

dour (*pron.* dŏŏr) *adj.* grim, determined.

dove *n.* a kind of pigeon. *n.* **dovecote** a box in which doves breed. *n.* **dovetail** a joint used in woodwork of alternate mortises and tenons like doves' tails.

down (1) *n.* 1. the first soft feathers of a young bird. 2. soft fluffy hair.

down (2) *n.* an open grassy upland. *n. pl.* **the downs** grassy uplands in South East England.

down (3) *adv.* 1. passing to a lower level, as *down the hill.* 2. deep into, as *down at the bottom of the sea.* prep. **down** along, as *down the road.* adj. **down** from a city, as *the down train from London.* v. **down** to put down, as *he downed his opponent.*

downcast sad.

downfall ruin, disgrace.

downhearted miserable.

downpour very heavy rain.

downright sincere.

downstage towards the footlights on a stage.

to go downhill to go to ruin, to become worse.

dowry *n.* money or property brought by a woman to her husband on marriage.

doze *v.* to be half-asleep (**dozing, dozed**). *n.* **doze** a light sleep.

dozen *n.* a set of twelve things.

drab *adj.* 1. of a grey-brown colour. 2. dull, monotonous. *n.* **drabness**.

draft *n.* (in the U.S.A. the word **draught** is usually spelled **draft**). 1. a rough sketch or plan, as *an architect's first draft of a building.* 2. a group of men called up to serve in one of the armed services. *v.* **draft** to sketch out.

drag *v.* 1. to pull along. 2. to be slow and dull, as *time dragged* (**dragging, dragged**). *n.* **drag** 1. a net for pulling along below water. 2. a kind of brake used on carts.

dragon *n.* an imaginary monster breathing out fire.

dragonfly *n.* a long insect with glittering blue or green wings (*pl.* **dragonflies**).

dragoon *n.* a soldier on horseback.

drain *v.* 1. to draw off water. 2. to flow off. 3. to cut ditches in land so that rainwater can flow away. 4. to empty, as *to drain a glass,* or *to drain a treasure-chest of money.* n. **drain** a ditch, sewer, or pipe for draining. n. **drainage** a network of drains.

drake *n.* a male duck.

drama (*pron.* drah'ma) *n.* 1. a play, especially a play full of action. 2. (in newspapers) an exciting human story. *adj.* **dramatic** 1. belonging to drama. 2. exciting.

dramatist *n.* a play-wright.

dramatize *v.* to make into a play or drama (**dramatizing, dramatized**).

drank *past* of **drink**.

drastic *adj.* extreme, powerful, as *a drastic action.*

draught (*pron.* drahft) *n.* **1.** a chilly stream of air. **2.** a catch of fish. **3.** the depth of a boat in water. **4.** a drink or dose of medicine (the word is sometimes spelled **draft**, especially in the U.S.A.). *adj.* **draughty.** *n.* **draughtiness.**

draughts *n. pl.* a game played by two players with 12 pieces, or draughtsmen, each, on a chequer-board of 64 squares (known in Canada and the U.S.A. as *chequers*).

draughtsman *n.* **1.** a man who draws plans in an engineering office. **2.** a piece in draughts.

draw *v.* **1.** to pull steadily. **2.** to take out, as *to draw money from a bank*. **3.** to attract, as *to draw attention to*. **4.** to sketch with pen, pencil, or crayon. **5.** to finish a game without either side winning (**drawing, drew, drawn**). *n.* **draw 1.** the picking of a ticket in a lottery. **2.** a tie between two teams. *n.* **drawing** a sketch in pencil.
to draw a blank to have no success.
to draw the line to set a limit.
to draw up to make up, to compose.

drawback *n.* a disadvantage, a weakness.

drawbridge *n.* a bridge over a moat leading to a castle, which can be drawn up.

drawer *n.* a sliding box in a desk, table, or dressing-table.

drawl *v.* to speak in a slow lazy way.

dread *n.* great fear, horror. *v.* **dread** to fear something may happen. *adj.* **dreadful** horrible.

dream *n.* **1.** a vivid picture imagined during sleep. **2.** something expected or hoped for, as *a dream of wealth*. *v.* **dream** to have a vision while asleep (**dreaming, dreamed** or **dreamt** *pron.* dremt). *adj.* **dreamy** vague. *adv.* **dreamily.**

dreary *adj.* gloomy, dull. *n.* **dreariness.**

dredge *v.* to scoop up mud to deepen a channel in a river (**dredging, dredged**). *n.* **dredger 1.** a boat which dredges. **2.** a pot having a lid with holes, used to sprinkle flour or sugar.

dregs *n. pl.* grains of dirt or powder settling at the bottom of a liquid.

drench *v.* to soak, to make very wet.

dress *n.* **1.** clothes. **2.** a frock. *v.* **dress 1.** to put on clothes. **2.** to prepare, as *to dress a chicken*. **3.** to attend to, as *to dress a wound*. **4.** to draw up a line of men, as in the order '*By the right! Dress!*' *n.* **dressing 1.** putting on clothes. **2.** a bandage. **3.** sauce or seasoning added to food.
to dress someone down to talk to him severely.

dresser *n.* a chest of drawers or sideboard.

dressing-table *n.* a piece of furniture with drawers and a mirror.

drew *past* of **draw.**

dribble *v.* **1.** (of water) to trickle. **2.** (of a baby) to let saliva drop from the mouth. **3.** (of a ball game) to push the ball forward with light taps (**dribbling, dribbled**).

dried *past* of **dry.**

drift *n.* **1.** a pile of blown snow or sand. **2.** material floating on water, as *driftwood*. *v.* **drift 1.** to pile up in heaps. **2.** to be carried along by air or water currents.

drill *v.* **1.** to bore holes with a tool. **2.** to sow seeds in rows by machine. **3.** to train any living creature by exercises. *n.* **drill 1.** a tool for boring holes. **2.** a machine for sowing seeds. **3.** exercises of a military kind.

drily *adv.* in a dry calm tone of voice.

drink *v.* **1** to swallow a liquid. **2.** to take in through the eyes or mind, as *to drink in what someone says* (**drinking, drank, drunk**). *n.* **drink** liquid for drinking.

drip *v.* to fall in drops, or let fall in drops, as *this tap drips* (**dripping, dripped**). *n.* **dripping 1.** a falling of water in drops. **2.** the fat from roast meat.

drive *v.* **1.** to push or urge forward forcefully. **2.** to guide and control, as *to drive a car*. **3.** (in golf) to hit a ball from the tee. **4.** to carry to a finish, as *to drive a bargain with someone* (**driving, drove, driven**). *n.* **drive 1.** a trip in a vehicle. **2.** a road leading to a large house. **3.** a rounding-up of cattle. **4.** energy, as *Mr Brown has plenty of drive*.

5. an organized activity, as *a drive to raise funds* or *a whist drive*. *n.* **driver** 1. someone who drives. 2. a golf-club for hitting from the tee.

dromedary *n.* a one-humped camel (*pl.* **dromedaries**). See **camel**.

drone *n.* 1. the male honey-bee which does no work. 2. someone who does no work but depends on others. 3. a low humming sound. *v.* **drone** to make a low humming noise.

droop *v.* to hang down, to sag. *n.* **droop** a hanging.

drop *v.* 1. to fall or let fall to a lower place. 2. to give up or abandon, as *to drop an inquiry*. 3. to speak casually, as *to drop a hint* (**dropping, dropped**). *n.* **drop** 1. a round spot of liquid. 2. a small amount of liquid. 3. a fall. 4. the amount of a fall, as *a big drop*.

to drop in to arrive unexpectedly without notice.

drought (*pron.* drowt) *n.* a long period without rain.

drove (1) *n.* a herd of animals being driven. *n.* **drover** a cattle dealer or driver.

drove (2) *past* of **drive**.

drown *v.* 1. to suffocate under water. 2. to overwhelm or overpower, as *the noise of the waterfall drowned his voice*.

drowsy *adj.* dozy, sleepy. *n.* **drowsiness**.

drudge *n.* someone who does heavy dull work. *n.* **drudgery** dull monotonous work.

drug *n.* 1. a medicine or substance used in making medicine. 2. a substance which it becomes a habit to take, as cocaine. *v.* **drug** to make unconscious with a drug (**drugging, drugged**). *n.* **druggist** someone who sells drugs. *n.* **drug-store** (in U.S.A.) a chemist's shop also selling stationery and light refreshments.

Druid *n.* a priest of the ancient Gauls and Britons.

drum *n.* 1. a musical instrument with stretched skins which are beaten with the fingers or sticks. 2. the hollow part of the ear behind the skin in the ear passage. 3. a cylinder or barrel. *v.*

drum to tap with the fingers or feet (**drumming, drummed**). *n.* **drummer** 1. someone who plays the drum. 2. (in North America) a travelling salesman.

drunk *past participle* of **drink**. *adj.* **drunk** intoxicated, affected by alcohol.

dry *adj.* 1. not wet. 2. sarcastic, as *a dry remark*. 3. uninteresting, as *a dry lecture* (*comparative* **drier,** *superlative* **driest**). *v.* **dry** to make dry (**drying, dried**). *n.* **dryness**. *adv.* **drily**.

dry battery an electric battery with no liquid.

dry dock a dock which can be emptied for a ship to be repaired.

cut and dried all arranged beforehand.

dual *adj.* double, for two uses, as *a dual carriageway is a double road, one for traffic each way*.

dubious (*pron.* dyōō'bi.us) *adj.* doubtful, uncertain.

duchess *n.* a noblewoman, the wife or widow of a duke.

duck (1) *n.* 1. a female water-bird (*masc.* **drake**). 2. (in cricket) no score. *n.* **duckling** a young duck.

duck (2) *v.* 1. to dip someone in water. 2. to bend down suddenly to avoid being hit.

to play ducks and drakes to throw away money.

due *adj.* 1. owing, as *money due to me*. 2. expected, as *he is due to arrive today*. 3. proper, right, as *with due respect to you*. *adv.* **due** exactly, as *he went due north*. *n.* **due** a toll, a payment, as *a harbour due*.

due to owing to, as a result of.

in due course later, in course of time.

duel *n.* a fight with weapons arranged between two people.

duet *n.* music for two players or singers.

duke *n.* a nobleman of highest rank (*fem.* **duchess**).

dull *adj.* 1. blunt, as *a dull knife*. 2. slow to learn, as *a dull scholar*. 3. uninteresting, as *a dull talk*. 4. not sunny, as *a dull day*. *adv.* **dully**. *n.* **dullness**.

duly (*pron.* dyōō'li) *adv.* at the proper time, as expected, as *he duly arrived*.

dumb *adj.* unable to speak, silent. *n.* **dumbness**. *adv.* **dumbly**. *adj.* **dumbfounded** dumb with surprise.

dummy *n.* 1. a tailor's model. 2. a model or imitation of the real thing (*pl.* **dummies**).

dune *n.* a small hill of sand near the sea.

dungeon *n.* an underground prison.

duplicate *n.* an exact copy. *v.* **duplicate** to make a copy or copies. *n.* **duplicator** a machine for making copies of writing or typewriting.

durable *adj.* long-lasting, hard-wearing. *n.* **durability**.

duration *n.* the time a thing lasts, as *the duration of the war was five years.*

during *prep.* in the time of, as *during his stay.*

dusk *n.* twilight. *adj.* **dusky** dark or half-dark.

dust *n.* fine powder which may float in air. *v.* **dust** 1. to remove this powder from clothes or furniture with a brush or cloth. 2. to sprinkle, as *to dust pastry with sugar. n.* **duster.** *adj.* **dusty**.

duty *n.* 1. some task one feels bound to do, as *it is our duty to be kind to animals.* 2. one of the tasks belonging to a certain position, as *one of the duties of a sea-captain.* 3. a government tax on certain articles, such as wine and tobacco (*pl.* **duties**). *adj.* **dutiful** obedient, attending to his duties, as *a dutiful son.*

dwarf *n.* 1. any living thing much smaller than usual. 2. (in fairy tales) a little man, usually bearded (*pl.* **dwarfs**). *v.* **dwarf** to make something seem small, as *the large house dwarfs the shed near by.*

dwell *v.* 1. to live in a place. 2. to talk about at length, as *he dwelt on his travels* (**dwelling, dwelt** or **dwelled**). *n.* **dwelling** a house.

dwindle *v.* to become smaller (**dwindling, dwindled**).

dye *n.* a stain used to colour cloth and other materials. *v.* **dye** to stain (**dyeing, dyed**). *n.* **dyer** someone who uses dyes.

dying *present participle* of **die.**

dyke see **dike.**

dynamite *n.* an explosive used for blasting rock.

dynamo *n.* a machine for making electricity (*pl.* **dynamos**).

E

each *pronoun* or *adj.* every single one, as *each of the boys* or *each boy.*

eager *adj.* keen, anxious to have or to do, as *they were eager to start. adv.* **eagerly**. *n.* **eagerness.**

eagle *n.* 1. a very large bird of prey. 2. a gold coin of the U.S.A., worth ten dollars.

ear (1) *n.* a spike of corn.

ear (2) *n.* 1. one of the two parts of the body through which we hear. 2. a sense of hearing, as *she has a good ear for music. n.* **ear-drum** the skin across the entrance to the middle ear.

to be all ears to listen carefully.

to turn a deaf ear to refuse to listen.

earl *n.* a British nobleman below a marquis in rank (*fem.* **countess**).

early *adj.* or *adv.* in good time, near the beginning of the day, as *an early start* or *early in the day* (*comparative* **earlier**, *superlative* **earliest**).

earn *v.* to gain money or some reward by giving service. *n. pl.* **earnings** wages.

earnest *adj.* sincere, serious.

in earnest determined, sincere.

earth *n.* 1. the world. 2. soil, the ground. 3. an animal's burrow, as *the fox has gone to earth.* 4. an electrical connection leading to the ground, as *the earth connection on a radio set.*

earthen *adj.* made of clay. *n.* **earthenware** pottery.

earthquake *n.* a shaking of the earth.

earthworm *n.* the common worm.

earwig *n.* a brown creeping insect.

ease *n.* 1. rest, comfort. 2. freedom from pain or worry. *v.* **ease** 1. to set free from pain or worry, as *to ease someone's mind.* 2. to remove tightness or pressure, as *to ease a rope* or *ease a load into a new position* (**easing, eased**). *adj.* **easy** 1. comfortable. 2. not difficult (*comparative* **easier**, *superlative* **easiest**). *adv.* **easily**. *n.* **easiness**.

easy-going idle, gentle, without effort.

to ease off to slacken off.

to stand at ease to stand with feet apart.

easel *n.* a support for a blackboard or picture.

easily, easiness see **ease**.

east *n.* one of the four points of the compass, the direction in which the sun rises, opposite to *west*. *adj.* **east** 1. in the direction of the east, as *the east side of a church*. 2. from the east, as *an east wind*. *adv.* **east** in the direction of the east, as *he went east*.

easterly towards the east, (of a wind) from the east.

eastern belonging to the east.

eastward, eastwards to the east.

the East the countries to the east of western Europe, the Orient.

the Far East the countries of eastern Asia.

Easter *n.* the Christian Festival in memory of the rising of Jesus Christ after his death, held on the Sunday after Good Friday, on one of the dates between March 21st and April 26th.

Easter egg a coloured or chocolate egg given as a present at Easter.

easy see **ease**.

eat *v.* 1. to take food through the mouth. 2. to corrode, as *acid eats into metal*. 3. to wear away, as *water eats into limestone* (**eating, ate** *pron.* et *or* ayt, **eaten**).

to eat your heart out to brood silently over your troubles.

to eat your words to admit being wrong.

eaves *n. pl.* the overhanging edges of a roof.

eavesdropper *n.* someone who secretly listens to a conversation between other people.

ebb *n.* the going out of the tide. *v.* **ebb** 1. for the tide to go out. 2. to fall off, to lessen, as *trade is ebbing*.

at a low ebb in poor condition.

ebony *n.* a hard black wood.

eccentric (*pron.* ek.sen'trik) *adj.* peculiar, odd, unusual, as *an eccentric old man. n.* **eccentricity**.

echo *n.* 1. the reflection of sound from a wall or cliff. 2. the repeating of something, as *the echo of an old rumour* (*pl.* **echoes**). *v.* **echo** 1. to throw back sound. 2. to repeat, as *you are echoing my opinions* (**echoing, echoed**).

eclipse *n.* a cutting off of light, as *when the earth moves between the sun and the moon it throws its shadow on the moon, and so causes an eclipse of the moon; when the moon comes between the earth and the sun, there is an eclipse of the sun. v.* **eclipse** to outshine, to do better than (**eclipsing, eclipsed**).

economical *adj.* thrifty, avoiding waste.

economize *v.* to save, to spend or use as little as possible (**economizing, economized**).

economy *n.* saving, using the least, thrift (*pl.* **economies**).

edge *n.* 1. the rim or border of anything. 2. the sharp side of a blade. *v.* **edge** 1. to move bit by bit. 2. to move sideways (**edging, edged**). *adv.* **edgeways** sideways.

to be on edge to be irritable.

to set someone's teeth on edge to irritate, annoy, or repel.

edging *n.* a border or fringe.

edible *adj.* fit to eat, as *edible fish*.

edifice (*pron.* ed'i.fis) *n.* a large building.

edit *v.* to prepare news and written matter for publication (**editing, edited**).

edition *n.* all the copies of a book or paper printed at one time.

editor *n.* the person who edits a book, magazine, or newspaper.

editorial *n.* the leading article of a newspaper.

educate *v.* 1. to teach or train someone. 2. to instruct, especially someone young (**educating, educated**).

education *n.* teaching, training, schooling. *adj.* **educational** concerning education.

eel *n.* a snake-like fish which can be eaten.

eerie *adj.* weird, strange, uncanny.

effect *v.* to make, to bring about, as *to effect an improvement. n.* **effect** a result, as *my holiday has had a good effect on my health* (note: do not confuse with **affect**).

effective *adj.* 1. able to produce results, as *effective work* or *an effective action.* 2. striking, as *an effective display*.

efficient *adj.* able to do things well. *n.* **efficiency**. *adv.* **efficiently** capably.

effort *n.* trouble or energy spent in getting something done. *adj.* **effortless** easy.

to make an effort to try hard.

egg (1) *n.* an oval object laid by birds, reptiles, fish, and insects, containing the germ of the young. *n.* **egg-cup** a holder for a boiled egg.

a bad egg a worthless person.

to put all your eggs in one basket to risk everything in one venture.

egg (2) *v.* (used with **on**) to urge, as *Fred egged Bert on to jump the ditch* (**egging, egged**).

egoist, egotist (*pron.* eg'ō.ist *or* eg'ō.tist) *n.* someone who thinks too much of himself, a selfish person.

eiderdown *n.* a quilt stuffed with feathers from the eider-duck.

eight *adj.* or *n.* one more than seven, represented by 8 or VIII. *adj.* or *n.* **eighteen** ten more than eight. *adj.* or *n.* **eighty** ten times eight. *adj.* **eightieth** next after seventy-ninth.

piece of eight an old Spanish coin.

either (*pron.* ī'THer *or* ee'THer) *adj.* or *pronoun* one of two, one or the other, as *either of the two may go.* *conj.* **either** (with **or**), as *either he pays or he does not go.*

elaborate (*pron.* e.lab'o.rit) *adj.* complicated, worked out in great detail, as *an elaborate drawing.*

eland *n.* a South African antelope with twisted horns.

elapse *v.* (of time) to go by, as *years elapsed before I saw him* (**elapsing, elapsed**).

elastic *n.* a rubber strip or band. *adj.* **elastic** full of springiness. *n.* **elasticity** (*pron.* e.las.tis'i.ti).

elbow *n.* the joint where the arm bends. *v.* **elbow** to push people aside with the elbows.

elbow-room plenty of space.

elder (1) *n.* a tree with white flowers. *n.* **elderberry** the berry of the elder tree.

elder (2) *adj.* the older of two people (*comparative* of **old**). *n.* **elder** 1. an older person. 2. an official in certain churches. *adj.* **elderly** old. *adj.* **eldest** the oldest.

elect *v.* to choose by voting. *n.* **election** choosing people for a committee or for Parliament by voting.

electric *adj.* concerned with or worked by electricity, as *an electric motor.* *adj.* **electrical**.

electrician *n.* a man who deals with anything electrical.

electricity *n.* a force carried by a metal conductor such as copper, producing light, heat, or motion.

electrify *v.* 1. to charge with electricity. 2. to startle, to excite, as *the sudden goal electrified the crowd* (**electrifying, electrified**).

electrocute *v.* to kill with an electric shock (**electrocuting, electrocuted**).

elegance *n.* refinement, good taste.

elegant *adj.* refined, in good taste.

element *n.* 1. a part, as *service to others is an important element of Scouting.* 2. (in chemistry) a simple chemical which cannot be broken down into anything simpler, as *oxygen, carbon, and hydrogen are elements.* 3. the heating unit of an electric iron or fire.

elementary *adj.* simple, easy, as *an elementary book on science.*

elephant *n.* the largest living land animal. The African elephant has larger ears than the Indian elephant and is almost untameable.

a white elephant anything whose upkeep costs more than it is worth. The kings of Siam used to give white elephants to those they wished to ruin, as the elephants were so costly to feed.

elevate *v.* to raise (**elevating, elevated**).

elevation *n.* 1. raising to a higher level. 2. height, as *the elevation of a point on a map above sea level.* 3. a drawing of the side of a building or object.

elevator *n.* 1. (in North America) a lift. 2. a storehouse for grain.

eleven *adj.* or *n.* one more than ten, represented by 11 or XI. *adj.* or *n.* **eleventh** next after tenth.

elf *n.* a small fairy. *pl.* **elves**. *adj.* **elfish**.

eligible (*pron*.el'i.ji.bl) *adj*. 1. able to take part, qualified, as *eligible for a competition*. 2. suitable, desirable. *n*. **eligibility**.

eliminate *v*. to get rid of, to remove (**eliminating, eliminated**). *n*. **elimination** removal, putting aside.

elk *n*. 1. the largest kind of deer. 2. (in America) the wapiti.

elm *n*. a tree with brittle branches.

elocution *n*. the art of speaking well in public.

elope *v*. to run away secretly with a lover (**eloping, eloped**). *n*. **elopement**.

eloquence *n*. fine, forceful, easy-flowing speech. *adj*. **eloquent** (of speech) forceful and easy in a way that stirs an audience.

else *adj*. referring to some other person, as *give it to someone else*. *adv*. **else** otherwise, as *what else is there to do?*

elsewhere *adv*. in some other place.

elves *plural* of **elf**.

emancipate *v*. to set free (**emancipating, emancipated**). *n*. **emancipation** setting free, as *the emancipation of slaves*.

embankment *n*. 1. a bank of earth carrying a road or railway above low ground. 2. a raised roadway or bank at the side of a river to prevent the water overflowing.

embark *v*. to go or put on board ship. *n*. **embarkation**.
to embark on to begin, as *to embark on a new venture*.

embarrass *v*. 1. to make someone confused or ill at ease, as *to embarrass someone by poking fun at him*. 2. to hinder, as *Auntie's luggage and umbrella embarrassed her n*. **embarrassment**.

embassy (*pron*. em'ba.si) *n*. 1. the post of ambassador. 2. the official house of an ambassador. 3. a group of people sent on some mission abroad (*pl*. **embassies**).

ember *n*. a red-hot piece of coal or wood.

emblem *n*. a sign or a badge that stands for some idea or movement, as *the cross is the emblem of Christianity*.

embrace *v*. 1. to hug someone with affection. 2. to take up with enthusiasm (some new hobby or interest). 3. to include, as *Europe embraces part of Soviet Russia* (**embracing, embraced**).

embroider *v*. (in needlework) to make designs on cloth with coloured thread.

emerald *n*. 1. a green precious stone. 2. a shade of bright green.

emerge *v*. to appear, to come out into the open, as *the Scouts emerged from the wood* (**emerging, emerged**). *n*. **emergence**.

emergency *n*. an unexpected happening requiring immediate attention (*pl*. **emergencies**).

emigrant *n*. a person who leaves one country to settle in another.

emigrate *v*. to leave one country to settle in another (**emigrating, emigrated**). *n*. **emigration**.

eminence *n*. 1. fame, as *Charles Dickens reached eminence as an author*. 2. a piece of high ground, a hillock. 3. the title given to a cardinal, who is addressed as *your eminence*.

eminent *adj*. famous, outstanding, as *an eminent scientist*. *adv*. **eminently**.

emotion *n*. a strong feeling of love, joy, grief, anger, excitement or some other state of mind. *adj*. **emotional** readily moved by emotion.

emperor *n*. the ruler of an empire (*fem*. **empress**).

emphasis *n*. 1. extra attention or importance given to something, as *emphasis will be given to road safety*. 2. extra force given to certain words or syllables when speaking, to make the meaning clearer or more forceful (*pl*. **emphases**).

emphasize *v*. 1. to give extra attention or importance to. 2. to give extra force to words or syllables when speaking (**emphasizing, emphasized**).

emphatic *adj*. forceful, decided, as *an emphatic reply to a question*. *adv*. **emphatically**.

empire *n*. 1. a country ruled over by an emperor. 2. a group of countries under one king or queen.

employ v. 1. to pay someone for working. 2. to use, as *to employ a machine to lift loads* (**employing, employed**). n. **employment** work.

employee n. someone who is paid to work.

employer n. someone who pays others to work for him.

empress n. feminine of **emperor**.

empty adj. 1. containing nothing. 2. unoccupied, as *an empty room*. 3. foolish, meaningless, as *empty threats* or *empty hopes*. v. **empty** 1. to take everything out. 2. to become vacant, as *the cinema emptied* (**emptying, emptied**). n. **emptiness**.

empty-handed carrying nothing.

empty vessels make most noise those who do least often talk most.

emu (*pron.* ee'myoo) n. an Australian bird like an ostrich but smaller (*pl.* **emus**).

emulate (*pron.* em'yoo.layt) v. to try to equal someone or even do better (**emulating, emulated**). n. **emulation** rivalry.

emulsion n. milk-like mixture of oil and water.

enable v. to make possible, as *light enables us to see* (**enabling, enabled**).

enact v. 1. (in a play) to take the part of, as *Joan enacted Peter Pan in the play*. 2. to make a government bill into a law. n. **enactment**.

enamel n. 1. hard glossy paint. 2. any hard glossy coating, as on the outer surface of teeth. v. **enamel** to cover with a hard glossy coat (**enamelling, enamelled**).

enchant v. 1. to charm, to delight, as *Susan was enchanted with the play*. 2. to bewitch, to cast a spell on. n. **enchantment**.

encircle v. to surround (**encircling, encircled**).

enclose v. 1. to shut in, as *to enclose land with a fence*. 2. to put inside an envelope or parcel, as *to enclose money with a letter* (**enclosing, enclosed**).

enclosure n. 1. land fenced in. 2. something put in an envelope with a letter.

encore (*pron.* ong.kaw') *interjection* a French word meaning 'again!', called by an audience wanting a song or act to be repeated. n. **encore** 1. a call for a performer to be heard again. 2. an extra song or piece of music given by a performer. v. **encore** to call for a performer to return.

encounter n. 1. an unexpected meeting. 2. a battle. v. **encounter** 1. to meet unexpectedly. 2. to meet in battle.

encourage v. 1. to give someone hope and courage to face a difficult task. 2. to egg on, to coax, as *do not encourage the dog to follow* (**encouraging, encouraged**). n. **encouragement**.

encroach v. 1. to go forward beyond a boundary, as *weeds have encroached on the garden beds*. 2. to invade someone's rights, as *she encroached on my spare time by asking me to help her*.

encyclopaedia or **encyclopedia** n. a book or set of books, with information on every subject in articles arranged in alphabetical order.

end n. 1. the last part, as *the end of the day*. 2. aim, purpose, as *they worked with an end in view*. 3. death, as *General Wolfe met his end at Quebec*. v. **end** to finish. n. **ending** a finish. adj. **endless** without end.

at a loose end having nothing to do.

at the end of one's tether desperate, having done everything possible.

to keep one's end up to avoid defeat, as in cricket to keep the wicket from being knocked down.

to make both ends meet to keep out of debt.

endeavour v. to try, to make an effort, as *they endeavoured to reach the drowning boy*. n. **endeavour** an attempt, as *an endeavour to win*.

endow v. 1. to leave money for some person or cause. 2. to grant some gift, as *the good fairy endowed the princess with beauty*. n. **endowment**.

endurable adj. bearable.

endurance n. power to bear or to last, as *the marathon race is a test of endurance*.

endure v. 1. to bear some hardship patiently. 2. to last a long time, as *the mountains will endure when we have died* (**enduring, endured**).

enemy *n.* a person or nation fighting against another, a foe (*pl.* **enemies**).

energetic *adj.* very active, full of life.

energy *n.* 1. ability to do work. 2. force or power, as *a man of energy* (*pl.* **energies**).

engage *v.* 1. to take part in, as *to engage in* (*or be engaged in*) *a hobby.* 2. attract, as *to engage someone's attention.* 3. to promise, as *to engage to finish some work.* 4. to betroth, as *the king engaged his daughter to the prince.* (**engaging, engaged**). *n.* **engagement** 1. taking part. 2. a battle. 3. a promise. 4. a betrothal.

engaged *adj.* 1. busy. 2. betrothed.

engaging *adj.* attractive, as *an engaging manner.*

engine *n.* a machine harnessing energy to do useful work, as *a steam engine.*

engineer *n.* a man in charge of an engine, or concerned with machinery. *n.* **engineering** the construction and handling of machinery.

engrave *v.* 1. to cut or carve on metal or stone. 2. to impress deeply as *his words are engraved on my mind* (**engraving, engraved**). *n.* **engraver.**

enjoy *v.* to take pleasure in (**enjoying, enjoyed**). *adj.* **enjoyable** giving pleasure. *n.* **enjoyment.**

enlarge *v.* 1. to make larger. 2. (in photography) to make a large print from a smaller negative. 3. (with **on** or **upon**) to talk or write more fully, as *the traveller enlarged upon his adventures* (**enlarging, enlarged**). *n.* **enlargement.**

enlighten *v.* to instruct, to make a subject clearer, as *Dick enlightened me about stamps.*

enlist *v.* 1. to join one of the armed forces. 2. to gain, to bring in, as *to enlist help. n.* **enlistment.**

enmity *n.* hatred, ill-will.

enormous *adj.* huge, gigantic.

enough *adj.* sufficient, as much as or as many as needed.

enough is as good as a feast sufficient of anything is all one needs.

enquire see **inquire.**

enrage *v.* to make very angry (**enraging, enraged**).

enrich *v.* to make rich. *n.* **enrichment.**

enrol or **enroll** *v.* 1. to enlist. 2. to be admitted as a member of a society. 3. to put on a roll or list (**enrolling, enrolled**). *n.* **enrolment** or **enrollment.**

ensign *n.* 1. a naval or military flag. 2. many years ago, a junior officer in the British army. 3. a junior officer in the United States navy.

blue ensign flag of a British passenger ship.

red ensign flag of the British Merchant Navy.

white ensign flag of the British Royal Navy.

enslave *v.* to make a slave of (**enslaving, enslaved**).

ensure *v.* to make sure, to make certain, as *to ensure that all is well* (**ensuring, ensured**).

enter *v.* 1. to go or come in. 2. to join (a club, society, or competition). 3. to put in (a show or competition). 4. to set down in a book. *n.* **entry.** See **entry.**

to enter into to take an active part in.

enterprise *n.* 1. readiness to do new and exciting things, as *John is full of enterprise.* 2. a daring undertaking or adventure. *adj.* **enterprising** bold and ready to try new things.

entertain *v.* 1. to receive and welcome a visitor. 2. to amuse people by performing before them, as *Brenda entertained us with a song. n.* **entertainer** a performer at a concert or gathering. *n.* **entertainment** a performance.

enthusiasm *n.* keenness, eagerness. *adj.* **enthusiastic.**

enthusiast *n.* a person full of enthusiasm.

entice *v.* to tempt, to attract, as *to entice a shy animal with food* (**enticing, enticed**). *adj.* **enticing** tempting.

entire *adj.* the whole of anything, as *the entire world. adv.* **entirely** completely. *n.* **entirety.**

in its entirety completely.

entitle *v.* 1. to give a title to, as *she is entitled 'Lady'.* 2. to give a claim or a right to, as *this coupon entitles you to a free sample* (**entitling, entitled**).

entrails *n. pl.* the bowels or insides of an animal.

entrance (1) (*pron.* en'tranz) *n.* 1. a way in, a doorway or gateway. 2. going in, as *entrance is free.*

entrance (2) (*pron.* en.trahnz') *v.* to charm, to delight (**entrancing, entranced**). *adj.* **entrancing**.

entrant *n.* someone who enters, as *Fred was an entrant for the painting competition.*

entreat *v.* to beg earnestly. *n.* **entreaty** an earnest request.

entry *n.* 1. coming in, as *Harry made a splendid entry on to the stage in the play.* 2. a way in, an entrance, as *entry to the ground is by the main gate.* 3. something written and recorded in a book (*pl.* **entries**).

entwine *v.* to fasten round, as *the tree is entwined with creeper* (**entwining, entwined**).

envelop (*pron.* en.vel'op) *v.* to wrap round and cover, as *the house was enveloped in smoke* (**enveloping, enveloped**). *n.* **envelopment**.

envelope (*pron.* en've.lōp *or* on've.lōp) *n.* 1. a paper covering for a letter. 2. the gas bag of a balloon.

enviable *adj.* to be envied.

envious *adj.* envying, wanting something that belongs to someone else.

environment, environs *n.* and *n. pl.* surroundings.

envy *n.* 1. a desire for something that belongs to someone else, jealousy. 2. something or somebody arousing envy, as *Jean's watch was the envy of her friends.* *v.* **envy** to feel envious (**envying, envied**).

epaulette *n.* a shoulder piece on a uniform.

epic *n.* a long poem of stirring deeds. *adj.* **epic** famous, heroic.

epidemic *n.* a widespread attack of disease.

episode *n.* 1. an incident in a series of events. 2. one part of a story.

epistle *n.* 1. a letter. 2. one of the letters of the apostles in the New Testament.

epitaph *n.* the writing on a gravestone.

epoch (*pron.* ee'pok) *n.* a special period in history, as *in the glacial epoch most of the world was covered with ice.*

equal *adj.* 1. the same in number, amount, or value, as *my weight is equal to yours.* 2. well-balanced, as *an equal match between two teams.* 3. fit, prepared, as *he was equal to the task.* *n.* **equal** someone of the same rank, or just as good, as *this batsman has no equal.* *v.* **equal** to be the same as (**equalling, equalled**). *adv.* **equally**. *n.* **equality**. *v.* **equalize** to make equal (**equalizing, equalized**).

equal to the occasion able to deal with an unexpected happening.

equation (*pron.* e.kway'zhun) *n.* (in mathematics) a number of quantities put equal to another number of quantities, as $4 + 5 = 6 + 3$.

equator *n.* (in geography) an imaginary circle passing round the earth, at equal distance at every point from the North and South poles. *adj.* **equatorial** concerning the equator.

equilateral *adj.* (of a figure in geometry) having all its sides equal, as *an equilateral triangle.*

equilibrium *n.* balance, as *a tight-rope walker must keep his equilibrium.*

equip *v.* to provide with everything needed, as *to equip a ship with fuel and food* (**equipping, equipped**). *n.* **equipment** supplies, an outfit.

equivalent (*pron.* e.kwiv'a.lent) *adj.* equal in value to, as *a metre is equivalent to a hundred centimetres.*

era (*pron.* ee'ra) *n.* a long period of time in history, as *the prehistoric era.*

erase *v.* to rub out (**erasing, erased**). *n.* **eraser** something which rubs out, as an india-rubber.

erect *adj.* upright, as *he stood erect.* *v.* **erect** to set up, to build, as *to erect a monument.* *n.* **erection** 1. setting up. 2. a building.

ermine (*pron.* er'min) *n.* 1. the stoat. 2. the white winter fur of the stoat with its black-tipped tail, used for ceremonial robes.

erosion *n.* a gradual wearing away.

err *v.* 1. to make mistakes. 2. to do wrong or fall into sin (**erring, erred**).

errand *n.* a small journey to deliver or collect a message or parcel.
a fool's errand a wasted journey.
errant *adj.* 1. wandering, roving. 2. sinning.
a knight errant a knight in search of adventure.
erratic *adj.* irregular, unreliable, as *an erratic clock* or *the erratic walk of a small child*.
error *n.* a mistake.
erupt *v.* to burst out. *n.* **eruption**.
escalator *n.* a moving staircase.
escapade *n.* a wild frolic, a piece of mischief.
escape *v.* 1. to get free from prison, danger, etc. 2. to avoid, danger, work, punishment, etc. (**escaping, escaped**). *n.* **escape** 1. getting free. 2. avoidance. 3. a leakage. 4. an outlet. 5. a fireman's ladder, a *fire escape*.
escort *n.* 1. a guard of soldiers or ships giving protection to others. 2. a gentleman accompanying a lady and looking after her. *v.* **escort** to accompany and protect.
especial *adj.* very special. *adv.* **especially** particularly, as *this cake is especially good*.
espionage *n.* spying, using spies.
esquire *n.* 1. (in the Middle Ages) a knight's attendant. 2. a title of respect written after a man's name, as *Tom Smith Esquire*, or *Tom Smith Esq.* (note: it is incorrect to write *Mr Tom Smith Esq.*).
essay (*pron.* es'ay) *n.* a written composition.
essence *n.* 1. a strong flavouring or scent. 2. the chief part of anything, as *fair play is the essence of sportsmanship*.
essential *adj.* really necessary, as *it is essential that you come*. *adv.* **essentially**.
establish *v.* 1. to set up, as *to establish a business*. 2. to prove, as *to establish someone's guilt*. *n.* **establishment** 1. a setting up. 2. an institution, business, or house, as *an old establishment*.
estate *n.* 1. lands or property belonging to a landowner. 2. rank or position, as *a man of high estate*.

esteem *v.* to think well of. *n.* **esteem** high regard, honour, as *a man of esteem*.
estimate *v.* to reckon, to calculate, to consider (**estimating, estimated**). *n.* **estimate** 1. an opinion. 2. a calculation of what something will cost, as *an estimate for painting a house*. *n.* **estimation** opinion.
estuary *n.* the mouth of a river where it enters the sea.
eternal *adj.* everlasting. *adv.* **eternally** always.
eternity *n.* everlasting time.
ether (*pron.* ee'ther) *n.* 1. a liquid used to make people unconscious before an operation. 2. the upper air, the sky.
etiquette (*pron.* et'i.ket) *n.* all the rules of manners and good behaviour.
evacuate *v.* 1. to leave, as *to evacuate a dangerous place in wartime*. 2. to cause to leave, to empty, as *the soldiers evacuated all civilians from the village* (**evacuating, evacuated**).
evacuee *n.* someone removed from a dangerous place.
evade *v.* 1. to slip away from, as *the name evades my mind*. 2. to shirk, as *to evade a duty* (**evading, evaded**). *n.* **evasion**. See **evasion**.
evaluate *v.* to say how much a thing is worth (**evaluating, evaluated**). *n.* **evaluation**.
evangelist *n.* 1. a travelling preacher. 2. one of the four writers of the New Testament gospels.
evaporate *v.* 1. to turn into vapour. 2. to concentrate a liquid by driving off water, as *to evaporate milk* (**evaporating, evaporated**).
eve *n.* 1. a poetical word for evening. 2. the day before, as *Christmas eve* or *the eve of one's birthday*.
even *adj.* 1. smooth, level. 2. equal, as *an even score in a game*. 3. able to be divided by 2, as *8 is an even number*. 4. calm, as *an even temperament or manner*. *v.* **even** to make level. *adv.* **even** 1. exactly, as *even so*. 2. still, as *even now*. 3. (used for strength), as *even you would not do it*.
to be even with to be revenged on.
evening *n.* the end of the day.

event *n.* 1. a happening. 2. one of the items in a sports programme. *adj.* **eventful** full of happenings.

eventual *adj.* final. *adv.* **eventually** at last.

ever *adv.* 1. always, as *I am ever with you.* 2. at any time, as *if ever you pass drop in.* 3. on record, as *the biggest ever.*

evergreen *adj.* always green and unfading.

every *adj.* 1. each one, as *every boy is here.* 2. the utmost, as *you will have every consideration. pronoun* **everybody, everyone** each person. *adj.* **everyday** common, as *an everyday event. n.* **everything** each thing. *adv.* **everywhere** in every place.

every man jack every single one.

evidence *n.* information which proves something, or throws further light on a case.

evident *adj.* obvious, clearly seen. *adv.* **evidently.**

evil *adj.* bad, harmful, sinful. *n.* **evil** 1. wickedness. 2. misfortune, as *may no evil afflict you.*

evolution *n.* 1. a gradual change and development, as *the evolution of ships from the galley to the modern liner.* 2. the theory that living things have gradually developed through the ages from simple forms of life. *adj.* **evolutionary.**

ewe *n.* a female sheep.

ex- *prefix* former, one-time, as *an ex-champion* or *an ex-president.*

exact *adj.* correct, just right. *v.* **exact** to demand, to obtain by threats, as *to exact obedience* or *to exact money. adv.* **exactly** just right.

exacting *adj.* 1. hard to please, as *an exacting master.* 2. requiring much careful effort, as *an exacting task.*

exaggerate *v.* to make things seem worse, better, or greater than they are, to overstate a story (**exaggerating, exaggerated**). *n.* **exaggeration** over-emphasis.

examination *n.* 1. a close look, an inspection. 2. a test.

examine *v.* 1. to look at closely, to inspect. 2. to test with questions (**examining, examined**). *n.* **examiner** someone who examines.

to cross-examine to ask questions of a witness in a court.

example *n.* 1. (in arithmetic) a practice sum to show how to do a new method. 2. a model, someone to be copied, as *Jack is an example to the other boys.* 3. a warning, as *Tom was punished as an example to the others.*

to make an example of to punish (someone) as a warning to others.

excavate *v.* to dig out, to unearth, as *to excavate some prehistoric remains* (**excavating, excavated**). *n.* **excavation.**

exceed *v.* 1. to go beyond, as *to exceed the speed limit in a car.* 2. to be greater than, as *this paper exceeds the size required. adv.* **exceedingly** very, greatly, as *I am exceedingly pleased.*

excel *v.* 1. to be very good, as *Bob excels in running.* 2. to be better than, as *Jim excels John at painting* (**excelling, excelled**).

excellence *n.* great worth, high quality.

excellent *adj.* very good, of great value.

except *v.* to leave out, not to include. *prep.* **except** leaving out, as *they are all here except Bert. n.* **exception** 1. what is left out. 2. what is unusual, as *I usually go, but today is an exception—I shall stay. adj.* **exceptional.**

to take exception to to object to, to take offence.

excess *n.* an extra amount, more than needed, as *the excess was thrown away. adj.* **excessive** too much.

in excess of more than, as *the bill was in excess of the amount expected.*

to excess too much, as *he eats to excess.*

exchange *v.* to give one thing in return for another (**exchanging, exchanged**). *n.* **exchange** 1. a building where business is done, as *a stock exchange.* 2. a telephone headquarters, *a telephone exchange.*

exchequer *n.* a country's treasury.

excite *v.* to cause bustle and activity, to stir up (**exciting, excited**). *adj.* **excitable** easily excited. *n.* **excitement**

commotion, an emotional stir. *adj.* **exciting** thrilling.

exclaim *v.* to cry out with excitement.

exclamation *n.* a sudden cry. *n.* **exclamation mark** a written or printed sign (!) to mark excitement.

exclude *v.* to keep out, to shut out (**excluding, excluded**).

exclusive *adj.* 1. shutting out others, as *we have an exclusive right to use this path.* 2. limited to certain people, as *an exclusive club.*

excommunicate *v.* to punish someone by not allowing him any longer to be a member of a church (**excommunicating, excommunicated**).

excursion *n.* a pleasure-trip.

excusable *adj.* forgivable, pardonable.

excuse (*pron.* eks.kyōoz¹) *v.* 1. to forgive. 2. to set free from, to let off, as *Dick was excused homework for tonight* (**excusing, excused**). *n.* **excuse** (*pron.* eks.kyōos¹) 1. an explanation. 2. an apology.

execute *v.* 1. to carry out, as *to execute a command.* 2. to put to death (**executing, executed**). *n.* **execution**.

executioner *n.* a man who puts criminals to death.

exempt *adj.* free from service or duty, as *a doctor is exempt from service on a jury. n.* **exemption**.

exercise *v.* 1. to give practice to, or train. 2. to use, as *to exercise care.* 3. to take physical training, as *to exercise in a gymnasium* (**exercising, exercised**). *n.* **exercise** 1. training. 2. a piece of work for practice on a lesson.

exert (*pron.* egz.ert¹) *v.* to use (with energy and effort), as *to exert authority* or *exert oneself to catch a bus. n.* **exertion**.

exhaust (*pron.* egz.awst¹) *v.* 1. to use up completely, as *to exhaust someone's patience.* 2. to tire, as *this running is exhausting me* (**exhausting, exhausted**). *n.* **exhaust** (on a gas, petrol, or oil engine) the pipe leading off the used gases.

exhausted *adj.* very tired. *n.* **exhaustion**.

exhibit *v.* 1. to put on show, as *to exhibit paintings.* 2. to show, to reveal,

as *to exhibit signs of wear. n.* **exhibition** a show.

exile *v.* to banish, to make someone leave his country (**exiling, exiled**). *n.* **exile** 1. banishment. 2. a person who is exiled.

exist *v.* 1. to live, as *he exists on little food.* 2. to be, to occur, as *disease exists here. n.* **existence** living, being.

exit *n.* 1. a way out, as *the exit of a cinema.* 2. a going off, as *the actor made his exit.*

expand *v.* to swell out, to grow larger.

expanse *n.* a wide space.

expansion *n.* increase, enlargement.

expect *v.* 1. to look forward to, to await, as *I expect to see you tomorrow.* 2. to suppose, to think something will happen, as *I expect it will snow. n.* **expectation**.

expedition *n.* 1. a special journey of an adventurous kind. 2. quickness, speed, as *he departed with expedition. adj.* **expeditious** speedy.

expel *v.* 1. to turn someone out of a school or club for bad conduct. 2. to drive out, as *to expel rats from a barn* (**expelling, expelled**). *n.* **expulsion**. See **expulsion**.

expend *v.* to spend or use up, as *to expend energy in searching for something. n.* **expenditure**.

expense *n.* cost in money, time, or energy. *adj.* **expensive** costly, dear.

experience *n.* 1. knowledge gained by doing and seeing. 2. an unusual happening, as *it was an experience to see the zoo. v.* **experience** to feel, to go through, as *to experience great joy* (**experiencing, experienced**). *adj.* **experienced** practised, skilful.

experiment *n.* a test to find something new, or to prove something. *v.* **experiment** to try out things. *adj.* **experimental**.

expert *adj.* skilful, knowing a great deal about some subject. *n.* **expert** someone who knows much about something.

expire *v.* 1. to breathe out (*n.* **expiration**). 2. to come to an end, as *the dog licence expires today* (*n.* **expiration**). 3. to die (*n.* **expiry**).

explain v. 1. to give the meaning of, as to explain one's words. 2. to give reasons for, as to explain why one is late.

explanation n. 1. the meaning of. 2. a reason.

explode v. 1. to blow up. 2. to break out, as to explode with laughter. 3. to destroy some old belief, as Galileo exploded the belief that the sun moves round the earth (**exploding, exploded**). n. **explosion**. See **explosion**.

exploit (pron. eks'ploit) n. a bold deed. v. **exploit** (pron. eks.ploit') to use for one's own ends, as to exploit a discovery to make a fortune.

exploration n. a journey of discovery, travelling for discovery.

explore v. 1. to search and examine, as to explore a cave. 2. to travel for discovery on land or sea (**exploring, explored**). n. **explorer**.

explosion n. a sudden bursting out. See **explode**.

explosive n. something which explodes. adj. **explosive** liable to explode.

export (pron. eks.port') v. to send goods to another country to be sold. n. **export** (pron. eks'port) or n. pl. **exports** the goods sent out.

expose v. 1. to lay bare or show up, as the ebbing tide exposed the rocks or to expose a fraud. 2. to take a photograph on, as to expose a film (**exposing, exposed**). n. **exposure**. See **exposure**.

exposure n. 1. being uncovered or unprotected, as exposure to the cold. 2. a showing up. 3. the taking of a photograph on a film.

express v. 1. to put into words, as a great writer expresses his thoughts well. 2. to show, as Mary's face expressed her feelings. adj. **express** clear, definite, as an express command. n. **express** a fast train. n. **expression** 1. putting feelings into words. 2. a way of saying things. 3. a look on a face.

to express oneself to show one's feelings by words, or some action.

exquisite adj. very delicate and beautiful.

extend v. 1. to hold out or stretch out, as to extend your hand in friendship

or the lake extends beyond the horizon. 2. to lengthen, as to extend a holiday by some weeks. n. **extension**. See **extension**.

extension n. 1. stretching out or enlarging. 2. an addition, as an extension to a factory.

extensive adj. very large or long.

extent n. size, space, or length.

exterior n. the outside. adj. **exterior** outer.

exterminate v. to destroy (**exterminating, exterminated**). n. **extermination**.

external adj. outside. adv. **externally**.

extinct adj. no longer alive, as an extinct volcano or the dodo is an extinct bird.

extinguish v. to put out a light, fire, life, or some feeling such as hope.

fire extinguisher a metal container filled with chemicals to put out a fire.

extra adj. more than usual, as extra homework. n. **extra** 1. an additional amount. 2. a special edition of a newspaper. adv. **extra** especially, as the train went extra slowly.

extract (pron. eks.trakt') v. 1. to draw out, as to extract a tooth. 2. to obtain, as to extract gold from ore or to extract a promise from someone. n. **extract** (pron. eks'trakt) a piece taken from the whole, as an extract from a book or meat extract is the essence of meat. n. **extraction**.

extraordinary adj. very unusual.

extravagance (pron. eks.trav'a.gans) n. reckless waste. adj. **extravagant** carelessly wasteful.

extreme adj. 1. the greatest, as extreme joy. 2. the farthest, as the extreme edge. adv. **extremely**. n. **extremity** (pl. **extremities**).

to go to extremes to go too far.

eye n. 1. the part of an animal which enables it to see. 2. being able to see with understanding, as Joan has an eye for colour. 3. anything like an eye, as the ring for a hook in a hook and eye. v. **eye** to look at closely (**eyeing, eyed**).

an eye for an eye an injury given in return for an injury.

eye-opener something to marvel at.

in the public eye with everyone watching.

in one's mind's eye in imagination.

to open someone's eyes to point out.

to see eye to eye to agree.

with an eye to intending to.

eyeball *n.* the movable ball of the eye.

eyebrow *n.* the hairy ridge over the eye.

eyelash *n.* one of the hairs on an eyelid.

eyelid *n.* the cover of skin over an eye.

eyesight *n.* the power to see.

eyesore *n.* an ugly sight.

eyewitness *n.* someone who sees an accident or crime.

F

fable *n.* 1. a fanciful story. 2. a short story with a moral. *adj.* **fabulous** beyond belief, as *he had fabulous riches.*

fabric *n.* 1. cloth. 2. a building. 3. a framework.

face *n.* 1. the front of one's head. 2. the front of anything, as of a building, clock, or the numbered side of a playing card. *n.* **face** to look towards, to stand opposite (**facing, faced**).

to face the music to stand the consequences of what you do.

to pull a long face to look dismal.

to put a good face on to appear happy although you feel unhappy.

to save your face to avoid being made to look foolish.

to set your face against to oppose.

two-faced deceitful, false.

fact *n.* a real thing, something true.

as a matter of fact actually.

factor *n.* 1. an agent. 2. (in arithmetic) one of the smaller numbers into which a larger number can be split. Thus *2, 3, 4, and 6 are all factors of 12.*

factorize *v.* to split a number into its factors (**factorizing, factorized**).

factory *n.* a place where goods are made (*pl.* **factories**).

fade *v.* 1. to grow paler. 2. to die away, as *the sound faded* (**fading, faded**).

Fahrenheit *n.* a scale on a thermometer invented by a scientist of that name, with 32 degrees as the freezing point of water, and 212 degrees as the boiling point.

fail *v.* 1. to be unsuccessful. 2. not to do something one ought, as *to fail in one's duty. n.* **failure**.

without fail with certainty, surely.

failing *n.* a bad habit or fault.

faint *v.* to lose consciousness. *adj.* **faint** weak, pale.

faint-hearted cowardly, timid.

fair (1) *adj.* 1. light in colour, as *a fair skin.* 2. beautiful, as *a fair lady.* 3. just, as *a fair verdict.* 4. even, as *a fair match (for).* 5. medium, not bad, as *he has done fair work.* 6. bright and dry, as *fair weather. n.* **fairness**.

fair (2) *n.* a kind of country market with side-shows and amusements.

fairy *n.* a small imaginary being with magic powers (*pl.* **fairies**). *n.* **fairy-tale** a tale of fairies.

faith *n.* 1. trust. 2. belief in something. 3. a religious belief. *adj.* **faithful** loyal.

in good faith sincerely.

fall *v.* 1. to drop from a high place to a low one. 2. to die away or ebb, as *the wind fell* or *the tide fell.* 3. to be conquered, as *the fortress fell.* 4. to occur, as *my birthday falls on Monday* (**falling, fell, fallen**). *n.* **fall** 1. a drop. 2. (in North America) autumn, when leaves fall.

to fall back on to depend on reserves.

to fall in with to agree with.

to fall out with to quarrel with.

to fall through to come to nothing.

false *adj.* 1. untrue, wrong. 2. faithless, as *a false friend.* 3. sham, artificial, as *false teeth. adv.* **falsely**.

falsehood *n.* a lie, an untruth.

falter (*pron.* fawl'ter) *v.* 1. to stumble or hesitate. 2. to speak hesitantly.

fame *n.* having a high reputation, glory.

familiar *adj.* 1. well-known, as *a familiar face.* 2. very friendly, as *a familiar way of speaking to someone. n.* **familiarity**.

family *n.* 1. parents and children. 2. the children of two parents. 3. a group of things of the same kind (*pl.* **families**).

famine *n.* great shortage, starvation.

famished *adj.* very hungry.

famous *adj.* 1. well-known to the public. 2. of high reputation.

fan *n.* 1. anything which can be moved rapidly to make a cooling draught, as *an electric fan* or *a paper fan of olden days.* 2. a keen supporter of some hobby or sport. *v.* **fan** 1. to waft or blow a cool current of air. 2. to spread out like an opening fan, as *troops fanning across a plain* (**fanning, fanned**).

fanatic (*pron.* fa.nat'ik) *n.* someone with extreme opinions. *adj.* **fanatical**. *n.* **fanaticism**.

fancy *v.* 1. to imagine. 2. to wish for (**fancying, fancied**). *adj.* **fancy** decorated, ornamental. *n.* **fancy** imagination.

fanciful *adj.* 1. imaginary. 2. decorated.

fang *n.* the long sharp tooth of an animal or the poison-tooth of a snake.

fantastic *adj.* unreal, fanciful, queer.

far *adj.* distant, a long way off (*comparative* **farther** or **further**, *superlative* **farthest** or **furthest**). *adv.* **far** 1. a long way, as *to go far.* 2. very much, as *he is far bigger.*

  far-fetched exaggerated.

  far-reaching having a great effect.

  far-sighted wise.

  the Far East the eastern part of Asia.

fare (1) *v.* to get on, as *Robert fared well at his new school* (**faring, fared**).

fare (2) *n.* 1. the price of a journey. 2. food, as *the table was loaded with good fare.*

farewell *n.* a parting wish, a good-bye.

farm *n.* cultivated land, or land for animals, with house and buildings. *v.* **farm** to cultivate land. *n.* **farmer** a man who farms. *n.* **farmhouse** the farmer's house. *n.* **farmyard**.

farther see **far**.

farthing *n.* a quarter of a penny, now no longer in use as a British coin.

fascinate (*pron.* fas'i.nayt) *v.* to charm, to hold spell-bound (**fascinating, fascinated**). *n.* **fascination** charm.

fashion *n.* 1. a style set by leaders of dress. 2. a way of doing something, as *he did his work in a clumsy fashion.* *adj.* **fashionable** in the style of the day.

fast (1) *adj.* 1. firm, tight, as *a fast knot.* 2. quick, as *a fast train.* 3. (of a clock) ahead of time. 4. (of a dye) not affected by washing. *adv.* **fast** 1. tightly, as *to hold fast.* 2. quickly, as *to go fast.*

fast (2) *v.* to go without food. *n.* **fast** going without food.

fasten *v.* to tie, to make tight. *n.* **fastener** a clasp. *n.* **fastening** something to hold tight.

fat *adj.* 1. plump, swollen, as *a fat dog.* 2. oily, greasy, rich (*comparative* **fatter,** *superlative* **fattest**). *n.* **fat** the greasy substance on meat. *adj.* **fatty**. *n.* **fatness**.

  to live on the fat of the land to live well.

fatal *adj.* 1. leading to death, as *a fatal illness.* 2. disastrous, ending in ruin, as *a fatal mistake.* *adv.* **fatally**.

fate *n.* a power guiding life over which one has no control, as *John tried hard, but fate was against him.* *adj.* **fateful** all-important.

father *n.* 1. a man who is a parent. 2. a Roman Catholic priest. 3. a man who starts some great development, as *George Stephenson is the father of the railway.* *adj.* **fatherly** like a father.

father-in-law *n.* the father of someone's husband or wife.

fathom *n.* a measure of sea-depth, equal to 6 feet (1·829 metres) *v.* **fathom** to get to the bottom of.

fatigue (*pron.* fa.teeg') *n,* tiredness. *adj.* **fatiguing** tiring.

fatten *v.* to make fat or grow fat (**fattening, fattened**).

faucet *n.* (in the U.S.A.) a water-tap.

fault *n.* 1. a mistake. 2. a weakness of character, as *David has one fault; he soon loses his temper.* 3. (in tennis) a serving stroke which does not send the ball into the right place. *adj.* **faultless** perfect. *adj.* **faulty** not perfect.

  at fault 1. blameworthy. 2. at a loss.

favour *n.* 1. a kindness, as *to do a favour.* 2. a gift, as *to grant a favour.* 3. good will, as *to regard with favour.* *v.* **favour** 1. to help, to be on the side of. 2. to do a kindness to.

  in favour of on the side of.

favourable *adj.* helpful.

favourite *n.* 1. someone much liked. 2. the entrant in a race that is expected by most people to win. *adj.* **favourite** most liked.

fawn (1) *n.* a young deer.

fawn (2) *n.* a light biscuit colour.

fear *n.* a feeling of alarm because of possible danger. *v.* **fear** to be afraid of. *adj.* **fearful** 1. terrible. 2. timid. *adv.* **fearfully**. *adj.* **fearsome** terrible. *adj.* **fearless** brave.

feast *n.* 1. a rich meal, a banquet. 2. a religious festival. *v.* **feast** to eat a rich meal.

feat *n.* a deed of skill and courage.

feather *n.* one of the plumes of a bird. *v.* **feather** 1. to cover with feathers. 2. (in rowing) to let the blade of an oar skim lightly over the water. *adj.* **feathery** like feathers.

a feather in your cap an achievement.

birds of a feather people of similar tastes.

to feather your nest to make money.

feature *n.* 1. a prominent mark, as *the tower is a feature of the view*. 2. a part of the face. 3. an important part of an entertainment or an important newspaper article. *v.* **feature** to be prominent (**featuring, featured**).

February *n.* the second month of the year.

federal *adj.* concerning a federation or union of states, especially the United States of America.

federation *n.* a union of states.

fee *n.* the price charged for help or advice, as *a lawyer's fee*.

feeble *adj.* weak and frail. *n.* **feebleness**.

feed *v.* to give or eat food (**feeding, fed**).

feel *v.* 1. to touch. 2. to find or know by touch, as *to feel your way*. 3. to be touched by emotion, as *to feel glad*. 4. to hold an opinion, as *to feel that something is wrong* (**feeling, felt**). *n.* **feel** a touch, a feeling.

feeler *n.* one of the two thin rods on an insect's head.

feeling *n.* 1. sense of touch. 2. emotion.

feet see **foot**.

feign (*pron.* fayn) *v.* to pretend, as *to feign illness*.

fell (1) *past* of **fall**.

fell (2) *n.* a hill.

fell (3) *v.* to cut down, as *to fell a tree*.

fellow *n.* 1. a man or boy, as *he is a good fellow*. 2. a member of a learned society. 3. a companion, as *a fellow-country-man*.

felt (1) *past* of **feel**.

felt (2) *n.* a cloth made of compressed wool or fur.

female *n.* a girl or woman, or a living creature of the same sex (*masc.* **male**). *adj.* **female**.

feminine *adj.* belonging to women or females (*masc.* **masculine**).

fen *n.* a low wet land, a marsh.

fence *n.* a railing or barrier to enclose land. *v.* **fence** 1. to enclose land. 2. to fight with swords or foils in the sport of fencing (**fencing, fenced**). *n.* **fencing**.

to sit on the fence not to take sides in a dispute.

fender *n.* 1. a metal fireguard or kerb. 3. a protective pad or bar on a ship, car, or train.

fern *n.* a plant with long green fronds.

ferocious *adj.* fierce. *n.* **ferocity** fierceness.

ferret *n.* a kind of white polecat. *v.* **ferret** 1. to hunt with a ferret. 2. to search and dig out, as *to ferret out a secret* (**ferreting, ferreted**).

ferry *v.* to carry goods or people across water by boat for payment (**ferrying, ferried**). *n.* **ferry** 1. a place where such a boat travels. 2. a boat used for ferrying (*pl.* **ferries**).

fertile *adj.* 1. (of land) able to produce good crops. 2. (of an egg) able to be hatched. *n.* **fertility**.

fertilize *v.* to make fertile, to enrich, as *to fertilize soil to produce better crops*. *n.* **fertilizer** chemicals used to fertilize soil.

festival *n.* a celebration with music and plays.

festive *adj.* joyful. *n.* **festivity** a joyful occasion (*pl.* **festivities**).

fetch 1. to bring, as *please fetch my coat*. 2. to bring in money, as *the house fetched a good price* (**fetches, fetching, fetched**). *adj.* **fetching** attractive.

fête (*pron.* fayt) *n.* 1. a festival. 2. an outdoor party, as *a garden fête.*

fetter *n.* a chain for the foot. *v.* **fetter** to bind with chains.

feud *n.* a long quarrel between people or families.

feudal *adj.* concerning the system of the Middle Ages in which land was leased in return for military or other service. *n.* **feudalism.**

fever *n.* 1. illness in which the patient is very hot. 2. nervous excitement, as *they waited for the news in a fever of excitement. adj.* **feverish** 1. hot and sick. 2. burning with excitement.

few *adj.* and *n.* not many, only a small number.

fez *n.* a Turkish hat with a tassel.

fiancé (*pron.* fee.ahn'say) *n.* a man who is engaged to be married (*fem.* **fiancée** a woman engaged to be married).

fibre *n.* a small thread. *adj.* **fibrous** made of fibre, or like a fibre.

fiction *n.* 1. a story which is not true. 2. books about imaginary people, novels.

fictitious *adj.* imaginary, not true.

fiddle *n.* a violin. *v.* **fiddle** 1. to play the violin. 2. to play with something aimlessly (**fiddling, fiddled**).

fidget *v.* to move restlessly (**fidgeting, fidgeted**). *adj.* **fidgety** restless.

field *n.* 1. an enclosed piece of land. 2. the scene of some great action, as *a battle-field.* 3. a region, as *a coal-field.* *v.* **field** (in cricket or baseball) to catch or return the ball. *n.* **fielder** someone who fields in a game.

field-glasses *n. pl.* long-distance glasses for use in the open.

field-marshal *n.* an army officer of highest rank.

fierce *adj.* savage, wild. *adv.* **fiercely** savagely.

fiery *adj.* 1. like fire, in flames. 2. hot-tempered.

fifteen *adj.* and *n.* one more than fourteen, represented by 15 or XV. *adj.* **fifteenth.**

fifth *adj.* the last of five. *adv.* **fifthly.**

fifty *n.* five times ten. *adj.* **fiftieth.**

fig *n.* a soft brown or green fruit growing on fig trees in warm countries.

fight *v.* to take part in a battle or struggle (**fighting, fought**). *n.* **fight** a battle. **to fight shy of** to be afraid of and avoid.

figure *n.* 1. a shape or outline, as *the figure of a man in mist.* 2. a design or illustration in a book. 3. a number, as *the figure two. v.* **figure** 1. to play a part in. 2. to reckon (*figuring, figured*).

figure-head *n.* 1. the figure carved on the bow of an old sailing ship. 2. a person who appears to be in charge, but who really has no influence.

filament *n.* 1. a thread. 2. the fine wire in an electric lamp.

file (1) *n.* 1. a line of people one behind another, as *to walk in single file.* 2. a box in which papers are kept in order. *v.* **file** to arrange papers in files (**filing, filed**).

file (2) *n.* a rough-faced iron tool for smoothing wood or metal. *v.* **file** to use a file (**filing, filed**).

fill *v.* 1. to make or become full. 2. to occupy or take up, as *to fill the position of captain. n.* **fill** as much as fills, as *the dog had its fill of meat. n.* **filling** anything used to fill a hole, as *a filling in a hollow tooth.*

filly *n.* a young mare (*pl.* **fillies**).

film *n.* 1. a thin skin or coating, as *a film of ice.* 2. a celluloid strip on which photographs are taken. 3. a motion picture as shown in a cinema. *v.* **film** 1. to coat with a thin skin. 2. to photograph for a motion picture.

film star a leading player in a film.

filter *v.* to remove solid particles from liquid by pouring it through cloth, paper, or wire mesh. *n.* **filter** material through which liquids are poured to remove solid particles.

filth *n.* loathsome disgusting dirt. *adj.* **filthy.**

fin *n.* 1. one of the parts of a fish's body which help it to swim. 2. part of the tail of an aeroplane, or the rear end of a car.

final *adj.* the last, coming at the end. *adv.* **finally** last of all.

finance *n.* the management of money. *adj.* **financial** concerned with money.

financier *n.* a man skilled in money matters.

finch *n.* one of several kinds of small birds, such as the goldfinch, linnet, chaffinch, or bullfinch.

find *v.* 1. to come across, to discover. 2. to learn by experience, as *to find certain work hard*. 3. to supply, as *to find the food for an expedition* (**finding, found**). *n.* **find** a valuable or interesting discovery.

to find fault to object to.

fine (1) *n.* money paid as a penalty for breaking a rule or the law. *v.* to demand money as a penalty (**fining, fined**).

fine (2) *adj.* 1. sunny and dry. 2. excellent, as *a fine catch*. 3. thin, sharp, as *a fine point*. 4. showy, as *fine clothes*. 4. sensitive, as *fine feelings*.

finger *n.* 1. one of the members of the hand. 2. a part of a glove into which a finger fits. *v.* **finger** to touch with the fingers (**fingering, fingered**).

to have at one's finger-tips to know well.

with a finger in the pie with a share in the matter.

finger print *n.* a copy of the ridges on a finger tip.

finish *v.* to come to an end, or bring something to an end. *n.* **finish** the end. *adj.* **finished** 1. ended. 2. polished and touched up, as *this furniture is nicely finished*.

fiord, fjord (*pron.* feeord) *n.* a long narrow inlet of the sea in Norway.

fir *n.* an evergreen tree bearing cones.

fire *n.* 1. the heat and light of something burning. 2. the explosion of weapons, as *the fire of rifles*. 3. passion and enthusiasm, as *a speaker full of fire*. *v.* **fire** 1. to set fire to. 2. to discharge a gun. 3. to bake, as *to fire pottery*. 4. to fill with enthusiasm, as *to fire a man to do his utmost* (**firing, fired**).

between two fires given two dangerous choices.

to set the Thames on fire to do something outstanding.

fire-arm *n.* a weapon which can shoot.

fire-brigade *n.* an organized group of firemen.

fire-engine *n.* a vehicle equipped for putting out fires.

fire-escape *n.* a means of escape from a burning building.

fireman *n.* 1. a man who helps to put out fires. 2. a man who shovels coal on a locomotive.

fireplace *n.* the place in a house where the fire burns.

firework *n.* a small explosive set off on festive occasions.

firm (1) *adj.* 1. fixed, not easily moved. 2. loyal, as *a firm friend*. *n.* **firmness**.

firm (2) *n.* 1. a group of business partners. 2. the name under which a group of businessmen trade together.

first *adj.* 1. earliest, before all others, as *we were first*. 2. chief, most important, as *first prize*. *adv.* **first** before all else, as *he sat down first*. *adv.* **firstly** in the first place.

first aid immediate treatment after an accident.

first-class *adj.* of the best quality.

first-hand *adj.* straight from the person concerned, as *first-hand information*.

firth *n.* a river mouth, as *the Firth of Forth*.

fish *n.* a cold-blooded animal living in the sea, which breathes through gills and has a scaly body (*pl.* **fish** or **fishes**). *adj.* **fishy** 1. like a fish. 2. (slang) very doubtful, as *a fishy story*. *n.* **fishery** a place where fishing is done (*pl.* **fisheries**).

fisherman *n.* a man who makes his living catching fish (*pl.* **fishermen**).

fishmonger *n.* a man who makes his living selling fish.

fist *n.* a closed or clenched hand.

fit (1) *n.* a sudden attack of illness, laughter, etc. *adj.* **fitful** in sudden gusts, as *a fitful wind*.

by fits and starts not regular, now and then.

fit (2) *adj.* 1. suitable, as *this boy is fit for the job*. 2. healthy, as *John felt very fit after his holiday* (*comparative* **fitter**, *superlative* **fittest**). *v.* **fit** 1. to provide, as *to fit a man with clothes*. 2. to prepare, as *training to fit a man for his work*. 3. to be of the right size, as *these gloves fit well* (**fitting, fitted**). *n.* **fit** adjustment, as *this lid is a good fit*. *n.* **fitting** 1. a trying-on, as *the fitting of a suit*. 2. a movable part of a house or shop, such as a curtain-rail or hanging light.

fitter *n.* 1. (in engineering) a man who assembles the parts of a machine. 2. a man who fits clothes.

fitting *adj.* suitable, appropriate.

five *adj.* and *n.* one more than four, represented by the sign 5 or V.

fix *v.* 1. to fasten, as *to fix a stamp on a letter*. 2. to decide, as *to fix on a date for a visit*. 3. to repair a thing and put it right. *adj.* **fixed** placed firmly. *adv.* **fixedly**.

in a fix in difficulties.

fixture *n.* 1. something fixed firmly. 2. a date for a match.

fizz *v.* to froth and bubble. *n.* **fizz** a hissing sound. *adj.* **fizzy** bubbly.

fjord see **fiord**.

flabby *adj.* 1. soft and feeble. 2. hanging loose, as flabby flesh. *n.* **flabbiness**.

flag (1) *n.* 1. a cloth with a design fastened to a pole. 2. a large paving stone. *v.* **flag** to signal with a flag (**flagging, flagged**).

flag of truce a white flag to stop fighting while talks are held.

flag (2) *v.* to droop with weariness or through lack of food or water (**flagging, flagged**).

flagrant (*pron.* flay'grant) *adj.* wicked in an open deliberate way, as *flagrant behaviour*.

flagship *n.* the ship of an admiral, bearing his flag.

flake *n.* a small chip, as *a flake of stone*. *v.* **flake** to cut into flakes (**flaking, flaked**).

flame *n.* a tongue of burning gas. *v.* **flame** to burn with a bright light (**flaming, flamed**).

flank *n.* 1. the side, as *a cow's flank*. 2. the outer wing of a line of soldiers. *v.* **flank** to stand by the side, as *trees flank the road*.

flannel *n.* a soft woollen cloth. *n. pl.* **flannels** a suit or trousers made of flannel.

flap *v.* 1. for something broad to wave with a smacking sound, as *the clothes flap in the wind*. 2. to move up and down, as *a bird flaps its wings* (**flapping, flapped**).

flare *n.* a blazing light used as a signal. *v.* **flare** to burst into flames, as *the match flared in the darkness* (**flaring, flared**).

to flare up to show sudden anger.

flash *n.* 1. a sudden light. 2. a moment of time, as *it all happened in a flash*. 3. a quick burst, as *a flash of anger*. *v.* **flash** 1. to give sudden light. 2. to pass suddenly, as *to flash by*. *adj.* **flashy** showy.

a flash in the pan a sudden effort which soon dies.

flask *n.* 1. a flat leather or metal bottle to hold a liquid or powder. 2. a narrow-necked bottle used in science.

flat *adj.* 1. level, smooth. 2. horizontal. 3. without taste, as *a flat flavour*. 3. below the correct musical pitch, as *a flat tone*. 4. positive, as *a flat refusal* (*comparative* **flatter,** *superlative* **flattest**). *n.* **flat** 1. (in music) half a tone lower than the natural tone, shown by the sign ♭, as *E flat* (*E♭*) *is half a tone lower than the note E*. See **sharp**. 2. a suite of rooms in a house, on one floor. *n.* **flatness**.

flatten *v.* to make flat.

flatter *v.* to praise someone with words one does not really mean, to praise too much. *n.* **flattery**.

flavour *n.* the particular taste of something, as *the flavour of pineapple*. *v.* **flavour** to give a special taste to food. *n.* **flavouring**.

flaw *n.* a small crack, a fault, as *a flaw in glass*.

flax *n.* a tall plant with a blue flower, from whose fibres linen is made. *adj.* **flaxen** pale as flax.

flea *n.* a small jumping insect which sucks blood.

a flea-bite a tiny amount.

a flea in one's ear a sharp scolding.

fled *past* of **flee**.

flee *v.* to run away (**fleeing, fled**).

fleece *n.* a sheep's woollen coat. *v.* **fleece** 1. to shear a sheep. 2. to rob someone of all he has (**fleecing, fleeced**). *adj.* **fleecy** soft as a fleece.

fleet (1) *n.* a number of ships or cars together.

fleet (2) *adj.* swift, fast-moving. *n.* **fleetness**.

flesh *n.* 1. the soft part of your body. 2. meat. 3. the soft part of fruit. *adj.* **fleshy**.

flew *past* of **fly**.

flexible *adj.* 1. easily bent. 2. adaptable, as *the rule is flexible*. *n.* **flexibility**.

flick *v.* to tap lightly, as *to flick a crumb from a table*. *n.* **flick** a light tap.

flicker *v.* to shine unsteadily, as *a candle flame flickers in a draught*. *n.* **flicker** a quick movement, as *the flicker of an eyelid*.

flight *n.* 1. passing through the air, as *the flight of a bird*. 2. a journey in an aeroplane. 3. a running away from danger. 4. a number of aeroplanes flying together. 5. a series of steps. *n.* **flight-lieutenant** a Royal Air Force rank equal to that of an army captain.

flinch *v.* to draw back from something unpleasant.

fling *v.* to throw away, to hurl (**flinging, flung**). *n.* **fling** 1. a throw. 2. a Highland Scottish dance.

flint *n.* a very hard rock which gives off sparks when struck with steel. **flint-hearted** hard and cruel.

flippant *adj.* spoken in a light-hearted disrespectful way, as *a flippant remark*.

flipper *n.* the flattened leg of a seal, walrus, penguin, or turtle.

flirt *v.* 1. to throw lightly, as *to flirt a piece of paper*. 2. to pretend to make love. 3. to play or dabble with, as *to flirt with an idea*. *n.* **flirtation**.

flit *v.* to move lightly from place to place (**flitting, flitted**).

float *v.* 1. to rest on the surface of a liquid. 2. to launch, as *to float a ship* or *float a new company*. *n.* **float** a piece of cork or wood used to hold up a fishing hook or net.

flock *n.* a group of birds or animals, as *a flock of sheep*. *v.* **flock** to crowd together.

floe *n.* a large area of floating ice.

flog *v.* to beat with a whip or stick (**flogging, flogged**). *n.* **flogging** a beating.

to flog a dead horse to waste time on something which is not worth while.

flood *n.* 1. a great overflowing of water. 2. an outburst, as *a flood of tears*. *v.* **flood** to overflow.

flood-lights *n. pl.* powerful lights used at night.

flood-lit *adj.* (of a building) lit by flood-lights.

floor *n.* 1. the bottom surface of a room or building. 2. any storey of a building, as *the ground floor* or *the second floor*. *v.* **floor** 1. to knock someone to the floor. 2. to take aback, as *the reply floored him*. *n.* **flooring** floor covering.

flop *v.* 1. to fall or drop down heavily. 2. (slang) to collapse, as *the runner flopped in the third lap* (**flopping, flopped**). *n.* **flop** (*slang*) a failure.

floral *adj.* concerning flowers.

florin *n.* an old British coin worth two shillings (10p).

florist *n.* someone who lives by selling flowers.

flotilla *n.* a small fleet.

flounce *n.* a gathered strip sewn round the edge of a skirt. *v.* **flounce** to move away impatiently (**flouncing, flounced**).

flounder (1) *v.* to struggle clumsily, as *to flounder through some difficult work* or *flounder in a marsh*.

flounder (2) *n.* a flat fish.

flour *n.* meal obtained from wheat. *adj.* **floury**.

flourish (*pron.* flur'ish) *v.* 1. to grow well, to prosper. 2. to wave about, as *to flourish a stick*. *n.* **flourish** a bold curve in writing.

flour-mill *n.* a mill where flour is ground.

flow *v.* 1. to move smoothly along. 2. to hang loosely, to wave, as *flowing hair*. 3. (of the tide) to rise.

flower *n.* 1. a plant which produces a bloom. 2. the blossom of a plant. 3. the best, as *the flower of the nation's young men*. *v.* **flower** to burst into bloom. *adj.* **flowery** elaborate, fancy, as *a flowery way of speaking*.

flown *past participle* of **fly**.

flue *n.* a pipe or chimney.

fluent *adj.* able to talk easily, as *a fluent speaker*. *n.* **fluency**.

fluid *n.* a liquid. *adj.* **fluid** able to flow like a liquid. *n.* **fluidity**.

flung *past* of **fling**.

flush *v.* 1. to blush. 2. to wash out with water, as *to flush a drain*. *n.* **flush** 1. a flow of water. 2. a blush. *adj.* **flush** even, as *to make one surface flush with another*. *adj.* **flushed** red-faced, excited.

fluster *v.* to make someone confused. *adj.* **flustered** bewildered.

flute *n.* 1. a musical wood-wind instrument. 2. a groove down the pillar of a building. *adj.* **fluted** grooved.

flutter *v.* 1. to flap quickly, as *a moth flutters its wings*. 2. to move about in excitement.

flux *n.* 1. movement and change. 2. a resin used in soldering metals.

fly (1) *n.* one of several kinds of winged insects, especially the ordinary housefly, or an imitation used for fishing (*pl.* **flies**).

a fly in the ointment a fault in something good.

fly (2) *v.* 1. to move through the air on wings. 2. to rush, as *to fly for protection*. 3. to cause to fly, as *to fly a kite*. 4. to burst, as *the glass flies into pieces* (**flies, flying, flew, flown** *pron.* flōn). *n.* **flier** someone who flies.

to fly in the face of to defy.

with flying colours with flags waving, with success.

fly-catcher *n.* 1. a bird which eats insects. 2. a sticky paper band which traps insects.

flying-fox *n.* a large bat.

foal *n.* a young horse or ass.

foam *n.* froth on sea-water, or something like it.

fo'c'sle (*pron.* fōk'sl) *n.* a short form of *forecastle*.

focus *n.* 1. the point at which the rays through a lens or burning-glass meet. 2. a centre of interest, as *Tom was the focus of attention* (*pl.* **focuses** or **foci**). *v.* **focus** to bring to a point, to concentrate, as *to focus attention on something* (**focusing, focused**).

foe *n.* an enemy.

fog *n.* a thick mist. *adj.* **foggy**.

fog-horn *n.* a warning signal during fog.

foil (1) *v.* to defeat the tricks of an enemy, as *we foiled their attempts to ambush us*.

foil (2) *n.* 1. a thin sheet of metal, as *tin foil*. 2. a fencing sword.

fold (1) *n.* an enclosure for sheep.

fold (2) *v.* to double something over. *n.* **fold** the crease caused by folding. *n.* **folder** an envelope of thin card for holding papers.

-fold (3) a *suffix* meaning 'many times', as *four-fold means four times as many*.

foliage *n.* the leaves of a plant or tree.

folk (*pron.* fōk) *n.* people. *adj.* **folk** national, as *a folk-dance* or *folk-song*.

follow *v.* 1. to go after, as *to follow a trail*. 2. to go behind, as *to follow a guide*. 3. to obey, as *to follow advice*. 4. to understand, as *to follow what someone says*.

following *n.* a group of followers, as *the rebel leader had a large following*.

folly *n.* foolishness (*pl.* **follies**).

fond *adj.* 1. loving. 2. (with **of**) liking greatly.

fondle *v.* to handle lovingly (**fondling, fondled**).

font *n.* a stone basin in a church to hold holy water for baptizing.

food *n.* what plants and animals take in to make them grow. *n.* **foodstuff** nourishment, provisions.

fool *n.* a silly person. *v.* **fool** to trick someone.

foolhardy *adj.* very rash, too bold. *n.* **foolhardiness**.

foolish *adj.* not wise. *n.* **foolishness**.

foot *n.* 1. the part of the body on which any living creature stands. 2. the base, the lowest part. 3. a measure of length equal to 12 inches (30·5 cm). 4. a division in a line of poetry (*pl.* **feet**).

to foot the bill to pay the account.

to have one foot in the grave to be very old and infirm.

to put one's best foot forward to step out.

to put one's foot in it to make an awkward mistake.

to set on foot to start something going.

football *n.* 1. a game played with a large leather ball by two teams. 2. the ball used in the game.

footlights *n. pl.* the lights at the front of a stage.

footnote *n.* a printed note at the foot of a page in a book.

footprint *n.* the mark of a foot.

footstep *n.* the sound of a foot.

for *prep.* 1. in the place of, as *'A stands for apple'.* 2. because of, as *for this reason.* 3. going to, as *the bus for Dover.* 4. during, as *he went for two days.* 5. intending, as *to go for a walk.* *conj.* **for** because, as *I will go, for it is late.*

for all that in spite of everything.

forage *v.* to search for food (**foraging, foraged**).

forbade *past* of **forbid**.

forbid *v.* to order not to, to refuse to allow (**forbidding, forbade, forbidden**).

forbidding *adj.* threatening, unpleasant.

force *n.* 1. power, might, strength. 2. a body of men, as *a police force.* *v.* **force** 1. to push or pull violently, as *to force open a door.* 2. to compel, as *to force a decision.* 3. to make plants grow rapidly, as *to force tomatoes in a greenhouse* (**forcing, forced**). *adj.* **forceful** impressive, with force. *adj.* **forcible** using force.

the forces the armed services.

to force the pace to speed things up.

ford *n.* a place where a river can be crossed on foot. *v.* **ford** to cross a river on foot.

fore *adj.* in front. *n.* **fore** the front, as *to the fore.*

fore- a *prefix* meaning in front, as *a forecourt is a space in front of a building.*

forearm *n.* the arm between elbow and wrist.

forecast *v.* to say beforehand what will most likely happen, as *to forecast the weather* (**forecasting, forecast**). *n.* **forecast** a statement of what will probably happen later.

forecastle (*pron.* fōk's'l) *n.* the crew's quarters of a ship at the bow. The word is sometimes shortened to **fo'c'sle.**

forefinger *n.* the finger nearest the thumb.

foreground *n.* the part of a picture or landscape at the front.

forehead *n.* the part of the face above the eyes.

foreign *adj.* 1. belonging to another country, as *a foreign port.* 2. strange, unusual, as *his views are foreign to me.* *n.* **foreigner** someone who belongs to another country.

foreman *n.* a man in charge of a group of workmen (*pl.* **foremen**).

foremost *adj.* 1. at the front. 2. chief, leading.

forenoon *n.* morning, before noon.

foresight *n.* seeing what might happen, and providing for it, as *Father showed foresight in taking his umbrella.*

forest *n.* a large area of land covered with trees.

forester *n.* a man who works in a forest.

forestry *n.* the management of forests.

foretaste *n.* a sample of what is to come.

foretell *v.* to prophesy, to say what might happen (**foretelling, foretold**).

forethought *n.* wise planning for the future.

forever *adv.* always.

foreword *n.* a preface or introduction to a book.

forfeit (*pron.* for'fit) *n.* a penalty, a fine. *v.* **forfeit** to lose some right or opportunity as a penalty, as *Joan forfeited her chance of being on the team by her absence.* (**forfeiting, forfeited**). *n.* **forfeiture.**

forge (1) *n.* 1. a blacksmith's fire for softening iron. 2. a smithy. *v* **forge** 1. to shape metal. 2. to imitate writing for a dishonest purpose, as *to forge a signature* (**forging, forged**).

forge (2) *v.* to push on steadily (**forging, forged**).

forger *n.* a person who copies handwriting for a dishonest purpose.

forgery *n.* 1. a false signature. 2. any copy to be used dishonestly (*pl.* **forgeries**).

forget *v.* not to remember (**forgetting, forgot, forgotten**). *adj.* **forgetful** liable to forget.

to forget oneself to be rude or angry or forget one's manners.

forget-me-not *n.* a small blue flower.

forgive v. to pardon, to overlook a fault (**forgiving, forgave, forgiven**). n. **forgiveness**.

fork n. 1. a small object for carrying food to the mouth. 2. a gardening tool with prongs. 3. a place where a road branches into two. 4. a part of a tree where it branches. adj. **forked** divided into branches.

forlorn adj. alone, neglected.

a forlorn hope a last desperate chance.

form n. 1. a shape. 2. a kind, as *a form of fish*. 3. a class in school. 4. a bench. 5. fitness, as *he is in good form*. 6. a printed paper to be filled in. v. **form** 1. to shape, to create, as *to form a scarecrow from old rags*. 2. to make, as *several companies form a battalion*.

formal adj. stiff and ceremonious. n. **formality** ceremony.

formation n. 1. forming something. 2. a body of troops, ships, etc.

former adj. earlier in time, as *a former pupil of the school*. adv. **formerly** once, earlier.

formidable adj. powerful, terrifying.

formula n. 1. a rule, a recipe, as *early to bed and early to rise is a formula for success*. 2. (in chemistry) symbols showing how a substance is made up, as *the formula for water is H_2O*. (pl. **formulae** or **formulas**.)

forsake v. to desert, to give up, as *to forsake a sinking ship* (**forsaking, forsook, forsaken**).

forsook past of **forsake**.

fort n. a strong place built for defence.

forth adv forward, as *to go forth*.

forthcoming adj. approaching, as *a forthcoming wedding*.

forthright adj. straightforward, as *a forthright man*.

forthwith adv. at once, as *I will come forthwith*.

fortification n. a strong place, a fort.

fortify v. to strengthen (**fortifying, fortified**).

fortnight n. two weeks. adv. **fortnightly** every two weeks.

fortress n. a fort, a strong place.

fortunate adj. lucky. adv. **fortunately**.

fortune n. 1. chance, luck, as *he won not by skill but by good fortune*. 2. great wealth, as *he inherited a fortune*. 3. future fate, as *the gypsy tells fortunes*.

forty adj. and n. ten times four, represented by the sign 40 or XL. adj. **fortieth**.

forty winks a short sleep.

forward or **forwards** adv. ahead, as *they went forward*. adj. **forward** 1. at the front, as *a forward player*. 2. early, as *forward crops*. 3. advanced, clever for his age, as *a forward scholar*.

fossil n. the remains or impression of an ancient animal or plant found in rock.

foster 1. to bring up, as *to foster young chicks*. 2. to encourage, as *to foster an idea*.

foster-parent someone who brings up a foster-child as his own, though not related to it.

fought past of **fight**.

foul adj. 1. dirty, disgusting, as *a foul smell*. 2. unfair, as *foul play*. 3. stormy, as *foul weather*. v. **foul** 1. to make dirty. 2. to hit, as *the ship fouled the buoy*. 3. to break a rule in football such as using hands to the ball or tackling too vigorously. n. **foul** the breaking of a rule. adv. **foully**.

found (1) past of **find**.

found (2) v. to set up, to start, as *to found a home for the aged* (**founding, founded**).

foundation n. 1. the base of a building. 2. the creating or setting up of an institution. n. pl. **foundations** the base on which a building rests.

foundation-stone a stone at the base of a new building, laid with public ceremony.

foundry n. a place where metal is melted and moulded (pl. **foundries**).

fountain n. a jet of water.

fountain-head n. a source or origin.

fountain-pen n. a pen with its own ink supply.

four adj. and n. one more than three, represented by the sign 4 or IV. adj. **fourth**. n. **fourteen** one more than thirteen. adj. **fourteenth**.

on all fours on hands and knees.

fowl n. a bird, especially a domestic hen (masc. **cock**, fem. **hen**). n. **fowler** someone who hunts and traps birds.

fox *n.* a reddish-brown dog-like wild animal, noted for slyness. *v.* **fox** to trick someone.

foxglove *n.* a wild plant with bell-shaped flowers.

foxhound *n.* a hound for hunting foxes.

fox-terrier *n.* a small black and white dog.

foyer (*pron.* fwa'yay) *n.* an entrance hall to a cinema, theatre, etc.

fraction *n.* 1. part of a whole, as *Dick saved only a fraction of his pocket money.* 2. (in arithmetic) part of a whole number, as *three-quarters is a fraction.*

decimal fraction part of a whole number in the form of a decimal, as $0·45$.

improper fraction a fraction which is more than one, as five thirds or $\frac{5}{3}$.

proper fraction a fraction which is less than one, as five eighths or $\frac{5}{8}$.

vulgar fraction any fraction which is not a decimal fraction.

fracture *n.* 1. a break. 2. the breaking of a bone.

fragile *adj.* frail, easily broken.

fragment *n.* a small part broken off.

fragrance *n.* a sweet smell.

fragrant *adj.* sweet-smelling.

frail *adj.* 1. delicate, weak, as *a frail old lady.* 2. brittle, fragile, as *a frail vase. n.* **frailty.**

frame *n.* 1. a skeleton, as *the human frame* or *the frame of a building.* 2. a border, as *a picture frame. v.* **frame** 1. to put a frame round, as *to frame a picture or a window.* 2. to compose, to put together, as *to frame rules, to frame a letter,* or *to frame a plan* (**framing, framed**).

a frame of mind a state of mind.

frank *adj.* plain-spoken, saying what one thinks. *n.* **frankness** openness, plain speech.

frantic *adj.* wild with anger, fear, etc. *adv.* **frantically** wildly, as *she waved frantically.*

fraud *n.* 1. a swindle, trickery. 2. a man who cheats.

fraudulent *adj.* dishonest.

fray (1) *n.* a commotion, a noisy fight.

fray (2) *v.* to wear away, as *frayed nerves* or *frayed cuffs* (**fraying, frayed**).

freak *n.* something out of the ordinary, as *this whirlwind is a freak. adj.* **freakish** unusual.

freckle *n.* a brown spot on the skin. *adj.* **freckled** spotted with freckles.

free *adj.* 1. loose, not shut up, at liberty. 2. generous, as *he is free with his money.* 3. at no cost, as *a free ticket.* 4. without, as *free of tax. v.* **free** to set free (**freeing, freed**). *adv.* **free** 1. loose, as *he set the bird free.* 2. at no cost, as *he went in free. n.* **freedom.**

free fight a fight open to all.

free-hand (of a drawing) drawn without instruments.

free kick (in football) a kick at the ball awarded by the referee.

free trade trade without duties or taxes.

freeze *v.* 1. to be very cold. 2. to become ice. 3. to stand still, as *a hunter freezes on seeing game* (**freezing, froze, frozen**).

freight (*pron.* frayt) *n.* cargo or goods, on ship or train. *n.* **freighter** a cargo ship.

French *adj.* belonging to France.

French leave absence without permission.

French polish a varnish rubbed into furniture.

French window a glazed door opening on to a garden.

frequency *n.* 1. the rate at which something happens, as *the frequency of one's heart beat.* 2. common occurrence, as *I welcomed the frequency of his visits.*

frequent (*pron.* free'kwent) *adj.* happening often, as *frequent rain. v.* **frequent** (*pron.* free.kwent') to visit often, as *to frequent a café. adv.* **frequently.**

fresh *adj.* 1. new, recent. 2. not stale or faded, as *fresh milk* or *fresh flowers. n.* **freshness.**

freshen *v.* to make fresh (**freshening, freshened**).

fret *v.* 1. to fidget. 2. to worry over trifles (**fretting, fretted**). *adj.* **fretful** restless and vexed.

fretsaw *n.* a fine-bladed saw to cut plywood.

fretwork n. woodwork done with a fretsaw.

friar n. a member of a religious brotherhood, a monk. n. **friary** a monastery.

friction n. 1. rubbing. 2. (in engineering) the rubbing between moving parts of a machine. 3. quarrels between people who disagree.

Friday n. the sixth day of the week. n. **Good Friday** the Friday before Easter, the day of the Crucifixion.

friend n. someone known and liked by another. adj. **friendly** kindly. n. **friendliness**. n. **friendship**.

fright n. a scare, sudden fear. adj. **frightful** dreadful. adv. **frightfully**.

frighten v. to alarm, to cause fright. adj. **frightening** terrifying.

frill n. an edging or ruffle of lace or cloth.

fringe n. 1. an edging of loose threads. 2. hair cut low across the forehead.

frivolous adj. light-hearted, silly.

fro adv. away from, as in to and fro.

frock n. a female dress, a monk's gown.

frog n. a small animal which jumps and lives partly in the water.

frolic v. to play merrily, to have fun (**frolicking, frolicked**). n. **frolic** merry play. adj. **frolicsome**.

from prep. 1. out of, as he came from London. 2. between one point and another, as from one to two o'clock. 3. because of, as he died from fever.

front n. the foremost part, as the front of a train. v. **front** to face, as my bedroom fronts the road. adj. **frontal** at the front.

frontier n. 1. the boundary between two countries. 2. the furthermost part of a new country that has been settled.

frontispiece n. a picture at the front of a book.

frost n. 1. frozen dew. 2. a temperature to freeze water, as we had three degrees of frost. adj. **frosty**.

frosted adj. looking as if covered with frost, as frosted glass.

frostbite n. sores caused by frost. adj. **frostbitten**.

froth n. foam, masses of bubbles.

frown n. a wrinkling of the forehead. v. **frown** 1. to wrinkle the forehead.

2. to show disapproval, as to frown on swearing.

froze, frozen past of **freeze**.

frugal adj. wasting little, sparing. adv. **frugally**. n. **frugality**.

fruit n. 1. the fleshy food, containing the seed, that follows the blossom on a tree or bush. 2. any produce, as the fruit of labour or the fruits of the earth. adj. **fruitful** productive. adj. **fruitless** wasted. n. **fruiterer** a fruitseller.

frustration n. a feeling of being baffled.

frustrate v. 1. to disappoint, to baffle. 2. to defeat, as to frustrate someone's plans (**frustrating, frustrated**). n. **frustration**.

fry v. to cook in oil or fat (**frying, fried**).

out of the frying pan into the fire out of one difficulty into a greater one.

fuel n. 1. anything used for burning in a fire or boiler, such as coal or coke. 2. material for giving energy to a motor, as petrol, gas, or diesel-oil. v. **fuel** to supply with fuel (**fuelling, fuelled**).

fugitive (pron. fyoo'ji.tiv) n. someone fleeing from danger or justice.

fulfil v. 1. to complete, to carry out, as to fulfil a task. 2. to satisfy, as to fulfil a wish (**fulfilling, fulfilled**). n. **fulfilment**.

full adj. 1. filled completely. 2. the greatest, as full honours or full speed ahead. 3. loose-fitting, in folds, as this dress is full. adv. **fully** completely. n. **fullness** or **fulness**.

full moon the whole shape of the moon to be seen.

full stop 1. a punctuation mark. 2. a complete stop.

full swing in full activity.

fully fledged fully developed.

full-blooded adj. vigorous.

fumble v. 1. to handle awkwardly, as to fumble a catch at cricket or baseball. 2. to grope about, as to fumble in the dark (**fumbling, fumbled**).

fume n. smoke, or gas. v. **fume** 1. to give off smoke. 2. to get into a rage (**fuming, fumed**).

fun n. amusement, merriment, play.

function n. 1. the purpose of a thing, as the function of a knife is to cut. 2. a ceremony, as *the mayor has many functions to attend*. *v.* **function** to work, as *this machine functions well*.

fund *n.* 1. a supply, a store, as *a fund of humour*. 2. a store of money put by for a special purpose, as *a holiday fund*.

funeral *n.* a burial service. *adj.* **funereal** (*pron.* fyoo.nee're.al) concerned with a burial, gloomy.

fungus *n.* a plant such as a mushroom or toadstool (*pl.* **fungi** *pron.* fung'jī or **funguses**).

funnel *n.* 1. the chimney of a ship or locomotive. 2. (in science) a wide-mouthed glass tube for pouring liquids into narrow openings.

funny *adj.* humorous, causing laughter (*comparative* **funnier,** *superlative* **funniest**).

fur *n.* the soft hairy coat of some animals. *adj.* **furry** made of fur.

furious *adj.* full of anger or violence, as *a furious storm*.

furl *v.* to roll up, as *to furl a flag*.

furlong *n.* a distance of one-eighth of a mile. Approximately 200 metres.

furnace *n.* a closed fireplace to heat water for a boiler, or to melt ore or metals.

furnish *v.* 1. to fit up with furniture and fittings, as *to furnish a house*. 2. to provide, to supply, as *to furnish campers with food*.

furnishings *n. pl.* furniture and fittings.

furniture *n.* the movable goods in a house.

furrier *n.* someone who sells furs.

furrow *n.* 1. a shallow trench made by a plough. 2. a wrinkle, a groove. *adj.* **furrowed**.

further *adj.* 1. *comparative* of **far**. 2. more distant, as *the further end*. 2. extra, as *further help. adv.* **further** to a greater distance, as *he walked further*.

furthermore *adv.* also, in addition.

furthermost *adj.* furthest, most distant.

furthest *adj. superlative* of **far**, most distant.

fury *n.* fierce rage, violence, as *the fury of the gale*.

fuse *v.* 1. to melt by heat. 2. to melt together two substances (**fusing, fused**).

n. **fuse** 1. a slow-burning cord fastened to a firework or explosive. 2. an electrical safety device of an easily melted piece of wire placed in the circuit.

fuse-box *n.* (in electricity) a box containing fuses.

fuselage (*pron.* fyoo'ze.lij *or* fyoo'ze.-lahzh) the body of an aeroplane.

fuss *n.* commotion, bother. *adj.* **fussy.** *n.* **fussiness**.

future *n.* what is still to come. *adj.* **future** still to be.

the future tense (in grammar) the tense showing what will happen, as *we shall go*.

-fy *suffix* meaning to make, as *clarify*—to make clear, or *solidify*—to make solid.

G

gabble *v.* to talk too fast to be understood (**gabbling, gabbled**).

gable *n.* the triangular end of a roof.

gadget *n.* a neat little tool or instrument.

gag *n.* 1. something pushed into someone's mouth to prevent him talking. 2. a quick humorous remark by an actor. *v.* **gag** to silence someone by force (**gagging, gagged**).

gaiety *n.* merriment, liveliness.

gaily *adv.* merrily, happily.

gain *v.* 1. to earn, to win, as *to gain money*. 2. to become more, as *this has gained in value. n.* **gain** profit, increase.

to gain ground to make progress.

gala (*pron.* gay'la *or* gah'la) *n.* 1. a festival. 2. a social function for sport or entertainment, as *a swimming gala*.

gale *n.* a very strong wind, but less than a hurricane or tempest.

gallant *adj.* brave, chivalrous. *n.* **gallantry**.

galleon *n.* a large Spanish sailing-ship with a high poop and several decks.

gallery *n.* 1. a long passage in an old house. 2. (in a cinema or theatre) a balcony (*pl.* **galleries**).

art gallery a building in which pictures are displayed to the public.

galley *n.* 1. an ancient ship moved by sails and oars. 2. a ship's kitchen (*pl.* **galleys**).

galley-slave a slave forced to row in a galley.

gallon *n.* a liquid measure equal to 8 pints (4·5 litres). In the U.S.A. a gallon is five-sixths of a British gallon.

gallop *n.* the fastest speed of a horse. *v.* **gallop** (of a horse) to run at full speed (**galloping, galloped**).

gallows *n.* a wooden structure on which criminals are hanged.

galvanized *adj.* 1. coated with another metal, as *galvanized iron.* 2. roused into action.

gamble *v.* 1. to play for money. 2. to take a risk for some possible gain (**gambling, gambled**). *n.* **gamble** a risk.

game *n.* 1. play or sport. 2. wild creatures hunted for food. 3. a wild bird served at a meal. *adj.* **game** brave, plucky, as *a game fighter.*

big game the larger wild animals.

the game is not worth the candle what you gain is not worth the trouble or expense.

to make game of to poke fun at.

to play the game to be fair and honest.

game-keeper *n.* a man who protects wild creatures kept for hunting.

gander *n.* a male goose.

gang *n.* 1. a group of persons acting together, perhaps for a bad purpose, as *a gang of robbers.* 2. a team of men working under a foreman, as *a railway repair gang.*

gangster *n.* a member of a criminal gang.

gangway *n.* 1. a passage between rows of seats. 2. a movable bridge between a ship and the landing stage.

gaol (*pron.* jail) *n.* a prison. Often spelled jail. *n.* **gaoler** a prison warder.

gap *n.* an opening or space in a wall, hedge, etc.

gape *v.* 1. to open wide. 2. to stare open-mouthed. *adj.* **gaping** wide-open, staring.

garage (*pron.* ga'rij *or* ga'rahzh) *n.* a building where motor-cars are kept or repaired.

garbage *n.* rubbish, waste matter.

garbled *adj.* muddle in telling, as *Robert gave a garbled story of his accident.*

garden *n.* 1. a piece of cultivated land attached to a house. 2. a public space for rest and pleasure.

to lead someone up the garden path to mislead him deliberately.

gardener *n.* a man who works in a garden.

gargle *v.* to gurgle liquid in your throat without swallowing, to wash away germs (**gargling, gargled**). *n.* **gargle** a throat wash.

garland *n.* a crown of flowers or leaves.

garlic *n.* a strong-smelling plant like an onion, used in cooking.

garment *n.* any piece of clothing such as a dress or coat.

garnish *v.* to decorate food, as *roast turkey garnished with cranberries.*

garret *n.* a small room at the top of a house, an attic.

garrison *n.* soldiers occupying a fort or town. *v.* **garrison** to occupy with soldiers.

garter *n.* 1. an elastic band to hold up a stocking. 2. the badge of the highest order of knighthood in Britain, as *a Knight of the Garter. n.* **garter-snake** a non-poisonous snake with yellow stripes running down its back, common in North America.

gas *n.* 1. one of several substances like air. 2. coal-gas used for heating and lighting. 3. a mixture of nitrous oxide and oxygen, used by dentists to make one unconscious. 4. a poisonous gas used in warfare (*pl.* **gases**). 5. (in the U.S.A.) a short word for **gasolene.** *v.* **gas** to make someone unconscious, or ill, with a gas (**gassing, gassed**).

gaseous *adj.* in the form of a gas.

gasholder, gasometer *n.* a tank for storing gas at a gasworks.

gash *n.* a cut or slash. *v.* **gash** to cut, to slash.

gasolene, gasoline *n.* (in the U.S.A.) petrol.

gasp *v.* to open the mouth breathing deeply for air. *n.* **gasp** a quick gulp of air.

gastric *adj.* belonging to the stomach, as *gastric juice helps food to digest.*

gate *n.* 1. a hinged frame in the opening of a wall, hedge, etc. 2. all the people who pay to see a sports event, as *there* *was a record gate at the match.* **3.** all the money paid by people at a sports event, as *the visiting team was paid a third of the gate.*

gateway *n.* an opening in a wall or fence.

gather *v.* **1.** to collect, as *to gather nuts.* **2.** to come together, as *a crowd gathers.* **3.** to draw up in folds, as *to gather curtains.* **4.** to conclude, as *I gather he will not return.* **5.** (of a sore) to form pus, as *the abscess gathered.*

gathering *n.* **1.** a crowd of people. **2.** a getting together, as *a gathering of the clans.* **3.** an inflamed sore forming pus.

gaudy *adj.* showy and bright in a vulgar way (*comparative* **gaudier,** *superlative* **gaudiest**). *n.* **gaudiness.**

gauge (*pron.* gayj) *n.* **1.** a measuring instrument, as *a rain gauge.* **2.** (in metalwork) the thickness of a wire or metal sheet. **3.** (in woodwork) a tool for scratching a line parallel with the edge of a piece of wood. **4.** the distance between railway lines, as *British railway lines have a gauge of 1·435 metres.* *v.* **gauge** **1.** to measure. **2.** to judge, to estimate, as *to gauge the width of a ditch* (**gauging, gauged**).

gaunt *adj.* **1.** lean, haggard. **2.** desolate.

gauntlet *n.* **1.** an iron glove worn by knights in the Middle Ages. **2.** a man's long leather glove.

to run the gauntlet a punishment where the victim runs between two rows of men who strike him.

to throw down the gauntlet to issue a challenge as knights of old did in throwing down their gloves.

gauze *n.* thin transparent fabric.

gauze wire (in science) a mat of woven iron wire placed over a Bunsen burner to spread heat.

gave *past* of **give.**

gay *adj.* **1.** merry, bright. **2.** showy, full of colour, as *a gay dress.* See **gaiety** and **gaily.**

gaze *v.* to stare, to look at steadily (**gazing, gazed**). *n.* **gaze** a steady look.

gazelle *n.* a small antelope of Africa and Asia.

gazetteer *n.* a list of geographical names in alphabetical order.

gear *n.* **1.** a toothed wheel fitting into other *gear wheels* of different sizes to make them move quickly or slowly. **2.** tools or equipment. **3.** clothes.

in gear with gear wheels fitting together so that an engine can move a load.

out of gear with gear-wheels not touching so that an engine cannot move a load.

gear-box *n.* the box in a motor-car which holds gear-wheels linked to the engine, which can be used to make the car move faster or slower.

gear-lever *n.* a rod by which a driver of a motor vehicle selects the gear he requires.

geese *plural* of **goose.**

gem *n.* a precious stone, a jewel.

general *n.* an army commander between a colonel and a field-marshal in rank. *adj.* **general** **1.** concerning everybody, as *a general election.* **2.** widespread, usual, as *a general belief.* **3.** chief, as *postmaster-general.* *adv.* **generally** usually.

in general usually, as a rule.

generate *v.* to produce, as *a dynamo generates electricity* (**generating, generated**).

generation *n.* **1.** production. **2.** people born at about the same time, as *the present-day generation.*

generator *n.* a machine for producing electricity, a dynamo.

generosity *n.* unselfishness.

generous *adj.* unselfish, giving freely.

genesis *n.* creation. *n.* **Genesis** the first book of the Bible.

genial *adj.* kindly, cheerful. *adv.* **genially.**

genie (*pron.* jee'ni) *n.* (in Arabian fairytales) a demon spirit.

genius (*pron.* jee'ni.us) *n.* **1.** extreme cleverness. **2.** a very gifted person (*pl.* **geniuses**).

genteel *adj.* very polite and refined.

Gentile *n.* a biblical word for anyone who is not Jewish.

gentle *adj.* **1.** mild, soothing, as *a gentle voice.* **2.** gradual, as *a gentle slope.* *n.* **gentleness.** *adv.* **gently.**

gentleman, gentlewoman *n.* a man or woman of good birth, or kind and well-mannered.

genuine *adj.* 1. real, true, as *genuine pearls*. 2. sincere, well-meant, as *a genuine welcome*.

geography *n.* the study of the earth and its peoples. *adj.* **geographical**.

geology *n.* the study of the rocks and materials of the earth. *adj.* **geological**.

geometry *n.* the part of mathematics concerned with lines, angles, and solids. *adj.* **geometrical**.

germ *n.* 1. the beginning of life. 2. a seed. 3. a harmful microbe.

germinate *v.* (of a seed) to sprout (**germinating, germinated**). *n.* **germination**.

gesture (*pron.* jes'tyur) *n.* 1. a movement of face or limb to show feeling, as *to throw up the hands as a gesture of despair*. 2. a friendly act, as *he sent me a letter of good wishes as a courteous gesture*.

get *v.* 1. to obtain, as *to get a letter*. 2. to become, as *to get ready*. 3. to reach, as *to get a book off a shelf*. 4. to persuade, as *to get someone to do something* (**getting, got**).

to get away with to manage successfully.

to get off 1. to get away. 2. to escape (from punishment, etc.).

to get on 1. to succeed. 2. to continue.

to get on with someone to associate in a friendly way with him.

to get over 1. to recover from an illness. 2. to overcome a difficulty.

to get round 1. to persuade someone. 2. to evade a difficulty.

geyser (*pron.* gay'zer) *n.* 1. a hot spring, as in New Zealand, gushing up from the ground. 2. a gas or electric water-heater (usually *pron.* gee'zer).

ghastly *adj.* horrible. *n.* **ghastliness**.

ghost *n.* 1. the supposed spirit of a dead person. 2. a faint appearance. *adj.* **ghostly**.

giant *n.* 1. (in fairy-tales) a man of enormous size. 2. anything gigantic. See **gigantic**.

giddy *adj.* dizzy, light-headed (*comparative* **giddier,** *superlative* **giddiest**). *adv.* **giddily**. *n.* **giddiness**.

gift *n.* 1. a present. 2. a natural ability, as *a gift for singing*.

do not look a gift horse in the mouth do not criticize a gift.

gifted *adj.* skilful, clever.

gigantic *adj.* enormous, like a giant. See **giant**.

giggle *v.* to titter, to laugh in an excited way (**giggling, giggled**).

gill (1) (*pron.* gil) *n.* the breathing organ of a fish or frog.

gill (2) (*pron.* jil) *n.* a liquid measure equal to one-quarter of a pint (0·142 litres

gilt *n.* a thin layer of gold or gold paint.

to take the gilt off the gingerbread to make something less attractive, from an old custom of gilding gingerbread at fairs.

gin (*pron.* jin) *n.* 1. a trap. 2. an alcoholic drink.

ginger *n.* a tropical root ground to a hot spicy powder for flavouring food.

gipsy see **gypsy**.

giraffe *n.* a long-necked African animal.

girder *n.* a strong beam holding up a weight, as *the girder of a roof*.

girdle *n.* 1. a belt, a sash. *v.* **girdle** to surround (**girdling, girdled**).

girl *n.* 1. a female child. 2. a young woman. 3. a female servant. *adj.* **girlish** 1. like a girl. 2. belonging to a girl.

Girl Guide a member of the world organization for girls founded by Lord Baden-Powell.

girth *n.* 1. a band round a horse holding the saddle in place. 2. the distance round anything, as *the girth of a tree*.

gist (*pron.* jist) *n.* the main point, as *the gist of a story*.

give *v.* 1. to hand over, to deliver. 2. to pay, as *to give a high price*. 3. to yield, as *the beam gives under the weight of the roof* (**giving, gave, given**).

to give and take to be tolerant.

to give in to surrender.

to give out 1. to let it be known. 2. to run short. 3. to distribute.

to give up to surrender.

to give oneself away to betray oneself.

glacial *adj.* concerning glaciers.

glacier *n.* a slow-moving river of ice.

glad *adj.* pleased (*comparative* **gladder,** *superlative* **gladdest**). *adv.* **gladly.** *v.* **gladden** to please. *n.* **gladness** happiness.

glade *n.* an open space in a wood or forest.

gladiator *n.* (in ancient Rome) a man who fought in the arenas in public.

glamour *n.* charm, enchantment. *adj.* **glamorous** charming, beautiful.

glance *v.* 1. to look at for a moment. 2. (with **off**) to bounce off at a sharp angle, as *the stone glanced off the side of the wall* (**glancing, glanced**). *n.* **glance** a quick look.

a glancing blow a blow at a sharp angle.

gland *n.* any organ in the body which gives out a fluid, as *sweat glands.*

glare *n.* 1. a dazzling light. 2. a fierce stare. *v.* **glare** 1. to dazzle. 2. to stare fiercely (**glaring, glared**). *adj.* **glaring** 1. dazzling. 2. very obvious, as *a glaring mistake.*

glass *n.* 1. a transparent brittle substance. 2. a tumbler. 3. a mirror. *n. pl.* **glasses** spectacles. *adj.* **glassy** like glass.

glass-house *n.* a greenhouse.

glaze *v.* to fit with glass, or finish with a glossy surface (**glazing, glazed**). *adj.* **glazed** glossy or glassy, as *glazed eyes.*

gleam *n.* a small ray of light. *v.* **gleam** to shine dimly.

glean *v.* 1. to gather bits of corn after the harvest. 2. to pick up scraps of information, as *Frank gleaned what news he could of the accident. n. pl.* **gleanings** scraps.

glee *n.* merriment. *adj.* **gleeful** delighted.

glen *n.* a narrow valley with a stream.

glide *v.* 1. to slip smoothly along. 2. to travel through air in a plane with no engine (**gliding, glided**). *n.* **glide** a smooth movement.

glider *n.* an aircraft with no engine.

glimmer *n.* a tiny ray of light. *v.* **glimmer** to shine faintly. See **gleam.**

glimpse *v.* to catch sight of (**glimpsing, glimpsed**). *n.* **glimpse** a quick glance at.

glint *n.* a sparkle, as *a glint of anger in someone's eye. v.* **glint** to sparkle.

glisten *v.* to shine, to gleam.

glitter *v.* to sparkle, to flash, as *diamonds glitter. n.* **glitter** brilliance, sparkle.

gloat *v.* to gaze with greedy joy on, as *a bird of prey gloats on its victim.*

globe *n.* 1. a ball, a sphere. 2. a map of the earth in the shape of a ball.

gloom *n.* 1. darkness. 2. sadness, depression. *adj.* **gloomy** (*comparative* **gloomier,** *superlative* **gloomiest**).

glorify *v.* to praise, to pay honour to (**glorifying, glorified**). *n.* **glorification.**

glorious *adj.* 1. worthy of praise. 2. magnificent.

glory *n.* splendour, fame, honour. *v.* **glory** (with **in**) to take pride in (**glorying, gloried**).

gloss *n.* a shine on a surface. *v.* **gloss** 1. to make smooth. 2. (with **over**) to cover some flaw, as *to gloss over someone's mistake. n.* **glossiness.**

glove *n.* a covering for the hand.

the velvet glove gentle words and a pleasant manner.

to throw down the glove to challenge.

glow *v.* 1. to give heat and light without flames. 2. to be flushed with warmth or excitement. *n.* **glow** 1. warmth. 2. redness. 3. a flush of excitement.

glow-worm *n.* a beetle which glows in the dark.

glucose *n.* 1. sugar from fruit. 2. (in Canada) corn-syrup made from cornstarch.

glue *n.* a sticky substance used to fasten things together. *v.* **glue** to stick with glue (**glueing, glued**). *adj.* **gluey.**

glum *adj.* silent and gloomy.

glut *n.* too large an amount, as *a glut of coffee in Brazil.*

glutton *n.* a greedy person. *adj.* **gluttonous.**

gnarled (*pron.* narld) *adj.* knotted, twisted.

gnash *v.* to grind one's teeth in anger.

gnat *n.* a small blood-sucking fly.

gnaw (*pron.* naw) *v.* to bite away gradually, as *rats gnaw through a board.*

gnome (*pron.* nōm) *n.* a dwarf or goblin.

gnu (*pron.* nyoo) *n.* a South African antelope.

go *v.* 1. to move away, to leave. 2. to be in motion, as *this clock goes*. 3. to last, as *this will go a long way*. 4. to be lost, as *my purse has gone*. 5. to become, as *to go pale* (**going, went, gone**). *n.* **go** 1. a try, as *have a go!* 2. (*slang*) energy, as *he has plenty of 'go'*.

to go all out to do one's utmost.

to go for 1. to attack. 2. to go and get.

to go halves to share equally.

to go in for to take up as a hobby.

to go off 1. to go away. 2. to explode. 3. to go bad.

to go one better to do even better.

to go over to revise.

to go slow to work slowly in protest.

to go the whole hog to go to the fullest.

to go to the wall to get pushed aside.

to go under to fail.

goal *n.* 1. an aim. 2. the posts between which a ball must be sent in football, hockey, etc. *n.* **goal-keeper** a player in goal.

goat *n.* a hairy horned animal which gives milk.

gobble *v.* to eat greedily (**gobbling, gobbled**).

goblet *n.* a drinking cup with no handle.

goblin *n.* a dwarf or gnome.

god *n.* a being with superhuman power (*fem.* **goddess**). *n.* **God** the Creator. *adj.* **godly** pious.

godfather, godmother *n.* a person who promises to look after a child's religious training at his baptism.

goggles *n. pl.* eye-glasses worn for protection.

gold *n.* a precious yellow metal. *adj.* **golden**.

golden-wedding fiftieth wedding anniversary.

goldfish *n.* a small red fish.

goldsmith *n.* a man who makes articles of gold.

golf *n.* a game played on a *golf-course* or *golf-links* with a ball and long-handled clubs.

gondola (*pron.* gon'do.la) *n.* a long light rowing boat used in Venice. *n.*

gondolier a man who rows a gondola.

gone *past* of **go**.

gong *n.* a metal disc which sounds when struck.

good *adj.* 1. excellent, right, as *a good deed*. 2. suitable, as *a good opportunity*. 3. well-behaved, as *a good girl*. 4. kind, as *a good master*. 5. early, as *in good time*. 6. enjoyable, as *to have a good time* (*comparative* **better**, *superlative* **best**). *n.* **good** what is right, the opposite of **bad**. *n.* **goodness** virtue, excellence.

Good Friday see **Friday**.

good humour a contented frame of mind.

good nature kindness.

to make good to prove to be a success.

good-bye *n.* farewell.

goods *n. pl.* 1. property, possessions. 2. materials carried by ship or train.

goodwill *n.* friendliness to others.

goose *n.* (*masc.* **gander**) a large, web-footed bird (*pl.* **geese**).

all his geese are swans he thinks all his ideas are good ones.

gooseberry *n.* a bush fruit (*pl.* **gooseberries**).

gopher *n.* 1. a North American ground squirrel. 2. a land tortoise.

gorge *n.* 1. the throat. 2. a narrow valley. *v.* **gorge** to eat greedily (**gorging, gorged**).

gorgeous *adj.* magnificent, as *a gorgeous view*.

gorilla *n.* the largest kind of ape.

gorse *n.* a prickly yellow-flowered shrub.

gosling *n.* a young goose.

gospel *n.* the teachings of Jesus; one of the four Gospels of the New Testament.

gossip *n.* 1. idle chatter. 2. a person fond of chatter.

got *past* of **get**.

gouge *n.* a curved chisel *v.* **gouge** to scoop out (**gouging, gouged**).

govern *v.* to rule, to control. *n.* **government** 1. rule or control. 2. a group of people who have power to rule.

governess *n.* a woman paid to teach children in their own home.

governor *n.* 1. a person who rules or governs. 2. a device on a steam-engine to control its speed.

governor-general *n.* the representative of Great Britain in a dominion.

gown *n.* 1. a woman's dress. 2. a loose robe.

grab *v.* to snatch (**grabbing, grabbed**). *n.* **grab** 1. a sudden snatch. 2. a crane with a scoop.

grace *n.* 1. charm, an easy manner. 2. favour, as *by someone's good grace*. 3. extra time, as *he is given a month's grace to pay*. 4. a short prayer at a meal. 5. a title given to a duke or an archbishop, who are addressed as *your grace*. *v.* **grace** to honour, as *will you grace us with your presence?* *adj.* **graceful** charming.

with a good grace willingly.

with a bad grace unwillingly.

gracious *adj.* kindly, charming.

grade *n.* 1. degree of quality, as *fruit of a higher grade*. 2. step, level, as *Tom is now working at a higher grade*. 3. (in North American schools) a class marking a different year of work, as *Anne is in the fifth grade*. 4. a slope, as *a grade of one in six*. *v.* **grade** to sort out according to quality (**grading, graded**).

gradient *n.* 1. a slope. 2. the steepness of a slope, as *a gradient of one in eight means the slope rises one metre for every eight metres along the level*.

gradual *adj.* by degrees, gentle and slow. *adv.* **gradually** little by little.

graduate *v.* 1. to receive a university degree. 2. to mark into regular divisions, as *to graduate a ruler or a thermometer* (**graduating, graduated**). *n.* **graduate** someone who has received a university degree. *n.* **graduation**.

grain *n.* 1. seed of corn, rice, etc. 2. a particle of dust or sand. 3. the markings of wood fibres.

to go against the grain to go against one's natural feelings.

grammar *n.* the study of the right use of words. *adj.* **grammatical** according to grammar. *n.* **grammar school** (in England and Wales) a secondary school for pupils over 11 years studying to an advanced level.

gramme *n.* a metric unit of mass.

gramophone *n.* a machine for producing sounds from a record

granary *n.* a grain store (*pl.* **granaries**).

grand *adj.* 1. magnificent, important, as *a grand display*. 2. chief, as *a grand duke*. 3. complete, as *the grand total*.

grandchild *n.* a son or daughter's child.

grandparent *n.* a father or mother's parent.

grandstand *n.* a main sports stand.

granite *n.* very hard rock.

grant *v.* 1. to give, as *to grant a favour*. 2. to admit, as *I grant you are right*. *n.* **grant** a gift, a favour.

to take for granted to suppose one may do something or believe something, without first making sure.

grape *n.* fruit growing in bunches on a *grape-vine*.

grapefruit *n.* fruit like a large orange.

graph *n.* a line drawn on squared paper, which gives information, as *a graph showing the classroom temperature day by day*.

grasp *v.* 1. to seize, as *to grasp a rope*. 2. to understand, as *to grasp a problem*.

grasping *adj.* 1. seizing. 2. greedy.

grass *n.* the green plant of lawns and meadows. *adj.* **grassy** covered with grass.

to let the grass grow under one's feet to waste time.

grasshopper *n.* a jumping insect.

grass-snake *n.* a harmless snake.

grate (1) *n.* a fire holder, a fireplace.

grate (2) *v.* 1. to rub into little pieces, as *to grate cheese*. 2. to rub with a harsh sound. 3. to irritate, as *the sound grates on my nerves* (**grating, grated**).

grateful *adj.* thankful. *adv.* **gratefully**.

grating *n.* 1. rubbing. 2. an iron grid.

gratis (*pron.* gray'tis) *adv.* without charge.

gratitude *n.* thankfulness to a helper.

grave (1) *n.* a hole in the earth to bury someone.

grave (2) *adj.* serious, solemn.

gravedigger *n.* a man who digs graves.

gravel *n.* small pebbles and sand.

gravestone *n.* a stone at the head of a grave.

graveyard *n.* a burial ground.

gravitation n. the force drawing things towards the earth's centre. See **gravity**.

gravity n. 1. gravitation. 2. seriousness, as *they discussed the matter with great gravity*.
the force of gravity the force drawing things towards the earth's centre, gravitation.

gravy n. cooked meat juices.

gray see **grey**.

graze (1) v. 1. to eat grass. 2. to put out to grass (**grazing, grazed**).

graze (2) v. to touch in passing, and scrape the skin (**grazing, grazed**).

grease n. thick fat. v. **grease** to put grease on (**greasing, greased**). adj. **greasy**.

great adj. 1. large, long. 2. important, as *a great day*. 3. distinguished, as *a great actor*. n. **greatness**.

great-grandfather n. a grandfather's father.

great-grandson n. a grandson's son.

great-hearted adj. generous.

greed n. a selfish desire for more. adj. **greedy** selfishly wanting more. n. **greediness**.

green n. 1. the colour of grass. 2. a stretch of grass, as *the village green* or *a putting green*. n. pl. **greens** green vegetables. n. **greenness**.

greengrocer n. a man who sells fruit and vegetables.

greenhouse n. a heated glass-house for plants.

greet v. to welcome. n. **greeting**.

grew past of **grow**.

grey (sometimes spelled **gray**) n. a colour between black and white. adj. **greyish** partly grey. n. **greyness**.

greyhound n. a racing dog.

grid n. 1. a frame of iron bars, a grating. 2. a network of high-powered cables supplying electricity, *the electrical grid*.

gridiron n. 1. a cooking grid of iron bars. 2. (in North America) a football field.

grief n. deep sorrow.
to come to grief to end in disaster.

grievance n. a deep-felt wrong, as *Bob had a grievance, feeling that he was blamed unjustly*.

grieve v. 1. to feel grief or sorrow. 2. to cause grief or pain to friends (**grieving, grieved**).

grill v. 1. to cook on a gridiron. 2. to question keenly. n. **grill** food cooked on a gridiron.

grim adj. stern, cruel. adv. **grimly**.

grime n. dirt embedded in face or hands. adj. **grimy** dirty.

grin v. to smile broadly (**grinning, grinned**). n. **grin** a wide smile.

grind v. 1. to crush to powder. 2. to sharpen, as *to grind scissors*. 3. to rub together, as *to grind one's teeth*. 4. to act as a tyrant, as *to grind people down* (**grinding, ground**).

grindstone n. a wheel of sandstone or emery for sharpening tools.
to keep someone's nose to the grindstone to make him work hard.

grip n. 1. a firm hold. 2. (in the U.S.A.) a travelling bag. v. **grip** 1. to hold tightly. 2. to hold one's interest, as *to be gripped by an exciting play* (**gripping, gripped**).

grit n. 1. a particle of sand or gravel. 2. courage, pluck. v. **grit** to grind, as *to grit one's teeth* (**gritting, gritted**). adj. **gritty**.

grizzly n. a large North American bear.

groan n. a sound of pain or disappointment. v. **groan** 1. to make a low sound of pain. 2. to be overloaded, as *the table groaned with food*.

grocer n. a man who sells tea, butter, etc. n. **grocery** a grocer's shop. n. pl. **groceries** goods sold by a grocer.

groom n. 1. a servant who looks after horses. 2. a bridegroom. v. **groom** 1. to look after a horse. 2. to make oneself clean and smart, as *Bob is always well groomed*. n. **groomsman** the bridegroom's 'best man' at a wedding.

groove n. a narrow channel in wood, metal, etc.

grope v. to feel for blindly, as *Tom groped for his torch in the dark* (**groping, groped**).

gross adj. 1. coarse, vulgar, as *gross talk*. 2. fat, as *a man of gross appearance*. 3. great, as *a gross mistake*. 4. full total, as *a gross profit*, compared with *the net profit* after expenses have been paid out. *n.* **gross** 1. the full amount. 2. twelve dozen or 144. *n.* **grossness** coarseness, fatness.

ground (1) *past* of **grind**.

ground (2) *n.* 1. the earth's surface. 2. a reason, as *grounds for complaint*. 3. a place where some action takes place, as *a football ground*, *a battle-ground*, or *a fair-ground*. *v.* **ground** 1. (of a boat) to run aground. 2. (of aircraft) to keep to the ground, as *all aircraft were grounded* (**grounding, grounded**). *adj.* **groundless** without cause, as *a groundless objection*.

to gain ground to make progress.

to stand one's ground not to give way.

groundhog *n.* the woodchuck, a kind of rat.

ground-nut *n.* the peanut or monkey-nut.

grounds *n. pl.* 1. reasons. 2. gardens round a large house. 3. sediment, as *coffee grounds*.

group *n.* a number of people or things together. *v.* **group** to arrange together. *n.* **group-captain** an airforce officer, equal to an army colonel in rank.

grouse *n.* 1. a moorland game bird (*pl.* grouse). 2. a grumble. *v.* **grouse** to grumble (**grousing, groused**).

grove *n.* a small wood.

grovel *v.* to cringe, to humble oneself in fear (**grovelling, grovelled**).

grow *v.* 1. to become bigger, to increase, to develop. 2. to cultivate, to produce, as *to grow crops*. 3. to be cultivated, as *potatoes grow in the fields* (**growing, grew, grown**). *n.* **grown-up** an adult, someone fully grown.

growl *v.* to make an angry noise in the throat.

growth *n.* 1. growing. 2. increase in size. 3. what has grown, as *a growth of moss on a tree*.

grub *n.* a soft insect larva, as a caterpillar. *v.* **grub** to root out of the soil (**grubbing, grubbed**).

grudge *n.* a feeling of ill-will against someone. *v.* **grudge** to give resentfully, as *Tom grudged Sam the gift* (**grudging, grudged**). *adv.* **grudgingly** unwillingly, resentfully.

gruel *n.* thin porridge.

gruelling *adj.* exhausting, as *a gruelling race*.

gruesome *adj.* horrible, bloodcurdling.

gruff *adj.* rough or surly in manner or voice.

grumble *v.* to find fault, to complain (**grumbling, grumbled**).

grunt *n.* the noise made by a pig or hog. *v.* **grunt** to make a noise like a pig or hog.

guarantee *n.* a promise that something bought is of good quality, and will be put right if it develops a fault within a certain time. *v.* **guarantee** to make a promise about something (**guaranteeing, guaranteed**).

guard *v.* to watch over, to protect. *n.* **guard** 1. protection, watchfulness. 2. an escort of men for protection. 3. a man in charge of a railway train. *adj.* **guarded** 1. protected. 2. cautious, as *a guarded reply to a question*.

on one's guard careful, looking out.

off one's guard unprepared, unawares.

guardian *n.* keeper, protector.

guerilla (*pron.* ge.ril'a) *n.* one of a gang of armed men carrying on warfare although not regular soldiers.

guess *v.* to give an opinion without being certain. *n.* **guess** a belief held without definite reason. *n.* **guesswork** opinions formed by guessing.

guest *n.* a visitor whom one entertains.

guidance *n.* advice, being shown how. See **guide**.

guide *n.* 1. someone who leads the way, or gives help and advice. 2. a book which gives directions, as *a railway guide*. *v.* **guide** 1. to show the way. 2. to advise or give instructions (**guiding, guided**). See **guidance**. *n.* **Guide** a Girl Guide. See **girl**.

guided missile *n.* a radio-controlled rocket.

guild *n.* a society of people in the same trade, especially in medieval times. *n.* **guildhall** a large hall where guilds used to meet.

guile *n.* deceit, cunning. *n.* **guileless** without guile.

guillotine *n.* a machine for beheading people.

guilt *n.* wrongdoing. *adj.* **guilty** having done wrong or committed a crime.

guinea *n.* an old British gold coin worth twenty-one shillings (£1·05).

guinea-pig *n.* a small animal about the size of a rat, kept as a pet.

guitar (*pron.* gi.tahr[1]) *n.* a wooden musical instrument with six strings plucked by hand.

gulf *n.* 1. a very large bay, as *the Gulf of Mexico.* 2. a deep rift or gap. 3. a big difference, as *the gulf between the Cavaliers and the Roundheads.*

gull *n.* a grey-white seabird.

gulp *v.* to swallow quickly.

gum (1) *n.* red flesh round the teeth.

gum (2) *n.* 1. a sticky liquid. 2. a gum tree, which gives off a sticky fluid. 3. chewing-gum. *v.* **gum** to fasten with gum (**gumming, gummed**). *adj.* **gummy**.

gun *n.* 1. a cannon, rifle, or revolver in which a bullet or shell is fired by explosive. 2. a tool for squeezing grease or oil into machinery, as *a grease-gun.* **to stick to your guns** to stand by what you say.

gunpowder *n.* an explosive mixture used in cartridges and fireworks.

gunwale or **gunnel** *n.* the top edge of a ship's side.

gurgle *v.* (of a liquid) to make a bubbling sound (**gurgling, gurgled**).

gush *n.* 1. the bursting out of a liquid. 2. a flow of talk which is not sincere. *adj.* **gushing**.

gust *n.* a sudden rush of wind, anger, etc. *adj.* **gusty**.

gutter *n.* a channel, under a roof or at the roadside, for drawing off water.

guttural *adj.* throaty, as *the guttural growl of a dog* or *a word with a guttural sound.*

guy *n.* 1. a supporting rope or wire, as *a tent guy.* 2. a stuffed imitation of Guy Fawkes. 3. (in the U.S.A.) a fellow. *v.* **guy** to mock or make fun of someone (**guying, guyed**).

gymnasium *n.* a large room fitted for physical exercises (*pl.* **gymnasiums** or **gymnasia**).

gymnastics *n. pl.* body exercises.

gypsy, gipsy *n.* a member of a dark-skinned race of people who originally came from India (*pl.* **gypsies, gipsies**).

H

habit *n.* 1. a usual custom, as *it was his habit to get up early.* 2. a practice, as *he had a habit of twitching his nose.* 3. dress, as *a riding-habit.*

habitant (*pron.* French: ab'ee.tahn) *n.* a native of Canada of French descent (*pl.* **habitants**).

habitation *n.* a dwelling-place.

hack *v.* to chop, to cut roughly. *n.* **hack** a blow.

had *past* of **have**.

haddock *n.* a fish used for food.

hag *n.* an ugly old woman.

haggard *adj.* thin and care-worn.

haggle *v.* to argue over a price (**haggling, haggled**).

hail (1) *n.* frozen rain. *n.* **hailstone** a piece of hail.

hail (2) *v.* to shout a greeting. **hail-fellow-well-met** very friendly. **to hail from** to come from.

hair *n.* 1. one of the fine fibres growing from the skin of a living creature. 2. the covering of a person's head. *adj.* **hair-raising** frightening. *adj.* **hairy**. *n.* **hairiness**. **a hair's breadth** a very small space. **not to turn a hair** not to be frightened. **to split hairs** to argue over trifles.

hair-dresser *n.* someone who cuts and styles hair.

hairpin *n.* a bent wire for fastening hair. **a hairpin bend** a turn in a road so sharp that the road doubles back.

half *n.* 1. one of two equal parts. 2. (in football) a half-back (*pl.* **halves**). *adj.* made up of half, as *a half share.* *adv.* **partly** as *half frozen.* *adj.* **half-hearted** not very keen. See **halve**

half-breed, half-caste *n.* someone with parents of different races.

half-brother, half-sister *n.* a brother, or sister, having the same father or mother only as another brother or sister.

half-crown *n.* an old British silver coin worth two shillings and sixpence(12½p).

half-mast *n.* a position where a flag is flown as a signal of distress.

halfpenny *n.* a British bronze coin (*pl.* **halfpence**).

hall *n.* 1. the entrance space of a building, *the entrance hall.* 2. a large room, as *a dance hall.* 3. a large building, as *a town hall.* 4. an old mansion.

hallmark *n.* a mark stamped on gold and silver articles to show their date and maker.

hallelujah, halleluiah (*pron.* hal.e.-loo'ya) an *interjection* meaning 'Praise God'.

hallow *v.* to make holy. *n.* **Hallowe'en** 'holy evening', the eve of All Saints Day (November 1st).

hallucination (*pron.* hal.oo.sin.ay'shun) *n.* something imagined, a delusion.

halo (*pron.* hay'lo) *n.* a ring of light round the moon in frosty weather, or round pictures of saints' heads (*pl.* **haloes**).

halt (1) *adj.* crippled. *adj.* **halting** 1. limping. 2. hesitant, as *a halting speech.*

halt (2) *v.* to stop for a time. *n.* **halt** a stop.

halve *v.* to divide in half (**halving, halved**).

to go halves to divide equally between two.

ham *n.* a pig's thigh prepared for eating.

hamlet *n.* a small village.

hammer *n.* 1. a tool for driving in nails, or breaking coal, etc. 2. the striking part of a clock or piano. 3. the part of a gun which hits the cartridge. *v.* **hammer** to hit hard.

hammer-and-tongs with great energy.

hammock *n.* a swinging couch hung by cords.

hamper (1) *n.* a large basket.

hamper (2) *v.* to hinder, to get in someone's way.

hand *n.* 1. the end of the arm. 2. one of the pointers of a clock. 3. a direction, as *left-hand* or *right-hand.* 4. a measure of the height of a horse, equal to 10 centimetres. 5. a worker in a factory or on a ship. 6. a deal of cards, as *I have a good hand.* 7. consent to marriage, as *to ask for a lady's hand.* 8. a performer, as *I am a poor hand at typing.* *v.* **hand** to pass on, to pass round. *adj.* **hand-made** made by hand.

at hand very close.

hand and glove with closely connected with.

hand over fist rapidly.

hands down easily.

hands up! surrender.

off one's hands out of one's care.

old hand an experienced person.

on all hands on every side.

on hand ready.

out of hand out of control.

show of hands a vote by raising hands.

to get one's hand in to get used to.

to wash one's hands of to take no further responsibility for.

upper hand control (of).

handbag *n.* a light bag carried by hand.

handcuffs *n. pl.* bracelets to fasten a prisoner.

handful *n.* one hand full (*pl.* **handfuls**).

handicap *n.* 1. a disadvantage imposed on good runners in a race to make the race more equal. 2. a race in which handicaps are imposed. 3. a disadvantage. *v.* **handicap** to place at a disadvantage (**handicapping, handicapped**).

handicraft *n.* work needing skill with the hands.

handkerchief *n.* a cloth for wiping the nose (*pl.* **handkerchiefs**).

handle *n.* the part of a tool or machine which is held. *v.* **handle** 1. to hold or move by hand. 2. to deal with, as *Mr Brown handles the accounts* (**handling, handled**). *n.* **handlebar** the steering part of a bicycle.

handsome *adj.* 1. good-looking. 2. generous, as *a handsome gift.*

handsome is as handsome does judge a man by what he does, not by what he seems.

handy *adj.* 1. clever with the hands. 2. convenient to use, or conveniently near, as *a handy shop* (*comparative* **handier,** *superlative* **handiest**). *n.* **handyman** a man who does little jobs.

hang *v.* 1. to fasten or be fastened so that a thing swings. 2. to drag, as *time hangs heavily.* 3. to listen carefully, as *to hang on every word* (**hanging, hung**). 4. to put someone to death by suspending him by the neck with a rope (**hanging, hanged**). *n.* **hanger** a support. *n.* **hanging** an execution by hanging. *n. pl.* **hangings** draperies, curtains.

to hang about to loiter.

to hang back to be unwilling.

to hang fire to be a long time happening.

hangar *n.* a shed for aircraft.

hansom *v.* a Victorian two-wheeled cab.

haphazard *adj.* unplanned, left to chance.

happen *v.* 1. to take place. 2. to chance, as *I happened to be there. n.* **happening** an event.

happy *adj.* 1. content, cheerful. 2. lucky, as *by a happy chance* or *a happy find* (*comparative* **happier,** *superlative* **happiest**). *n.* **happiness**.

happy-go-lucky easy-going.

harass *v.* to worry, to pester. *adj.* **harassed**.

harbour *n.* 1. a sheltered place for ships. 2. any refuge. *v.* **harbour** to shelter.

hard *adj.* 1. firm, not soft, as *hard stone.* 2. difficult, as *a hard sum.* 3. tiring, as *hard work.* 4. harsh, as *a hard master.* 5. not easy to lather with soap, as *hard water. adv.* **hard** fully, as *work hard. v.* **harden** to make or become firm. *n.* **hardness** being hard.

hard-and-fast very strict, as *a hard-and-fast rule.*

hard by close by.

hard-headed business-like.

hard-hearted cruel.

hard put to it in difficulty.

hardly *adv.* 1. scarcely, as *he is hardly in time.* 2. harshly, as *he treats his dog hardly.*

hardship *n.* suffering, misfortune.

hardy *adj.* able to stand hardship or extreme cold.

hare *n.* an animal like a large rabbit.

to run with the hare and hunt with the hounds to try to be on both sides in a quarrel.

hare-brained *adj.* foolish, rash.

harem (*pron.* ha'reem) *n.* 1. the women's part of a Mohammedan house. 2. the women of such a house.

harm *v.* to injure, to damage. *n.* **harm** damage. *adj.* **harmful** causing harm. *adj.* **harmless** not doing harm.

harmonica *n.* a mouth organ.

harmony *n.* 1. the blending of musical sounds, as *the choir sang in harmony* 2. agreement among people, as *harmony exists between the nations. adj.* **harmonious** pleasant, friendly. *v.* **harmonize** to agree, to blend well (**harmonizing, harmonized**).

harness *n.* the equipment fastening a horse to a carriage or plough, or used for riding. *v.* **harness** 1. to fasten straps on a horse. 2. to make natural power do useful work, as *to harness the tides to make electricity.*

harp *n.* a large musical instrument, played by plucking the strings. *n.* **harpist**.

to harp on to nag, to mention constantly.

harpoon *n.* a spear with a rope, shot from a gun, to catch whales. *n.* **harpoonist**.

harsh *adj.* 1. rough. 2. cruel, severe.

harvest *n.* 1. a crop. 2. the time of the gathering of a crop. 3. the result of hard work. *v.* **harvest** to gather a crop. *n.* **harvester** a reaping machine.

hash *n.* 1. a dish of chopped meat and vegetables. 2. a mess.

to make a hash of to cause a muddle.

hassock *n.* a cushion to kneel on.

haste *n.* great speed, hurry. *v.* **hasten** 1. to hurry. 2. to urge on. *n.* **hastiness**. *adj.* **hasty** 1. hurried. 2. quick-tempered, as *hasty words.*

hat *n.* a head-covering.

to talk through one's hat to talk nonsense.

hatch (1) *n.* 1. a trapdoor. 2. the cover of a hatchway in a ship's deck. *n.* **hatchway** a deck-opening on a ship, leading below.

hatch (2) *v.* 1. to bring chicks from eggs by warmth. 2. to plan in secret, as *to hatch a plot. n.* **hatch** a brood of young birds.

hatchet *n.* a small axe.

to bury the hatchet to make peace.

hate *v.* to dislike intensely (**hating, hated**). *n.* **hate** a strong dislike. *adj.* **hateful**. *n.* **hatred** enmity.

hatter *n.* a man who makes men's hats (note: a *milliner* makes ladies' hats).

mad as a hatter very mad.

hat-trick *n.* (in a game) taking three wickets, or scoring three goals, etc., in succession.

haughty *adj.* proud, contemptuous. *n.* **haughtiness**.

haul *v.* to drag, to pull. *n.* **haul** 1. a pull. 2. a catch of fish. *n.* **haulage**. *n.* **haulier** a carrier.

to haul over the coals to scold.

haunch *n.* the part of the body behind the hips (*pl.* **haunches**).

haunt *v.* 1. to visit a place often. 2. to visit and trouble someone constantly, as *the memory of the accident haunts me*. *n.* **haunt** a meeting place, a den. *adj.* **haunted** often visited, or supposed to be visited by ghosts.

have *v.* 1. to own, to hold. 2. to experience, as *to have a bad dream*. 3. to be forced, as *I have to do it*. 4. to allow, as *I will not have dogs here*. 5. to show, as *have mercy on me*. 6. to deceive, as *he had me there* (**having, had**). The word is used as an extra verb to form other tenses, as *I have been, I had been, I shall have been*.

to have on 1. to wear. 2. to hoax someone.

to have up to bring to court.

haven *n.* a harbour, a place of refuge.

haversack *n.* a bag slung over the shoulders holding food for travel.

havoc *n.* ruin, destruction.

haw *n.* a hawthorn berry.

hawk (1) *n.* a bird of prey.

hawk (2) *v.* to sell goods from a van or cart. *n.* **hawker** (note: a *pedlar* sells goods from door to door).

hawser *n.* a small cable.

hawthorn *n.* a small tree which blossoms in May.

hay *n.* grass cut and dried for animal food. *n.* **hayrick** or **haystack** a large pile of stored hay.

to make hay while the sun shines to get things done while one can.

hazard *n.* a risk, danger. *v.* **hazard** to risk.

haze *n.* slight mist or smoke. *adj.* **hazy** 1. misty. 2. confused in mind. *n.* **haziness**.

hazel *n.* 1. a bush bearing nuts. 2. reddish-brown in colour.

he *pronoun* referring to a man or boy (*fem.* **she**).

head *n.* 1. the top part of the body. 2. the top or front part of anything, as *a masthead* or *the head of a procession*. 3. chief. 4. a cape, as *Beachy Head*. 5. (of a pier) the end out at sea, the *pierhead*. *adj.* **head** chief, or at the top, as *the head boy of a school*. *v.* **head** to lead, to go, as *to head north* or *to head a procession*.

head over heels in a complete somersault.

to bring to a head to bring to a climax.

to give someone his head to let him do as he likes.

to lose one's head to get into a panic.

headache *n.* a pain in the head.

heading *n.* a title.

headland *n.* land jutting out to sea.

headline *n.* a newspaper title in bold print.

headlong *adj.* head first, hasty.

head-on *adj.* (of a collision) front to front.

headquarters *n.* the head office.

headstrong *adj.* obstinate, wilful.

headway *n.* progress.

heal *v.* to make well again.

health *n.* 1. being well in mind and body. 2. a toast drunk as a compliment, as *let us drink the health of the Queen*. *adj.* **healthy** free from illness. *n.* **healthiness**.

heap *n.* a pile. *v.* **heap** to pile up.

hear *v.* 1. to pick up a sound through the ears. 2. to listen to. 3. to learn, as *I hear that he is ill* (**hearing, heard**).

heard *past* of **hear**.

hearing *n.* the ability to pick up sounds.

hard of hearing almost deaf.

hearsay *n.* rumours, everyday talk.

hearse *n.* a car for carrying a coffin.

heart *n.* 1. the organ which pumps blood round the body. 2. the centre or chief part, as *that is the heart of the problem.* 3. love, as *he gave her his heart.* 4. interest, as *his heart is in his work.* 5. courage, as *he is a boxer full of heart.* 6. one of the suits of playing-cards.

after one's own heart greatly to one's liking.

in good heart in good spirits.

to learn by heart to memorize.

to set one's heart on to want very much.

to take heart to pluck up courage.

to take to heart to think over seriously.

heartbreaking *adj.* causing sorrow.

hearten *v.* to encourage.

heartfelt *adj.* sincere.

hearth *n.* a fireplace.

heartless *adj.* cruel, unfeeling.

hearty *adj.* strong, sincere. *adv.* **heartily.**

heat *n.* 1. hotness, warmth, high temperature. 2. an elimination event held before the final of a race. *v.* **heat** to make hot. *n.* **heater.**

heath *n.* 1. moorland. 2. heather.

heathen *n.* a worshipper of idols.

heather *n.* a very small moorland shrub.

heave *v.* 1. to lift with an effort. 2. to utter, as *to heave a sigh of relief.* 3. to rise and fall. 4. to come, as *he hove in sight* (**heaving, heaved** or **hove, heaved**).

heaven *n.* 1. the home of God and the saints. 2. a place of happiness. *n. pl.* **heavens** the sky. *adj.* **heavenly.**

heavy *adj.* 1. having great weight. 2. severe, as *heavy rain* or *a heavy fine.* 3. serious, as *a heavy book.* 4. sad, as *a heavy heart.* 5. slow, as *heavy progress.* *n.* **heaviness.**

Hebrew *n.* 1. a Jew. 2. the language of the Hebrews, the language in which the Old Testament was written.

hectare *n.* A metric unit of area measurement equal to 10,000 m² (2·5 acres).

hedge *n.* a boundary of close-set bushes. *v.* **hedge** 1. to shut in with a hedge. 2. to answer an awkward question in a vague way (**hedging, hedged**).

hedgehog *n.* a small, prickly animal.

heed *v.* to pay attention to. *adj.* **heedless** not attending.

heel (1) *v.* (with **over**) to lean on one side, as *the yacht heeled over.*

heel (2) *n.* the back underside of a foot, shoe, or stocking.

down at heel shabby.

to show a clean pair of heels, to take to one's heels to run away.

heifer (*pron.* hef'er) *n.* a young cow (*masc.* bullock).

height *n.* 1. how high a thing is. 2. a high piece of ground, as *the Heights of Abraham in Canada.*

heir (*pron.* air) *n.* a man or boy who inherits money or property from a dead person (*fem.* **heiress**).

heiress (*pron.* air'es) *n. feminine* of **heir.**

heirloom (*pron.* air'loom) *n.* an article handed down in a family through the years.

held *past* of **hold.**

helicopter *n.* an aircraft with large propellors which enable it to rise vertically and hover over any point.

hell *n.* a place of wickedness and misery. *adj.* **hellish.**

hello *interjection* a greeting or cry of surprise.

helm *n.* 1. the tiller or wheel for steering a ship. 2. a helmet. *n.* **helmsman** a steersman.

helmet *n.* a strong covering to protect the head.

help *v.* 1. to assist. 2. to keep from doing, as *I cannot help it. n.* **help** 1. support, aid. 2. a servant, as *a daily help. n.* **helper** someone who helps. *adj.* **helpful** useful. *adj.* **helpless** weak, without help. *n.* **helping** a portion of food at a meal. *adv.* **helpfully.**

hem *n.* an edge of cloth doubled over and sewn. *v.* **hem** to sew a folded edge (**hemming, hemmed**).

to hem in to surround and enclose.

hemisphere *n.* 1. half of a sphere. 2. half the world.

northern hemisphere the half of the world north of the equator.

southern hemisphere the half of the world south of the equator.

western hemisphere the half of the

world which includes North and South America.

eastern hemisphere the half of the world which includes Asia, Europe, Africa, and Australia.

hen *n.* a female bird (*masc.* **cock**).

hence *adv.* 1. from here, from now. 2. therefore.

henceforth *adv.* from now on.

her *pronoun* and *adj.* derived from **she** (*masc.* **him**). *possessive pronoun* **hers**, as *this is hers. pronoun* **herself**.

herald *n.* (in olden days) an announcer, a bearer of messages. *v.* **herald** to announce.

heraldic *adj.* relating to heraldry.

heraldry *n.* the study of coats-of-arms and family histories.

herb *n.* a plant used in medicine or in cookery.

herd *n.* 1. a group of cattle or other animals. 2. a crowd of people. *v.* **herd** to crowd together. *n.* **herdsman** a man in charge of cattle.

here *adv.* in this place, to this place, **neither here nor there** not to the point, of no importance.

hereafter *adv.* after this.

hereby *adv.* in this way.

hereditary *adj.* passing down from parents to their young ones.

heredity *n.* the way in which parents pass down the qualities of their bodies and minds to their young ones.

heretic (*pron.* her'e.tik) *n.* someone who holds an unusual belief, against authority.

herewith *adv.* with this.

heritage *n.* something handed down by ancestors, as *we have a heritage of freedom and justice.*

hermit *n.* someone who lives alone, shut off from other people.

hero *n.* 1. a brave man or boy. 2. someone who is thought highly of. 3. the chief character of a book or play (*pl.* **heroes**; *fem.* **heroine**).

heroic *adj.* 1. very brave. 2. about a hero, as *a heroic tale. n.* **heroism**.

heroine *n.* a brave woman or girl. See **hero**.

heron *n.* a large wading-bird.

herring *n.* a fish used for food.

hers see **her**.

herself *pronoun* 1. a strong way of saying **she**, as *she herself went.* 2. a reflexive form of **she**, as *she hurt herself.*

hesitancy *n.* uncertainty, indecision.

hesitant *adj.* undecided, wavering.

hesitate *v.* 1. to be uncertain or doubtful. 2. to wait undecided (**hesitating, hesitated**). *n.* **hesitation**.

hew *v.* to chop with an axe (**hewing, hewed, hewn** or **hewed**). *n.* **hewer** someone who hews.

hewn *past* of **hew**.

hibernate *v.* to pass the winter in sleep like the squirrel (**hibernating, hibernated**).

hiccup *n.* a quick noisy movement in the throat. *v.* **hiccup** to make a noise of hiccups (**hiccuping, hiccuped**).

hid *past* of **hide** (2).

hide (1) *n.* an animal's skin.

hide (2) *v.* 1. to put something out of sight. 2. to keep oneself out of sight. 3. to keep secret, as *to hide the truth* (**hiding, hid, hidden** or **hid**). *n.* **hide** a hiding-place used by hunters or bird-watchers. *n.* **hide-out** a refuge.

hideous *adj.* very ugly, horrible.

high *adj.* 1. far up, as *a high mountain.* 2. well up, as *a high tide.* 3. great, as *a high price* or *a high wind.* 4. important, chief, as *a man of high rank.* 5. tainted, as *this meat is high. adv.* **high** up above, as *the bird flew high. adv.* **highly** greatly, as *highly honoured.*

High Mass a mass with music and ceremony.

high school a secondary school.

high seas 1. the open sea. 2. stormy seas.

highly-strung very sensitive.

the Highlands northern Scotland.

highness *n.* the title of a prince.

high-pitched *adj.* shrill, treble.

highway *n.* a public road. *n.* **highwayman** a robber on the highways.

hike *n.* a journey on foot. *v.* **hike** to go for a journey on foot (**hiking, hiked**).

hill *n.* a mound, a small mountain, high land. *adj.* **hilly**. *n.* **hillock** a little hill. *n.* **hillside** a hill slope.

hilt *n.* the handle of a sword.
up to the hilt heavily, as *up to the hilt in debt.*

him *pronoun* derived from **he** (*fem.* **her**). *pronoun* **himself**.

hind *adj.* at the back, as *a horse's hind legs* (*comparative* **hinder**, *superlative* **hindmost**).

hinder *v.* to stop something or make it difficult, as *to hinder a man from working.*

hindrance *n.* an obstacle.

Hindu, Hindoo *n.* a believer in **Hinduism**, an Indian religion.

hinge *n.* a metal joint about which a door or a lid swings. *v.* **hinge** 1. to hang on a hinge. 2. to depend on, as *that hinges on the money he has* (**hinging, hinged**).

hint *n.* a helpful or tactful suggestion. *v.* **hint** to suggest tactfully.

hip *n.* 1. the joint at the top of the thigh. 2. the fruit of the rose.

hippopotamus *n.* a large thick-skinned African animal (*pl.* **hippopotamuses**).

hire *v.* 1. to use something for a while and pay for the use, as *to hire a taxi.* 2. to employ, as *to hire a gardener* (**hiring, hired**). *n.* **hire-purchase** buying an article by weekly or monthly payments.
to hire out to let out for hire.

his *pronoun* and *adj.* the possessive form of **he**, belonging to **him**.

hiss *v.* to make a noise like the letter S.

historian *n.* a man who studies history.

historic *adj.* having an interesting history, as *a historic castle.*

historical *adj.* connected with history.

history *n.* the study of past events.

hit *v.* to strike, to knock (**hitting, hit**). *n.* **hit** 1. a blow. 2. a success, as *the play was a hit.*
hard hit badly affected.
hit-or-miss haphazard.
to hit the nail on the head to mention the most important thing.
to hit upon to come across by chance.

hitch *v.* 1. to fasten with a loop, as *to hitch a horse to a post.* 2. to move up with a jerk. *n.* **hitch** 1. a jerk. 2. an upset in arrangements, as *a hitch in our plans.* 3. a knot, as *a clove-hitch.*

hitch-hike to travel with lifts on the way.

hither *adv.* here, as *come hither.*

hive *n.* 1. a wooden house for bees. 2. busy place, as *this scout hut is a hive of activity.*

hoar *adj.* white, as *hoar-frost. adj.* **hoary** grey with age.

hoard *n.* a secret store or pile of valuables. *v.* **hoard** to pile up in a secret place, as *a miser hoards his money.*

hoarding *n.* a wooden fence for displaying posters.

hoarse *adj.* (of a voice) husky and rough. *n.* **hoarseness** huskiness.

hoax *n.* a practical joke. *v.* **hoax** to deceive.

hobble *v.* to walk lamely and unsteadily (**hobbling, hobbled**). *n.* **hobble** an awkward walk.

hobby *n.* a favourite pastime, such as aero-modelling (*pl.* **hobbies**).

hobo *n.* a tramp (*pl.* **hobos** or **hoboes**).

hockey *n.* a game played by two teams of eleven players, each having a curved stick to hit the ball.

hoe *n.* a long pole with a short blade at the end, used by gardeners for loosening soil. *v.* **hoe** to use a hoe (**hoeing, hoed**).

hog *n.* a pig (*fem.* **sow**).

hoist *v.* to raise, as *to hoist a flag.*

hold (1) *n.* the space for a ship's cargo.

hold (2) *v.* 1. to grasp, as *to hold a cup.* 2. to have, to keep, as *he holds a high position.* 3. to contain, as *this box holds matches.* 4. to keep back. 5. to carry on, as *to hold a meeting.* 5. to defend successfully, as *to hold a castle which is being attacked.* 6. to remain unbroken, as *the rope holds* (**holding, held**). *n.* **hold** 1. a grasp. 2. a support, as *a foothold.* 3. power over, as *to have a hold over someone.*
to hold forth to speak in public.
to hold up 1. to raise. 2. to cause delay. 3. to rob by threats.

hole *n.* 1. an opening. 2. a hollow, a pit.

holiday *n.* a day free from work.

holiness *n.* saintliness.
His Holiness a title of the Pope.

hollow *n.* 1. a hole. 2. a valley. *v.* **hollow** to scoop out. *adj.* **hollow** 1. empty within, as *a hollow tooth*. 2. false, untrue, as *a hollow promise*. *n.* **hollowness**.

holly *n.* a prickly evergreen shrub.

hollyhock *n.* a tall flowering plant.

holy *adj.* sacred, concerning God (*comparative* **holier,** *superlative* **holiest**).

the Holy Land Palestine.

homage *n.* 1. respect. 2. (in feudal times) the pledge of loyalty by a vassal to his lord.

home *n.* any dwelling-place for a family, old people, cats, etc. *adj.* **home** belonging to one's district, as *the home team*. *adj.* **homing** going home, as *a homing pigeon*. *adj.* **homely** 1. simple and comfortable. 2. (in the U.S.A.) plain.

to bring home to somebody to make him realize.

to strike home to impress.

Home Secretary *n.* the government minister who deals with law and order in Britain.

homesick *adj.* longing to be home.

homespun *adj.* plain, made at home.

homeward *adj.* towards home.

homework *n.* work done at home.

honest *adj.* 1. never cheating or stealing. 2. truthful. *n.* **honesty** fair dealing.

honey *n* sticky food made by bees. *n.* **honeycomb** rows of wax cells in which honey is stored.

honeymoon *n.* a newly wed couple's holiday.

honorary (*pron.* on'er.er.i) *adj.* 1. serving without pay, as *an honorary secretary receives no payment*. 2. (of a university degree) given as an honour, without passing examinations.

honour (*pron.* on'er) *n.* (spelt **honor** in the U.S.A.) 1. high regard, as *Mr Smith is held in honour*. 2. glory, fame, as *he did it for the honour of the school*. 3. honesty, fair dealing, as *he is a man of honour*. *adj.* **honourable** fair and honest.

Your Honour a title of respect, especially for a County Court judge.

hood *n.* 1. a covering for the head, usually attached to a coat. 2. a coloured top to a university gown. 3. a folding cover for a car or baby-carriage. 4. (in

the U.S.A.) the bonnet of a motor-car. *adj.* **hooded**.

hoof *n.* the horny part of the foot of a horse or cow (*pl.* **hoofs** or **hooves**).

hook *n.* a bent piece of metal made to catch or hold something, as *a fish-hook* or *a curtain-hook*. *v.* **hook** to catch or fasten by a hook. *adj.* **hooked**.

hook-and-eye a hook and metal eye for fastening a dress.

by hook or by crook one way or another.

hooligan *n.* a ruffian. *n.* **hooliganism**.

hoop *n.* a wooden or metal ring for holding together the staves of a barrel, for acrobats to jump through in a circus, etc.

hoot *v.* 1. to jeer. 2. to sound a motorhorn. 3. to make a noise like an owl. *n.* **hooter** a factory siren.

hooves see **hoof**.

hop (1) *n.* a trailing plant whose cones are used to flavour beer.

hop (2) *v.* to jump like a sparrow, or to jump on one leg (**hopping, hopped**). *n.* **hop** a short jump. *n.* **hopscotch** a hopping game.

hope *v.* to wish something will happen (**hoping, hoped**). *n.* **hope** 1. a wish. 2. confidence, as *we all have plenty of hope*. *adj.* **hopeful** expecting something with confidence. *adj.* **hopeless** without hope.

horizon *n.* the line where earth and sky, or sea and sky, seem to meet.

horizontal *adj.* flat, parallel to the ground. *adv.* **horizontally**. See **vertical**.

horn *n.* 1. a hard pointed growth on the heads of cows, etc. 2. the substance of which this growth is made. 3. an animal's horn used for holding things, as *a powder-horn* or *drinking-horn*. 4. a musical wind-instrument. 5. a warning signal, as *a fog-horn* or *motor horn*. *adj.* **horned** having horns. *adj.* **horny** like horn.

the horns of a dilemma two equally unpleasant ways out of a difficulty.

hornet *n.* a large kind of wasp.

hornpipe *n.* a lively sailors' dance.

horrible *adj.* dreadful, awful. *adv.* **horribly**.

horrid *adj.* nasty, terrible.

horrify *v.* to fill with horror (**horrifying, horrified**).

horror *n.* fear, terror.

horse *n.* an animal used for riding and drawing loads (*fem.* **mare**).

to ride the high horse to be arrogant and aloof.

horsepower *n.* a unit of engine-power.

horticulture *n.* the study of gardening. *adj.* **horticultural**.

hose *n.* 1. stockings, socks. 2. a long flexible pipe for water.

hospitable *adj.* friendly and kind to guests.

hospital *n.* a building in which sick or injured people are cared for.

hospitality *n.* friendly and generous treatment of guests.

host (1) *n.* an army, a great crowd.

host (2) *n.* 1. anyone who entertains guests (*fem.* **hostess**). 2. an innkeeper.

Host (3) *n.* in the Roman Catholic church, the consecrated bread of the Mass.

hostage *n.* someone kept prisoner as a pledge until certain promises have been fulfilled.

hostel *n.* 1. a home for students. 2. a hiker's resting-place. 3. an inn.

hostess *feminine* of **host** (2).

hostile *adj.* unfriendly, war-like.

hostility *n.* enmity, warfare.

hot *adj.* 1. full of heat, as *hot water*. 2. full of passion, as *hot words*. 3. strong to taste, as *hot mustard* (*comparative* **hotter,** *superlative* **hottest**).

hot cross bun a bun marked with a cross, eaten on Good Friday.

in hot water in trouble.

hot-headed *adj.* rash.

hot-tempered *adj.* quick to take offence.

hotel *n.* a large building with many rooms for travellers and holiday-makers.

hound *n.* a hunting-dog. *v.* **hound** to chase and worry.

hour *n* 1. sixty minutes or the twenty-fourth part of the day. 2. the time shown by a clock. *adj.* **hourly** every hour.

at the eleventh hour at the last moment.

hour-glass *n.* an instrument for measuring time, in which sand runs for an hour.

house *n.* 1. a building in which people live. 2. an inn, a *public house*. 3. a theatre audience, as *the play attracted a full house*. 4. a business firm. *v.* **house** (*pron.* howz) to provide house, to give shelter, to store (**housing, housed**).

to bring down the house to receive loud applause in a theatre.

house-boat *n.* a riverside boat to live in.

housebreaker *n.* a burglar.

housefly *n.* the common fly.

household *n.* all the people of a house.

householder *n.* the owner or tenant of a house.

housekeeper *n.* a woman paid to manage a house.

housemaid *n.* a female servant in a house.

housewife *n.* the mistress of a house.

hove *past* of **heave**.

hovel *n.* a poor cottage, a hut.

hover *v.* to keep in the air over one spot, as *the helicopter hovered over the ship*.

how *adv.* 1. in what way, as *how will he go?* 2. to what extent, as *how deep is it?* 3. in what condition, as *how are you?*

however *adv.* 1. in what way, as *however did he manage? conj.* **however** and yet, as *I feel sure, however I may be wrong*.

howl *n.* a long wailing cry.

hub *n.* 1. the centre of a wheel. 2. any centre, as *the city is a hub of activity*.

huddle *v.* to press close together (**huddling, huddled**). *n.* **huddle** a close pack, a crowd.

hue *n.* a colour.

a hue and cry a loud shouting after someone who is being chased.

hug *v.* 1. to clasp close in the arms. 2. to keep close to, as *to hug the edge of a road* (**hugging, hugged**).

huge *adj.* enormous. *adv.* **hugely**.

hull *n.* a ship's frame.

hum *v.* 1. to make a noise like a bee. 2. to make a tune down the nose. 3. to bustle with activity, as *the village hummed with excitement* (**humming, hummed**). *n.* **hum** a buzzing sound.

human *adj.* belonging to mankind. *n.*
human a man, woman, or child. *adv.*
humanly in a human way, as *I will do
what is humanly possible.*
humane *adj.* kind, merciful.
humanity *n.* 1. all people. 2. human
kindness, as *show humanity to the
suffering.*
humble *adj.* 1. meek, as *a humble man.*
2. small and poor, as *a humble cottage.*
v. **humble** to make a proud person
humble (**humbling, humbled**). *adv.*
humbly modestly.
humbug *n.* 1. a fraud. 2. a kind of peppermint. *v.* **humbug** to deceive (**hum-
bugging, humbugged**).
humiliate *v.* to cover with shame
(**humiliating, humiliated**). *n.* **humil-
iation.**
humility *n.* modesty, meekness.
humour *n.* 1. fun. 2. a state of mind, as *to
be in a bad humour. adj.* **humorous**
laughable.
a sense of humour ability to see the
funny side of anything.
hump *n.* a large bulge, especially on the
back, as *a camel's hump.*
hunchback *n.* a person with a lump on
his back.
hundred *n.* ten times ten, or its sign 100
or C. *adj.* **hundredth.**
hundredweight *n.* a British weight of
112 lbs. (50 kg), or a North American
weight of 100 lbs. (45 kg).
hunger *n.* 1. lack of food, starvation. 2. a
craving for food. *v.* **hunger** to crave for
food.
hungry *adj.* wanting food. *adv.* **hung-
rily.**
hunt *v.* 1. to chase after, in order to catch
or kill, as *to hunt lions.* 2. (with **for**) to
seek, to search for, as *to hunt for one's
shoes. n* **hunt** a chase, hunting. *n.*
hunter someone who hunts, or a horse
used for hunting. *n.* **huntsman** someone hunting with hounds.
to hunt down to chase and catch.
to hunt up to search out.
hurdle *n.* 1. a fence of laths or twigs. 2. a
movable fence for jumping over.
hurl *v.* to throw with all one's strength.
hurrah, hurray *interjection* a cheer.
hurricane *n.* a violent windy storm.

hurry *v.* 1. to move fast. 2. to urge others
to move fast, as *the captain hurried his
men along* (**hurrying, hurried**). *n.*
hurry haste. *adj.* **hurried** hasty, as *a
hurried breakfast.* **to hurry up** to go
faster.
hurt *v.* 1. to cause pain or injury. 2. to
wound someone's feelings, as *I hurt his
pride* (**hurting, hurt**). *n.* **hurt** pain,
harm. *adj.* **hurtful.**
hurtle *v.* to rush, to dash (**hurtling,
hurtled**).
husband *n.* a married man (*fem.* **wife**).
v. **husband** to manage carefully and
with thrift, as *the explorers husbanded
their food.*
hush *interjection* keep quiet! *v.* **hush** 1.
to calm, to quieten. 2. to become
quiet.
to hush up to conceal, as *to hush up a
crime.*
husk *n.* the outer shell of a seed.
husky (1) *adj.* 1. (of the voice) hoarse.
2. strong.
husky (2) *n.* a sledge-dog.
hustle *v.* 1. to push roughly. 2. to work
fast (**hustling, hustled**). *n.* **hustle**
great activity.
hut *n.* a wooden shed or rough shelter.
hutch *n.* a box for rabbits (*pl.* **hutches**).
hyaena, hyena *n.* a dog-like wild animal
of Africa and Asia.
hydraulic *adj.* worked by water, as *a
hydraulic lift.*
hydro- *prefix* connected with water, as
*hydro-electric power refers to elec-
tricity obtained from water-power.*
hydrogen *n.* the lightest of all gases. *n.*
hydrogen bomb a very powerful bomb
in which atomic energy is produced
from hydrogen.
hygiene *n.* 1. the study of good health.
2. the practice of cleanliness and good
health. *adj.* **hygienic** concerning cleanliness and good health.
hymn *n.* a song of praise to God. *n.*
hymnal a book of hymns.
hyphen *n.* a short dash (-) used to join
two words, as in *ice-age.*
hypnotize *v.* for a *hypnotist* to send
someone into a trance in which he
obeys suggestions put to him. *adj.*
hypnotic. *n.* **hypnotism.**

hypocrite (*pron.* hip'ō.krit) *n.* someone who pretends to be good, when he is not.

hysteria, hysterics *n.* a nervous state in which a person laughs or cries uncontrollably.

I

I *pronoun* referring to oneself (*p* . **we**).

ice *n.* 1. frozen water. 2. ice cream. *v.* **ice** 1. to cover with ice. 2. to cover with icing, as *to ice a cake* (**icing, iced**). *adj.* **icy** 1. covered with ice. 2. very cold, as *an icy wind.* 3. cold in manner, as *an icy look. adv.* **icily**.

cuts no ice is of no importance.

to break the ice to open conversation.

ice-age *n.* a period long ago when much of the earth was covered with ice.

iceberg *n.* a floating mass of ice.

ice-box *n.* (in North America) a refrigerator.

ice-hockey *n.* a game like hockey played on ice.

ice-rink *n.* a skating rink.

icicle *n.* a hanging piece of ice.

icing *n.* a sugar coating for cakes.

idea *n.* 1. a thought, a picture in one's mind. 2. a plan, as *a clever idea.*

ideal *n.* an idea or picture in mind of something perfect, as *Mary's ideal of a lovely doll. adj.* **ideal** perfect, as *an ideal house. adv.* **ideally** if everything were perfect.

identical *adj.* exactly alike, as *identical twins.*

identify *v.* to recognize as the same, as *Bob identified the pen which was found as his own* (**identifying, identified**). *n.* **identification**.

identity *n.* 1. sameness, as *to recognize the identity of some lost property which has been found.* 2. who someone is, as *Mr Brown proved his identity to the police.*

idiocy (*pron.* id'i.os.i) *n.* feeble-mindedness.

idiot *n.* a person of weak mind, a fool. *adj.* **idiotic** foolish.

idle *adj.* 1. not working. 2. lazy. *v.* **idle** to waste time (**idling, idled**). *n.* **idleness**. *adv.* **idly**. *n.* **idler** a lazy person.

idol *n.* an image which is worshipped.

idolize *v.* to be very fond of (**idolizing, idolized**).

if *conj.* 1. on condition, as *I will do it if you wish.* 2. whether, as *I wonder if he went.* 3. should it happen, as *if I need help I will tell you.*

igloo *n.* an Eskimo snow hut.

ignite *v.* to set on fire, or to catch fire (**igniting, ignited**).

ignition *n.* 1. burning. 2. the explosion of gases in a petrol or gas engine.

ignorant *adj.* 1. without learning, knowing little. 2. unaware, not told, as *I was ignorant of what you wanted. n.* **ignorance**.

ignore *v.* to pretend not to notice, as *I ignored the remark* (**ignoring, ignored**).

ill *adj.* 1. unwell, sick. 2. bad, harmful, as *an ill wind* (*comparative* **worse**, *superlative* **worst**). *n.* **illness** sickness.

ill-feeling dislike.

ill-will enmity.

illegal *adj.* not lawful. Opposite of **legal**.

illegible *adj.* impossible to read. Opposite of **legible**.

illiterate *adj.* unable to read or write. Opposite of **literate**.

illogical *adj.* falsely reasoned. Opposite of **logical**.

illuminate *v.* 1. to light up. 2. to decorate with lights. 3. to throw light on a difficulty (**illuminating, illuminated**). *n.* **illumination**.

illusion *n.* something that seems different from what it really is.

optical illusion a deception depending on some trick of light.

illustrate *v.* to explain by pictures, diagrams, or examples (**illustrating, illustrated**). *n.* **illustration** 1. a picture. 2. an example.

image *n.* 1. a likeness such as a picture, a reflection in a mirror, or in water. 2. a picture thrown on to a screen. *n.* **imagery** images.

imagine *v.* 1. to suppose, as *let us imagine you were me.* 2. to form a picture in one's mind (**imagining,**

imagined). *adj.* **imaginable** what can be imagined. *adj.* **imaginary** unreal. *n.* **imagination** the ability to form pictures in the mind, fancy. *adj.* **imaginative** full of imagination.

imitate *v.* to copy (**imitating, imitated**). *n.* **imitation** 1. copying. 2. a copy. *adj.* **imitation** not real, as *imitation pearls*. *adj.* **imitative** copying. *n.* **imitator** someone who imitates.

immaculate *adj.* pure, clean, unstained.

immediate *adj.* 1. needing to be done now, as *an immediate task*. 2. instant, as *an immediate reply*. 3. close, near, as *my immediate friends*. *adv.* **immediately** at once.

immense *adj.* huge, gigantic. *adv.* **immensely** enormously. *n.* **immensity** vastness, as *the immensity of the task*.

immerse *v.* 1. to plunge into a liquid. 2. to be wrapped in or absorbed in, as *he was immersed in study* (**immersing, immersed**). *n.* **immersion**.

immersion heater an electric heater placed in water to heat it.

immigrant *n.* a foreigner who comes in to a country to settle.

immigrate *v.* to come into a country to settle (**immigrating, immigrated**). *n.* **immigration**.

immoral *adj.* evil, wicked. Opposite of **moral**. *n.* **immorality** wickedness.

immortal *adj.* everlasting. Opposite of **mortal**. *n.* **immortality**.

immovable *adj.* fixed, not able to be moved. Opposite of **movable**.

immune *adj.* not liable to, free from, as *Anne seems to be immune from colds*. *n.* **immunity**.

impact *n.* a collision.

impartial *adj.* fair, not favouring anyone unjustly, as *a judge must always be impartial*. *adv.* **impartially**. *n.* **impartiality**.

impassable *adj.* not able to be passed through, as *heavy snow made the roads impassable*.

impatient *adj.* 1. restless, fidgety. 2. not able to endure, as *Dick was always impatient with unfairness*. *n.* **impatience**.

impenetrable *adj.* not able to be entered or forced through, as *an impenetrable jungle*.

imperfect *adj.* not perfect. Opposite of **perfect**. *n.* **imperfection** a fault.

imperial *adj.* concerning an empire or an emperor.

impersonal *adj.* not referring to one person.

impersonate *v.* 1. to imitate, to mimic. 2. for an actor to play a stage part, as *to impersonate a king* (**impersonating, impersonated**). *n.* **impersonation**.

impertinent *adj.* impudent. *n.* **impertinence**.

impetuous *adj.* impulsive, acting without thought. *n.* **impetuosity**.

implement *n.* a tool. *v.* **implement** to carry out, as *to implement a plan*.

implore *v.* to plead, to beg (**imploring, implored**).

imply *v.* 1. to hint at without saying it, as *he nodded to imply that he agreed*. 2. to mean, as *success implies hard work* (**implying, implied**).

import (*pron.* im.pōrt') *v.* to bring in from abroad, as *to import tea*. Opposite of **export**. *n. pl.* **imports** (*pron.* im'ports) goods brought in from abroad. *n.* **importation**.

important *adj.* of great interest, value, or concern. *n.* **importance**.

imposing *adj.* impressive, stately.

imposition *n.* a punishment or burden laid on someone.

impossible *adj.* not possible. *n.* **impossibility** something which cannot be done.

imposter *n.* a deceiver, a fraud.

impractical *adj.* not practical.

impress (*pron.* im.pres') *v.* 1. to stamp a mark. 2. to make an effect on someone's mind, as *we were impressed by the speech*. *n.* **impress** (*pron.* im'pres) a mark made by pressure.

impression *n.* 1. a mark made by pressure. 2. an effect on the mind.

impressive *adj.* making an effect on the mind, as *an impressive display*.

imprint (*pron.* im.print') *v.* to print words or marks. *n.* **imprint** (*pron.* im'print) a mark, a stamp, as *the imprint of an inky finger*.

imprison v. to put in prison. n. **imprisonment**.

improbable adj. unlikely.

impromptu adj. done without preparation, as an impromptu speech.

improve v. to make better or become better (**improving, improved**). n. **improvement**.

imprudent adj. rash, not cautious. Opposite of **prudent**.

impudent adj. rude, disrespectful. n. **impudence**.

impulse n. 1. a throb of energy, a pulse, as the impulse of an engine. 2. a sudden wish, as to act on impulse.

impulsive adj. acting by sudden desire, without thought. n. **impulsiveness**.

in prep. 1. contained by, as in a tin, in a week, or in other words. 2. made of, as a statue in stone. adv. **in** 1. into, as to walk in. 2. at home, as he is in.

in- prefix 1. not, as incapable. 2. into, as income.

inaccessible (pron. in,ak.ses'i.bl) adj. out of reach, not easy to get at. Opposite of **accessible**.

inaccurate adj. not exact. Opposite of **accurate**. n. **inaccuracy**.

inadequate adj. not enough. n. **inadequacy**.

inanimate adj. lifeless, dead.

inaudible adj. not able to be heard, as an inaudible whisper. Opposite of **audible**.

inborn adj. natural, inherited, as an inborn love of music.

incapable adj. not able, not having the power. Opposite of **capable**. adv. **incapably**.

incense (1) (pron. in.sens') v. to make angry (**incensing, incensed**).

incense (2) (pron. in'sens) n. a spice burned in churches to give a pleasant smell.

inch n. the twelfth part of one foot in length (25 mm) (pl. **inches**). v. **inch** to creep along slowly.

every inch every bit.

incident n. a particular event, a happening.

incite v. to stir up, as to incite a crowd (**inciting, incited**). n. **incitement**.

inclination n. 1. a slope. 2. a desire, a preference, as an inclination for sweet food.

incline (pron. in.klin') v. 1. to lean. 2. to have a wish for, as I feel inclined to go out (**inclining, inclined**). n. **incline** (pron. in'klin) a slope.

include v. to contain, to count in (**including, included**). n. **inclusion**.

inclusive adj. counting in what is mentioned, as May the 21st to the 27th inclusive.

income n. money that comes in from earnings, investments, business, and property. n. **income-tax** tax paid on income.

incompetent adj. not capable of doing one's work as it should be done. Opposite of **competent**.

incomprehensible adj. beyond understanding, as Latin is incomprehensible to John.

inconspicuous adj. hardly to be noticed. Opposite of **conspicuous**.

inconvenience n. trouble, irritation, as it is an inconvenience to call at the Post Office. v. **inconvenience** to put to trouble, as do not let me inconvenience you (**inconveniencing, inconvenienced**). adj. **inconvenient** troublesome.

increase (pron. in.krees') v. to make greater or become greater, as Jack's height has increased. n. **increase** (pron. in'krees) a growth in size. **on the increase** growing larger.

incredible adj. unbelievable. adv. **incredibly**.

incubate v. to hatch out eggs in a warm box (**incubating, incubated**). n. **incubator** a warm box for hatching eggs without a hen.

incur v. to bring on oneself some trouble or burden, as to incur a punishment, fine, or a debt (**incurring, incurred**).

incurable adj. not able to be cured.

indebted adj. (with **to**) in someone's debt. n. **indebtedness**.

indecent adj. not modest, shocking. Opposite of **decent**.

indecision n. hesitation. adj. **indecisive** hesitant.

indeed adv. really, in fact.

indefinite *adj.* vague, uncertain. Opposite of **definite**.

indelible *adj.* unable to be rubbed out, as *indelible ink*.

independence *n.* complete freedom, self-government.

independent *adj.* 1. deciding for oneself, as *Peter has an independent mind*. 2. not connected with others, as *an independent business*.

index *n.* 1. a list of subjects in a book, placed at the end of the book in alphabetical order. 2. the forefinger, the *index finger* (*pl.* **indexes** or **indices** *pron.* in'di.seez).

Indian *n.* 1. a native of India. 2. an original native of America, a *Red Indian*.

indicate *v.* to show, to be a sign of, to point out, as *a clear sky indicates fine weather* (**indicating, indicated**). *n.* **indication** a sign. *n.* **indicator** a pointer, a timetable, as *a railway train indicator*.

indifferent *adj.* 1. not caring, as *I am indifferent whether I win or lose*. 2. moderate, as *he is an indifferent swimmer*. *n.* **indifference**.

indigestible *adj.* not easy to digest.

indigestion *n.* painful digestion of food.

indignant *adj.* angry at some wrong.

indignation *n.* anger at cruelty or unfairness.

indirect *adj.* not direct, roundabout, as *an indirect route* or *an indirect answer to a question*. Opposite of **direct**. *adv.* **indirectly**.

indiscreet *adj.* tactless, unwise, as *indiscreet talk*. Opposite of **discreet**.

indispensable *adj.* essential, not to be without, as *Jennifer's help is indispensable*.

indisposed *adj.* 1. slightly ill, as *Auntie is indisposed*. 2. unwilling, as *Bert is indisposed to help*. *n.* **indisposition** 1. illness. 2. unwillingness.

indistinct *adj.* not clearly seen or heard.

individual *n.* 1. a single person or thing. 2. one of a group. *adj.* **individual** single, separate, as *each house has its individual name*. *adv.* **individually**.

indivisible *adj.* not able to be divided, as *ten is indivisible by six without a remainder*.

indoor *adj.* inside, as *indoor decoration*. *adv.* **indoors** inside, as *he went indoors*.

indulge *v.* to give way to a wish or desire, as *to indulge a wish for sweets* (**indulging, indulged**). *adj.* **indulgent** lenient. *n.* **indulgence**.

industrial *adj.* connected with industry.

industrious *adj.* hard-working.

industry *n.* 1. hard work. 2. making goods or manufactures (*pl.* **industries**).

inequality *n.* dissimilarity, difference.

inevitable *adj.* unavoidable, bound to happen, as *the crash was inevitable*.

inexpensive *adj.* cheap, reasonably-priced.

inexperience *n.* newness, lack of practice.

inexplicable *adj.* mysterious, not able to be explained. *adv.* **inexplicably**.

infancy *n.* being an infant.

infant *n.* a baby or young child. *adj.* **infantile** babyish.

infantry *n.* foot-soldiers.

infect *v.* 1. to give germs to someone. 2. to cause a feeling to spread, as *to infect someone with one's own enthusiasm*. *n.* **infection** an illness passing to many people. *adj.* **infectious**.

inferior *adj.* 1. less important. 2. poorer in value or quality. *n.* **inferior** someone of lower rank. *n.* **inferiority** being inferior.

infernal *adj.* belonging to hell.

infidel *n.* an unbeliever, a heathen.

infinite *adj.* endless, beyond measure. *adv.* **infinitely**.

infinity *n.* a number, distance, or time too great for measurement ; endlessness.

infirm *adj.* feeble in body or mind. *n.* **infirmity**.

infirmary *n.* a hospital.

inflame *v.* 1. to excite. 2. to cause a hot swelling (**inflaming, inflamed**). *adj.* **inflamed** red and swollen.

inflammable *adj.* easily catching fire, as *paraffin is inflammable*.

inflammation *n.* a painful swelling.

inflate *v.* to fill with air or gas, as *to inflate a tyre* or *a balloon* (**inflating, inflated**). *n.* **inflation**.

inflict (something on someone) *v.* to lay a burden, pain, or a punishment on, as to *inflict a fine on a motorist*. *n.* **infliction**.

influence *n.* 1. unseen power, as *the influence of a magnet on a piece of iron*. 2. personal power, as *Tom is an influence for good*. *v.* **influence** to have an effect on, to persuade (**influencing, influenced**). *adj.* **influential** having influence, powerful.

influenza *n.* a feverish cold.

inform *v.* to tell, to instruct. *n.* **informer** someone who gives information.

informal *adj.* free-and-easy, without ceremony.

information *n.* knowledge, instruction, news.

informative *adj.* instructive.

infuriate *v.* to make very angry (**infuriating, infuriated**). *adj.* **infuriating** maddening.

ingenious *adj.* 1. cleverly thought out, as *an ingenious plan*. 2. clever at inventing, as *Dick is an ingenious boy*.

ingenuity *n.* cleverness at inventing.

ingot *n.* a bar of moulded metal.

ingratitude *n.* lack of gratitude or thankfulness.

ingredient *n.* one of the things in a mixture.

inhabit *v.* to live in (**inhabiting, inhabited**). *adj.* **inhabited** lived in.

inhabitant *n.* a dweller.

inhale *v.* to breathe in (**inhaling, inhaled**).

inherit *v.* 1. to receive by will from someone who has died, as *to inherit money*. 2. to receive from one's ancestors, as *Anne has inherited her mother's sweetness*. *n.* **inheritance** something handed down.

inhospitable *adj.* unfriendly to strangers, not welcoming. *adv.* **inhospitably**.

inhuman *adj.* cruel, devilish. *n.* **inhumanity**.

iniquity *n.* wickedness, sin (*pl.* **iniquities**).

initial *n.* the first letter of a word or name, as *John Smith's initials are J. S.* *adj.* **initial** first, as *the initial cost was great*. *v.* **initial** to mark with one's initials (**initialling, initialled**).

initiative *n.* 1. the first move, the lead, as *Bob's team took the initiative and scored the first goal*. 2. ability to think for oneself, as *Sam has plenty of initiative*.

inject *v.* to force in through a syringe, as *the doctor injected a fluid into Tom's arm*. *n.* **injection**.

injure *v.* to damage, to hurt (**injuring, injured**).

injurious (*pron.* in.joo'ri.us) *adj.* harmed.

injury *n.* hurt, harm (*pl.* **injuries**).

injustice *n.* unfairness. Opposite of **justice**.

ink *n.* writing-fluid. *adj.* **inky**. *n.* **inkpot** a pot to hold ink.

inkling *n.* a hint, a small suspicion.

inlaid *adj.* with pieces set in the surface to form a design, as *inlaid wood*. See **inlay**.

inland (*pron.* in'land) *adj.* in the country, as *an inland town*. *adv.* **inland** (*pron.* in.land') in country districts, away from the sea, as *the invaders travelled inland*.

inlet *n.* a narrow arm of the sea.

inmate *n.* a person living in a hospital or prison.

inmost *adj.* short for **innermost**, farthest in.

inn *n.* a public house for travellers to stay in. *n.* **innkeeper** a person who keeps an inn.

inner *adj.* inside, farther in. *adj.* **innermost** most inward.

innings (in North America **inning**) *n.* (in some ball games) the batsman's turn to play.

innocent *adj.* 1. not guilty, blameless. 2. simple, harmless, as *innocent play*. *n.* **innocence**.

innumerable *adj.* numerous, countless.

inoculate *v.* to inject into the body as a safeguard against disease (**inoculating, inoculated**). *n.* **inoculation**.

inquest *n.* an inquiry by coroner and jury into the cause of a sudden death.

inquire (sometimes spelt **enquire**) *v.* to ask questions, to get to know (**inquiring, inquired**).

inquiry *n.* 1. a question. 2. an investigation (*pl.* **inquiries**).

inquisitive *adj.* curious, questioning. *n.* **inquisitiveness**. *adv.* **inquisitively**.

insane *adj.* mad, senseless. *n.* **insanity**.

insanitary *adj.*. liable to cause ill-health.

insatiable (*pron.* in,say'sha.bl) *adj.* not able to be satisfied, as *an insatiable appetite*.

inscribe *v.* to write, to engrave, as *to inscribe a name on a watch* (**inscribing, inscribed**).

inscription *n.* writing, engraving.

insect *n.* a small creature such as a bee, ant, or fly, with six legs and three parts to its body.

insecticide *n.* a chemical to kill insects.

insecure *adj.* not firm, unsafe.

insensitive *adj.* unfeeling, as *insensitive to pain*. Opposite of **sensitive**. *n.* **insensitivity**.

inseparable *adj.* not to be separated, as *two inseparable friends*.

insert *v.* to put into, as *to insert a coin in a slot machine*. *n.* **insertion**.

inside *adj.* interior, as *an inside wall*. *adv.* **inside** within, as *to stay inside*. *n.* **inside** the inner part, as *the inside of the box*. *prep.* **inside** on the inner side, as *inside a house*.

inside-left (or **right**) in football, a player to the left (or right) of the centre-forward.

inside information secret knowledge.

insight *n.* ability to see into the heart of things.

insignificant *adj.* very small, unimportant. *n.* **insignificance**.

insincere *adj.* pretended, not sincere.

insipid *adj.* tasteless, as *insipid food*.

insist *v.* to persist, to hold strongly, as *Joan insisted that she was right*. *adj.* **insistent** persistent. *n.* **insistence**.

insolent *adj.* rude, impudent. *n.* **insolence**.

insoluble *adj.* 1. not able to be dissolved. 2. (of a mystery or problem) not able to be explained.

insomnia *n.* sleeplessness.

inspect *v.* to examine carefully. *n.* **inspection**.

inspector *n.* 1. someone who inspects. 2. a police officer below a superintendent in rank.

inspiration *n.* 1. a good influence, a good example to others. 2. a sudden good idea.

inspire *v.* to encourage, to fill with ambition or noble ideas (**inspiring, inspired**).

instability *n.* unsteadiness.

install (sometimes spelt **instal**) *v.* 1. to fix in position, as *to install a new cooker*. 2. to put an important person in office with ceremony, as *to install a new chairman*. *n.* **installation**.

instalment *n.* 1. a part of a serial story. 2. a part payment of the cost of something bought under hire-purchase. See **hire-purchase**.

instance *n.* an example, a particular case. *v.* **instance** to give as an example. **for instance** as an example.

instant *n.* 1. a moment. 2. a day of this month, as *in business letters 16th instant* (or *inst.*) means the 16th of this month. *adj.* **instant** immediate, as *this needs instant attention*. *adv.* **instantly** at once.

instantaneous *adj.* immediate, done at once.

instead *adv.* in the place of.

instep *n.* the arched part of the foot.

instinct *v.* an urge to do something without reasoning, as *pigeons fly home by instinct*. *adj.* **instinctive** by a natural urge. *adv.* **instinctively** by nature.

institute *v.* to establish, to set up, as *to institute a new set of rules* (**instituting, instituted**). *n.* **institute** 1. a society. 2. a building for education.

institution *n.* 1. a building used for some public service, as *an institution for the blind*. 2. an old custom, as *it has become an institution to eat pancakes on Shrove Tuesday*. 3. a society. 4. a beginning.

instruct *v.* 1. to teach. 2. to give an order. *n.* **instruction** 1. teaching. 2. an order. *n* **instructor**.

instructive *adj.* informative.

instrument *n.* 1. a tool. 2. anything producing music, as a flute or a piano.

insubordinate *adj.* rebellious. *n.* **insubordination**.

insufficient *adj.* not enough. *n.* **insufficiency**.

insulate v. to wrap in material which will not let heat or electricity escape (**insulating, insulated**). n. **insulation** covering with insulating material.

insulator n. any material, such as plastic or rubber, which does not let electricity escape.

insult (*pron.* in'sult) n. rudeness to anyone. v. **insult** (*pron.* in.sult') to be rude to someone or show contempt. adj. **insulting** rude.

insurance n. money paid out in small amounts, by the insured person, to guard against heavy loss.

insure v. 1. to make sure, to ensure. 2. to pay money each year to an insurance company, in return for which the company pays for loss by death, fire, etc.

intake n. something taken in, as *a quick intake of breath.*

intellect n. the power of the mind to reason, intelligence. adj. **intellectual** concerning the mind.

intelligence n. ability to learn and reason. adj. **intelligent** quick to learn, sensible.

intend v. to mean, to have in mind. adj. **intended** planned.

intense adj. extreme, very strong, as *an intense wish.* n. **intensity** strength.

intensive adj. long and thorough, as *the police made an intensive search for the child.*

intent adj. eager, absorbed, as *Mary was intent on her drawing.* n. **intent** purpose, intention, as *it was his intent to stay.*

to all intents and purposes for all that matters.

intention n. purpose, a plan. adj. **intentional** done on purpose. adv. **intentionally.**

inter- *prefix* between, as *international means between nations.*

interchange v. to exchange (**interchanging, interchanged**). adj. **interchangeable** able to be exchanged.

interest n. 1. attention, curiosity, eagerness to know more. 2. benefit, as *it is in her interest to work hard.* 3. payment made by a bank for lending them money. v. **interest** to arouse attention. adj. **interesting.**

interfere v. to meddle, to get mixed up in (**interfering, interfered**). n. **interference.**

interior n. 1. the inside. 2. the inland part of a country. adj. **interior** inside, inner.

interlude n. 1. an interval. 2. something performed during an interval.

intermediate adj. in between two things.

intermittent adj. on and off, stopping and starting, as *intermittent laughter.*

internal adj. inside, as *internal trade is trade within a country.* adv. **internally.**

international adj. between nations, as *an international peace treaty.*

interpret v. 1. to explain. 2. to translate a foreign language (**interpreting, interpreted**). n. **interpretation** 1. an explanation. 2. a translation.

interpreter n. someone who translates from another language and explains what a foreigner is speaking or writing.

interrogate v. to question someone (**interrogating, interrogated**). n. **interrogation.**

interrupt v. to break in upon, to cause a stoppage. n. **interruption.**

intersperse v. to scatter here and there among other things (**interspersing, interspersed**).

intertwine v. to twist together (**intertwining, intertwined**).

interval n. 1. a space between things. 2. a pause in time, as *an interval of ten minutes during the school morning.*

intervene v. to go between, to interfere, as *the teacher intervened in the fight between two boys.* n. **intervention.**

interview n. a private talk arranged between two people, where one is seeking information from the other. v. **interview** to have a private discussion with someone.

intestines n. pl. the bowels.

intimacy n. closeness, friendliness.

intimate adj. close, friendly. v. **intimate** to say, to state (**intimating, intimated**). n. **intimation** a statement, a suggestion.

intimidate v. to bully, to frighten by threats (**intimidating, intimidated**). n. **intimidation.**

into *prep.* 1. to the inside of. 2. to the form of, as *day changed into night.*

intolerable *adj.* more than one can bear.

intolerance *n.* impatience with the rights and opinions of others.

intolerant *adj.* not prepared to consider the opinions of others.

intoxicated *adj.* drunk with alcohol. *n.* **intoxication**.

intrepid *adj.* bold, fearless.

intricate *adj.* complicated, difficult, as *an intricate sum.*

intrigue (*pron.* in'treeg) *n.* a scheme, a plot. *v.* **intrigue** to plot (**intriguing, intrigued**).

introduce *v.* 1. to bring in, to try, as *the firm introduced a new method of book-keeping.* 2. to make one person known to another, as *I introduced John to Mr Smith* (**introducing, introduced**).

introduction *n.* 1. a bringing in or trial of something new. 2. making one person known to another. 3. the foreword at the beginning of a book.

intrude *v.* to enter, or go forward, without invitation (**intruding, intruded**). *n.* **intrusion**.

intuition (*pron.* in.tyoo.ish'un) *n.* knowing something instantly without thought or reasoning. *adj.* **intuitive** known by intuition.

invade *v.* to march into, to enter with an army (**invading, invaded**). *n.* **invasion**.

invalid (*pron.* in'va.lid) *n.* a person who is ill or disabled.

invaluable *adj.* above any price, very valuable.

invariable *adj.* never changing. *adv.* **invariably** constantly, uniformly.

invasion see **invade**.

invent *v.* 1. to create or think out something new. 2. to make up or imagine, as *to invent a false tale. n.* **invention** 1. something new that has been created. 2. a made-up story, a lie. *n.* **inventor**.

inventive *adj.* good at inventing.

inverse *adj.* the opposite way round, as *the numbers 3, 2, 1, are in inverse order to the numbers 1, 2, 3.*

invert *v.* to turn upside down, as *to invert the fraction $\frac{3}{4}$ to make $\frac{4}{3}$.*

inverted commas marks ('...') used to show that someone is speaking, as *'Not yet,' said Jim.*

invest *v.* 1. to put money into a business for profit. 2. to put official robes or signs of office on someone, as *to invest a president of a society with his chain of office.* 3. to grant, to endow, as *to invest someone with authority. n.* **investment** money invested.

investigate *v.* to inquire into, as *to investigate a crime* (**investigating, investigated**). *n.* **investigation**. *n.* **investigator** someone who makes an inquiry.

invigorate *v.* to refresh, to give strength to, as *sea air invigorates me* (**invigorating, invigorated**). *adj.* **invigorating**.

invincible *adj.* unconquerable. *n.* **invincibility**.

invisible *adj.* not able to be seen. *n.* **invisibility**.

invitation *n.* a polite request to someone. See **invite**.

invite *v.* 1. to ask someone politely to go with you, or to do something. 2. to attract, as *the sunshine invites me to go out* (**inviting, invited**). *adj.* **inviting** tempting, attractive, as *these cakes are very inviting.*

invoice *n.* a bill, a list of goods.

involve *v.* 1. to entangle or become entangled, as *the prince was involved in a plot.* 2. to include, to lead to, as *this involves hard work* (**involving, involved**). *adj.* **involved** complicated.

inward *adj.* or *adv.* towards the inside.

iodine *n.* a chemical substance used as an antiseptic.

irate *adj.* angry.

ire *n.* anger.

irksome *adj.* dull, wearying.

iron *n.* 1. a grey metal in the form of *wrought iron* which is soft and can be hammered into shape when hot, or *cast iron* which is brittle. 2. a heated mass of iron for smoothing cloth. *v.* **iron** to smooth cloth with an iron.

iron lung a machine for pumping air into a patient's lungs.

too many irons in the fire too many plans at one time.

to rule with a rod of iron to rule sternly.

iron-foundry *n.* a place where iron is cast.

ironmonger *n.* a man who sells iron goods.

irregular *adj.* not regular, even, or smooth. *n.* **irregularity**.

irresistible *adj.* not to be resisted, overwhelming, as *an irresistible attack*.

irresolute *adj.* hesitating, undecided. Opposite of **resolute**.

irresponsible *adj.* untrustworthy, not capable of carrying out a duty properly. *n.* **irresponsibility**.

irreverent *adj.* without respect for sacred things. Opposite of **reverent**.

irrigate *v.* to water land by channels dug in the ground (**irrigating, irrigated**). *n.* **irrigation**.

irritable *adj.* bad-tempered. *n.* **irritability**. *adv.* **irritably**.

irritate *v.* 1. to annoy or anger. 2. to make skin sore or inflamed (**irritating, irritated**). *adj.* **irritating** annoying. *n.* **irritation**.

Islam *n.* the Mohammedan religion.

island *n.* a piece of land with water round it. *n.* **isle** or **islet** a small island.

isolate *v.* to place by itself, as *to isolate someone who has an infectious disease* (**isolating, isolated**). *n.* **isolation** separation.

issue *v.* 1. to send out, as *to issue an order*. 2. to flow out, as *water issues from a tap* (**issuing, issued**). *n.* **issue** 1. a flowing out. 2. a publication, as *an issue of a magazine*. 3. a result, as *the issue was uncertain*. 4. a problem, as *they discussed the issue*.

isthmus *n.* a narrow strip of land joining two larger masses.

it *pronoun* referring to a thing. *possessive pronoun* and *adj.* **its** belonging to it, as *the dog wears its collar* (note: do not confuse **its** with **it's**, which is short for *it is*). *pronoun* **itself** referring to it, as *the dog shook itself*.

italics *n. pl.* a style of printing or writing, as *this is in italics*.

itch *n.* a tickling feeling on the skin. *v.* **itch** 1. to have a tickling feeling. 2. to have a desire for something.

item *n.* a single thing on a list. 2. a small piece of news in a newspaper.

ivory *n.* the substance of which elephants' tusks are made. *adj.* **ivory** 1. made of ivory. 2. the colour of ivory.

ivy *n.* an evergreen climbing plant.

J

jab *v.* to stab, to prick (**jabbing, jabbed**).

jack *n.* 1. an instrument for lifting a car or some other load. 2. a small flag. 3. a picture playing-card, the knave.

jack-in-the-box a toy in which a small figure jumps up when the box is opened.

jack of all trades a man who tries many kinds of work.

every man jack everyone.

Union Jack the British flag.

jackal *n.* a dog-like wild animal.

jackdaw *n.* a black bird like a crow.

jacket *n.* 1. a short coat. 2. a covering.

Jacobean (*pron.* jak.o.bee'an) *adj.* belonging to the reign of King James I, as *Jacobean furniture*.

Jacobite *n.* a supporter of King James II.

jaded *adj.* tired, weary.

jagged (*pron.* jag'id) *adj.* torn and rough.

jaguar (*pron.* jag'yoo.ar) *n.* a South American animal like a leopard.

jail, jailer see **gaol, gaoler**.

jam (1) *n.* a preserve made of fruit and sugar.

jam (2) *v.* 1. to squeeze, to press together. 2. to cause radio interference, as *to jam a foreign radio station* (**jamming, jammed**). *n.* **jam** 1. a squeeze, a blocking-up. 2. a difficult situation, as *he is in a jam*.

jamboree *n.* an international meeting of Boy Scouts.

janitor *n.* a caretaker or doorkeeper.

January *n.* the first month of the year.

jar (1) *n.* a container of pottery or glass.

jar (2) *v.* 1. to make an irritating grating sound. 2. to irritate. 3. to send a shock through (nerves, etc.) (**jarring, jarred**).

jaunt *n.* a short trip.

jaunty *adj.* gay, care-free. *adv.* **jauntily**.

javelin *n.* a light spear thrown by hand.

jaw *n.* 1. the chin and lower part of the face. 2. either of the ridges of bone in which teeth are fixed. *n.* **jawbone** the bone of the jaw.

jazz *n.* lively music with a strong rhythm.

jealous *adj.* 1. envious of someone's success or possessions. 2. displeased because someone is loved more than you. *n.* **jealousy.**

jeep *n.* a light military car.

jeer *v.* to make fun of, to laugh at unpleasantly.

jelly *n.* a soft food made from gelatine (*pl.* **jellies**). *adj.* **jellied** covered with jelly, as *jellied eels.*

jellyfish *n.* a jelly-like sea creature.

jerk *n.* a quick tug. *v.* **jerk** to pull or tug suddenly. *adj.* **jerky** *n.* **jerkiness.**

jerkin *n.* a man's sleeveless leather jacket.

jersey *n.* a knitted pullover worn by men and children. See **jumper.**

jest *n.* a joke, a merry trick.

jester *n.* a joker.

jet (1) *n.* a stream of liquid or gas issuing from an opening, or a nozzle through which liquid or gas spurts.

jet (2) *n.* a black, shiny mineral used to make ornaments.

jet (3) *n.* short for 'jet-propelled aircraft', pushed forward by streams of hot gases.

jetty *n.* a small pier running from land to sea.

Jew *n.* a Hebrew or one whose religion is Judaism (*fem.* **Jewess**). *adj.* **Jewish.**

jewel *n.* a precious stone.

jeweller a seller of jewels.

jewellery or **jewelry** jewels.

jib *n.* 1. a triangular sail at the front of a ship. 2. the arm of a crane. *v.* **jib** to refuse or be unwilling to do something, as *Tom jibbed at wearing his coat* (**jibbing, jibbed**).

jig *n.* a lively dance. *v.* **jig** to dance a jig (**jigging, jigged**).

jigsaw *n.* a fretsaw or thin-bladed saw for cutting sheets of wood.

jigsaw-puzzle a picture cut into small pieces by a jigsaw, which have to be fitted together again.

jingle *n.* a tinkling sound. *v.* **jingle** to clink or tinkle (**jingling, jingled**).

job *n.* 1. a piece of work. 2. a duty. 3. an occupation. *adj.* **jobbing** doing odd jobs, as *a jobbing gardener.*

jockey *n.* a man who rides race-horses (*pl.* **jockeys**). *v.* **jockey** 1. to jostle someone out of the way. 2. to trick someone.

jog *v.* 1. to push, to shake. 2. (of a horse) to move at a slow trot (**jogging, jogged**). *n.* **jog** a jerk.

join *v.* 1. to put together, to fasten. 2. to mix with other people, as *to join a group.* *n.* **join** a joint.

joiner a man who does the woodwork in buildings.

joinery woodwork.

joint *n.* 1. a place where two parts meet and join. 2. a large piece of meat for cooking. *adv.* **jointly** together.

joke *n.* something said or done to cause a laugh, a funny story. *v.* **joke** to make funny remarks (**joking, joked**).

jolly *adv.* full of fun (*comparative* **jollier,** *superlative* **jolliest**). *n.* **jollity** fun.

jolt *n.* a sudden jerk. *v.* **jolt** to shake sharply.

jostle *v.* to push roughly (**jostling, jostled**).

jot *n.* a tiny piece. *v.* **jot** to write down a quick note (**jotting, jotted**). *n.* **jotter** a note-book.

journal (*pron.* jer'nal) *n.* 1. a diary or book in which daily notes are made. 2. a magazine or newspaper.

journalism the business of writing for or publishing newspapers and magazines.

journalist a reporter who writes for newspapers or magazines.

journey *n.* a trip or excursion (*pl.* **journeys**). *v.* **journey** to travel (**journeying, journeyed**).

joust (*pron.* jowst *or* jōost) *n.* a medieval fight between knights on horseback. *v.* **joust** to tilt on horseback.

jovial *adj.* merry, jolly. *adv.* **jovially.**

joy *n.* delight, pleasure. *adjs.* **joyful, joyous.** *advs.* **joyfully, joyously.**

jubilant *adj.* rejoicing, triumphant. *n.* **jubilation.**

jubilee *n.* the celebration of an anniversary.

silver jubilee celebration of a 25th anniversary.

diamond jubilee celebration of a 60th anniversary.

Judaism *n.* the Jewish religion.

judge *n.* 1. someone who presides over a higher court of law. 2. someone who decides the winner of a race or competition. 3. an expert, as *Sheila is a good judge of pastry.* *v.* **judge** to give a decision (**judging, judged**). *n.* **judgment** or **judgement** a decision, an opinion.

judicial *adj.* concerning a judge or court of justice, as *a judicial verdict.*

judicious *adj.* carefully judged, wise, as *a judicious decision.* *adv.* **judiciously**.

jug *n.* a tall container for liquids.

juggle *v.* to entertain people with balancing tricks (**juggling, juggled**). *n.* **juggler**.

juice *n.* the liquid in fruits and in meat. *adj.* **juicy**. *n.* **juiciness**.

juke-box *n.* a coin-in-the-slot machine playing gramophone records.

July *n.* the seventh month of the year.

jumble *n.* a muddle, a confused mass, as *a jumble of clothing.*

jumble sale a sale of second-hand goods for a good cause.

jump *v.* 1. to spring up, as *to jump up from a chair.* 2. to leap over, as *to jump a fence.* *n.* **jump** 1. a leap. 2. an obstacle to be jumped over, as *the jumps in an obstacle race.*

to jump a claim to seize land claimed by someone else.

jumper *n.* 1. someone who jumps. 2. a woman's knitted pullover.

junction *n.* a place where railway lines meet.

June *n.* the sixth month of the year.

jungle *n.* tropical land thickly covered with trees and plants.

junior *adj.* 1. younger. 2. in a lower position, as *the junior partner in a firm.* 3. for younger persons, as *the junior football team.* *n.* **junior** 1. a younger person. 2. someone in a lower position.

junk (1) *n.* valueless rubbish.

junk (2) *n.* a Chinese sailing-ship.

jurisdiction *n.* authority, legal power.

juror *n.* a member of a jury.

jury *n.* a group of twelve persons who decide in a court of law whether an accused person is guilty or not (*pl.* **juries**).

just (1) *adj.* fair, right, as *a just decision.*

just (2) *adv.* 1. barely, as *he has just left.* 2. exactly, as *the money is just right.*

just now at present.

just then a moment ago.

justice *n.* fairness.

to do justice to oneself to do one's best.

Justice of the Peace (in England) a magistrate who tries small offences.

justify *v.* to defend, to say why something that has been done was right, as *Tom justified his absence from the Scout meeting* (**justifying, justified**). *adj.* **justifiable** shown to be right. *n.* **justification** defence, as *there is no justification for what you have done.*

jut *v.* to stick out (**jutting, jutted**).

juvenile *adj.* 1. young. 2. suitable for young people, as *juvenile books.* *n.* **juvenile** a young person.

K

kangaroo *n.* an Australian animal.

kayak (*pron.* kī'ak) *n.* an Eskimo canoe.

keel *n.* a length of wood or steel stretching from bow to stern along the bottom of a ship.

on an even keel balanced, steady.

keen *adj.* 1. sharp, as *a keen knife.* 2. eager, as *a keen Scout.* *n.* **keenness** 1. sharpness. 2. enthusiasm.

keep (1) *n.* the inner strong part of a fort.

keep (2) *v.* 1. to hold. 2. to go on, as *to keep moving.* 3. to store or be stored, as *these eggs will keep,* or *he keeps fish* (**keeping, kept**). *n.* **keep** the cost of food, as *to earn one's keep.* *n.* **keeper** someone who takes charge, as *a park-keeper.* *n.* **keeping** care, as *it is left in your keeping.*

keep your temper do not get angry.

to keep in mind to remember.

to keep on to continue.

to keep one's hand in to practise often.

to keep time (of a clock) to show time correctly; (in music) to follow the time of the music.

to keep up to support, to continue doing.

to keep up appearances to make a good outward show no matter how difficult it is.

keepsake *n.* something kept in memory of someone.

keg *n.* a small cask, as *a keg of rum.*

ken *n.* knowledge, as *beyond his ken. v.* **ken** to know, as *do you ken John Peel?*

kennel *n.* a shelter for a dog.

kept *past* of **keep**.

kerb *n.* the stone edge of a pavement.

kernel *n.* the inner part of a nut or grain.

kettle *n.* a metal container with handle and spout for boiling water.

a fine kettle of fish an awkward situation.

key *n.* 1. a small piece of shaped metal for opening the lock of a door, or for winding a clock. 2. a lever on a piano or a typewriter which is pressed down to produce an effect. 3. the answer to a problem, as *this footprint is the key to the murder.* 3. musical pitch, as *a high key* or *a low key,* or *music in the key of A sharp. adj.* **key** important, as *a key man* or *a key industry.*

keyed-up tense with excitement.

keyboard *n.* the line of keys on a piano.

keynote *n.* the most important part of a matter.

keystone *n.* the wedge-shaped stone at the top of an arch.

khaki (*pron.* kah¹ki) *n.* 1. yellowish-brown. 2. a uniform of this colour.

kick *v.* 1. to hit with the foot. 2. (of a gun) to jump back when fired.

kick-off the start of a football match.

to kick over the traces to rebel.

kid *n.* a young goat, or its skin made into leather.

kidnap *v.* to steal a child, or carry off someone by force (**kidnapping, kidnapped**). *n.* **kidnapper.**

kidney *n.* one of two glands in the body carrying waste matter from the blood to the bladder (*pl.* **kidneys**).

kill *v.* to put to death, to destroy. *n.* **killer** someone, something which kills.

kill-joy a gloomy depressing person.

to kill time to pass time.

to kill two birds with one stone to get two results from doing one thing.

kiln *n.* a furnace or oven, as *a brick-kiln* for baking bricks, or *a hop-kiln* for drying hops.

kilogramme *n.* a unit of mass in the metric system, equal to 1,000 grammes.

kilometre *n.* a distance in the metric system equal to 1,000 metres or five-eighths of a mile.

kilt *n.* a pleated tartan skirt worn by Scottish Highlanders.

kin, kindred, or **kinsfolk** *n. pl.* relatives. *n.* **kinship** relationship. See **kith**.

next of kin nearest relatives.

kind (1) *n.* a sort, a variety.

kind (2) *adj.* gentle, friendly. *adv.* **kindly** in a kind way (*comparative* **kindlier,** *superlative* **kindliest**). *adj.* **kind-hearted** friendly. *adj.* **kindly** gentle, friendly. *n.* **kindness**.

kindergarten *n.* a school for very young children.

kindliness *n.* friendliness. See **kind**.

kindred see **kin**.

king *n.* 1. a ruler of a country (*fem.* **queen**). 2. a playing-card with the picture of a king. 3. a piece in draughts (chequers) or chess. *adj.* **kingly** like a king.

kingdom *n.* a country ruled by a king or queen.

kingfisher *n.* a bright coloured fish-eating river bird.

kinsfolk, kinship see **kin**.

kiosk (*pron.* kee¹osk) *n.* 1. a small stall for selling things. 2. a box, as *a telephone kiosk.*

kipper *n.* a dried, smoked herring.

kirk *n.* a Scottish church.

kiss *v.* 1. to touch with the lips. 2. to touch gently. *n.* **kiss** a touch with the lips.

kit *n.* 1. an outfit or equipment. 2. a set of parts, as *an aero-modelling kit. n.* **kit-bag** a long canvas bag used by a serviceman.

kitchen *n.* a room where meals are cooked.

kite *n.* 1. a light frame covered with paper or cloth, flown in the air with a string. 2. a kind of hawk.
kith *n.* neighbours, friends. See **kin**.
kith and kin friends and relatives.
kitten *n.* a young cat.
kiwi *n.* a New Zealand bird with no tail and undeveloped wings.
knack *n.* easy skill, a way of doing something.
knapsack *n.* a canvas haversack.
knave *n.* a rogue, a rascal. *n.* **knavery**. *adj.* **knavish**.
knead *v.* to mix flour and water into dough.
knee *n.* the middle joint of the leg. *n.* **knee-cap** a bone over the knee.
kneel *v.* to bend the knee, to rest on the knees (**kneeling, knelt**).
knew *past* of **know**.
knickers *n. pl.* undergarments over the thighs; briefs, shorts.
knife *n.* a cutting tool with a handle and blade (*pl.* **knives**). *v.* **knife** to stab with a knife (**knifing, knifed**).
knight *n.* 1. a man bearing the title 'Sir', next in rank below a baronet. 2. in the Middle Ages, a man raised to certain rank in return for military service. 3. a piece with a horse's head in the game of chess. *adj.* **knightly** brave, chivalrous.
knight-errant a knight seeking adventure.
knighthood the rank of knight.
knit *v.* to weave wool or silk thread into garments with long needles (**knitting, knitted**). *n.* **knitting** material being knitted.
knives *plural* of **knife**.
knob *n.* the round handle of a door or drawer.
knock *v.* to strike, to tap sharply. *n.* **knock** a sharp blow. *n.* **knocker** 1. someone who knocks. 2. a doorstriker.
knock-kneed with knees turned inwards.
knock-out (in boxing) a finishing blow.
to knock off to stop work.
to knock out (in boxing) to strike a person unconscious.

knot (1) *v.* to tie together two strings or ropes (**knotting, knotted**). *n.* **knot** 1. the place where two strings or ropes are tied. 2. a hard lump in a piece of wood. *adj.* **knotted** tied in knots.
knotty hard, as *a knotty puzzle*.
knot (2) *n.* (of ships) a speed of one seamile (or nautical mile) per hour, a seamile being 2 kilometres (note: we do not speak of 'knots *per hour*', for a knot is one sea-mile per hour).
know *v.* 1. to be aware of, to understand. 2. to recognize, as *I know that man*. 3. to experience, as *he has known better times* (**knowing, knew, known**). *adj.* **knowing** cunning, as *a knowing look*. *adv.* **knowingly** on purpose, as *he did it knowingly*. *n.* **knowledge** 1. information. 2. understanding. 3. skill. *adj.* **knowledgeable** full of information.
know-all someone who thinks he understands everything.
know-how expert knowledge.
to know the ropes, to know what is what to know all about a matter.
knuckle *n.* a finger-joint.
to knuckle under to give way.
koala (*pron.* kō.a'la) *n.* an Australian animal like a small bear.
kookaburra *n.* an Australian bird which makes a laughing noise.
Koran (*pron.* kor.ahn') *n.* the holy scriptures of the Mohammedans.
kraal *n.* a South African native village.

L

label *n.* a small tag or slip of paper bearing a name or description. *v.* **label** to fasten a label on (**labelling, labelled**).
laboratory *n.* a scientific workshop (*pl.* **laboratories**).
laborious *adj.* 1. needing much work, as *a laborious job*. 2. hard-working, as *a laborious scholar*.
labour *n.* hard work. *v.* **labour** to work. *n.* **labourer** an unskilled workman.
labour of love work done for pleasure, not payment.
lace *n.* 1. a fine net-like pattern of woven threads. 2. a cord threaded through

holes, as *a shoe-lace*. *v* **lace** to fasten with a string through holes (**lacing, laced**).

lack *v.* to be without, to need.

lacquer *n.* a varnish of resin dissolved in spirit.

lad *n.* a boy, a youth (*fem.* **lass**).

ladder *n.* 1. a set of rungs or steps between two poles. 2. a broken thread in a stocking.

ladle *n.* a long-handled serving spoon.

lady *n.* 1. a gentlewoman (*masc.* **gentleman**). 2. a title given to the wife of a lord or knight (*pl.* **ladies**). *adj.* **ladylike** refined. *n.* **ladyship** a title, as *your ladyship.*

lady-bird *n.* a small red flying beetle (*pl.* **lady-birds**).

lag *v.* to fall behind (**lagging, lagged**).

lagoon *n.* a shallow lake separated from the sea by a narrow reef.

laid *past* of **lay**.

lain *past participle* of **lie**.

lair *n.* a wild beast's den.

laird *n.* a Scottish landowner.

lake *n.* 1. a large sheet of water surrounded by land. 2. a crimson colour.

lamb *n.* a young sheep, and its meat.

lame *adj.* 1. limping with a hurt leg or foot. 2. poor, as *a lame story*. *v.* **lame** to make someone limp (**laming, lamed**). *n.* **lameness**.

lament *v.* to mourn, to show grief. *n.* **lament** a song of mourning. *n.* **lamentation**.

lamp *n.* a glass globe containing a light.

lamp-post *n.* a post holding a street-lamp.

lance *n.* a long spear once used by cavalry soldiers. *n.* **lancer** a cavalry soldier with a lance. *n.* **lance-corporal** a soldier between a private and a corporal in rank.

land *n.* 1. the part of the earth's surface above the sea. 2. soil. 3. a country. *v.* **land** 1. to go ashore, or bring ashore, from a ship. 2. to finish up, as *to land in gaol*. *n.* **landing** 1. going ashore. 2. a descent from an aeroplane. 3. a platform at the top of a stairway.

land-breeze *n.* a breeze blowing from land to sea.

landing-stage *n.* a platform where passengers land from a ship.

landlord *n.* the owner of a rented house, inn, or estate (*fem.* **landlady**).

landlubber *n.* a sailor's name for a person who lives on land.

landmark *n.* a striking object such as a hilltop, which gives a traveller his position.

landscape *n.* a wide view.

landslide *n.* a fall of earth down a hill.

lane *n.* a path or small country road.

language *n.* 1. human speech. 2. a nation's speech, as *the Dutch language*.

lantern *n.* a glass case with a light inside.

lap (1) *v.* to lick up liquid, like a dog (**lapping, lapped**).

lap (2) *n.* 1. the top of someone's thighs when sitting, as *the dog sat in her lap*. 2. once round a race-track.

lap-dog *n.* a very small dog.

lapse *n.* a careless mistake. *v.* **lapse** 1. to slip gently, as *to lapse into a doze*. 2. to make a mistake. 3. to come to an end, as *the time for keeping the library book has now lapsed* (**lapsing, lapsed**).

larceny *n.* the crime of stealing, theft.

lard *n.* purified pig's fat, used in cooking.

larder *n.* a small food-store, a pantry.

large *adj.* great in size, big (*comparative* **larger**, *superlative* **largest**). **at large** free, at liberty.

largely *adv.* for the most part, almost all, as *it is largely true*.

lariat *n.* a rope with a noose for catching cattle, a lasso.

lark (1) *n.* a merry frolic, a joke.

lark (2) *n.* a singing bird, a *skylark*.

larva *n.* an insect grub, such as a caterpillar (*pl.* **larvae** *pron.* lahr'vee).

lash *v.* 1. to whip. 2. to beat upon, as *the sea lashed the rocks*. 3. to tie firmly, as *they lashed the flag to the masthead*. *n.* **lash** 1. a stroke of a whip. 2. the thong of a whip. 3. a hair from the eyelid, an *eyelash*. *n.* **lashing** a whipping.

lass *n.* a girl (*pl.* **lasses**. *masc.* **lad**).

lasso *n.* a rope with a noose for catching cattle (*pl.* **lassos**). *v.* **lasso** to catch with a lasso (**lassoing, lassoed**).

last (1) *adj.* after all others, the latest (*superlative* of **late**). *adv.* **last** at the end, as *he came last in the race. n.* **last** the one at the end.

at last finally.

at long last after a long time.

the last word the most expert, as *this book is the last word on tennis.*

last (2) *v.* to endure, to wear, to continue, as *the food lasted several days. adj.* **lasting** going on for a long time, as *lasting joy.*

latch *n.* a door-catch or gate fastening.

late *adj.* 1. behind time, as *the train is late.* 2. far on in time, as *a late hour of the day* (comparative **later** or **latter**, *superlative* **latest**). 3. dead, as *the late king. adv.* **late** behind time, as *he came late. adv.* **lately** recently.

of late recently.

lath *n.* a thin strip of wood.

lathe *n.* a machine which spins wood or metal round while it is being cut or shaped.

lather *n.* 1. soap froth. 2. the white sweat of horses. *v.* **lather** to cover with soapy foam.

Latin *n.* the language of the ancient Romans.

latitude *n.* 1. the distance of a place on the earth's surface north or south of the equator, measured in degrees. 2. freedom, as *the boys were given plenty of latitude to wander where they wished.*

latter *adj.* 1. later. 2. the second of two (compared with the *former* which is the first of two). See **late.**

laugh *n.* a loud 'ha-ha' of amusement or scorn. *v.* **laugh** to make sounds of amusement or scorn. *adj.* **laughable** amusing, silly. *n.* **laughter.**

laughing-stock someone who makes himself ridiculous.

to laugh to scorn to jeer at.

to laugh up your sleeve to laugh secretly.

launch (1) *n.* a large motor-driven boat (*pl.* **launches**).

launch (2) *v.* 1. to float a newly-built boat. 2. to set going, as *to launch a new business.*

laundry *n.* 1. a business undertaking the washing and ironing of clothes. 2. clothes to be laundered (*pl.* **laundries**).

laurel *n.* an evergreen shrub, whose leaves were used in days of old for crowns of honour.

lava (*pron.* lah'va) *n.* molten stone from volcanoes.

lavatory *n.* a place for washing oneself; a water-closet (*pl.* **lavatories**).

lavender *n.* a plant with scented flowers and leaves.

lavish *adj.* generous, abundant, as *lavish praise.*

law *n.* 1. a rule made by a government. 2. the power of government, as *the law does not permit begging.* 3. a rule, as *the laws of football.* 4. (in science) something that is always true, as *'metals conduct electricity' is a law. adj.* **law-abiding** obeying the law. *adj.* **lawful** allowed by law. *adv.* **lawfully.** *adj.* **lawless** not regarding the law.

to lay down the law to say what you think very strongly.

to take the law in one's own hands to act on one's own in place of the law.

lawn *n.* a carefully mown plot of grass. *n.* **lawn-mower** a machine for mowing a lawn.

lawsuit *n.* a case tried in a law court.

lawyer *n.* a man who knows and practises law.

lay *v.* 1. to put down. 2. (of a bird) to drop an egg into a nest (**laying, laid**) (note: do not confuse with **lay** *past* of **lie**).

to lay bare to open for all to see.

to lay by to store for future use.

to lay hold of to seize.

to lay in, to lay up to store up.

to lay into to fight fiercely against.

to lay waste to destroy.

layer *n.* a coating, as *a layer of paint.*

lazy *adj.* avoiding work (*comparative* **lazier,** *superlative* **laziest**). *adv.* **lazily.** *n.* **laziness.**

lea *n.* a stretch of grass, a meadow.

lead (1) (*pron.* leed) *v.* to go in front, to show the way (**leading, led**). *n.* **lead** 1. the first place, as *to take the lead.* 2. a distance ahead, as *a lead of many metres.* 3. a strap to hold a dog. *n.* **leader** someone who leads. *n.* **leadership.**

leading-article the chief article of a newspaper.

leading man, leading lady the principal actor in a play.

to lead astray to lead in the wrong direction.

to lead someone a dance to cause someone unnecessary trouble.

lead (2) (*pron.* led) *n.* a heavy grey metal. *adj.* **leaden** heavy, like lead.

leaf *n.* 1. a flat green growth on a plant or tree. 2. a sheet of paper printed on both sides in a book (*pl.* **leaves**). *adj.* **leafy** covered with leaves.

to take a leaf from someone's book to copy someone's example.

to turn over a new leaf to change for the better.

leaflet *n.* a pamphlet, a printed paper with a message.

league (1) *n.* 1. an alliance or union of people or nations. 2. a group of sports teams which play against one another.

league (2) *n.* an old measure of distance, about 5 kilometres.

leak *n.* a small hole or crack through which gas or liquid escapes. *v.* **leak** for gas or liquid to escape. *n.* **leakage**. *adj.* **leaky**.

lean (1) *adj.* 1. thin. 2. without fat. *n.* **leanness**.

lean (2) *v.* 1. to slant. 2. to rest against, as *the ladder leans against a wall* (**leaning, leaned** or **leant**). *adj.* **leaning** slanting, as *the leaning tower of Pisa. n.* **lean-to** a shed leaning against a building.

leap *v.* 1. to spring upwards. 2. to jump over, as *to leap a fence* (**leaping, leaped** or **leapt**). *n.* **leap** a jump.

leap-frog a game in which players jump over one another.

leap-year every fourth year, containing 366 days.

to look before you leap to think before acting.

learn *v.* to discover or get to know new facts or ways of doing things (**learning, learned** or **learnt**). *n.* **learning** knowledge. *adj.* **learned** (*pron.* lern'ed) wise.

to learn by heart to memorize.

lease *v.* to let a building or land to someone for a certain time in return for rent (**leasing, leased**). *n.* **lease** 1. a written agreement leasing a building or land to someone. 2. the time the agreement lasts, as *a ten-year lease.*

least *adj.* (*superlative* of **little**) smallest. *n.* **least** the smallest.

at least anyhow, at any rate.

leather *n.* an animal's skin, tanned and made ready for shoes, gloves, etc. *adj.* **leathery** like leather.

leave (1) *v.* 1. to go away from, as *to leave home.* 2. to depart, as *he left without speaking.* 3. to give away property in a will, as *his uncle left him his money* (**leaving, left**).

leave (2) *n.* 1. permission, as *I was given leave to stay.* 2. a farewell, as *Jack took his leave at ten o'clock.* 3. freedom from duty, as *the sailors were on leave.*

French leave leave without permission.

lecture *n.* 1. a talk given to a group of people or students. 2. a scolding. *v.* **lecture** to give a talk (**lecturing, lectured**). *n.* **lecturer**.

led *past* of **lead**.

ledge *n.* a narrow shelf, as *a window ledge.*

ledger *n.* a business account-book.

lee *n.* the side sheltered from the wind.

leech *n.* a blood-sucking worm once used by doctors to bleed patients (*pl.* **leeches**).

leek *n.* a vegetable with a thick white stem, tasting like an onion.

leer *n.* a sly glance. *v.* **leer** (often with **at**) to give a sly evil glance at someone.

leeward *adj.* and *adv.* (referring to a side) sheltered from the wind, as *they walked along the leeward side of the hill.*

leeway *n.* a sideways drift of a boat caused by the wind.

to make up leeway to make up time or distance lost.

left (1) *past* of **leave**.

left (2) *n.* the opposite of right. *adj.* **left** of the left, or to the left, as *the left fork of a road. adj.* **left-handed** 1. only able to use the left-hand well. 2. having two meanings, as *a left-handed compliment.*

leg *n.* 1. one of the limbs on which a living creature walks. 2. something like a leg, as *a chair leg.*
leg-pull a joke.
leg side (in cricket) the left side of the batsman as he faces the bowler.
leg before wicket (L.B.W.) (in cricket) the batsman being out as he stopped the ball hitting the wicket with his leg.
not a leg to stand on no defence at all.
on your last legs completely exhausted.
legacy *n.* money or property left in a will (*pl.* **legacies**).
legal *adj.* 1. concerning the law, as *a legal document.* 2. allowed by law, as *a legal right. n.* **legality**. *adv.* **legally**.
legend *n.* an ancient story which is probably not true, as *the legend of King Arthur and his knights. adj.* **legendary**.
legible (*pron.* lej'i.bl) *adj.* readable, clear, as *legible writing.*
legion *n.* 1. a large body of Roman soldiers. 2. a military corps, as *the French Legion.* 3. a great number. *n.* **legionary**.
legitimate *adj.* lawful, proper, as *Janet has a legitimate excuse for being late.*
leisure *n.* spare time. *adj.* and *adv.*
leisurely slowly and without hurry.
lemon *n.* 1. a pale-yellow sour fruit. 2. *a* pale-yellow colour.
lemonade a drink made from sugar and lemon juice.
lemon curd, lemon cheese a paste made from lemon, eggs, and butter.
lend *v.* to let someone have something for a time (**lending, lent**).
length *n.* 1. the distance of a thing from end to end. 2. a piece, as *a length of cloth. v.* **lengthen** to make longer. *adj.*
lengthy long.
at full length stretched out.
at length in great detail, at last.
lengthways along the length.
to go to any lengths to do anything possible.
to keep someone at arm's length to be cool and distant to him.
lenience *n.* mildness, mercy.
lenient *adj.* mild, forgiving.

lens *n.* 1. a curved glass used in cameras, telescopes, and spectacles. 2. the part of the eye which focuses light on the screen at the back (*pl.* **lenses**).
lent (1) *past* of **lend**.
Lent (2) *n.* the time between Ash Wednesday and Easter Sunday, held in the Christian Church as a period of fasting. *adj.* **Lenten** concerning Lent.
leopard *n.* a spotted wild animal, found in Africa and Asia.
leper *n.* a person suffering from leprosy.
leprosy *n.* a very bad skin disease.
less *adj.* (*comparative* of **little**) 1. smaller, fewer. 2. not so important. *adv.* **less** not so much, as *they had less than they wanted.*
-less *suffix* without, as *hatless* or *worthless.*
lessen *v.* to make smaller or become smaller.
lesser *n.* the smaller, as *the lesser of the two.*
lesson *n.* 1. a period of time in which something is taught or learnt, as *a History lesson.* 2. an example, as *let that be a lesson to you!* 3. a Bible-reading in church.
let *v.* 1. to allow, as *let him stay.* 2. to hire out for payment, as *we will let this house* (**letting, let**).
to let down to lower, to betray.
to let off to fire off, to set free.
to let well alone to leave as it is for fear of doing worse.
-let *suffix* small, as *a piglet is a small pig.*
letter *n.* 1. one of the signs in an alphabet. 2. a long message written to someone. *n. pl.* **letters** learning, as *a man of letters. n.* **lettering** a series of letters.
letter-box *n.* a post office box for mail, a slot in a house-door for letters.
lettuce *n.* a plant with large leaves used in salads.
level *adj.* 1. smooth and flat. 2. of the same height. *v.* **level** to make smooth and flat (**levelling, levelled**).
sea-level at the same height as the sea.
level-crossing *n.* a place where railway lines cross a road.
level-headed *adj.* calm.

lever *n.* a bar which helps you to move something heavy, a crowbar.

levy *v.* to raise money or an army by force (**levying, levied**). *n.* **levy** taxes or soldiers raised by force (*pl.* **levies**).

liability *n.* 1. responsibility, as *he has a liability for any damage he causes.* 2. being liable. *n. pl.* **liabilities** debts.

liable *adj.* 1. responsible for, as *a cashier is liable for his money.* 2. in danger of, as *he is liable to be found out.* 3. likely to, as *Dick is liable to lose his temper.*

liar *n.* someone who tells lies.

liberal *adj.* 1. broad-minded, free. 2. generous, plentiful, as *a liberal helping of pudding.* *n.* **liberal** a member of a political party. *n.* **liberality**. *adv.* **liberally**.

liberate *v.* to set free (**liberating, liberated**). *n.* **liberation**.

liberty *n.* freedom.

at liberty free.

to take liberties with someone to be too familiar with him.

librarian *n.* someone in charge of a library.

library *n.* 1. a collection of books. 2. a room or building for books (*pl.* **libraries**).

licence *n.* 1. a permit, as *a driving licence* or *a television licence.* 2. great freedom (note: do not confuse with the verb **license**).

license *v.* to grant a permit, as *this shop is licensed to sell tobacco* (**licensing, licensed**) (note: do not confuse with the noun **licence**).

lick *v.* 1. to wet with the tongue, as *to lick a stamp.* 2. to touch, as *the flames licked the wood.*

to lick into shape to improve something.

licorice see **liquorice**.

lid *n.* 1. the movable top of a tin, bottle, or box. 2. a movable skin over the eye, an *eyelid.*

lie (1) *v.* to tell an untruth in order to deceive someone (**he lies, lying, lied**). *n.* **lie** an untruth.

lie (2) *v.* 1. to rest in a flat position. 2. to stretch out, as *the valley lies before them* (**he lies, lying, lay, lain**) (note:

do not confuse *lie* with *lay.* To *lie* down is not the same as to *lay* down. See **lay**.)

the lie of the land the state of affairs.

to lie to (of a ship) to stop facing the wind.

to take it lying down to take an insult or injury without hitting back.

lieutenant (*pron.* lef.ten'ant, in the U.S.A. lyoo.ten'ant) *n.* a man below a captain in rank (in the army), or below a lieutenant-commander (in the navy).

life *n.* 1. the ability to grow and develop. 2. a human being, as *many lives were saved.* 3. the years of living, as *all my life I worked hard.* 4. energy, as *Jack is full of life* (*pl.* **lives**). *adj.* **lifeless** dead, not moving.

life-and-death very critical.

lifelike looking a perfect copy.

lifelong lasting a lifetime.

for the life of me though my life depended on it.

lifebelt *n.* a belt to hold one up in water.

lifeboat *n.* a boat specially built for the rescue of shipwrecked people.

lifebuoy *n.* a floating buoy to which shipwrecked people can cling.

lifeguard *n.* 1. a soldier bodyguard. 2. a swimmer who keeps watch on bathers.

lift *v.* to raise or to rise. *n.* **lift** a hoist or elevator which moves from floor to floor of a building.

light (1) *n.* 1. brightness which enables one to see things. 2. a source of brightness, such as the sun or a lamp. 3. understanding, as *this clue throws new light on the mystery.* *v.* **light** to set fire to, or to fill with light (**lighting, lit**). *adj.* **light** (of a colour) pale in tone. *v.* **lighten** to make or become bright. *n.* **lighting** the lamps which light a place, as *the lighting was bright.*

lighting-up time the hours during which vehicles are obliged to be lit.

light (2) *adj.* 1. not heavy. 2. made for small loads, as *a light van.* *n.* **lightness** being light. *v.* **lighten** to make lighter.

light-fingered clever at stealing.

light-handed empty-handed.

light-headed frivolous.

light-hearted gay.

to make light of to pretend a matter is not serious.

lighter *n.* a *cigarette-lighter* for lighting cigarettes.

lighthouse *n.* a tower by the sea with a light to warn ships.

lightning *n.* the flashing of electricity in a thunderstorm.

lightning-conductor a metal rod fixed to a building to give lightning safe passage to the earth.

lightship *n.* a ship stationed by sandbanks with a warning light.

like (1) *v.* 1. to be fond of, as *I like meat.* 2. to prefer, as *which would you like?* (**liking, liked**). *adj.* **likable** or **likeable** pleasing. *n.* **liking** fondness for.

like (2) *adj.* 1. similar to, as *he looks like you.* 2. in the mood for, as *I felt like sleeping. n.* **like** equal, as *I have not seen his like before. adj.* **likely** suitable, as *a likely place to stay at.*

lilac *n.* a flowering shrub.

lily *n.* a flower growing from a bulb (*pl.* **lilies**).

limb *n.* 1. an arm or leg. 2. a tree branch.

lime (1) *n.* a white powder obtained when chalk or limestone is burnt in a kiln. *n.* **limestone** a soft white rock.

lime (2) *n.* a tree bearing small fruits from which *lime-juice* is obtained.

limerick *n.* a humorous poem five lines long.

limit *n.* a boundary or point one cannot pass. *adj.* **limited** kept to a limit, as *I have a limited amount of money to spend. n.* **limitation** something which fixes a limit. *adj.* **limitless** without limit.

limp (1) *v.* to walk lamely. *n.* **limp** a hobble.

limp (2) *adj.* flabby, drooping.

line *n.* 1. a long narrow mark. 2. a row, as *a line of trees.* 3. a rope, cord, or wire, as *a clothes-line.* 4. a single railway track, the *'up' line* or the *'down' line* (note: in Britain, the 'up' line leads into a city, and the 'down' line leads out). 5. a travel route, as an *air-line.* 6. a way of doing things, as *they worked on those lines. adj.* **linear** of length, concerning lines.

hard lines bad luck.

to draw the line to refuse to go beyond a certain point.

to read between the lines to find a hidden meaning in what is written.

linen *n.* 1. cloth made of flax fibres. 2. articles made of this cloth, as *household linen.*

liner *n.* a large passenger ship or aircraft.

linesman *n.* 1. (in football or tennis) someone who watches to see if the ball crosses the boundary line. 2. a man who examines railway or telephone lines.

linger *v.* to wait behind, to loiter, to stay.

link *n.* 1. a loop in a chain. 2. a fastener, as *the cuff-link of a shirt.*

links *n. pl.* a golf-course.

linnet *n.* a small, brown song-bird.

linoleum *n.* a floor-covering made of canvas, cork, and linseed oil.

linseed *n.* flax seed. *n.* **linseed oil** oil from crushed flax seed.

lion *n.* a wild animal of Africa and southern Asia (*fem.* **lioness**).

lion-hearted brave.

lion's share the largest share.

lip *n.* 1. a fleshy edge of the mouth. 2. any edge, as *the lip of a cup.*

lip-reading a deaf person's way of understanding what people say by watching their lip movements.

a stiff upper lip firm self-control.

lipstick *n.* a stick of red grease-paint for reddening the lips.

liquefy *v.* to make liquid (**liquefies, liquefying, liquefied**).

liquid *n.* a substance like water which can be poured.

liquidate *v.* 1. to pay off a debt. 2. to close down a business. 3. (*slang*) to destroy (**liquidating, liquidated**). *n.* **liquidation.**

liquor *n.* alcoholic liquid.

liquorice (sometimes spelled **licorice**) *n.* a black substance made from a plant root, used as a sweet.

lisp *v.* to pronounce *s* and *z* as *th*, as 'thothage' for 'sausage'. *n.* **lisp** a lisping speech.

list (1) *n.* 1. a column of names. 2. a catalogue.

list (2) *v.* (of a ship) to tilt to one side. *n.* **list** the leaning over of a ship.

listen v. to hear and attend to. n. **listener**.

listen in to listen to the radio, to overhear.

lit past of **light**.

literacy n. being able to read.

literal adj. 1. exact, as a literal description. 2. using the actual words, as a literal account. adv. **literally** exactly, as it is literally impossible to read his writing.

literary adj. concerning literature or authors.

literate adj. able to read, educated.

literature n. 1. the good books and poems of a language. 2. writing on one subject, as the literature of swimming.

litre (pron. lee'ter) (spelled **liter** in the U.S.A.) n. a unit of volume in the metric system equal to about 1¾ pints.

litter (1) n. 1. a stretcher. 2. a portable couch used by the Romans.

litter (2) n. 1. waste paper and other rubbish. 2. an animal's young ones born at one time. 3. straw for bedding animals.

little adj. small, short (comparative **less** or **lesser**, superlative **least**). adv. **little** not much, as he spoke little.

little by little gradually.

to make little of 1. to say a thing is not important. 2. to not understand something.

live (1) (pron. liv) v. to be, to have life, to dwell, as to live in a hotel (**living, lived**). adj. **livable** (with **in**) fit to live in.

live and let live be tolerant.

to live up to one's ideals to live in a good way one has set oneself.

live (2) (pron. līv) adj. 1. alive, not dead. 2. full of electricity, as a live wire. 3. not struck, as a live match. adj. **lively** energetic. n. **liveliness** energy.

livelihood n. a means of support or living, as he depends on farming for his livelihood.

liver n. a large organ in the body which helps in the digestion of food.

livestock n. farm animals.

livid adj. 1. very pale (with anger). 2. (of a bruise) blue.

living adj. 1. alive. 2. in use, as French is a living language. n. **living** 1. a way of earning money, as farming is my living. 2. a way of life, as a hard living. 3. (in England) a church position held by a clergyman.

lizard n. a small reptile with four legs.

llama n. a South American animal related to a camel.

load n. a bundle of goods to be carried, a cargo or weight. v. **load** 1. to place goods on to an animal or vehicle. 2. to put a cartridge or shell into a gun.

loaf (1) n. a lump of bread (pl. **loaves**).

loaf (2) v. to pass time in idleness.

loam n. rich soil.

loan n. 1. something lent. v. **loan** to lend.

loath or **loth** (pron. lōth) adj. unwilling. **nothing loth** willing.

loathe (pron. lōTH) v. to detest. n. **loathing** great dislike. adj. **loathsome** detestable.

lob v. 1. to toss gently, or bowl underhand at cricket. 2. to knock a ball high in the air (**lobbing, lobbed**).

lobe n. the lowest part of the ear.

lobster n. a shell-fish with eight legs and two large claws, black before boiling and red when boiled.

lobster-pot a basketwork cage for catching lobsters.

local adj. 1. concerning a particular place, as a local guide-book. 2. affecting one part of the body, as a local pain. n. **locality** a district. adv. **locally**.

locate v. 1. to find the position of, as to locate gold. 2. to be situated, as the school is located in the High Street (**locating, located**).

loch (pron. loCH) n. a Scottish lake.

lock (1) n. a curl or tress of hair.

lock (2) n. 1. a door or lid fastening worked by a key. 2. the firing part of a gun. v. **lock** to fasten up with a key. **locksmith** a man who makes locks.

lock (3) n. a part of a river or canal, enclosed by lock gates, in which a boat can be raised or lowered to a different level.

locker n. a small, locked cupboard.

locomotive n. a railway engine.

locust n. a grasshopper of Africa and Asia which destroys crops.

lodge *v.* 1. to stay with someone as a visitor. 2. to deposit something for safety, as *to lodge a package in a bank.* 3. to put before an official, as *to lodge a complaint.* 4. to become firmly fixed, as *the bullet lodged in a tree* (**lodging, lodged**). *n.* **lodge** 1. a small house at the entrance to a large house. 2. a beaver or otter's burrow.

loft *n.* a room just under the roof of a house.

lofty *adj.* 1. very tall. 2. noble, as *lofty ideals. n.* **loftiness.**

log *n.* 1. part of a tree trunk ready for sawing. 2. a ship's diary or *log-book. v.* **log** to make an entry in a log-book (**logging, logged**).

logic *n.* careful reasoning. *adj.* **logical.**

loin *n.* the part of the body between the lowest rib and the thigh-bone, on either side.

lollipop *n.* a large sweet to be sucked.

lone *adj.* alone, by oneself, as *the lone cowboy.*

lonely *adj.* 1. alone. 2. without friends. 3. feeling sad and alone. *n.* **loneliness.**

long (1) *adj.* having much length or taking much time, as *a long road* or *a long journey. adv.* **long** for a long time, as *I thought long before I went.*

long-bow a bow nearly 2 metres long.
long-winded boring, with a lot to say.
in the long run in the end.

long (2) (with **for**) *v.* to yearn for, to pine for. *n.* **longing** a strong wish.

longitude (*pron.* lon'ji.tyōod *or* long'gi.-tyōod) *n.* the distance of a place, measured in degrees, east or west of Greenwich in London.

look *v.* 1. to watch, to gaze. 2. to examine carefully. 3. to face, as *the house looks on the sea.* 4. to seem, as *it looks as if it will rain. n.* **look** 1. a glance. 2. an appearance. 3. an expression. *n. pl.* **looks** appearance, beauty.
look sharp! be quick!
to look after to care for.
to look down on to despise.
to look forward to await with pleasure.
to look into to examine.
to look up 1. to find in a book. 2. to find where someone lives and visit him.
to look up to to respect.

looking-glass *n.* a mirror.

look-out *n.* a watch, as *a sharp look-out,* or a position for watching.

loom (1) *n.* a machine for weaving cloth.

loom (2) *v.* to appear dimly out of the dark, or out of fog.

loop *n.* a twist in a string or rope, a noose. *v.* **loop** to make a loop or noose.

loophole *n.* 1. a slit in a castle wall to fire through. 2. a way of escape.

loose (*pron.* lōōs) *adj.* 1. not fastened or tight, as *a loose hinge* or *loose soil.* 2. not in a packet, as *sugar sold loose.* 3. vague, as *Jack had only a loose idea of what he wanted. adv.* **loosely.** *n.* **looseness.**
at a loose end having nothing much to do.
to break loose to get free.
to let loose to set free, to let out (note: do not confuse **loose** with **lose**).

loosen *v.* to make loose or become loose.

loot *n.* plunder taken from an enemy. *v.* **loot** to plunder.

lop *v.* to chip off, as twigs or branches from a tree (**lopping, lopped**).
lop-sided with one side lower than the other.

lord *n.* 1. a ruler or master. 2. (in Britain) a nobleman who sits in the *House of Lords.* 3. a title given to a Lord Mayor, bishop, or judge. *adj.* **lordly** like a lord. *n.* **lordship** the title given to a lord, who is addressed as *your lordship.*
Lord's Prayer the prayer of Jesus in St Matthew chapter 6.
Lord's Supper the last supper of Jesus with the disciples.

lorry *n.* a large motor wagon or truck (*pl.* **lorries**).

lose (*pron.* lōōz) *v.* 1. not to have because of theft, accident, or carelessness, as *to lose a purse.* 2. to miss, as *to lose the way.* 3. not to win, as *to lose a match* (**losing, lost**). *n.* **loser** someone who loses.
to lose ground to lose an advantage.
to lose sight of to overlook, to forget.
to lose one's head to get into a panic (note: do not confuse **lose** with **loose**).

loss *n.* 1. the losing of something. 2. the thing lost, as *the loss of a purse.*
to be at a loss to be puzzled.
lost *past* of **lose.**
lot *n.* 1. a large number. 2. (loosely) the whole amount, as *take the lot!* 3. a share. 4. fortune, fate, as *his was a hard lot.* 4. a method of deciding something by draw, as *they drew lots to decide who should go.* 5. an article at an auction sale.
loth see **loath.**
lotion *n.* a soothing liquid for the skin.
lottery *n.* a money-making scheme in which many numbered tickets are sold, and a few win prizes (*pl.* **lotteries**).
loud *adj* noisy.
loud-speaker the part of a radio set from which sound comes.
lounge *v.* to move or rest in a lazy way (**lounging, lounged**). *n.* **lounge** a sitting-room with easy chairs.
love *n.* 1. affection, very strong liking. 2. no score in certain games such as tennis. *v.* **love** to hold in deep affection (**loving, loved**). *adjs.* **lovable, loving.** *n.* **lover** someone with a great liking for a person or thing, as *a lover of music.*
no love lost (between two people) they have no liking for each other.
lovely *adj.* beautiful (*comparative* **lovelier,** *superlative* **loveliest**). *n.* **loveliness** beauty.
low (1) *adj.* 1. not high, as *a low hill.* 2. small, as *a low number.* 3. at the bottom of the scale, as *a low note.* 4. poor, as *to have a low opinion of. adj.* **lowly** humble. *n.* **lowliness.**
the Low Countries Holland and Belgium.
to lay low to kill, to destroy.
to lie low to lie in hiding.
low (2) *v.* to moo like a cow.
low-down *adj* mean, unworthy.
lower *v.* to let down or bring down. *adj.* **lower** less high, smaller, *comparative* of **low.**
lowland *n.* flat low-lying country.
low-spirited *adj.* cast down.
loyal *adj.* faithful and true to friends and country. *adv.* **loyally.** *n.* **loyalty.**
lubricant *n.* oil or grease for a machine.

lubricate *v.* to oil or grease machinery (**lubricating, lubricated**). *n.* **lubrication.**
lucid (*pron.* lōō'sid) *adj.* clear, easy to understand.
luck *n.* chance, fortune. *adj.* **lucky** successful by good chance. *adv.* **luckily** by good fortune.
down on one's luck having bad fortune.
ludicrous (*pron.* lōō'di.krus) *adj.* absurd.
luggage *n.* a traveller's bags.
lukewarm *adj.* 1. not very warm. 2. half-hearted, as *a lukewarm welcome.*
lull *n.* a period of calm in a storm. *v.* **lull** to quieten, to calm.
lullaby *n.* a cradle-song (*pl.* **lullabies**).
lumber *n.* 1. timber, felled trees. 2. useless junk. *v.* **lumber** to move awkwardly, as *the heavy cart lumbered down the lane.* *n.* **lumberman, lumberjack** a man who fells trees and cuts lumber.
luminous *adj.* giving out light, glowing.
lump *n.* 1. a piece of anything. 2. a swelling on the skin. *adj.* **lumpy.**
lunacy *n.* madness.
lunar *adj.* concerning the moon.
lunar month a period of twenty-eight days, compared with a *calendar month* of thirty or thirty-one days.
lunatic *n.* a mad person. *adj.* **lunatic** mad, as *a lunatic plan.*
lunch *n.* 1. the midday meal. 2. something to eat half-way through the morning (*pl.* **lunches**). *n.* **luncheon** another word for lunch.
lung *n.* one of an animal's two breathing organs.
lurch *v.* to roll or stagger, to sway.
to leave in the lurch to desert, to forsake.
lurk *v.* to lie in ambush, to prowl stealthily.
luscious *adj.* sweet and delicious.
lush *adj.* juicy, refreshing, as *lush grass for cattle grazing.*
lust *n.* a strong desire. *v.* **lust** (with **for**) to want strongly. *adv.* **lustily** strongly. *adj.* **lusty** strong.
lute *n.* an old musical instrument with strings plucked by hand.
luxurious *adj.* 1. very comfortable. 2. expensive and rich.

luxury *n.* something expensive and en-joyable, but not really necessary (*pl.* **luxuries**).

lying *present participle* of **lie**.

lynch *v.* to hang someone without trial.

lynx *n.* a kind of wild cat.

lynx-eyed with keen sight.

lyric *n.* 1. the words of a song. 2. a poem set to music. *adj.* **lyrical**.

M

macaroni *n.* long tubes of flour paste, to be boiled and eaten.

mace *n.* 1. a spiked war-club. 2. a staff carried before a mayor or Speaker, as a sign of his authority.

machine *n.* 1. an engine. 2. a combina-tion of wheels and levers to do work.

machinery *n.* 1. engines and machines. 2. the working part of an engine.

mackerel *n.* a sea-fish like a herring (*pl.* **mackerel**).

mad *adj.* 1. insane, without reason. 2. carried away with emotion, as *mad with anger* (*comparative* **madder,** *super-lative* **maddest**). *adv.* **madly**. *n.* **mad-ness**.

madam *n.* 1. a polite way of addressing a lady. 2. the start of a letter to a lady, '*Dear Madam*' (*pl.* **mesdames** *pron.* may'dam).

madden *v.* to make mad.

made *past* of **make**.

Madonna *n.* the Virgin Mary.

magazine *n.* 1. a weekly or monthly publication having pictures, stories, and articles. 2. a storehouse for ammuni-tion. 3. the cartridge-chamber of a rifle.

maggot *n.* the grub or larva of an insect, such as a house-fly. *adj.* **maggoty** full of maggots.

magic *n.* the ability to do things which seem impossible by conjuring, witch-craft, or the help of demons. *adj.* **magical** using magic. *n.* **magician** a wizard.

magistrate *n.* a Justice of the Peace who judges small cases of crime in a local court.

magnet *n.* 1. a bar of iron or steel which draws iron or steel towards it. 2. any attractive person or thing. *adj.* **mag-netic** attractive.

magnetism *n.* power of attraction.

magnetize *v.* 1. to attract. 2. to cause iron or steel to become a magnet (**magnetizing, magnetized**).

magnificent *adj.* splendid, wonderful. *n.* **magnificence**.

magnify *v.* to make something seem larger (**magnifies, magnifying, mag-nified**). *n.* **magnification** enlarge-ment.

magpie *n.* a black-and-white bird re-lated to the crow.

mahogany *n.* a tropical American tree giving hard, reddish-brown wood.

Mahommedan see **Mohammedan**.

maid *n.* 1. a girl. 2. a female servant.

maiden *n.* a girl. *adj.* **maiden** first, as *a maiden voyage of a new liner.*

maiden over (in cricket) an over in which no runs are scored.

mail (1) *n.* armour, especially chain armour, used in olden times. *adj.* **mailed**.

mail (2) *n.* letters and parcels sent by post. *v.* **mail** to send by post.

maim *v.* to cripple some living thing.

main *adj.* chief, most important. *n.* **main** the sea, as *to sail the Spanish Main. adv.* **mainly**.

in the main on the whole.

with might and main with all one's strength.

mainland *n.* the main mass of land, not an island.

mainmast *n.* the chief mast of a ship.

mainstay *n.* the chief support.

maintain *v.* 1. to support. 2. to keep going. 3. to hold strongly to an opinion, as *he maintained that he was right. n.* **maintenance**.

maize *n.* Indian corn.

majestic *adj.* magnificent, noble.

majesty *n.* great power and dignity.

Majesty the title of a king and queen who are addressed as *Your Majesty* (*pl.* **majesties**).

major *adj.* greater. Opposite of **minor** or **lesser**. *n.* **major** an army officer, next above a captain.

majority *n.* 1. the greater number or part, as *the majority of the class were boys.* 2. the number of votes by which the winner leads over his nearest rival. 3. the legal age at which one becomes a man or woman, the age of twenty-one, as *Jack has reached his majority.*

make *v.* 1. to build, produce, create. 2. to gain, as *to make a profit.* 3. to appoint, as *they made him captain.* 4. to amount to, as *that makes a large sum of money.* 5. to force (to), as *I will make you do it* (**making, made**). *n.* **make** a brand, a model, as *this is a good make of car. n.* **maker** someone who makes a thing.

to make amends to make up for.

to make believe to pretend.

to make good to prove a success.

to make much of to make a fuss of.

to make out 1. to argue. 2. to pretend. 3. to just be able to see. 4. to draw up (a list).

to make sure of to be certain of.

to make the best (or most) of to use to the best advantage.

to make up one's mind to decide.

makeshift *adj.* temporary, serving until something better can be used, as *a makeshift ladder.*

malady *n.* an illness, a disease (*pl.* **maladies**).

malaria *n.* a tropical illness caused by mosquito bites.

male *adj.* belonging to the same sex as men or boys, masculine. *n.* **male** a man, boy, or male animal such as a ram, bull, cock, etc. (*fem.* **female**).

malice *n.* ill-will, a wish to harm others.

malicious *adj.* full of spite.

mallet *n.* 1. a wooden hammer. 2. a long wooden stick used in polo and croquet.

malnutrition *n.* having too little food, or the wrong kind of food.

malt *n.* barley, partly sprouted, used in brewing.

maltreat *v.* to ill-treat. *n.* **maltreatment**.

mamma *n.* a child's name for mother.

mammal *n.* an animal that suckles its young.

mammon *n.* wealth, wordly riches.

mammoth *n.* a prehistoric animal like a huge elephant. *adj.* **mammoth** huge.

man *n.* 1. the human race. 2. a male human being over twenty-one years of age. 3. a male servant (*pl.* **men**). *v.* **man** to supply with men, as *to man a boat* (**manning, manned**). *adj.* **manly** like a man. *n.* **manliness** being like a brave man. **manhood** being a man.

man in the street an ordinary man.

man-of-the-world a man with experience of the world.

manage *v.* 1. to take charge of, as *to manage a shop.* 2. to control, as *to manage a horse.* 3. to succeed in doing, as *he managed to swim ashore* (**managing, managed**). *adj.* **manageable** able to be managed. *n.* **manager** someone who takes charge of a business or hotel (*fem.* **manageress**).

management *n.* 1. control. 2. people in charge of a shop, hotel, etc.

man-at-arms *n.* an armed soldier (*pl.* **men-at-arms**).

mandarin *n.* 1. a Chinese official of high rank. 2. a small orange.

mandolin, mandoline *n.* a musical instrument with six or eight strings plucked by hand.

mane *n.* the long hair on the neck of a horse or lion.

manger *n.* a trough or rack holding hay or other food for horses or cattle.

mangle (1) *n.* a machine with rollers for squeezing wet clothes.

mangle (2) *v.* to spoil by cutting and hacking (**mangling, mangled**).

manhole *n.* an opening for a man to enter a tank or sewer.

mania *n.* 1. madness. 2. a strong mad desire, as *a mania for buying clothes.*

manicure *n.* the care of the hands and finger-nails (note: *chiropody* is the care of the feet and toe-nails). *n.* **manicurist** someone who practises manicure.

manipulate *v.* 1. to use tools with one's hands cleverly. 2. to manage affairs cleverly and to advantage (**manipulating, manipulated**). *n.* **manipulation**.

mankind *n.* all people.

manna *n.* (in the Bible) the food of the Israelites in the desert.

mannequin (*pron.* man'i.kin) *n.* a woman employed to show off new clothes.

manner *n.* 1. the way in which something occurs or is done. 2. a style, a custom. *n. pl.* **manners** behaviour. *adj.* **mannerly, well-mannered** courteous, polite.

by no manner of means not at all.

mannerism *n.* some odd habit of speech or behaviour, as *Mr Jones has a mannerism of rubbing his hands when he is speaking.*

man-of-war *n.* a warship.

manor *n.* in olden times, a large estate belonging to a lord.

manse *n.* a Scottish minister's house.

mansion *n.* a very large house.

manslaughter *n.* killing a person unlawfully, but without planning to do so.

mantel *n.* a shelf above a fireplace, the *mantelshelf* or *mantelpiece.*

mantle *n.* a loose cloak.

manual *adj.* done by hand, as *manual work. n.* **manual** a handbook explaining how to do something.

manufacture *v.* to produce goods in quantity in a factory (**manufacturing, manufactured**). *n.* **manufacture** 1. large quantity production. 2. the goods made.

manure *n.* a substance, such as animal droppings, added to land to make it more fertile.

manuscript *n.* a book or paper written by hand.

Manx *adj.* concerning the Isle of Man.
Manx cat a tail-less cat found in the Isle of Man.

many *adj.* and *n.* a great number (*comparative* **more,** *superlative* **most**).

map *n.* a drawing representing some part of the earth's surface. *v.* **map** to draw a map (**mapping, mapped**).
map-reading gaining information from a map.

maple *n.* a Canadian tree with broad leaves.

mar *v.* to damage, to spoil (**marring, marred**).

marble *n.* 1. a form of limestone used for statues and buildings. 2. a small glass or clay ball used by boys in the game of *marbles.*

March (1) *n.* the third month.
mad as a March hare like a hare which in the breeding time jumps as if mad.

march (2) *v.* 1. to walk in step like soldiers. 2. to make someone walk, as *they marched the prisoner to his cell. n.* **march** 1. a walk in step. 2. the distance covered by marching. 3. music for soldiers to march to.
forced march a rapid march.
march past a review of troops.

mare *n.* the female of a horse, donkey, or zebra.
mare's nest a discovery of no importance.

margarine (*pron.* mahr'ga.reen *or* mahr'-ja.reen) *n.* imitation butter.

margin *n.* 1. an edge, a border. 2. the blank edge to a page of a book. *adj.* **marginal.**

marigold *n.* a bright orange garden flower.

marine *adj.* concerning the sea, as *marine plants. n.* **marine** a soldier who serves in the navy.
tell it to the marines a way of saying 'I don't believe it'.

mariner *n.* a sailor.

marionette *n.* a puppet worked by strings (note: a *glove puppet* is worn on the hand).

mark *n.* 1. a scratch or blot. 2. a sign, as *a laundry mark.* 3. a target. 4. an examination score. *v.* **mark** 1. to scratch, stain, or make a mark. 2. to notice. 3. to judge the value of a test. *adj.* **marked** noticeable, graded. *adv.* **markedly** noticeably.
off the mark off to a good start.
to mark time to stay in one place.
up to the mark 1. up to standard. 2. in good health.

market *n.* 1. a public building or place where goods are sold. 2. the business of buying and selling, as *a market in tea* or *the foreign market was weak today. v.* **market** to sell. *adj.* **marketable** able to be sold.

market-garden *n.* land growing produce for market.

market-place *n.* a place where a market is held.

market-town *n.* a country town with a large market.

marmalade *n.* jam made of oranges or lemons.

maroon (1) *n.* a dark red colour.

maroon (2) *v.* to leave someone alone on a desert island.

marquee (*pron.* mar.kee¹) *n.* a large tent.

marriage *n.* a wedding ceremony.

marrow *n.* the fat in the hollow part of bones. 2. vegetable like a huge cucumber.

marry *v.* 1. to become husband and wife. 2. to join together as husband and wife (**marrying, married**).

Mars *n.* the Roman god of war. 2. the planet nearest to the earth.

marsh *n.* swampy ground. *adj.* **marshy**.

marshal *n.* 1. an officer of highest rank, as a *field-marshal* or an *air-marshal*. 2. (in North America) a police or fire brigade chief officer. *v.* **marshal** to arrange in order (**marshalling, marshalled**).

martial *adj.* war-like, military.

martial law military rule in times of riot.

martyr *n.* a person who suffers death for his beliefs. *n.* **martyrdom**.

marvel *n.* a wonderful thing. *v.* **marvel** to wonder at, as *to marvel at a conjuror* (**marvelling, marvelled**). *adj.* **marvellous** amazing.

mascot *n.* a lucky charm, or a pet which is kept to bring luck.

masculine *adj.* belonging to the male sex, manly.

mash *n.* 1. a soft pulp. 2. bran and water for horses. *v.* **mash** to crush into a pulp.

mask *n.* a covering to protect or hide the face. *v.* **mask** 1. to put a mask over the face. 2. to hide emotions, as *to mask a feeling of surprise*.

mason *n.* a worker in stone. *n.* **masonry** stonework.

mass (1) *n.* 1. a large lump or quantity. 2. the greater part, as *the mass of the people were pleased*. 3. the quantity of matter which a body contains. *v.* **mass** to collect, to gather, as *the people massed outside the prison. adj.* **massive** huge.

mass production a method of producing goods on a large scale.

Mass (2) *n.* the celebration of Holy Communion in the Roman Catholic church.

massacre *n.* killing in large numbers.

massage (*pron.* ma.sahzh¹) *n.* rubbing the muscles as a cure for aches and stiffness. *v.* **massage** to rub the body (**massaging, massaged**).

massive *adj.* great and heavy.

mast *n.* a pole to hold up the sails of a ship, a radio aerial, or a flag.

masthead the top of a mast.

master *n.* 1. a man who takes charge. 2. a male teacher. 3. the captain of a merchant ship. 4. an expert or skilled craftsman. *n.* **Master** 1. a title given to a young boy. 2. someone who holds a university degree, as a *Master of Arts*. *adj.* **master** chief. *v.* **master** 1. to overcome. 2. to become an expert.

masterful *adj.* with a commanding manner.

masterly *adj.* expert.

masterpiece *n.* an exceptionally good piece of work.

mastery *n.* power, expert skill.

mastiff *n.* a big powerful dog.

mat *n.* 1. a piece of material to cover a floor. 2. a small piece of cloth for a table, as *a table-mat. v.* **mat** to tangle (**matting, matted**). *adj.* **matted** thick and tangled. *n.* **matting** material used for mats.

matador *n.* the man who kills the bull in a bull-fight.

match (1) *n.* a small tipped splinter of wood which lights when rubbed (*pl.* **matches**).

match-box a box to hold matches.

matchwood very thin wood.

match (2) *v.* to be similar to, to agree with, as *her hat matches her coat. n.* **match** 1. something similar to or agreeing with. 2. an equal in a game, as *he is my match at tennis*. 3. a game, as *a football match* (*pl.* **matches**).

mate *n.* 1. a companion. 2. a husband or wife. 3. an officer in the Merchant Navy below the rank of captain. *v.* **mate** (of people) to marry, (of animals) to pair (**mating, mated**).

material *n.* 1. the substance of which anything is made. 2. a piece of cloth. *adj.* **material** important.

maternal (*pron.* ma.ter'nl) *adj.* concerning a mother, motherly, as *maternal love. n.* **maternity** motherhood.

mathematics *n.* the study of numbers and measurement. *adj.* **mathematical** *n.* **mathematician** someone expert in mathematics.

matinée (*pron.* mat'i.nay) *n.* an afternoon concert or other performance.

matrimony *n.* marriage. *adj.* **matrimonial**.

matron *n.* 1. an elderly married woman. 2. a woman in charge of the nursing in a hospital, or the household management of a boarding school. *adj.* **matronly** like a dignified elderly woman.

matter *n.* 1. the material a thing is made of. 2. pus from a sore. 3. business, an affair, as *it is an important matter. v.* **matter** to be important, as *this matters to me.*

matter-of-fact ordinary, not imaginative.

as a matter of course in the ordinary way.

as a matter of fact in actual fact.

no matter it is not important.

mattress *n.* the soft, springy underpart of a bed.

mature *adj.* full-grown, ripe, fully developed. *v.* **mature** to develop fully **(maturing, matured)** *n.* **maturity**.

mauve (*pron.* mōv) *n.* a light purple colour.

maxim *n.* a guiding rule, as *'honesty is the best policy' is a good maxim.*

maximum *n.* 1. the greatest. 2. the highest point (*pl.* **maxima**). Opposite of **minimum**.

may (1) *auxiliary verb.* 1. to be allowed to, as *she may go.* 2. to be possible, as *it may be so* (*past* **might**).

May (2) *n.* the fifth month.

May-day the 1st of May.

mayflower *n.* the hawthorn.

mayor *n.* the head of the government of a borough or city. *n.* **mayoress** a mayor's wife, or a lady who represents her.

maypole *n.* a pole to dance round on May-day.

maze *n.* 1. a confusing network of passages. 2. a puzzle.

me *pronoun* a form of **I**.

meadow *n.* a field of grass.

meal *n.* 1. grain ground to coarse flour. 2. an occasion for eating food. 3. the food eaten.

mean (1) *adj.* 1. poor, worth little. 2. miserly; as *Tom is too mean to spend any money.* 3. nasty, as *a mean trick. n.* **meanness**.

mean (2) *n.* the middle amount or middle point, the average. See **average**. *advs.* **meantime, meanwhile** during this time. *n. pl.* **means** 1. the cause, as *a means of escape.* 2. riches, as *a man of means.*

by all means certainly.

by any means in any way possible.

by no means certainly not.

mean (3) *v.* 1. to intend, to have in mind. 2. to signify, as *these black clouds mean rain.* 3. to intend for a certain person or purpose, as *this present is meant for you* **(meaning, meant)**. *n.* **meaning** 1. what is meant. 2. an intention. *adj.* **meaning** full of expression, as *a meaning glance. adj.* **meaningless** without meaning.

measles *n.* an infectious illness.

measure *n.* 1. the size or quantity of something. 2. something which tells the size or amount, as a *tape-measure.* 3. an action, as to *take measures to reduce crime.* 4. a slow dance. *v.* **measure** 1. to find the size or amount, as *to measure some cloth.* 2. to ration something in fixed amounts **(measuring, measured)**. *adj.* **measurable** able to be measured. *adj.* **measured** slow and regular, as *he walked with measured steps. n.* **measurement**.

in some measure to some extent.

to measure one's length to fall flat.

meat *n.* animal flesh used for food. *adj.* **meaty** full of meat.

mechanic *n.* a worker using tools and machinery.

mechanical *adj.* 1. concerning machinery. 2. worked by machinery as *a mechanical toy.* 3. done without thinking, as *to work in a mechanical way. adv.* **mechanically.**

mechanism *n.* the working parts of a machine, as *the mechanism of a clock.*

medal *n.* a piece of metal, often attached to a ribbon, given as a reward.

medallion *n.* a large medal or an ornament like a medal.

meddle *v.* to interfere (**meddling, meddled**). *adj.* **meddlesome** fond of interfering.

media see **medium.**

mediaeval or **medieval** (*pron.* med.i.-ee'vl) *adj.* concerning the Middle Ages, from about A.D. 600 to A.D. 1500.

medical *adj.* concerning medicine or doctors, as a *medical student.*

medicine *n.* 1. a liquid or powder which helps to cure an illness. 2. the study of healing the sick.

meditate *v.* to reflect, to think carefully about (**meditating, meditated**). *n.* **meditation.**

medium (1) *adj.* middle, average. *n.* **medium** 1. the middle, the average. 2. the means or the method by which something is done, as *we send letters by the medium of the post office* (*pl.* **media**).

medium (2) *n.* a person who claims to receive messages from spirits (*pl.* **mediums**).

meek *adj.* patient, gentle, mild. *n.* **meekness.**

meet *v.* 1. to come together, to join. 2. to come across, as *he met difficulties* (**meeting, met**). *n.* **meet** a meeting for hunting. *n.* **meeting** a gathering, a coming across.

to meet someone half-way to come to an agreement with him.

megaphone *n.* a large speaking-trumpet.

melancholy *adj.* sad and downcast.

mellow *adj.* 1. ripe, as *mellow fruit.* 2. rich in colour or sound. *v.* **mellow** to become wise and understanding through age.

melodious *adj.* tuneful, pleasant to hear.

melodrama *n.* a very exciting play. *adj.* **melodramatic** very sensational.

melody *n.* 1. a pleasant tune. 2. the part of a song containing the main tune (*pl.* **melodies**).

melon *n.* a very large fruit.

melt *v.* 1. to become liquid with heat. 2. to disappear, as *mist melts in the sun.* 3. to soften, as *his heart melted with pity* (**melting, melted**).

member *n.* 1. someone who belongs to a group or society. 2. an arm or a leg. *n.* **membership** being a member of a group.

memorable *adj.* remarkable, worth remembering.

memorial *n.* a statue or a monument in memory of something. *adj.* **memorial** in memory of someone, as *a memorial service.*

memorize *v.* to learn by heart (**memorizing, memorized**).

memory *n.* 1. the ability to remember. 2. something remembered (*pl.* **memories**).

menace *v.* to threaten (**menacing, menaced**). *n.* **menace** a threat. *adj.* **menacing.**

menagerie *n.* a collection of wild animals for show.

mend *v.* 1. to repair or put right. 2. to get better, as *her health mended.*

on the mend getting better.

menial *adj.* poor, humble, as *menial work.*

mental *adj.* concerning the mind, done in the head, as *mental arithmetic. adv.* **mentally.**

mentality *n.* mental character, intelligence, as *he is a man of high mentality.*

mention *v.* to make a remark about, to speak about casually, as *do not mention it to anyone.*

menu (*pron.* men'yoo) *n.* in a café or hotel, a list of foods to be served.

mercantile *adj.* concerned with trade, as *the mercantile marine is a fleet of trading ships.*

mercenary (*pron.* mer'se.nar.i) *adj.* concerning money, as *he has a mercenary mind and thinks only of money. n.* **mercenary** a hired soldier (*pl.* **mercenaries**).

merchandise *n.* goods bought and sold.

merchant *n.* a man who trades on a big scale. *n.* **merchantman** a trading ship.

merciful see **mercy**.

mercury n. quicksilver, a heavy silvery metal used in thermometers and barometers.

mercy n. 1. forgiveness or kindness to someone in one's power or whom one could hurt. 2. a blessing, as *it is a mercy she was not hurt.* adj. **merciful** showing forgiveness and pity. adj. **merciless** cruel, showing no pity.

at the mercy of in the power of.

mere (1) n. a lake, a large pool.

mere (2) adj. only, nothing but, as *a mere trifle.* adv. **merely** simply, as *I merely asked.*

merge v. to unite, to become one, as *the two shops merged into one big store* (**merging, merged**). n. **merger** a union of two or more firms into one.

merit n. 1. what one deserves, as *they were paid according to their merits.* 2. worth, as *work of great merit.* v. **merit** to deserve, as *to merit praise* (**meriting, merited**). adj. **meritorious** deserving praise.

in order of merit the best first.

mermaid n. a maiden, in fairy-tales, like a fish from the waist downwards.

merry adj. laughing, full of fun (*comparative* **merrier**, *superlative* **merriest**). adv. **merrily**. n. **merriment** fun, gaiety.

merry-go-round wooden horses at a fair on which children sit and are whirled round.

mesh n. one of the openings in a net. v. to bring together two gear-wheels so that one engages the other (*pl.* **meshes**).

mesmerize v. to hypnotize, to force one's will on someone (**mesmerizing, mesmerized**). n. **mesmerism**. See **hypnotize**.

mess n 1. a dirty muddle. 2. a soldiers' or officers' canteen. v. **mess** 1. to dirty. 2. to eat together in a group. adj. **messy**.

message n. a notice sent from one person to another.

messenger n. a person who does an errand or takes a message.

Messiah n. Jesus Christ.

metal n. a substance such as iron, lead, or tin. adj. **metallic** made of metal.

meteor n. a shooting star, which is matter from outer space burning up in the earth's atmosphere.

meteorological adj. concerning the weather.

meteorology n. the study of weather. n. **meteorologist** a man who studies weather.

meter n. a machine which measures gas, electricity, or water.

method n. 1. a way of doing something, a system, a plan, as *the class learned a new method of multiplying fractions.* 2. orderly arrangement, as *Dick set out his stamps with method.* adj. **methodical** orderly and careful.

Methodism n. a Protestant religious denomination founded by John Wesley in the eighteenth century. n. **Methodist** a follower of Methodism.

metre (1) n. the rhythm or pattern of the sounds in poetry or music.

metre (2) n. a measure of length in the metric system, equal to 39·37 inches.

metric adj. concerning measurement.

metric system the system of measurement based on the *metre*. Length is measured in *metres* (m), mass (weight) in *grammes* (g) and volume (or liquid) in *litres* (l).

mew n. the cry of a cat or seagull. v. **mew**.

microbe n. a tiny germ causing disease.

microphone n. an electrical instrument which picks up sounds to be sent through a loudspeaker.

microscope n. an instrument with lenses to make tiny objects appear much larger. adj. **microscopic** too small to be seen except through a microscope.

mid adj. middle, as *mid-winter*.

midday n. noon.

middle n. the centre, halfway between the two ends or edges.

middle-aged about fifty years old.

Middle Ages the time in history between about A.D. 600 and A.D. 1500.

midnight n. twelve o'clock at night.

midshipman n. a junior naval officer below a sub-lieutenant.

midst prep. in the middle of. n. **midst** the middle.

might (1) *past* of **may**.
might-have-been something that could possibly have happened.
might (2) *n*. power, strength. *adj*. **mighty** powerful (*comparative* **mightier,** *superlative* **mightiest**).
migrate *v*. 1. to move to another district or country. 2. (of birds) to fly to a warmer climate each winter, returning in spring (**migrating, migrated**). *n*. **migration**. *adj*. **migratory** in the habit of migrating, as *the swallow is a migratory bird*.
mild *adj*. 1. not extreme, as *a mild climate*. 2. gentle, as *a mild breeze*. *adv*. **mildly**.
mildew *n*. a white fungus growth on damp things.
mile *n*. a length of 1760 yards (1·6 km). *n*. **mileage** 1. distance in miles. 2. (in North America) a travelling allowance at so much a mile. **milestone** *n*. a stone marking a distance in miles.
nautical mile a mile at sea equal to 6080 feet (1,852m).
militant *adj*. war-like.
military *adj*. concerning the army or war, as *a military depot*.
milk *n*. a white fluid with which cows and some other animals feed their young. *adj* **milky**. *n*. **milkiness**.
milk-and-water feeble.
milkman *n*. a man who sells milk.
milksop a soft weak person.
Milky Way the mass of stars clustered together like a white cloud in the sky.
mill *n*. 1. machinery for grinding corn, as a *flour mill*, or for cutting timber, as *a saw-mill*. 2. a large factory, as *a cotton mill*. *v*. **mill** 1. to crush or roll by machine. 3. to move about restlessly, as *the crowd milled in the street*. *n*. **miller** a man in charge of a flour mill.
to go through the mill to gain experience painfully.
millilitre *n*. a thousandth part of a litre.
millimetre *n*. a thousandth part of a metre.
milliner *n*. a woman who makes or sells ladies' hats (note : a *hatter* makes men's hats only). *n*. **millinery** the making of ladies' hats.

million *n*. a thousand thousand or 1,000,000.
millionaire *n*. a rich man with over one million pounds or dollars.
millpond *n*. a pond supplying water to a mill.
millstone *n*. one of the grinding stones of a mill.
mimic *v*. to imitate someone, making fun of his voice and manner (**mimicking, mimicked**). *n*. **mimic** an imitator. *n*. **mimicry**.
minaret *n*. a tall thin tower of a Mohammedan mosque or temple.
mince *v*. to chop into tiny pieces (**mincing, minced**). *n*. **mince** minced meat. *adj*. **mincing** silly, affected, as *to walk with mincing steps*.
not to mince matters, not to mince one's words to speak straight out, to speak frankly.
mincemeat *n*. a mixture of minced fruit, suet, and spice, used in *mince-pies*.
mind *n*. 1. the ability to think. 2. intelligence. 3. memory, as *to keep in mind*. 4. opinion, as *to speak one's mind*. *v*. **mind** 1. to guard, to take care of, as *to mind a baby*. 2. to be careful, as *mind what you do*. 3. to be concerned about, as *I mind what he says*.
absent-minded with thoughts far away.
in two minds undecided.
out of one's mind mad.
presence of mind readiness in an emergency.
to bear in mind to remember.
to make up one's mind to decide.
to mind one's p's and q's to be careful what one says or does.
mine (1) *pronoun* belonging to me, the possessive form of the pronoun **I**.
mine (2) *n*. 1. a tunnel in the earth from which coal or ore is dug. 2. a great store, as *he is a mine of information*. 3. an underground tunnel beneath an enemy's position, filled with explosives. 4. a floating bomb to destroy ships. *n*. **miner** a man who works in a mine.
mine-layer a ship which lays floating mines in wartime.

mineral *n.* 1. a substance obtained by mining. 2. a fizzy drink, short for *mineral-water*.

mingle *v.* to mix, as *they mingled with the crowd* (**mingling, mingled**).

miniature *adj.* copied on a small scale, as *a miniature car for a small boy*. *n.* **miniature** a very small painting or copy.

minimum *n.* the least possible. *adj.* **minimum** the least (*pl.* **minima**). Opposite of **maximum**.

minister *n.* 1. a clergyman. 2. a head of a government department, as the *Foreign Minister*. *v.* **minister** (with **to**) to attend to, to serve, as *to minister to the sick and the aged*. *n.* **ministration**.

ministry *n.* 1. service to others. 2. the profession of clergyman, as *the Baptist ministry*. 3. a government department, as *the Ministry of Labour*.

mink *n.* an animal like a weasel with valuable fur.

minor *n.* a person under the age of twenty-one years. *adj.* **minor** smaller, less important, as *a minor accident*.

minority *n.* 1. being under twenty-one years of age, as *Tom is in his minority*. 2. the smaller of two parts, as *only a minority were against the plan; the majority were in favour*.

minster *n.* 1. an abbey church. 2. a cathedral.

minstrel *n.* a singer of olden days.

mint (1) *n.* a strongly-scented plant used in cooking.
mint-sauce a sauce of vinegar and chopped mint.

mint (2) *n.* a place where coins are made, as *the Royal Mint in London*.

minus *n.* the subtraction sign (−), as 10 − 6 = 4. *prep.* **minus** without, as *minus a leg*.

minute (1) (*pron.* min'it) *n.* 1. the sixtieth part of an hour. 2. (in measuring angles) the sixtieth part of a degree.

minute (2) (*pron.* mī.nyōōt') *adj.* 1. tiny, as *a minute speck*. 2. very exact, as *a minute description*.

miracle *n.* a happening outside the ordinary laws of nature, a marvel. *adj.* **miraculous**.

mirage (*pron.* mi.rahzh') *n.* a trick of light, by which in hot countries one sees things which are really elsewhere, due to the heat affecting the air.

mirror *n.* a looking-glass. *v.* **mirror** to reflect an image from water or glass.

mis- *prefix* wrongly, as *misfit*, to fit badly, or *misjudge*, to judge wrongly.

misadventure *n.* an unlucky happening.

misbehave *v.* to behave badly (**misbehaving, misbehaved**). *n.* **misbehaviour**.

miscellaneous (*pron.* mis.e.lay'ni.us) *adj.* mixed, made up of different kinds, as *a miscellaneous collection of toys*. *n.* **miscellany** a jumble.

mischief *n.* 1. harm, damage. 2. annoying behaviour. 3. thoughtless tricks. *adj.* **mischievous** (*pron.* mis'chi.vus) fond of mischief.

misdeed *n.* a bad action, a crime.

miser *n.* a man who hoards money greedily. *adj.* **miserly**.

miserable *adj.* 1. unhappy, downcast. 2. poor and wretched.

misery *n.* 1. great unhappiness. 2. wretchedness.

misfire *n.* (of an explosive) to fail to go off (**misfiring, misfired**).

misfit *n.* 1. something which does not fit, as *this coat is a misfit*. 2. someone not suitable for his work.

misfortune *n.* bad luck.

misgiving *n.* doubt, suspicion, as *they had misgivings about the new plan*.

mishap *n.* an unfortunate accident.

mislay *v.* to forget where something has been left, as *Sheila mislaid her purse* (**mislaying, mislaid**).

mislead *v.* to give someone a wrong idea or the wrong information, as *Jean misled us into thinking the party was today* (**misleading, misled**).

misplace *v.* to put in the wrong place (**misplacing, misplaced**).

Miss (1) *n.* the title of a girl or unmarried woman, as *Miss Sheila Jones* (*pl.* **Misses**).

miss (2) *v.* 1. to fail to find, reach, hit, catch, or hear something. 2. to notice someone is not present, as *we missed Joan at the ball*. 3. to be sorry someone is absent or dead, as *Tom misses his mother*. *n.* **miss** 1. a failure to hit, catch, etc. 2. an escape.

missile n. something fired or thrown, as a shell or bullet.

guided missile a rocket or shell directed by radio.

missing adj. lost, not to be found.

mission n. 1. an important errand. 2. a group of people sent on some special business abroad. 3. an important operation in warfare. 4. a religious organization for spreading the Gospel.

missionary n. someone who spreads the Gospel in some foreign land (pl. **missionaries**).

mist n. water particles in the air, haziness. adj. **misty**. n. **mistiness**.

mistake n. something done or said wrongly, an error. v. **mistake** 1. to understand something wrongly. 2. to confuse one person or thing with another, as I mistook your pen for mine (**mistaking, mistook, mistaken**).

mistaken adj. wrong, not understood rightly, as a mistaken belief.

mister n. a man's title, written Mr for short, as Mr John Bell.

mistletoe n. an evergreen plant with white berries which grows on certain trees.

mistook past of **mistake**.

mistress n. 1. a woman in charge of a house. 2. a woman teacher. 3. a very skilled woman, as she is mistress of her trade.

mistrust v. not to trust, to doubt. n. **mistrust** doubt, suspicion. adj. **mistrustful**.

misunderstand v. not to understand, to mistake the meaning of (**misunderstanding, misunderstood**).

misunderstanding n. 1. a disagreement, a quarrel. 2. a wrong belief, a mistaken idea.

misunderstood past of **misunderstand**.

misuse (pron. mis.yo͞oz') v. to use wrongly (**misusing, misused**). n. **misuse** (pron. mis.yo͞os') the wrong use of something, ill-treatment.

mite n. 1. a tiny insect. 2. a small coin mentioned in the Bible (the widow's mite). 3. a small child.

mitre n. 1. a hat worn by bishops and archbishops. 2. (in woodwork) a joint with slanting edges used at corners of boxes.

mitten n. a glove covering the four fingers all together, or leaving the fingers bare.

mix v. 1. to stir together. 2. for people to move among one another. 3. to mistake one thing for another, as to mix two addresses. adj. **mixed** made up of different kinds. n. **mixture**.

a good mixer someone sociable who gets on well with others.

mix-up confusion.

moan v. to make a noise of pain or sorrow. n. **moan** a low noise of pain.

moat n. a deep ditch round a castle.

mob n. an unruly crowd. v. **mob** to attack in big numbers (**mobbing, mobbed**).

mobile adj. 1. movable, as mobile artillery. 2. moving about, as mobile police patrols. n. **mobility**.

moccasin n. 1. a soft leather shoe worn by North American Indians. 2. a poisonous snake of the U.S.A.

mock v. to make fun of, to jeer at. n. **mockery**.

mocking-bird an American bird which imitates other birds.

mock-turtle soup soup like turtle soup but made of calf's head.

model n. 1. a small copy, as a model of a train. 2. a good example, as Dick is a model of what a Scout should be. 3. someone who poses for an artist, or who shows off clothes. 4. a style, as the Spring models are in the shops. v. **model** 1. to make models. 2. to pose, or show off dresses (**modelling, modelled**). adj. **model** 1. a good example, as a model Girl Guide. 2. copied, as a model train. n. **modelling** making models, or showing off dresses.

moderate (pron. mod'er.ayt) v. to become calmer, as the storm is moderating (**moderating, moderated**). adj. **moderate** (pron. mod'er.it) medium, average, fairly good, as Jean's work is moderate.

modern adj. up to date. Opposite of **old-fashioned**.

modest adj. 1. not showy or boastful, quiet and shy. 2. small, as a modest wage. n. **modesty**.

Mohammedan *n.* a follower of Mohammed. *adj.* **Mohammedan** concerning Mohammed or his religion. *n.* **Mohammedism** the religion of Mohammed as written in the holy book of the Mohammedans, the Koran.

moist *adj.* slightly wet. *v.* **moisten** to dampen. *n.* **moisture**.

molasses *n.* syrup made from sugar.

mole (1) *n.* a dark spot on the skin.

mole (2) *n.* a small burrowing animal which leaves *molehills* on the ground.

to make a mountain of a molehill to make a fuss of nothing.

molten *adj.* melted, as *molten metal*.

moment *n.* 1. an instant of time. 2. importance, as *this is a matter of some moment*.

momentary *adj.* for a moment.

momentum *n.* the force of a moving body, as *the bicycle gained momentum as it sped downhill*.

monarch *n.* a king, queen, or sovereign.

monarchy *n.* rule by a monarch.

monastery *n.* a house in which monks live (*pl.* **monasteries**). *adj.* **monastic** concerning monks.

Monday *n.* the day after Sunday.

money *n.* coins and paper-notes used for buying (*pl.* **moneys** or **monies**).

mongoose *n.* a ferret-like animal of India which kills snakes (*pl.* **mongooses**).

mongrel *n.* an animal (especially a dog) of mixed breed.

monitor *n.* 1. a schoolboy or girl with special duties. 2. a small battleship. 3. a large lizard.

monk *n.* a man devoted to religion who lives with other monks in a monastery (*fem.* **nun**).

monkey *n.* an animal living in the trees of tropical forests (*pl.* **monkeys**).

monkey-nut a peanut or African groundnut.

monkey-wrench an adjustable spanner.

to monkey with to play the fool with.

mono- *prefix* one, single, as *a monorail is a railway with cars hanging from one rail*.

monogram *n.* someone's initials woven into a pattern.

monologue *n.* a speech by one actor in a play.

monopoly *n.* the sole possession of, or right to sell, certain goods.

monotonous *adj.* always the same, dull and boring.

monotony *n.* dullness, sameness.

monsoon *n.* a wind blowing over the Indian Ocean bringing heavy rain to the land in summer.

monster *n.* 1. anything deformed or ugly. 2. a huge frightening creature.

monstrous *adj.* 1. huge and ugly. 2. wicked, as *a monstrous crime*. *n.* **monstrosity** an ugly or wicked thing.

month *n.* one of the twelve parts of the year.

calendar month one of the twelve parts of the year, varying from twenty-eight to thirty-one days.

lunar month a period of twenty-eight days, from one new moon to the next, making thirteen in one year.

monument *n.* a statue or building in memory of someone or something.

monumental *adj.* 1. concerning a monument, as *a monumental mason makes monuments*. 2. huge, impressive.

mood *n.* a state of mind, temper, as *Father is in a good mood*.

moon *n.* 1. the satellite moving round the earth every twenty-eight days. 2. a satellite moving round a planet, as *Jupiter has nine moons*.

moonbeam, moonlight light from the moon.

once in a blue moon very rarely.

moor (1) *n.* open waste land covered with grass and heather. *n.* **moorland**.

moor (2) *v.* to fasten a ship with cable or anchor. *n. pl.* **moorings** a ship's anchorage.

moose *n.* a North American deer like the elk (*pl.* **moose**).

mop *n.* a bundle of rags at the end of a stick, used for cleaning. *v.* **mop** to use a mop (**mopping, mopped**).

moral *n.* a lesson from a story or happening, as *the moral Billy learnt from the story was always to tell the truth*. *adj.* **moral** good, decent, as *to live a moral* *life. n. pl.* **morals** behaviour, as *a man of fine morals. n.* **morality** good conduct. *adv.* **morally.**

morale *n.* good spirits, as *the troops were in a state of high morale.*

more *adj* 1. greater, as *take more care.* 2. extra, as *he ate one more cake* (*superlative* **most**).

once more again.

moreover *adv.* besides, in addition.

morning *n.* the time before noon.

morris-dance *n.* an English country dance.

morrow *n.* the next day, tomorrow.

Morse code *n.* a system of sending signals by dots and dashes, invented by Samuel Morse.

morsel *n.* a tiny piece of food, as *a morsel of cheese.*

mortal *n.* a human being. *adj.* **mortal** deadly, as *a mortal injury. adv.* **mortally** causing death, as *mortally wounded. n.* **mortality** death.

mortar *n.* 1. a mixture of lime, sand, and water, used for laying bricks. 2. a bowl in which substances are crushed or mixed. 3. a short cannon.

mortuary *n.* a place where the bodies of people who are killed in accidents are kept.

mosaic *n.* a design made of small pieces of coloured glass or stone.

Moslem. See **Muslim.**

mosque *n.* a Mohammedan place of worship.

mosquito *n.* a gnat which in hot countries carries malaria fever (*pl.* **mosquitoes**).

moss *n.* a small plant growing as a thin green covering on damp places. *adj.* **mossy** covered with moss.

most *adj.* and *n.* the greatest amount, as *John has most of the apples* (*superlative* of **much** and **many**). *adv.* **mostly** chiefly.

moth *n.* 1. an insect like a butterfly which flies by night. 2. an insect which lays eggs in clothes.

moth-ball a strong-smelling ball which drives moths away from clothes.

moth-eaten eaten by moths' grubs.

mother *n.* a female parent. *v.* **mother** to care for like a mother. *adj.* **motherly** like a mother. *n.* **motherhood** being a mother.

mother-in-law the mother of a husband or of a wife (*pl.* **mothers-in-law**).

mother-of-pearl the lining of an oyster shell, used for making buttons.

mother tongue one's own language.

motherland one's own country.

motion *n.* movement. *adj.* **motionless** still.

motive *n.* the reason for doing something, as *the motive for a crime. adj.* **motive** causing movement, as *the motive power of steam or electricity.*

motor *n.* 1. a machine that makes something move. 2. a motor-car or automobile. *adj.* **motor** worked by a motor as *a motor-cycle* or *a motor-boat. n.* **motorist** a driver of a motor-car.

motto *n.* an inspiring saying or slogan such as 'never yield' (*pl.* **mottoes**).

mould *n.* 1. mildew, a fungus growing in damp places. *adj.* **mouldy.**

mould (2) *n.* 1. a hollow pattern or shape into which molten metal is poured to cast it into a shape. 2. a similar mould for jellies.

moulding *n.* 1. something moulded. 2. an ornament on a building.

moult *v.* for animals or birds to cast off fur or feathers at certain seasons. *n.* **moult** the seasonal shedding of fur or feathers, by certain animals or birds.

mound *n.* a heap of earth or stones, a small hill.

mount *v.* 1. to climb, as *to mount stairs.* 2. to get on to, as *to mount a horse.* 3. to fix, as *to mount a picture on cardboard. n.* **mount** 1. a high hill. 2. a cardboard backing for a picture. 3. a horse for riding.

mountain *n.* a very high hill. *adj.* **mountainous** having many mountains. *n.* **mountaineer** a man who climbs mountains.

mourn *v.* to feel deep sorrow. *adj.* **mournful** sorrowful. *n.* **mourner** someone at a funeral.

in mourning dressed in funeral clothes.

mouse *n.* a small, long-tailed gnawing animal (*pl.* **mice**). *adj.* **mousy** like a mouse.

moustache *n.* hair on a man's top lip.

mouth *n.* 1. the opening in the head for speaking and eating. 2. any opening, as *the mouth of a river or cave* (*pl.* **mouths** *pron.* mowTHz). *n.* **mouthful** (*pl.* **mouthfuls**).

down in the mouth downhearted.

living from hand to mouth living from day to day with nothing kept for the future.

mouth-organ *n.* a musical wind-instrument played with the mouth.

mouthpiece *n.* 1. the part of a wind-instrument put in the mouth. 2. some-one who speaks for others.

move *v.* 1. to pass from place to place. 2. to set in motion. 3. to arouse through emotion, as *anger moved him.* 4. to propose at a meeting, as *Mr Smith moved a vote of thanks to the speaker* (**moving, moved**) 1. a change from place to place. 2. some action that has taken place. *adj.* **movable** able to be moved. *n. pl.* **movables** goods, furniture. *n.* **movement** 1. change. 2. a united effort, as *a movement for more hospitals.* 3. the working parts of a clock or watch.

moving *adj.* pathetic, touching, as *a moving scene in a play.*

mow *v.* to cut grass or corn with a scythe or machine (**mowing, mowed, mowed** or **mown**). *n.* **mower** a machine which mows, a man who mows.

much *adj.* and *n.* a great deal (*comparative* **more**, *superlative* **most**).

to make much of to make a fuss of.

too much for too clever or strong for.

mud *n.* wet soil. *adj.* **muddy**.

mud-guard a cover for a wheel to stop mud from flying up.

muddle *n.* confusion. *v.* **muddle** to cause confusion (**muddling, muddled**).

muffle *v.* 1. to wrap up for warmth. 2. to deaden the sound of a drum or bell by wrappings (**muffling, muffled**). *n.* **muffler** a scarf.

mug *n.* a thick cup with a handle.

mule *n.* 1. an animal half donkey and half horse. 2. a stubborn person. 3. a cotton-spinning machine. *adj.* **mulish** obstinate.

multi- *prefix* many, as *multi-coloured*, many-coloured.

multiple *adj.* having many parts. *n.* **multiple** a number which contains another number an exact number of times, as *15 is a multiple of 5.*

lowest common multiple (L.C.M.) the smallest number into which other numbers will divide, as *the lowest common multiple of 5, 8, and 10 is 40.*

multiple store one of a number of shops owned by the same firm.

multiply *v.* 1. to increase, as *the worms are multiplying on the lawn.* 2. to increase a quantity a number of times, as *3 multiplied by 2 equals 6* (**multiplying, multiplied**). *n.* **multiplication**.

multitude *n.* a great crowd.

mum *adj.* silent.

mumble *v.* to speak softly and indistinctly (**mumbling, mumbled**).

mummy (1) *n.* a dead body preserved by embalming, especially in ancient Egypt.

mummy (2) *n.* a child's word for mother.

mumps *n.* a swelling of the neck.

munch *v.* to chew in a noisy way.

municipal *adj.* concerning a town or city, as *a municipal park.*

murder *n.* the unlawful and deliberate killing of a human being. *v.* **murder** to kill someone unlawfully and deliberately. *n.* **murderer** (*fem.* **murderess**). *adj.* **murderous** intending to murder.

murky *adj.* dim and gloomy.

murmur *n* 1. a low indistinct sound, or a low humming sound, as *the murmur of bees.* 2. a grumble. *v.* **murmur** to make a low sound (**murmuring, murmured**).

muscle *n.* a tissue found in various parts of the body which causes limbs to move. *adj.* **muscular**.

muse (1) *v.* to think deeply, or to be lost in thought (**musing, mused**).

Muse (2) *n.* in ancient Greek stories, one of the nine goddesses of the arts.

museum *n.* a building for displaying rare and interesting objects.

mush *n.* a soft mixture like porridge. *adj.* **mushy**.

mushroom *n.* an umbrella-shaped fungus plant which grows quickly and can be cooked and eaten.

music *n.* the art of making a succession of pleasing sounds. *adj.* **musical**. *n.* **musician** a person who composes or plays music.

musical box a box which gives out music when wound up, or by turning a handle.

musical comedy a light play with music and songs.

muskeg *n.* (in Canada) a swamp or marsh.

musket *n.* an old-fashioned smooth-bore gun.

musketeer *n.* a soldier who carried a musket.

musk-rat *n.* a North American animal like a water-rat, a musquash.

Muslim *n.* a follower of Mohammed, a Moslem. See **Mohammedan**.

muslin *n.* 1. a soft cotton cloth. 2. (in North America) a heavier cotton cloth used for sheets.

musquash see **musk-rat**.

mussel *n.* a shellfish with a double dark blue shell.

Mussulman *n.* a Mohammedan.

must *v.* used before another verb, meaning 'forced to' or 'ought to', as *I must do it* or *you must come and visit us*.

mustang *n.* an American prairie horse.

mustard *n.* a yellow powder made from the seeds of the mustard-plant, used as a seasoning for food.

musty *adj.* stale, smelling of damp. *n.* **mustiness**.

mute *adj.* dumb, speechless. *n.* **mute** 1. a dumb person. 2. a clip or muffle to soften the sound of a musical instrument.

mutineer *n.* someone who rebels against those in authority, and joins a mutiny.

mutiny *n.* a rebellion of soldiers or sailors against their officers (*pl.* **mutinies**). *adj.* **mutinous** taking part in a mutiny.

mutter *v.* 1. to speak in a low indistinct voice. 2. to grumble in low tones.

mutton *n.* meat from a sheep.

mutual *adj.* shared or exchanged between two people, as *mutual hatred, each hating the other. adv.* **mutually**.

muzzle *n.* 1. the jaws and nose of an animal. 2. a leather cover over an animal's jaws. 3. the open end of a gun. *v.* **muzzle** 1. to tie up the jaws of an animal. 2. to suppress a person or a newspaper from giving opinions, as *to muzzle the press* (**muzzling, muzzled**).

my *adj.* belonging to me.

myself *pron.* concerning me, as *I hurt myself*.

mysterious *adj.* full of mystery, secret.

mystery *n.* something secret or unexplained, as *it is a mystery how he opened the locked door* (*pl.* **mysteries**).

mystic, mystical *adj.* mysterious.

mystify *v.* to puzzle, to bewilder (**mystifying, mystified**).

myth *n.* a legend, an imaginary story of olden times. *adj.* **mythical** *n.* **mythology** a study of, or collection of, ancient tales.

N

nab (*slang*) *v.* to grab (**nabbing, nabbed**).

nag (1) *n.* a poor kind of horse.

nag (2) *v.* to pester or scold, to worry constantly (**nagging, nagged**).

nail *n.* 1. the horny end of a finger or toe. 2. a small metal spike to be driven into wood. *v.* **nail** to fasten with nails.

to hit the nail on the head to state the most important point of a matter.

naïve (*pron.* nah.eev') *adj.* simple, innocent, as *a naïve remark*.

naked *adj.* unclothed, bare.

with the naked eye without the help of glasses.

name *n.* 1. what a person or thing is called. 2. reputation, character, as *Mr White has a good name. adv.* **namely** that is to say.

namesake someone with the same name as someone else.

nap (1) *n.* a short sleep. *v.* **nap** to sleep for a while (**napping, napped**).
to be caught napping to be caught unawares.
nap (2) *n.* the short hairs on some cloths.
nape *n.* the back of the neck.
napkin *n.* 1. a small cloth or paper square to· spread on the lap while eating. 2. a small towel pinned round a baby (a *diaper* in North America).
narcissus *n.* a spring flower which grows from a bulb (*pl.* **narcissuses** or **narcissi**).
narrate *v.* to describe, to tell a story (**narrating, narrated**). *n.* **narrative** a story.
narrow *adj.* 1. small in width, as *a narrow gate*. 2. not understanding or sympathetic, as *a narrow-minded man*.
narrow escape a close escape.
nasal *adj.* 1. concerning the nose. 2. sounding from the nose, as *a nasal voice*.
nasturtium *n.* a plant with red or yellow flowers.
nasty *adj.* 1. dirty, unpleasant, as *a nasty mess*. 2. serious, as *a nasty cut* (*comparative* **nastier,** *superlative* **nastiest**). *adv.* **nastily.** *n.* **nastiness**.
nation *n.* a country and its people.
national *adj.* concerning a nation.
national anthem the official song of a nation.
nationality *n.* the fact of belonging to a nation, as *he is of British nationality*.
nationalize *v.* for the government to make some great industry belong to the nation and not to private firms, as *in Britain the railways are nationalized* (**nationalizing, nationalized**). *n.* **nationalization**.
native *n.* someone belonging to a place by birth, as *he is a native of Bristol. adj.* **native** belonging by birth, as *my native land*.
nativity *n.* birth.
the Nativity the birth of Christ.
natural *adj.* 1. found in nature, as *a natural talent* or *natural pearls*. 2. inborn, as *it is natural for ducks to swim.* 3. (in music) not sharp or flat, as *the note 'B natural'. adv.* **naturally** 1. as one would expect, as *naturally I thanked*

him. 2. by nature, as *she was naturally good at sewing*.
naturalist *n.* a man who studies plants and animals.
nature *n.* 1. the world and all things not made by man. 2. the character of a thing, as *it is a lion's nature to be cruel*. 3. sort, kind, as *things of that nature do not interest me*.
naught *n.* nothing, nought. See **nought**.
to come to naught to fail.
naughty *adj.* badly behaved. *n.* **naughtiness**.
nautical *adj.* concerning ships, sailors, or the sea.
naval *adj.* concerning the navy, as *a naval battle*.
nave *n.* the central part of a church.
navigable *adj.* 1. (of a river) deep enough for ships to sail over. 2. (of a boat) seaworthy.
navigate *v.* to guide a ship or aircraft (**navigating, navigated**). *n.* **navigation** sailing, steering. *n.* **navigator** someone who directs the course of a ship or aircraft.
navy *n.* a country's warships with their crews (*pl.* **navies**).
navy blue dark blue.
nay *adv.* an old word for 'no'.
neap *adj.* low.
neap tide a low tide about the first and last quarter of the moon.
near *adj.* 1. not far off. 2. closely related, as *a near relative*. 3. on the left side, as *the near front wheel of a car* (*comparative* **nearer,** *superlative* **nearest**). *adv.* **near** close. *v.* **near** to draw near. *adj.* **near-by** very close. *adv.* **nearly** closely. *n.* **nearness**.
near at hand close by.
Near East Turkey, Palestine, and near-by countries.
near miss a narrow escape.
near-sighted *adj.* only able to see clearly things which are near.
neat *adj.* 1. clean and tidy. 2. carefully finished.
necessary *adj.* what has to be done.
necessity *n.* something one cannot do without, as *food is a necessity* (*pl.* **necessities**). *v.* **necessitate** to force, to compel.

necessity is the mother of invention one is forced to be inventive when the need is great.

neck *n.* the part of the body that supports the head.

neck and neck side by side in a race.

neck or nothing risking all to win.

necklace *n.* a string of beads or pearls round the neck.

nectar *n.* 1. (in Greek stories) the wine of the gods. 2. the sweet juice of flowers, collected by bees for honey.

need *v.* to require. *n.* **need** 1. a want, as *there is a need for more hospitals.* 2. poverty, distress, as *this poor man is in great need. adj.* **needful** necessary. *adj.* **needless** not necessary.

needy poor, requiring help.

if need be if necessary.

needle *n.* 1. a thin, sharp spike of steel with a hole (or 'eye') used for sewing, or a longer, thicker spike without an eye used for knitting. 2. a mounted magnetized pointer to show the magnetic north. 3. a metal pointer on a measuring instrument. 4. anything sharp and pointed, as *a pine needle.*

negative *adj.* 1. saying 'no', as *a negative reply.* 2. less than nothing, to be subtracted or taken away, as *−4 is a negative number. n.* **negative** 1 (in electricity) of the opposite charge to *positive.* 2. (in photography) the picture on the film, in which black and white are reversed, and from which the positive or print is made.

neglect *n.* not doing what ought to be done, lack of attention. *v.* **neglect** not to take care of, as *to neglect a bicycle. adj.* **neglectful.**

negligence *n.* lack of care.

negligent *adj.* careless.

negligible *adj.* too small to require attention, as *the small leak in the boat is negligible.*

negotiate *v.* 1. to discuss and make some arrangement, as *to negotiate a business deal.* 2. to get over an obstacle, as *the horse negotiated the jump* (**negotiating, negotiated**). *n.* **negotiation.**

Negro *n.* a black-skinned man of African race (*fem.* **Negress,** *pl.* **Negroes**).

neigh *v.* to make a noise like a horse. *n.* **neigh** the noise made by a horse.

neighbour *n.* someone who lives nearby.

neighbourly friendly.

neighbouring near by.

neighbourhood the district around.

neither (*pron.* nī'THer *or* nee'THer) *adj.* not one or the other. *conj.* **neither** nor, as *she did not come, neither did she write.* (Note : **neither** may be followed by **nor,** as *neither she nor I would go.* The word **either** is followed by **or,** as *either Tom or Mary will go.*)

neon *n.* a gas which gives a red glow when electricity passes through it, used in *neon lamps.*

nephew *n.* the son of a brother or sister (*fem.* **niece**).

nerve *n.* 1. one of the fibres carrying feelings to and from the brain to all parts of the body. 2. courage, as *John faced the angry dog with plenty of nerve. v.* **nerve** to gather courage, as *Anne nerved herself to dive into the water* (**nerving, nerved**). *adj.* **nerveless** without strength. *adj.* **nervous** timid. *n.* **nervousness.**

to get on one's nerves to irritate.

nest *n.* 1. a home made by birds for their young. 2. a breeding-place made by wasps, a *wasps' nest.* 3. a group of tables fitting within one another, a *nest of tables. n.* **nestling** a young bird in its nest.

to feather one's nest to get rich by any means.

nestle *v.* to press snugly and warmly against someone or something (**nestling, nestled**).

net (1) *n.* 1. a fabric of string or wire, with large spaces between the strings or wires. 2. a piece of this fabric, as a *tennis net,* a *fishing net,* a woman's *hair-net,* or a *mosquito net* for keeping out mosquitoes in hot countries. *v.* **net** to catch in a net (**netting, netted**).

net (2) or **nett** *adj.* remaining after allowances are made, as *the net profit is what remains after expenses are paid.*

netball *n.* a ball game between two teams, seven players a side, in which the ball is thrown into a net.

nett see **net**.

netting *n*. a piece of net, as *wire-netting*.

nettle *n*. a plant with stinging hairs. *v*. **nettle** to vex someone (**nettling, nettled**).

neuter *adj*. neither masculine nor feminine.

neutral *adj*. 1. taking no side in a quarrel or in a war. 2. having little colour, as *grey is a neutral colour*. 3. mid-way between extremes, neither good nor bad, strong nor weak, acid nor alkaline. *n*. **neutrality** being neutral.

neutralize *v*. to make something harmless and not active, as *to neutralize a poison with medicine* (**neutralizing, neutralized**).

never *adv*. not once, not ever.

nevermore never again.

nevertheless however.

new *adj*. 1. never known or seen before. 2. not old, fresh. *n*. **newness** freshness.

new moon the moon when a crescent of light can first be seen.

New World North and South America.

new-fangled new, but of little value.

newcomer *n*. someone just arrived.

news *n*. information about what has just happened.

newsagent *n*. a newspaper-seller.

newsboy *n*. a boy who delivers papers.

newspaper *n*. a daily or weekly paper containing news.

news-reel *n*. a cinema film showing news in pictures.

newt *n*. a small animal like a lizard, but developed from newt-spawn and living on land and water.

next *adj*. 1. nearest, as *the next village*. 2. the one after, as *the next day*. *adv*. **next** immediately after, as *we came next*.

next door in the next house.

next of kin the nearest relatives.

nib *n*. a metal pen-point.

nibble *v*. to take small bites (**nibbling, nibbled**).

nice *adj*. 1. pleasant, as *a nice day*. 2. careful, exact, as *he has a nice sense of duty* (*comparative* **nicer**, *superlative* **nicest**). *adv*. **nicely**. *n*. **nicety** exactness, as *it fits to a nicety*.

nick *n*. a slit, a small slot.

in the nick of time just in time.

nickel *n*. 1. a silvery metal used in alloys. 2. (in North America) a five-cent piece.

nickname *n*. a familiar name given in place of the real one, as *Harry Clark was known by the nickname of 'Nobby'*.

niece *n*. the daughter of a brother or sister (*masc*. **nephew**).

night *n*. the time between sunset and sunrise. *adv*. **nightly** every night.

nightdress, nightshirt *ns*. garments worn in bed.

nightingale *n*. a bird whose song is often heard at night.

nightmare *n*. a frightening dream.

nil *n*. nothing, as *the score was two–nil*.

nimble *adj*. quick and active. *adv*. **nimbly**. *n*. **nimbleness**.

nine *n*. one more than eight, represented by 9 or IX. *adj*. **ninth**.

nine days' wonder an exciting event which is soon forgotten.

nineteen *n*. one more than eighteen, represented by 19 or XIX. *adj*. **nineteenth**.

ninety *n*. ten times nine, represented by 90 or XC. *adj*. **ninetieth**.

nip *v*. 1. to pinch. 2. to damage by frost or wind (**nipping, nipped**).

no *n*. 1. a refusal. 2. a vote against (*pl*. **noes**). *adv*. **no** not at all, as *I am no better*.

nobility *n*. 1. greatness of character. 2. people of high rank and noble birth, as dukes and earls.

noble *n*. a man of high rank. *adj*. **noble** 1. great of character. 2. to be admired, as *a noble sight*. *n*. **nobleman** a noble.

noble-minded good and generous.

nobody *pronoun* no one. *n*. **nobody** a person of no importance.

nod *n*. a quick up-and-down shake of the head. *v*. **nod** 1. to say 'yes' with a nod. 2. to be half asleep. (**nodding, nodded**).

Noel *n*. 1. Christmas. 2. a Christmas carol.

noise *n*. a sound, a disturbance. *adj*. **noisy** (*comparative* **noisier**, *superlative* **noisiest**). *n*. **noisiness**. *adj*. **noiseless** silent.

nomad *n.* a member of a tribe wandering from place to place in search of food. *adj.* **nomadic**.

nominate *v.* to put forward someone's name at an election (**nominating, nominated**). *n.* **nomination**.

non- *prefix* not; thus *non-stop* means not stopping, as *a non-stop bus service*.

none *pronoun* no one, not any.

nonsense *n.* foolishness, silly talk. *adj.* **nonsensical**.

nook *n.* a sheltered corner.

to search in every nook and cranny to look everywhere.

noon, noonday, noontide *n.* midday.

noose (*pron.* nōōs) *n.* 1. a loop made with a slip-knot which tightens when pulled. 2. a snare to catch wild animals.

nor *conj.* and not, used after **neither** (note: **nor** is used after **neither,** and **or** after **either**).

normal *adj.* ordinary, as usual. *adj.* **normally**.

normal school (in North America) a training-college for teachers.

north *n.* 1. one of the four compass points, to the left of a person facing the sunrise. 2. the part of the country lying to the north, as *the north of Britain*. *adj.* **north** 1. concerning the north. 2. from the north, as *a north wind*. *adj.* **northerly** (*pron.* norTH'er.li) from the north. *adj.* **northern** to, of, or from the north. *adv.* **northwards** to the north.

northeast half-way between north and east.

northern lights a greenish light sometimes seen in the north sky, called the Aurora Borealis.

north pole the northern end of the axis about which the earth spins.

north star the Pole Star, very nearly over the north pole.

northwest half-way between north and west.

nose *n.* the part of the face through which one smells.

to cut off one's nose to spite one's face to harm oneself in a fit of temper.

to keep one's nose to the grindstone to work very hard.

to turn up one's nose at to refuse with contempt.

nostril *n.* one of the two openings in the nose.

not *adv.* a word meaning refusal or denial.

notable *adj.* 1. remarkable, as *a notable event*. 2. distinguished, as *a notable visitor*. *adv.* **notably** particularly.

notch *n.* a nick, a small cut (*pl.* **notches**). *v.* **notch** to make a small cut.

note *n.* 1. a written reminder, short letter, or notice. 2. a piece of paper-money, as *a bank-note*. 3. a musical sound, or a sign on a sheet of music standing for a sound. 4. importance, reputation, as *he is a man of some note*. *v.* **note** to pay attention to, to notice (**noting, noted**). *adj.* **noted** well-known. *adj.* **noteworthy** worthy of notice.

note-book *n.* a small book in which to write notes.

note-paper *n.* writing-paper for letters.

nothing *n.* 1. not anything. 2. (in arithmetic) a nought, zero.

to come to nothing to prove a failure.

notice *n.* 1. an announcement. 2. a warning, as *the cook gave a week's notice that she would leave*. *v.* **notice** to see, to observe (**noticing, noticed**). *adj.* **noticeable** easily seen.

notice-board a board for notices.

to take notice to pay attention.

notify *v.* to let it be known (**notifying, notified**). *n.* **notification**.

notion *n.* an idea, a belief, a fancy. *n. pl.* **notions** (in North America) small articles, such as pins and tape.

notorious *adj.* well-known for being bad, as *a notorious criminal*. *n.* **notoriety**.

notwithstanding *prep.* in spite of.

nougat (*pron.* noo'ga) *n.* a sweet containing chopped nuts.

nought *n.* nothing, zero.

noun *n.* a word used to name a person or thing, as *pen, Tom, and colour are nouns*.

nourish *v.* 1. to feed. 2. to encourage, as *to nourish the will to do good*. *n.* **nourishment** food and drink. *adj.* **nourishing** providing food.

novel (1) *n.* a long story, in a book, about imaginary people. *n.* **novelist** a writer of novels.

novel (2) *adj.* new, unusual. *n.* **novelty** something new.

November *n.* the eleventh month.

novice *n.* 1. a learner, a beginner. 2. a monk or nun who has just entered a monastery or nunnery.

now *adv.* at the present time.

nowadays *adv.* in these times.

nowhere *adv.* in no place.

nozzle *n.* a spout at the end of a pipe or hose.

nucleus *n.* the core or centre, as *the nucleus of an atom is the centre about which the electrons revolve* (*pl.* **nuclei** *pron.* nyōō'klee.ī). *adj.* **nuclear** concerning the nucleus.

nudge *v.* to push someone gently with the elbow to attract attention (**nudging, nudged**). *n.* **nudge** a slight push.

nugget *n.* a rough lump, as *a nugget of gold.*

nuisance *n.* something that causes annoyance.

numb *adj.* without feeling, as *numb with cold.*

number *n.* 1. a word or set of numerals saying how many, as *eighty-four* or *number 84.* 2. many, as *a number of people were there.* 3. one issue of a newspaper or magazine. *v.* **number** 1. to give numbers, as *the pages of a book are numbered.* 2. to amount to, as *the pupils of the school number over 400.* 3. to count in, as *we number him among our friends. adj.* **numberless** more than can be counted.

times without number very often.

numeral *n.* a figure, as *1, 2, 3,* or *I, II, III,* are *numerals.*

numerator *n.* the top number of a fraction, as *in $\frac{7}{8}$ the number 7 is the numerator* (*number 8 is the denominator*).

numerical *adj.* concerning numbers.

in numerical order arranged in order of numbers.

numerous *adj.* very many.

nun *n.* a woman under vows in a convent.

nurse *n.* a woman who looks after those who cannot care for themselves, as sick people, old people, wounded soldiers, or babies. *v.* **nurse** 1. to care for the helpless. 2. to hold a baby or a pet in the arms. 3. to tend young plants (**nursing, nursed**). *n.* **nursing** looking after the helpless.

nursery *n.* 1. a room or building where very young children sleep and play. 2. a place where young plants are tended (*pl.* **nurseries**). *n.* **nurseryman** a man who tends young trees and plants.

nut *n.* 1. a fruit with a hard shell, such as a *walnut,* or *coconut.* 2. a piece of metal with a threaded hole which can be screwed on to a bolt. *adj.* **nutty** with nuts, as *nutty flavoured. n.* **nutcracker(s)** a pair of hinged metal arms for cracking nuts.

nutmeg *n.* the kernel of an East Indian nut used for spice.

nuzzle *v.* to press the nose against, as *a dog will nuzzle one's hand* (**nuzzling, nuzzled**).

nylon *n.* a fibre made artificially from chemicals, woven into stockings and cloth or made into brush bristles.

O

oak *n.* a slow-growing tree with hard wood, bearing acorns. *adj.* **oaken** made of oak.

oak-apple or **oak-gall** a swelling on an oak tree caused by a grub.

oar *n.* 1. a long pole with a flattened end used for rowing. 2. someone who uses an oar, as *he is the best oar in the boat. n.* **oarsman** someone who rows.

to rest on one's oars to stop trying.

oasis (*pron.* ō.ay'sis) *n.* a place in a desert where there is water and where trees grow (*pl.* **oases**).

oath (*pron.* ōth) *n.* 1. a solemn statement, sometimes made with a hand on the Bible. 2. a swear-word (*pl.* **oaths** *pron.* ōTHz).

oatmeal *n.* ground oats.

oats *n. pl.* grain from which oatmeal is made.

obedient *adj.* obeying, doing as one is told. *n.* **obedience.**

obey *v.* to do as one is told, to follow guidance (**obeying, obeyed**).

object (1) (*pron.* ob.jekt') (with **to**) *v.* to complain, to be against. *n.* **objection** 1. a reason against something. 2. a feeling of dislike. *adj.* **objectionable** not liked, unpleasant.

object (2) (*pron.* ob'jekt) *n.* 1. a thing that can be seen. 2. a target or aim, as *his object was to win the match.*

no object of no importance, as *we will deliver anywhere, distance no object.*

obligation *n.* 1. a duty. 2. a promise.

oblige *v.* to compel, as *I felt obliged to attend the funeral* (**obliging, obliged**). *adj.* **obliging** helpful, as *Sam is a most obliging boy.*

oblique (*pron.* ob.leek') *adj.* slanting.

oblong *n.* a four-sided figure longer than wide. *adj.* **oblong** longer than wide.

obscene *adj.* filthy, not decent.

obscure *adj.* 1. dim, dark, as *an obscure corner.* 2. not easy to understand, as *his meaning is obscure.* 3. hidden away, as *an obscure cottage in the hills.* *v.* **obscure** to darken or hide, as *the tree obscures the window* (**obscuring, obscured**). *n.* **obscurity.**

observant *adj.* quick to notice.

observation *n.* 1. noticing or watching. 2. a remark.

observatory *n.* a building where the stars are observed through a telescope.

observe *v.* 1. to notice, to watch. 2. to celebrate, as *to observe armistice day.* 3. to remark. 4. to obey, as *to observe the rules of a game* (**observing, observed**). *n.* **observation.**

obsolete *adj.* out of date.

obstacle *n.* something in the way, an obstruction.

obstacle race a race over obstacles at a sports meeting.

obstinate *adj.* stubborn, holding firmly to an opinion or to some action. *n.* **obstinacy.**

obstruct *v.* 1. to block up, as *dirt obstructs a pipe.* 2. to get in the way, to hinder, as *snow obstructed the car.* *n.* **obstruction.**

obtain *v.* to get, to gain.

obvious *adj.* plain to be seen, evident.

occasion *n.* 1. an event, a particular time. 2. a cause, as *there is no occasion for being angry.*

occasional *adj.* happening now and then. *adv.* **occasionally.**

occupant *n.* a person who lives in a house, or holds a place or position.

occupation *n.* 1. a person's employment. 2. being in possession of a house or place.

occupy *v.* 1. to live in. 2. to take possession of, as *the troops occupied the town.* 3. to hold, as *he occupied the post of Town Clerk.* 4. to fill in, as *my hobby occupies most of my time* (**occupying, occupied**).

occur 1. to happen. 2. to be found, as *this word often occurs in the book.* 3. to enter one's mind, as *it occurred to me to visit him* (**occurring, occurred**). *n.* **occurrence.**

ocean *n.* one of the five great seas, the *Atlantic, Pacific, Indian, Arctic, or Antarctic oceans.* *adj.* **oceanic** concerning an ocean.

ochre (*pron.* ō'ker) *n.* a shade of yellow.

o'clock *adv.* short for *of the clock.*

octave *n.* (in music) a distance of eight notes on a scale, as from middle C to the C above, or *the notes doh, ray, me, fah, soh, la, te, doh make an octave.*

October *n.* the tenth month.

octopus *n.* a soft sea-creature with eight arms fitted with suckers (*pl.* **octopuses**).

odd *adj.* 1. not even, not exactly divisible by two, as *7 is an odd number.* 2. one of a pair, as *an odd sock.* 3. and a few more, as *the scouts numbered fifty odd.* 4. casual, as *odd jobs.* 5. queer, as *an odd fellow.* *n.* **oddity** a queer thing. *n. pl.* **odds** chances, as *the odds are that Harry will win.*

odds and ends bits left over.

ode *n.* a poem.

odious (*pron.* ō'di.us) *adj.* hateful.

odour *n.* a scent or smell. *adj.* **odorous.**

of (*pron.* ov) *prep.* 1. from, as *out of school.* 2. belonging to, as *the roof of the church.* 3. holding, as *a bag of corn.* 4. made from, as *a sheet of glass.* 5. about, as *I heard of her.*

off (*pron.* of) *adv.* 1. away, as *he went off.* 2. out of action, as *the current is off.* 3. completely, as *the work is finished off.* 4. stopping suddenly, as *he broke off what he was saying.* *prep.* **off** away from, as *he lifted the lid off the pan.* *adj.* **off** 1. not on, as *his hat was off.* 2. on the right side, as *the off front wheel of a car.*

off colour not well.

offhand casual, without thinking.

offshoot a branching off.

offside (in football) between the ball and the other team's goal.

well off, badly off rich, poor.

offence (in the U.S.A. spelled **offense**) *n.* 1. a sin, crime, or breaking of rules. 2. attack, as *rifles are weapons of offence.*

to give offence to hurt someone's feelings.

to take offence to feel offended.

offend *v.* 1. to annoy or make angry. 2. to do wrong. *n.* **offender.**

offensive *adj.* 1. insulting. 2. disgusting. 3. for attack, as *offensive weapons.* *n.* **offensive** an attack in warfare.

offer *n.* 1. a proposal, as *an offer of marriage.* 2. money offered, as *he increased his offer.* *v.* **offer** to put forward or hold out, as *to offer help.* *n.* **offering** a gift.

office *n.* 1. an official position or duty, as *the office of chairman of a council.* 2. a place from which a business or firm is managed.

officer *n.* 1. a person who holds a public position, as *a police officer.* 2. someone in command, as *an army officer.*

official *n.* a person who holds a public post. *adj.* **official** 1. concerning an office. 2. coming from someone in authority, as *official news.* *adv.* **officially.**

offspring *n.* children, or the descendants of animals.

often *adv.* many times.

ogre *n.* (in fairy-tales) a man-eating giant.

oil *n.* a greasy liquid from plants, animals, or minerals.

ointment *n.* a grease to help heal a cut or wound.

okra *n.* an African or West Indian plant whose pods are used as a vegetable.

old *adj.* 1. having lived or existed for a long time, as *an old house.* 2. having lived a certain time, as *baby is two years old* (*comparative* **older** or **elder,** *superlative* **oldest** or **eldest.** See **elder.**)

old-fashioned, old-time, old-world out of date.

olden days times of long ago.

olive *n.* 1. a Mediterranean tree with an oily yellow-green fruit. 2. the fruit, or the colour of the fruit.

olive branch a symbol of peace.

olive oil oil pressed from olives used on salads and for cooking.

Olympic Games *n. pl.* international contests held every four years since 1896. The old Greek contests were held at Olympia.

omelet or **omelette** *n.* eggs beaten up and fried.

omen *n.* a sign of good or bad fortune for the future.

ominous *adj.* threatening harm, as *ominous clouds before a storm.*

omission *n.* 1. leaving something out. 2. something not done or left out. See **omit.**

omit *v.* to leave out or leave undone (**omitting, omitted**). *n.* **omission.** See **omission.**

omnibus *n.* an older name for bus (*pl.* **omnibuses**).

on *prep.* on top of. *adv.* **on** continuing, as *to go on.*

onside (in games) opposite to **offside.**

once *adv.* 1. one time, as *I once went to Paris.* 2. in the past, as *there was once an old tree here.* 3. as soon as, as *once you cross the bridge you must turn left.*

at once now.

once in a while now and then.

once upon a time at a time long ago.

one *adj.* single, as *one goal.* *n.* **one** a single person or thing.

oneself yourself

onion *n.* a strong-smelling bulb used as a vegetable.

onlooker *n.* a watcher, a spectator.

only *adj.* single, as *Susan is an only child.* *adv.* **only** merely, as *I only did my duty.*

conj. **only** but, as *I wanted to play only I had work to do.*

onset *n.* 1. an attack. 2. a beginning, as *the onset of rain.*

onslaught *n.* a fierce attack.

onward *adj.* forward, as *the onward movement of the army. adv.* **onward, onwards** forward, as *to move onward.*

ooze *v.* to leak, to flow slowly through, as *oil oozed from the crack* (**oozing, oozed**). *n.* **ooze** mud, slime.

opaque (*pron.* ō.payk¹) *adj.* not letting light through. Opposite of **transparent**. *n.* **opaqueness**.

open *adj.* 1. letting things through, not shut. 2. free for all to enter, as *an open competition.* 3. wide and clear, as *the open sky* or *the open moors. v.* **open** 1. to unfasten, as *to open a gate.* 2. to start, as *to open a bank account* or *open a bazaar. adv.* **openly** hiding nothing. *n.* **openness** sincerity. *n.* **opening** 1. making open. 2. a gap, a way in or out. 3. a beginning.

open-handed generous.

open secret a secret which many people know.

to have an open mind to be ready to hear both sides of a matter.

opera *n.* a play set to music. *adj.* **operatic**.

operate *v.* 1. to work, as *to operate a machine.* 2. to cut part of the body to cure a disease (**operating, operated**). *n.* **operation** 1. a way of working. 2. treatment of a disease by cutting. 3. a military or naval action.

opinion *n.* a belief, a point of view.

public opinion what most people think.

opossum *n.* a small American tree animal, which pretends to be dead when in danger.

opponent *n.* someone on the opposite side in a fight or game.

opportunity *n.* 1. a good chance, as *I have had no opportunity to inquire.* 2. a favourable time, as *this is your opportunity to win success.*

oppose *v.* to fight, work, speak, or in any way act against someone or something (**opposing, opposed**).

opposite *adj.* 1. facing one, on the other side. 2. very different, as *we have opposite ideas on the subject. n.* **opposite** the contrary, as *'rough' is the opposite of 'smooth'.*

opposition *n.* 1. resistance, acting against. 2. the party not in power in Parliament, *Her Majesty's Opposition.*

oppress *v.* 1. to govern severely or cruelly. 2. to weigh heavily on, as *his troubles oppressed him. n.* **oppression**.

optic, optical *adj.* concerning eyesight, as *the optic nerve leads from the eye to the brain* and *we look through optical instruments such as telescopes.*

optician *n.* a man who sells eyeglasses and optical instruments.

optimism *n.* being cheerful and looking on the bright side of things. Opposite of *pessimism.*

optimist *n.* a cheerful person who looks on the bright side and sees everything hopefully. *adj.* **optimistic**. *adv.* **optimistically**.

option *n.* the right to choose, as *you have the option to take it or leave it.*

optional *adj.* free to be chosen, as *fancy dress was optional at the ball.* Opposite of **compulsory**.

or *conj.* suggesting a choice, as *this or that.*

oral *adj.* spoken, not written, as *an oral message.* See also **verbal**. *adv.* **orally**.

orange *n.* a reddish-yellow fruit, and the tree on which it grows. *n.* **orangeade** a drink made from orange juice.

orang-utan (*pron.* o.rang¹-oo.tan¹) *n.* a large ape from Borneo.

orator *n.* a great public speaker.

orbit *n.* the path followed by a planet or satellite round the earth or sun.

orchard *n.* a garden of fruit trees.

orchestra *n.* a band of musicians playing together. *adj.* **orchestral**.

orchid (*pron.* or¹kid) *n.* a very beautiful flower.

ordain *v.* 1. to decide, to order. 2. to appoint or consecrate someone as a Christian minister.

ordeal *n.* a painful experience.

order *n.* 1. tidiness, regular arrangement. 2. good condition, as *the car is in working order.* 3. good government, as *law* *and order.* 4. a command, instructions, as *an army order* or *a grocery order.* 5. a society, as *the order of Oddfellows.* 6. a decoration, as *the Order of the Garter.* *v.* **order** 1. to command. 2. to arrange. *adj.* **orderly** well-arranged, well-behaved.

in alphabetical order in the order A, B, C, etc.

in order that so that.

made to order made by request.

orderly *n.* 1. a soldier who waits on an officer. 2. a hospital attendant.

ordinary *adj.* usual, commonplace. *adv.* **ordinarily.**

ore *n.* rock and earth containing metal.

organ *n.* 1. a large musical instrument with pipes and a piano keyboard, worked by air. 2. part of a human being or living thing with a special use, as *an ear is an organ of hearing.*

organization *n.* 1. management, arrangement. 2. a society, business, or group of people working together.

organize *v.* 1. to arrange in an orderly way. 2. to get a group of people to work together for some special purpose, as *to organize a bazaar* (**organizing, organized**).

Orient *n.* the countries of the East. *adj.* **Oriental.**

origin *n.* the beginning, a starting-point.

original *adj.* 1. first, earliest, as *my original plan was to go by train.* 2. not copied, new, as *an original idea. adv.* **originally** at first. *n.* **originality** ability to think out new ideas.

ornament *n.* something beautiful and decorative, as a brooch or a vase. *adj.* **ornamental.**

ornate *adj.* very decorated, over-decorated.

ornithology *n.* the study of birds. *n.* **ornithologist** one who studies birds.

orphan *n.* a child whose parents are dead. *n.* **orphanage** a home for orphans.

orthodox *adj.* thinking and behaving as most other people do, showing no originality.

oscillate (*pron.* os'i.layt) *v.* to swing to and fro (**oscillating, oscillated**). *n.* **oscillation.**

ostrich *n.* a very large South African bird which cannot fly, bred for its feathers.

other *adj.* 1. different, not the same, as *I have other things to do.* 2. extra, as *I have one other sister.* 3. opposite, as *the other side of the road.*

otherwise *adv.* 1. differently, as *she thought otherwise.* 2. or else, as *go now, otherwise you will be late.*

otter *n.* a large fish-eating water animal.

ought *v.* 1. to be obliged, as *I ought to go now.* 2. to be expected, as *this ought to be enough.*

ounce *n.* one sixteenth of a pound weight (28 grammes).

our *adj.* belonging to us, as *our house. pronoun* **ours** belonging to us, as *this is ours. pronoun* **ourselves** a strong way of saying *we,* as *we ourselves will help.*

out *adv.* 1. away, as *he is out.* 2. at an end, as *the money gave out* or *the fire is out.* 3. outside, as *to leave out.* 4. prominent, as *it stands out.* 5. loudly, as *he called out.*

out and out complete, as *he is an out and out fool.*

out of bounds in a forbidden place.

out of date old-fashioned.

out of hand out of control.

out of one's mind mad.

out of pocket losing money.

out of the way unusual.

outback *n.* (in Australia) the lonely parts of the country far inland.

outbreak *n.* 1. a bursting out. 2. a riot. 3. an epidemic, as *an outbreak of disease.*

outburst *n.* a bursting out, an explosion, as *an outburst of anger.*

outcast *n.* someone driven from home, or shunned by others.

outcome *n.* a result.

outcry *n.* a loud cry, an uproar.

outdo *v.* to do better than others (**outdoing, outdid, outdone**).

outdoor *adj.* in the open air, as *outdoor sports. adv.* **outdoors** in the open air, as *I went outdoors.*

outer *adj.* on the outside. Opposite of **inner.**

outfit n. a set of clothes or equipment n. **outfitter** someone who sells outfits.

outgrow v. 1. to become too big for, as to outgrow a dress. 2. to lose as one grows older, as Pamela outgrew her shyness (**outgrowing, outgrew, outgrown**).

outgrowth n. something growing out, as an outgrowth of suburbs round a city.

outing n. a short excursion, a day trip.

outlaw n. a wandering robber or bandit outside the protection of the law.

outlay n. money spent, as an outlay of money on new clothes.

outlet n. a way out, an opening.

outline n. 1. a line showing the shape of an object. 2. a short description. v. **outline** 1. to draw the outer edge of an object. 2. to describe in a few words (**outlining, outlined**).

outlook n. 1. a view, as an outlook from a window 2. a point of view, as Charles has a cheerful outlook on life. 3. a forecast of what is likely to happen, as a weather outlook for the next day.

outlying adj. distant, away from the main centre of things, as an outlying farm.

outnumber v. to be more than, as the Red Indians outnumbered the white settlers.

outpost n. 1. a small body of soldiers on guard in front of the main army. 2. the place where this guard is stationed. 3. a small colony of settlers.

output n. the amount produced by a factory, etc.

outrage n. a shocking crime. adj. **outrageous**.

outright adv. 1. completely, as he sold his shop outright. 2. openly, as he spoke outright about his troubles. 3. at once, as he was killed outright. adj. **outright** thorough, as an outright scandal.

outset n. the beginning, as it was clear from the outset that he would win.

outshine v. to do better than, as Carol outshines the other girls at Art (**outshining, outshone**).

outside n. the outer part. Opposite of **inside**. adj. **outside** outer, as the outside wall. adv. **outside** outdoors as he went outside. prep. **outside** or the outer side, as the mat lay outside the door.

outsider n. someone avoided by others because he does not belong to their society or group.

outskirts n. pl. the outer edge of a town

outspoken adj. open, saying freely what one thinks.

outstanding adj. 1. standing out, exceptional. 2. (of a debt) unpaid.

outward adj. 1. going away, as outward bound. 2. showing, visible. adv. **outward, outwards** towards the outside as to lean outward. adv. **outwardly** on the surface.

outwit v. to beat someone by cleverness (**outwitting, outwitted**).

outworn adj. worn out, out of date.

oval adj. egg-shaped.

ovation n. applause, cheers, as the singer was given a great ovation.

oven n. a box-shaped space for baking or drying.

over prep. and adv. 1. above, as the bird flew over the trees. 2. more than, as it took him over an hour by bus. 3. down as it fell over. 4. across, as he went over the bridge. 5. finished, as the concert is over. 6. too much, as we have some money over. 7. through, as think it over n. **over** (in cricket) a change-over of fielders and bowler after every six balls bowled.

overalls n. pl. a loose garment worn over a suit to keep it clean.

overawe v. to fill someone with awe (**overawing, overawed**).

overbalance v. to topple over (**overbalancing, overbalanced**).

overboard adv. over a ship's side.

overcast adj. (of the sky) cloudy, dark

overcharge v. to charge too much (**overcharging, overcharged**).

overcoat n. a heavy outer coat.

overcome v. to defeat, to get the better of (**overcoming, overcame, overcome**).

overdo v. to carry too far, to exaggerate to cook too much (**overdoing, overdid, overdone**). adj. **overdone** cooked too much, carried too far.

overdue *adj.* behind time, as *the train is overdue* or *payment of this bill is overdue*.

overestimate *v.* to put too high a value on, as *I overestimated his chances of winning* (**overestimating, overestimated**).

overflow *v.* to flow over. *n.* **overflow** 1. a flood. 2. a waste pipe to draw off extra water.

overgrown *adj.* 1. grown too big. 2. covered, as *this ground is overgrown with nettles.*

overhand *adj.* (in ball games) thrown, bowled, or swung with the arm coming over the shoulder, as *an overhand stroke in tennis.*

overhang *v.* to stick out (**overhanging, overhung**). *n.* **overhang** a piece sticking out.

overhaul *v.* 1. to catch up and overtake, as *to overhaul another runner in a race.* 2. to examine and repair, as *to overhaul a bicycle.*

overhead *adv.* high above, as *the sun shines overhead. adj.* **overhead** up above, as *an overhead archway. n. pl.* **overheads** yearly business expenses.

overhear *v.* to hear by chance a conversation which one was not intended to hear (**overhearing, overheard**).

overjoyed *adj.* delighted.

overlap *v.* to cover partly, as *tiles on a roof overlap each other* (**overlapping, overlapped**).

overload *v.* to load or fill too much.

overlook *v.* 1. to look down on, as *the church on the hill overlooks the town.* 2. to miss seeing, not to notice, as *to overlook a mark on a dress.* 3. to forgive, as *to overlook a fault.*

overnight *adv.* for one night, as *he stayed overnight at the hotel. adj.* **overnight** through the night, as *the overnight express train.*

overrun *v.* to swarm over, as *ants overran the pantry* (**overrunning, overran, overrun**).

overseas *adv.* across the sea.

overseer *n.* a foreman, a superintendent.

oversight *n.* a slip made by forgetfulness or failure to notice.

overtake *v.* to catch up with, to come upon (**overtaking, overtook, overtaken**).

overthrow *v.* to push over, to defeat (**overthrowing, overthrew, overthrown**).

overtime *n.* extra work done after ordinary working hours.

overture *n.* 1. music played before the start of an opera or musical play. 2. a friendly offer made in order to reach an agreement with someone.

overturn *v.* 1. to upset, to turn over. 2. to defeat, to overthrow, as *to overturn a government.*

overwhelm *v.* to crush completely. *adj.* **overwhelming** crushing.

owe *v.* 1. to be in debt, to have to make payment. 2. to be obliged to, as *I owe you my good fortune* (**owing, owed**). **owing to** because of.

owl *n.* a night bird of prey, with a hooting call.
owlet a young owl.

own (1) *v.* 1. to have, to possess. 2. to admit, as *I own that I was wrong. n.* **owner** someone who owns. *n.* **ownership** owning.
to own up to confess.

own (2) *adj.* belonging to, as *his own coat.*
on one's own by oneself.
to get one's own back to get revenge.
to hold one's own not to give in.

ox *n.* an animal of the cow family (*pl.* **oxen**).

oxygen *n.* one of the gases in the air, very necessary for life.

oyster *n.* a shell-fish used for food.

ozone *n.* a form of oxygen.

P

pace *n.* 1. a stride or step, or the length of the step. 2. speed, as *to walk at a fast pace. v.* **pace** 1. to walk to and fro. 2. to measure in paces. 3. (in racing) to set a pace (**pacing, paced**).

pace-maker someone who sets a pace for another runner.
to keep pace with to keep up with.
to set someone through his paces to test him to see what he can do.

pacific *adj.* peaceful.

pacifist *n.* someone who believes war is always wrong. *n.* **pacifism**.

pacify *v.* to calm someone, to restore peace (**pacifying, pacified**).

pack *n.* 1. a bundle. 2. a set of cards. 3. a group of hounds, wolves, etc. hunting together. 4. a mass of broken ice, an *ice-pack*. *v.* **pack** 1. to put into a bundle, or to put clothes into a travelling case. 2. to press close together, as *they all packed into the car*. 3. to fill a crack or leak with material.

package *n.* a bundle.

packet *n.* 1. a small parcel. 2. a mail-boat.

packing *n.* 1. making a pack. 2. material to protect goods sent away.

to send someone packing to send him off at once because he is not wanted.

pad *n.* 1. a small soft cushion. 2. soft material soaked in ink for use with a rubber stamp, an *ink-pad*. 3. sheets of writing-paper fastened together on one edge, a *writing-pad*. 4. the soft under-part of a dog's or cat's paw. 5. (in cricket) a leg-guard. *v.* **pad** to stuff with soft material (**padding, padded**). *n.* **padding**.

paddle *n.* a short, broad-bladed oar used for a canoe. *v.* **paddle** 1. to move a canoe with a paddle. 2. to walk in water bare-footed (**paddling, paddled**).

paddock *n.* a small field.

paddy-field *n.* a rice-field.

padlock *n.* a removable hanging lock fitted with a hinged arm.

pagan (*pron.* pay'gan) *n.* a heathen. *n.* **paganism**.

page (1) *n.* 1. a uniformed boy-servant in a hotel. 2. (in the Middle Ages) a boy attending a knight. 3. a boy carrying the bride's train at a wedding.

page (2) *n.* one side of a written or printed sheet of paper.

pageant (*pron.* paj'ant) *n.* a procession or show in costume. *n.* **pageantry** a display, a show.

paid *past* of **pay**.

pail *n.* a bucket. *n.* **pailful** (*pl.* **pailfuls**).

pain *n.* an ache, suffering of mind or body. *adj.* **painful**. *adv.* **painfully**. *adj.* **painless**. *adv.* **painlessly**.

painstaking very careful, thorough.

paint *n.* a liquid used with a brush for colouring. *v.* **paint** 1. to cover with paint. 2. to make a picture with paint. 3. to describe in words, as *Helen painted a glowing picture of her school*. *n.* **painter** someone who paints. *n.* **painting** a painted picture.

painter *n.* a rope for fastening a boat.

pair *n.* 1. a set of two of the same kind, as *a pair of gloves*. 2. an article made of two parts, as *a pair of scissors*. *v.* **pair** to arrange in pairs.

palace *n.* a very large and splendid house, the official home of a king or other ruler, or of a bishop.

palatial *adj.* magnificent, like a palace.

pale *adj.* dim, weak in colour. *v.* **pale** to turn white or a pale colour (**paling, paled**).

palette *n.* a board on which an artist mixes his colours.

paling *n.* a wooden fence.

palisade *n.* a strong wooden fence round a fort. *n. pl.* **palisades** (in North America) cliffs overhanging a river.

palm (1) *n.* the inside of the hand between wrist and fingers.

to palm off to pass on to someone something worthless.

palm (2) *n.* a tree growing in warm countries with long fern-shaped leaves at the top. *adj.* **palmy** rich. *n.* **Palm Sunday** the Sunday before Easter.

palsy (*pron.* pawl'zi) *n.* a paralysis of part of the body.

paltry *adj.* small, worthless.

pampas *n. pl.* the treeless grassy plains of South America.

pamper *v.* to spoil someone by over-kindness.

pamphlet *n.* a thin, paper-covered booklet.

pan *n.* a metal dish with a handle, used in cooking, as a *frying-pan* or a *saucepan*.

a flash in the pan a fine start which leads to nothing.

pancake a thin round cake of fried batter.

pandemonium *n.* wild disorder.

pane *n.* a sheet of window-glass.

panel *n.* 1. a piece of wood sunk into a door or wall. 2. a list of jurymen or doctors ready for service.

panelling *n.* a row of panels on a wall.

pang *n.* a sudden sharp pain.

panic *n.* a sudden, uncontrollable fear. **panic-stricken** struck with sudden fear.

panorama *n.* 1. a wide view. 2. a changing or unfolding scene passing before one's eyes.

pansy *n.* a garden flower with flat velvety blossoms (*pl.* **pansies**).

pant *v.* to puff, to gasp for breath. *n. pl.* **pants** (*slang*) trousers.

panther *n.* 1. a leopard. 2. a North American puma or cougar.

pantomime *n.* 1. (in Britain) a musical play based on a fairy-tale. 2. (in the U.S.A.) mime or play without words.

pantry *n.* a storeroom for food in a house (*pl.* **pantries**).

papacy *n.* the position of Pope.

papal *adj.* concerning the Pope.

paper *n.* 1. material to be written or printed on, or used for wrapping. 2. a newspaper. *v.* **paper** to cover with paper, as *to paper a wall*.

paper-chase *n.* a sport in which runners follow a trail of paper.

paper-weight *n.* a small weight to prevent papers from being scattered.

papoose *n.* a Red Indian's child.

par *n.* being equal, the same level, as *with regards to brains John is on a par with Dick*.

below par worse than usual, especially in health, as *Joan is feeling below par*.

parable *n.* a short story which points out some lesson, especially a story which Jesus told.

parachute *n.* an arrangement which opens out like an umbrella, to save an airman who jumps from his plane. *n.* **parachutist**.

parade *n.* 1. an assembly of soldiers for inspection. 2. a procession. 3. a promenade. *v.* **parade** 1. to turn out for inspection. 2. to make a display or to march in procession (**parading, paraded**).

paradise *n.* 1. heaven, where the souls of good people go after death. 2. a state of happiness.

paraffin *n.* 1. an inflammable oil, used for heating and lighting, also called *kerosene*. 2. a wax used for making candles.

paragraph *n.* a short section of a piece of writing.

parallel *adj.* the same distance apart at all points, as *railway lines are parallel*.

parallelogram *n.* a four-sided figure whose opposite sides are parallel and equal.

paralyse *v.* to make someone helpless and unable to move (**paralysing, paralysed**). *n.* **paralysis** loss of power to move, through disease or fear.

parapet *n.* a low wall on the edge of a bridge, flat roof, trench, fort, etc.

parasite *n.* 1. a plant or animal living on another, as *the mistletoe is a parasite living on an oak tree*. 2. someone who does no work, but lives on another person's generosity. *adj.* **parasitic**.

parcel *n.* a small wrapped-up package. *v.* **parcel** to make up into a package (**parcelling, parcelled**).

parch *v.* to dry up. *adj.* **parched** dried.

parchment *n.* 1. the thin skin of a sheep or goat prepared so that one can write on it. 2. a document on such a skin.

pardon *v.* 1. to forgive, to set free from punishment. 2. to excuse. *n.* **pardon** forgiveness. *adj.* **pardonable** excusable.

pare *v.* to peel, to cut off the outside, as *to pare an apple* or *to pare a piece of wood* (**paring, pared**).

parent *n.* a father or mother.

parentage *n.* ancestors of one or two generations back, as *he is of noble parentage*.

parish *n.* 1. a district in the charge of a clergyman. 2. a part of a country. 3. (in the U.S.A.) a congregation.

park *n.* 1. an enclosed piece of land with trees and shrubs for the public's enjoyment. 2. a large piece of land round a country mansion. *v.* **park** to leave in a safe place for a time.

car-park a place for motor-cars to be left for a while.

parliament *n.* 1. a council made up of people who have been elected to make a country's laws. 2. (in Great Britain) the House of Commons and the House of Lords. *adj.* **parliamentary**.

Act of Parliament a law passed by Parliament.

parole *n.* the word of honour given by a prisoner of war that he will not escape if given some freedom.

parrot *n.* a brightly coloured tropical bird.

parsley *n.* a plant whose leaves are used in cooking.

parsnip *n.* a vegetable like a pale carrot.

parson *n.* a minister or clergyman. *n.* **parsonage** a parson's house.

part (1) *n.* 1. a share, a bit. 2. a character in a play, as *the part of Macbeth.* 3. a side, as *Norah took Jim's part in the argument. adv.* **partly** not entirely.

for my part as far as I am concerned.

for the most part mostly.

part-time for part of the time, as *part-time work.*

to take part in to help in.

part (2) *v.* to separate. *n.* **parting** 1. a leave-taking. 2. a dividing line of hair on the head.

to part company to stop going with someone.

partial *adj.* 1. in part only, as *Mr Smith has a partial share in the business.* 2. fond of, as *Tom is partial to jelly.* 3. favouring one side, as *the referee was not fair, for he was partial to one team. adv.* **partially** in part only.

participate *v.* (with **in**) to take part in (**participating, participated**). *n.* **participation**.

particle *n.* a tiny bit, as *a particle of dust.*

particular *adj.* 1. special, as *I have a particular job to do.* 2. very careful, as *Sylvia is particular about her writing. n. pl.* **particulars** details, as *I will write down the particulars on the form. adv.* **particularly** especially, as *be particularly careful.*

in particular especially.

partition *n.* 1. a dividing up, as *the partition of Germany into East Germany and West Germany.* 2. a thin wall between two rooms. *v.* **partition** to divide into parts.

partner *n.* 1. someone sharing in a business. 2. a husband or wife. 3. someone dancing with another, or playing a game on the same side, as *a dancing partner,* or *a tennis partner. n.*

partnership common ownership, or the joining of people in some game or activity.

partridge *n.* a game-bird like a small pheasant.

party *n.* 1. a group of people working together, or having the same political opinions. 2. a social gathering, as *a tea-party* (*pl.* **parties**).

pass *v.* 1. to go by or beyond, as *to pass the bus stop.* 2. to hand on, as *please pass the mustard.* 3. to put through, as *to pass a law.* 4. to get through, as *to pass an examination* (**passing, passed**). (Note: do not confuse **passed** and **past**. **passed** is only used as a verb, as *I have passed.* See **past**.)

n. **pass** 1. a narrow mountain passage. 2. a permit to leave or enter a place. 3. success in an examination. *adj.* **passable** 1. able to be crossed. 2. fairly good. *adv.* **passably**.

to come to pass to happen.

to pass out to go out, to faint.

to pass over to ignore, to overlook.

passage *n.* 1. a way through, a corridor or lane. 2. a voyage. 3. a few paragraphs of a book.

a bird of passage a migrating bird. Someone always on the move.

passenger *n.* a traveller in a train, ship, bus, etc.

passer-by *n.* someone walking past (*pl.* **passers-by**).

passion *n.* a strong feeling, as of love, hate, or enthusiasm. *adj.* **passionate**. *adv.* **passionately**.

The Passion Christ's sufferings on the cross.

passive *adj.* not resisting an attack, submitting. Opposite of **active**. *adv.* **passively**.

Passover *n.* a Jewish feast, in memory of the destroying angel killing the first-born of the Egyptians but passing over those of the Israelites (see Exodus, chapter XII).

passport *n.* a document allowing one to travel in a foreign country.

password *n.* a secret word to give to a sentry.

past *n.* 1. time gone by. 2. someone's former life, as *he has a wicked past.*

adj. **past** gone by, as *the past week.* *adv.* **past** by, as *I went past.* *prep.* **past** beyond, as *she is past all hope.* (Note : do not confuse with **passed.** See **pass.**) **a past master** a skilful expert.

paste *n.* 1. a sticky mixture for fastening papers together. 2. a sticky mixture of meat or fish for eating, as *fish-paste.* 3. imitation jewellery. *v.* **paste** to stick with paste (**pasting, pasted**).

pastel *n.* a soft, coloured crayon.

pastime *n.* an amusement or game.

pastry *n.* baked flour-paste and fat used for pies and tarts.

pasture *n.* grassland for grazing cattle. *n.* **pasturage** pasture-land.

pasty (1) (*pron.* pas'ti) *n.* a pie.

pasty (2) (*pron.* pays'ti) *adj.* 1. like paste. 2. pale.

pat *v.* to tap gently with the hand (**patting, patted**). *n.* **pat** 1. a slight tap. 2. a small lump, as *a pat of butter.* *adj.* **pat** quick and ready, as *the reply came pat.*

patch *n.* 1. a small piece of material to cover a hole. 2. a small area, as *a patch of ground* (*pl.* **patches**). *v.* **patch** to put a patch on. *adj.* **patched** having a patch. *adj.* **patchy** having several patches.

patchwork a cloth made up of coloured patches.

patent *n.* a government permit allowing an inventor to be the only person making or selling his invention for a number of years. *v.* **patent** to get a patent. *n.* **patentee** the holder of a patent.

paternal *adj.* 1. fatherly. 2. on the father's side of the family, as *a paternal grandmother.* *adv.* **paternally.**

path *n.* a track, a narrow lane (*pl.* **paths** *pron.* pahThz). *n.* **pathway** a narrow footpath or track.

pathetic *adj.* causing pity.

patience *n.* 1. being patient, being calm and uncomplaining. 2. a card game.

patient *adj.* calm, steady, and persistent in face of trouble and difficulty. *n.* **patient** a person in a doctor's care.

patriot *n.* someone who loves his country. *adj.* **patriotic** loving and serving one's country. *n.* **patriotism.**

patrol *v.* to walk round guarding and watching (**patrolling, patrolled**). *n.* **patrol** 1. soldiers patrolling. 2. a group of six Boy Scouts under a leader. *n.* **patrolman** (in the U.S.A.) a police-man on duty.

patron *n.* 1. a regular customer. 2. some-one who supports artists by buying their works. *adj.* **patron** protecting, acting as guardian, as *a patron saint.* *n.* **patronage** acting as patron.

patter *n.* 1. a succession of light taps, as *the patter of hail on a roof.* 2. quick talk, as *the patter of a comedian.* *v.* **patter** to make a series of quick sounds.

pattern *n.* 1. a model to be copied. 2. a design, as *the pattern in a curtain.*

pause *v.* to stop for a while, to wait (**pausing, paused**). *n.* **pause** a short stop, a rest.

pave *v.* to cover with flat stones (**paving, paved**). *n.* **paving** material to pave a road.

pavement *n.* a paved footpath (in the U.S.A. a *sidewalk*).

pavilion *n.* 1. a building for the players on a sports ground. 2. a large tent.

paw *n.* the foot of an animal having claws. *v.* **paw** 1. to scrape with a paw. 2. (of horses) to scrape the ground with a hoof.

pawn (1) *v.* to leave an article with a *pawnbroker* in return for money, the article being returned when the money is paid back. *n.* **pawnshop** a shop where articles can be pawned.

pawn (2) *n.* the piece of lowest value in chess.

pay *v.* 1. to give money for articles bought, or for work done. 2. to give something other than money, as *to pay a visit* or *to pay a compliment.* 3. (with **out**) to let out, as *to pay out a rope* (**paying, paid**). *adj.* **payable** due to be paid. *n.* **payment.**

to pay through the nose to pay heavily.

pea *n.* a plant bearing pods containing round seeds used for food.

peace *n.* 1. quietness, calm. 2. freedom from war. *adj.* **peaceful.** *adv.* **peace-fully.** *adj.* **peaceable** loving peace. *adv.* **peaceably.**

to hold one's peace to keep quiet.

peach *n.* a juicy stone-fruit.

peacock *n.* a large bird with green and blue feathers and a fan-like tail (*fem.* **peahen**).

peak 1. a pointed mountain top. 2. the front part of a cap. 3. the highest amount, as *the work reached its peak in the afternoon. adj.* **peaked** having a peak.

peal *n.* 1. a loud sound of thunder, bells, laughter, etc. 2. a tune played on a set of church bells. *v.* **peal** to play church bells.

peanut *n.* a monkey-nut or African ground-nut, with a yellow husk and reddish nut.

pear *n.* a fruit like an apple but longer.

pearl *n.* a valuable gem found in oysters and mussels. *n.* **mother-of-pearl** the shiny lining of shell-fish containing pearls, used for making buttons, etc.

peasant *n.* (on the continent of Europe and in Asia) a countryman (*pl.* **peasants** or **peasantry**).

peat *n.* dried turf used as fuel.

pebble *n.* a small round stone. *adj.* **pebbly** full of pebbles.

peck (1) *v.* (of a bird) to strike or pick seeds with the beak.

peck (2) *n.* a dry measure equal to a quarter of a bushel.

peculiar *adj.* 1. strange, queer. 2. special, individual, as *Tom has his own peculiar way of writing. n.* **peculiarity**.

pedal *n.* a lever worked by foot. *v.* **pedal** to work a lever by foot (**pedalling, pedalled**).

pedestal *n.* the base of a statue, lamp, etc.

pedestrian *n.* a walker.
pedestrian crossing a road-crossing for walkers.

pedigree *n.* a list of ancestors. *adj.* **pedigree** thorough-bred, as *a pedigree spaniel.*

pedlar *n.* a man who goes from house to house carrying things to sell (note: a *pedlar* carries things to sell : a *hawker* sells things from a cart).

peel *n.* the skin or rind of a fruit or vegetable. *v.* **peel** to strip off skin or bark.

peep *v.* 1. to take a quick look, to take a sly look through a hole. 2. to appear for a short time, as *the sun peeped through the clouds.* 3. to make a noise like a chick. *n.* **peep** a quick sly look.

peer (1) *v.* 1. to look closely at. 2. to look intently, as *they peered into the darkness.*

peer (2) *n.* 1. an equal, as *he was tried by his peers.* 2. a nobleman (*fem.* **peeress**).

peerage *n.* 1. the rank of nobleman. 2. all noblemen.

peg *n.* a small wood or metal pin, as a *tent-peg,* a *hat-peg,* or a *clothes-peg. v.* **peg** to fix with pegs (**pegging, pegged**).

a square peg in a round hole, or **a round peg in a square hole** someone not suitable for his job.

to take down a peg to humble someone.

pelican *n.* a large water-bird with a pouch under its long lower beak.

pellet *n.* a little ball, as *a shotgun pellet* or *a paper pellet.*

pelt (1) *v.* to throw many things at, as *to pelt with snowballs* or *hail is pelting down.*

pelt (2) *n.* the raw skin of an animal.

pen (1) *n.* an enclosure for animals or birds, as a *duck-pen. v.* **pen** to shut in (**penning, penned**).

pen (2) *n.* an instrument for writing with ink, either a *pen-nib* in a *pen-holder,* or a *fountain-pen.*

penal *adj.* concerning punishment.
penal servitude imprisonment with hard labour.

penalize *v.* 1. to punish. 2. (in a game) to give a penalty against (**penalizing, penalized**).

penalty *n.* 1. a punishment. 2. (in games) a handicap against one side for breaking a rule (*pl.* **penalties**).

penance *n.* a punishment one chooses to undergo to make up for some sin or wrong-doing.

pence *n. pl.* pennies.

pencil *n.* a thin stick of black graphite lead, or coloured chalk, encased in wood and used for writing. *v.* **pencil** to use a pencil (**pencilling, pencilled**).

pendulum *n.* a swinging weight which makes a clock keep time (*pl.* **pendulums**).

penetrate *v.* to pierce, to go into, to soak into, to see into (**penetrating, penetrated**). *n.* **penetration**. *adj.* **penetrating** sharp, keen.

penguin *n.* a large black-and-white sea-bird which cannot fly, found only near the South Pole.

peninsula *n.* a long strip of land, almost surrounded by water. *adj.* **peninsular**.

penitent *adj.* being sorry for some wrong one has done. *n.* **penitence**.

penknife *n.* a pocket-knife (*pl.* **penknives**).

pennant *n.* a long, narrow flag.

penniless *adj.* without a penny, very poor.

penny *n.* a British bronze coin worth one-hundredth of a pound, (in North America) one cent (*pl.* **pennies** or **pence**).

penny-farthing an old type of bicycle with a large front wheel and a small back wheel.

penny wise but pound foolish saving small amounts but wasting large sums.

pension *n.* a regular allowance of money paid to someone because of old age, injury, or some other cause. *n.* **pensioner** someone receiving a pension.

Pentecost *n.* 1. Whitsunday. 2. a Jewish festival the fiftieth day after the Passover.

people *n. pl.* 1. persons, the general public. 2. a nation, as *the Swiss people*.

pepper *n.* a sharp-tasting spice made from East Indian berries ground to powder. *v.* **pepper** to pelt with shot. *adj.* **peppery** (of a person) hot-tempered.

peppermint *n.* a mint plant whose oil is used for flavouring sweets.

per *prep.* 1. by, as *per letter post*. 2. in each, as *forty kilometres per hour*.

per cent in each hundred.

perceive *v.* 1. to see, to notice. 2. to understand (**perceiving, perceived**). See **perception**.

percentage *n.* a proportion of each hundred, as *a percentage of twelve means*

twelve parts in a hundred, or *a large percentage of the boys were early means many boys were early*. See **per cent**, under **per**.

perception *n.* 1. power of observing, as *an eagle is a bird of keen perception*. 2. power of understanding, as *he is a man of great perception*.

perch (1) *n.* a fresh-water fish.

perch (2) *n.* 1. a rod or branch for a bird to sit on. 2. a measure of length equal to 5 metres. *v.* **perch** to sit on a perch.

percussion *n.* a noisy striking or clash. **percussion instruments** drums, cymbals, etc.

perennial *adj.* 1. lasting through the year or years. 2. (of plants) many years; compare **annual** and **biennial**.

perfect (*pron.* per'fekt) *adj.* without fault, complete. *v.* **perfect** (*pron.* per.-fekt') to finish or make perfect. *n.* **perfection**.

perforate *v.* to make holes in. *adj.* **perforated** pierced with holes, as *a perforated sheet of stamps*.

perform *v.* 1. to do, to carry out, as *to perform a duty*. 2. to entertain people, as *to perform on the piano*. *n.* **performance** 1. doing. 2. an entertainment.

perfume (*pron.* per'fyoom) *n.* a pleasant scent. *v.* **perfume** (*pron.* per.fyoom') to make scented (**perfuming, perfumed**).

perhaps *adv.* possibly, it may be.

peril *n.* danger. *adj.* **perilous** dangerous.

perimeter *n.* the outside edge of an area.

period *n.* a length of time, as *a period of wet weather*. *adj.* **periodic** happening at regular times, as *the periodic appearance of the new moon*.

periodical *n.* a magazine published at regular times. *adj.* **periodical** at regular intervals.

periscope *n.* a long tube, fitted with mirrors, enabling a man in a submarine to see what is happening above.

perish *v.* to die or decay.

perishable *adj.* easily spoiled, liable to decay, as *soft fruits are perishable*.

permanent *adj.* lasting, fixed, changeless. *n.* **permanence**.

permission *n.* consent, freedom to do something.

permit (*pron.* per.mit[1]) *v.* to allow, to give consent (**permitting, permitted**). *n.* **permit** (*pron.* per[1]mit) a licence, written permission.

perpendicular *adj.* upright, at right angles. *n.* **perpendicular** a line at right angles to another line or surface.

perpetual *adj.* never-ending. *adv.* **perpetually** constantly.

perpetuate *v.* 1. to make something last for a long time. 2. to see that something is not forgotten, as *to perpetuate someone's memory* (**perpetuating, perpetuated**).

perplex *v.* to puzzle, as *Tom was perplexed by the sum. n.* **perplexity.**

persecute *v.* to keep on ill-treating someone, especially for religious reasons (**persecuting, persecuted**). *n.* **persecution** continuous ill-treatment. *n.* **persecutor** someone who persecutes.

perseverance *n.* keeping on trying, working hard.

persevere *v.* to keep on trying, to work hard and continuously (**persevering, persevered**). *adj.* **persevering** trying hard.

persist *v.* to keep on doing something, to continue. *adj.* **persistent** keeping on, obstinate. *n.* **persistence.**

person *n.* 1. a human being. 2. the human body.

personage *n.* an important person.

personal *adj.* 1. belonging to one person, as *one's personal luggage.* 2. concerning one person, as *personal remarks. adv.* **personally** 1. in person, as *I went there personally.* 2. as far as I am concerned, as *personally, I do not like it.*

personality *n.* 1. the special character of a person. 2. a famous person (*pl.* **personalities**).

personnel *n.* the people engaged in a firm, factory, or some service, as *the personnel of the fire brigade.*

perspective *n.* a way of drawing or painting so that distant things seem distant and small, while near things seem near and large.

in perspective according to perspective, in proportion.

perspire *v.* to sweat (**perspiring, perspired**). *n.* **perspiration.**

persuade *v.* to win someone over to one's way of thinking by argument (**persuading, persuaded**). *n.* **persuasion.** *adj.* **persuasive.**

perturb *v.* to cause worry, to make uneasy. *n.* **perturbation** uneasiness.

perverse *adj.* stubborn in doing wrong. *n.* **perversion** a turning from good to evil. *n.* **perversity** persistent wrongdoing.

pessimism *n.* always thinking the worst of everything. *n.* **pessimist** someone who takes a gloomy view of life and expects the worst to happen. *adj.* **pessimistic.**

pest *n.* 1. a troublesome person or thing. 2. a disease.

pet *n.* a favourite bird, animal, or child. *v.* **pet** to treat lovingly (**petting, petted**).

a pet aversion something particularly disliked.

petal *n.* one of the coloured parts of a flower.

petition *n.* a written request to someone in authority, signed by many people.

petrol *n.* refined petroleum used as motor-fuel, gasolene.

petroleum *n.* a heavy brown mineral oil from the depths of the earth.

petticoat *n.* an underskirt.

petty *adj.* small, unimportant. *n.* **pettiness.**

petty officer a naval rank equal to an army corporal or sergeant.

pew *n.* a long wooden bench in a church.

pewter *n.* an alloy of tin and lead used for tankards and plates.

phantasy see **fantasy.**

phantom *n.* a ghost, a spirit.

pharmacy *n.* 1. the making of drugs and medicines. 2. a chemist's or druggist's shop. *adj.* **pharmaceutical** concerning pharmacy.

phase *n.* 1. a particular appearance of the moon, as *the new moon is the moon in its first phase.* 2. a stage of development, as *the egg is the first phase of a chicken's life.*

pheasant *n.* a game-bird.

phenomenon *n.* 1. any happening in nature, as *rainfall is a phenomenon*. 2. a remarkable event (*pl.* **phenomena**). *adj.* **phenomenal**.

philately *n.* stamp-collecting. *n.* **philatelist** a stamp-collector.

philosophy *n.* the study and love of knowledge. *n.* **philosopher** 1. a student of philosophy. 2. someone who takes things calmly, and follows his reason rather than his emotions. *adj.* **philosophical** *adv.* **philosophically**.

phone *n.* a short word for **telephone**.

photograph *n.* a picture taken by exposing sensitive film to light, in a camera.

photography *n.* the taking of photographs. *n.* **photographer**. *adj.* **photographic**.

phrase *n.* part of a sentence.

physic *n.* medicine.

physical *adj.* 1. concerning the world around us, as *wind and water-power are physical forces*. 2. concerning the human body, as *physical fitness*. *adv.* **physically**.

physician *n.* a doctor.

physics *n.* the science of heat, light, mechanics, magnetism, and electricity.

physique (*pron.* fi.zeek') *n.* the development of the body, as *Dick has a splendid physique*.

pianist *n.* a person who plays the piano.

piano *n.* a musical instrument with iron wires struck by hammers operated by keys.

pick (1) *v.* 1. to take up or take off with the fingers, as *to pick fruit*. 2. to choose, as *to pick a library book*. 3. to pierce or break open, as *to pick a hole* or *pick a lock*.

pick-pocket a thief who steals from pockets.

to pick up to lift, to call for someone, to learn.

pick (2) *n.* a heavy pointed tool for breaking up roads, as a *pickaxe*, or for breaking ice, as an *ice-pick*.

pickle *n.* 1. (often in the plural) vegetables preserved in vinegar. 2. salt water or vinegar for preserving meat or vegetables. *v.* **pickle** to preserve in vinegar or salt water (**pickling, pickled**).

in a pickle in trouble.

picnic *n.* a pleasure-trip by a few people with an outdoor meal. *v.* **picnic** to have a picnic (**picnicking, picnicked**).

pictorial *adj.* 1. illustrated. 2. like a picture, as *a pictorial description*.

picture *n.* 1. a drawing, painting, or photograph. 2. a likeness, as *he is the picture of his father*. *n. pl.* **the pictures** (*slang*) the cinema.

pie *n.* meat or fruit baked in pastry.

piebald *adj.* (of a horse) of two colours, especially black and white.

piece *n.* 1. a part of anything, a bit, as *a piece of bread*. 2. a single thing, as *a piece of music* or *a piece of advice*. 3. one of the men in a board-game, as *a chess piece*.

piecemeal bit by bit.

piece of eight an old Spanish dollar bearing the figure eight.

to give someone a piece of one's mind to scold.

pied *adj.* of mixed colours, piebald.

pier *n.* 1. a roadway stretching from the shore out to sea, at the end of which is a landing-stage for ships. 2. one of the pillars supporting a bridge.

pierce *v.* 1. to run through, to penetrate, to stab. 2. to enter, as *the needle pierced Joan's finger* (**piercing, pierced**). *adj.* **piercing** shrill, penetrating, as *a piercing cry*.

piety *n.* holiness, reverence.

pig *n.* a farm animal raised for pork and bacon, a swine, a hog. *n.* **piggery** a place where pigs are kept. *n.* **piglet** a small pig.

pig-headed obstinate.

to buy a pig in a poke to buy something before seeing it.

pigeon *n.* a bird which coos like a dove. **pigeon-hole** a small box-like division for papers in a desk.

pigmy see **pygmy**.

pigsty *n.* a place where pigs are kept (*pl.* **pigsties**).

pigtail *n.* a long plait of hair.

pike (1) *n.* a fierce fresh-water fish.

pike (2) *n.* a spear with a steel head.

pile (1) *n.* a large stake driven into soft ground by a *pile-driver*, to act as a firm foundation.

pile (2) *n.* a heap, as *a pile of sand. v.* **pile** to form a heap (**piling, piled**).

pile (3) *n.* the short hairs or nap on cloth or a carpet.

pilgrim *n.* a traveller on foot to a holy place. *n.* **pilgrimage** a pilgrim's journey.

Pilgrim Fathers the Puritans from England who landed in Massachusetts in 1620.

pill *n.* a pellet of medicine.

pillar *n.* 1. an upright post. 2. a tall monument.

pillar-box a street letter-box.

pillion *n.* a passenger seat on a motor-cycle.

pillow *n.* a cushion for the head, used in a bed.

pilot *n.* 1. a man who comes on board and steers a ship into port. 2. a man who operates the controls of an aeroplane.

pilot-officer a junior Air Force officer.

pimple *n.* a small swelling on the skin.

pin *n.* a small piece of wire with a head at one end and a point at the other, used as a fastener. *v.* **pin** to fasten with a pin (**pinning, pinned**). *n.* **pinpoint** the point of a pin.

pinafore *n.* a little apron for a girl.

pincers *n. pl.* 1. a tool for gripping nails. 2. the claws of a crab or lobster.

pinch *v.* 1. to nip or squeeze. 2. to make thin, as *his face was pinched with hunger. n.* **pinch** 1. a squeeze. 2. a small amount, as *a pinch of salt.*

at a pinch if really necessary.

to take a story with a pinch of salt to believe it to be exaggerated.

pine (1) *n.* an evergreen tree with cones and leaves like needles.

pine (2) *v.* 1. to long for. 2. to waste away with grief (**pining, pined**).

pineapple *n.* a large tropical fruit.

pink *n.* 1. a very pale red colour. 2. a garden flower. *adj.* **pink** of a very pale red.

the pink of condition the peak, or best, of health.

pint *n.* a liquid measure (0·57 litres).

pioneer *n.* someone who goes first and prepares the way for others, a settler, an explorer, an inventor. *v.* **pioneer** to explore and prepare the way.

pious *adj.* religious, reverent. See **piety**.

pip *n.* 1. the seed of a fruit. 2. the spot on a playing card.

pipe *n.* 1. a tube to carry away water or gas. 2. a tube for blowing musical notes, as an *organ-pipe*. 3. a little bowl with a stem for tobacco-smoking. 4. a bird's shrill cry. *v.* **pipe** 1. to run off water through a pipe. 2. to play a tune on a pipe (**piping, piped**). *n.* **piper** a man who plays a tune on bagpipes.

the pipes bagpipes.

piracy *n.* attack and robbery at sea.

pirate *n.* a sea-robber.

pistol *n.* a small gun fired from one hand.

piston *n.* the part of an engine which slides up and down (or to and fro) in the cylinder. *n.* **piston-rod** the rod fastened to the piston.

pit (1) *n.* 1. a hole in the ground, either a mine-shaft or a hole for trapping animals. 2. part of the ground-floor of a theatre behind the stalls. 3. a hollow, as *an armpit*.

pitfall a trap, a hole covered with branches for an animal to fall into.

pithead the top of a mine-shaft.

pit (2) *v.* to set against, as *to pit one's wits against an enemy* (**pitting, pitted**).

pitch (1) *n.* thick, black coal-tar.

pitch (2) *v.* 1. to set up, as *to pitch a tent*. 2. to throw, as *to pitch a ball*. 3. to plunge, as *to pitch forward*. 4. (in music) to set the key, as *to pitch a tune an octave higher. n.* **pitch** 1. a ground on which a match is played. 2. a selling-place, as *the ice-cream man has a pitch on the seashore*. 3. the high or low tone of a voice or musical note. 4. (in cricket) the distance between wickets.

pitched battle a battle on chosen ground.

pitcher (1) *n.* (in baseball) the player who throws or pitches the ball.

pitcher (2) *n.* a large jug.

pitchfork *n.* a long fork for tossing hay.

piteous *adj.* arousing pity.

pitfall *n.* a trap. See **pit**.

pith *n.* 1. the soft white substance in the stems of some plants. 2. the main part, as *the pith of a speech*. *adj.* **pithy** full of meaning, as *a pithy remark*.

pitiable *adj.* deserving pity. *adv.* **pitiably**.

pitiful *adj.* 1. full of pity, as *a pitiful look*. 2. sad, deserving pity, as *a pitiful sight*. 3. contemptible, as *pitiful meanness*. *adv.* **pitifully**.

pitiless *adj.* showing no pity, cruel.

pity *n.* a feeling of sorrow for other people's suffering or troubles. *v.* **pity** to feel sorry for (**pitying, pitied**).

pivot *n.* a little rod or pin on which a wheel or something similar turns. *v.* **pivot** to turn round a pivot (**pivoting, pivoted**).

pixie or **pixy** *n.* a small fairy.

placard *n.* a poster, a large notice. *v.* **placard** to put up posters.

place *n.* a position, point, or particular building, as *a place of worship*. *v.* **place** to hand in, to put (**placing, placed**).

out of place unsuitable.

to take place to happen.

plague *n.* 1. a deadly and widespread disease. 2. a nuisance. *v.* **plague** to annoy (**plaguing, plagued**).

plaice *n.* a flat sea-fish.

plaid (*pron.* plad) *n.* a long woollen tartan cloth worn across the shoulder and chest by Scottish Highlanders.

plain (1) *adj.* 1. clear, obvious, as *it is plain that he is honest*. 2. simple, ordinary, as *plain cooking* or *plain clothes*. 3. frank, as *plain words*. 4. not beautiful, as *she is very plain*. *n.* **plainness**.

plain (2) *n.* a stretch of level country.

plaintive *adj.* mournful, sad. *adv.* **plaintively**.

plait (*pron.* plat) *n.* a length of interwoven hair or straw. *v.* **plait** to weave into a plait.

plan *n.* 1. a drawing showing the layout of a building, town, etc., as seen from above. 2. an arrangement, a scheme. *v.* **plan** 1. to arrange to do something. 2. to make a drawing or plan (**planning, planned**).

plane (1) *n.* a carpenter's tool for smoothing wood. *v.* **plane** to smooth with a plane (**planing, planed**).

plane (2) *n.* 1. a level surface. 2. a short word for **aeroplane**.

planet *n.* one of the large bodies in space which move round the sun. *adj.* **planetary** concerning a planet. (note: Saturn, Jupiter, Uranus, Neptune, Venus, Earth, Mars, Mercury, and Pluto are planets. The comets and meteors are not planets.)

plank *n.* a long flat piece of timber. *v.* **plank** (in North America) to cook on a plank, as *to plank fish*.

to walk the plank to be forced by pirates to walk along a plank into the sea.

plant *n.* 1. a living thing growing from soil with leaves, stem, and roots. 2. all the machinery in a factory, as *a tractor plant*. *v.* **plant** 1. to sow seeds or put plants into the soil. 2. to put down firmly, as *to plant a table against a wall*.

plantation *n.* a place where many trees are planted.

planter *n.* the owner of a plantation of tea, rubber, etc.

plaque *n.* a metal plate fixed to a wall, with words engraved on it.

plaster *n.* 1. a paste of sand, lime, and water spread on the walls and ceilings of new buildings. 2. a cloth spread with a substance for healing cuts and sores, placed over the cut. *v.* **plaster** 1. to cover with plaster. 2. to spread on thickly.

plastic *adj.* easily shaped or moulded. *n.* **plastic** a chemically made substance which can be moulded into a great variety of things for the home, etc.

plate *n.* 1. a shallow dish for holding food. 2. household articles of gold and silver. 3. a flat sheet of metal or glass. 4. a full-page book illustration, as *the book has several coloured plates*. 5. (in baseball) the home base where the batter stands. *v.* **plate** to coat with metal (**plating, plated**). *n.* **plateful** (*pl.* **platefuls**).

plate-glass good quality glass for shop windows and mirrors.

plateau (*pron.* pla.tō') *n.* a raised area of flat land (*pl.* **plateaux** or **plateaus** *pron.* pla.tōz').

platform *n.* a raised level surface, as *a railway station platform* or *a platform in a hall.*

platinum *n.* a heavy silvery very precious metal.

platoon *n.* a group of about sixty soldiers, one quarter of a company.

platypus *n.* an Australian furry water-animal, which has a duck's bill and lays eggs.

plausible *adj.* seeming to be true, although it may not be, as *a plausible story.*

play *v.* 1. to have fun or amusement, or to take part in a game. 2. to act, as *to play the hero on the stage.* 3. to produce music from an instrument, as *to play the violin.* 4. to set going, as *to play a trick* or *play water on a fire* (**playing, played**). *n.* **play** 1. a game or amusement. 2. a stage performance. 3. loose movement, as *there is plenty of play in this handbrake. adj.* **playful** lively, full of fun.

to play the game to play fairly.

to play up to play hard.

to play up to to flatter someone.

playground *n.* a ground to play in.

plaything *n.* a toy.

plea *n.* 1. an excuse. 2. an appeal, an urgent request. 3. (in law) an accused person's defence.

plead *v.* 1. to beg, to ask earnestly. 2. to offer as an excuse, as *Bob pleaded he was late because he overslept.* 3. (in law) to reply to a charge, as *the accused man pleaded guilty.*

pleasant *adj.* nice, pleasing. *n.* **pleasantness.**

please *v.* 1. to give pleasure, as *the gift pleased me.* 2. to like, as *do as you please.* 3. used in polite requests, as *please pass the salt* (**pleasing, pleased**). *adj.* **pleasing** pleasant.

pleasure *n.* enjoyment, delight. *adj.* **pleasurable** giving pleasure.

pleat *n.* a double fold in a skirt, etc. *v.* **pleat** to fold in pleats.

pledge *v.* 1. to give a solemn promise. 2. to drink a toast. 3. to give an article as security in return for money (**pledging, pledged**). *n.* **pledge** 1. a promise. 2. a toast. 3. something given as a guarantee.

plenty *n.* a full supply, an abundance. *adj.* **plentiful** abundant, more than enough. *adj.* **plenteous** in full supply.

pliable *adj.* easily bent.

pliers *n.* a pair of pincers with long jaws for bending wire, etc.

plight *n.* a state or condition, as *the shipwrecked men were in a desperate plight.*

Plimsoll line *n.* a mark on the side of a ship to show how far the ship may be loaded with safety.

plod *v.* 1. to walk slowly and heavily, to trudge. 2. to keep on working hard (**plodding, plodded**).

plot *n.* 1. a piece of land. 2. the main outline of a story. 3. a secret plan. *v.* **plot** 1. to plan secretly. 2. to mark out a position on a plan (**plotting, plotted**).

plough (in the U.S.A. spelt *plow*) *n.* a farm machine for turning over soil. *v.* **plough** 1. to turn over soil with a plough. 2. to push through, as *to plough one's way through heavy snow.*

the Plough a group of stars also called the Great Bear.

plover *n.* a shore or marsh bird, the lapwing.

pluck *n.* 1. to pick, snatch, or pull. 2. to pull all the feathers off, as *to pluck a hen. n.* **pluck** 1. a sharp pull. 2. courage. *adj.* **plucky** brave.

to pluck up courage to become bold with an effort.

plug *n.* 1. a stopper for the outlet of a sink or bath, or for some other hole. 2. an electrical connection fitted with pins. 3. a fitting in the cylinder head of a petrol engine, to fire the petrol mixture electrically, a *sparking-plug. v.* **plug** to stop up a hole with a plug (**plugging, plugged**).

plum *n.* a soft fruit with a stone.

plumage (*pron.* plōōm'ij) *n.* a bird's feathers.

plumb *adj.* upright, vertical. *v.* **plumb** to measure depth, as *to plumb the depth of the sea.*

plumb-line a lead weight at the end of a string to test whether a wall is upright.

plumber *n.* a man who fits and repairs pipes, taps, etc. *n.* **plumbing.**

plume *n.* a feather worn as an ornament. *v.* **plume** to boast, to feel proud, as *Alan plumed himself on his cleverness* (**pluming, plumed**).

plump *adj.* round and fat. *v.* **plump** 1. to drop suddenly, as *to plump into a chair.* 2. (with **for**) to vote for.

plunder *v.* to steal by force. *n.* **plunder** booty.

plunge *v.* 1. to dive, as *Harry plunged into the water.* 2. to dash, as *Tom plunged into the crowd* (**plunging, plunged**). *n.* **plunge** a dash forward, a dive.

to take the plunge to act, after hesitating.

plural *adj.* more than one.

plus *prep.* added to, as *4 plus 5 equals 9. n.* **plus** the addition sign $+$.

ply (1) *v.* 1. to travel to and fro, as *the ferry-boats ply between the two landing stages.* 2. to attack persistently, as *they plied him with questions.* 3. to offer again and again, as *they plied him with food.* 4. to work at steadily, as *they plied themselves to their task* (**plying, plied**).

ply (2) *n.* a layer, as *five-ply wood.*

plywood *n.* several layers of wood glued together.

poach (1) *v.* to cook an egg without the shell in boiling water.

poach (2) *v.* to hunt or fish on someone's land without permission.

pocket *n.* 1. a small bag fitted to the clothes. 2. (in billiards or snooker) one of the six nets on the table. 3. thin air causing an aeroplane to drop, an *air-pocket. adj.* **pocket** 1. for the pocket, as *a pocket-book.* 2. small, as *pocket-sized. v.* **pocket** to put in the pocket (**pocketing, pocketed**).

to be out of pocket to have lost money.

pod *n.* a long seed-case.

poem *n.* a piece of fine writing, whose lines have a certain number of syllables and usually rhyme.

poet *n.* a man who writes poems (*fem.* **poetess**).

poetic *adj.* concerning poetry.

poetry *n.* 1. the writing of poems. 2. the work of a poet.

point *n.* 1. a sharp end. 2. a dot. 3. a particular place. 4. reason, purpose, as *that is the point of doing it.* 5. the important part, as *the point of a story.* 6. a position on a compass. *v.* **point** 1. to show the way, or draw attention to. 2. to aim, as *to point a gun.* 3. to face. *n. pl.* **points** movable parts of railway lines allowing a train to be switched to another line. *adj.* **pointed** with a point.

point-blank 1. fired from close range. 2. straight to the point.

point of view a way of looking at things.

pointer *n.* 1. a stick to point to a blackboard or map. 2. a breed of dog.

poise (*pron.* poyz) *n.* 1. balance. 2. self-confidence. *v.* **poise** to balance (**poising, poised**).

poison *n.* a substance which when swallowed or absorbed kills or harms a living thing. *v.* **poison** to harm or kill with poison. *adj.* **poisonous**.

poke *v.* 1. to jab with a finger or stick. 2. to stick out. *n.* **poke** a jab.

to poke fun at to joke about.

poker *n.* 1. a metal rod to stir a fire. 2. a card game.

polar *adj.* concerning the North or South Pole.

pole (1) *n.* 1. a very long round piece of wood, as *a flag-pole.* 2. a measure of length equal to 5 metres.

pole (2) *n.* 1. either end of the earth's axis, *the North Pole* or *the South Pole.* 2. either end of a magnet.

Pole Star a star almost directly over the North Pole.

police *n.* the men and women in blue uniform who keep law and order. *n.* **policeman** a man of the police.

police force all policemen and police-women.

policy *n.* 1. a plan, a way of doing something, as *it is a good policy to save for the future.* 2. an agreement with an insurance company (*pl.* **policies**).

polish *v.* to make something shiny by rubbing. *n.* **polish** 1. glossiness. 2. wax or liquid to make a polish. 3. good manners.

to polish off to finish.

polite *adj.* good-mannered. *n.* **politeness** courtesy, good manners.

politics *n. pl.* all the activities of governing a country. *adj.* **political** concerned with government. *n.* **politician** a man active in politics.

poll *n.* 1. an election. 2. the votes given at an election. *v.* **poll** 1. to vote or receive a vote. 2. to cut off the top of a tree.

pollen *n.* yellow powder on the stamens of flowers.

pollination *n.* the carrying of pollen from one flower to another to produce seeds.

polo *n.* a game like hockey played by two teams of four men each, mounted on ponies.

pomegranate *n.* a fruit with a hard skin and many seeds.

pommel *n.* 1. a round knob on a sword hilt. 2. the raised front of a saddle. *v.* **pommel** (also spelled **pummel**) to beat with the fists (**pommelling, pommelled**).

pomp *n.* great show, splendour.

pompous *adj.* too full of importance. *n.* **pomposity**.

pond *n.* a small lake or pool.

ponderous *adj.* heavy, clumsy.

pony *n.* a horse of a small breed (*pl.* **ponies**).

pool (1) *n.* a small pond, a deep part of a river, or a puddle.

pool (2) *v.* to put money, food, or ideas into a general fund. *n.* **pool** 1. a general fund. 2. a game like billiards.

poop *n.* 1. the stern of a ship. 2. a raised deck at the stern of a ship.

poor *adj.* 1. having little money. 2. not good. 3. humble, as *a poor cottage*. *adj.* **poorly** not well.

pop *n.* a small sharp sound. *v.* **pop** 1. to make a small quick sound. 2. to appear suddenly, as *to pop out* (**popping, popped**).

pop-corn baked Indian corn.

Pope *n.* the head of the Roman Catholic church.

poplar *n.* a tall tree.

poppy *n.* a wild or garden flower (*pl.* **poppies**).

popular *adj.* 1. of the people, as *popular opinion*. 2. liked by most people, as *a popular boy*. *n.* **popularity** being liked by many people.

population *n.* the number of people in a country or town.

porcelain *n.* china, earthenware made from the finest clay.

porch *n.* a covered entrance.

porcupine *n.* an animal like a large hedgehog, with protective spines or quills.

pore (1) *n.* a tiny hole in the skin.

pore (2) *v.* (with **over**) to examine closely, as *to pore over a map* (**poring, pored**).

pork *n.* pig's flesh or meat.

pork-pie a pie containing chopped pork.

porous *adj.* full of tiny holes or pores.

porpoise *n.* a sea-animal like a small whale.

porridge *n.* oatmeal boiled with water.

port (1) *n.* a harbour, or town with a harbour.

port (2) *n.* the left side of a ship as one faces the front or bow. Opposite to **starboard**.

port (3) *n.* a red wine.

portable *adj.* easily carried, as *a portable radio*.

porter *n.* 1. a man who carries market goods. 2. a man who carries luggage at a railway station. 3. (in North America) a railway sleeping-car attendant. 4. a hotel door-keeper.

port-hole *n.* a small, round ship's window.

portion *n.* a part or share. *v.* **portion** to divide into shares.

portrait *n.* a picture of someone.

portray *v.* 1. to draw or paint a likeness of someone. 2. to describe in words.

pose *v.* 1. to take up a position for a portrait. 2. to pretend to be what one is not. 3. to ask, as *to pose a question* (**posing, posed**). *n.* **pose** 1. a position taken up for a portrait. 2. a pretence. *n.* **poser** a difficult question.

position *n.* 1. a place or situation. 2. how one stands, sits, or lies, as *a comfortable position*. 3. a job or rank, as *he holds a good position in a bank*.

positive *adj.* certain, definite. *n.* **positive** 1. more than nothing, signified by the mark +. 2. (in photography) the finished photograph made from the film (the negative). 3. (in electricity) one of the terminals of a battery. Opposite of **negative**. *adv.* **positively** definitely.

posse (*pron.* pos'i) *n.* in the U.S.A. a number of men who were called by the sheriff to help him.

possess *v.* to have as one's own. *n.* **possession** 1. having as one's own. 2. property which one owns. 3. control. *n. pl.* **possessions** property. *adj.* **possessive** controlling, owning. *n.* **possessor**.

possibility *n.* what might happen (*pl.* **possibilities**).

possible *adj.* concerning what might happen, or what can be done, as *a possible mistake. adv.* **possibly** perhaps.

possum *n.* short for opossum, a small American animal.

to play possum to pretend to be ill or dead.

post (1) *n.* an upright pole or pillar, as a *gate-post. v.* **post** to stick on a wall or board, as *to post up a notice.*

post (2) *n.* the mail, the delivery of letters and parcels. *v.* **post** to send letters and parcels by post (in the U.S.A. to mail). *adj.* **postal**.

post-haste with the greatest speed.

post (3) *n.* 1. a station or position of duty, as *every soldier was at his post.* 2. a job or rank, as *the post of treasurer. v.* **post** to place in position, as *to post a guard.*

postage *n.* money paid for posting.

postage-stamp *n.* a stamp on a letter or parcel.

postal order *n.* paper money to be sent by post.

postcard *n.* a card sent by post.

poster *n.* a large notice or placard.

posterity *n.* future generations, our descendants.

postman *n.* a man who delivers letters and parcels.

postmark *n.* the mark cancelling a stamp.

post-office *n.* a shop selling stamps and postal orders, and receiving parcels for the post.

postpone *v.* to put off until later, as *the meeting was postponed* (**postponing, postponed**). *n.* **postponement**.

postscript *n.* (often shortened to **P.S.**) something added to a letter after it has been signed.

posture *n.* the way one holds oneself when standing or sitting, as *an upright posture.*

pot *n.* a round container, as a *jam-pot, teapot,* or *plant-pot. v.* **pot** to put in a pot (**potting, potted**). *adj.* **potted** in a pot, as *potted meat.*

potting shed a garden shed where plants are potted.

potato *n.* a vegetable grown for food (*pl.* **potatoes**).

potent *adj.* powerful, strong.

potter (1) *n.* a man who makes things of clay. *n.* **pottery** 1. articles made of baked clay. 2. the place where such things are made.

potter (2) *v.* to work in a haphazard lazy way.

pouch *n.* a small bag, as *a tobacco-pouch.*

poultice *n.* a dressing of hot, moist bread or meal put on a sore as a cure.

poultry *n.* birds reared for food, as hens or ducks.

pounce *v.* (with **on**) to swoop or leap on (**pouncing, pounced**). *n.* **pounce** a sudden swoop.

pound (1) *n.* 1. a measure of weight equal to 16 ounces (approximately 0·454 kilogrammes). 2. a unit of British money equal to 100 new pence.

pound (2) *v.* 1. to beat, to thump, as *to pound a door with one's fist.* 2. to smash to pieces.

pour *v.* 1. for a liquid to flow or fall in quantity, as *the rain poured down.* 2. to make flow, as *to pour out milk from a jug.*

it never rains but it pours bad luck comes in quantity.

to pour cold water on an idea to try to kill an idea with discouraging words.

pout *v.* to push out one's lips in a sulky way.

poverty *n.* being very poor.

powder *n.* any fine dust-like substance, as *face-powder* or *gunpowder. v.*

powder 1. to crush to powder. 2. to use powder, as *to powder one's face*. *adj.* **powdery** like powder.

power *n.* 1. strength, force, as *the power of steam*. 2. being able to do something, as *the power to govern*. 3. a great nation, as *a treaty between the powers*. *adj.* **powerful**. *adv.* **powerfully**. *adj.* **powerless**.

power-house, power-station *ns.* a building where electricity is produced.

practical *adj.* 1. able to be carried out, as *a practical plan*. 2. wise through experience, as *a practical gardener*. 3. good at making things, as *a practical boy*. *adv.* **practically** almost.

a practical joke a trick played on someone.

practice *n.* 1. a custom, a habit. 2. regular exercise, as *piano practice*. 3. the business of a doctor, as *Dr Smith has a practice in town* (note: do not confuse the spelling of *practice* (noun) with **practise** (verb)).

practise *v.* 1. to do regularly, as *he practises with the violin each day*. 2. to work as a doctor, as *to practise medicine* (**practising, practised**). *adj.* **practised** experienced (note: do not confuse the spelling of *practise* (verb) with **practice** (noun)).

prairie *n.* a stretch of grassland in North America.

prairie-dog a small animal of North America.

prairie-wolf a coyote, a small North American wolf.

praise *v.* 1. to speak well of a person or thing. 2. to sing hymns to God (**praising, praised**). *n.* **praise** words praising someone. *adj.* **praiseworthy** deserving praise.

prance *v.* 1. (of a horse) to jump about on the hind legs. 2. to strut about (**prancing, pranced**).

prank *n.* a mischievous trick.

prattle *v.* to babble like a child (**prattling, prattled**).

pray *v.* 1. to speak to God. 2. to ask earnestly for some favour (**praying, prayed**)

prayer *n.* 1. speaking to God. 2. a request.

pre- *prefix* before, as *pre-war* or *pre-fabricated*.

preach *v.* 1. to give a sermon. 2. (with **at**) to nag someone. *n.* **preacher**.

precarious *adj.* uncertain, risky.

precaution *n.* care taken beforehand to avoid danger, as *lifebelts are a precaution against drowning*. *adj.* **precautionary**.

precede *v.* 1. to go before. 2. to be earlier in time, as *Monday precedes Tuesday*. 3. to be of higher rank (**preceding, preceded**). *n.* **precedence**.

precious *adj.* very valuable.

precious stones jewels, gems.

precipice *n.* a steep cliff or hill.

precise *adj.* exact, accurate, very particular. *adv.* **precisely**. *n.* **precision**.

precocious *adj.* developed very early, too wise for one's age, as *Tommy is very precocious; he knows more than most boys*. *n.* **precocity**.

predicament *n.* an unpleasant situation.

predict *v.* to prophesy what will happen. *n.* **prediction**.

predominant *adj.* greatest, strongest, chief.

prefabricated *adj.* made beforehand.

preface *n.* an introduction to a book.

prefect *n.* someone in authority over others, especially a senior pupil in a school.

prefer *v.* 1. to like one thing better than another. 2. to put forward a claim or request (**preferring, preferred**). *adj.* **preferable** better. *adv.* **preferably** for choice, as *go soon, preferably tomorrow*. *n.* **preference** choice.

prefix *n.* a syllable put before a word to change its meaning, as in '*dis*honest' or '*un*fold'. *v.* **prefix** to put before.

prehistoric *adj.* before the times of recorded history.

prejudice *n.* an unfair opinion formed before all the facts are known.

preliminary *adj.* going first, before the main event, as *preliminary heats before Sports Day*.

prelude *n.* 1. an introduction. 2. music played before the main music of a concert.

premature *adj.* too soon, before the proper time.

premier adj. chief, first.

the Premier the Prime Minister.

premises n. pl. a building with its grounds.

premium n. 1. money paid for insurance. 2. a reward.

premonition n. a feeling that something is going to happen.

preoccupied adj. lost in thought.

preparation n. 1. being ready or making ready. 2. a medicine. 3. (often shortened to **prep**) a schoolchild's period for preparing work.

preparatory adj. preparing.

prepare v. to get ready or make ready (**preparing, prepared**). n. **preparedness** being ready.

preposition n. (in grammar) a word showing a relationship between two nouns or pronouns in a sentence, such as the word 'over' in he walked over the bridge.

preposterous adj. absurd.

prescribe v. to order, to advise, as a doctor prescribes medicine (**prescribing, prescribed**).

prescription n. a doctor's written order for medicine.

presence n. 1. being present, nearness, as to sign a form in the presence of a witness. 2. appearance, as he is a man of distinguished presence.

presence of mind ability to act quickly and coolly at a time of danger.

present (1) (pron. prez'ent) adj. here and now, as my present job or I am present. adv. **presently** soon.

at present now.

present-day modern.

present (2) (pron. prez'ent) n. a gift.

present (3) (pron. pre.zent') v. 1. to give, as to present a prize or present a play. 2. to introduce one person to another, as to present Mrs Smith to Mrs Jones. 3. to show, as he presented a woeful appearance. adv. **presentable** fit to be seen. n. **presentation** 1. act of giving. 2. an introduction.

preservative n. a substance which prevents rot or decay, as tar is a preservative for wood.

preserve v. 1. to keep safe. 2. to keep food from going bad, by salting, pickling, etc. (**preserving, preserved**). n. **preserve** a natural park where wild animals can live undisturbed. n. pl. **preserves** jam, marmalade, bottled fruit. n. **preservation** protection.

preside v. to be chairman at a meeting (**presiding, presided**).

president n. 1. chairman or chief official. 2. the head of a republic. n. **presidency** being president.

press v. 1. to push or squeeze, as to press a button. 2. to force, as to press an attack. 3. to push on, to smooth, as to press clothes. 4. to urge on someone, as to press a demand. n. **press** 1. a push or squeeze. 2. a crowd. 3. a machine for printing. 4. the newspaper industry. adj. **pressing** urgent, as pressing business.

press-gang (in days gone by) a group of naval men who took men by force for the navy.

to go to press for a newspaper to start printing.

pressure n. 1. a steady push, force. 2. influence, authority, as to bring pressure on the council to repair a road.

pressure-cooker a strong metal pan to cook things under steam pressure.

prestige n. fame, reputation.

presumably adv. probably.

presume v. 1. to suppose, to take for granted, as I presume he is at home. 2. to dare, as he presumed to tell me I was wrong. 3. to take advantage of, as to presume on someone's goodness (**presuming, presumed**).

presumption n. 1. something taken for granted. 2. impertinence. adj. **presumptuous**.

pretence n. pretending, a false show, as he made a pretence of not knowing.

pretend v. to make believe, to claim wrongly.

pretender n. someone who claims a title, as a pretender to a throne.

pretty adj. 1. charming, attractive. 2. fairly, as a pretty large amount. adv. **prettily**. n. **prettiness**.

prevail v. 1. to be stronger, to get the better of. 2. to be widespread, as grey skies prevail in winter. 3. (with **on**) to persuade, as *to prevail on someone to open a bazaar.*

prevailing *adj.* widespread, commonest, as *the prevailing wind blows from the south-west.*

prevalent *adj.* common, widespread, as *greenflies are prevalent on the roses this year. n.* **prevalence.**

prevent *v.* to stop something happening, or someone from doing something. *n.* **prevention** stopping. *adj.* **preventive** stopping something. *adj.* **preventable** able to be stopped, as *some kinds of accidents are preventable.*

previous *adj.* 1. earlier, as *a previous year.* 2. next before, as *the previous day.*

prey *n.* 1. an animal hunted by another for food, as *mice are the prey of owls.* 2. a victim, as *she became the prey of nervous fears. v.* **prey** (with **upon**) 1. to hunt smaller creatures. 2. to worry, as *his losses preyed upon his mind.*

bird of prey a bird, like an eagle, which hunts smaller creatures.

price *n.* the cost of anything. *v.* **price** to ask the price of, or place a price on (**pricing, priced**). *adj.* **priceless** too valuable to have a price.

prick *v.* to stab with a sharp point. *n.* **prick** a tiny hole, as *a pinprick.*

to prick up one's ears to listen intently.

prickle *n.* a thorn. *v.* **prickle** to cause a tingling on the skin (**prickling, prickled**). *adj.* **prickly.**

pride *n.* 1. satisfaction at doing something well, as *Tom takes a pride in his work.* 2. too high an opinion of oneself, conceit, as *pride comes before a fall. v.* **pride** to take pleasure in, as *he prided himself on his neatness* (**priding, prided**).

priest *n.* a clergyman, a minister of religion *(fem.* **priestess**). *n.* **priesthood** 1. the position of priests. 2. all priests.

prig *n.* a conceited person. *adj.* **priggish.**

prim *adj.* neat and proper, too nicely behaved.

primary *adj.* 1. first, as *a primary school is one for young children.* 2. chief, as *primary colours are the main colours*

from which others are made by mixing. *adv.* **primarily** firstly, mainly.

prime *adj.* 1. first, as *the prime minister.* 2. best, as *prime meat. n.* **prime** the best time, as *he was in the prime of life.*

primitive *adj.* 1. belonging to the earliest times, as *primitive man.* 2. simple, as *a primitive hut.*

primrose *n.* a pale-yellow spring flower.

prince *n.* 1. the son of a king or queen. 2. the ruler of a small country *(pl.* **princes**, *pron.* prin'sez, *fem.* **princess**, *pron.* prin.ses¹). *adj.* **princely** concerning a prince, noble.

Prince of Wales the eldest son of a British sovereign.

principal *adj.* chief, as *Paris is the principal city of France. n.* **principal** 1. the head of a college, or business. 2. money in the bank which gives interest. *adv.* **principally** chiefly.

principle *n.* 1. a rule to guide one's conduct, as *'honesty is the best policy' is a sound principle.* 2. a scientific rule or law.

print *v.* 1. to press a mark on something, such as inked type on paper. 2. to write using letters copied from printed ones. 3. to make a photograph from a negative film. *n.* **print** a mark left by pressure, as *a footprint. n.* **printer** someone who prints from type. *n.* **printing.**

prior (1) *adj.* 1. earlier, as *a prior engagement.* 2. (with **to**) before, as *prior to your coming.*

prior (2) *n.* the head of a monastery *(fem.* **prioress**).

priority *n.* first position in importance, as *this work has priority and must be done now.*

priory *n.* a house for monks or nuns *(pl.* **priories**).

prism *n.* a three-sided piece of glass which splits light into colours.

prison *n.* a gaol, a building in which criminals are kept. *n.* **prisoner.**

privacy *n.* 1. being away from others. 2. secrecy.

private *adj.* 1. not public, for one or two people only, as *a private talk.* 2. hidden from the public, as *a private garden. n.* **private** a soldier of lowest rank.

private school a school not under the control of the government or other public authority.

privilege *n.* a favour granted to one or a few people only, as *the school prefects had certain privileges.*

prize *n.* 1. a reward. 2. something won in a competition. 3. a captured enemy ship. *v.* **prize** to value highly, as *Nora prizes her cat* (**prizing, prized**).

prize-fight a boxing match for money.

pro- *prefix* for, on the side of, as *this man is pro-Russian.*

probability *n.* what is likely to happen, what might be expected.

probable *adj.* to be expected, likely to happen or be true. *adv.* **probably** very likely.

probation *n.* a testing period.

to put on probation to set a guilty person free for a trial period, instead of sending him to prison, to see if he can behave himself.

probe *v.* to search thoroughly, as *to probe a wound for a bullet* (**probing, probed**). *n.* **probe** an instrument for probing a wound.

problem *n.* a matter hard to decide, a question or difficulty to be answered.

procedure *n.* a way of doing something, as *the detective followed his usual procedure.*

proceed *v.* to continue, to go forward.

proceedings *n. pl.* 1. business done at a meeting, or a record of the business. 2. legal action, as *to take proceedings against someone.*

proceeds (*pron.* prō'seedz) *n. pl.* profits, or money taken.

process *n.* 1. a method of manufacture, as *a new process of making glass.* 2. progress, as *the house is in process of being built.* *v.* **process** to treat in a special way, as *to process cloth to make it waterproof.*

procession *n.* a large number of people moving in a long column on some special occasion.

proclaim *v.* to announce publicly.

proclamation *n.* a public announcement.

prod *v.* to poke, to urge on (**prodding, prodded**).

prodigal *adj.* wasteful, extravagant, as *the prodigal son* in the Bible story.

produce (*pron.* pro.dyo͞os') *v.* to bring forth, to show, to make, as *bees produce honey* or *to produce a ticket from one's pocket* (**producing, produced**). *n.* **produce** (*pron.* pro'dyo͞os) something made, grown, or produced. *n.* **producer** 1. a manufacturer. 2. someone who makes a film or organizes a play.

product *n.* 1. something produced, a result. 2. the amount obtained when numbers are multiplied together, as *the product of 2 × 3 × 4 is 24.*

production *n.* 1. making or growing things. 2. the things produced, as *the production of a factory.*

productive *adj.* producing something, fruitful. *n.* **productivity.**

profession *n.* 1. a statement. 2. an occupation, like that of doctor or lawyer, requiring a good education and training.

professional *adj.* concerning a profession. *n.* **professional** a sportsman who receives payment, as *a professional at football or golf.*

professor *n.* a teacher of highest rank at a university or college.

proficient *adj.* skilful, trained.

profile *n.* 1. an outline. 2. the side view of a face.

profit *n.* gain, money made by selling a thing for more than was paid for it. *adj.* **profitable** making a profit.

profound *adj.* 1. very deep, as *profound thought.* 2. deeply felt, as *profound joy.* 3. difficult, as *a profound problem.*

programme *n.* (in the U.S.A. spelt **program**) 1. a plan. 2. a list of items at a concert.

progress (*pron.* prō'gres) *n.* 1. forward movement, as *the progress of an expedition.* 2. growth, as *the progress of a business.* 3. improvement, as *the progress of an invalid.* *v.* **progress** (*pron.* prō.gres') to go forward, to improve. *n.* **progression.**

progressive *adj.* 1. moving forward. 2. ready to improve and adopt new ideas, as *a progressive business.* *adv.* **progressively** steadily, as *he became progressively better.*

prohibit *v.* to forbid, not to allow. *n.* **prohibition** 1. forbidding. 2. forbidding the sale of alcoholic drink.

project (*pron.* proj'ekt) *n.* a plan, a scheme. *v.* **project** (*pron.* prō.jekt') 1. to throw. 2. to throw pictures on a screen. 3. to jut forward. *n.* **projection** 1. throwing. 2. something sticking out. 3. a plan drawn on paper.

projectile *n.* a shell, bullet, or rocket fired from a gun.

projector *n.* an apparatus for throwing pictures on a screen.

prolong *v.* to make longer, as *to prolong a holiday. n.* **prolongation**.

promenade (*pron.* prom.e.nahd') *n.* a wide road along the sea front where people can stroll. *v.* **promenade** to walk about (**promenading, promenaded**).

prominent *adj.* 1. standing out, noticeable. 2. distinguished, famous, as *a prominent musician. n.* **prominence**.

promise *v.* 1. to say one will or will not do something. 2. to show signs of, as *it promises to be a good concert* (**promising, promised**). *n.* **promise** 1. giving one's word. 2. a reason for hoping, a sign of better things to come, as *Tom's work shows promise. adj.* **promising** giving hope.

promote *v.* 1. to raise to a higher position. 2. to support some scheme, as *to promote a bazaar* (**promoting, promoted**). *n.* **promotion**.

prompt *adj.* quick, immediate, as *a prompt start. v.* **prompt** 1. to urge on, as *we prompted him to start.* 2. to whisper to an actor who has forgotten his words. *n.* **promptness** quickness.

prone *adj.* 1. liable to, as *he is prone to forgetfulness.* 2. lying face downwards, as *he was stretched prone on the floor.*

prong *n.* one of the spikes of a fork.

pronoun *n.* a word used instead of a noun, as *he, it, which, who.*

pronounce *v.* 1. to say the sound of a word clearly and correctly, as *how do you pronounce c-h-a-o-s?* (**pronouncing, pronounced**). *n.* **pronunciation**. 2. to announce, as *to pronounce the sentence on a guilty criminal. n.* **pronouncement**.

pronunciation *n.* the way one sounds a word when speaking, as *he has a clear pronunciation.*

proof *n.* 1. something that shows beyond doubt that a thing is true, as *I have proof that you took the apples.* 2. a test, as *they put his statement to the proof.* 3. a sample print taken by a printer or photographer.

-proof *suffix* strong enough to withstand, as *waterproof* or *bullet-proof*

prop *n.* a support, a post, as *a miner's pit-prop. v.* **prop** to hold up (**propping, propped**).

propaganda *n.* stories and opinions spread deliberately to bring other people to one's point of view.

propel *v.* to drive forward (**propelling, propelled**).

propeller *n.* a revolving shaft with blades to drive a ship or aeroplane.

proper *adj.* 1. suitable, right, as *this is the proper way to do it.* 2. correctly behaved, as *Miss Jones is always very proper.* *adv.* **properly** rightly, thoroughly.

proper fraction a fraction less than a whole number, as $\frac{1}{2}$, $\frac{7}{8}$, or $\frac{2}{3}$.

proper noun the particular name of a person or thing, as *Doris* or *London.*

property *n.* 1. things one owns, possessions. 2. houses and buildings, as *he is a property-owner.* 3. a quality, what a thing is or does, as *a magnet has the property of attracting iron* (*pl.* **properties**).

prophecy (*pron.* prof'e.si) *n.* something forecast about the future (*pl.* **prophecies**) (note : do not confuse the spelling with that of the verb **prophesy**).

prophesy (*pron.* prof'e.sī) *v.* to say what is going to happen in the future (**prophesying, prophesied**, (note : do not confuse the spelling with that of the noun **prophecy**).

prophet *n.* 1. a man who tells what will happen in the future. 2. (in the Bible) a man who tells people God's plans and wishes (*fem.* **prophetess**). *adj.* **prophetic**.

proportion *n.* 1. part, share, as *we spend a large proportion of our time at school.* 2. one amount compared with another, as *make the mixture in the proportion of three parts of sand to one of cement.* *adj.* **proportional** in the right proportion.

proportions *n. pl.* size, measurements, as *a field of big proportions.*

proposal *n.* 1. a suggestion, a plan. 2. an offer of marriage.

propose *v.* 1. to put forward a suggestion or plan. 2. to make an offer of marriage (**proposing, proposed**). *n.* **proposition** a suggestion.

proprietor *n.* a property-owner (*fem.* **proprietress**).

propulsion *n.* driving forward, as *the propulsion of an aeroplane by jet engines.*

prose *n.* writing which is not poetry.

prosecute *v.* 1. to bring someone before a court of law. 2. to carry out, as *to prosecute a search* (**prosecuting, prosecuted**). *ns.* **prosecution, prosecutor**.

prospect (*pron.* pros'pekt) *n.* 1. a view. 2. something to look forward to, as *the prospect of a holiday.* 3. something to expect, as *a prospect of thunder.* *v.* **prospect** (*pron.* pros.pekt') to search for gold or oil. *n.* **prospector**.

prosper *v.* to do well, to succeed, to get rich. *adj.* **prosperous** doing well, rich. *n.* **prosperity** good fortune.

protect *v.* to guard, to shield. *n.* **protection** safe-keeping, defence. *n.* **protector** a defender.

protein (*pron.* prō'teen) *n.* a body-building foodstuff, found in meat, eggs, and fish.

protest (*pron.* prō.test') 1. to object to. 2. to state firmly, as *Dick protested he was right.* *n.* **protest** (*pron.* prō'test) a strong complaint or objection. *n.* **protestation**.

Protestant *n.* one of those who separated from the Church of Rome at the time of the Reformation in the sixteenth century.

protractor *n.* an instrument for measuring angles.

protrude *v.* to stick out (**protruding, protruded**).

proud *adj.* 1. conceited. 2. dignified, as *she was too proud to complain.* 3. feeling pleased, as *he was proud of his*

success. 4. splendid, as *a proud sight.* *adv.* **proudly**. See **pride**.

prove *v.* 1. to find proof, to show that something is true. 2. to turn out to be, as *Jennifer proved a good painter.* 3. to test, as *to prove a new motor* (**proving, proved**). See **proof**.

proverb *n.* a wise old saying, as *look before you leap.* *adj.* **proverbial** well-known.

provide *v.* 1. to supply. 2. to prepare for, as *to provide for illness.* 3. to ensure, as *the law provides that all men receive equal justice* (**providing, provided**).

provided that on condition that.

providence *n.* care for the future

Providence God, as *to trust in Providence.*

provident *adj.* careful for the future, thrifty.

province *n.* 1. a division of a country, as *Brittany is a province of France.* 2. a field of study or knowledge, as *Greek history was the professor's special province.* *n. pl.* **provinces** the part of a country outside the capital. *adj.* **provincial** concerning the provinces.

provision *n.* preparation, arrangements, as *we made provision for cold weather.* *n. pl.* **provisions** food.

provisional *adj.* for the time being.

provoke *v.* 1. to arouse, as *my remark provoked a smile.* 2. to stir to anger, as *he was provoked by the threat* (**provoking, provoked**).

provost *n.* 1. the chief magistrate or mayor of a Scottish town. 2. the head of a college.

prow *n.* the front part of a boat.

prowl *v.* to go about silently in search of something to eat or steal.

prudent *adj.* cautious, careful. *n.* **prudence** not taking risks, careful planning. *adv.* **prudently**.

prune (1) *n.* a dried plum.

prune (2) *v.* to cut short the branches of a tree or bush (**pruning, pruned**).

pry *v.* 1. to peep inquisitively. 2. to force open with a lever (**prying, pried**).

psalm (*pron.* sahm) *n.* a sacred song, as in the *Book of Psalms* in the Old Testament.

psychologist *n.* someone who studies psychology.

psychology *n.* the study of the mind. *adj.* **psychological.**

public *adj.* concerning the people or for the people, as a *public park, public service,* or *public announcement. adv.* **publicly.**

public-spirited working for the general good.

public school (in Britain) a private secondary school whose pupils often live in the school.

publican *n.* 1. (in Britain) an inn-keeper. 2. (in the Bible) a tax-collector.

publication *n.* 1. publishing. 2. a book or magazine.

publicity *n.* advertisements, making things widely known.

publicize *v.* to advertise, to make widely known (**publicizing, publicized**).

publish *v.* 1. to make books, magazines, or sheets of music for sale. 2. to make widely known. *n.* **publisher** a man who produces books, etc., for sale.

pucker *v.* to wrinkle. *adj.* **puckered** wrinkled, in creases, as *he gazed with puckered brows.*

pudding *n.* soft boiled food served as a sweet.

puddle *n.* a small pool of muddy water.

puff *n.* 1. a quick blow of breath, smoke, gas, steam, or wind. 2. a light pastry filled with jam or cream. 3. a soft pad for use with powder, a *powder-puff. v.* **puff** 1. to give out a puff of breath, gas, etc. 2. to swell up. *adj.* **puffy** swollen.

puffin *n.* a sea-bird with a coloured beak.

pull *v.* 1. to draw forcibly, as *to pull a cart.* 2. to pluck, as *to pull flowers to pieces. n.* **pull** a tug, a heavy movement.

to pull oneself together to gain control of oneself.

to pull one's weight to do one's share of the hard work.

pullet *n.* a young hen.

pulley *n.* a grooved wheel fitted with a rope for pulling up weights (*pl.* **pulleys**).

pullover *n.* a woollen jersey.

pulp *n.* 1. the fleshy part of fruit. 2. any soft wet mass. *v.* **pulp** to make into pulp. *adj.* **pulpy.**

pulpit *n.* a kind of raised desk in church for the preacher.

pulse *n.* the throbbing of the blood in an artery, especially in the wrist. *v.* **pulse** to throb (**pulsing, pulsed**).

puma (*pron.* pyoo'ma) *n.* an American wildcat, a cougar, or mountain lion.

pummel see **pommel.**

pump *n.* a machine for raising liquids, or for forcing liquids or gases through a pipe. *v.* **pump** to work a pump.

pumpkin *n.* a large fruit like a melon.

pun *n.* a play upon words, as when the traveller was told : 'Beware of the bear ! Bear left !'

punch (1) *v.* 1. to hit with the fist. 2. to stamp a hole in, as *to punch a ticket. n.* **punch** 1. a blow with a fist. 2. a machine or tool for stamping metal, leather, etc.

punch (2) *n.* a strong drink made from spirits and lemon.

punctual *adj.* prompt, on time. *n.* **punctuality.** *adv.* **punctually.**

punctuate *v.* 1. to put full-stops, commas, etc. in sentences. 2. to interrupt, as *the speech was punctuated by cheers* (**punctuating, punctuated**). *n.* **punctuation.**

puncture *n.* a small hole made with something pointed. *v.* **puncture** to prick, as *to puncture a tyre* (**puncturing, punctured**).

punish *v.* to make a wrong-doer suffer for his fault or crime. *adj.* **punishing** very exhausting, as *a punishing struggle. n.* **punishment.**

capital punishment the death penalty.

punt *n.* a flat-bottomed boat moved by a pole. *v.* **punt** 1. to push a boat with a pole. 2. to kick a ball dropped from the hands.

puny (*pron.* pyoo'ni) *adj.* small and weak.

pup *n.* a puppy, a young dog.

pupa (*pron.* pyoo'pa) *n.* a cocoon or chrysalis, the stage reached by an insect after it has ceased to be a grub or caterpillar (*pl.* **pupae** *pron.* pyoo'pee).

pupil (1) *n.* someone who is being taught.

pupil (2) *n.* the black centre of the eye.
puppet *n.* 1. a doll worked by strings.
2. a doll which fits over the hand and is worked by the fingers, a *glove-puppet*. 3. someone who always does what others tell him. *n.* **puppetry** the use of puppets.
puppy *n.* a young dog (*pl.* **puppies**).
purchase *v.* to buy (**purchasing, purchased**). *n.* **purchase** 1. buying. 2. the thing bought. 3. a grip, as *a purchase on a rope. n.* **purchaser** buyer.
pure *adj.* 1. clean, as *pure water.* 2. unmixed, as *pure coffee. adv.* **purely**. *n.* **purity**.
purify *v.* to clean, to make pure (**purifying, purified**). *n.* **purification**.
purl *v.* to knit with stitches which are opposite to **plain**.
purple *n.* the colour formed by mixing red and blue. *adj.* **purplish** like purple.
purpose *n.* an intention, plan, aim. *adj.* **purposeful** deliberate. *adj.* **purposeless** aimless. *adv.* **purposely** deliberately.
purr *n.* the sound a cat makes.
purse *n.* a small money-bag.
purser *n.* a ship's officer who looks after money.
pursue *v.* to chase, to follow (**pursuing, pursued**). *n.* **pursuer**.
pursuit *n.* 1. a chase. 2. an occupation.
push *v.* 1. to press against. 2. to urge on, as *they pushed the plan for a new library. n.* **push** 1. a thrust. 2. (*slang*) energy, ability to get things done, as *Dick has plenty of push*.
put *v.* 1. to place in position, as *to put coal on a fire.* 2. to express in words, as *to put a plan to a meeting* (**putting, put**).
to be put out to be offended.
to put by to save.
to put off to delay.
to put someone in his place to snub.
to put to death to kill.
to put to the test to try out.
to put to sea to start a voyage.
to put two and two together to form an opinion from certain facts.
to put up with to make the best of.
putrid *adj.* decayed, rotten.
putt *v.* (in golf) to strike a ball gently towards the hole when on the green. *n.* **putter** the club used to putt.
putty *n.* a paste of whiting and oil used for fixing glass in frames. *v.* **putty** to fix with putty (**puttying, puttied**).
puzzle *n.* a difficult question, an interesting problem to solve for fun, as *a crossword puzzle. v.* **puzzle** to bewilder (**puzzling, puzzled**).
pygmy or **pigmy** *n.* a dwarf (*pl.* **pygmies**).
pyjamas (in the U.S.A. **pajamas**) *n. pl.* a sleeping-suit.
pylon *n.* a tall steel tower.
pyramid *n.* a solid figure with triangular sides which meet at a point at the top, as *the pyramids of Egypt*.
python *n.* a large snake which crushes its prey.

Q

quack *n.* the cry of a duck.
quadrangle *n.* 1. a four-sided figure, a rectangle. 2. a four-sided space surrounded by buildings.
quadrilateral *n.* any four-sided figure.
quadruped *n.* a four-footed animal.
quaint *adj.* pleasantly old-fashioned.
quake *v.* to shake, to tremble (**quaking, quaked**).
qualify *v.* 1. to pass an examination or test in order to become entitled to some post or honour, as *to qualify to become a doctor.* 2. to modify a remark and make it less sweeping, as *the teacher qualified his remark that the boys had done badly, and said that only some had done badly* (**qualifying, qualified**). *adj.* **qualified** trained, as *a qualified teacher. n.* **qualification**.
quality *n.* 1. value, worth, as *cloth of poor quality.* 2. something that makes one thing different from another, as *hardness and brilliance are the chief qualities of a diamond* (*pl.* **qualities**).
quandary *n.* difficulty, doubt.
quantity *n.* an amount (*pl.* **quantities**).
quarantine *n.* keeping apart persons and animals from others (especially in a ship from a foreign country) until it is certain they are free from any infection.

quarrel *n.* an angry argument or disagreement. *v.* **quarrel** to argue bitterly, or fall out with a friend (**quarrelling, quarrelled**). *adj.* **quarrelsome** fond of quarrelling.

quarry (1) *n.* an opening in the earth or a hillside from which stone is cut. *v.* **quarry** to obtain slate or stone from the earth (**quarrying, quarried**).

quarry (2) *n.* a hunted animal or bird.

quart *n.* a liquid measure equal to two pints or a quarter of a gallon (1·137 litres).

quarter *n.* 1. a fourth part. 2. a district of a town or city, often where people of the same race or occupation live, as *the Chinese quarter* or *the artists' quarter in Paris.* 3. direction, as *ants swarmed from every quarter.* 4. mercy, as *the enemy gave no quarter. v.* **quarter** 1. to divide into four parts, as *to quarter an apple.* 2. to find food and lodging for, as *to quarter troops. n. pl.* **quarters** 1. lodgings. 2. the front or back of an animal, as the *fore-quarters* or the *hind-quarters. adv.* **quarterly** every three months or quarter-year.

quarter-deck the officers' deck of a ship.

quarter-master an army officer in charge of stores.

at close quarters very near.

to show no quarter to show no mercy.

quartet or **quartette** *n.* 1. a group of four singers or musicians. 2. music for four players or singers.

quartz *n.* a hard mineral.

quaver *v.* to quiver, to tremble. *n.* **quaver** 1. a tremble. 2. (in music) a note equal in length to half a crotchet.

quay (*pron.* kee) *n.* a place for ships to load and unload.

queen *n.* 1. a king's wife, or a woman ruler. 2. a playing-card. 3. a piece in chess. 4. the fully developed female bee. *adj.* **queenly.**

queer *adj.* 1. strange, unusual. 2. unwell.

quell *v.* to put down, as *to quell a revolt.*

quench *v.* 1. to put out, as *to quench a fire.* 2. to satisfy, as *to quench one's thirst.*

query *n.* a question, a question mark (?)

(*pl.* **queries**). *v.* **query** to ask a question (**querying, queried**).

quest *n.* a search.

question *n.* 1. a query, a request for information. 2. a problem, as *that is a big question to decide. v.* **question** 1. to ask a question. 2. to doubt, as *I question whether he is right.*

question-mark a mark (?) which should always be put at the end of a sentence asking a question.

beyond question without doubt.

out of the question impossible.

questionable *adj.* doubtful.

queue (*pron.* kyoo) *n.* a line of waiting people or cars. *v.* **queue** to wait one's turn in a line of people (**queueing** or **queuing, queued**).

quibble *v.* to avoid answering an awkward question, or to avoid telling the truth, by a clever playing with words (**quibbling, quibbled**).

quick *adj.* fast, rapid, hasty. *n.* **quick** the sensitive skin under the nails. *adv.* **quickly** *n.* **quickness.**

quick-witted with an alert mind.

quicken *v.* to move faster, to hasten.

quicklime *n.* lime made by heating limestone, used in making mortar.

quicksand *n.* loose, wet sand in which one can sink.

quicksilver *n.* mercury, a liquid metal.

quiet *adj.* 1. noiseless, peaceful. 2. not bright, as *a quiet colour.* 3. calm, as *a quiet sea. n.* **quiet** peace, stillness. *v.* **quieten** to make quiet. *n.* **quietness.**

quill *n.* 1. a large feather. 2. a pen made from a feather, once used for writing. 3. a spine of a porcupine or hedgehog.

quilt *n.* a thick padded bed-cover.

quinine (*pron.* kwi.neen') *n.* a bitter medicine made from the bark of a South American tree.

quintet or **quintette** *n.* 1. a group of five singers or musicians. 2. music for five players or singers.

quire *n.* twenty-four sheets of paper.

quit *v.* to give up, to leave (**quitting, quitted**). *n.* **quitter** (in North America) someone who gives up easily.

quite *adv.* 1. completely, as *you are quite wrong.* 2. somewhat, fairly, as *your homework is quite good.*

quits *adj.* even, level, as *we are quits.*

quiver (1) *v.* to shake.

quiver (2) *n.* a case for arrows.

quiz *n.* a game or competition to see who knows most. *v.* **quiz** 1. to ask many questions. 2. to make fun of (**quizzing, quizzed**).

quoit *n.* a ring thrown over a peg in the game of *quoits.*

deck quoits a game played with a rope ring over a net.

quota *n.* 1. a share. 2. a limited amount of foreign goods allowed into a country.

quotation *n.* 1. repeating someone's exact words. 2. a passage repeated, as *a quotation from Shakespeare.* See **quote.**

quotation marks marks (' . . . ') used before and after a quotation or spoken passage.

quote *v.* 1. to repeat someone's exact words. 2. to name a price for some article (**quoting, quoted**). See **quotation.**

quotient *n.* the answer one gets when one number is divided by another, as *when 15 is divided by 5 the quotient is 3.*

R

rabbi *n.* a Jewish priest.

rabbit *n.* a small animal which burrows in the ground.

rabbit-hutch a box for a rabbit to live in.

rabbit-warren a number of holes where rabbits live.

rabble *n.* a noisy crowd.

raccoon or **racoon** *n.* a North American furry animal with a ringed tail, a *coon.*

race (1) *n.* 1. a contest of speed. 2. a channel of water to a mill-wheel, a *mill-race.* 3. a groove in a wheel holding ball-bearings, a *ball-race.* *v.* **race** 1. to compete against others in speed. 2. (with **after**) to chase (**racing, raced**). *n.* **racing.**

race (2) *n.* living things of the same kind, of the same descent, as *the human race.* *adj.* **racial** concerning a race of people.

rack *n.* 1. a frame on which to hang

things. 2. an old instrument of torture. *v.* **rack** to torment.

to rack one's brains to try to remember or to solve a problem.

racket (1) *n.* 1. a noise, a din. 2. a dishonest plan for getting money.

racket (2) or **racquet** *n.* a bat with a network of catgut used in tennis and other games.

racoon see **raccoon.**

racy *adj.* lively, bright, as *he writes in a racy style.*

radar *n.* an apparatus which uses the reflection of radio waves to detect ships or aeroplanes at night or in fog.

radiant *adj.* 1. sending out rays across space, as *radiant heat.* 2. bright, shining, as *a radiant smile.* *n.* **radiance.**

radiate *v.* 1. to send out in rays, as *to radiate heat, light, or X-rays.* 2. to spread out in every direction, as *wires radiate from the telephone exchange* (**radiating, radiated**). *n.* **radiation.**

radiator *n.* 1. a grid of hot-water pipes for heating a room. 2. a part at the front of a motor-car for cooling the engine.

radical *adj.* going to the roots, extreme, as *radical changes.*

radio *n.* 1. wireless, the sending and receiving of music and speech without wires. 2. a receiving set (*pl.* **radios**).

radiogram a radio set and a record-player in a cabinet.

radioactive giving off X-rays like uranium and some other rare metals.

radish (*pron.* rad'ish) *n.* a small plant, eaten in salads.

radium *n.* a rare metal which gives off X-rays.

radius *n.* a straight line from the centre to the edge, or circumference, of a circle (*pl.* **radii**).

raffia *n.* palm-fibre woven to make baskets and mats.

raffle *n.* making money by selling numbered tickets, which are later drawn for prizes.

raft *n.* logs or planks tied together to make a platform floated on water.

rafter *n.* one of the slanting beams holding up a roof.

rag (1) *n.* a piece of old cloth. *adj.* **ragged** worn and tattered.

rag (2) *v.* to tease someone (**ragging, ragged**).

rage *n.* violent anger. *v.* **rage** to be very angry (**raging, raged**).

raid *n.* a sudden quick attack.

rail *n.* 1. a wooden or metal bar, as *a hand-rail on a stairway,* or *a fence rail attached to the upright posts.* 2. a railway line. *v.* **rail** (with **off**) to enclose with a fence. *n.* **railing** a fence of rails.

railroad *n.* (in North America) a railway.

railway *n.* a track of steel rails for trains. **railway crossing** a place where a road crosses a railway without a bridge.

rain *n.* water falling in drops from the clouds. *v.* **rain** 1. to fall in drops of water. 2. to fall like rain, as *curses rained upon him from the angry mob.* *adj.* **rainy**.

to rain cats and dogs to rain heavily. **to save for a rainy day** to save for bad times.

rainbow *n.* a coloured arch in the sky in rainy weather.

raincoat *n.* a waterproof coat.

rainfall *n.* the amount of rain falling in a certain place during a certain time.

raise *v.* 1. to lift up. 2. to build. 3. to bring up, as *to raise children.* 4. to breed or grow, as *to raise chickens.* 5. to collect, as *to raise money* (**raising, raised**).

raisin *n.* a small, dried grape.

rajah *n.* an Indian prince (*fem.* **ranee**).

rake (1) *n.* a farm or garden tool with a row of spikes at the end of a pole. *v.* **rake** to use a rake (**raking, raked**).

rake (2) *n.* slope, as *the rake of a ship's mast.*

rally *v.* 1. to get together again, as *the general rallied his men who had scattered.* 2. to improve after an illness (**rallying, rallied**). *n.* **rally** 1. a meeting. 2. (in tennis) a number of quick shots across the net (*pl.* **rallies**).

ram *n.* 1. a male sheep (*fem.* **ewe**). 2. (in olden days) a beam for battering the gate of a fort. *v.* **ram** 1. to crash into. 2. to stuff into, to cram (**ramming, rammed**).

ramble *v.* 1. to stroll, to wander. 2. to talk in an aimless way (**rambling,**

rambled). *n.* **rambler** 1. a walker in the country. 2. a climbing plant.

ramp *n.* a short slope.

rampart *n.* a wall around a fort.

ran *past* of **run**.

ranch *n.* (in America) a cattle-farm. *n.* **rancher** the owner of a ranch.

random *adj.* chance, haphazard, as *a random guess.*

at random by chance.

rang *past* of **ring**.

range *n.* 1. a line, as *a range of hills.* 2. a variety, as *a range of goods.* 3. a place for shooting-practice, a *rifle range.* 4. the distance one can shoot, shout, etc., as *to be within range.* 5. a stove, as a *kitchen-range.* 6. (in North America) grazing land for cattle. *v.* **range** 1. to stand in a row. 2. to vary, as *the scores range from 1 to 10.* 3. to wander (**ranging, ranged**).

ranger *n.* 1. a wanderer. 2. a senior Girl Guide. 3. a forest warden.

rank (1) *n.* 1. a row, as *the front rank.* 2. an important position, as *he holds the rank of major.* *v.* **rank** to put in order of importance. *n. pl.* **ranks** ordinary soldiers.

rank and file ordinary soldiers or people.

rank (2) *adj.* 1. strong, coarse. 2. extreme, as *rank folly.*

ransom *n.* a price paid by his friends for a prisoner to be set free. *v.* **ransom** to pay ransom.

to hold to ransom to keep a prisoner until ransom is paid.

rap *n.* a quick light blow, a tap. *v.* **rap** to tap (**rapping, rapped**).

rapid *adj.* fast, quick. *n. pl.* **rapids** a part of a river where the current flows swiftly. *n.* **rapidity** swiftness.

rapier *n.* a long, thin fencing-sword.

rapt *adj.* lost in thought or wonder, as *Joan sat rapt watching the play.*

rapture *n.* great pleasure, delight. *adj.* **rapturous** delighted.

rare *adj.* 1. scarce, not often seen. 2. thin, as *the air on Mount Everest is rare.* 3. (in North America) underdone, as *rare meat.* *adv.* **rarely** not often.

rarity *n.* 1. scarceness. 2. a scarce object (*pl.* **rarities**).

rascal *n.* a rogue, a dishonest person.

rash (1) *adj.* hasty, reckless. *n.* **rashness**

rash (2) *n.* a number of spots on the skin.

rasp *n.* 1. a rough file. 2. a grating sound. *v.* **rasp** to make a harsh, grating sound.

raspberry *n.* a soft, juicy berry (*pl.* **raspberries**).

rat *n.* a gnawing animal like a large mouse.

to smell a rat to suspect something.

rate *n.* 1. speed, as *to move at a fast rate.* 2. amount, as *the birth-rate of a town tells us the number of births for every thousand people. n. pl.* **rates** money that every house-owner or business firm pays to the local council each year. *v.* **rate** to value, to consider, as *I rate Tom a better swimmer than Jack* (**rating, rated**).

rather *adv.* 1. more gladly, as *he would rather ride than walk.* 2. a little, as *he felt rather tired.*

ratio (*pron.* ray'shi.ō) *n.* the proportion of one quantity to another, as *there is a ratio of three boys to two girls in our class* (*pl.* **ratios**).

ration (*pron.* rash'un) *n.* a fixed share, as *each man had his ration of food. v.* **ration** to share out fairly.

rattle *v.* to make a number of quick sounds, to clatter (**rattling, rattled**). *n.* **rattle** 1. a number of quick sounds. 2. a baby's toy.

rattlesnake *n.* a poisonous snake whose tail rattles.

rave *v.* to talk like a madman (**raving, raved**).

raven *n.* a large, black bird.

ravenous (*pron.* rav'en.us) *adj.* very hungry.

ravine (*pron.* ra.veen') *n.* a very deep valley.

raw *adj.* 1. uncooked, as *raw potatoes.* 2. untreated, as *raw wool.* 3. cold, as *a raw day.* 4. sore, as *raw hands.* 5. untrained, as *raw soldiers.*

ray *n.* a thin beam, a gleam, as *a ray of light* or *a ray of hope.*

raze *v.* to destroy entirely, as *to raze a fort* (**razing, razed**).

razor *n.* an instrument with a sharp blade for shaving.

re- *prefix* again, as *to re-write* or *re-make.*

reach *v.* 1. to arrive at, as *the train reached the station.* 2. to stretch to, as *the procession reached the length of the street.* 3. (with **for**) to stretch out the hand, as *to reach for a book. n.* **reach** a stretching out of the hand.

react (*pron.* ree.akt') *v.* to show a result, as *his illness reacted to treatment. n.* **reaction.**

to react against to rebel against.

read (*pron.* reed) *v.* 1. to look at words and understand their meaning, or to say them aloud. 2. to understand what an instrument has to tell, as *to read a thermometer* (**reading, read** *pron.* red). *adj.* **readable** easy to read. *n.* **reading.**

to read between the lines to see a hidden meaning.

ready *adj.* 1. prepared, willing. 2. on hand, as *ready money.* 3. quick, as *he has a ready wit. adv.* **readily.** *n.* **readiness.**

ready reckoner a book of tables to help work out sums quickly.

ready-made made beforehand.

real *adj.* 1. true, not imaginary. 2. not artificial, as *real pearls. adj.* **realistic** life-like. *n.* **reality** actual fact. *adv.* **really** as a matter of fact, truly.

in reality in fact.

realize *v.* 1. to be aware, to see clearly. 2. to gain, as *to realize an ambition.* 3. to make a profit. *n.* **realization.**

realm *n.* a kingdom.

reap *v.* 1. to cut down and gather, as *to reap the harvest.* 2. to gain, to receive a reward.

rear (1) *n.* the back part.

rear-admiral an officer next below a vice-admiral.

to bring up the rear to march last in a troop.

rear (2) *v.* 1. to bring up, to breed. 2. (of a horse) to stand on the hind-legs. 3. to raise, as *the bull reared its head.*

reason *n.* 1. an explanation. 2. ability to think things out, as *to use one's reason to solve a puzzle. v.* **reason** 1. to think something out. 2. to argue, to persuade. *n.* **reasoning.**

by reason of because of.

reasonable *adj.* 1. sensible, as *a reasonable plan.* 2. moderate, as *a reasonable amount. adv.* **reasonably.**

reassure *v.* to remove doubts and give confidence to someone (**reassuring, reassured**).

rebel (*pron.* reb'l) *n.* someone who fights the government or those in power. *adj.* **rebel** against the government, as *a rebel troop. v.* **rebel** (*pron.* re.bel') to revolt (**rebelling, rebelled**). *n.* **rebellion** a revolt. *adj.* **rebellious.**

rebuke *v.* to scold or blame (**rebuking, rebuked**). *n.* **rebuke** a scolding.

recall *v.* 1. to call back again. 2. to remember, as *I recall his name.*

recede *v.* to move back (**receding, receded**). *adj.* **receding** sloping back.

receipt *n.* 1. the receiving of a thing, as *on receipt of the goods I will send payment.* 2. a signed note confirming that money has been received. *n. pl.* **receipts** all money received.

receive *v.* 1. to be given. 2. to entertain, as *to receive a visitor.*

receiver *n.* 1. someone who receives. 2. a radio set which receives broadcasts. 3. a telephone earpiece.

recent *adj.* just happened, new. *adv.* **recently.**

reception *n.* 1. the receiving of anything. 2. the way someone is received, as *a warm reception.* 3. a big party to honour someone, as *a wedding reception.*

receptionist *n.* someone who receives visitors to a hotel, surgery, etc.

recipe (*pron.* res'i.pi) *n.* a list of materials for a cake, medicine, etc.

recital *n.* 1. a story. 2. an entertainment, as *a recital of music.*

recitation *n.* repeating a poem from memory in public.

recite *v.* 1. to tell a story. 2. to repeat a poem from memory in public (**reciting, recited**).

reckless *adj.* rash, careless of danger. *n.* **recklessness.**

reckon *v.* 1. to count. 2. to consider, to believe, as *we reckon him the best in the team.* 3. to rely, as *we reckon on you for help.*

reckoning *n.* 1. a calculation. 2. a bill.

reclaim *v.* 1. to bring back land into use, as *to reclaim waste land or land from the sea.* 2. to demand back. *n.* **reclamation.**

recline *v.* to lean back, to rest (**reclining, reclined**).

recognition *n.* 1. recognizing. 2. admitting, as *recognition of someone's rights.*

recognize *v.* 1. to know again. 2. to admit, as *to recognize the truth of a remark* (**recognizing, recognized**). *adj.* **recognizable.**

recoil *v.* 1. to spring back, as *a gun recoils when fired.* 2. to shrink back, as *to recoil with fear.*

recollect *v.* to remember. *n.* **recollection.**

recommend *v.* 1. to speak well of, as *to recommend a new shop.* 2. to advise, as *I recommend you to see a lawyer. n.* **recommendation.**

reconcile *v.* 1. to make friends again after a quarrel. 2. to become used to, as *I am reconciled to being away from home* (**reconciling, reconciled**). *n.* **reconciliation.**

reconnaissance (*pron.* re.kon'i.sens) *n.* (in warfare) exploring the enemy's position.

reconnoitre (*pron.* rek.o.noi'ter) *v.* (in warfare) to explore round.

record (*pron.* rek'ord) *n.* 1. a written account. 2. a gramophone disc. 3. a best performance. *v.* **record** (*pron.* re.kord') 1. to write down. 2. to show, as *the gas-meter records the gas used.* 3. to make a gramophone record.

off the record (of information) given in private, not to be published.

to break a record to do better than ever before.

recount *v.* 1. to count again. 2. to tell a story. *n.* **recount** a second count of votes at an election.

recover *v.* 1. to get back again something that was lost. 2. to get well after an illness. *n.* **recovery** getting back, or getting well again.

recreation *n.* amusement, play.

recruit *n.* a man who has just joined the Army or other service, a new member. *v.* **recruit** to enlist new members.

rectangle *n.* an oblong with its four angles all right angles.

rectify *v.* to put right (**rectifying, rectified**).

rector *n.* 1. a clergyman or priest in charge of a parish. 2. the principal of a college or school.

rectory *n.* the house of a rector.

recur *v.* 1. to happen again, as *his illness recurred.* 2. to come back to mind (**recurring, recurred**). *n.* **recurrence** a further happening. *adj.* **recurrent**.

red *n.* the colour of blood. *adj.* **red** of this colour (*comparative* **redder,** *superlative* **reddest**). *v.* **redden** to go red or make red.

a red herring something not to the point brought into a discussion to change its course.

Red Cross a world organization for helping wounded soldiers.

red-currant a small red berry.

Red Ensign the flag of the British merchant navy.

Red Indian an American Indian.

red-letter day an important day.

red-tape tape used in government offices, a sign of official power.

to catch red-handed to catch someone in the act of doing wrong.

redouble *v.* 1. to double a second time. 2. to try harder, as *Ian redoubled his efforts.*

reduce *v.* 1. to make less, as *to reduce speed.* 2. to put into a lower rank, as *to reduce a corporal to a private* (**reducing, reduced**). *n.* **reduction** lessening, as *a reduction in price.*

reed *n.* 1. a tall grass growing near water. 2. a vibrating part of the mouthpiece of a musical wind-instrument.

reef (1) *n.* a dangerous ridge of rock just below the surface of the sea.

reef (2) *n.* part of a ship's sail that can be rolled.

reef-knot a knot for tying two ropes so that they cannot slip.

reek *v.* to smell strongly.

reel (1) *n.* a spool or bobbin.

to reel off to speak quickly.

reel (2) *n.* a Scottish dance.

reel (3) *v.* to stagger, to feel dizzy.

refer *v.* 1. to speak of, as *Bill often refers to his school.* 2. to turn to, to consult, as *Janet refers to a timetable to see when the bus is due.* 3. to turn a matter over to someone else, as *let us refer it to the police* (**referring, referred**).

referee *n.* a judge or umpire in a game.

reference *n.* 1. referring to something, a mention. 2. a testimonial or written report on someone's character.

reference-book a book which you consult for information, such as a dictionary.

with reference to in connection with.

refine *v.* to purify (**refining, refined**).

refinery *n.* a factory for refining.

refit *v.* to make ready, as *to refit a ship* (**refitting, refitted**).

reflect *v.* 1. to throw back rays of light, sound, etc. 2. to give a picture as a mirror does. 3. to throw, as *Ann's good manners reflect credit on her parents.* 4. to think over carefully. *n.* **reflection**.

reflector *n.* anything that reflects, as *a red reflector at the rear of a bicycle.*

reform *v.* 1. to make better. 2. to live a better life. *n.* **reform** an improvement. *n.* **reformation** changing something to improve it.

refrain (1) *v.* to hold back from doing, as *he refrained from speaking.*

refrain (2) *n.* the chorus of a song.

refresh *v.* to give new life to, to make fresh again. *n.* **refreshment** 1. being refreshed. 2. food and drink.

refrigerator *v.* a very cold store-cupboard for food.

refuge *n.* a shelter in time of danger.

refugee *n.* someone who has fled to another country for safety.

refund *v.* to pay back money.

refuse (1) (*pron.* re.fyōoz') *v.* to say 'no'. *n.* **refusal** saying 'no'.

refuse (2) (*pron.* ref'yōos) *n.* rubbish.

regain *v.* to win back.

regal *adj.* royal. *adv.* **regally** royally.

regard *v.* 1. to look at. 2. to consider, as *I regard Charles as a good player.* 3. to like, to respect, as *I regard him highly. n.* **regard** 1. a look. 2. careful thought. 3. respect. *n. pl.* **regards** respects, good wishes.

with regard to concerning.

regarding *prep.* concerning.

regardless *adj.* with no care for, as *regardless of risk.*

regatta *n.* a series of races for yachts and small boats.

regent *n.* someone who rules in place of a king or queen.

regiment *n.* a group of soldiers under the command of a colonel.

region *n.* a district, a large area, as *tropical regions. adj.* **regional.**

register *n.* 1. a list of names. 2. a machine used in a shop to show how much money is taken, a *cash register. v.* **register** 1. to write one's name in a book. 2. to show, as *to register a smile.*

registrar *n.* a man who keeps records, as *a registrar of births, deaths, and marriages.*

registry *n.* an office where records are kept.

regret *n.* sorrow. *v.* **regret** to feel sorry (**regretting, regretted**). *adj.* **regretful.** *adj.* **regrettable** causing sorrow, unfortunate.

regular *adj.* 1. steady, even, as *the regular beat of one's pulse.* 2. professional, as *a regular soldier. n.* **regularity.** *adv.* **regularly.**

regulate *v.* to keep in proper order, as *to regulate a watch* (**regulating, regulated**). *n.* **regulation** 1. a rule. 2. control.

rehearsal *n.* a practice performance.

rehearse *v.* to practise before a public performance (**rehearsing, rehearsed**).

reign *v.* to rule. *n.* **reign** the period of a king's or queen's rule.

rein *n.* a leather strap fastened to a bridle to guide a horse.

reindeer *n.* a deer living in northern countries (*pl.* **reindeer**).

reinforce *v.* to strengthen, as *reinforced concrete is concrete strengthened with steel. n.* **reinforcement.**

reject *v.* to refuse, to throw aside. *n.* **rejection.**

rejoice *v.* to be very glad, to make glad (**rejoicing, rejoiced**). *n.* **rejoicing** celebration, joy.

rejoin *v.* 1. to meet again, as *I will rejoin you later.* 2. to reply.

relate *v.* 1. to describe. 2. to be connected, as *the coal and gas industries are related.*

relation *n.* 1. a connection. 2. someone connected by birth or marriage. *n.* **relationship.**

relative *n.* a relation, one of the same family. *adj.* **relative** 1. connected with. 2. compared with, as *travel by rail is slow relative to travel by air. adv.* **relatively.**

re-lay *v.* to lay again, as *to re-lay a floor covering* (**re-laying, relaid**).

relay *v.* to pass on a radio message, as *the radio station relayed a programme from another station* (**relaying, relayed**).

relay-race a race between two or more teams in which each runner runs part of the way in turn.

release *v.* to set free (**releasing, released**).

relent *v.* to become less severe. *adj.* **relentless** without mercy.

reliable *adj.* dependable. *n.* **reliability.** *adv.* **reliably.**

reliance *n.* trust. *adj.* **reliant** trusting.

relic *n.* something from a past age, as *fossils are prehistoric relics.*

relief *n.* 1. freedom from worry or pain. 2. help for those in distress. 3. the rescue of a besieged town. 4. taking over someone's duty, as *the relief of a guard.* 5. a way of carving or painting so that the main figures are raised from the background, as *a carving in relief* or *a map drawn in relief.*

relieve *v.* 1. to lessen pain or worry. 2. to help those in distress. 3. to rescue a besieged town. 4. to take over someone's duty. 5. to take something away, as *to relieve a man of his coat* (**relieving, relieved**).

religion *n.* 1. the worship of God and belief in Him. 2. one of the ways of worship, as *the Moslem religion. adj.* **religious** concerning religion, holy.

relish *n.* 1. enjoyment, as *Jean swims with relish.* 2. a sauce or pickle. *v.* **relish** to enjoy.

reluctant *adj.* unwilling. *n.* **reluctance** unwillingness. *adv.* **reluctantly.**

rely (with **on**) v. to depend on, to trust (**relying, relied**). n. **reliance**. See **reliance**.

remain v. to stay behind or be left behind. n. pl. **remains** 1. what is left. 2. ruins, as *Roman remains*. 3. a dead body.

remainder n. 1. what is left over or left behind. 2. (in arithmetic) what is left after subtracting, as *9 with 5 taken away leaves a remainder of 4.*

remark v. 1. to say something casually, by the way. 2. to notice. n. **remark** a comment, a few words.

remarkable adj. very unusual.

remedy n. a cure for an illness (pl. **remedies**). v. **remedy** to cure (**remedying, remedied**).

remember v. 1. to keep in mind, not to forget. 2. to bring back to mind.

remembrance n. 1. a memory. 2. a souvenir or keepsake.

remind v. to bring back to memory.

reminder n. something to remind one.

remit v. 1. to send money. 2. to cancel a fine or punishment, to pardon (**remitting, remitted**).

remnant n. a small piece left over, as *a remnant of cloth.*

remnant sale a sale of odds and ends.

remorseless adj. cruel, pitiless.

remote adj. 1. far away, as *a remote friend*. 2. slight, as *a remote chance.*

remove v. 1. to take away, take off, or take out, as *to remove stains from a cloth*. 2. to dismiss, as *to remove an official from his post*. 3. to change one's house (**removing, removed**). n. **remove** a step, as *this is only one remove from mutiny*. n. **removal** a moving, a taking away. adj. **removable**.

rend v. to tear, to split (**rending, rent**).

render v. 1. to give, to put forward, to offer, as *to render thanks*. 2. to translate into another language, as *to render French into English*. 3. to melt and purify, as *to render lard.*

rendezvous (pron. ron'day.voo) n. a French word for 'meeting-place'.

renew v. 1. to start afresh. 2. to make as new. 3. to continue, as *to renew a loan* or *renew a demand*. n. **renewal**.

renounce v. to give up a claim, to refuse to accept, as *the prince renounced his father's throne* (**renouncing, renounced**).

renovate v. to repair and make as new, as *to renovate an old boat* (**renovating, renovated**). n. **renovation**.

renown n. fame. adj. **renowned** famous.

rent (1) n. 1. money paid regularly for the use of a house, television set, etc. 2. a tear in cloth. v. **rent** to pay or receive rent. n. **rental** money paid as rent.

rent (2) past of **rend**.

repaid past of **repay**.

repair v. to mend. n. **repair** 1. the mending of something. 2. condition, as *in good repair.*

repay v. to pay back (**repaying, repaid**). n. **repayment**.

repeal v. to cancel, to do away with, as *to repeal a law.*

repeat v. 1. to say or do something again. 2. to recite from memory. adv. **repeatedly** several times.

repel v. 1. to force back. 2. to cause disgust, as *this dirt repels me* (**repelling, repelled**).

repent v. to be sorry for some wrong one has done. n. **repentance**. adj. **repentant**.

repertoire (pron. rep'er.twahr) n. the full list of plays or songs which an actor or musician is able to perform.

repetition n. a repeating of something.

replace v. 1. to put back. 2. to take the place of or put in the place of, as *to replace a broken cup with a new one* (**replacing, replaced**). n. **replacement**.

replenish v. to fill up again, as *to replenish a stock of oil.*

replica n. an exact copy, as *the artist painted a replica of a picture he had once done.*

reply v. to answer (**replying, replied**). n. **reply** an answer (pl. **replies**).

report v. 1. to describe, to tell about. 2. to turn up for duty, as *he reported to the foreman as fit for work*. n. **report** 1. a written account. 2. gossip, rumour. 3. a loud bang.

reporter n. someone who collects news and writes for newspapers.

represent v. 1. to stand for, as *the athlete represented his country in the Olympic Games.* 2. to show, as *this painting represents a storm at sea.* 3. to act a part, as *Mary represents Joan of Arc in the play.* n. **representation.**

representative n. 1. someone who is chosen to speak for other people. 2. a commercial traveller, an agent for a firm.

repress v. to put down or keep down. n. **repression.** adj. **repressive** harsh.

reprieve v. to delay a sentence of punishment (**reprieving, reprieved**). n. **reprieve** a putting off of punishment.

reprimand v. to scold someone severely.

reprint v. to print further copies of a book.

reproach v. to blame. n. **reproach** blame. adj. **reproachful.**
beyond reproach blameless.

reproduce v. 1. to make a copy. 2. to bear young ones (**reproducing, reproduced**). n. **reproduction.** adj. **reproductive.**

reproof n. a scolding.

reprove v. to scold (**reproving, reproved**).

reptile n. an animal like a snake or tortoise which crawls and lays eggs.

republic n. a nation ruled by its people and their elected leader, a president. adj. **republican** concerning a republic. n. **Republican** (in U.S.A.) member of the party which opposes the Democrats.

repugnant adj. unpleasant. n. **repugnance.**

repulse v. 1. to push back. 2. to snub someone (**repulsing, repulsed**). n. **repulsion** dislike.

repulsive adj. disgusting.

reputation n. what people say and think of one.

reputed adj. considered, believed, as *he is reputed to be rich.*

request v. to ask a favour, as *to request advice.* n. **request** 1. the asking of a favour, as *a request for a book.* 2. the favour asked for, as *he granted the request.*

require v. to need, to want (**requiring, required**). n. **requirement.**

rescue v. to save from harm (**rescuing, rescued**). n. **rescuer.**

research n. a careful study to gain new information.

resemble v. to be similar to (**resembling, resembled**). n. **resemblance** a likeness.

resent v. to be annoyed at, as *Tom resents anyone teasing him.* n. **resentment.** adj. **resentful.**

reservation n. 1. caution, holding back. 2. a seat booked beforehand. 3. an area of land for certain people only, as *an Indian reservation.*

reserve v. 1. to keep back for later use. 2. to book a place in advance. n. **reserve** 1. something kept for future use. 2. an extra member of a team. 3. shyness.

reservoir (pron. rez'er.vwahr) n. a store of water or other liquid.

reside v. to dwell (**residing, resided**).

residence n. the place where one lives.

resident n. a person living in a place, as *he is a resident of London.*

residential adj. having a number of pleasant houses, as *a residential district.*

resign v. 1. to give up a position, as *the cabinet minister resigned.* 2. to submit, as *the prisoner resigned himself to his sentence.* n. **resignation** 1. giving up a job. 2. submitting to fate. adj. **resigned** patient, making no complaint.

resin n. a brown gum from pine or fir trees. adj. **resinous** like resin.

resist v. to struggle against. n. **resistance.** adj. **resistant** resisting.

resolute adj. firm, determined. adv. **resolutely.**

resolution n. 1. firmness. 2. something one has decided to do, as *a New Year resolution.*

resolve v. to decide (**resolving, resolved**). n. **resolve** a firm decision.

resort v. (with **to**) to turn to for help, as *he resorted to a disguise to escape.* n. **resort** 1. help. 2. a holiday place, as *a seaside resort.*
in the last resort when all else fails.

resound v. 1. to echo and ring with sound. 2. to be much talked about, as *a resounding success.*

resource *n.* cleverness in getting out of difficulties. *n. pl.* **resources** wealth. *adj.* **resourceful** quick-witted.

respect *v.* to think highly of, to honour. *n.* **respect** 1. high opinion. 2. a certain point, as *in this respect I do not agree.* *adj.* **respectful** showing respect.

respectable *adj.* decent, of good character. *n.* **respectability**.

respective *adj.* individual, as *they returned to their respective homes.* *adv.* **respectively** concerning each one, as *Tom, Joan, and Dick were first, second, and third respectively.*

respiration *n.* breathing.

artificial respiration a way of forcing air into the lungs of someone who is unconscious.

respond *v.* to answer, to react, as *they responded with cheers.*

response *n.* an answer, as *the response to an appeal for money* or *the response of a car to the brakes.*

responsible *adj.* 1. in charge and having to take the blame if anything goes wrong. 2. trustworthy. *n.* **responsibility** (*pl.* **responsibilities**).

rest (1) *n.* 1. being still, peace, calmness. 2. a prop to lean against, as a *book-rest.* 3. a pause in music. *v.* **rest** 1. to be still, to stop working, to lie down. 2. to depend on, as *it rests with you whether we go on.*

rest (2) *n.* what remains, as *the rest of the day.*

restaurant *n.* a public dining-room.

restore *v.* 1. to put back. 2. to repair or make well again, as *the sea air and sunshine restored her to good health.* *n.* **restoration**.

restrain *v.* to hold back, to keep in check. *n.* **restraint** a check, self-control, as *he showed great restraint when he was insulted.*

restrict *v.* to keep within narrow limits. *n.* **restriction** an order, law, or restraint which keeps one in check.

result *n.* an effect, the end of a happening, the answer to a sum.

resume *v.* to go on again, to begin again after stopping (**resuming, resumed**).

resumption *n.* resuming, continuing again.

resurrect *v.* to bring back to life. *n.* **resurrection**.

the Resurrection Christ's rising from the grave.

retail (*pron.* ree.tayl') *v.* to sell goods in shops. *adj.* **retail** (*pron.* ree'tayl) concerning the selling of goods in small quantities in shops. Opposite of **wholesale**. *n.* **retailer** a shopkeeper.

retain *v.* to keep, to hold.

retard *v.* to delay, to slow up.

retina *n.* a sensitive skin at the back of the eye which enables us to see.

retinue *n.* the attendants of someone of high rank.

retire *v.* 1. to go back, to retreat. 2. to go to bed. 3. to give up work. *n.* **retirement**.

retiring *adj.* quiet, shy.

retort (1) *n.* a sharp reply. *v.* **retort** to make a sharp reply.

retort (2) *n.* a glass flask with a bent neck used in science.

retouch *v.* to improve a painting or photograph by one or two last touches.

retrace *v.* to go back the same way (**retracing, retraced**).

retreat *v.* to be forced to go back. *n.* **retreat** 1. a going back. 2. a quiet place of rest.

retrieve *v.* to get something back again, to rescue (**retrieving, retrieved**). *n.* **retriever** a breed of dog trained to bring back shot game.

return *v.* to go, come, give, or send back. *n.* **return** 1. a going or coming back. 2. a profit, as *he made a good return on the sale of ice-cream.*

by return by the next post back.

reunion *n.* a meeting or gathering of friends who have not met for some time.

reveal *v.* to bring out something hidden, to show.

reveille (*pron.* re.val'i) *n.* a bugle call in camp to waken everyone.

revel *v.* 1. to make merry. 2. to delight in (**revelling, revelled**). *n.* **revel** merry-making.

revelation *n.* making known some secret, something made known.

revelry *n.* merry-making.

revenge *n.* repaying harm for harm. *v.* **revenge** to pay someone back for harm done. *adj.* **revengeful** full of revenge.

revenue *n.* money received, income.

revere *v.* to respect. *n.* **reverence** respect. *adj.* **reverent** respectful.

reverend *n.* a title given to a clergyman, often written *Rev.* for short.

reverse *v.* 1. to turn inside out, upside down, or back to front. 2. to cause backward movement, as *to reverse a car* (**reversing, reversed**). *n.* **reverse** a defeat. *adj.* **reversible** able to be reversed. *n.* **reversal** a turning the other way round.

review *v.* 1. to look over again. 2. to inspect. *n.* **review** 1. an inspection. 2. a newspaper or magazine article describing a book, play, etc. 3. a magazine.

revise *v.* 1. to read something again and alter it. 2. to change after some thought, as *to revise one's views. n.* **revision**.

revival *n.* 1. a return to life. 2. putting fresh energy into something. 3. a new performance of an old play.

revive *v.* 1. to bring or come back to new life. 2. to produce again an old play (**reviving, revived**).

revolt *n.* a rebellion. *v.* **revolt** 1. to rise in rebellion. 2. to disgust, as *this food revolts me. adj.* **revolting** disgusting.

revolution *n.* 1. a turning round, as *the revolution of a wheel round an axle.* 2. an uprising of people against those in power. *adj.* **revolutionary** bringing great changes.

revolve *v.* to spin round (**revolving, revolved**).

revolver *n.* a pistol which can fire several shots at one loading.

revue *n.* a variety entertainment.

reward *n.* a prize or payment. *v.* **reward** to give something in return for a favour or good work.

rheumatism *n.* a painful disease of the joints. *adj.* **rheumatic**.

rhinoceros *n.* a large thick-skinned African animal with one or two horns on its nose (*pl.* **rhinoceroses**).

rhododendron *n.* an evergreen flowering shrub.

rhubarb *n.* a plant whose red stalks are eaten.

rhyme *n.* the last syllables of the lines of a poem sounding alike, as *'Like an army defeated The snow hath retreated'. v.* **rhyme** to make a rhyme (**rhyming, rhymed**).

nursery rhyme a poem for small children.

rhythm *n.* 1. a regular beat or flow of words or sounds. 2. a regular movement, as *the rhythm of the tides. adj.* **rhythmic**.

rib *n.* 1. one of the curved bones from the spine which protect the lungs. 2. a curved timber at the side of a ship. *adj.* **ribbed** with ridges like ribs.

ribbon *n.* a narrow strip of material, as a *hair-ribbon* or a *typewriter ribbon*.

rice *n.* white grain from a tropical plant used as food.

rich *adj.* 1. having plenty of money or property. 2. plentiful, as *a rich harvest.* 3. costly, as *rich presents.* 4. full of good things, as *a rich cake. n. pl.* **riches** wealth. *n.* **richness**. *adv.* **richly** fully, as *he richly deserves to be punished.*

rickshaw *n.* a two-wheeled carriage pulled by a man, used in Japan and China.

rid *v.* to get free of, as *to rid a garden of weeds* (**ridding, ridded**). *n.* **riddance**. **a good riddance** satisfactory that something is removed.

to get rid of to do away with.

riddle (1) *n.* a puzzling question.

riddle (2) *n.* a large sieve to sift soil or cinders. *v.* **riddle** 1. to use a riddle. 2. to fill with small holes, as *to riddle with bullets* (**riddling, riddled**).

ride *v.* 1. to travel on a horse or vehicle. 2. to be carried by, as *the boat rides the waves* (**riding, rode, ridden**). *n.* **ride** a journey on a horse or vehicle.

riding-school a school or stable where one may learn to ride a horse.

ridge *n.* 1. a long hill or mountain. 2. the top of a slope or furrow.

ridicule *v.* to make fun of (**ridiculing, ridiculed**). *n.* **ridicule** mockery. *adj.* **ridiculous** absurd.

rifle (1) *n.* a gun with a grooved barrel.

rifle (2) *v.* to search and steal, as *to rifle a shop* (**rifling, rifled**).

rift n. a split, a crack.

rig v. 1. to fit a ship with sails and ropes. 2. to clothe someone. 3. to make, as to rig up a shed (**rigging, rigged**). n. **rig** the style of a ship's sails.

rigging n. a ship's ropes and sails.

right n. 1. the opposite of **left**. 2. what is good, the opposite of **wrong**. 3. a proper claim, as a right to some land. adj. **right** good, true, correct. v. **right** to put right, as to right an injustice. n. pl. **rights** what one is entitled to.

right angle an angle of 90 degrees, the angle of a square.

right of way the right to use a road or path.

righteous adj. honest, good. n. **righteousness**.

rightful adj. just, lawful.

rightly adv. truly, fairly.

rigid (pron. rij'id) adj. stiff, firm. n. **rigidity**.

rigour n. sternness, strictness. adj. **rigorous** stern.

rim n. the edge of a cup, bowl, or wheel.

rime n. frost.

rind n. the outer skin or peel.

ring (1) n. 1. a circular shape, a hoop. 2. an enclosure, as a boxing-ring. v. **ring** to fit with a ring. adj. **ringed** 1. fitted with a ring. 2. surrounded.

ring (2) v. 1. to sound a bell or sound like a bell. 2. to sound, as his words ring true (**ringing, rang, rung**). n. **ring** the sound of a bell, a ringing sound.

ringleader n. the leader of a gang.

rink n. 1. a sheet of ice for skating. 2. a floor for roller-skating.

rinse v. to wash lightly in clean water (**rinsing, rinsed**). n. **rinse** a quick wash in clean water.

riot n. 1. a noisy disturbance. v. **riot** to cause a disorder. adj. **riotous**.

to run riot 1. to act in a wild way. 2. (of plants) to grow in wild confusion.

rip v. to tear, as to rip a dress on a nail (**ripping, ripped**). n. **rip** a tear.

rip-cord a cord for opening a parachute.

ripe adj. 1. ready to be picked and eaten. 2. ready, as ripe for mischief. v. **ripen** to grow ripe. n. **ripeness**.

ripple n. a tiny wave. v. **ripple** to move in ripples (**rippling, rippled**).

rise v. 1. to get up or move up. 2. to stretch up, as the mountain rises high above the valley. 3. to slope up, as the ground rises. 4. to rebel, as the people rose against the government (**rising, rose, risen**). n. **rise** 1. an increase. 2. a small hill. n. **rising** 1. getting up. 2. a rebellion.

to give rise to to lead to.

to rise to the occasion to deal with a difficulty capably and well.

risk n. a chance of harm or loss. v. **risk** to take a chance. adj. **risky** (comparative **riskier**, superlative **riskiest**).

rite n. a solemn religious ceremony.

ritual n. a rite, a way of worship. adj. **ritual** concerning a ceremony, as a ritual dance.

rival n. a competitor, someone trying for the same prize as someone else. v. **rival** to compete with someone (**rivalling, rivalled**). n. **rivalry**.

river n. a large stream of water.

river-bed the sandy bottom of a river.

rivet n. a small bolt for fastening metal plates together, one end of the bolt being hammered flat. v. **rivet** to fasten with rivets (**riveting, riveted**). n. **riveter** a man who fastens plates with rivets.

road n. a highway along which people can travel. n. pl. **roads** an anchorage for ships. n. **roadway**.

roam v. to wander, to travel about.

roan v. a mixed colour of some horses and cattle, usually brown sprinkled with white.

roar n. a deep sound as made by a lion, heavy traffic, or a roar of laughter. v. **roar** 1. to make a deep sound. 2. to laugh loudly.

roast v. to cook in an oven or before a fire. n. **roast** meat cooked in an oven.

rob v. to steal (**robbing, robbed**). n. **robber** a thief. n. **robbery** stealing (pl. **robberies**).

robe n. a long, flowing dress or gown. v. **robe** to put on a robe or dress (**robing, robed**).

robin n. a bird with a red breast.

robot (*pron.* rō'bot) *n.* 1. a mechanical man. 2. a traffic signal.

robust *adj.* strong and healthy.

rock (1) *v.* to move backwards and forwards, to sway.
rocking-chair a chair which rocks.
rocking-horse a child's wooden horse which rocks.

rock (2) *n.* a mass of stone. *adj.* **rocky** full of rocks, as *rocky ground*.

rocket *n.* a firework, shell, or cylinder shot into the air by the backward thrust of burning gases.

rod *n.* 1. a stick of wood or metal. 2. a measure of length equal to 5 metres.

rode *past* of **ride**.

rodent *n.* a gnawing animal such as a rat or rabbit.

rodeo (*pron.* rō.day'ō) *n.* 1. (in North America) a round-up of cattle. 2. an exhibition of cowboy's skill in handling cattle and horses.

roe (1) *n.* a cluster of fish's eggs.

roe (2) *n.* a small deer.

rogue (*pron.* rōg) *n.* 1. a swindler. 2. a mischievous person. *n.* **roguery** 1. cheating. 2. playfulness.

rôle *n.* a part played by an actor or actress, as *Tom played the rôle of pirate in the school play*.

roll *v.* 1. to move along by turning over. 2. to wrap round, as *to roll up a carpet*. 3. to rock and sway, as *the ship rolled*. 4. to rumble, as *the thunder rolled*. *n.* **roll** 1. a turning over and over. 2. something in the shape of a cylinder, as *a sausage roll* or *a roll of cloth*. 3. a list of names. 4. a long deep sound.
roll-call the calling of names from a list.
roller 1. a cylinder. 2. a long wave.
roller-skate a skate with wheels.
rolling-pin a roller for pressing dough.

Roman *adj.* concerning Rome or ancient Rome.
roman numerals the numbers I, II, III, etc.

romance *n.* an imaginary story of love or adventure.

romantic *adj.* imaginative, full of feeling.

romp *v.* to jump about in play.

roof *n.* the top covering of a house, bus, cave, etc. (*pl.* **roofs**). *n.* **roofing** a roof.

rook *n.* 1. a large, black bird. 2. a chess piece. *n.* **rookery** a place where rooks live.

room *n.* 1. a living-space in a building. 2. space. *adj.* **roomy** spacious (*comparative* **roomier,** *superlative* **roomiest**). *n.* **roominess**.

roost *n.* a perch on which a bird rests. *v.* **roost** to rest on a perch. *n.* **rooster** a farmyard cock.

root *n.* 1. the part of a plant which grows in the ground. 2. a cause, as *the root of a problem*.
to take root to grow strongly.

rope *n.* a thick cord of several strands.
rope-ladder a ladder made of ropes.
to know the ropes to know what to do.

rosary *n.* 1. a string of beads used to count prayers. 2. a series of prayers. 3. a rose-garden (*pl.* **rosaries**).

rose (1) *n.* 1. a flower growing on a thorny bush. 2. a pink colour. *adj.* **rosy** pink (*comparative* **rosier,** *superlative* **rosiest**).

rose (2) *past* of **rise**.

rot *n.* decay. *v.* **rot** to decay (**rotting, rotted**). *adj.* **rotten** decayed, going bad.

rotate *v.* to revolve or make revolve (**rotating, rotated**). *n.* **rotation** 1. turning round. 2. following one after another.
in rotation in turn.

rouge *n.* red powder or paste for colouring ladies' cheeks.

rough *adj.* 1. uneven, not smooth. 2. violent, stormy, as *a rough sea*. 3. unfinished, as *a rough sketch*. 4. harsh, as *a rough voice*. *v.* **roughen** to make rough. *adv.* **roughly**. *n.* **roughness**.
rough and ready done anyhow.

round *adj.* shaped like a circle or ball. *n.* **round** 1. a series of regular calls, as *a newsboy's round*. 2. a burst, as *a round of applause*. 3. a period of boxing. 4. a part-song. 5. a single bullet or shell. *v.* **round** 1. to bring in, as *to round up cattle*. 2. to go round, as *the yacht rounded the buoy*. *adv.* **round** in a circle, as *to turn round*. *prep.* **round** on all sides of, as *a garden round a house*.
to bring round to revive.
to round off to complete.

roundabout *n.* 1. a circular traffic island where roads meet. 2. a merry-go-round. *adj.* **roundabout** not direct or straightforward.

rouse *v.* to waken, to stir up (**rousing, roused**). *adj.* **rousing** stirring, as *a rousing tune.*

rout *v.* to defeat and drive back in disorder. *n.* **rout** a disorderly retreat.

route (*pron.* ro͞ot) *n.* a way of getting to a place, a way that is regularly used, as *the bus route goes past the town hall.*

routine *n.* a regular way of doing something, as *a daily routine of housework.*

rove *v.* to wander, to ramble (**roving, roved**). *n.* **rover** 1. a wanderer. 2. a pirate. 3. a senior Boy Scout.

row (1) (*pron.* rō) *n.* a line of things.

row (2) (*pron.* rō) *v.* to move a boat with oars.

row (3) (*pron.* row) *n.* (*slang*) a quarrel, a disturbance.

royal *adj.* concerning a king or queen. *adv.* **royally** in a royal way. *n.* **royalty** the royal family. *n.* **royalist** a supporter of the royal family.

rub *v.* 1. to move one thing against another. 2. to wipe, to polish (**rubbing, rubbed**).

to rub someone the wrong way to irritate him by saying or doing the wrong thing.

rubber *n.* 1. an elastic substance used to make tyres, tubes, etc. 2. soft indiarubber used to rub out marks.

rubbish *n.* 1. waste matter. 2. nonsense.

ruby *n.* a red jewel (*pl.* **rubies**).

rudder *n.* a flat piece of wood or metal hinged at the back of a ship or aeroplane and used for steering.

rude *adj.* 1. bad-mannered. 2. rough, as *a rude shed.* 3. uncivilized, as *rude savages. n.* **rudeness**.

ruff *n.* a starched, pleated collar worn in olden times.

ruffian *n.* a rough bully.

ruffle *v.* 1. to wrinkle, to crumple. 2. to vex someone (**ruffling, ruffled**).

rug *n.* a small floor mat.

Rugby football *n.* football played with an oval ball which can be handled.

rugged (*pron.* rug'id) *adj.* rough, strong.

ruin *n.* 1. destruction. 2. downfall, as *idleness caused his ruin.* 3. a decayed old building. *v.* **ruin** 1. to destroy. 2. to make someone lose all his money. *n.* **ruination.** *adj.* **ruinous** causing ruin.

rule *n.* 1. a law, a regulation. 2. government. 3. the usual custom, as *we walk to school as a rule.* 4. a ruler of wood or metal. *v.* **rule** 1. to govern. 2. to decide, as *the committee ruled that the fee should be increased.* 3. to draw lines with a ruler (**ruling, ruled**). *n.* **ruling. as a rule** usually.

ruler *n.* 1. someone who governs. 2. a wooden or metal strip for drawing lines and measuring.

ruling *n.* a decision.

rum (1) *n.* a spirit made from sugarcane.

rum (2) *adj.* (*slang*) queer, odd, unusual.

rumble *v.* to make a deep, rolling sound (**rumbling, rumbled**). *n.* **rumble** a deep sound.

ruminate *v.* 1. to chew the cud, like a cow. 2. to think deeply over something (**ruminating, ruminated**).

rumour *n.* a story which passes from person to person and which may or may not be true.

rumple *v.* to crease, to make untidy (**rumpling, rumpled**).

run *v.* 1. to run quickly. 2. to stretch, as *a good road runs between the two villages.* 3. to spread, as *this paint runs easily.* 4. to manage, as *he runs a grocer's shop.* 5. to chance, as *to run a risk* (**running, ran, run**). *n.* **run** 1. a race. 2. a trip. 3. (in cricket and baseball) a single score. 4. the time a play lasts, as *this play has had a long run.* 5. free use of, as *to have the run of a house*

running commentary a continuous report.

to run out of to have none left.

to run over 1. to practise. 2. to knock over with a vehicle.

to run through 1. to practise. 2. to use up.

runaway *n.* an escaping horse or man.

run-down *adj.* in bad health.

rung *n.* one of the steps of a ladder.

runner-up *n.* the one next after the winner.

runway *n.* a concrete path for aeroplanes.

rural *adj.* concerning the countryside.

ruse (*pron.* rooz) *n.* a trick, a fraud.

rush (1) *v.* to dash, to move quickly.

rush (2) *n.* a marsh-plant with tall leaves.

russet *adj.* of a reddish-brown colour.

rust *n.* a reddish-brown coating on iron and steel exposed to dampness and air. *adj.* **rusty** (*comparative* **rustier,** *superlative* **rustiest**). *n.* **rustiness.**

rustic *adj.* 1. concerning the country, rural. 2. roughly made, as *a rustic seat.*

rustle *v.* 1. to make a soft crackling sound, as *the dead leaves rustled.* 2. (in the U.S.A.) to steal cattle (**rustling, rustled**). *n.* **rustle** a faint sound.

rut *n.* a deep track made by a wheel.

ruthless *adj.* cruel, pitiless.

rye *n.* a grain used for food.

S

Sabbath *n.* a day of rest, Saturday among Jews, and kept by Christians on Sunday.

sabotage (*pron.* sab'ō.tahzh) *n.* the damaging of machinery by men with a grievance.

sack (1) *n.* a large bag of coarse cloth.

sack (2) *v.* to rob and plunder.

sacrament *n.* a solemn religious ceremony, such as Baptism or Holy Communion.

sacred *adj.* holy, devoted to God.

sacrifice *n.* 1. an offering to God. 2. (in the Roman Catholic church) the Mass. 3. the giving up of something valuable for someone else's benefit. *v.* **sacrifice** 1. to make an offering to God. 2. to give up something for someone's benefit. (**sacrificing, sacrificed**). *adj.* **sacrificial.**

sacrilege *n.* disrespect or ill-treatment of something holy. *adj.* **sacrilegious.**

sad *adj.* sorrowful, unhappy (*comparative* **sadder,** *superlative* **saddest**). *n.* **sadness.** *v.* **sadden** to make sad.

saddle *n.* 1. a seat for the rider of a horse or bicycle. 2. a piece of meat with part of the backbone and ribs, as *a saddle of mutton.* *v.* **saddle** 1. to put a saddle on a horse. 2. to load, as *saddled with troubles* (**saddling, saddled**).

safe (1) *adj.* 1. out of danger. 2. reliable, as *a safe driver. adv.* **safely.** *n.* **safety.**

safe (2) *n.* a strong metal case for valuables.

safeguard *n.* something which gives protection.

safety-lamp *n.* a miner's lamp which will not cause an explosion.

safety-pin *n.* a bent pin with a guarded point.

sag *v.* to droop in the middle (**sagging, sagged**).

sage *n.* a herb used in cooking.

sago *n.* starch from an East Indian tree, used in puddings.

said *past* of **say.**

sail *n.* 1. a sheet of canvas to catch the wind and make a ship move. 2. a trip in a boat. 3. an arm of a windmill. *v.* **sail** 1. to travel in a ship or steamer. 2. to glide smoothly, as *the arrow sailed through the air. n.* **sailor** a member of a ship's crew.

saint *n.* a holy man or woman. *adj.* **saintly** like a saint. *n.* **saintliness.**

sake *n.* benefit, cause, purpose, as *he did it for my sake* or *for the sake of the school.*

salad *n.* a mixture of vegetables served raw.

salary *n.* regular payment for work, usually paid monthly (*pl.* **salaries**). *adj.* **salaried** paid a salary (note: a *wage* is usually paid weekly).

sale *n.* 1. the selling of something. 2. a selling of goods at specially low prices, or by auction. *n.* **salesman** a man whose business it is to sell things (*pl.* **salesmen**).

saliva *n.* spit.

sallow *adj.* pale yellow in colour.

sally *n.* 1. a sudden rush out, as *a sally of soldiers from a besieged fort.* 2. a clever remark (*pl.* **sallies**). *v.* **sally** to rush out and attack (**sallying, sallied**).

salmon *n.* a large fish with pink flesh (*pl.* **salmon**). *adj.* **salmon** coloured pink like salmon flesh.

salon *n.* an exhibition hall or art gallery.

saloon *n.* 1. a sitting-room in a hotel or ship. 2. (in the U.S.A.) a public house.

salt *n.* 1. white crystals used to flavour food. 2. the name given to many chemicals. 3. an old sailor. *n.* **saltiness**. *adj.* **salty**.

the salt of the earth the really good people.

to take with a pinch of salt to have doubts whether something one is told is really true.

salt-cellar *n.* a small dish for salt.

salute *n.* 1. a greeting. 2. a sign of respect to an officer made with the hand. 3. a firing of cannon. *v.* **salute** 1. to greet. 2. for a soldier to raise a hand in respect to an officer. 3. to fire cannon in welcome (**saluting, saluted**).

salvage *v.* goods saved from waste or destruction. *v.* **salvage** 1. to save from waste. 2. to raise a sunken ship (**salvaging, salvaged**).

salvation *n.* 1. saving someone from danger or sin. 2. safety.

salvo *n.* a firing of guns in salute (*pl.* **salvoes**).

same *adj.* alike, equal, unchanged. *n.* **sameness**.

all the same nevertheless.

sample *n.* a small part taken from the whole to show what the rest is like. *v.* **sample** to test a part of something to see what the whole is like (**sampling, sampled**).

sanatorium *n.* a hospital.

sanctify *v.* to make holy, to free from sin (**sanctifying, sanctified**).

sanction *n.* permission, as *Jean left school early with the teacher's sanction.* *v.* **sanction** to agree to.

sanctuary *n.* 1. a sacred place. 2. a shelter or place of refuge, as *a bird sanctuary* (*pl.* **sanctuaries**).

sand *n.* tiny grains of earth or rock. *adj.* **sandy** 1. covered with sand. 2. the colour of sand.

sandal *n.* a low shoe fastened with straps.

sand-dune *n.* a sandy ridge on the seashore.

sandpaper *n.* sand-coated paper used for polishing.

sandstone *n.* soft rock which easily crumbles to sand.

sandwich *n.* two slices of buttered bread with meat, paste, or jam between.

sane *adj.* not mad, of a sound mind.

sanitary *adj.* 1. concerning health and cleanliness. 2. clean, healthy. *n.* **sanitation** cleanliness, especially good drainage.

sanity *n.* soundness of mind. Opposite of **madness**.

Santa Claus *n.* Father Christmas.

sap *n.* the watery liquid in plants and trees.

sapling *n.* a young tree.

sapphire *n.* a deep-blue jewel.

sarcasm *n.* a sneering remark. *adj.* **sarcastic** bitter, sneering. *adv.* **sarcastically**.

sardine *n.* a small fish kept in oil for food.

sash (1) *n.* a broad ribbon worn round the waist or over the shoulder.

sash (2) *n.* a window-frame.

Satan *n.* the devil.

satchel *n.* a schoolbag.

satellite *n.* 1. a small planet moving round a larger one. 2. a man-made 'moon' shot from the earth and moving round it.

satisfaction *n.* pleasure, contentment.

satisfactory *adj.* pleasing, satisfying.

satisfy *v.* 1. to please someone by giving him what he wishes. 2. to convince, as *to satisfy someone that one is speaking the truth* (**satisfying, satisfied**).

saturate *v.* to soak completely (**saturating, saturated**). *n.* **saturation**.

Saturday *n.* the seventh day of the week.

Saturn *n.* a large planet with rings around it.

sauce *n.* 1. a liquid added to food to make it taste better. 2. stewed fruit, as *apple sauce*. 3. impudence. *adj.* **saucy** impudent.

saucepan *n.* a metal cooking-pan.

saucer *n.* a dish to hold a cup.

saunter *v.* to stroll idly.

sausage *n.* minced meat in a skin.

savage *adj.* wild, fierce, uncivilized. *n.* **savage** a wild primitive person. *n.* **savagery** cruelty.

save v. 1. to rescue from harm or danger. 2. to put by, as *to save money*. 3. to avoid wasting, as *to save time or trouble*.
to save up to put by, to store.
to save one's face to avoid losing one's dignity.
savings n. pl. money saved.
saviour n. someone who rescues.
the Saviour Jesus Christ.
savour n. a taste. adj. **savoury** tasty, salty (not sweet).
saw (1) n. a steel blade with cutting-teeth. v. **saw** to cut with a saw (**sawing, sawed, sawed** or **sawn**).
saw (2) *past* of **see**.
sawdust n. powdered wood made by sawing.
sawmill n. a place where wood is sawn.
say v. to speak, to tell (**saying, said**).
saying n. a proverb.
scab n. a crust over a sore.
scaffold n. a platform on which criminals are executed.
scaffolding n. a framework of poles and planks round a building which is being built or repaired.
scald v. 1. to burn with hot liquid or steam. 2. to clean pans with boiling water. n. **scald** a burn caused by scalding.
scale (1) n. one of the pans on a pair of balances. n. pl. **scales** balances.
scale (2) n. one of the thin plates on the skin of a fish or reptile.
scale (3) n. 1. a series of musical notes in order. 2. a ruler. 3. the number of times the drawing of an object is less than the object itself.
scale (4) v. to climb, as *to scale some rocks* (**scaling, scaled**).
scalp n. the skin and hair on top of the head. v. **scalp** to cut off the scalp, as Red Indians once did.
scamp n. a rascal. v. **scamp** to do hasty work.
scamper v. to run about.
scan v. to examine carefully (**scanning, scanned**).
scandal n. 1. a public disgrace. 2. unkind gossip. adj. **scandalous** disgraceful. n. **scandal-monger** someone who spreads scandal.

scanty adj. little, hardly enough.
scapegoat n. an innocent person who is made to take the blame for others.
scar n. the mark left after a wound or burn has healed. v. **scar** to mark with a scar (**scarring, scarred**).
scarce adj. in short supply. adv. **scarcely** hardly ever, barely. n. **scarcity**.
scare v. to frighten (**scaring, scared**). n. **scare** a fright, an alarm.
scarecrow n. a dummy figure to frighten birds.
scarf n. a length of cloth worn round the neck (pl. **scarfs** or **scarves**).
scarlet n. a bright red colour.
scathing adj. bitter, harsh, as *a scathing remark*.
scatter v. to throw, to fall, to run, in all directions. adj. **scattered** spread out here and there, as *scattered leaves on a lawn*.
scene n. 1. a view. 2. a place where something happened, as *the scene of a battle*. 3. a part of a stage play. 4. stage scenery. 5. a show of temper, as *there was a dreadful scene when Margaret was found out*.
scenery n. 1. a landscape. 2. a painted backcloth for a play.
scent n. 1. a smell, especially a pleasant smell. 2. a perfume. v. 1. to put perfume on. 2. to smell out, to suspect, as *I scent trouble*.
sceptic (pron. skep'tik) n. someone who doubts what he is told. adj. **sceptical**. n. **scepticism**.
sceptre (pron. sep'ter) n. a short staff carried by a king or queen as a sign of authority.
schedule (pron. shed'yool or in the U.S.A. sked'yool) n. a list, a time-table.
scheme (pron. skeem) n. a plan, an arrangement, a plot. v. **scheme** 1. to make a plan. 2. to plot (**scheming, schemed**). adj. **scheming**.
scholar n. 1. a pupil at school. 2. a student. 3. a very learned man. adj. **scholarly** learned.
scholarship n. 1. learning. 2. money or a free place awarded to a successful scholar.

scholastic *adj.* concerning schools or scholars.

school *n.* 1. a place where boys and girls are taught. 2. a university department, as *a school of medicine.* 3. a shoal of whales or porpoises. *v.* **school** to teach. *n.* **schooling** teaching, learning. *ns.* **schoolbook, schoolboy, schoolmaster, schoolmistress, school-teacher.**

science *n.* 1. the complete study of a subject. 2. a study of some branch of nature, as *chemistry, botany, and astronomy are sciences. adj.* **scientific** using the methods of science.

scientist *n.* someone who studies a science.

scissors *n. pl.* a small pair of cutting blades pivoted together.

scoff *v.* to jeer at, to mock.

scold *v.* to find fault with in an angry way.

scone *n.* a small, round, flat cake.

scoop *n.* 1. a small shovel for flour or sugar. 2. important news reported by a newspaper before other newspapers. *v.* **scoop** to shovel with a scoop.

scooter *n.* 1. a wheeled toy driven along by the foot. 2. a small motor-cycle, a *motor-scooter.*

scope *n.* 1. opportunity, as *this job gives me plenty of scope.* 2. range, limit, as *that job is outside the scope of my work.*

scorch *v.* to burn slightly, to singe.

score (1) *n.* twenty, as *a score of apples.*

score (2) *n.* 1. a mark, a cut. 2. a total number of points or goals made in a game. 3. a written piece of music for an orchestra. *v.* **score** 1. (in games) to make a point or goal. 2. to keep a record of points made in a game 3. to mark or cut. *n.* **scorer** someone who records the points made in a game.

to score off someone to win an advantage over him.

scorn *n.* contempt. *v.* **scorn** to despise. *adj.* **scornful.** *adv.* **scornfully.**

scorpion *n.* a small, stinging creature with claws and eight legs.

scoundrel *n.* a wicked man.

scour (1) *v.* to clean by rubbing hard with powder or some material.

scour (2) *v.* to search energetically, as *they scoured the hillside for the prisoner.*

scourge (*pron.* skerj) *v.* to whip. *n.* **scourge** a whip, a punishment, a plague.

scout *n.* a man sent out to find what he can about an enemy. *v.* **scout** to act as a scout.

Boy Scout a member of the organization founded by Lord Baden-Powell in 1908.

Girl Scout (in North America) the same as a British Girl Guide.

scowl *v.* to frown and look angry. *n.* **scowl** a sullen frown.

scramble *v.* 1. to crawl on hands and knees. 2. to rush to be first for something. 3. to beat up eggs and cook them in milk and butter (**scrambling, scrambled**). *n.* **scramble** 1. a climb. 2. a wild rush.

scrap *n.* a small bit. *v.* **scrap** to throw away as useless (**scrapping, scrapped**). *adj.* **scrappy** not well finished.

scrap-book *n.* a book into which pictures are pasted.

scrape *v.* 1. to scratch, drag, or rub. 2. to make a grating noise. 3. to get together with difficulty, as *to scrape money together* (**scraping, scraped**). *n.* **scrape** 1. a scratch, a scraping. 2. an awkward difficulty.

scrap-heap *n.* a pile of waste material.

scratch *v.* 1. to mark with a sharp point. 2. to rub a sore. 3. to cancel, as *to scratch a game.* 4. (with **out**) to remove, as *to scratch out a written word. n.* **scratch** 1. a mark, a slight cut. 2. a scraping sound.

to start from scratch 1. to start from the beginning. 2. for all to start equal.

scrawl *n.* scribble, bad writing. *v.* **scrawl** to scribble.

scream *n.* a shrill shriek. *v.* **scream** to make a shrill cry.

screech *n.* a shrill noise.

screen *n.* 1. a covered framework or curtain to hide something or to keep out draughts. 2. a white sheet on which films are shown. 3. a large sieve. *v.*

screen 1. to hide or shelter. 2. to pass through a sieve. 3. to throw a picture on a screen.

screw *n.* 1. a metal pin with a spiral thread. 2. a ship's propeller. *v.* **screw** 1. to fasten with a screw. 2. to twist, as *to screw up one's face*. *n.* **screwdriver** a tool for tightening screws. **to screw up one's courage** to try to be brave.

scribble *v.* to write or draw badly, to scrawl (**scribbling, scribbled**). *n.* **scribble** untidy writing or drawing.

scribe *n.* 1. a writer. 2. a Jewish teacher of the laws.

script *n.* 1. a style of handwriting. 2. (in radio) the written speech which a speaker is about to read.

scripture *n.* 1. a sacred book. 2. the Bible. *adj.* **scriptural**.

scroll *n.* a parchment or paper roll.

scrub (1) *v.* to clean by rubbing hard with soap and water (**scrubbing, scrubbed**).

scrub (2) *n.* 1. poor shrubs. 2. poor land on which only small bushes grow. *adj.* **scrubby** poor, undersized.

scruff *n.* the back of the neck.

scrum, scrummage *n.* (in Rugby football) a struggle for the ball by the forwards packed together.

scruple *n.* 1. a very small weight. 2. a feeling of doubt and hesitation as to what is the right thing to do.

scrutinize *v.* to examine very carefully (**scrutinizing, scrutinized**).

scrutiny *n.* a close examination.

scuffle *n.* a confused struggle. *v.* **scuffle** to struggle and fight (**scuffling, scuffled**).

scull *n.* a light oar. *v.* **scull** 1. to move a boat forward with a single oar over the boat's stern. 2. to move a boat with a pair of light oars.

sculptor *n.* a man who carves statues and figures (*fem.* **sculptress**).

sculpture *n.* 1. the art of carving figures. 2. a piece of carving in wood or stone.

scum *n.* dirt, froth, or slime, on the top of a liquid such as pond water.

scurvy *n.* a skin disease. *adj.* **scurvy** mean, as *a scurvy trick*.

scuttle (1) *v.* to hurry away (**scuttling, scuttled**).

scuttle (2) *n.* a trap-door in a ship's deck. *v.* **scuttle** to sink a ship by letting water in (**scuttling, scuttled**).

scuttle (3) *n.* a coal-bucket.

scythe *n.* a large, curved blade at the end of a long handle for mowing grass. *v.* **scythe** to mow with a scythe (**scything, scythed**).

sea *n.* 1. a stretch of salt water. 2. a great number, as *a sea of heads*. **all at sea** in a muddle.

sea-dog *n.* an old sailor.

seafaring *adj.* travelling by sea.

sea-gull *n.* a fish-eating sea bird.

seal (1) *n.* a sea animal with flippers and a furry skin.

seal (2) *n.* a design stamped on wax. *v.* **seal** 1. to fasten tightly. 2. to put a wax seal on a document. 3. to settle, as *to seal a bargain*. **under sealed orders** sailing under secret orders.

sea-level *n.* the surface of the sea from which heights of land are measured.

sealing-wax *n.* wax used to make a seal.

sea-lion *n.* a large seal.

seam *n.* 1. the line where two pieces of cloth are sewn together. 2. a thin layer, as *a seam of coal*.

search *v.* 1. to look for everywhere. 2. to examine. *n.* **search** a looking round, an examination. *adj.* **searching** piercing, as *a searching look*.

searchlight *n.* a powerful light used in warfare.

search-warrant *n.* a document giving a policeman the right to enter a building.

sea scout *n.* a Boy Scout trained as a sailor.

season *n.* 1. one of the four main periods of the year, as *the seasons of summer, autumn, winter, and spring*. 2. a special time, as *the cricket season*. *v.* **season** 1. to improve by storing, as *to season wood*. 2. to add salt or pepper, as *to season food*. **in season** fit for eating, as *raspberries are in season now*.

season ticket a ticket which can be used over again for a period of time, on trains, buses, for entertainments, etc.

seasonable *adj*. happening at the right season, as *snow is seasonable at Christmas*.

seasonal *adj*. happening at a certain season of the year, as *harvesting is seasonal work*.

seasoning *n*. something like pepper or spice to make food tastier.

seat *n*. 1. something to sit on. 2. a centre, as *a seat of learning*. 3. a mansion, as *a country seat*.

seaweed *n*. a plant growing by or in the sea.

seaworthy *adj*. fit for the sea.

secluded *adj*. away from others, quiet and out of sight, as *a secluded village*.

seclusion *n*. being secluded.

second (1) *n*. the sixtieth part of a minute of time, or of a minute of an angle (note: sixty minutes of an angle equal one degree).

second (2) *n*. 1. the one after the first. 2. a man who helps a boxer, or who helps a fighter in a duel. *adj*. **second** next to the first. *v*. **second** to support a proposal put by someone at a meeting.

secondary *adj*. coming after the first.

second-hand *adj*. not new.

secondly *adv*. in the second place.

second-rate *adj*. not of the best quality.

secrecy *n*. being secret, mystery, as *he moved with an air of secrecy*.

secret *adj*. private, hidden. *n*. **secret** information kept to oneself.

secret service spying for a government.

secretary *n*. 1. someone who writes letters for an employer. 2. someone who does this work for a club or society. *adj*. **secretarial**.

secrete (*pron*. se.kreet') *v*. 1. to hide from view, as *to secrete a document*. 2. to give off a juice or liquid, as *rubber trees secrete a sticky fluid*. *n*. **secretion**.

sect *n*. a group of people who worship in their own special way.

section *n*. 1. a separate part, a division. 2. the appearance of a thing if it were cut straight through.

secure *adj*. 1. free from worry or danger, safe. 2. firmly fastened, as *the gate is secure*. *v*. **secure** 1. to make firm or safe. 2. to obtain, as *to secure employment* (**securing, secured**). *n*. **security** 1. safety. 2. a valuable which is held back until a debt is paid off.

sedate *adj*. quiet and serious. *adv*. **sedately**.

sediment *n*. dirt or powder settling at the bottom of a liquid.

see (1) *v*. 1. to look at, to watch. 2. to understand, as *I see what he means*. 3. to make sure, as *I will see that he does it*. 4. to find out, as *I will see what can be done* (**seeing, saw, seen**).

to see eye to eye with to agree with.

to see something through to see that it is finished.

to see through something or someone not to be deceived by it (or him).

see (2) *n*. a district under a bishop's authority.

the Holy See Rome, as the Pope is the bishop of Rome.

seed *n*. 1. a little grain from which a new plant grows. 2. offspring, young ones.

seedling *n*. a young plant grown from seed.

seek *v*. 1. to search for. 2. to try, as *Tom seeks to be higher in the class* (**seeking, sought** *pron*. sort).

seem *v*. to appear to be. *adv*. **seemingly** apparently.

seep *v*. to trickle through slowly.

seer *n*. someone who foretells the future.

see-saw *n*. a plank balanced at the middle with someone at each end moving up and down.

seethe *v*. 1. to boil. 2. to be very angry or excited (**seething, seethed**).

seize *v*. to grasp, to take hold of (**seizing, seized**).

seizure *n*. 1. a sudden grasp. 2. a fit.

seldom *adv*. not often.

select *v*. to choose carefully. *adj*. **select** carefully chosen, as *select fruit*. *n*. **selection**.

self *n*. one's own person (*pl*. **selves**).

self-confidence *n*. belief in oneself.

self-conscious *adj*. thinking too much of oneself when among others, embarrassed.

self-control *n*. control of one's emotions.

self-defence *n.* protecting oneself.

self-government *n.* national independence.

self-importance *n.* having big ideas about oneself.

selfish *adj.* caring only for oneself. *n.* **selfishness**.

self-sacrifice *n.* giving up something one values for the sake of others.

self-starter *n.* an electric motor for starting an engine.

sell *v.* to exchange for money (**selling, sold**).

semi- *prefix* half.

semicircle *n.* half a circle.

semicolon *n.* a punctuation mark (;) showing a pause in a sentence.

senate *n.* a governing council. **Senate** the Upper House in the U.S.A., Canada, and Australia.

senator *n.* a member of the Senate.

send *v.* to make to go (**sending, sent**). **send-off** a farewell.

to send someone to Coventry to refuse to speak to him.

senior *adj.* older, of higher rank. *n.* **senior** a person older or higher in rank. *n.* **seniority**.

sensation *n.* 1. a feeling, as *a sensation of relief*. 2. excitement. 3. the cause of excitement, as *the new fashion was a sensation*. *adj.* **sensational** exciting.

sense *n.* 1. one of the powers we use to make contact with the outside world, seeing, hearing, touching, smelling, and tasting. 2. understanding, wisdom, as *Mary has the good sense to know how to behave*. 3. meaning, as *I do not understand the sense of his remark*. 4. feeling, as *a sense of duty*. *v.* **sense** to be aware of, as *he sensed he was unpopular* (**sensing, sensed**). *adj.* **senseless** 1. unconscious. 2. foolish. *n.* **senselessness**.

sensible *adj.* 1. full of good sense, as *a sensible idea*. 2. noticeable, as *a sensible coolness*. 3. aware, as *he was sensible of a change*. *adv.* **sensibly**.

sensitive *adj.* easily hurt, easily affected. *n.* **sensitivity**.

sent *past* of send.

sentence *n.* 1. a punishment given by a judge to a prisoner. 2. a number of words which make a complete statement. *v.* **sentence** for a judge to condemn a prisoner to be punished (**sentencing, sentenced**).

sentiment *n.* a strong feeling, as *sentiments of hate or love*.

sentimental *adj.* 1. arousing feelings or emotions, as *a sentimental film*. 2. easily moved to feel love or pity, as *a sentimental woman*. *adv.* **sentimentally**.

sentinel *n.* a soldier on guard.

sentry *n.* a sentinel (*pl.* **sentries**).

separate *v.* to part or set apart (**separating, separated**). *adj.* **separate** apart, not joined. *n.* **separation**. *adv.* **separately**.

September *n.* the ninth month.

septic *adj.* infected with germs.

sequel *n.* what follows as a result, as *the sequel to the story was that the hero married the heroine*.

sequence *n.* a number of happenings one after the other.

serenade *n.* romantic music played at night by a lover outside his lady's window. *v.* **serenade** to play a serenade for someone (**serenading, serenaded**).

serene *adj.* calm, peaceful. *adv.* **serenely**. *n.* **serenity**.

serf *n.* in the Middle Ages, a slave sold with the land on which he worked. *n.* **serfdom**.

sergeant (*pron.* sar'jent) *n.* a non-commissioned officer next above a corporal, or a policeman next above a constable. *n.* **sergeant-major** a rank next above a sergeant.

serial *n.* a story which appears in parts, week by week, in a magazine or on film.

series *n.* a number of events one after the other, as *a series of accidents* (*pl.* **series**).

serious *adj.* 1. solemn, thoughtful. 2. sincere, not joking. 3. important, grave. *n.* **seriousness**.

sermon *n.* 1. a talk on religion given in church. 2. a serious talk, a warning.

serpent *n.* a snake.

servant *n.* someone employed in a house, *a domestic servant*, or in some public work, *a public servant* or *a civil servant.*

serve *v.* 1. to work for others. 2. to wait on others at table. 3. (in tennis) to make the opening stroke. 4. to act (as), as *this box will serve as a table* (**serving, served**).

service *n.* 1. employment. 2. duty with the armed forces. 3. worship in church. 4. a religious ceremony. 5. a set of dishes for a meal, as *a dinner service.* 6. making the opening stroke at tennis. *adj.* **serviceable** useful.

serviette *n.* a table-napkin.

session *n.* 1. a meeting of a court or council. 2. a series of meetings.

set *v.* 1. to place, to put. 2. to become stiff, as *the jelly sets.* 3. (of the sun) to go down out of sight. 4. to put in place, as *to set a broken bone* (**setting, set**). *n.* **set** 1. a group of things of the same kind. 2. an apparatus, as *a radio set.* 3. (in tennis) a series of games in one part of a match. *adj.* **set** 1. fixed, as *a set purpose.* 2. made beforehand, as *a set speech.*

to set forth to start forward.

to set one's heart on to want greatly.

to set one's teeth to become determined.

to set upon to attack.

setback *n.* a defeat, a check.

set square *n.* a triangular piece of plastic or wood helping one to draw lines at different angles.

settee *n.* a long seat with a back, a sofa.

setting *n.* 1. the background and furniture for a play. 2. the frame in which jewels are fixed. 3. music for the words of a song.

settle (1) *v.* 1. to decide. 2. to come to rest. 3. to sink. 4. to pay an account. 5. to start a colony (**settling, settled**). *n.* **settlement**.

settler *n.* someone who lives in a new colony.

seven *n.* one more than six, represented by 7 or VII. *ns.* **seventeen, seventy**. *adjs.* **seventh, seventeenth, seventieth**.

in the seventh heaven very happy.

sever *v.* to cut off, to break off (**severing, severed**). *n.* **severance**.

several *adj.* 1. few, more than two but not many. 2. separate, different, as *they went home along their separate ways.*

severe *adj.* 1. strict, harsh. 2. serious, as *a severe cold.* 3. hard, as *a severe winter. adv.* **severely.** *n.* **severity**.

sew *v.* to stitch with needle and thread (**sewing, sewed, sewn** or **sewed**).

sewing machine a machine for sewing cloth.

sewage *n.* water and waste carried away by sewers.

sewer *n.* an underground drain for carrying away water and waste.

sewerage *n.* a network of sewers.

sewn *past* of **sew**.

sex *n.* being male or female, as *a man is of the male sex, and a woman is of the female sex. adj.* **sexual** concerning sex.

shabby *adj.* 1. old and worn. 2. poorly clothed. 3. mean, as *a shabby trick.*

shack *n.* a rough wooden hut.

shackles *n. pl.* iron rings on a prisoner's wrists or ankles. *v.* **shackle** to put shackles on.

shade *n.* 1. partial darkness. 2. something to cut off a strong light, as *a sunshade.* 3. (in the U.S.A.) a window blind. 4. the depth of a colour, as *a light shade of red. v.* **shade** 1. to keep off strong light. 2. to sketch the shadows in a picture (**shading, shaded**).

shadow *n.* a patch of shade. *v.* **shadow** 1. to darken. 2. to follow closely, as *they shadowed the thief. adj.* **shadowy**.

shady *adj.* 1. giving shade. 2. (*slang*) dishonest.

shaft *n.* 1. a long handle. 2. a passage leading to a mine. 3. a ray, as *a shaft of light.*

shaggy *adj.* with rough, uncombed hair.

shake *v.* 1. to move quickly to and fro. 2. to tremble, as *to shake with fear* (**shaking, shook, shaken**). *adj.* **shaky** *n.* **shakiness**.

shall *v.* used with other verbs: 1. to form the future tense, as *I shall stay.* 2. to show determination, as *you shall go!* (but *I will go!*).

shallow *adj.* not deep.

sham *n.* a pretence, an imitation. *adj.* **sham** not real, as *sham pearls*. *v.* **sham** to pretend, as *to sham illness* (**shamming, shammed**).

shamble *v.* to walk with shuffling feet (**shambling, shambled**).

shame *n.* 1. a painful feeling of having done something wrong or foolish. 2. disgrace. *v.* **shame** 1. to bring shame on. 2. to make someone feel shame (**shaming, shamed**). *adj.* **shameful** disgraceful.

shamefaced showing shame.

to put to shame to do so well that others are ashamed of themselves.

shampoo *n.* a hair wash, a powder for washing the hair. *v.* **shampoo** to wash the hair with soft soap (**shampooing, shampooed**).

shamrock *n.* a plant like the clover.

shanty *n.* 1. a hut. 2. a sailor's song (*pl.* **shanties**).

shape *n.* 1. the appearance or outline of a thing. 2. a mould or something made in a mould. 3. condition, as *the wounded man is in bad shape*. *v.* **shape** to model (**shaping, shaped**). *adj.* **shapely** of a good shape. *n.* **shapeliness**.

share *n.* 1. one person's portion of something divided. 2. (in business) money invested in a business. *v.* **share** 1. to divide out. 2. to have in common, as *to share an umbrella* (**sharing, shared**).

share-holder a man who has shares in a business.

shark *n.* a large fierce fish.

sharp *adj.* 1. cutting, piercing, biting. 2. keen, as *sharp eyes*. 3. quick, fierce, as *a sharp walk* or *a sharp temper*. 4. (in music) raised half a note higher, as *F sharp* (*F♯*) *is half a note higher than F*. *n.* **sharpness**.

sharpen *v.* to give a keen edge or a fine point to (**sharpening, sharpened**). *n.* **sharpener** something that sharpens.

shatter *v.* to break into pieces.

shave *v.* 1. to remove hair with a razor. 2. to pass very close to (**shaving, shaved**). *n.* **shave** a removal of hair with a razor. *n. pl.* **shavings** thin slices of wood cut off.

a close shave a narrow escape.

shawl *n.* a square piece of material used as a wrap.

she *pronoun* referring to a female.

sheaf *n.* a bundle of corn or papers (*pl.* **sheaves**).

shear *v.* to cut off (wool) with large scissors, as *to shear sheep* (**shearing, sheared, shorn**). *n. pl.* **shears** large cutters, as *garden shears*.

sheath (*pron.* sheeth) *n.* a cover, as for a sword blade or knife. *v.* **sheathe** (*pron.* sheeTH) to put in a sheath (**sheathing, sheathed**).

shed (1) *n.* a hut, an out-house.

shed (2) *v.* to throw off, to let fall (**shedding, shed**).

sheep *n.* 1. an animal reared for wool and its flesh, *mutton*. 2. a timid person (*pl.* **sheep**, *masc.* **ram**, *fem.* **ewe**, *young one* **lamb**). *adj.* **sheepish** shy, bashful. *n.* **sheepishness**.

sheepfold, sheep-pen an enclosure for sheep.

the black sheep of a family a member of a family who gets into disgrace.

sheer *adj.* 1. complete, as *sheer stupidity*. 2. very steep, as *the sheer face of a cliff*. 3. pure, as *sheer silk*.

sheet *n.* 1. a large, thin piece or wide area, as *a sheet of cloth* or *a sheet of water*. 2. a rope fastened to a sail.

sheik or **sheikh** *n.* an Arab chief.

shelf *n.* a board or ledge for holding things (*pl.* **shelves**).

shell *n.* 1. a hard case or covering. 2. a metal case filled with explosives. *v.* **shell** 1. to remove the shell, as *to shell peas*. 2. to fire at with shells.

shell-fish a water animal with a shell, as an oyster or winkle.

shelter *v.* a place that gives protection or cover. *v.* **shelter** to protect.

shelve *v.* 1. to put on a shelf. 2. to put off, to delay, as *to shelve a plan*. 3. to slope gently (**shelving, shelved**).

shepherd *n.* a man who looks after sheep (*fem.* **shepherdess**).

sheriff *n.* 1. a chief officer of the law in a county. 2. (in Scotland) a judge.

sherry *n.* a Spanish wine.

shew see **show**.

shield *n.* 1. a flat plate of iron carried on the left arm by soldiers in olden days for protection. 2. any protection. v. **shield** to shelter from harm.

shift v. to change position. n. **shift** 1. a change, a removal. 2. a group of men working together during certain hours, as *the day shift* or *the night shift*. 3. a trick, a dodge.

shiftless lazy.

shifty deceitful.

to shift for oneself to manage on one's own.

shilling n. a silver coin worth five new pence.

shimmer v. to gleam, to quiver with light.

shin n. the front of the leg below the knee. v. **shin** to climb (**shinning, shinned**).

shine v. 1. to give out light, to sparkle (**shining, shone**). 2. to polish (**shining, shined**). n. **shine** 1. brightness. 2. polish.

shingle n. 1. pebbles on a beach. 2. a wooden roof-tile.

shiny adj. bright (*comparative* **shinier**, *superlative* **shiniest**).

ship n. a vessel which sails the seas. v. **ship** 1. to carry by ship. 2. (in North America) to send goods by rail or road (**shipping, shipped**).

shipment n. goods carried by ship.

shipping n. 1. sending goods by ship. 2. all the ships of a country.

shipshape adj. tidy and orderly.

shipwreck n. a ship lost at sea.

shipyard n. a place where ships are built.

shire n. a county, as *Ayrshire*.

shirk v. to avoid unpleasant work or a duty. n. **shirker**.

shirt n. an undergarment worn by men and boys. n. **shirt-waist** (in North America) a woman's blouse.

shiver v. to tremble, to shake, to break up. n. **shiver** a trembling.

shoal n. a large group of fish.

shock (1) n. 1. a sudden blow. 2. a sudden numbness due to bad news or illness. 3. a sharp pain caused by an electric current. v. **shock** to cause anger or horror, as *the accident shocked the onlookers*. adj. **shocking** painfully surprising, revolting.

shock (2) n. 1. a pile of corn sheaves. 2. a mass of untidy hair.

shoddy adj. poor, badly made.

shoe n. 1. a covering for the foot reaching to the ankle. 2. a crescent-shaped iron bar nailed to a horse's hoof. 3. the part of a brake which rubs against the wheel. v. **shoe** to put on a shoe (**shoeing, shod**).

shoe-lace a lace for fastening shoes.

shone past of **shine**.

shook past of **shake**.

shoot v. 1. to fire a bullet, shell, etc. 2. to send forward quickly, as *to shoot a football at the goal*. 2. to sprout, to burst out. 3. to film a scene (**shooting, shot**). n. **shoot** a small twig.

shooting-star a meteor flashing across the sky.

shop n. 1. a building where goods are sold. 2. a place where goods are made or repaired, a *workshop*. v. **shop** to buy from shops (**shopping, shopped**). n. **shopper**.

shopkeeper n. a person who keeps a shop.

shop-soiled adj. not quite clean through being kept in a shop.

shore n. land at the edge of a sea or lake.

shorn past participle of **shear**.

short adj. 1. small in length or time. 2. lacking in weight or money. 3. angry, curt, as *a short answer*. 4. crumbly, as *short pastry*. n. **shortage** being short. v. **shorten** to make short. adv. **shortly** soon.

in short in a few words.

the long and short of it in a few words.

shortbread n. crumbly sweet cake.

short-circuit n. a leakage of electricity.

shorthand n. a method of quick writing, using small signs for words.

short-handed adj. short of helpers.

shorts n. pl. short trousers.

short-sighted adj. 1. only able to see things that are near. 2. not taking count of the future.

short-tempered adj. easily made angry.

shot (1) n. 1. the firing of a gun. 2. a lead pellet (*pl.* **shot**). 3. a shooter, as *he is a good shot*. 4. a heavy metal ball thrown in sport.

shot (2) *past* of **shoot**.

shotgun *n*. a gun that fires cartridges containing pellets.

should 1. *past* of **shall**. 2. ought to.

shoulder *n*. the part of the body where the arm joins the trunk. *v*. **shoulder** to take on, to bear.

shoulder-blade one of the two flat bones at the top of the back.

to give the cold shoulder to to snub. **to put one's shoulder to the wheel** to make a great effort.

shout *n*. a loud call. *v*. **shout** to call loudly.

shove *v*. to push roughly. *n*. **shove** a strong push.

shovel *n*. a kind of spade for moving coal, cinders, etc. *v*. **shovel** to move with a shovel (**shovelling, shovelled**).

show or **shew** *v*. 1. to let people see, to exhibit. 2. to explain, as *to show how to do a sum*. 3. to point out, as *to show the way* (**showing, shown** or **showed, shown**). *n*. **show** 1. an exhibition, a display. 2. a play, a performance. *adj*. **showy** bright, splendid.

a show of hands a vote made by holding up hands.

to give the show away to give away a secret.

to show off to try to impress.

to show up 1. to stand out. 2. to make someone look foolish.

shower *n*. 1. a short fall of rain. 2. a bath under a spray of water. *v*. **shower** 1. to rain for a short time. 2. to give in plenty, as *to shower gifts on someone*. *adj*. **showery**.

showman *n*. a man who stages shows for money.

shred *v* to cut into strips (**shredding, shredded**). *n*. **shred** a strip, a small piece.

shrew *n*. 1. a mouse-like animal. 2. a bad-tempered woman.

shrewd *adj*. sharp-witted, keen. *n*. **shrewdness**.

shriek *n*. a shrill cry. *v*. **shriek** to scream.

shrill *adj*. piercing, as *a shrill cry*. *n*. **shrillness**.

shrimp *n*. a small shell-fish.

shrine *n*. a sacred place.

shrink *v*. 1. to become smaller. 2. to draw back in fear (**shrinking, shrank, shrunk**). *n*. **shrinkage**. *adj*. **shrunken**.

shrivel *v*. to wither, to wrinkle (**shrivelling, shrivelled**).

shroud *n*. 1. a cloth round a dead body. 2. a covering, as *a shroud of mist on a hill*. *v*. **shroud** to hide.

shrub *n*. a bush with many branches coming from the ground.

shrubbery *n*. a place planted with shrubs.

shrug *v*. to move the shoulders to show doubt or surprise (**shrugging, shrugged**).

shrunk, shrunken see **shrink**.

shudder *v*. to tremble with fear or cold. *n*. **shudder** a shake of the body.

shuffle *v*. 1. to walk with dragging feet. 2. to mix playing-cards before dealing them (**shuffling, shuffled**).

shun *v*. to avoid (**shunning, shunned**).

shunt *v*. to move a train to another line.

shut *v*. to close (**shutting, shut**).

to shut down to close (a business).

to shut one's eyes to to pretend not to see.

shutter *n*. 1. a cover for a window. 2. a camera lens cover which moves when the trigger is pressed to let light through.

shuttle *n*. 1. (in weaving) a wooden bobbin which carries thread to and fro. 2. (in a sewing-machine) a sliding metal holder carrying the thread. *v*. **shuttle** to move to and fro.

shuttlecock *n*. a cork with feathers stuck in it, used in badminton.

shy (1) *adj*. timid, nervous (*comparative* **shyer**, *superlative* **shyest**). *adv*. **shyly**.

to fight shy of to keep away from.

shy (2) *v*. 1. to throw. 2. for a horse to rear up in fright (**he shies, shying, shied**).

coconut shy a fairground side-show where balls are thrown at coconuts.

sick *adj*. ill, vomiting. *n*. **sickness**. *v*. **sicken** to become unwell. *adj*. **sickly** weak.

side *n*. 1. an edge. 2. a surface. 3. a team or group of people in a contest. *v*. **side** (with the word **with**) to join a side (**siding, sided**).

sideboard *n.* a piece of dining-room furniture.

side-car *n.* a small carriage at the side of a motor-cycle.

side-show *n.* a small show at a fair.

siding *n.* a side line on a railway.

sidle *v.* to move sideways towards someone in a timid way (**sidling, sidled**).

siege *n.* the surrounding of a fort or town by an enemy.

sieve *n.* a round frame with a mesh to separate coarse powders from fine, etc. *v.* **sieve** to use a sieve (**sieving, sieved**).

sift *v.* 1. to use a sieve to separate fine things from coarse. 2. to examine carefully, as *to sift truth from falsehood*.

sigh *v.* 1. to breathe heavily to show love or sorrow. 2. (with **for**) to long for.

sight *n.* 1. the ability to see. 2. the thing seen, as *the sunset was a fine sight*. 3. device to help aim a gun. *v.* **sight** 1. to aim a gun. 2. to see suddenly. *n. pl.* **sights** places of interest, as *the sights of London.*

sightseer *n.* a tourist.

sightseeing *n.* seeing places of interest.

sign *n.* 1. a mark or movement with a special meaning. 2. a notice-board. *v.* **sign** 1. to make a sign. 2. to put one's signature at the end of a letter.

to sign on to engage or be engaged for work.

signal *n.* 1. a sign giving a message. 2. (on a railway) a movable arm or a light signing a train to stop or drive on. *v.* **signal** to send a message with a signal (**signalling, signalled**). *adj.* **signal** remarkable, as *a signal success*.

signature *n.* a person's name written by himself.

signature-tune a special tune which an entertainer always uses for his performances.

signet *n.* a seal.

significant *adj.* 1. full of meaning, as *a significant glance*. 2. important, as *a significant event*. *n.* **significance**.

signpost *n.* a direction post at a crossroads.

silent *adj.* quiet, noiseless. *n.* **silence**.

silencer something to quieten a gun or engine.

silk *n.* the thread of silkworms woven into cloth. *adj.* **silken** or **silky** like silk.

silkworm *n.* a caterpillar that spins silk.

sill *n.* a ledge below a window or door.

silly *adj.* foolish, stupid (*comparative* **sillier**, *superlative* **silliest**). *n.* **silliness**.

silt *n.* river mud. *v.* **silt** to choke a rivermouth with silt.

silver *n.* 1. a precious metal. 2. money made of silver. *v.* **silver** to coat with silver. *adj.* **silvery** like silver.

silver-plated coated with silver.

silver wedding the twenty-fifth anniversary of a wedding.

similar *adj.* nearly alike. *n.* **similarity**.

simmer *v.* to boil gently.

to simmer down to calm down.

simple *adj.* 1. easy, as *a simple question*. 2. plain, as *a simple dress*. 3. foolish, as *a simple man*. 4. innocent, as *a simple child*. 5. not complicated, as *a simple fracture of a bone*. *adv.* **simply**.

simplicity *n.* being simple.

simplify *v.* to make something simpler (**simplifying, simplified**). *n.* **simplification**.

simultaneous *adj.* happening at the same time. *adv.* **simultaneously**.

sin *n.* a wicked action. *v.* **sin** to do evil (**sinning, sinned**). *n.* **sinner** someone who sins. *adj.* **sinful**.

since *adv.* 1. from that past time to the present, as *he came once, but I have not seen him since*. 2. ago, as *he has been gone long since*. *conj.* because, as *I did not write since you were told what to do*.

sincere *adj.* true, real, not false. *adv.* **sincerely**. *n.* **sincerity**.

sinew *n.* 1. a tough cord joining muscle to bone. 2. strength. *adj.* **sinewy** strong.

sing *v.* to make musical sounds with the voice (**singing, sang, sung**). *n.* **singer**.

singsong a flat tone of voice.

singe *v.* to scorch (**singeing, singed**).

single *adj.* 1. one only. 2. for one only, as *a single bed*. 3. for one way only, as *a single ticket*. 4. unmarried, as *a single man*. *v.* **single** to pick out one, as *to single out an apple from a basket* (**singling, singled**). *adv.* **singly** one by one.

single-handed by oneself alone.

to walk in single file to walk one behind another.

singular *adj.* 1. strange, unusual. 2. (in grammar) referring to one only. Opposite of **plural**. *adv.* **singularly** unusually.

sinister *adj.* evil-looking, threatening.

sink (1) *v.* 1. to go down or go under. 2. to make go down, as *to sink a well* (**sinking, sank, sunk**).

sink (2) *n.* a basin fixed under a tap.

sinner see **sin**.

sip *v.* to drink in small amounts (**sipping, sipped**).

siphon *n.* 1. a bent tube for drawing liquid from one container to another. 2. a bottle of soda-water from which the liquid is forced by gas, *a soda-siphon*.

sir *n.* a polite way of addressing a man (*fem.* **madam**). *n.* **Sir** the title of a knight (*fem.* **Lady**).

sire *n.* 1. a father. 2. a male parent of an animal (*fem.* **dam**). 3. a title used in speaking to a king.

siren *n.* 1. a warning hooter. 2. (in old Greek legends) a woman who attracts men to their doom by her singing.

sister *n.* 1. a daughter of the same parents as another (*masc.* **brother**). 2. a nun. 3. a senior nurse.

half-sister a girl or woman with only one parent the same as that of another.

sister-in-law the wife of a brother, or the sister of a husband or wife (*pl.* **sisters-in-law**).

sit *v.* 1. to be seated, to perch. 2. to be a member of a council or jury. 3. to hang, as *his coat sits well on him* (**sitting, sat**).

sitting pretty being in a favourable position compared with someone else.

to sit tight to keep still.

site *n.* a place, a plot of ground.

sitting-room *n.* a room to sit in.

situated *adj.* placed.

situation *n.* 1. a place. 2. employment, as *a situation in a bank*

six *n.* one more than five, written as 6 or VI. *ns.* **sixteen, sixty** *adjs.* **sixth, sixteenth, sixtieth**.

at sixes and sevens in confusion.

six of one and half a dozen of another both sides the same.

sixpence *n.* a British silver coin (worth $2\frac{1}{2}$ new pence).

size (1) *n.* the bigness of a thing.

sizable or **sizeable** fairly big in size.

to size up to come to an opinion about someone.

size (2) *n.* a weak glue used as a varnish for paper.

sizzle *v.* to hiss with heat, as *bacon sizzles in a pan* (**sizzling, sizzled**).

skate (1) *n.* a steel blade fastened to a boot for gliding on ice, or a set of steel balls fastened to a boot for rolling on a floor. *v.* **skate** to use skates (**skating, skated**).

skating-rink a stretch of ice or a wooden floor intended for skating.

to skate on thin ice to be in a situation needing much caution.

skate (2) *n.* a large, flat fish.

skeleton *n.* the bony framework of a human being or animal.

skeleton key a key which will open many locks.

a skeleton in the cupboard an unpleasant hidden secret.

sketch *n.* 1. a rough plan or drawing. 2. a short play. *v.* **sketch** 1. to give a rough outline. 2. to draw in a few lines. *adj.* **sketchy** thin, rough.

skewer *n.* a pin for holding meat firm.

ski (*pron.* skee *or* shee) *n.* one of a pair of long wooden runners fastened to the foot for moving over snow (*pl.* **skis**). *v.* **ski** to travel with skis (**skiing, skied** *pron.* skeed *or* sheed). *n.* **skier**.

skid *v.* for a moving vehicle to slip sideways suddenly (**skidding, skidded**). *n.* **skid** 1. a sudden slip sideways. 2. a kind of brake on a cart-wheel.

skilful *adj.* clever, expert, *adv.* **skilfully**.

skill *n.* cleverness at doing something.

skilled *adj.* able to do something well.

skim *v.* 1. to take the top off a liquid, as *to skim the cream off milk*. 2. to read quickly, as *to skim through a book*. 3. to glide on the surface, as *a canoe* *skimming over a lake* (**skimming, skimmed**).

skim-milk milk with the cream removed.

skin *n.* 1. the thin outer covering of the body of a human being or animal. 2. the peel or rind of a fruit or vegetable. *v.* **skin** to take off the skin (**skinning, skinned**).

skip *v.* 1. to jump lightly. 2. to pass over, as *to skip parts of a book* (**skipping, skipped**).

skipper *n.* a ship's captain.

skirmish *n.* a fight between small groups.

skirt *n.* 1. the lower part of a dress. 2. a garment hanging below the waist. *v.* **skirt** to go along the edge of, as *to skirt a hill.*

skittles *n. pl.* game in which balls are bowled at wooden pins.

skull *n.* the bony case holding the brain.

skunk *n.* a furry American animal which can give off a very unpleasant smell.

sky *n.* the space above the earth (*pl.* **skies**).

sky-blue a light blue.

skylark *n.* a European song-bird.

skyline *n.* the horizon, the outline of buildings.

sky-rocket *n.* a firework shooting very high.

skyscraper *n.* a very tall building.

slab *n.* a flat thick piece.

slack *adj.* 1. loose. 2. careless, as *slack work.* 3. not busy, as *trade is slack. v.* **slack** to be lazy. *n.* **slackness**. *n.* **slacker** a lazy person.

slacken *v.* 1. to loosen. 2. to be less active.

slag *n.* cinders or scale left in a furnace.

slain *past* of **slay**.

slake *v.* to quench with water, as *to slake one's thirst* or *to slake quicklime* (**slaking, slaked**).

slam *v.* to shut or throw down noisily (**slamming, slammed**). *n.* **slam** a noisy shutting of a door.

slander *v.* to speak evil of someone falsely. *adj.* **slanderous**.

slang *n.* a popular word or expression which is not good English, as *'use your loaf'* is slang for *'use your brain'.*

slant *n.* a slope, a tilt. *v.* **slant** to tilt. *adj.* **slanting** tilted.

slap *v.* to hit with the palm of the hand (**slapping, slapped**).

slapdash *adj.* hasty, careless.

slash *v.* to strike with a knife or sword. *n.* **slash** a slit or cut.

slate *n.* 1. a grey rock that splits into thin sheets. 2. a small sheet of this rock used for roofing. *v.* **slate** 1. to cover with slate. 2. to scold (**slating, slated**).

slaughter *v.* to kill in big numbers. *n.* **slaughter** a great killing.

slave *n.* a human being owned by a master. *v.* **slave** to work very hard (**slaving, slaved**). *n.* **slavery**. *adj.* **slavish** like a slave, humble.

slave-driver a hard master.

slay *v.* to kill (**slaying, slew, slain**).

sled or **sledge** *n.* a platform on runners for moving over snow.

sledge-hammer *n.* a heavy hammer used by blacksmiths.

sleek *adj.* smooth and glossy.

sleep *v.* to rest with closed eyes and unconscious mind (**sleeping, slept**). *n.* **sleep** deep rest. *adj.* **sleepless** without sleep. *adj.* **sleepy** wanting to sleep.

sleeper *n.* 1. someone who sleeps. 2. a sleeping-car. 3. one of the wooden beams to which railway lines are fastened.

sleeping-car *n.* a railway carriage with bunks in which to sleep.

sleep-walker *n.* someone who walks while asleep.

sleet *n.* rain and snow, or rain and hail, falling together.

sleeve *n.* the part of a garment which covers tha arm. *adj.* **sleeveless** without sleeves.

to laugh up one's sleeve to laugh to oneself.

sleigh *n.* a sledge.

slender *adj.* very thin, narrow.

slept *past* of **sleep**.

slew (1) *past* of **slay**.

slew (2) *v.* to swing round.

slice *n.* 1. a thin flat piece cut off. 2. a share. *v.* **slice** to cut into slices (**slicing, sliced**).

slick *adj.* 1. smooth. 2. smooth-tongued, speaking in a friendly but insincere way.
slid *past* of **slide**.
slide *v.* to glide smoothly along (**sliding, slid**). *n.* **slide** 1. a slip, a glide. 2. a stretch of ice for sliding. 3. a photograph on glass to be shown on a screen. 4. a girl's hair-clip.
slight *adj.* 1. very little, unimportant. 2. weak and frail, as *a slight old lady*. *v.* **slight** to treat without respect, to snub. *n.* **slight** an impolite act. *adv.* **slightly** rather, a little.
slim *adj.* slender, thin. *v.* **slim** to lessen one's weight by eating less (**slimming, slimmed**).
slime *n.* sticky mud. *adj.* **slimy**.
sling *n.* 1. a loop over the shoulder to hold up an injured arm. 2. a rope or chain to hold a load. 3. a strip of leather used in olden days as a weapon to throw stones. *v.* **sling** 1. to throw, to fling. 2. to hold in a sling (**slinging, slung**).
slink *v.* to creep about in a sly way (**slinking, slunk**).
slip *v.* 1. to move quietly. 2. to slide. 3. to move to one side. 4. to escape (**slipping, slipped**). *n.* **slip** 1. a slide. 2. a mistake, as *he made a slip in adding*. 3. a loose cover, as *a pillow-slip*. 4. a piece of paper. *adj.* **slippery** easy to slide on, smooth.
a slip of the tongue a hasty remark.
to give someone the slip to escape quietly.
to slip up 1. to lose one's balance. 2. to make a mistake.
slip-knot *n.* a movable knot.
slipper *n.* a soft, indoor shoe.
slipshod *adj.* careless.
slipway *n.* a slope down which a ship is launched.
slit *n.* a long cut or narrow opening. *v.* **slit** to gash, to cut lengthways (**slitting, slit**).
slog *v.* 1. to hit hard at. 2. to work hard (**slogging, slogged**).
slogan (*pron.* slō'gan) *n.* a catchy sentence used in advertising, as *drink more milk*.
slop *v.* to spill a liquid (**slopping, slopped**). *n. pl.* **slops** dirty water. *adj.* **sloppy** messy.

slope *n.* something higher at one end than the other, as a field or path. *v.* **slope** to tilt (**sloping, sloped**).
slot *n.* a slit, groove, or narrow opening. *adj.* **slotted** fitted with a slot.
slouch *v.* to walk with bent head and drooping shoulders.
slovenly *adj.* careless, untidy. *n.* **slovenliness**.
slow *adj.* 1. taking a long time. 2. (of a clock) behind time. 3. dull in learning. *adv.* **slowly**. *n.* **slowness**.
slow-motion film one showing movement on the screen very slowly.
sludge *n.* soft mud.
slug (1) *n.* 1. a snail with no shell. 2. a small pellet.
slug (2) *v.* (in North America) to strike with the fist (**slugging, slugged**).
sluggish *adj.* slow-moving.
slum *n.* a poor overcrowded district with old houses.
slumber *v.* to sleep. *n.* **slumber** sleep.
slump *v.* 1. to fall heavily, as *to slump into a chair*. 2. for prices or trade to fall. *n.* **slump** a sudden fall in prices or trade.
slung *past* of **sling**.
slunk *past* of **slink**.
slur *v.* 1. to sound words indistinctly. 2. to pass over lightly (**slurring, slurred**). *n.* **slur** a reproach, an insulting remark.
slush *n.* half-melted snow, watery mud.
sly *adj.* underhand, secretive (*comparative* **slyer**, *superlative* **slyest**). *adv.* **slyly**. *n.* **slyness**.
on the sly secretly.
smack (1) *v.* 1. to hit with the palm of the hand. 2. to make a noise with the lips. *n.* **smack** 1. a blow with the open hand. 2. a noise made with the lips. 3. a taste, a flavour.
smack (2) *n.* a small fishing-boat.
small *adj.* little, not big.
small talk talk about unimportant things.
the small hours very early morning.
the small of the back the lowest part of the back.
small-arms *n. pl.* rifles, swords, revolvers.
small-minded *adj.* narrow in outlook.
smallpox *n.* a disease which marks the skin.

smart v. to feel sore, to have one's feelings hurt. n. **smart** 1. soreness. 2. hurt feelings. adj. **smart** 1. clever. 2. fashionable. 3. quick, as a smart walk. n. **smartness**.

smarten v. to make smarter.

smash v. to break into pieces. n. **smash** 1. a breaking into pieces. 2. a hard stroke at tennis.

smear v. to mark with something sticky. n. **smear** a sticky dab.

smell n. 1. a scent or odour. 2. one of the five senses, the sense of smell. v. **smell** 1. to notice something through the nose. 2. to give off a smell (**smelling, smelt** or **smelled**). adj. **smelly** with a bad smell.

smelling-salts strong-smelling crystals or a liquid to revive fainting persons.

smelt (1) past of **smell**.

smelt (2) v. to obtain metal from ore in a furnace.

smile v. to look pleased or happy (**smiling, smiled**). n. **smile** a pleased look on one's face. adj. **smiling** with a pleased look.

smite v. to hit hard.

smith n. a worker in metal, as a blacksmith, locksmith, or goldsmith.

smithy (pron. smiTH'i) n. a blacksmith's shop.

smock n. an outer garment like a loose shirt.

smog n. a dense fog of smoky vapour.

smoke n. 1. a black cloud from something burning. 2. breathing in tobacco fumes, as he had a smoke. v. **smoke** 1. to give off smoke. 2. to breathe in tobacco fumes (**smoking, smoked**). n. **smoking**. adj. **smoky** (comparative **smokier**, superlative **smokiest**).

smoke-screen n. a cloud of smoke to hide ships or troops in war.

smooth adj. 1. even, not rough. 2. pleasant, as a smooth manner. v. **smooth** 1. to make level or even. 2. to calm, as to smooth an angry man. n. **smoothness**.

smote past of **smite**.

smother v. 1. to choke or suffocate. 2. to cover, as John was smothered in dirt.

smoulder v. to burn slowly without flame.

smudge n. 1. a dirty mark. 2. (in North America) a very smoky fire. v. **smudge** to smear (**smudging, smudged**).

smug adj. very pleased with oneself. n. **smugness**.

smuggle v. to take goods into or out of a country secretly and illegally (**smuggling, smuggled**). ns. **smuggler, smuggling**.

smut n. a speck of soot or dirt. adj. **smutty**.

snack n. a light quick meal.

snag n. 1. a branch or point sticking out. 2. a difficulty.

snail n. a small slimy creature with a shell on its back.

snake n. a long, legless reptile. n. **snaky**.

snake-charmer n. a man who trains snakes to sway to music.

snap v. 1. to break suddenly. 2. to make a sudden bite at. 3. to make a quick angry remark, as he snapped at me angrily. 4. to take a quick photograph (**snapping, snapped**). n. **snap** 1. a sudden breaking. 2. a spring-catch. 3. a spell of bad weather, as a cold snap. 4. a quick photograph. adj. **snappy** quick, lively.

snapshot n. a quick photograph.

snare n. a wire loop as a trap for animals.

snarl v. to growl. n. **snarl** an angry growl.

snatch v. 1. to grab. 2. to tug at something. n. 1. a sudden grab. 2. a small song.

sneak v. 1. to creep quietly. 2. to give someone away by telling tales. n. **sneak** 1. a mean person. 2. a telltale.

sneer v. to show contempt or scorn. n. **sneer** a scornful look or remark.

sneeze v. to sound 'atishoo' through the nose (**sneezing, sneezed**). n. **sneeze** a sudden blowing of air through the nose.

sniff v. 1. to draw in air through the nose. 2. to smell cautiously. n. **sniff** 1. a cautious smell at something. 2. a little noise made with the nose.

snigger v. to giggle. n. **snigger** a nervous laugh.

snip v. 1. to cut a little bit off. 2. to cut with short strokes (**snipping, snipped**). n. **snip** a bit cut off.

snipe v. to shoot at an enemy from a hiding-place (**sniping, sniped**). n. **sniper**.

snivel v. 1. to run at the nose. 2. to cry in a quiet, whining way (**snivelling, snivelled**).

snob n. someone who looks down on those who are not wealthy or important. n. **snobbery**. adj. **snobbish**.

snoop v. to pry in a sly way.

snooze v. to doze (**snoozing, snoozed**).

snore v. to breathe noisily while asleep (**snoring, snored**).

snort v. to breathe noisily through the nose in anger.

snout n. an animal's nose and mouth.

snow n. frozen water vapour which falls in white flakes. v. **snow** 1. for snow to fall. 2. to fall as thick as snow, as *invitations snowed upon her.* adj. **snowy**.

snowbound held up by snow, as *snowbound travellers.*

snowed up blocked by snow.

snowdrift n. a bank of drifted snow.

snowdrop n. a small white winter flower.

snowflake n. a single bit of snow.

snow-plough n. (in the U.S.A. spelt **snow-plow**) a machine to clear roads or railway tracks of snow.

snow-shoe n. a shoe shaped like a tennis racket and used for walking over deep snow.

snub v. to be rude and unfriendly to someone (**snubbing, snubbed**). n. **snub** a rude and unfriendly act.

snub-nosed adj. having a short, stubby nose.

snuff n. powdered tobacco which is sniffed to cause sneezing and clear the head. v. **snuff** 1. to sniff at. 2. to put out a small light, as *to snuff a candle with the fingers.*

snuffle v. to breathe noisily through the nose.

snug adj. warm and cosy.

snuggle v. to press warmly and cosily against, as *a baby snuggles against its mother* (**snuggling, snuggled**).

so adv. 1. as much, as *you are not so heavy as I am.* 2. thus, as *so he thinks.*

conj. **so** therefore, as *I feel tired, so I shall rest.*

so-called said to be.

so to speak in other words.

soak v. 1. to absorb, as *the paper soaks up water.* 2. to make very wet, as *the rain has soaked us.*

soap n. a substance making a lather with water, used for washing. adj. **soapy**.

soap-suds n. foamy lather.

soar v. 1. to rise like a bird. 2. to rise quickly, as *the price of sugar has soared lately.*

sob v. 1. to weep with gulps of breath. 2. to breathe gulps of air, as *the tired runner sobbed for breath* (**sobbing, sobbed**). n. **sob** 1. a gulp of air. 2. a noise of weeping.

sober adj. 1. not drunk. 2. calm, serious. adv. **soberly** calmly.

soccer n. short for Association Football, a game played by two teams of eleven players who kick a ball towards the opponents' goal.

sociable adj. fond of company. adv. **sociably** n. **sociability**.

social adj. 1. having to do with living in a group, as *ants are social insects.* 2. friendly, companiable, as *a social gathering.* n. **social** a friendly gathering. n. **socially**.

social services all the public services which benefit a town or city.

socialism n. the belief that all industries should belong to the public or the government. n. **socialist** someone who believes in socialism.

society n. 1. people as a whole. 2. people of rank or fashion. 3. a club whose members share some interest or hobby. 4. companionship, as *I like Joan's society.*

sock n. a short stocking.

socket n. a hole into which something fits, as *a socket for an electric plug.*

sod n. a piece of earth with grass growing from it.

soda n. a chemical used in washing, *washing-soda,* or in baking, *bicarbonate of soda.*

soda-fountain a counter where pop and similar drinks are sold.

soda-water fizzy water full of carbon-dioxide gas.

sofa *n.* a long, padded seat with arms and a backrest.

soft *adj.* 1. not hard. 2. weak, not strong. 3. gentle, mild. *n.* **softness**.

soften *v.* to make soft.

soggy *adj.* soaked with water.

soil (1) *n.* earth, the ground.

soil (2) *v.* to make dirty, as *to soil clothes*.

solar *adj.* having to do with the sun, as *the solar system is the sun and all its planets*.

sold *past* of **sell**.

solder *n.* a metal alloy which melts easily and is used for joining other metals together.

soldier *n.* a man who serves in an army.

sole (1) *n.* the underside of a foot or shoe. *v.* **sole** to put a new sole on a boot or shoe (**soling, soled**).

sole (2) *n.* a flat fish.

sole (3) *adj.* single, alone, one only. *adv.* **solely**.

solemn *adj.* grave, serious, reverent. *adv.* **solemnly**. *n.* **solemnity**.

solicitor *n.* a lawyer who advises people and defends them in a lower court of law.

solid *adj.* 1. firm and hard. 2. made of the same material right through, as *this bar is of solid gold*. *n.* **solidity**.

solidify *v.* to become solid (**solidifying, solidified**).

solitary *adj.* single, alone, lonely.

solitude *n.* 1. loneliness. 2. a lonely place, as *the solitude of the desert*.

solo *n.* 1. a piece of music sung or played by one person. 2. a card game (*pl.* **solos**). *n.* **soloist** someone who sings or plays by himself.

solution *n.* 1. a liquid with something dissolved in it. 2. the answer to a problem, as *the solution of a crime*.

solve *v.* to find the answer to a problem (**solving, solved**).

sombre *adj.* gloomy, dark.

sombrero (*pron.* som.bray'rō) *n.* a South American wide-brimmed felt hat.

some *pronoun* a few. *adj.* **some** a certain (person or thing), as *some girl has taken it*.

somebody *pronoun* 1. some person. 2. an important person, as *he thinks he is somebody*.

somehow *adv.* in some way.

somersault *v.* to turn head over heels.

sometime *adv.* at some time.

sometimes *adv.* now and then.

somewhere *adv.* at some unknown place.

son *n.* someone's male child.

son-in-law someone's daughter's husband (*pl.* **sons-in-law**).

song *n.* 1. words set to music for singing. 2. the musical notes of a bird.

sonnet *n.* a poem of fourteen lines.

soon *adv.* 1. in a short time, early. 2. willingly, as *I would as soon watch as play*.

sooner or later at some time in the future.

soot *n.* the black powder in smoke.

soothe *v.* to quieten, to comfort. *adj.* **soothing** comforting.

sophisticated *adj.* wise in the ways of the world, experienced. Opposite of **simple**.

sorcerer *n.* a wizard (*fem.* **sorceress**). *n.* **sorcery**.

sordid *adj.* dirty, unpleasant.

sore *adj.* painful, tender. *adv.* **sorely** 1. painfully. 2. greatly, as *help was sorely needed*. *n.* **soreness**.

sorrow *n.* sadness, grief.

sorry *adj.* 1. unhappy for what has happened. 2. wretched, as *Tom was in a sorry state* (*comparative* **sorrier**, *superlative* **sorriest**).

sort *n.* a kind, a variety, as *there are all sorts of sweets in the shop*. *v.* **sort** to separate into groups of a kind, as *to sort stamps into countries*.

out of sorts not feeling well.

sought *past* of **seek**.

soul *n.* 1. the spirit within a person. 2. a person, as *she is a brave old soul*. 3. a centre of energy, as *he was the life and soul of the party*.

soulful full of feeling.

soulless hard, unfeeling.

soul-stirring stirring the feelings.

sound (1) *adj.* 1. healthy. 2. undamaged, as *these oranges are sound*. 3. deep, as *a sound sleep*. 4. reliable, as *a man* *of sound character.* 5. thorough, as *he has had a sound training.* n. **soundness**.

sound (2) *n.* a noise, something heard. *v.* **sound** 1. to make a noise, as *sound the trumpet!* 2. to give an impression, as *that sounds good.*

sound (3) *v.* 1. to test the depth of water. 2. to find out what someone thinks, as *I will sound father about his plans.* n. **sounding**.

sound (4) *n.* a water-channel joining two lakes or seas.

soup *n.* a liquid food made by boiling meat and vegetables.

sour *adj.* 1. having a bitter taste like vinegar. 2. bad-tempered, as *a sour face.* adv. **sourly**. n. **sourness**.

source *n.* 1. a spring from which a river flows. 2. the beginning or origin of anything.

south *n.* 1. the point of the compass lying to the right as one faces the rising sun. Opposite of **north**. 2. the part of a country lying to the south. *adj.* **south** belonging to the south, coming from the south, as *a south wind.*

south-east the compass point midway between south and east.

south-west the compass point midway between south and west.

southerner (*pron.* suTH'er.ner) someone from the south.

southwards towards the south.

the South Pole the southern end of the earth's axis.

souvenir (*pron.* soo.ve.neer') *n.* something one keeps in remembrance of a person or place.

sovereign *n.* 1. a king or queen. 2. a British gold coin (no longer in circulation) originally worth £1. *adj.* **sovereign** highest in authority. n. **sovereignty** highest power.

sow (1) *n.* a female pig or hog (*masc.* **boar**).

sow (2) (*pron.* sō) *v.* to set seeds (**sowing, sowed, sowed** or **sown**).

space *n.* 1. the distance between things, room to be filled. 2. a length of time. *adj.* **spacious** roomy.

space-ship *n.* an enclosed cabin in which astronauts orbit the earth or travel to other planets.

space-travel *n.* travel in a space-ship.

spade *n.* 1. a tool for digging. 2. a card in one of the four suits of playing-cards.

span *n.* 1. the distance between the outstretched thumb and little finger. 2. the full length of a thing in distance or time, as *the span of a bridge,* or *the span of a man's life.* 3. an arch of a bridge. 4. (in North America and South Africa) a pair of horses or oxen used to pull a vehicle. *v.* **span** to stretch across, as *the electric cable spanned the valley* (**spanning, spanned**).

spank *v.* to smack with the hand or a slipper.

spanner *n.* a tool for moving nuts on bolts, a wrench.

spar (1) *n.* a ship's mast or wooden crosspiece.

spar (2) *v.* to practise boxing (**sparring, sparred**).

sparring partner a man who gives a boxer practice.

spare (1) *adj.* 1. extra, kept for use later. 2. lean, as *a tall spare boy.* n. **spare** 1. an extra part. 2. an extra tyre. 3. (in North America) in a game of bowls or skittles, knocking down all the pins with one ball to spare.

spare (2) *v.* 1. to use in small amounts. 2. to give what one does not need, as *to spare someone some matches.* 3. to be merciful to, as *to spare someone's feelings* (**sparing, spared**).

not to spare oneself to work very hard.

spare the rod and spoil the child if a child is not punished when he needs it then his character is spoiled.

spark *n.* 1. a speck of burning matter. 2. a small electric flash. 3. a trace, as *he has not a spark of humour in him.* v. **spark** to give out sparks.

sparking-plug *n.* (in North America, **spark-plug**) one of the plugs in a petrol or gas engine which fires the explosive mixture.

sparkle *v.* to glitter, to flash (**sparkling, sparkled**).

sparrow *n.* a small, brownish bird.

sparrow-hawk *n.* a small bird of prey which feeds on sparrows.

sparse *adj.* scanty, thinly scattered. *adv.* **sparsely.**

spasm *n.* a sudden twitch of the muscles. *adj.* **spasmodic** happening now and then, uneven.

spat (1) *past* of **spit.**

spat (2) *n.* (in North America) a slight slap, sprinkle, or quarrel.

spate *n.* a flood, as *the river is in spate.*

spatter *v.* to splash with liquid or mud.

spawn *n.* the eggs of fish, frogs, or other water creatures.

speak *v.* to talk, to say (**speaking, spoke, spoken**).
to speak one's mind to say what one really thinks.

speaker *n.* 1. someone who speaks. 2. the chairman who keeps order in the House of Commons, or in the United States House of Representatives.

spear *n.* a long weapon with a steel point. *v.* **spear** to stab with a spear.

special *adj.* of a particular kind, unusual, exceptional. *adv.* **specially** particularly.

specialist *n.* an expert with special knowledge of some subject.

speciality *n.* something very special, as *Smith's fruit tarts are a speciality.*

specialize *v.* to follow one particular study, as *Professor Brown specializes in ancient Chinese languages* (**specializing, specialized**). *n.* **specialization.**

species (*pron.* spee'sheez) *n.* 1. a sort, a kind. 2. a group of living things of the same general kind, as *all kinds of horses belong to the same species* (*pl.* **species**).

specific *adj.* definite, exact, as *I gave him specific instructions.* *adv.* **specifically.**

specification *n.* an exact account of how something is to be done, and the materials to be used, as *the specification for making a model aeroplane.*

specify *v.* to say or write down clearly what is required, as *we specified that the work should be finished by the end of May* (**specifying, specified**).

specimen *n.* a sample, one thing taken from a batch.

speck *n.* a tiny bit, a small spot.

speckle *n.* a small spot. *v.* **speckle** to mark with small spots (**speckling, speckled**).

spectacle *n.* a sight, a fine show.

spectacles *n. pl.* lenses in a frame worn to improve the eyesight.

spectacular *adj.* showy, wonderful to see.

spectator *n.* an onlooker, a watcher.

spectre *n.* a ghost.

spectrum *n.* the band of colours seen in a rainbow, a water-drop, or a glass prism.

speculate *v.* 1. to wonder, to guess. 2. to buy goods hoping to sell them later at a profit (**speculating, speculated**). *n.* **speculation.**

sped *past* of **speed.**

speech *n.* 1. ability to speak. 2. the way one speaks, as *Jean's speech is good, she speaks clearly.* 3. a talk to an audience. *adj.* **speechless** unable to speak.

speed *n.* fast movement. *v.* **speed** to move quickly (**speeding, sped** or **speeded**). *adj.* **speedy.**

speedometer *n.* an instrument for measuring speed.

speedway *n.* a racing track for motorcycles or cars.

spell (1) *v.* to name or write the letters of a word in their order (**spelling, spelt** or **spelled**).
spelling-bee a spelling competition.

spell (2) *n.* 1. magic words. 2. a short period, as *to do a spell of work.*
spellbound fascinated, enchanted.

spelt *past* of **spell.**

spend *v.* to use up money, time, or energy (**spending, spent**).

spendthrift someone who wastes money.

spent *past* of **spend.**

sphere (*pron.* sfyair) *n.* any object shaped like a ball, a globe. *adj.* **spherical** like a sphere.

sphinx (*pron.* sfingks) *n.* 1. a monster supposed by the ancient Greeks to have a human head and the body of a lion, like the large statue of the Sphinx in Egypt. 2. a quiet mysterious person.

spice *n.* a substance for flavouring food, such as ginger, nutmeg, or pepper. *adj.* **spicy.**

spider *n.* a small, eight-legged creature which spins a web to trap flies.

spied *past* of **spy.**

spike *n.* 1. a sharp point. 2. an ear of corn, or the head of a flowering plant. *v.* **spike** to pierce with a spike. *adj.* **spiky.**

spill (1) *v.* to overflow, to let a liquid or powder fall out of a container (**spilling, spilt** or **spilled**). *n.* **spill** a fall.

spill (2) *n.* a strip of wood or twisted paper for use as a lighter.

spilt *past* of **spill.**

spin *v.* 1. to make threads, as *to spin cotton* or *a spider spins a web.* 2. to turn round quickly, as *to spin a top* or *to spin on one's heels.* 3. to tell slowly, as *to spin a long story* (**spinning, spun**). *n.* **spin** 1. a quick turn. 2. a short ride, as *a spin in a car.*

spinach (*pron.* spin'ij) *n.* a vegetable whose leaves are cooked and eaten.

spinal *adj.* concerning the backbone or spine.

spindle *n.* a thin rod about which something turns.

spine *n.* 1. the backbone. 2. a large thorn. 3. a spike of a hedgehog or porcupine. *adj.* **spineless** 1. having no backbone. 2. lacking courage. *adj.* **spiny** having spines.

spinster *n.* an unmarried woman (*masc.* **bachelor**).

spiral *n.* a curve shaped like a clock-spring or the thread of a screw.

spire *n.* a tower tapering to a point.

spirit *n.* 1. a person's soul. 2. a ghost. 3. energy, liveliness, as *Dick is a boy with plenty of spirit.* 4. the real meaning, as *he helped others in the spirit of a good Christian.* 5. strong drink containing plenty of alcohol. *adj.* **spirited** lively.

in high spirits with lively good humour.

spiritual *adj.* concerning the spirit, God, or religion. *adv.* **spiritually.**

spit (1) *v.* 1. to throw saliva from the mouth. 2. to throw anything from the mouth, as *to spit out orange pips* (**spitting, spat**).

spit (2) *n.* 1. a metal rod on which meat is roasted. 2. a strip of land reaching into the sea.

spite *n.* ill-will, a grudge. *adj.* **spiteful.**

in spite of although, even allowing for.

splash *v.* to spatter with liquid. *n.* **splash** 1. a spattering of liquid. 2. a daub.

splendid *adj.* magnificent, brilliant. *n.* **splendour.**

splice *v.* to join the ends of two ropes by twining the strands together. *n.* **splice** a joint made in this way.

splint *n.* a piece of wood to hold a broken bone in position.

splinter *n.* a small chip of wood, glass, or metal.

split *v.* 1. to crack or break open length-ways. 2. to divide (**splitting, split**). *n.* **split** a crack.

to split hairs to argue about small differences.

to split the difference to reach agreement by each side giving way and meeting half-way.

splutter *v.* 1. to spit or make spitting sounds. 2. to talk in a very excited way.

spoil *v.* 1. to damage, to make worse. 2. to plunder, as *the soldiers spoiled the city* (**spoiling, spoiled** or **spoilt**). *n.* **spoil** plunder, booty.

spoiled, spoilt *past* of **spoil.**

spoke (1) *n.* one of the bars from the hub to the rim of a wheel.

spoke (2) *past* of **speak.**

spokesman *n.* a man who speaks on behalf of others.

sponge *n.* 1. a kind of sea-animal fastened to the bed of warm seas, whose soft skeleton is used for washing and cleaning. 2. a kind of cake like a sponge. *v.* **sponge** 1. to wash with a sponge. 2. to be always begging from others (**sponging, sponged**). *adj.* **spongy.**

to throw up the sponge to give up a struggle.

spontaneous *adj.* occurring naturally and of its own accord, not forced. *n.* **spontaneity.**

spool *n.* a small reel or bobbin on which thread or wire is wound.

spoon *n.* a little bowl at the end of a handle for stirring or eating food. *n.* **spoonful** (*pl.* **spoonfuls**).

spoor *n.* the track of a wild animal.

sporran *n.* a purse worn in front of a kilt.

sport *n.* a game, amusement, or athletic contest.

sportsman *n.* 1. a man taking part in sport. 2. a good loser. *n.* **sportsmanship**.

spot *n.* 1. a small mark or stain. 2. a particular place, as *this is the spot where it happened.* *v.* **spot** 1. to mark with spots. 2. to notice (**spotting, spotted**). *adj.* **spotless** free from spots. *adj.* **spotted** marked with spots.

spotlight *n.* a bright beam of light shining on one spot.

spouse (*pron.* spowz) *n.* a husband or wife.

spout *n.* a pipe or tube through which a liquid flows. *v.* **spout** (of a liquid) to gush out.

sprain *v.* to twist a muscle. *n.* **sprain** a painful twist of a muscle.

sprang *past* of **spring**.

sprat *n.* a very small sea-fish.

a sprat to catch a mackerel something small given in the hope of getting something large in return.

sprawl *v.* 1. to sit or lie with one's limbs spread out. 2. to spread out, as *new buildings sprawl over the countryside.*

spray (1) *n.* a twig or cluster of flowers.

spray (2) *n.* 1. a watery mist. 2. a bottle from which scent can be blown, a *scent-spray.* *v.* **spray** to scatter liquid in fine drops (**spraying, sprayed**).

spread *v.* 1. to unfold, to open out, as *to spread a cloth.* 2. to cover a wider area, as *the fog is spreading.* 3. to pass from person to person, as *to spread a disease* (**spreading, spread**). *n.* **spread** 1. a cover for a bed, a *bedspread.* 2. a feast set out on a table.

spree *n.* a gay time.

sprightly *adj.* lively, gay (*comparative* **sprightlier,** *superlative* **sprightliest**).

spring *v.* 1. to jump, to start suddenly. 2. to follow from, as *success springs from boldness.* 3. to start, as *to spring a leak* or *spring a trap* (**springing, sprang, sprung**). *n.* **spring** 1. a leap. 2. a stream of water from the ground. 3. a compressed metal spiral which opens out as the pressure is removed, as *a clock-spring* 4. the season following winter. *adj.* **springy** elastic.

spring-balance *n.* an instrument fitted with a spring and used to measure weights.

springboard *n.* a springy diving-board.

springbok *n.* a South African deer.

spring tide *n.* a very high tide.

springtime *n.* the season of spring.

sprinkle *v.* to scatter powder or small drops (**sprinkling, sprinkled**). *n.* **sprinkle** a light shower.

sprint *v.* to run at full speed for a short time. *n.* **sprint** a short race run at full speed.

sprout *v.* to begin to grow. *n.* **sprout** a young shoot.

Brussels sprouts very small cabbages on a single stem.

spruce (1) *adj.* neat, tidy, smart.

spruce (2) *n.* a kind of fir-tree.

sprung *past* of **spring**.

spun *past* of **spin**.

spur *n.* 1. a spiked wheel on a horseman's boot to urge a horse on faster. 2. anything that urges one on, as *the desire for fame is a spur.* 3. a mountain peak. *v.* **spur** to urge on with a spur (**spurring, spurred**).

on the spur of the moment suddenly, without thought.

to win one's spurs to win honour.

spurn *v.* to push aside or refuse with scorn.

spurt *v.* to gush out, to squirt out. *n.* **spurt** 1. a sudden gushing out. 2. a sudden effort, as *to make a spurt at the end of a race.*

sputnik *n.* a Russian name given to their first satellite launched in 1957.

spy *n.* someone who secretly watches others or gains information in an enemy country. *v.* **spy** 1. to watch secretly. 2. to catch sight of. 3. to gain information secretly about an enemy (**spying, spied**).

squabble *v.* to quarrel noisily about some small matter (**squabbling, squabbled**).

squad *n.* a small group of soldiers.

squadron *n.* a group of warships under the command of an admiral, or of aeroplanes under the command of a squadron-leader.

squalid *adj.* dirty, uncared-for. *n.*
squalor dirt, wretchedness.

squall *n.* a short, sudden wind. *v.* **squall**
to cry out loudly.

squalor see **squalid.**

squander *v.* to waste money or goods
foolishly.

square *n.* 1. a figure with four equal
sides and four right angles. 2. a four-
sided open space in a city or town. 3. an
instrument for drawing right angles.
4. (in arithmetic) the result obtained by
multiplying a number by itself, as *16
is the square of 4. adj.* **square** 1. shaped
like a square. 2. fair, honest, as *a square
deal.* 3. full, as *a square meal. v.* **square**
1. to make square. 2. to straighten, as
to square one's shoulders. 3. to multiply
a number by itself, as *to square 5 to
make 25.* 4. to balance, as *to square an
account.* 5. (*slang*) to bribe someone
(**squaring, squared**). *adv.* **squarely.**
all square both sides equal in a game.
square metre a square each side of
which is a metre.

squash *v.* to squeeze, to crush. *n.*
squash 1. a crush. 2. a drink made from
crushed fruit, as *lemon squash.* 3. a
game played with rackets and a ball in
a walled court, *squash-rackets.*

squat *v.* 1. to sit on one's heels, to
crouch. 2. to live on land or in a building without permission (**squatting,
squatted**). *adj.* **squat** short and
thick. *n.* **squatter** 1. someone who
lives on land or in a building without
right. 2. (in Australia) a farmer who
settles on undeveloped land.

squaw *n.* a Red Indian's wife.

squeak *n.* a small, high-pitched sound.
v. **squeak** to make a high-pitched noise.

squeal *n.* a high-pitched cry. *v.* **squeal**
to utter a shrill cry.

squeeze *v.* to press hard, to crush
(**squeezing, squeezed**). *n.* **squeeze**
a crush, a hug.

squib *n.* a small firework.

squint *v.* 1. to look in different ways with
each eye. 2. to glance quickly at. *n.*
squint 1. a cross-eyed look. 2. a quick
peep.

squire *n.* 1. (in England) a country
gentleman. 2. (in the U.S.A.) a local

judge. 3. (in olden days) a knight's
attendant, an *esquire.*

squirm *v.* to wriggle.

squirrel *n.* a bushy-tailed animal which
lives in trees.

squirt *v.* to force out liquid in a fine
stream. *n.* **squirt** a thin stream of
liquid.

stab *v.* to wound with a pointed weapon
(**stabbing, stabbed**). *n.* **stab** a sharp
blow with a pointed weapon.

stability *n.* steadiness.

stabilize *v.* to make firm or steady
(**stabilizing, stabilized**). *n.* **stabiliza-
tion.**

stable (1) *adj.* firm, steady.

stable (2) *n.* a building for horses.

stack *n.* 1. a large pile, as *a stack of
bricks.* 2. a tall chimney. *v.* **stack** to
pile up in an orderly heap.

stadium *n.* a sports ground with seats
around it (*pl.* **stadia** or **stadiums**).

staff (1) *n.* a stick or pole (*pl.* **staffs** or
staves).

staff (2) *n.* a group of people working
together under a leader, as *a school
staff* or *a staff of officers* (*pl.* **staffs**).

stag *n.* a male deer (*fem.* **hind**).

stage *n.* 1. a platform in a hall. 2. the
distance between two stopping-places
in a journey. 3. a point in the development of something, as *the model Jack
is making is now at an advanced stage.*
v. **stage** to produce on a stage, as *to
stage a play* (**staging, staged**).
by easy stages in short spells, with
rests.
on the stage acting in the theatre.

stage-coach *n.* a coach which, in
olden days, did regular journeys in
stages.

stage-fright *n.* nervousness before an
audience.

stagger *v.* 1. to walk unsteadily, to reel
from side to side. 2. to astonish, as *to
stagger someone with some news.* 3. to
fix at different intervals, as *to stagger
holidays so that not all people take
holidays at the same time.*

stagnant *adj.* still, motionless, as *stagnant water.*

stain *n.* 1. a blot, a mark. 2. a dye for
colouring wood, etc. *v.* **stain** 1. to make

a blot. 2. to dye wood or other material.
adj. **stainless** 1. without stain. 2. not
easily stained, as *stainless steel.*

stair *n.* one of a set of steps.

staircase, stairway *ns.* a set of steps
with a rail.

stake *n.* 1. a pointed post fixed in the
ground. 2. money put on a bet. *v.* **stake**
1. to mark out with stakes, as *to stake
out a plot of land.* 2. to wager money in
a bet (**staking, staked**).

at stake to be risked, in danger.

stalactite *n.* a piece of limestone hanging from the roof of a cave.

stalagmite *n.* a piece of limestone rising from the floor of a cave.

stale *adj.* not fresh. *n.* **staleness.**

stalk (1) *n.* the stem of a leaf, fruit, or
flower.

stalk (2) *v.* 1. to walk with long, slow
steps. 2. to hunt an animal stealthily.

stall *n.* 1. a place in a stable or cattle-
shed for an animal. 2. a table in a
market, a *market-stall.* 3. a ground-floor
seat in a theatre or cinema. 4. a seat in
the choir of a church. 5. a covering for
a sore finger, a *finger-stall. v.* **stall** (of
an engine) to lose speed and stop.

stallion *n.* a male horse (*fem.* **mare**).

stalwart *adj.* strong, sturdy, brave.

stamen *n.* the part of a flower bearing
pollen.

stamina *n.* endurance, lasting-power.

stammer *v.* to repeat a sound nervously
when speaking, to stutter.

stamp *n.* 1. a mark or design pressed
on something. 2. a tool for making such
a mark, as *a date-stamp.* 3. a small piece
of gummed paper bought at a post office
as a receipt for posting a letter or
parcel. 4. a thump on the ground with
the foot. *v.* **stamp** 1. to thump the
ground with the foot. 2. to label or mark
with a stamp.

to stamp out to destroy completely.

stampede *n.* a mad rush of frightened
people or animals, a panic. *v.* **stampede** to rush away madly in a group
(**stampeding, stampeded**).

stance *n.* the way one stands, as *the
stance of a batsman at cricket.*

stand *v.* 1. to be on one's feet, or rise
to one's feet. 2. to be in a certain place.

3. to bear, to endure, as *I can stand it no
longer.* 4. to mean, to signify, as
G.P.O. stands for General Post Office
(**standing, stood**). *n.* **stand** 1. a
position, a place where goods are sold
in the street. 2. a platform or lines of
seats from which to watch a game.
3. a piece of furniture to hang things
on, a *hat-stand.* 4. a halt in a retreat, as
the retreating troops made a stand. 5.
(in North America) a growing crop, as
a stand of corn.

to stand by 1. to support. 2. to wait
until called.

to stand for to represent.

to stand up for to support.

to stand up to to face bravely.

standard *n.* 1. a flag, as *a regimental
standard.* 2. a post, as *a lamp-standard.*
3. a rule or example of good conduct, as
he is a man of high standards. 4. a unit
of length, volume, or quantity, as *the
standard metre is 100 cm long.* 5. a
level, as *a high standard of living.*

standardize *v.* to make things all of one
size or kind, as *to standardize the bolts
in a machine* (**standardizing, stan-
dardized**). *n.* **standardization.**

standing *n.* 1. duration, as *a habit of
long standing.* 2. reputation, position,
as *a musician of high standing.*

standpoint *n.* a point of view.

standstill *n.* a complete stop.

staple (1) *n.* 1. a U-shaped piece of
metal driven into wood. 2. a piece of
bent wire to hold papers together.

staple (2) *adj.* chief, as *rice is the staple
food of China.*

star *n.* 1. a distant world or heavenly
body which appears as a point of light.
2. an asterisk (*) used in printing. 3. a
famous actor or other performer. *v.*
star to present or appear as a first-rate
performer, as *the film stars Gary Grey*
(**starring, starred**). *adj.* **starry** like
a star.

star-gazer an astronomer, an astrologer, a dreamy person.

starboard *n.* the right side of a ship,
looking towards the bow. Opposite of
port.

starch *n.* a white substance found in
grain and potatoes, used in laundry-

work for stiffening clothes. *v.* **starch** to stiffen with starch. *adj.* **starchy.**

stare *v.* to look at with a fixed gaze (**staring, stared**). *n.* **stare** a fixed look.

starfish *n.* a sea-animal shaped like a star.

starling *n.* a small, dark, insect-eating bird.

start *v.* 1. to begin, as *to start work.* 2. to set out, as *he started from home.* 3. to jump suddenly, as *Sandra started with surprise. n.* **start** 1. a beginning. 2. a lead, as *Tom was given a start of ten metres in the race.* 3. a sudden jump of surprise or fear. *n.* **starter** 1. someone who starts a race. 2. a small, electric motor used to start a larger motor. **to start up** (an engine) to set going. **to start with** in the first place.

startle *v.* to scare, to frighten suddenly (**startling, startled**).

starve *v.* to suffer or die from hunger, or to cause some living creature to suffer or die from hunger (**starving, starved**). *n.* **starvation.**

state (1) *n.* 1. a condition, as *to be in a happy state of mind.* 2. pomp and ceremony, as *the Prince was received with great state.* 3. a nation. 4. one of a group of districts under one government, as *the United States of America. adj.* **stately** majestic. *n.* **stateliness** dignity.

state (2) *v.* to say firmly, to declare, as *the law states that every driver of a car must have a licence* (**stating, stated**).

statement *n.* something said or written.

statesman *n.* someone experienced in government. *adj.* **statesmanlike** wise and skilful. *n.* **statesmanship.**

station *n.* 1. a place, a position, as *the sentry took up his station by the gate.* 2. a building for members of some organization, as a *fire-station* or a *police station.* 3. a stopping place on a railway, a *railway station.* 4. a rank in life, as *a man of high station.* 5. (in Australia) a sheep-farm. *v.* **station** to place in position.

stationary *adj.* fixed, standing still (note: do not confuse with **stationery**).

stationery *n.* writing-materials (note: do not confuse with **stationary**). *n.* **stationer** a person who sells stationery.

statistics *n. pl.* a series of numbers and facts set out to provide information about some subjects. *adj.* **statistical.**

statue *n.* the figure of a person or animal carved or cast in some material. *n.* **statuette** a small statue.

stature *n.* a person's height.

status (*pron.* stay'tus) *n.* rank, position.

statute *n.* a law. *adj.* **statutory** according to law.

staunch (or **stanch**) *adj.* strong, firm. *v.* **staunch** (or **stanch**) to stop a flow of blood.

stave (1) *n.* 1. a staff or stick. 2. one of the pieces of wood of which a cask or tub is made. 3. a verse of a poem. 4. the five lines with spaces between on which music is written (*pl.* **staves**). See **staff.**

stave (2) *v.* 1. (with **in**) to knock a hole in a box or ship. 2. (with **off**) to drive back, to hold off, as *to stave off an attack* (**staving, staved** or **stove**).

stay *v.* 1. to remain. 2. to put off, as *Jack stayed his departure* or *Mary stayed her hunger with some buns.* 3. to support, as *the mast was stayed with wires* (**staying, stayed**). *n.* **stay** 1. a stop, a visit. 2. a support.

stead *n.* place, as *I went in his stead.* **to stand one in good stead** to be useful.

steadfast *adj.* firm, steady.

steady *adj.* 1. standing firmly. 2. regular, constant, as *a steady fall of rain* (*comparative* **steadier,** *superlative* **steadiest**). *n.* **steadiness.**

steak *n.* a thick slice of meat for cooking.

steal *v.* 1. to take secretly from someone else, to rob. 2. to move secretly (**stealing, stole, stolen**). **to steal a march on someone** to gain an advantage over him secretly.

stealth (*pron.* stelth) *n.* acting secretly. *adj.* **stealthy.** *adv.* **stealthily.**

steam *n.* vapour from boiling water. *v.* **steam** 1. to give off steam. 2. to go by steam-power, as *the train steamed out of the station.* 3. to cook in steam. **steam-boat, steamer, steamship** a ship driven by steam.

steam-engine an engine driven by steam.

steam-roller a steam-engine used in road-making.

steel *n.* 1. a hard, strong metal made from iron. 2. a piece of steel used for sharpening knives. *adj.* **steely** like steel.

steep (1) *adj.* 1. having a sharp slope. 2. very high, as *a steep price. n.* **steepness**.

steep (2) *v.* to soak, to saturate.

steeple *n.* a church tower with a spire.

steeple-jack a man paid to climb tall spires and chimneys.

steeple-chase a horse-race across country over jumps.

steer (1) *v.* to guide a ship or vehicle with a rudder or wheel.

steer (2) *n.* a young ox.

stem (1) *n.* 1. a plant stalk, or a thin stalk holding flower, leaf, or fruit. 2. the front of a ship, as *the ship shook from stem to stern.*

stem (2) *v.* 1. to stop, to hold back, as *to stem an enemy's advance.* 2. to advance against, as *the boat stemmed the current.* 3. (with **from**) to be caused by, as *his failure stems from idleness* (**stemming, stemmed**).

stencil *n.* a sheet of metal or waxed paper with letters or a design cut out, brushed over with paint so that the letters appear on paper beneath. *v.* **stencil** to use a stencil (**stencilling, stencilled**).

step (1) *n.* 1. a single pace, or the distance covered by a pace. 2. a tread on a stairway. 3. the sound of a foot. 4. action, as *he took steps to put the matter right. v.* **step** to move the feet in walking or dancing (**stepping, stepped**).

in step putting one's foot down at the same time as other people who are marching.

out of step not in step.

to step out to walk quickly.

to step up 1. to mount. 2. to increase, as *the shop stepped up its sales.*

to take steps to follow a plan of action.

step- (2) *prefix* new relation gained when a parent remarries, as *his mother married again, so now he has a stepfather and a step-sister.*

steppe *n.* an immense, grassy, treeless plain, in Russia.

sterile *adj.* 1. unfruitful, barren. 2. free from germs. *n.* **sterility**.

sterilize *v.* 1. to make sterile. 2. to destroy germs in, as *to sterilize milk by boiling* (**sterilizing, sterilized**). *n.* **sterilization**.

sterling *n.* British money, as *a pound sterling. adj.* **sterling** pure, of good value, as *a man of sterling worth.*

stern (1) *adj.* strict, severe.

stern (2) *n.* the back part of a ship.

stew *v.* to cook food by boiling it slowly. *n.* **stew** stewed meat and vegetables.

steward *n.* 1. an attendant in a club, hotel, or ship. 2. someone who manages an estate (*fem.* **stewardess**).

stick *v.* 1. to stab. 2. to fasten or be fastened. 3. to bear, to endure, as *Charles could stick it no longer* (**sticking, stuck**). *n.* **stick** 1. a thin piece of wood. 2. a shaped piece of wood for playing hockey, a *hockey-stick.* 3. anything slender, as *a stick of chalk.* 4. a holder, as *a candle-stick.*

to stick at nothing to take every step.

sticking-plaster *n.* a plaster to put over cuts.

sticky *adj.* gummy, gluey (*comparative* **stickier,** *superlative* **stickiest**). *n.* **stickiness**.

a sticky wicket (from cricket) a difficult situation.

stiff *adj.* 1. not easily moved, firm. 2. strong, as *a stiff breeze.* 3. difficult, as *a stiff test.* 4. cold, haughty, as *a stiff manner. n.* **stiffness.** *adv.* **stiffly**.

stiffen *v.* to make stiff or become stiff. *n.* **stiffening** starch or size used to stiffen cloth.

stifle *v.* to smother (**stifling, stifled**).

stile *n.* a set of steps to help one climb over a wall or fence.

stiletto *n.* a thin dagger (*pl.* **stilettos**).

still (1) *adj.* 1. without movement, calm. 2. even now, as *it is still wet.* 3. yet, all the same, as *he hates me, but still I like him.* 4. even, as *this problem is still harder. conj.* **still** however, as *it is* *difficult, still I will try.* v. **still** to soothe, to make calm. n. **stillness**.

still (2) n. an apparatus for distilling whisky, etc.

stilted adj. stiff, not natural, as *a stilted manner*.

stimulant n. a drug or food to revive a person and give him energy.

stimulate v. to excite, to give energy to (**stimulating, stimulated**). n. **stimulation**.

sting n. a small, needle-like weapon which some insects and nettles have. v. **sting** to prick with a sting (**stinging, stung**).

stink n. a foul smell. v. **stink** to smell foul (**stinking, stank** or **stunk, stunk**).

stir v. 1. to move or make move. 2. to mix with a spoon. 3. to arouse feelings, as *the news stirred him to anger* (**stirring, stirred**). n. **stir** a shaking up, a commotion, as *his action caused a great stir*.

stirrup n. a rider's footrest hanging from a horse's saddle.

stitch n. 1. (in sewing and knitting) a complete movement of the needle to form a loop of thread. 2. a loop of thread made in this way. 3. a sharp pain in one's side. v. **stitch** to sew, to join with stitches.

a stitch in time saves nine a little work done in time saves much work later.

stoat n. a large kind of weasel, a small animal, brown in summer and white in winter.

stock n. 1. a wooden stump. 2. the handle of a rifle. 3. a supply, as *a stock of coal*. 4. the animals on a farm. 5. ancestors, as *he comes of farming stock*. 6. shares in a business. 7. a garden plant. 8. liquid from boiled bones used in making soup. v. **stock** to lay in a supply. n. pl. **stocks** a firm's money.

to take stock to count the goods in a shop.

to take stock of to consider carefully.

stockade n. a strong, wooden fence.

stock-exchange n. a building in which business men meet to deal with stocks.

stocking n. a close-fitting covering for the leg and foot.

stock-still adj. completely still, motionless.

stocky adj. short and sturdy.

stodgy adj. dull, uninteresting.

stoep (*pron.* stoop) n. a verandah or porch in front of a house in South Africa.

stoke v. to feed a fire (**stoking, stoked**). n. **stoker** a man who stokes a fire.

stole, stolen past of **steal**.

stolid adj. dull, not showing any feeling.

stomach n. a bag in the body into which food passes and is partly digested.

stone n. 1. a piece of rock. 2. a gem, a *precious stone*. 3. the hard seed of certain fruits, as a *plum-stone*. 4. a weight of 14 pounds (6·35 kg). v. **stone** 1. to throw stones at. 2. to remove stones from fruit, as *to stone cherries* (**stoning, stoned**). adj. **stony** 1. having stones, as *stony fruit*. 2. hard, as a *stony look*.

stone-deaf deaf as a stone.

stone walling defensive play, as in cricket.

to leave no stone unturned to do all that is possible.

stood past of **stand**.

stool n. a small seat without a back.

stoop v. 1. to bend forward. 2. to be mean enough to do something, as *to stoop to cheating*. n. **stoop** a bending forward.

stop v. 1. to cease. 2. to prevent or cut off, as *to stop a gas supply*. 3. to fill up a hole, as *to stop a leak*. 4. to remain, as *to stop at home* (**stopping, stopped**). n. **stop** 1. a halt, or halting-place. 2. a punctuation-mark, a *full-stop* (.).

stoppage n. the stopping of something.

stopper n. a plug in a bottle-mouth or pipe.

stop-press n. late news.

storage n. 1. keeping goods in store. 2. a storing-place.

store n. 1. a supply of goods. 2. a shop. v. **store** to put by for future use (**storing, stored**).

to set great store by to value greatly.

storehouse n. a place for storing goods.

storey n. a floor of a building and its rooms (*pl.* **storeys**).

stork *n.* a large wading-bird with long beak, neck, and legs.

storm *n.* 1. a violent outburst of bad weather. 2. a violent outburst of passion or excitement, as *a storm of applause*. *adj.* **stormy**.

a storm in a teacup much excitement about very little.

to take by storm to capture a fort or town by sudden attack.

story *n.* a tale (*pl.* **stories**).

stout *adj.* 1. fat. 2. strong, brave. *n.* **stout** a strong beer.

stout-hearted *adj.* brave, resolute.

stove *n.* a cooker or closed heater.

stow *v.* to pack away.

stowaway *n.* someone who hides in a ship or vehicle to travel in secret.

straddle *v.* 1. to stand with legs apart. 2. to sit with one leg on each side of, as *to straddle a fence* (**straddling, straddled**).

straggle *v.* to wander away. *n.* **straggler**.

straight *adj.* 1. in a direct line, not curved. 2. honourable, as *a man who is straight in his actions*. 3. blunt, frank, as *a straight talk*.

straight away or **straightway** at once.

to keep a straight face to keep from smiling.

straighten *v.* to put straight or become straight.

straightforward *adj.* direct, honest.

strain *v.* 1. to stretch tightly, as *to strain a rope*. 2. to use to the utmost, as *to strain one's ears* or *strain someone's patience*. 3. to sprain, as *to strain a muscle*. 4. to put through a sieve, as *to strain tea*. *n.* **strain** 1. tightness. 2. ill-health through worry or overwork, as *he suffers from strain*. 3. a sprain. 4. a tune. 5. a manner of speaking, as *they teased him, and he replied in the same strain*. 6. a breed, as *a certain strain of cattle*.

strainer *n.* a sieve.

strait *n.* (often *n. pl.* **straits**) a narrow sea-channel. *n. pl.* **straits** hardship, difficulty.

strand (1) *n.* the seashore. *adj.* **stranded** 1. (of a ship) driven ashore. 2. (of a person) lost without money or help.

strand (2) *n.* a single string, thread, or wire, in a rope or cable. 2. a lock of hair.

strange *adj.* 1. unfamiliar, unusual. 2. out of place, as *to feel strange in a new school. n.* **strangeness**.

stranger *n.* a person unknown, a foreigner.

strangle *v.* to choke, to kill by squeezing the throat (**strangling, strangled**). *n.* **strangulation**.

strap *n.* a strip of leather or cloth. *v.* **strap** to fasten with a strap (**strapping, strapped**). *adj.* **strapping** tall and strong.

stratosphere *n.* the upper layer of air, from 7 to 10 kilometres up.

straw *n.* dried stalks of corn.

strawberry *n.* the juicy red fruit of a low-growing plant (*pl.* **strawberries**).

stray *v.* to wander and become lost (**straying, strayed**).

streak *n.* 1. a stripe, as *a streak of paint*. 2. a tinge, a small amount, as *there is a streak of vanity in his nature. v.* **streak** 1. to mark with streaks. 2. to move quickly. *adj.* **streaky**.

stream *n.* 1. a small river. 2. a flow of air, water, or people. *v.* **stream** to flow, to gush.

streamer *n.* a long ribbon or paper decoration.

streamlined *adj.* shaped to cut smoothly through air or water, as *a streamlined submarine*.

street *n.* a road in a town lined with houses or shops.

the man in the street any ordinary man.

strength *n.* 1. being strong. 2. power.

strengthen *v.* to make stronger.

strenuous *adj.* 1. hard-working, as *a strenuous worker*. 2. energetic, as *a strenuous walk*.

stress *n.* 1. strain. 2. emphasis, importance, as *he laid stress on the need for caution. v.* **stress** to put emphasis on.

stretch *v.* 1. to pull at something and make it longer. 2. to reach, as *the field stretches to the river. n.* **stretch** 1. a period of time. 2. a space, as *a stretch of water*.

stretcher *n.* a frame covered with canvas for carrying an injured or sick person.

strew *v.* to scatter (**strewing, strewed, strewed** or **strewn**).

stricken *adj.* struck by misfortune.

strict *adj.* 1. severe, as *a strict master.* 2. exact, as *he gave a strict account of what he saw. n.* **strictness.**

stride *n.* a long pace. *v.* **stride** to walk with long steps (**striding, strode, stridden**).

strife *n.* quarrelling and fighting.

strike *v.* 1. to hit. 2. to rub, as *to strike a match.* 3. to come across, as *to strike gold.* 4. to go off in a certain direction, as *to strike west.* 5. to stop work because of a grievance. 6. to lower as a sign of defeat, as *to strike a flag* (**striking, struck**). *n.* **strike** 1. a stoppage of work because of a grievance. 2. (in baseball) an unsuccessful stroke, or a ball pitched which should have been hit. *adj.* **striking** attracting attention. *n.* **striker.**

to strike out, or **off**, to cross out, to push forward.

to strike up to start a song or tune.

string *n.* 1. a thin cord. 2. a stretched wire or gut on a musical instrument. 3. a number of things on a thread, as *a string of beads.* 4. a line of things, as *a string of horses. v.* **string** to tie with a string or put on a string (**stringing, strung**). *adj.* **stringy** full of strings.

strip *n.* a long, narrow piece. *v.* **strip** 1. to tear off. 2. to undress. 3. to rob of everything (**stripping, stripped**).

stripe *n.* 1. a long, narrow line or streak. 2. a strip sewn to the sleeve of a uniform to show the wearer's rank. *v.* **stripe** to mark with stripes (**striping, striped**).

strive *v.* to try hard, to struggle (**striving, strove, striven**).

stroke *n.* 1. a blow. 2. a movement in swimming. 3. a sudden attack of illness. 4. a sweep of a pen or paintbrush. 5. (in rowing) the oarsman nearest the stern, who sets the pace. *v.* **stroke** to rub gently (**stroking, stroked**).

stroll *n.* a gentle walk. *v.* **stroll** to go for a gentle walk.

strong *adj.* powerful.

stronghold *n.* a fort.

strove *past* of **strive.**

struck *past* of **strike.**

structure *n.* something built or put together. *adj.* **structural.**

struggle *v.* to fight, to try hard (**struggling, struggled**). *n.* **struggle** a fight, a contest.

strung *past* of **string.**

strut (1) *v.* to walk in a proud way (**strutting, strutted**). *n.* **strut** a proud way of walking.

strut (2) *n.* a prop, a support. *v.* **strut** to hold up a weight with a strut (**strutting, strutted**).

stub *n.* 1. a stump. 2. the short thick end of a pencil or cigarette. *v.* **stub** 1. to knock the foot against a hard object. 2. to put out a lighted cigar or cigarette (**stubbing, stubbed**). *adj.* **stubby** short and thick.

stubble *n.* stumps of cornstalks left after the harvest.

stubborn *adj.* obstinate, not easily giving way.

stuck *past* of **stick.**

stud (1) *n.* 1. a shaped piece of bone or metal for fastening a collar to a shirt. 2. a large-headed nail.

stud (2) *n.* a group of horses kept for breeding.

student *n.* someone who studies, especially at a college or university.

studio *n.* 1. an artist's workroom. 2. a room in which films are made or radio programmes are broadcast.

studious *adj.* 1. fond of study. 2. thoughtful, considerate, as *Tom helped the child with studious care.*

study *n.* 1. the learning of a subject. 2. a room in a house for reading and writing. 3. a close examination of something. 4. a careful drawing. *v.* **study** 1. to learn. 2. to examine closely (**studying, studied**).

stuff *n.* 1. material, cloth. 2. rubbish. *v.* **stuff** to pack tightly, to cram.

stuffing *n.* 1. material packed into a cushion or into upholstery. 2. bread crumbs and flavouring packed into a fowl for roasting.

stuffy *adj.* 1. lacking fresh air. 2. dull and uninteresting.

stumble *v.* 1. to trip over something and nearly fall. 2. (with **on**) to discover unexpectedly (**stumbling, stumbled**). *n.* **stumble** a trip, a wrong step.

stumbling-block a difficulty, an obstacle.

stump *n.* 1. a part left after the main part has been removed, as *the stump of a tree.* 2. one of the sticks which make the wicket at cricket. *v.* **stump** 1. (*slang*) to puzzle someone. 2. (in cricket) to get a batsman out by touching his wicket with the ball when he is outside his crease. 3. to walk in a heavy way. *adj.* **stumpy** short and thick.

stun *v.* to knock senseless, to daze with shock (**stunning, stunned**).

stunt (1) *v.* to hinder the growth of anything. *adj.* **stunted** small.

stunt (2) *n.* something which is done to attract attention.

stupefy *v.* to daze, to amaze (**stupefying, stupefied**).

stupendous *adj.* huge, astounding.

stupid *adj.* unintelligent, foolish. *n.* **stupidity.**

stupor *n.* a dazed state.

sturdy *adj.* strong, firm (*comparative* **sturdier**, *superlative* **sturdiest**). *n.* **sturdiness.**

stutter *v.* to stammer, to speak nervously. *n.* **stutter** a stammer.

sty (1) *n.* a place for pigs (*pl.* **sties**).

sty (2), **stye** *n.* a small pimple or sore on the eyelid (*pl.* **sties** or **styes**).

style *n.* 1. a way of doing something, as *he has an awkward style of speaking.* 2. a smart way, a fashion, as *this hat is the latest style. adj.* **stylish** fashionable.

sub- *prefix* under, as *submarine means 'under the sea'.*

subconscious *adj.* only partly conscious.

subdivide *v.* to divide a second time, as *twelve can be divided into two sixes, and each six can be subdivided into threes* (**subdividing, subdivided**). *n.* **subdivision.**

subdue *v.* 1. to overcome, to conquer. 2. to soften, to tone down. *adj.* **subdued** 1. conquered. 2. softened, as *subdued light.*

subject (1) (*pron.* sub'jekt) *n.* 1. a person under someone's rule. 2. a matter which is discussed or studied.

subject to 1. liable, as *I am subject to illness.* 2. dependent on, as *subject to your approval.*

subject (2) (*pron.* sub.jekt¹) *v.* 1. to bring under one's power. 2. (with **to**) to cause to experience, as *to subject someone to a hard test. n.* **subjection.**

sublime *adj.* noble, awe-inspiring.

submarine *n.* a warship which moves under water. *adj.* **submarine** under water, as *submarine plants.*

submerge *v.* to cover with water, to go under water, as *the seal submerged* (**submerging, submerged**). *n.* **submersion.**

submission *n.* a surrender, a giving in.

submissive *adj.* meek, humble.

submit *v.* 1. to give in, to surrender. 2. to offer for consideration, as *to submit a plan to someone for his opinion* (**submitting, submitted**).

subordinate *n.* someone of lower rank or importance.

subscribe *v.* (with **to**) 1. to pay money to help some cause. 2. to agree to, as *to subscribe to a plan* (**subscribing, subscribed**).

subscription *n.* money paid to help a cause.

subsequent *adj.* following, later.

subside *v.* to sink, to grow less (**subsiding, subsided**). *n.* **subsidence.**

subsidize *v.* to give grants of money to (**subsidizing, subsidized**).

subsidy *n.* a grant of money (*pl.* **subsidies**).

substance *n.* 1. matter, material. 2. wealth, as *he is a man of substance.* 3. the important part of anything, as *the substance of a book.*

substantial *adj.* 1. solid, strongly made. 2. real, not imaginary. 3. big, important. *adv.* **substantially.**

substitute *n.* a person or thing standing in place of another. *v.* **substitute** to put one in place of another (**substituting, substituted**). *n.* **substitution.**

subterranean *adj.* underground, secret.

subtle (*pron.* sut'l) *adj.* 1. delicate, slight, as *there is a subtle difference between the two words.* 2. clever, cunning, as *he has a subtle mind. adv.* **subtly.** *n.* **subtlety.**

subtract *v.* to take one number from another. *n.* **subtraction.**

suburb *n.* an outer district of a town or city. *adj.* **suburban** connected with a suburb, as *a suburban bus service.*

subway *n.* 1. an underground passage. 2. (in the U.S.A.) an underground railway.

succeed *v.* 1. to gain success. 2. to follow after, as *King Edward VII succeeded Queen Victoria.*

success *n.* 1. a win, a good result. 2. fame, wealth. *adj.* **successful** gaining success.

succession *n.* 1. a number of things following one after another. 2. the right to follow someone holding a position, as *the succession to a throne. adj.* **successive** following one after another. *n.* **successor** someone who inherits a title or property from another person.

succulent *adj.* juicy.

succumb *v.* 1. to give way. 2. to die.

such *adj.* 1. of that kind, as *it was on just such a day as this that I arrived.* 2. so much, as *it was such a surprise.*

suck *v.* 1. to draw into the mouth. 2. to roll in the mouth, as *to suck a sweet.* 3. to absorb, as *a sponge sucks up water.*

suckle *v.* to nurse at the breast (**suckling, suckled**).

suction *n.* 1. the act of sucking. 2. making things stick together by removing the air between them.

sudden *adj.* quick, unexpected. *adv.* **suddenly.**

suds see **soap.**

sue *v.* to claim against someone in a law-court (**suing, sued**).

suet *n.* hard animal fat.

suffer *v.* 1. to feel pain or grief. 2. to put up with, as *to suffer loss of money.* 3. to be harmed, as *do not let your work suffer by carelessness.* 4. to allow.

suffering *n.* pain, grief.

suffice *v.* to be enough (**sufficing, sufficed**).

sufficient *adj.* enough. *n.* **sufficiency.**

suffix *n.* a small part added to the end of a word, as *-ing is a suffix in the word 'working'.*

suffocate *v.* to choke by stopping the breathing, or through lack of air (**suffocating, suffocated**). *n.* **suffocation.**

sugar *n.* a sweet substance made from sugar-cane or sugar-beet. *v.* **sugar** to sprinkle with sugar. *adj.* **sugary** sweet. **sugar-beet** a kind of white beetroot. **sugar-cane** a tall, woody grass from whose sap sugar is obtained.

suggest *v.* 1. to put forward an idea, to propose. 2. to give an impression, as *his letter suggests that he is unhappy. n.* **suggestion** 1. a proposal. 2. an impression. *adj.* **suggestive** bringing an idea to mind.

suicide *n.* killing oneself deliberately. *adj.* **suicidal** so dangerous as to be like suicide.

suit *n.* 1. a set of clothes, armour, or playing-cards. 2. a law-court case. 3. a marriage proposal. *v.* **suit** to satisfy, to look well on, as *that coat suits you. adj.* **suitable** fitting, proper. *n.* **suitability. suit-case** a travelling case.

to follow suit to follow someone else's lead.

suitor *n.* 1. a man who wishes to marry a lady and woos her. 2. someone who makes a petition in a law-court.

sulk *v.* to be bad-tempered and silent. *adj.* **sulky** (*comparative* **sulkier,** *superlative* **sulkiest**). *n.* **sulkiness.**

sullen *adj.* angrily silent.

sulphur *n.* a yellow chemical found in the earth.

sultan *n.* a Mahommedan ruler (*fem.* **sultana**).

sultana (*pron.* sul.tahn'a) *n.* 1. a sultan's wife. 2. a small raisin.

sultry *adj.* hot and close. *n.* **sultriness,**

sum *n.* 1. the result of adding things together. 2. a problem in arithmetic. 3. an amount of money. *v.* **sum** (with **up**) to add up, to summarise (**summing, summed**).

summarize *v.* to go over the main points of an argument briefly (**summarizing, summarized**).

summary *n.* a brief account of the main points (*pl.* **summaries**). *adj.* **summary** quick, brief, as *a summary account of what happened.*

summer *n.* the warmest season.

summer-house a garden hut for summer use.

summer-time the summer months.

summit *n.* the top, the highest point.

summon *v.* to send for.

summons *n.* an order to appear in a law-court, a command (*pl.* **summonses**).

sumptuous *adj.* luxurious, costly.

sun *n.* the heavenly body which gives us heat and light. *v.* **sun** to bathe in the sun (**sunning, sunned**). *adj.* **sunny** (*comparative* **sunnier**, *superlative* **sunniest**).

sunbeam *n.* a ray of sunshine.

sunburn *n.* burning of the skin caused by the sun.

sundae *n.* an ice-cream with fruit and nuts.

Sunday *n.* the first day of the week.

sundial *n.* an instrument for telling the time from a shadow cast by the sun.

sundry *adj.* various, several.

all and sundry everyone.

sunflower *n.* a very large yellow flower.

sung *past* of **sing**.

sunk, sunken *past* of **sink**.

sunlight *n.* the light of the sun.

sunrise *n.* the first appearance of the sun at daybreak.

sunset *n.* the last appearance of the sun.

sunstroke *n.* an illness caused by the sun's heat.

sup *v.* 1. to sip. 2. to eat supper (**supping, supped**).

super- *prefix* over, more than, as *a supervisor watches over the work of others.*

superb *adj.* splendid.

supercilious *adj.* haughty, proud.

superficial *adj.* 1. on the surface, not deep, as *a superficial wound.* 2. not sincere, as *a superficial smile. adv.* **superficially**.

superfluous (*pron.* soo.per'floo.us) *adj.* more than is needed, not required. *n.* **superfluity**.

superhuman *adj.* more than one would expect from a human being, as *a superhuman effort to win.*

superintend *v.* to take charge of, to manage.

superintendent *n.* a person in charge.

superior *adj.* 1. higher in rank or quality. 2. (with **to**) better than, as *his work is superior to yours. n.* **superior** someone of higher rank. *n.* **superiority**.

superlative *adj.* 1. the best. 2. (in grammar) the greatest, the most, as *'lowest'* and *'most sensible'* are the superlative words for *'low'* and *'sensible'*.

supernatural *adj.* miraculous, not to be explained in any natural way.

supersonic *adj.* faster than sound.

superstition *n.* belief in luck, magic, and charms. *adj.* **superstitious**.

supervise *v.* to watch over machines or people to see that they work well (**supervising, supervised**). *n.* **supervision** control. *n.* **supervisor** someone who supervises.

supper *n.* the last meal of the day.

supplant *v.* to take the place of, as *motor-cars have supplanted horses.*

supple *adj.* easily bent, springy. *n.* **suppleness**.

supplement *n.* 1. something added to a thing to complete it. 2. an extra part of a newspaper or magazine. *adj.* **supplementary** additional.

supply *v.* to provide (**supplying, supplied**). *n.* **supply** a stock, an amount (*n. pl.* **supplies**). *n.* **supplier** someone who supplies something.

support *v.* 1. to hold up. 2. to help, as *to support a good cause.* 3. to provide for, as *to support an old mother. n.* **support** 1. a prop. 2. help, as *I will give you all the support you need. n.* **supporter** someone giving help and encouragement.

suppose *v.* 1. to imagine, as *let us suppose you are king.* 2. to take it to be true, as *suppose he is right* (**supposing, supposed**). *n.* **supposition** something supposed. *adv.* **supposedly** probably.

suppress *v.* 1. to put down, as *to suppress a revolt.* 2. to keep secret, as *to*

suppress news or *to suppress a yawn. n.*
suppression.
supremacy *n.* complete power.
supreme *adj.* above all others.
sure *adj.* 1. certain, as *he is sure to be there.* 2. safe, reliable, as *the goalkeeper has sure hands. adv.* **surely.**
sure-footed safe in walking, as *a sure-footed mountain goat.*
surf *n.* waves breaking on the shore.
surface *n.* 1. the outside of anything. 2. the top of a liquid. *v.* **surface** (of a submarine) to rise above water (**surfacing, surfaced**).
surge *v.* to rise and fall, or move forward like waves (**surging, surged**). *n.* **surge** a sweeping forwards.
surgeon *n.* a doctor who performs operations.
surgery *n.* 1. the carrying-out of operations by a doctor. 2. the room in which a doctor receives patients.
surgical *adj.* concerning surgery.
surly *adj.* bad-tempered, unfriendly (*comparative* **surlier,** *superlative* **surliest**).
surname *n.* a family name.
surpass *v.* 1. to go beyond, to exceed, as *Tom's success in the test was so great that it surpassed what he expected.* 2. to do better than, as *Harry surpassed Jim in the competition.*
surplice (*pron.* sur'plis) *n.* a wide-sleeved white gown worn by clergymen and choir-boys.
surplus *n.* what is left over after what is wanted has been taken.
surprise *n.* 1. an unexpected event. 2. the feeling of astonishment one has at an unexpected happening. *v.* **surprise** 1. to astonish. 2. to attack or come upon unexpectedly (**surprising, surprised**).
surrender *v.* to give up, to yield. *n.* **surrender** a giving-up, a yielding.
surround *v.* to enclose, to be all around.
surroundings *n. pl.* environment.
survey (*pron.* ser.vay') *v.* 1. to look at, to inspect. 2. (of land) to measure and make a plan. *n.* **survey** (*pron.* ser'vay) 1. an inspection. 2. a measuring and planning of land. *n.* **surveyor.**

survive *v.* 1. to remain alive, as *they survived after many dangers.* 2. to live longer than, as *she survived her cousins* (**surviving, survived**). *n.* **survival** surviving. *n.* **survivor** someone still alive after others have died.
suspect (*pron.* sus.pekt') *v.* 1. to think it likely, as *I suspect he went.* 2. to mistrust, to doubt, as *I suspect him. n.*
suspect (*pron.* sus'pekt) a person who is thought to be guilty. *adj.*
suspect (*pron.* sus'pekt) not to be trusted.
suspend *v.* 1. to hang up. 2. to hold back or put aside for a time, as *to suspend the date of a meeting.*
suspenders *n. pl.* 1. supports for socks or stockings. 2. (in the U.S.A.) supports for trousers, braces.
suspense *n.* doubt, uncertainty.
suspension *n.* suspending or being suspended.
suspension bridge *n.* a bridge held up by cables from towers at either end.
suspicion *n.* 1. doubt or mistrust about someone or something. 2. a very small amount.
suspicious *adj.* 1. feeling doubtful about. 2. causing doubt or mistrust.
sustain *v.* 1. to uphold, to bear up. 2. to suffer, as *to sustain an injury.*
swab (*pron.* swob) *n.* 1. a mop. 2. a small pad of cotton wool. *v.* **swab** to use a swab (**swabbing, swabbed**).
swaddle *v.* to wrap a baby in many clothes.
swaddling-clothes bandage-like clothes wrapped round a baby.
swagger *v.* to walk or behave in a boastful conceited way.
swallow (1) *v.* 1. to pass food or drink down the throat. 2. to absorb, to take in, as *the expenses swallowed our pocket money.*
swallow (2) *n.* a small blue-and-white bird with a forked tail.
swam *past* of **swim.**
swamp *n.* a marsh, boggy ground. *v.* **swamp** to flood with water, as *the sea swamped the boat. adj.* **swampy.**
swan *n.* a large water-bird.
swan-song the last work of a poet or musician.

swap or **swop** v. (*slang*) to exchange (**swapping, swapped** or **swopping, swopped**).

swarm (1) *n.* 1. a large number of insects. 2. a large group of bees. 3. a crowd. *v.* **swarm** to move in large numbers.

swarm (2) *v.* (with **up**) to climb, using hands and feet.

swarthy (*pron.* sworTH'i) *adj.* dark-skinned.

swathe v. to wrap in bandages (**swathing, swathed**).

sway *v.* 1. to rock to and fro unsteadily. 2. to influence people, as *the speaker swayed the crowd.*

swear *v.* 1. to make a solemn promise. 2. to use bad language (**swearing, swore, sworn**).

sweat *v.* perspiration, the moisture from hot skin. *v.* **sweat** to perspire.

sweater *n.* a heavy jersey.

sweep *v.* 1. to clean with a brush. 2. (with **up**) to clear away. 3. to move powerfully, as *the wave swept up the shore.* 4. to stretch in a curve, as *the road sweeps round the bay* (**sweeping, swept**). *n.* **sweep** a man who sweeps chimneys, a *chimney-sweep.*

sweet *adj.* 1. tasting like sugar. 2. fresh, pleasant. 3. kind, gentle, as *a sweet nature.* *n.* **sweetness.** *v.* **sweeten** to make sweet.

sweetheart *n.* a lover.

swell *v.* 1. to grow bigger or greater. 2. to bulge, to expand (**swelling, swelled, swollen** or **swelled**). *n.* **swell** a rise and fall of the sea.

to have a swelled head to be conceited.

swelling *n.* a swollen lump.

swerve *v.* to turn aside suddenly (**swerving, swerved**). *n.* **swerve** a sudden turn to one side.

swift (1) *adj.* fast, quick. *n.* **swiftness.**

swift (2) *n.* a bird like a swallow.

swill *v.* to dash water over. *n.* **swill** 1. a wash. 2. liquid food for pigs.

swim *v.* 1. to move through water using one's limbs. 2. to be bathed in, as *eyes swimming with tears.* 3. to feel dizzy (**swimming, swam, swum**). *n.* **swim**

a spell of swimming. *n.* **swimmer** someone who swims.

swindle *v.* to cheat (**swindling, swindled**). *n.* **swindle** a fraud. *n.* **swindler** someone who swindles.

swine *n.* a pig, a hog (*pl.* **swine**).

swineherd *n.* someone who looks after pigs.

swing *v.* 1. to move to and fro like a clock pendulum. 2. to change direction, as *the yacht swung to the north* (**swinging, swung**). *n.* **swing** a seat held by ropes or chains on which one can swing.

in full swing in full action.

swipe *n.* a swinging blow.

swish *v.* to cut through the air with a hissing sound.

switch *n.* 1. a lever for turning electricity on or off. 2. a thin stick or whip. 3. railway points for moving a train to another track. *v.* **switch** 1. to alter suddenly, as *to switch plans.* 2. to operate a switch, as *to switch on electric current.*

switchback *n.* a railway at a fun-fair with steep ups and downs.

switchboard *n.* a board at a telephone exchange with points for connecting callers.

swivel *n.* a joint which allows either part to turn freely. *v.* **swivel** to turn freely (**swivelling, swivelled**).

swoon *v.* to faint.

swoop *v.* to pounce, to sweep down.

at one fell swoop in one attack.

swop see **swap**.

sword *n.* a weapon with a long blade.

to cross swords with to fight or argue with.

to put to the sword to kill.

sword-fish *n.* a fish with a jaw like a sword.

swordsman *n.* a man using a sword.

swore, sworn *past* of **swear**.

swum *past* of **swim**.

swung *past* of **swing**.

syllable *n.* a part of a word which can be pronounced separately, as *the word tu-lip has two syllables.*

syllabus *n.* a list of subjects in a course of study (*pl.* **syllabi** or **syllabuses**).

symbol *n.* a sign, mark, or emblem that stands for something, as *a cross is the symbol of Christianity. adj.* **symbolical**.

symmetrical *adj.* well-balanced, so that one half of an object is exactly similar to the other half. *n.* **symmetry**.

sympathize *v.* to feel for others (**sympathizing, sympathized**).

sympathy *n.* 1. sharing the feelings of others. 2. feeling pity for someone else's troubles. *adj.* **sympathetic**.

symptom *n.* a sign, especially a change in the body which signals an approaching illness.

synagogue (*pron.* sin¹a.gog) *n.* a Jewish church, or a Jewish congregation.

synonym *n.* a word with the same meaning as another word, as *'little' is a synonym of 'small'. adj.* **synonymous** meaning the same.

synthetic *adj.* artificial, as *synthetic rubber*.

syphon see **siphon**.

syringe *n.* 1. (in medicine) a tube with a sharp needle for forcing liquid into the flesh. 2. (in gardening) a pump for spraying plants.

syrup *n.* a thick, sugary liquid. *adj. syrupy*.

system *n.* 1. an orderly group of things working together, as *the trains in a railway system* or *a system of rules.* 2. the human body, as *exercise is good for the system. adj.* **systematic** methodical, regular.

T

tabernacle *n.* 1. a church. 2. a small cupboard on an altar to hold the sacrament. **the Tabernacle** (in the Bible) a tent used by the Jews as a place of worship.

table *n.* 1. a piece of furniture with a broad top. 2. a list of facts or figures, as *a multiplication table*.

table-spoon a large spoon.

table-tennis a game played with bats and a celluloid ball.

to turn the tables to win after being defeated.

tableau (*pron.* tab¹lō) *n.* a scene made by people dressed in costume (*pl.* **tableaux** *pron.* tab¹lōz).

tablet *n.* 1. a small flat plate with writing on. 2. a small flat piece of medicine or soap.

taboo *adj.* forbidden, not to be touched.

tack *n.* 1. a small nail. 2. (in sewing) a loose stitch. 3. a movement of a sailing-ship going against the wind. *v.* **tack** 1. to use tacks for fixing. 2. (in sailing) to use tacks to go against the wind.

tackle *n.* 1. ropes and pulleys for lifting weights. 2. equipment, as *fishing tackle. v.* **tackle** 1. to stop an opposing player in a game. 2. to deal energetically with a difficulty (**tackling, tackled**).

tacky *adj.* sticky.

tact *n.* skill in keeping friendly with other people and not offending them. **tactful** using tact.

tactless not using tact.

tactics *n. pl.* the art of moving ships or troops to the best advantage in battle (note: *strategy* is the art of moving troops or ships in the best way in a *war*).

tadpole *n.* a young frog or toad in its first stage of development after leaving the spawn.

tag *n.* 1. a label. 2. a metal point at the end of a shoe-lace.

tail *n.* 1. the movable end of an animal, bird, or fish. 2. any end part, as *the tail of a queue or an aeroplane.* 3. the side of a coin opposite the side bearing the head.

to turn tail to run away.

tailor *n.* someone who makes suits and overcoats (*fem.* **tailoress**).

taint *n.* a stain, decay, infection. *v.* **taint** to spoil by touching with something bad.

take *v.* 1. to get hold of, to grasp. 2. to carry. 3. to act in some way, as *to take care* or *to take a photograph* (**taking, took, taken**).

to take after to look like.

to take heed to be careful.

to take in 1. to receive. 2. to understand. 3. to swindle.

to take it out of to act spitefully to, to tire.

to take off 1. to imitate. 2. (of an aeroplane) to start out. 3. to remove.

to take on to undertake, to engage.

to take over to take control of.

to take to to begin to like.

to take up to follow (a hobby), to admit (as a passenger).

talcum n. a toilet powder.

tale n. a story.

talent n. 1. special skill. 2. an ancient coin or weight. adj. **talented** having special skill.

talk v. to speak. n. **talk** speech. n. **talker** speaker. adj. **talkative** fond of talking.

to talk down to force someone to do something by constant talking.

to talk down to to speak to someone as if to a child.

to talk round, or **to talk someone into** to persuade someone by talking.

to talk shop to speak about one's work.

tall adj. 1. of more than usual height, as *a tall building.* 2. of a certain height, as *the man is 2 metres tall.*

tall story a story difficult to believe.

tally n. a score, a total number. v. **tally** to agree, as *his tale tallies with mine* (**tallying, tallied**).

talon n. a bird of prey's claw.

tame adj. 1. not wild. 2. dull, not interesting. n. **tameness.** adj. **tameable, tamable** able to be tamed.

tamper v. (with **with**) to meddle.

tan n. tree bark used for turning skins or hides into leather. v. **tan** 1. to turn skins into leather. 2. to become brown with the sun (**tanning, tanned**).

tandem n. a bicycle with two seats one behind the other.

tang n. a strong flavour.

tangerine (pron. tan.je.reen¹) n. a small orange.

tangible adj. real, able to be touched.

tangle n. a twisted muddle, as *a tangle of string.*

tank n. 1. a large container for a liquid. 2. a kind of armoured car on movable tracks.

tankard n. a large metal drinking-cup.

tanker n. a ship carrying oil.

tanner n. a person who tans hides.

tannery n. a place where hides are tanned.

tantalize v. to tease someone by letting him see something he cannot have (**tantalizing, tantalized**).

tantrum n. a fit of bad temper.

tap (1) n. 1. a screw or peg for regulating the flow of gas or liquid through a pipe. 2. (in the U.S.A. of a water-tap) a faucet. v. **tap** 1. to draw liquid from, as *to tap a barrel* or *tap a rubber-tree for latex to make rubber.* 2. to draw information from, as *to tap a telephone wire to overhear a message* (**tapping, tapped**).

tap-root the main root of a plant.

tap (2) v. to knock lightly (**tapping, tapped**). n. **tap** a slight knock.

tap-dancer someone who dances with taps of his shoe.

tape n. a long, narrow strip of cloth, paper or plastic.

taper n. a thin wax wick which can be lit. v. **taper** to become thinner towards the end.

tape-recorder n. a machine which records speech or music on a tape.

tapestry n. a cloth with a woven design to be hung on walls (pl. **tapestries**).

tar n. a thick, black liquid obtained from coal. v. **tar** to cover with tar (**tarring, tarred**). adj. **tarry.**

to spoil the ship for a ha'porth of tar to spoil something for want of a little extra attention.

target n. something to aim at.

tariff n. a list of prices, taxes, or charges.

tarnish v. to make dull or become dull, to lose brightness.

tarpaulin n. canvas made waterproof with tar.

tart (1) adj. sharp in taste, acid.

tart (2) n. an open fruit or jam pie.

tartan n. woollen cloth with a chequered pattern, originally worn by Scottish Highlanders.

task n. a piece of work to be done.

tassel n. a bunch of threads as an ornament hanging from a flag or uniform or used in decoration.

taste v. to eat or drink a little of something to try its flavour (**tasting,**

tasted). *n.* **taste** 1. one of the senses. 2. a flavour. 3. a liking, as *a taste for painting.* 4. good or bad judgement, as *Mary has poor taste. adj.* **tasteful** showing good judgement or taste. *adj.* **tasteless** showing bad taste. *adj.* **tasty** of good flavour.

tattered *adj.* torn, ragged.

in tatters in rags.

tattoo (1) *n.* 1. a signal to soldiers on a bugle or drum. 2. tapping with the fingers.

tattoo (2) *v.* to prick a design on the skin and rub in dye (**tattooing, tattooed**). *n.* **tattoo** a design pricked on the skin (*pl.* **tattoos**).

taught *past* of **teach**.

taunt *v.* to jeer at, to make unkind remarks to.

taut *adj.* stretched tightly. *v.* **tauten** to make taut.

tavern *n.* a public house.

tawdry *adj.* cheap, showy.

tawny *adj.* golden brown.

tax *n.* 1. money which has to be paid to the government. 2. a heavy burden (*pl.* **taxes**). *v.* **tax** 1. for the government to put a charge on something to bring in money. 2. to lay a burden on, as *to tax someone's strength.* 3. to accuse, as *to tax someone with lying. n.* **taxation**.

taxi *n.* a motor-car for hire (*pl.* **taxis**). *v.* **taxi** (of an aeroplane) to run along the ground (**taxiing, taxied**).

tea *n.* 1. a drink made from the dried leaves of the *tea-plant* which grows in Asia. 2. an afternoon meal at which tea is served. *ns.* **teacup, tea-leaf, teapot, tea-shop, teaspoon, teaspoonful** (*pl.* **teaspoonfuls**).

teach *v.* to show someone how to do something, to give lessons (**teaching, taught**). *n.* **teaching**.

teak *n.* a very hard wood.

team *n.* 1. a group of people working or playing together. 2. a group of animals working together, as *a team of oxen.*

team-work working together as a team to gain success.

tear (1) (*pron.* tyeer) *n.* a drop of water from the eye. *adj.* **tearful** crying. *n.* **teardrop** a tear.

tear (2) (*pron.* tayr) *v.* to pull apart, to

rip (**tearing, tore, torn**). *n.* **tear** a rip, a jagged slit.

tease *v.* 1. to annoy someone by making fun of him. 2. to unravel threads (**teasing, teased**).

technical *adj.* concerning machinery, science, and engineering. *adv.* **technically.** *n.* **technicality** a technical word.

tedious *adj.* boring, wearisome.

tee *n.* the place where the golf player starts to play each hole.

teenager *n.* someone between the ages of twelve and twenty.

teens *n. pl.* the years between twelve years of age and twenty.

teeth plural of **tooth**.

teethe *v.* to cut teeth (**teething, teethed**).

telegram *n.* a message sent by telegraph.

telegraph *n.* a means of sending messages along wires by electricity. *n.* **telegraphy** sending messages by telegraph. *adj.* **telegraphic**.

telephone *n.* an instrument for sending speech long distances using electricity along a wire. *n.* **telephonist** an operator at a telephone exchange.

telescope *n.* an instrument for making distant things seem larger. *adj.* **telescopic**.

television *n.* sending and receiving pictures by radio. *v.* **televise** to send pictures by television (**televising, televised**).

tell *v.* 1. to speak, to say. 2. to have an effect on, as *his illness is telling on him* (**telling, told**). *adj.* **telling** striking, as *his speech had a telling effect on the crowd.*

temper *n.* 1. mood, as *to be in a good temper.* 2. an angry mood. *v.* **temper** 1. to make a metal hard or flexible. 2. to make less severe.

to lose one's temper to fly into a rage.

temperament *n.* one's nature or personality. *adj.* **temperamental** changeable in mood.

temperance *n.* 1. moderation and self-control in all that one does. 2. not drinking alcoholic drinks.

temperate *adj.* 1. moderate. 2. (of climate) not very hot or cold.

temperature *n.* the amount of heat, as measured by a thermometer.

tempest *n.* a violent storm. *adj.* **tempestuous**.

temple (1) *n.* a large building for public worship.

temple (2) *n.* the part of the head above the cheek-bone.

temporary *adj.* lasting for a short time. *adv.* **temporarily**.

tempt *v.* to try to persuade, especially to do something wrong. *adj.* **tempting** attractive. *n.* **temptation**.

ten *n.* one more than nine, represented by 10 or X. *adj.* **tenth**. **tenfold** ten times.

tenacious *adj.* holding firm. *n.* **tenacity**.

tenant *n.* someone who pays rent for a building, house, or land. *n.* **tenancy** occupying a place.

tend (1) *v.* to look after, as *to tend a baby*.

tend (2) *v.* to be inclined to, as *John tends to be quick-tempered*.

tendency *n.* an inclination (*pl.* **tendencies**).

tender (1) *adj.* 1. soft, delicate, as *tender meat*. 2. gentle, as *a tender smile*. *n.* **tenderness**.

tender (2) *n.* 1. a wagon with coal and water for a locomotive. 2. a boat carrying supplies to a large ship. 3. someone who looks after something, as a *machine-tender*.

tender (3) *v.* to offer. *n.* **tender** a bid, an offer.

tenderfoot *n.* a newcomer, the lowest rank of Boy Scout or Girl Guide.

tenement *n.* a large building occupied by many families.

tennis *n.* a game played by two or four players with rackets and a ball.

tense (1) *adj.* strained, stretched, causing mental strain, as *a tense situation*. *n.* **tenseness** being tense.

tense (2) *n.* the form of a verb to show present, past, or future.

tension *n.* strain.

tent *n.* a canvas shelter held up by poles and ropes.

tentacle *n.* a feeler, as *the tentacle of an octopus*.

tepid *adj.* just warm, lukewarm.

term *n.* 1. a certain length of time. 2. part of a school year. 3. a word or name for something. *v.* **term** to call, to name. *n. pl.* **terms** conditions.

not on speaking terms not speaking to someone because of bad feeling.

on good (bad) terms with friendly (or unfriendly).

to come to terms with to make a bargain with.

terminal *n.* 1. (in the U.S.A.) the end of a railway line or bus route. 2. a holder for the end of an electric wire.

terminate *v.* to come to an end, or bring to an end (**terminating, terminated**). *n.* **termination**.

terminus *n.* the end of a railway line or bus route (*pl.* **terminuses** or **termini**).

terrace *n.* 1. a raised, flat bank of land. 2. a row of houses.

terrestrial *adj.* concerning the earth.

terrible *adj.* dreadful, arousing fear. *adv.* **terribly**.

terrier *n.* a small dog, as a *fox-terrier*.

terrific *adj.* 1. causing terror. 2. (*slang*) very big.

terrify *v.* to frighten greatly (**terrifying, terrified**).

territory *n.* a large stretch of land (*pl.* **territories**).

terror *n.* 1. great fear. 2. someone causing fear.

terrorize *v.* to fill with terror (**terrorizing, terrorized**).

terse *adj.* using few words, brief.

test *n.* an examination, a trial. *v.* **test** to examine.

test match (in cricket) a match between countries.

test pilot a pilot who tests aeroplanes.

testament *n.* a will saying who is to inherit money and goods.

Old Testament, New Testament the two main parts of the Bible.

testify *v.* to swear that something is true, to give evidence (**testifying, testified**).

testimonial *n.* 1. a statement about someone's character. 2. a gift given for good services.

tether v. to tie up an animal with a rope or chain.
at the end of one's tether at the end of one's endurance, desperate.
text n. 1. the printed words of a book. 2. a verse from the Bible, used in a sermon.
textbook n. a book for use in schools and colleges.
textile n. a cloth, woven material.
texture n. the way the threads of a cloth are woven.
than conj. compared with, as *he is bigger than I am.*
thank v. to tell someone how grateful one is. n. pl. **thanks** gratitude.
thanksgiving n. thanks offered to God. **Thanksgiving Day** a yearly feast day, celebrated in the U.S.A. on the last Thursday in November, and in Canada on the second Monday in October.
that adj. the one over there (pl. **those**). pronoun **that** which, as *the house that Jack built.*
thatch n. a covering or roof of straw.
thaw v. (of snow and ice) to melt due to warmer weather.
the the definite article pointing out a single thing.
theatre n. 1. a building where plays are acted. 2. a hospital room where operations are performed. adj. **theatrical** connected with the theatre, unnatural as if acting in a play.
theft n. stealing.
their adj. belonging to them, as *their house.* pronoun **theirs** belonging to them, as *these hats are theirs.*
them pronoun those persons or things. pronoun **themselves**.
then adv. 1. after that, as *he stopped and then he turned.* 2. at that time, as *he did it then.* conj. **then** therefore, as *there is then no need to go.*
thence adv. from there, as *he set off thence.* adv. **thenceforth** from that time.
theology n. the study of religion. adj. **theological** concerned with theology. n. **theologian**.
theoretical adj. worked out from theory, not from practice.
theory n. an explanation that one has thought out (pl. **theories**).

there adv. in or to that place, not here.
thereafter after that.
thereby in that way, near by.
therefore for that reason.
therein in that place, in that respect.
thereupon after which.
thermometer n. an instrument fo measuring temperature, either in degrees Celsius (Centigrade) or in degree of any temperature scale.
these plural of **this**.
they pronoun 1. plural of **he, she,** or **it** 2. people in general, as *what do they say?*
thick adj. 1. deep, fat, as *a thick slice o bread.* 2. not watery, as *thick porridge.* 3. dense, as *thick fog.* n. **thickness**.
through thick and thin through bad times and good.
thick-skinned not easily hurt o offended.
thicken n. to become thick.
thief n, someone who steals (pl. **thieves**).
thieve v. to steal (**thieving, thieved**).
thigh n. the part of the leg between the knee and the hip.
thimble n. a protective cover for the end of the finger when sewing.
thin adj. 1. shallow, with no depth. 2. watery, as *thin soup.* 3. slender, as *a thin rod.* 4. not dense, as *a thin veil* (comparative **thinner,** superlative **thinnest**). v. **thin** to grow thinner or make thinner (**thinning, thinned**). adv. **thinly.** n. **thinness**.
thing n. an object. pl. **things** personal belongings, as *I will pack my things.*
think v. to consider, to reflect (**thinking, thought**).
to think better of to change one's mind after second thoughts.
to think over to consider.
third adj. next after second.
third-rate of poor quality.
thirst n. a strong desire for drink. v. **thirst** 1. to want to drink. 2. to have a strong wish for. adj. **thirsty** (comparative **thirstier,** superlative **thirstiest**). adv. **thirstily**.
thirteen n. one more than twelve, represented by 13 or XIII. adj. **thirteenth**.

thirty *n.* one more than twenty-nine, represented by 30 or XXX. *adj.* **thirtieth**.

this *adj.* and *pronoun* the one here or nearest (*pl.* **these**).

thistle *n.* a prickly wild plant.

thorn *n.* 1. a sharp point on a plant stem, a prickle. 2. a shrub bearing thorns, as *a hawthorn*. *adj* **thorny** 1. bearing thorns. 2. difficult, painful, as *a thorny problem* (*comparative* **thornier**, *superlative* **thorniest**).

thorough *adj.* 1. complete, well done, as *a thorough inquiry*. 2. careful, as *he is thorough in his work*. *n.* **thoroughness**. *adv.* **thoroughly**.

thoroughbred *n.* an animal of pure breed.

those plural of **that**.

though *conj.* although, even if.

thought (1) *n.* 1. consideration, thinking. 2. an idea.

thought (2) *past* of **think**.

thoughtful *adj.* considerate, thinking deeply. *n.* **thoughtfulness**. *adv.* **thoughtfully**.

thoughtless *adj.* careless, not thinking. *n.* **thoughtlessness**. *adv.* **thoughtlessly**.

thousand *n.* ten hundreds, represented by 1000 or M. *adj.* **thousandth**.

thrash *v.* 1. to beat, to whip. 2. (or **thresh**) to beat the grain from wheat. 3. (with **out**) to talk for a long time about some matter.

thrashing (or **threshing**) **machine** a machine for thrashing grain.

thread *n.* 1. a twisted fibre. 2. the ridge on a screw or nut. *v.* **thread** 1. to put a thread through. 2. to pick one's way through, as *to thread one's way through a crowd*.

threadbare *adj.* worn and shabby.

threat *n.* a warning of trouble to come.

threaten *v.* to warn of coming trouble.

three *n.* one more than two, represented by 3 or III.

threepence, threepenny-bit *n.* an old British coin worth three pennies (about 1 new penny).

thresh see **thrash**.

threshold *n.* a doorway or door-sill.

threw *past* of **throw**.

thrift *n.* saving. *adj.* **thrifty** in the habit of saving (in North America) prosperous. *adj.* **thriftless** wasteful.

thrill *n.* a quiver of excitement.

throat *n.* the front part of the neck. *adj.* **throaty** hoarse.

throb *v.* to beat strongly (**throbbing**, **throbbed**). *n.* **throb** a beat.

throne *n.* a ceremonial chair for a king, queen, or bishop.

throttle *v.* to choke, to strangle (**throttling, throttled**). *n.* **throttle** a valve controlling the fuel or gas to an engine.

through *adv.* and *prep.* 1. from end to end or side to side. 2. because of. *adj.* **through** going all the way, as *a through train*.

throughout *prep.* all through.

throw *v.* to hurl, to fling (**throwing, threw, thrown**).

thrown *past* of **throw**.

thrush *n.* a song-bird.

thrust *n.* a push, a stab. *v.* **thrust** to push, to stab (**thrusting, thrust**).

thud *n.* a dull sound of one thing hitting another. *v.* **thud** to hit with a dull sound (**thudding, thudded**).

thumb *n.* the short, thick finger. *v.* **thumb** 1. to soil. 2. (with **through**) to handle, to turn over the pages, as *to thumb through a book*.

under someone's thumb in his power.

thump *v.* to beat with the fist. *n.* **thump** a heavy blow.

thunder *n.* the noise that follows lightning. *adj.* **thundery**.

thunderbolt *n.* lightning and thunder.

thunderstorm *n.* a storm with thunder.

thunderstruck *adj.* amazed.

Thursday *n.* the fifth day of the week.

thus *adv.* in this way, therefore.

tick *v.* 1. to make regular clicking sounds, as *a clock ticks*. 2. (with **off**) to check each item on a list with a mark.

to tick someone off to scold him.

ticket *n.* 1. a small piece of paper or card given in return for payment for a seat in a cinema, bus, etc. 2. a label showing a price.

tickle *v.* to stroke lightly, to cause a tingling feeling (**tickling, tickled**).

n. **tickle** a light stroking causing a tingling feeling. *adj.* **ticklish** 1. easily tickled. 2. dangerous, as *a ticklish position.*

tidal *adj.* concerning tides.

tide *n.* 1. the regular rise and fall of the sea. 2. anything like a tide, as *a tide of luck.* 3. a season, as *Christmastide* or *Eastertide.*

tidings *n. pl.* news.

tidy *adj.* neat, in good order (*comparative* **tidier,** *superlative* **tidiest**). *v.* **tidy** to make neat and orderly (**tidying, tidied**). *n.* **tidiness.**

tie *v.* 1. to fasten with a string or rope. 2. to bind, as *to tie someone to his word.* 3. (in a game) to draw, to be even (**tying, tied**). *n.* **tie** 1. a necktie. 2. a common interest, as *ties of friendship.* 3. a draw in a game. 4. (in North America) a railway sleeper.

tier (*pron.* teer) *n.* 1. one of several raised rows of seats. 2. a layer, as *a two-tier cake.*

tiger *n.* a striped wild animal (*fem.* **tigress**).

tight *adj.* 1. firm, packed close. 2. fully stretched. 3. hard to move, as *a tight stopper.* *n.* **tightness.** *v.* **tighten** to make or become tight.

a tight corner a difficult situation.

tight-rope *n.* a stretched rope on which acrobats walk.

tile *n.* a flat piece of baked clay for floors, walls, or roofs.

till (1) *n.* a shop-keeper's drawer for money.

till (2) *v.* to cultivate land. *n.* **tillage.**

till (3) *prep.* short for **until,** up to the time of.

tiller *n.* a long handle on the rudder of a boat.

tilt *v.* 1. to slope, to slant. 2. (in olden days) to charge with a lance. *n.* **tilt** 1. a slope. 2. a fight with lances between men on horseback.

at full tilt at full speed.

timber *n.* 1. wood for building. 2. trees for cutting. *adj.* **timbered** made of timber.

time *n.* 1. an interval. 2. a particular moment shown by a clock. 3. an age, as *in the time of Cromwell.* 4. a season, as

springtime. *v.* **time** to measure time, as *to time a race* (**timing, timed**). *adj.* **timely** in good time.

in time 1. after a while. 2. in step with music.

once upon a time at some time gone by.

on time punctually.

time-table a list of times.

timid *adj.* shy, fearful. *n.* **timidity.**

tin *n.* 1. a silvery white metal. 2. a metal container, a can, made of tinned iron. *v.* **tin** 1. to coat with tin, as *to tin iron.* 2. to put in a tin, as *to tin salmon* (**tinning, tinned**).

tinder *n.* dry material used for starting a fire.

tinge (*pron.* tinj) *v.* to colour slightly. *n.* **tinge** a slight colour, a slight amount.

tingle *v.* to smart, to have a prickling feeling (**tingling, tingled**).

tinker *n.* a man who mends pots and pans. *v.* **tinker** to meddle with something in a clumsy way.

tinkle *n.* a small, ringing sound. *v.* **tinkle** to make a small, ringing sound (**tinkling, tinkled**).

tinsel *n.* glittering strips of metal used for decoration.

tint *n.* a delicate shade of a colour. *v.* **tint** to colour slightly.

tiny *adj.* very small (*comparative* **tinier,** *superlative* **tiniest**).

tip (1) *n.* a pointed end, as *a finger-tip.*

tip (2) *v.* to tilt, to overturn (**tipping, tipped**). *n.* **tip** a place for rubbish.

tip (3) *n.* 1. a small gift of money to a waiter or servant. 2. a useful piece of advice. *v.* **tip** 1. to pass on information. 2. to give a waiter some money as a reward for service (**tipping, tipped**).

tiptoe *v.* to walk on the tips of one's toes (**tiptoeing, tiptoed**).

tire (1) see **tyre.**

tire (2) *v.* to grow tired or make tired (**tiring, tired**). *adj.* **tired** weary. *n.* **tiredness.** *adj.* **tireless** not easily tired. *adj.* **tiresome** troublesome, boring.

tissue *n.* 1. very thin cloth or paper. 2. the substance of which parts of plants and animals are made.

titbit *n.* a choice bit of food.

title *n.* 1. the name of a book, piece of writing, or film. 2. a word before a person's name to show his rank, as *Lord, Sir, or Mister.* 3. a championship, as *a boxing title.* *adj.* **titled** having a title.

titter *n.* a quiet giggle. *v.* **titter** to giggle.

to *prep.* in the direction of, as far as, until.

to and fro backwards and forwards.

toad *n.* an animal like a frog, but with a rougher skin.

toadstool *n.* a poisonous, mushroom-shaped fungus.

toast (1) *n.* bread browned by heat. *v.* **toast** to warm, to brown with heat.

toast (2) *n.* a drink in honour of someone. *v.* **toast** to drink to someone's health.

tobacco *n.* a plant whose leaves are dried and used for smoking. *n.* **tobacconist** someone who sells tobacco.

toboggan *n.* a kind of sledge used on snow.

today *adv.* and *n.* 1. (on) this day. 2. (at) the present time.

toddle *v.* to walk like a baby with short steps (**toddling, toddled**). *n.* **toddler** a small child.

toe *n.* 1. one of the five tips of the foot. 2. the front of a shoe or stocking.

to toe the line 1. to stand on the starting-line in a race. 2. to do as one is told.

toffee (in North America, **taffy**) *n.* candy made from sugar and butter.

together *adv.* 1. with each other, in company. 2. at the same time.

toil *n.* hard work. *v.* **toil** to work hard, to move with effort.

toilet *n.* 1. the process of washing and dressing. 2. a wash-place or lavatory.

token *n.* 1. a sign, a symbol. 2. a piece of metal or plastic used for money.

told *past* of **tell**.

tolerance *n.* willingness to let others think and do as they wish, without objecting. *adj.* **tolerant**.

tolerate *v.* to endure, to put up with (**tolerating, tolerated**). *n.* **toleration**.

toll (1) *n.* payment for the use of a road or bridge.

toll-gate a gate across a road where a toll is paid.

toll (2) *v.* to ring a bell slowly, as at a funeral.

tomahawk *n.* an axe used by North American Indians.

tomato *n.* a plant with juicy red fruit (*pl.* **tomatoes**).

tomb (*pron.* tōōm) *n.* a grave or vault for the dead.

tombstone a stone over a grave.

tomorrow *adv.* and *n.* (on) the day after today.

tomtom *n.* an Indian or African drum.

ton *n.* an Imperial measure of weight equal to 20 hundredweights. **tonnage** *n.* the weight of cargo a ship can carry.

tone *n.* 1. a sound or quality of a sound. 2. general character, as *the tone of a school.* 3. a shade of colour.

to tone down to soften in colour.

tongs *n. pl.* a tool with two hinged arms for lifting things, as *fire-tongs for lifting coal.*

tongue (*pron.* tung) *n.* 1. the fleshy organ in the mouth for licking and tasting. 2 a language.

to have one's tongue in one's cheek to say what one does not really mean.

to hold one's tongue to keep silent.

tongue-tied silent through shyness or fear.

tonic *n.* a medicine giving one fresh energy.

tonight *adv.* and *n.* (on) this night.

tonne *n.* metric weight equal to 1,000 kg.

tonsil *n.* one of the two fleshy lumps at the back of the mouth. *n.* **tonsilitis** swollen tonsils.

too *adv.* 1. also, as well. 2. more than enough, as *he went too far.*

tool *n.* a workman's instrument, as *a spade and a saw are tools.*

toot *n.* the sound of a horn or whistle.

tooth *n.* 1. one of the bony parts of the mouth. 2. anything like a tooth, as *a tooth of a saw or gear-wheel* (*pl.* **teeth**). *adj.* **toothed** having teeth. *n.* **toothache** a pain in a tooth.

armed to the teeth fully armed.

to escape by the skin of one's teeth to have a narrow escape.

to fight tooth and nail to fight desperately.

to have a sweet tooth to like sweet food.

toothbrush *n.* a brush for cleaning teeth.

top (1) *n.* the highest point, the upper side. *v.* **top** 1. to reach the top of. 2. to cut the top off (**topping, topped**). *adjs.* **top, topmost** the highest.

top-heavy having too much weight at the top.

top (2) *n.* a toy that can be made to spin.

topic *n.* a subject to talk or write about, a piece of news.

topical *adj.* concerning something happening at the time.

topple (with **over** or **down**) *v.* to wobble and fall (**toppling, toppled**).

tor *n.* a hilltop.

torch *n.* a light of flaming wood, or an electric light, carried in the hand.

tore, torn *past* of **tear.**

toreador *n.* a bullfighter.

torment (*pron.* tor'ment) *n.* great pain, suffering. *v.* **torment** (*pron.* tor.ment') to give pain to, to tease. *n.* **tormentor** someone who torments.

tornado (*pron.* tor.nay'dō) *n.* a violent whirlwind (*pl.* **tornadoes**).

torpedo *n.* a large, cigar-shaped, explosive shell which can travel under water, and is fired from a warship or submarine (*pl.* **torpedoes**). *v.* **torpedo** to hit with a torpedo (**torpedoing, torpedoed**).

torrent *n.* a rushing stream, a rapid flow. *adj.* **torrential** flowing madly.

tortoise *n.* a slow-moving animal covered with a large shell.

torture *v.* to cause extreme pain to someone (**torturing, tortured**). *n.* **torture** the causing of great pain.

toss *v.* 1. to throw up in the air. 2. to roll about. *n.* **toss** a fling, an upward throw.

to toss up to spin a coin to see whether heads or tails lies uppermost.

total *n.* 1. the whole amount. 2. the answer to an addition sum. *adj.* **total** complete, as *a total failure. v.* **total** to add (**totalling, totalled**). *adv.* **totally** completely, as *he is totally deaf.*

totem *n.* an animal's head carved on a pole, used by Red Indians as a badge of the tribe.

totter *v.* to stagger, to sway unsteadily.

touch *v.* 1. to feel with the fingers or some part of the body. 2. to affect, as *her words touched him.* 3. to refer to casually, as *he touched on the matter of payment. n.* **touch** 1. contact. 2. one of the five senses, the sense of feeling. *adj.* **touching** causing pity. *adj.* **touchy** irritable.

to touch up to improve something with small touches.

tough *adj.* 1. not easily broken or bent. 2. hard to chew. 3. able to stand hardship. 4. difficult, as *a tough problem. n.* **toughness**. *v.* **toughen** to make tough.

tour *n.* a journey from place to place. *v.* **tour** to make a tour. *n.* **tourist** a person making a tour.

tournament *n.* 1. (in olden days) a contest between knights on horseback. 2. (in modern times) a contest between a number of players.

tow *v.* to pull by a rope.

tow-path a path by a river or canal on which horses tow barges.

towards *prep.* 1. in the direction of. 2. regarding, as *how do you feel towards Jim?*

towel *n.* a cloth or paper for drying something wet.

tower *n.* a tall structure, sometimes part of a church or castle. *v.* **tower** to stand high above anything around. *adj.* **towering** very high.

town *n.* a collection of houses and other buildings, larger than a village but smaller than a city.

town hall the building from which the town is governed by the *town council.*

toy *n.* a plaything. *v.* **toy** to treat in a half-hearted way, as *to toy with one's food* or *toy with an idea.*

trace *v.* 1. to draw. 2. to copy a design on thin half-transparent paper laid over it. 3. to find out from inquiries, as *to trace a missing article* (**tracing,**

traced). *n.* **trace** 1. a track, a sign. 2. a small amount.

track *n.* 1. a series of marks on the ground left by feet or wheels. 2. a rough path. 3. a course for racing. 4. the course or path of something moving, as *the track of a torpedo.* 5. a railway line. **off the beaten track** unusual.

tract *n.* a large area, a region.

tractor *n.* a machine used for pulling ploughs or loads, a *farm tractor.*

trade *n.* 1. buying and selling. 2. an occupation requiring skilful use of tools, as *the trades of joiner or plumber.* *v.* **trade** to buy and sell (**trading, traded**).

trademark *n.* a design or name used for a particular kind of goods.

trader *n.* a man engaged in trade.

tradesman *n.* a shopkeeper, a skilled workman.

trade-union *n.* an association of workers in a particular trade.

trade-wind *n.* a wind near the equator blowing towards the equator.

tradition *n.* a story, custom, or way of doing something handed down from generation to generation. *adj.* **traditional**.

traffic *n.* the passing to and fro of vehicles, ships, or goods. **traffic signals** coloured street lights controlling traffic.

tragedy *n.* 1. a play with a sad ending. 2. a very sad event (*pl.* **tragedies**).

tragic *adj.* concerning tragedy, very sad. *adj.* **tragical**. *adv.* **tragically**.

trail *n.* 1. a track left by something moving. 2. a rough path. *v.* **trail** 1. to hunt something by following its track. 2. to drag along the ground. 3. to move wearily along, as *the cross-country runners trailed home.* 4. to sprawl about, as *the creeper trailed over the fence.*

trailer *n.* 1. a wagon pulled by a motor-vehicle. 2. a trailing plant.

train (1) *n.* 1. a railway-engine pulling a number of coaches or wagons. 2. a number of things following one after another, as *a train of ideas.* 3. the trailing part of a long dress carried by *train-bearers.*

train (2) *v.* 1. to teach or prepare some-one for a sporting event by repeated practice. 2. to cause something to grow in a certain way, as *to train a climbing plant.* 3. to aim a gun. *n.* **training** 1. education. 2. drill. *n.* **trainer** some-one who trains people or animals.

traitor *n.* someone who betrays his friends or country (*fem.* **traitress**).

tramp *v.* 1. to walk heavily. 2. to journey on foot, as *to tramp over the hills.* *n.* **tramp** 1. a journey on foot. 2. a wandering beggar. 3. a cargo boat trading between any ports where it can pick up cargo.

trample *v.* to tread underfoot (**trampling, trampled**).

trance *n.* a daze, an unnatural sleep.

tranquil *adj.* calm, quiet. *n.* **tranquillity**.

transact *v.* to carry on, to manage, as *to transact business.* *n.* **transaction** a business deal.

transfer (*pron.* trans.fer¹) *v.* 1. to move from place to place or person to person. 2. to copy a drawing (**transferring, transferred**). *n.* **transfer** (*pron.* trans¹fer) 1. a movement from place to place or from person to person. 2. a paper bearing a design which can be pressed on to some object.

transfix *v.* to pierce through. *adj.* **transfixed** as if turned to stone by fear or wonder.

transform *v.* 1. to change the shape or appearance of. 2. to change the voltage of electric current. *n.* **transformation** a change. *n.* **transformer** an appara-tus for changing the voltage of electric current.

transfusion *n.* the passing of blood from one person to another in order to save his life.

transit *n.* passing from place to place, being carried, as *the parcel was lost in transit.*

transition *n.* change, as *transition from a grub to an insect.*

translate *v.* to change from one language to another (**translating, translated**). *ns.* **translation, translator**.

transmission *n.* 1. sending out. 2. a radio broadcast.

transmit v. to send out, to pass on (**transmitting, transmitted**).

transmitter n. something that transmits, as a radio station or a telephone mouthpiece.

transparent adj. 1. allowing light through, as *glass is transparent*. 2. clear to see, as *a transparent lie*.

transplant v. to take up and plant in another place.

transport (*pron.* trans.pōrt¹) v. 1. to carry from one place to another. 2. (of criminals) to send away to another country. n. **transport** (*pron.* trans¹-pōrt) 1. carriage from place to place. 2. a ship for carrying troops. n. **transportation**.

trap n. 1. a snare, noose, or arrangement for catching birds or animals. 2. a plan for catching someone unawares. 3. an ambush. 4. a light carriage drawn by a horse. v. **trap** to catch by means of a trap (**trapping, trapped**).

trap-door n. a door in a floor or ceiling.

trapper n. someone who traps animals.

trash n. worthless rubbish. adj. **trashy**.

travel v. to make a journey (**travelling, travelled**). n. **travel** a journey. n. **traveller** 1. someone who travels. 2. someone who moves from place to place buying and selling goods.

traverse v. to go across (**traversing, traversed**).

trawl v. to fish with a wide-mouthed net. n. **trawl** a large, open-mouthed net. n. **trawler** a ship used for trawling.

tray n. a flat sheet of wood or metal on which light articles are carried, as a *tea-tray*.

treacherous adj. not loyal, not to be trusted. n. **treachery**.

treacle n. thick, dark syrup. adj. **treacly**.

tread v. to walk, to tramp on (**treading, trod, trodden**). n. **tread** 1. a footstep. 2. the outer part of a tyre bearing a pattern. 3. a step in a stair.

to tread in someone's footsteps to follow his lead.

treadle (*pron.* tred¹l) n. the part of a machine, such as a sewing-machine, worked by the foot.

treason n. betraying one's country. adj. **treasonable**.

high treason treason against king or country.

treasure n. 1. a store of wealth. 2. anything of great value. v. **treasure** 1. to store. 2. to value greatly (**treasuring, treasured**).

treasurer n. someone who looks after a society's or club's accounts.

treasury n. 1. a place where riches are kept. 2. a government department which manages a nation's money.

treat v. 1. to deal with. 2. to give medical care to, as *to treat an illness*. 3. to pay for someone else's pleasure. n. **treat** a pleasure given to someone. n. **treatment** the way something is dealt with.

treaty n. a written agreement between nations (*pl.* **treaties**).

treble adj. 1. three times. 2. (in music) having a high pitch. n. **treble** the highest part in music. v. **treble** to make three times as great (**trebling, trebled**).

tree n. a large woody plant with trunk and branches.

a family tree a diagram showing how different members of a family are related.

trek n. a long laborious journey. v. **trek** to travel slowly (**trekking, trekked**).

tremble v. to shiver with fear or cold (**trembling, trembled**).

tremendous adj. huge, awe-inspiring.

tremor n. a shaking, a quiver.

trench n. a long, narrow ditch.

trend n. a tendency, a direction, as *there is a trend towards rising prices*.

trespass v. 1. to go on someone's land without permission. 2. to take too much of someone's time or good nature. 3. to sin. n. **trespass** 1. going on land without permission. 2. a sin. n. **trespasser** someone who trespasses.

trestle n. one of a pair of wooden supports for holding a table-top.

trial n. 1. a test, as *a trial of strength between two wrestlers*. 2. the hearing of a law-court case. 3. trouble, annoyance, as *the rude boy is a trial to others*.

triangle n. 1. a three-sided figure. 2. a steel rod bent into the shape of a triangle, used as a musical instrument by striking it with a rod. *adj.* **triangular** like a triangle.

tribe *n.* a group of families living together under a chief. *adj.* **tribal** concerning a tribe.

tributary *n.* a river flowing into a larger river (*pl.* **tributaries**).

tribute *n.* 1. money paid by a weak country to a more powerful one. 2. praise, a compliment.

trick *n.* 1. a clever action to deceive someone. 2. a habit, as *she has a trick of blinking while speaking.* 3. one round of cards in a card-game. *v.* **trick** to deceive. *n.* **trickery** deception. *n.* **trickster** a swindler. *adj.* **tricky** unreliable, difficult (*comparative* **trickier,** *superlative* **trickiest**).

trickle *v.* to flow in a very thin stream (**trickling, trickled**). *n.* **trickle** a thin stream.

trifle *n.* 1. something small or of little value. 2. a sweet of sponge, jelly, and whipped cream. *v.* **trifle** to play with or take lightly (**trifling, trifled**). *adj.* **trifling** of no importance.

trigger *n.* a small lever which when pulled fires a gun.

trim *v.* 1. to make neat and tidy. 2. to clip the edges of a hedge, hair, etc. 3. to decorate a hat (**trimming, trimmed**). *adj.* **trim** neat, tidy (*comparative* **trimmer,** *superlative* **trimmest**).

trinity *n.* a group of three. **the Trinity** God the Father, Son, and Holy Ghost.

trinket *n.* a small ornament or jewel.

trio *n.* a group of three, especially three musicians.

trip *v.* 1. to move with quick light steps. 2. to stumble or cause to stumble. 3. to make a mistake or catch out in a mistake (**tripping, tripped**). *n.* **trip** 1. a quick step. 2. a stumble or mistake. 3. a short journey.

tripe *n.* part of a cow's stomach used for food.

triple *adj.* 1. having three parts. 2. three times as much.

triplets *n. pl.* three children born together of the same mother.

tripod *n.* a three-legged stand.

triumph *n.* a great victory or success. *v.* **triumph** to win success. *adj.* **triumphal** celebrating a victory, as *a triumphal song.* *adj.* **triumphant** rejoicing in success.

trivial *adj.* of no importance. *n.* **triviality**.

trod, trodden *past* of **tread**.

trolley *n.* a small handcart or truck (*pl.* **trolleys**).

trombone *n.* a musical instrument like a trumpet with a long, sliding piece.

troop *n.* a group of soldiers, animals, etc. *v.* **troop** for a crowd to move together, as *they trooped into the football ground.* *n. pl.* **troops** soldiers. *n.* **trooper** a cavalry soldier or Australian mounted policeman.

trophy *n.* something captured in war, or won in a competition (*pl.* **trophies**).

tropic *n.* one of the two imaginary circles round the earth marking the greatest distance north or south of the equator at which the sun is overhead—the *Tropic of Cancer,* and the *Tropic of Capricorn.* *adj.* **tropical** belonging to the tropics, as *tropical heat.*

the tropics the very hot zone round the equator between these two circles.

trot *v.* to run at an easy pace (**trotting, trotted**). *n.* **trot** a gentle run. *n.* **trotter** a pig's foot, or a sheep's foot.

trouble *n.* distress, disturbance, worry. *v.* **trouble** to worry, to cause distress (**troubling, troubled**). *adj.* **troublesome** disturbing, causing worry.

trough *n.* 1. a long, narrow, open box to hold water or food for animals. 2. the hollow between two waves. 3. anything shaped like a trough.

troupe *n.* a company of actors or performers.

trousers *n. pl.* a two-legged outer garment reaching from waist to ankles.

trousseau (*pron.* trōō'sō) *n.* a bride's outfit (*pl.* **trousseaux** or **trousseaus**).

trout *n.* a fresh-water fish (*pl.* **trout**).

trowel *n.* a small tool for spreading mortar or moving plants.

truant *n.* a pupil absent from school without permission. *n.* **truancy**.

truce *n.* a pause in warfare, agreed to by both sides.

truck *n.* a wagon, a lorry.

true *adj.* 1. real, genuine. 2. exact. 3. loyal, as *a true friend*. *adv.* **truly** really, in fact.

trump *n.* (in card games) a card of a suit of highest value. *v.* **trump** to play a trump card to win a trick.

a trump card a winning move.

trumpet *n.* 1. a musical wind instrument made of metal. 2. something like a trumpet, as an *ear-trumpet*. 3. a sound like that of a trumpet, as *the trumpet of an elephant*. *n.* **trumpeter** a trumpet-player.

to blow one's own trumpet to sound one's own praises.

truncheon *n.* a short stick carried by policemen.

trundle *v.* to roll or wheel along (**trundling, trundled**).

trunk *n.* 1. the main part of a tree or an animal's or person's body. 2. a large luggage box. 3. the long nose of an elephant. *n. pl.* **trunks** the short trousers of an athlete or swimmer.

trunk-call a long-distance telephone call.

truss *n.* 1. a support for a bridge or roof. 2. a bundle of straw or hay. *v.* **truss** to tie up or bind the limbs.

trust *n.* 1. faith, reliance. 2. something held for others, as *to hold land in trust*. 3. a group of business firms. *v.* **trust** to have faith in. *adjs.* **trustful, trusting** having faith in others. *adj.* **trustworthy, trusty** reliable.

trustee *n.* someone who looks after money or property for others.

truth *n.* what is true, what has actually happened. *adj.* **truthful** speaking the truth, true. *adv.* **truthfully.** *n.* **truthfulness.**

try *v.* 1. to make an attempt, to aim at. 2. to test, as *to try a new idea*. 3. to strain, as *this poor light tries my eyes*. 4. to judge in a law-court (**trying, tried**). *n.* **try** an attempt. *adj.* **trying** annoying, as *this noise is very trying*.

tub *n.* a large, open container. *adj.* **tubby** fat and round.

tube *n.* 1. a pipe. 2. a cylinder of soft metal for holding toothpaste, paint, etc. 3. an underground railway. 4. (in North America) a radio valve. *adj.* **tubular** like a tube. *n.* **tubing** a length of tube.

tuck *v.* 1. to fold tightly. 2. to put away out of sight. 3. to sew folds in cloth. 4. to wrap up closely. *n.* **tuck** 1. a fold in a garment. 2. (loosely) food.

tuck shop a shop where schoolboys buy sweets.

Tudor *n.* the family name of English kings from 1485 to 1603.

Tuesday *n.* the third day of the week.

tuft *n.* a little bunch of grass, hair, etc.

tug *v.* to pull hard and sharply (**tugging, tugged**). *n.* **tug** 1. a sharp pull. 2. a boat for towing.

tug-of-war a contest between two teams pulling a rope.

tuition *n.* teaching.

tulip *n.* a plant grown from a bulb.

tumble *v.* 1. to fall. 2. to upset, to ruffle (**tumbling, tumbled**). *n.* **tumble** a sudden fall.

tumbler *n.* 1. a drinking-glass. 2. an acrobat. 3. a kind of pigeon.

tumult *n.* an uproar, disorder. *adj.* **tumultuous** disorderly.

tundra *n.* a frozen Arctic desert.

tune *n.* a pleasant piece of music. *v.* **tune** to put notes in the correct pitch, as *to tune a violin* (**tuning, tuned**).

in tune (of music) in the correct pitch.

to change one's tune to alter one's way of talking.

tunic *n.* a jacket or belted frock.

tunnel *n.* an underground passage. *v.* **tunnel** to dig a tunnel (**tunnelling, tunnelled**).

turban *n.* a sash wound round a cap, worn in the East.

turbine *n.* an engine driven by steam, air, or water blowing against the blades of a wheel.

turbo-jet *n.* an air-liner's jet-propelled gas turbine.

turbo-prop *n.* an air-liner's jet engine whose turbine is linked with a propeller.

turbulent *adj.* violent, unruly.

turf *n.* grass-covered earth (*pl.* **turves** or **turfs**).

turkey *n.* a large bird reared for food.

turmoil *n.* confusion, commotion.

turn v. 1. to move round, to alter direction. 2. to change, to become. n. **turn** 1. a circular motion. 2. a change. 3. time for something, as *it is your turn*. 4. a short act on a stage.
 a good turn a good deed.
 to turn over a new leaf to make a fresh start.
 to turn turtle to capsize.
 to turn up to arrive unexpectedly.
turncoat n. a deserter.
turning-point n. a time when a big change occurs.
turnip n. a vegetable with a large round root.
turnstile n. a gate revolving in one direction only.
turpentine n. an oil from pine trees used in varnishes.
turret n. 1. a small tower on a building. 2. a revolving shelter on a warship containing guns.
turtle n. a large sea-tortoise.
 mock-turtle soup made of calf's head.
 turtle-dove a European dove.
tusk n. a very long tooth sticking from the mouth of an elephant or wild boar.
tutor n. a private teacher.
tweed n. rough, woollen cloth.
twelve n. one more than eleven, shown by 12 or XII. adj. **twelfth**.
twelvemonth a year.
twenty n. one more than nineteen, shown by 20 or XX. adj. **twentieth**.
twice adv. two times.
twig n. a small shoot from a tree or bush.
twilight n. the faint half-light before sunrise or after sunset.
twin n. one of two babies born at the same birth.
 twin-screw (of a ship) having two propellers.
twine n. twisted string. v. **twine** to twist round (**twining, twined**).
twinge n. a sudden pain.
twinkle v. to glitter, to sparkle (**twinkling, twinkled**).
 in the twinkling of an eye in a moment.
twirl v. to spin round.
twist v. 1. to wind round, to curve. 2. to change the shape of, to bend. n. **twist** a bend, a wrench.

twitch v. to move with a jerk. n. **twitch** a jerky movement of a muscle.
two n. one added to one, represented by 2 or II.
 two-faced false.
 twofold double.
tying see **tie**.
type n. 1. a kind, a class, as *a modern type of car*. 2. an example, as *he is a good type of soldier*. 3. raised letters or figures used for printing. 4. printed letters. v. **type** to write on a typewriter (**typing, typed**).
typewriter n. a machine for typing.
typewriting n. 1. using a typewriter. 2. writing produced by a typewriter.
typhoid n. a serious kind of fever.
typhoon n. a violent storm.
typical adj. what one would expect, characteristic. adv. **typically**.
typist n. someone who uses a typewriter.
tyrannize v. to rule with tyranny (**tyrannizing, tyrannized**).
tyranny n. 1. cruel power. 2. government by a cruel dictator. adjs. **tyrannical, tyrannous**.
tyrant n. a powerful and cruel ruler.
tyre or **tire** n. a rubber tube or metal band round the rim of a wheel.

U

udder n. the baglike part of a cow or other female animal which contains the milk.
ugly adj. 1. not pleasant to look at. 2. evil. 3. threatening, as *an ugly look*. (*comparative* **uglier,** *superlative* **ugliest**). n. **ugliness**.
ulterior adj. hidden, as *an ulterior motive*.
ultimate adj. final, last. adv. **ultimately**.
ultimatum (*pron.* ul.ti.may'tum) n. a final offer, given with threats.
ultra- *prefix* far more than usual, as *ultra-modern, ultra-fast, ultra-sensitive*.
umbrella n. a folding protection against rain or sun, held in the hand.
umpire n. a judge in a game or dispute.
un- *prefix* not, as *unreal*, not real, *unsafe*, not safe.

unable *adj.* not able.

unaccustomed *adj.* 1. not used to, as *Jim was unaccustomed to camping.* 2. unusual, as *an unaccustomed sight.*

unaffected *adj.* natural, not affected.

unanimous (*pron.* yoo.nan'i.mus) *adj.* all in agreement. *n.* **unanimity.**

unarmed *adj.* without weapons.

unassuming *adj.* modest.

unavailing *adj.* without effect, useless.

unavoidable *adj.* not to be escaped.

unaware *adj.* not noticing. **unawares** by surprise.

unbearable *adj.* more than one can bear.

unbecoming *adj.* not fit for, not suitable.

unbelief *n.* lack of faith. *n.* **unbeliever** someone without faith.

unbroken *adj.* continuous, not broken.

unburden *v.* 1. to get rid of a burden. 2. to relieve one's mind by talking over some worry.

uncalled-for *adj.* not necessary.

uncanny *adj.* strange, mysterious.

uncertain *adj.* doubtful, not certain. *n.* **uncertainty.**

uncle *n.* the brother of one's father or mother (*fem.* **aunt**).

unclean *adj.* dirty, diseased.

uncoil *v.* to unwind.

uncomfortable *adj.* not comfortable.

uncommon *adj.* not common, rare.

unconscious *adj.* 1. unaware, not realizing. 2. accidental, not meant, as *an unconscious mistake. n.* **unconsciousness.**

uncouple *v.* to disconnect (**uncoupling, uncoupled**).

uncouth *adj.* rough, clumsy.

uncover *v.* to lay bare, to take off the cover.

undecided *adj.* doubtful, hesitant.

undeniable *adj.* certain, unquestionable.

under *prep.* 1. beneath, less than. 2. beneath the heading of.

undercarriage *n.* the landing wheels of an aeroplane.

undercurrent *n.* 1. a movement under the surface. 2. a hidden feeling, as *an undercurrent of suspicion.*

underestimate *v.* to think too little of (**underestimating, underestimated**).

undergo *v.* to experience (**undergoes, undergoing, underwent, undergone**).

undergraduate *n.* a university student who has not yet taken a degree.

underground *adj.* 1. beneath the ground. 2. secret. *n.* **underground** an underground railway.

undergrowth *n.* shrubs and low plants in a wood.

underhand *adj.* sly, secret. *n.* **underhand** (in games) a ball bowled from under the shoulder.

underline *v.* to draw a line under.

underneath *prep.* and *adv.* below.

understand *v.* 1. to know, to get the meaning of. 2. to believe, as *I understand he is ill* (**understanding, understood**).

understanding *n.* 1. knowledge. 2. intelligence. 3. an agreement, as *the two girls had an understanding that they spent Sunday together.*

understood *past* of **understand.**

understudy *n.* an actor or actress who takes the part of one who is ill.

undertake *v.* 1. to set about a task. 2. to agree to do something (**undertaking, undertook, undertaken**).

undertaker *n.* someone who manages funerals.

undertaking *n.* 1. a task. 2. a promise, as *he gave an undertaking to stay.* 3. the management of funerals.

undertone *n.* a quiet voice.

undertook *past* of **undertake.**

underwear *n.* underclothes.

undesirable *adj.* not wanted.

undeveloped *adj.* not fully grown.

undid *past* of **undo.**

undo *v.* 1. to unfasten. 2. to destroy some good work (**undoing, undid, undone**).

undoing *n.* 1. unfastening. 2. ruin, as *pride was his undoing.*

undoubted *adj.* certain, not to be doubted. *adv.* **undoubtedly.**

undying *adj.* everlasting.

unearth *v.* to dig up, to find.

unearthly *adj.* weird, like nothing on earth.

uneasy *adj.* 1. worried. 2. uncomfortable. *adv.* **uneasily.** *n.* **uneasiness.**

unemployed *adj.* out of work. *n.* **unemployment.**

unequal *adj.* 1. not equal. 2. not capable enough, as *unequal to a task.*

unerring *adj.* making no mistake.

uneven *adj.* not even, not level.

uneventful *adj.* quiet, without anything happening, as *an uneventful day. adv.* **uneventfully.**

unexpected *adj.* sudden, not expected. *adv.* **unexpectedly.**

unfailing *adj.* reliable, never lacking.

unfair *adj.* not fair or just.

unfamiliar *adj.* strange, not familiar.

unfeeling *adj.* hard-hearted.

unfit *adj.* 1. not suitable. 2. in poor health.

unfold *v.* to spread out, to open up.

unforeseen *adj.* unexpected.

unforgettable *adj.* not to be forgotten.

unfortunate *adj.* unlucky.

unfurl *v.* to unfold.

ungainly *adj.* clumsy.

ungrateful *adj.* showing no gratitude.

unguarded *adj.* not guarded, careless.

unheard *adj.* not heard.

unheard of strange, never heard before.

uni- *prefix* one, as *unify* to make into one.

unicorn *n.* an imaginary animal like a horse with a horn on its forehead.

unified see **unify.**

uniform *adj.* 1. unchanging, as *the temperature has been uniform throughout the week.* 2. all the same, as *the wolves advanced with a uniform cautious step. n.* **uniform** a special dress worn by soldiers, the police, members of a school, etc. *n.* **uniformity.**

unify *v.* to unite, to make into one (**unifies, unifying, unified**).

union *n.* 1. uniting. 2. a joining. 3. a society of workers, a *trade-union.*

Union Jack the British flag.

unique (*pron.* yoo.neek¹) *adj.* the only one of its kind.

unit *n.* 1. a single thing or person. 2. a standard of measure, as *a gramme is a unit of mass.*

unite *v.* to join together (**uniting, united**). *adj.* **united** joined together.

unity *n.* 1. agreement. 2. the whole of anything. 3. the number one.

universal *adj.* 1. shared by all, as *universal joy.* 2. applying to the universe, as *a universal law. adv.* **universally** generally.

universe *n.* the whole of creation, all that exists.

university *n.* a place of learning which grants degrees to students, and where research is carried on.

unleavened *adj.* (of bread) made without yeast.

unless *conj.* if not, except when, as *I shall go unless it rains.*

unlikely *adj.* probably not going to happen.

unlimited *adj.* without limit.

unload *v.* 1. to take a load from. 2. to remove ammunition from a gun or revolver.

unlock *v.* to open a lock.

unlooked-for *adj.* unexpected.

unlucky *adj.* unfortunate.

unmanly *adj.* cowardly.

unmistakable *adj.* clear, evident.

unnatural *adj.* not natural.

unnecessary *adj.* not needed.

unpack *v.* to open, to take out of a case.

unparalleled *adj.* without equal, never seen before.

unpleasant *adj.* not pleasant, nasty.

unprofitable *adj.* not profitable, useless.

unravel *v.* to disentangle, to solve (a mystery) (**unravelling, unravelled**).

unrest *n.* uneasiness, restlessness.

unruly *adj.* hard to control.

unscrupulous (*pron.* un.skroo¹pyoo.-lus) *adj.* not caring about right and wrong.

unseemly *adj.* not respectable, as *unseemly behaviour.*

unsettle *v.* to disturb (**unsettling, unsettled**). *adj.* **unsettled** restless.

unsound *adj.* 1. rotten. 2. unreliable.

unspeakable *adj.* indescribable, as *unspeakable misery.*

unsuspected *adj.* not suspected.

unsuspecting *adj.* not aware of danger.

unthinkable *adj.* so bad it is not even to be thought of.

untie *v.* to undo, as *to untie a knot* (**unties, untying, untied**).

until *conj*. till, to the time when.
unto *prep*. to.
untold *adj*. 1. not told. 2. too great to count, as *untold riches*.
untruth *n*. a lie. *adj*. **untruthful** not telling the truth. *adv*. **untruthfully**.
unusual *adj*. not usual, strange.
unveil *v*. to uncover, to reveal.
unwary *adj*. careless.
unwieldy *adj*. awkward, clumsy.
unwise *adj*. foolish. *adv*. **unwisely**.
unworthy *adj*. 1. not worthy, as *it is unworthy of praise*. 2. poor, as *it is unworthy work*. *n*. **unworthiness**.
up *adv*. and *prep*. 1. to a higher place, as *he went up the hill*. 2. (of a river) towards the source, as *he rowed up the river*. 3. entirely, as *he ate up his food*. 4. on high, as *the aeroplane is up in the sky*.
it is all up it is all over.
to make it up to become friends again.
up against it faced with difficulties.
up in arms ready to fight.
ups and downs good and bad luck.
up-to-date modern.
upbringing *n*. a child's training.
upheaval *n*. 1. a great shaking or disturbance. 2. a great change.
uphill *adj*. 1. upwards. 2. difficult, as *he had an uphill task*.
uphold *v*. 1. to support, to help, as *to uphold a good cause*. 2. to defend, as *to uphold a friend in an argument* **(upholding, upheld)**.
upholster *v*. to fit covers, springs, and padding on to chairs and sofas. *n*. **upholsterer** someone who fits chairs and sofas with cushions and padding. *n*. **upholstery**.
upkeep *n*. keeping something in good condition, or the cost of it.
uplands *n*. *pl*. high land.
upon *prep*. on.
upper *adj*. higher.
upper-cut (in boxing) an upward blow.
to have the upper hand to have power over.
uppermost *adj*. highest.
upright *adj*. 1. standing up, erect. 2. honest.
uprising *n*. a revolt, a revolution.

uproar *n*. a noisy disturbance.
upset (*pron*. up.set[1]) *v*. 1. to overturn, as *to upset a cup*. 2. to disturb, as *his death upset her* **(upsetting, upset)**. *n*.
upset (*pron*. up'set) 1. an overturning. 2. a disturbance.
upside *n*. the upper side.
upside-down 1. with the top part at the bottom. 2. in confusion.
upstairs *adv*. on a higher floor.
upstream *adv*. against the current of a river.
upward or **upwards** *adv*. and *adj*. towards a higher position.
uranium *n*. a heavy radioactive metal from which nuclear power is obtained.
urban *adj*. concerning a town, not the country.
urchin *n*. a small, mischievous boy.
urge *v*. 1. to force, to drive on. 2. to persuade strongly **(urging, urged)**. *n*. **urge** a longing, a wish, as *Colin had an urge to go camping*.
urgent *adj*. needing attention at once. *n*. **urgency**.
urn *n*. 1. a large vase. 2. a large metal container in which tea or coffee is made.
us *pronoun* referring to me and others.
usage *n*. the way a thing is used, custom.
use (*pron*. yo͞oz) *v*. to make something serve a purpose **(using, used)**. *n*. **use** (*pron*. yo͞os) 1. being used. 2. power of using, as *he lost the use of a finger*. 3. value, as *what use is it?* *n*. **user** (*pron*. yo͞oz'er) someone who uses something. *adj*. **usable** able to be used. *adj*. **useful** helpful. *adj*. **useless** of no help. *adv*. **usefully**. *n*. **usefulness**.
usual *adj*. as generally happens, regular. *adv*. **usually**.
utensil *n*. a kitchen tool or article, as *pots and dishes are utensils*.
utility *n*. 1. usefulness. 2. (in North America) a gas or water company, etc.
utilize *v*. to use **(utilizing, utilized)**. *n*. **utilization**.
utmost *adj*. 1. farthest. 2. greatest.
utter *v*. to speak. *adj*. **utter** complete. *adv*. **utterly** completely, as *utterly false*.

V

vacancy *n.* 1. emptiness. 2. a position or post that needs to be filled (*pl.* **vacancies**).

vacant *adj.* empty.

vacation *n.* 1. leaving a place empty. 2. a holiday.

vaccinate (*pron.* vak'si.nayt) *v.* to give someone an injection to prevent him catching a disease (**vaccinating, vaccinated**). *n.* **vaccination**.

vacuum (*pron.* vak'yoom) *n.* an empty space with all the air removed.

vacuum cleaner a machine which removes dust from carpets and furniture.

vacuum flask a flask which keeps liquids hot for a long time.

vagabond *n.* a wanderer with no settled home, a tramp.

vagrant (*pron.* vay'grant) *n.* a vagabond, a tramp. *adj.* **vagrant** wandering.

vague *adj.* not clear, uncertain. *adv.* **vaguely.** *n.* **vagueness.**

vain *adj.* 1. conceited, too proud. 2. useless, not successful, as *a vain attempt to win.* 3. empty, idle, as *vain show. adv.* **vainly.**

in vain 1. unsuccessfully. 2. without respect, as *to take someone's name in vain is to speak of him without respect.*

vale *n.* a valley.

valet (*pron.* val'et *or* val'ay) *n.* a manservant who looks after his master's clothes, etc.

valiant *adj.* brave, heroic.

valley *n.* a stretch of low land between hills or mountains (*pl.* **valleys**).

valour *n.* great bravery. *adj.* **valorous** very brave.

valuable *adj.* worth much. *n. pl.* **valuables** jewellery, etc., which is worth much.

value *n.* the worth of a thing in money or usefulness. *v.* **value** 1. to have a good opinion of something or regard it with affection. 2. to estimate the worth of something (**valuing, valued**). *n.* **valuation.**

valve *n.* any arrangement which lets a liquid, gas, or electric current flow in one direction only, and does not allow a return flow.

vampire *n.* 1. a blood-sucking South American bat. 2. someone who forces money from others.

van (1) *n.* a covered wagon for delivering goods.

van (2) *n.* the front part of an army, fleet, of procession.

vandal *n.* someone who destroys beautiful things. *n.* **vandalism.**

vane *n.* a weathercock, a windmill's sail.

vanguard *n.* the front of an army or fleet.

vanish *v.* to disappear.

vanity *n.* conceit, too much pride.

vanquish *v.* to conquer, to overcome.

vantage *n.* an advantage.

vantage-point a commanding position.

vaporize *v.* to turn into vapour (**vaporizing, vaporized**). *n.* **vaporization.**

vapour *n.* 1. mist, fumes, or steam from a liquid. 2. a gas formed from a heated liquid.

variable *adj.* changeable, not staying the same.

variation *n.* a change, a difference from what is usual.

varied *adj.* of different kinds. See **vary**.

variety *n.* 1. change, difference. 2. a collection of different things, as *John has a variety of toys.* 3. a kind, as *there are several varieties of dog.* 4. entertainment with several kinds of acts (in North America called **vaudeville**) (*pl.* **varieties**).

various *adj.* of different sorts.

varnish *n.* a liquid containing dissolved gum for giving a smooth polish to wood. *v.* **varnish** to paint varnish on to wood.

vary *v.* to alter (**varies, varying, varied**).

vase *n.* an ornamental jar, often for holding flowers.

vassal *n.* (in feudal times) a servant or tenant who received protection and land from a lord in return for services and allegiance he gave.

vast *adj.* enormous, very big. *n.* **vastness.**

vat *n.* a large tank or tub.

vault (1) *n.* 1. an arched roof. 2. a cave or cellar with an arched roof.

vault (2) *v.* to jump over something using one's hands or a pole.

veal *n.* calf's meat.

veer *v.* to change direction, as *the wind veered from south to west.*

vegetable *n.* a plant (except fruit) grown for food. *adj.* **vegetable** concerning plant life.

vegetable marrow a long gourd used for food.

vegetarian *n.* someone who eats no meat, but only vegetable food.

vegetation *n.* plant life.

vehement (*pron.* vee'e.ment) *adj.* strong, full of passion, as *vehement words. n.* **vehemence.**

vehicle *n.* anything carrying passengers or goods.

veil *n.* a thin covering or net to hide the face or head. *v.* **veil** to hide or cover as with a veil.

vein *n.* 1. one of the tubes in the body which carry blood to the heart (note: an *artery* carries blood *from* the heart). 2. something like a vein, as the rib of a leaf or a streak of ore in a rock.

vellum *n.* fine parchment for writing on.

velocity *n.* speed, swiftness, rate of movement.

velvet *n.* a silk fabric with a short, thick pile. *adj.* **velvety** like velvet.

veneer *n.* 1. a thin layer of fine wood laid over poorer wood. 2. a show with nothing good behind it.

vengeance *n.* revenge.

venison *n.* deer's flesh.

venom *n.* 1. snake poison. 2. spite, hatred. *adj.* **venomous** full of venom.

vent *n.* an opening.

to give vent to to let out, to express.

ventilate *v.* to allow air to pass into, as *to ventilate a room* (**ventilating, ventilated**). *n.* **ventilation.** *n.* **ventilator** a grid for letting air into and out of a room.

ventriloquist *n.* a person who can make his voice seem to come from a doll or another person. *n.* **ventriloquism.**

venture *n.* a dangerous undertaking. *v.* **venture** to take a risk (**venturing, ventured**). *adj.* **venturesome** daring.

veranda or **verandah** *n.* a long, roofed porch along the side of a house.

verb *n.* a word in a sentence which says what is happening, as in the sentence *I met him,* 'met' is a verb.

verbal *adj.* spoken, as *a verbal message is one that is spoken not written. adv.* **verbally** by word of mouth, as *I let him know verbally.*

verdict *n.* 1. the decision of a magistrate or jury in a court of law. 2. any judgement.

verge *n.* 1. an edge. 2. a grass border. *v.* **verge** to be on the edge of (**verging, verged**).

verify *v.* to check, to make sure that something is true (**verifying, verified**). *n.* **verification.**

vermin *n.* a harmful or unpleasant animal or insect, a pest (*pl.* **vermin**).

versatile *adj.* able to do many things well. *n.* **versatility.**

verse *n.* 1. poetry. 2. a group of lines in a poem. 3. one of the divisions in a chapter of the Bible.

version *n.* 1. a description, as *Sheila gave her version of what happened.* 2. a translation.

versus *prep.* a Latin word meaning 'against', as *United versus the Rovers,* often shortened to *United v. Rovers.*

vertebrate *n.* an animal with a backbone.

vertical *adj.* upright, erect. *adv.* **vertically.**

very *adv.* extremely, as *he works very well. adj.* **very** real, exact, as *he is the very image of his father.*

vessel *n.* 1. a large ship. 2. a container for liquids. 3. a tube in an animal or plant through which a liquid passes, as a *blood-vessel.*

vest *n.* 1. a close-fitting undergarment. 2. (in the U.S.A.) a waistcoat.

vestibule *n.* 1. a small entrance hall. 2. (in North America) the covered entrance to a railway coach.

vestige *n.* a trace, a sign, as *there is not a vestige of reason for thinking that.*

vestry *n.* a room in a church where the clergy put on their robes.

veteran *n.* 1. someone with long experience, especially a soldier or sailor. 2. (in the U.S.A.) a soldier who has seen active service.

veterinary *adj.* concerned with the medical care of animals, as *a veterinary surgeon*.

veto *n.* a refusal to allow something, by someone in authority (*pl.* **vetoes**). *v.* **veto** to forbid (**vetoing, vetoed**).

vex *v.* to annoy, to make cross. *adj.* **vexatious** annoying. *n.* **vexation**.

a vexed question a difficult question to decide.

via *prep.* by way of, as *to fly from London to Madrid via Paris*.

viaduct *n.* a bridge carrying a road or railway over a valley.

vibrant *adj.* 1. throbbing, vibrating. 2. (of a person) full of enthusiasm.

vibrate *v.* to tremble, to quiver (**vibrating, vibrated**). *n.* **vibration**.

vicar *n.* 1. a clergyman in charge of a parish. 2. (in the Roman Catholic church) a bishop's deputy.

vicarage *n.* a vicar's house.

vice (1) *n.* 1. wickedness. 2. a bad habit.

vice (2) (in North America spelled **vise**) *n.* a clamp on a work-bench for holding things.

vice- (3) *prefix* in place of, as *vice-president*.

viceroy *n.* a man who rules a country or colony in the place of a king.

vice-versa (*pron.* vīˈsee-verˈsa) a phrase meaning the other way round, as *I praised Tom and vice-versa* (*Tom praised me*).

vicious (*pron.* vishˈus) *adj.* harmful, evil.

victim *n.* someone who dies or suffers either through accident or because of others.

victor *n.* a winner, a conqueror.

victorious *adj.* winning.

victory *n.* a win, a conquest (*pl.* **victories**).

victuals (*pron.* vitˈlz) *n. pl.* food.

vie (usually with **with**) *v.* to try to do better than, as *Jean vied with her friend to be top of the class* (**vying, vied**).

view *n.* 1. sight, as *the car came into view*. 2. scene, as *a wonderful view*. 3. opinion, as *in my view you are wrong*. *v.* **view** to look at.

in view of because.

with a view to with the intention of.

viewfinder *n.* (of a camera) the part which shows what the photograph will look like.

viewpoint *n.* 1. a place giving a good view. 2. a way of judging or thinking of things.

vigilant *adj.* watchful. *n.* **vigilance**.

vigorous *adj.* strong, full of energy. *n.* **vigour** energy.

vile *adj.* evil, very bad.

villa *n.* a large country house in its own grounds.

village *n.* a group of houses in the country, smaller than a town. *n.* **villager** someone who lives in a village.

villain *n.* a wicked person, a scoundrel. *adj.* **villainous**. *n.* **villainy** wickedness.

villein *n.* a serf in the Middle Ages.

vim *n.* energy, vigour.

vindicate *v.* to show that someone is innocent or right, after he has been wrongly accused (**vindicating, vindicated**). *n.* **vindication**.

vindictive *adj.* revengeful, spiteful. *n.* **vindictiveness**. *adv.* **vindictively**.

vine *n.* a climbing plant on which grapes grow.

vinegar *n.* a sour liquid used for flavouring salads, etc., and for pickling.

vineyard (*pron.* vinˈyard) *n.* a place where grapes are grown.

violent *adj.* very vigorous, very forceful. *n.* **violence**.

violet *n.* 1. a small plant with a bluish-purple flower. 2. a bluish-purple colour.

violin *n.* a four-stringed musical instrument played with a bow. *n.* **violinist** a violin player.

viper *n.* a poisonous snake, an adder.

virgin *n.* a maiden. *adj.* **virgin** pure, untouched, as *virgin snow*. *n.* **virginity** purity.

the Virgin Mary the mother of Jesus Christ.

virile *adj.* manly, active. *n.* **virility**.

virtual *adj.* really so, but not said in actual words, as *he made a virtual promise to go*. *adv.* **virtually** really, in effect, as *he virtually agreed to do it*.

virtue *n.* goodness, a good quality, as *patience is a virtue*. *adj.* **virtuous** good.

by virtue of because of.

visa (*pron.* veeˈza) *n.* a permit to enter a country.

viscount (*pron.* vī'kownt) *n.* a nobleman next below an earl (*fem.* **viscountess**).

vise see **vice**.

visible *adj.* able to be seen. *n.* **visibility** 1. being seen. 2. the clearness of the air. *adv.* **visibly**.

vision *n.* 1. the ability to see. 2. ability to plan ahead, as *he is a man with vision*. 3. a dream, something imagined.

visionary *n.* 1. a dreamer. 2. a person who has ideas.

visit *v.* to go and see. *n.* **visit** 1. a call to see someone or some place. 2. a stay with someone. *n.* **visitor**.

visor or **vizor** *n.* 1. (in old days) the movable part of a helmet, covering the face. 2. the peak of a cap.

visual *adj.* able to be seen or having to do with sight. *adv.* **visually**.

visualize *v.* to form a picture in the mind (**visualizing, visualized**).

vital (*pron.* vī'tal) *adj.* 1. concerning life, as *vital energy* or *a vital injury is one that destroys life*. 2. very important, as *a vital task*. *n.* **vitality** liveliness, energy. *adv.* **vitally**.

vitamin *n.* one of a number of substances in food called vitamins A, B, C, etc., which are needed for healthy growth.

vivacious (*pron.* vi.vay'shus) *adj.* lively, gay. *n.* **vivacity**.

vivid *adj.* bright, clear, lifelike.

vixen *n.* a female fox (*masc.* **fox**).

vizor see **visor**.

vocabulary *n.* 1. a list of words with their meanings. 2. the number of different words which a person uses.

vocal *adj.* concerning the voice. *adv.* **vocally**.

vocal chords muscles in the windpipe moving to make sounds.

vocation *n.* 1. occupation, trade. 2. an inner call to a dedicated way of life.

voice *n.* speech or song from the mouth. *v.* **voice** to put into words, to say, as *to voice one's opinions* (**voicing, voiced**).

void *adj.* empty, useless. *n.* **void** emptiness.

volcanic *adj.* concerning a volcano.

volcano *n.* a mountain with an opening reaching down into the earth up which molten rock may be thrown (*pl.* **volcanoes**).

volley *n.* a shower, a discharge, as *they threw a volley of stones* (*pl.* **volleys**). *v.* **volley** (in tennis) to hit a ball before it touches the ground (**volleying, volleyed**).

volt *n.* a unit of electric force.

voltage *n.* the number of volts at which an electric current is working.

voluble *adj.* talking a great deal. *adv.* **volubly**.

volume *n.* 1. a book, or one of a set of books. 2. the amount of space taken up by a thing, as *this box has a volume of 35 cubic centimetres*. 3. a large quantity, as *the car raised volumes of dust*.

voluntary *adj.* given or done freely, not compelled, as *a voluntary gift*. *adv.* **voluntarily**.

volunteer *n.* someone who offers to do something without being compelled. *v.* **volunteer** to offer to do something of one's own free will.

vomit *v.* 1. to be sick. 2. to throw up in large amounts, as *the ship's funnel vomited smoke* (**vomiting, vomited**).

vote *n.* a choice by ballot or a show of hands. *v.* **vote** 1. to choose by ballot, etc. 2. to grant something by vote, as *to vote someone a sum of money* (**voting, voted**). *n.* **voter** someone with the right to vote.

vouch (with **for**) *v.* to answer for, to guarantee.

voucher *n.* a receipt.

vow *n.* a solemn promise, a firm resolution.

vowel *n.* any one of the letters *a, e, i, o, u.*

voyage *n.* a long journey by water.

vulgar *adj.* rude, bad-mannered, in bad taste. *n.* **vulgarity**.

vulnerable *adj.* liable to injury, not protected.

vulture *n.* a large bird of prey that feeds on dead animals.

W

wad (*pron.* wod) *n.* 1. a soft pad. 2. a pile of banknotes or paper. *n.* **wadding** soft packing material.

waddle *v.* to walk like a duck (**waddling, waddled**).

wade *v.* to walk through water or mud (**wading, waded**).

wafer *n.* a thin biscuit as used with ice-cream.

waft *v.* to float lightly through air.

wag *v.* to move from side to side (**wagging, wagged**).

wage (1) *n.* payment for work, especially a weekly payment. See **salary**.

wage (2) *v.* to carry on, as *to wage war* (**waging, waged**).

wager *n.* a bet. *v.* **wager** to bet.

waggle *v.* to move from side to side, to wag (**waggling, waggled**).

wagon or **waggon** *n.* 1. a horse-drawn four-wheeled vehicle for carrying loads. 2. (in Britain) an open railway truck. *n.* **wagoner** a man who drives a wagon.

wail *n.* a long, mournful cry.

waist *n.* 1. the part of the body between the ribs and the hips. 2. (in the U.S.A.) a bodice. 3. the middle part of a ship.

waistcoat *n.* a sleeveless garment worn under a man's jacket.

wait *v.* 1. to stop in readiness for something to happen. 2. to serve at table. 3. (with **upon**) to attend to. *n.* **wait** a period of waiting.

to lie in wait to hide and then attack.

waiter *n.* a man serving at table (*fem.* **waitress**).

wake (1) *v.* 1. to stop sleeping. 2. to arouse, to stir up (**waking, woke** or **waked, waked** or **woken**). *n.* **wake** a watch, a vigil. *adj.* **wakeful** watchful.

wake (2) *n.* a holiday, a fair.

wake (3) *n.* the track left by a ship.

waken *n.* to awake.

walk *v.* to go on foot. *n.* **walk** 1. a journey on foot. 2. a roadway to walk on. 3. a position in society, as *people from all walks of life were there.*

wall *n.* a fence or side of a building made of brick, concrete, or stone. *v.* **wall** to build a wall round.

to go to the wall to fail.

with backs to the wall in a desperate position.

wallaby *n.* a small Australian kangaroo.

wallaroo *n.* a large Australian kangaroo.

wallet *n.* a leather pocket-case or bag.

wallow *v.* to roll about in mud or sand.

wallpaper *n.* printed paper pasted on the walls of a room.

walnut *n.* a nut with a crinkled shell, or the tree bearing the nut.

walrus *n.* a large sea-animal like a seal, but with long tusks.

waltz *n.* a smooth, graceful dance.

wan *adj.* pale, tired-looking.

wand *n.* a slender stick.

wander *v.* to roam about, to ramble. *n.* **wanderer**.

wane *v.* 1. to grow smaller, as *the full moon wanes as it changes to the last quarter.* 2. to grow weaker or of less importance (**waning, waned**).

want *v.* 1. to wish for. 2. to be without, to be in poverty. *n.* **want** scarcity, need. *n. pl.* **wants** needs, as *his wants were many.*

wanting *adj.* lacking, missing, not up to requirements.

war *n.* 1. a long fight. 2. an armed fight between nations. *v.* **war** to make war (**warring, warred**).

a cold war a struggle between nations without actual warfare.

on the warpath preparing for a fight.

warble *n.* a bird's song. *v.* **warble** to sing like a bird (**warbling, warbled**). *n.* **warbler** a singing bird.

ward *n.* 1. a young person in the care of a guardian chosen by a court. 2. a section of a town or city. 3. a section of a hospital. *v.* **ward** (with **off**) to keep away, as *to ward off a blow.*

-ward or **-wards** *suffix* in the direction of, as *homewards* or *inward.*

warden *n.* 1. a guard or keeper. 2. (in North America) a man in charge of a prison.

warder *n.* a prison officer.

wardrobe *n.* 1. a cupboard for clothes. 2. someone's stock of clothes.

ware *n.* manufactured goods, as *hardware* or *silverware. n. pl.* **wares** goods for sale.

warehouse *n.* a building for storing goods.

warfare *n.* being at war.

warily, wariness see **wary**.

warm *adj.* 1. moderately hot. 2. enthusiastic, as *a warm welcome. n.*

warmth. adv. **warmly**. adj. **warm-hearted** loving, kindly.

to become warm (in games) to get near to what is being looked for.

warn v. to caution someone of possible danger or trouble. n. **warning** a caution.

warp v. to become twisted, as *damp wood warps out of shape*. n. **warp** 1. a twist in wood. 2. the threads running lengthways in cloth (note: the threads running across are called the **weft**).

warrant n. 1. authority. 2. a document giving someone authority. 3. a reason for believing something. v. **warrant** 1. to give reason for, as *his words do not warrant his bad conduct*. 2. to guarantee, as *this jug is warranted to be of solid silver*.

warren n. a place where rabbits burrow, a *rabbit-warren*.

warrior n. a soldier.

warship n. an armed ship built for fighting.

wart n. a small, hard lump on the skin.

wary adj. cautious, on guard against danger. n. **wariness**. adv. **warily**.

wash v. 1. to clean with soap and water. 2. to flow against, as *the sea washed the cliffs*. 3. (with **away**) to carry away with water, as *the sea washed away part of the pier*. n. **wash** 1. cleaning with soap and water. 2. (in water-colour painting) a coat of paint. 3. some special liquid to be used, as *whitewash* or *eye-wash*.

washer n. a machine for washing clothes.

wasp n. a stinging insect. adj. **waspish** irritable.

wastage n. an amount lost in waste.

waste v. 1. to use something carelessly, using too much, or throwing some away. 2. to wear away, as *he was wasted with illness* (**wasting, wasted**). n. **waste** refuse, something not wanted. adj. **wasteful** causing waste.

to lay waste to destroy.

watch v. 1. to look at, to observe. 2. to be on guard. n. **watch** 1. being on the look-out. 2. part of a ship's crew being on duty. 3. a small timepiece. adj.

watchful alert. n. **watchfulness**. adv. **watchfully**.

watchman n. a man who guards a building.

watchword n. a password.

water n. the liquid which falls as rain. v. **water** 1. to sprinkle with water. 2. to dilute or weaken with water, as *to water lemon cordial*. 3. to give water to, as *to water a horse*. adj. **watery**.

to pour oil on troubled waters to calm an angry person.

water-colour n. a paint to be mixed with water.

watercress n. a water-plant used in salads.

waterfall n. a cascade of water.

waterfowl n. a bird that lives on and near water.

waterlogged adj. saturated with water.

water-melon n. a very large juicy fruit.

water-polo n. a game played in water between two teams of seven players.

waterproof, watertight adj. not allowing water to pass through. n. **waterproof** a raincoat.

watershed n. a hill or mountain from which rivers run down on both sides.

waterspout n. a column of water swept up by high winds.

wave v. 1. to move quickly to and fro, as *to wave a flag*. 2. to make waves, as *to wave hair* (**waving, waved**). n. **wave** 1. a ridge on water stirred by wind. 2. a sudden rise in amount of something, as a *heat-wave*. adj. **wavy** like waves.

waver v. 1. to be unsteady. 2. to hesitate.

wax (1) n. a solid substance which easily melts, as *beeswax, paraffin wax*, or *sealing wax*. adj. **waxen** like wax, made of wax.

wax (2) v. to grow larger. Opposite of **wane**.

way n. 1. a road or direction. 2. a manner, habit, or custom, as *this is my way of doing it*.

under way (of a ship) moving.

ways and means methods.

wayfarer n. a traveller on foot.

waylay v. to lie in wait for (**waylaying, waylaid**).

wayside *n.* the edge of a road.

wayward *adj.* obstinate, fond of doing things one's own way.

weak *adj.* lacking strength. Opposite of **strong**. *n.* **weakness**. *v.* **weaken** to grow weak or make weak.

weak-kneed *adj.* having a weak will.

weakling *n.* a weak creature.

weal (1) *n.* a scar made by a blow.

weal (2) *n.* well-being, prosperity.

wealth *n.* riches. *adj.* **wealthy** (*comparative* **wealthier**, *superlative* **wealthiest**).

weapon *n.* anything used to fight with.

wear *v.* 1. to dress in, as *to wear a hat*. 2. to show, as *to wear a frown*. 3. to use or rub away, as *to wear a carpet* (**wearing, wore, worn**). *n.* **wearer**.

to wear someone down to overcome him by persistence.

to wear out 1. to use up in wearing. 2. to make very tired.

weary *adj.* very tired (*comparative* **wearier**, *superlative* **weariest**). *n.* **weariness**. *adv.* **wearily**.

wearisome causing tiredness, boring.

weasel *n.* a long thin wild animal which attacks rabbits.

weather *n.* the climate at a particular place. *v.* **weather** 1. to wear away by wind and rain. 2. to come through successfully, as *to weather a storm*.

weather-beaten worn by wind and rain.

weather-cock, weather-vane a movable pointer on a building which shows which way the wind blows.

weather-forecast an estimate of the weather to be.

weave *v.* to make cloth by twisting threads across one another (**weaving, wove, woven**).

web *n.* 1. a network of threads. 2. the skin between the toes of water-birds. *adj.* **webbed** having webs. *n.* **webbing** a narrow fabric strip.

wed *v.* to marry (**wedding, wedded**). *n.* **wedding** a marriage ceremony.

silver, golden, diamond weddings the twenty-fifth, fiftieth, and sixtieth anniversaries.

wedge *n.* a tapered piece of wood or metal.

Wednesday *n.* the fourth day of the week.

Ash Wednesday the first day of Lent.

wee *adj.* very small, tiny.

weed *n.* a wild plant growing on cultivated land. *v.* **weed** to pull out weeds. *adj.* **weedy** 1. full of weeds. 2. thin, scraggy, as *a weedy man*. *n. pl.* **weeds** mourning clothes.

week *n.* a period of seven days. *adj.* **weekly** 1. lasting a week. 2. once a week.

week in week out for many weeks.

weekday *n.* any day except Sunday.

week-end *n.* Saturday and Sunday.

weep *v.* to cry (**weeping, wept**).

weft *n.* the threads running across cloth. Opposite of **warp**.

weigh *v.* 1. to measure how heavy a thing is by using scales. 2. to press down heavily. 3. to consider carefully, as *to weigh an argument*. 4. to raise (an anchor), as *the ship weighed anchor before sailing*.

weighing-machine *n.* a machine to weigh people or things.

weight *n.* 1. heaviness. 2. a piece of metal used to weigh things. 3. anything heavy, as *to hold papers down with a weight*. 4. importance, as *your opinion carries weight*. *adj.* **weighty** 1. heavy. 2. important.

weir *n.* a dam across a river.

weird *adj.* strange, uncanny.

welcome *adj.* received gladly, as *a welcome gift*. *n.* **welcome** a reception. *v.* **welcome** to receive gladly (**welcoming, welcomed**).

weld *v.* to join two pieces of metal together by hammering them while hot.

welfare *n.* well-being, good health and prosperity.

well (1) *n.* a shaft in the ground from which water or oil is drawn.

well (2) *adv.* 1. in a good way, as *he did it well*. 2. intimately, closely, as *I know him well*. *adj.* **well** in good health, as *is he well?* (*comparative* **better**, *superlative* **best**).

well-being welfare.

well-bred polite.

well-meaning intending well.

well-nigh almost.

went *past* of **go**.

wept *past* of **weep**.

were see **be**.

west *n.* the part of the sky where the sun sets. The opposite direction to **east**.

the West Europe and America, as compared with Asia.

the western hemisphere the half of the earth including North and South America.

westerly (direction) towards the west; (of a wind) from the west.

western concerning the west.

westward, westwards towards the west.

wet *adj.* soaked in liquid, not dry (*comparative* **wetter**, *superlative* **wettest**). *v.* **wet** to soak with liquid (**wetting, wet** or **wetted**).

a wet blanket a dismal person.

whale *n.* a large fish-like animal which lives in the sea, hunted for its oil. *n.* **whaler** a boat used to catch whales.

wharf *n.* a landing-stage to which ships can be moored (*pl.* **wharfs** or **wharves**).

what *adj.* which, as *at what time does the bus go? pronoun* **what** 1. which, as *what is it?* 2. such as, as *I will do what I can.*

whatever, whatsoever *pronoun* any, anything that, as *whatever he does is wrong.*

wheat *n.* a tall, grass-like plant, or its seed, from which flour is made.

wheedle *v.* to coax (**wheedling, wheedled**).

wheel *n.* a circular frame or disk which turns on an axle. *v.* **wheel** 1. to push on wheels, as *to wheel a pram.* 2. to turn round like a wheel, as *the troops wheeled to the right.*

wheelbarrow *n.* a small vehicle on one wheel pushed by hand.

wheeze *v.* to breathe with a whistling sound (**wheezing, wheezed**). *n.* **wheeze** a noisy breath.

when *adv.* 1. at what time, as *when do you go?* 2. at the moment that, as *it was five o'clock when he came. conj.* **when** 1. although, as *he played when he should have been working.* 2. at the time that.

whence *adv.* from which, as *the town whence he came.*

whenever *adv.* as often as required.

where *adv.* at, from, or to, what place.

whereabouts 1. in what place? 2. the place where a thing is.

whereas and yet.

wherefore 1. why? 2. therefore.

whereupon after which.

wherever at, to, or in whatever place.

whet *v.* to sharpen, as *to whet a knife*, or *the sound whetted my curiosity* (**whetting, whetted**).

whether *conj.* if, which of two, as *I do not know whether to go or stay.*

whey *n.* the watery part of milk when it has been curdled for making cheese.

which *pronoun* that, one of several, as *the hat which I bought. adj.* **which** what, as *which books are yours.*

whichever *pronoun* and *adj* which one of several.

whiff *n.* a slight puff, a faint smell, as *a whiff of smoke.*

while *n.* a period of time, as *a short while ago. conj.* **while** during the time when, as *he slept while I worked.*

once in a while now and then.

to while away the time to pass the time.

worth while worth the time spent.

whilst *conj.* while.

whim *n.* a passing fancy.

whimper *n.* a feeble cry of fear or pain.

whimsical *adj.* quaint. *adv.* **whimsically**.

whine *v.* 1. to make a long, drawn-out cry. 2. to complain continually (**whining, whined**).

whinny *n.* the neigh of a horse. *v.* **whinny** to neigh (**whinnying, whinnied**).

whip *n.* a lash attached to a rod. *v.* **whip** to beat with a whip (**whipping, whipped**).

whir or **whirr** *n.* a fluttering sound, as *the whir of birds' wings. v.* **whir** or **whirr** to buzz or flutter (**whirring, whirred**).

whirl *v.* to spin round rapidly.

whirlpool *n.* a strong, circular current of water.

whirlwind *n.* a powerful, circular swirl of air.

whisk *v.* to move quickly and lightly. *n.* **whisk** 1. a little brush. 2. a kitchen utensil for beating eggs or cream.

whiskers *n. pl.* the hair on a man's face or growing from the upper lip of a cat or other animal.

whisky (in Ireland spelled **whiskey**) *n.* a strong alcoholic spirit.

whisper *v.* to speak in a soft, low voice.

whist *n.* a card game for four people.

whistle *v.* to make a loud, shrill noise by blowing air from the mouth, or steam through a narrow pipe (**whistling, whistled**).

Whit see **Whitsun**.

white *n.* the colour of snow.
whiten to make white.
white elephant see **elephant**.
white feather a symbol of cowardice.
white flag a symbol of surrender.
white lie a small lie.
whitish fairly white.

whitewash *n.* a mixture of lime and water for coating walls and ceilings.

whither *adv.* where, to what place?

Whitsun *adj.* belonging to Whitsuntide, the period seven weeks after Easter.

whittle *v.* to cut or shape with a knife (**whittling, whittled**).

whizz or **whiz** *v.* to move quickly with a hissing sound (**whizzing, whizzed**).

who *pronoun* 1. which person or persons. 2. the person that, as *the man who came.*

whoever *pronoun* the person that, as *whoever said that was wrong.*

whole *adj.* entire, complete, as *the whole truth. n.* **whole** the total. *adv.* **wholly** entirely.
on the whole generally speaking.

wholehearted *adj.* enthusiastic.

wholesale *adj.* in large quantities.

wholesome *adj.* health-giving.

whom *pronoun* a form of **who**, as *to whom did you give it?*

whoop *n.* a shout of triumph.

whose *pronoun* a form of **who**, as *whose coat is it?*

why *adv.* for what reason, as *why did he go?*

wick *n.* a cord in a candle, or oil lamp, passing up oil to the flame.

wicked *adj.* bad, evil. *n.* **wickedness**.

wicket *n.* 1. a small gate or door. 2. (in cricket) a set of three stumps with bails on top, at either end of the pitch.

wicket-keeper (in cricket) the player who stands behind the wicket.

wide *adj.* 1. broad, measuring more than usual from side to side. 2. not near the target, as *the arrow flew wide of the mark. adv.* **widely** *n.* **widen** to make wide.

wide awake fully awake, alert.

widespread *adj.* spread out widely.

widow *n.* a woman whose husband is dead.

widower *n.* a man whose wife is dead.

width *n.* 1. being wide. 2. how wide a thing is.

wield *v.* 1. to use with the hands, as *to wield an axe.* 2. to use, as *to wield power over men.*

wife *n.* a married woman (*pl.* **wives**).

wig *n.* an artificial head of hair.

wigwam *n.* a North American Indian's home.

wild *adj.* 1. not tamed, not civilized. 2. rough, uncontrolled. *adv.* **wildly**. *n.* **wildness**.
like wildfire very quickly.

wilderness *n.* a wild, desert place.

wile *n.* a cunning trick. *n.* **wiliness** cunning.

wilful *adj.* 1. obstinate, as *a wilful mule.* 2. done on purpose, deliberate, as *wilful damage. adv.* **wilfully**. *n.* **wilfulness**.

will *n.* 1. the power of the mind to decide what to do, *will-power.* 2. a written statement in which someone says who is to have his property after his death. *v.* **will** used with another verb to mark the future, as *he will go.*

willing *adj.* ready, agreeable, as *I am willing to help. n.* **willingness**.

willow *n.* a tree which grows by water. *adj.* **willowy** slender and graceful.

wilt (1) *v.* to droop, to wither.

wilt (2) *v.* an old-fashioned word for *will* used with *thou*, as *wilt thou go?*

wily *adj.* cunning, crafty (*comparative* **wilier**, *superlative* **wiliest**).

win v. 1. to gain a victory. 2. to earn or reach with a struggle, as *to win someone's confidence* (**winning, won**). n. **win** a victory. n. **winner** someone who wins.

to win one's spurs to win honour.

to win someone over to gain his friendship.

wince v. to flinch, to draw back in sudden pain (**wincing, winced**).

wind (1) n. 1. moving air. 2. breath, as *a runner gets his second wind*. adj. **windy** (*comparative* **windier**, *superlative* **windiest**).

to take the wind out of someone's sails to embarrass him by doing something he was about to do.

wind (2) (*pron.* wind) v. 1. to twist about. 2. to roll round or wrap round. 3. to tighten a clock spring with a key (**winding, wound**).

windfall n. 1. fruit blown off a tree. 2. unexpected good luck.

wind-instrument n. a musical instrument which has to be blown.

windmill n. a mill worked by the wind.

window n. a glass-covered opening in a wall or roof to let in light and air.

windpipe n. the passage from throat to lung.

windscreen n. (in North America **windshield**) a protective sheet of glass in front of a motor-vehicle.

windward n. the direction from which the wind blows.

wine n. an alcoholic drink made from grape-juice or fruits.

wing n. 1. a limb of a bird, bat, or insect, used for flying. 2. a part of a building branching off the main part. 3. a side of a stage. adj. **winged** having wings.

wing-commander a Royal Air Force officer, next below a group-captain.

to take under one's wing to protect.

wink v. to close and open an eye quickly. **forty winks** a short nap.

winning adj. 1. successful. 2. charming, as *Tom has a winning manner*.

winnings n. pl. money won by gambling.

winter n. the coldest season of the year.

wintry adj. cold, like winter.

wipe v. to rub clean or dry (**wiping, wiped**). n. **wiper** something that wipes, as *a windscreen wiper*.

wire n. 1. a long metal thread. 2. (loosely) a telegram. v. **wire** 1. to fit with electric wires. 2. (loosely) to send a telegram (**wiring, wired**). n. **wiring** a system of wires passing electric current.

wireless n. radio.

wire-netting n. fencing made of interwoven wires.

wiry adj. tough, strong.

wisdom n. being wise, having good judgement and understanding.

wisdom tooth one of the extreme back teeth.

wise (1) adj. having knowledge, good judgement, and understanding. adv. **wisely**.

wise (2) n. way, manner, as *he did it in this wise*.

wish v. to want, to desire.

wisp n. a small handful, a small bit, as *a wisp of hay*.

wistful adj. longing, yearning. adv. **wistfully**. n. **wistfulness**.

wit n. 1. ability to make amusing smart remarks. 2. intelligence, reason (often *plural*), as *he used his wits to escape*.

at one's wits end not knowing what to do.

to have one's wits about one to be smart and alert.

witch n. a woman supposed to have magic powers (*masc.* **wizard**). n. **witchcraft** the magic used by witches.

with prep. 1. by the side of, accompanying, as *Jim went with Jack*. 2. possessing, as *the boy with the cap*. 3. from, as *baby did not like to part with her toys*. 4. through, because of, as *he jumped with fright*.

withdraw v. 1. to draw back from. 2. to remove (**withdrawing, withdrew, withdrawn**). n. **withdrawal**.

withdrew past of **withdraw**.

wither v. to dry up, to fade, to droop.

withheld past of **withhold**.

withhold v. 1. to hold back from, as *to withhold from crime*. 2. to refuse to give, as *to withhold a gift* (**withholding, withheld**).

within *adv.* inside, as *come within*. *prep.* **within** not beyond, as *within reach*.

without *adv.* outside. *prep.* **without** 1. not having, as *to travel without a ticket*. 2. so as not to, as *talk without waking the baby*.

withstand *v.* to stand against, to resist (**withstanding, withstood**).

withstood *past* of **withstand**.

witness *n.* 1. someone who has seen something happen, an *eye-witness*. 2. someone who gives evidence of what he knows in a court of law. 3. evidence, as *to bear witness against someone*. *v.* **witness** 1. to see something happen. 2. to give evidence in a court of law. 3. to put one's name on a document after someone's signature, as evidence that he has signed it.

witticism *n.* a smart, humorous remark.

witty *adj.* full of wit, clever and amusing. *adv.* **wittily**.

wives plural of **wife**.

wizard *n.* a magician.

woad *n.* a blue dye.

wobble *v.* to move unsteadily (**wobbling, wobbled**). *adj.* **wobbly**.

woe *n.* misery, deep sorrow. *adj.* **woeful** sorrowful.

woebegone *adj.* looking very miserable.

woke *past* of **wake**.

wold *n.* rolling country, a down.

wolf *n.* a wild grey animal like a dog (*pl.* **wolves**). *adj.* **wolfish** savage, like a wolf.

to cry wolf to raise a false alarm.

to keep the wolf from the door to keep oneself or one's family free from hunger.

Wolf Cub a junior Boy Scout.

woman *n.* a grown-up female human being (*pl.* **women**). *n.* **womanhood**. *adj.* **womanly**.

womb *n.* the organ in the female body which holds the young before birth.

won *past* of **win**.

wonder *n.* 1. a marvellous thing or happening. 2. amazement. *v.* **wonder** 1. to marvel. 2. to doubt, as *I began to wonder whether he could do it*. 3. to want to know, as *I wonder what it is*. *adjs.* **wonderful, wondrous** amazing.

won't short for 'will not'.

woo *v.* 1. to make love to. 2. to try to persuade. *n.* **wooer** a lover.

wood *n.* 1. a large number of trees growing together. 2. the hard part of a tree. *adjs.* **woody, wooded** covered with trees; **wooden** made of wood.

woodland *n.* land on which many trees grow.

woodpecker *n.* a bird that lives on the insects under the bark of trees.

woodwork *n.* the making of articles of wood.

wool *n.* the hair of sheep and other animals such as llamas and alpacas. *adjs.* **woollen, woolly** made of wool (*comparative* **woollier**, *superlative* **woolliest**).

wool-gathering absentmindedness.

word *n.* 1. a sound or group of printed letters with a meaning. 2. a message. 3. a promise, as *give me your word that you will come*.

to have words with to quarrel with.

wore *past* of **wear**.

work *n.* 1. an effort of body or mind. 2. occupation. 3. a book, piece of music, or other composition, as *she played some of Beethoven's works*. *v.* **work** 1. to labour. 2. to act, to produce a result, as *this plan works well*. *n. pl.* **works** 1. a factory. 2. the moving parts of a machine.

to have one's work cut out to have a hard task.

workable *adj.* able to work or be worked.

worker, workman, working-man *ns.* a man who does work.

workmanship *n.* skill in doing work.

workshop *n.* a place where things are made.

world *n.* 1. the earth. 2. a planet or star. 3. all the people on earth. *adj.* **worldly** concerning the world and the things in it.

the New World North America.

the Old World Europe.

world-wide all over the world.

worm *n.* a small thin crawling creature. *v.* **worm** 1. to wriggle, as *to worm one's way through a crowd*. 2. to squeeze, as *to worm information from someone*.

worm-cast a small pile of earth left by a worm.

worm-eaten full of small holes made by worms or grubs.

worn *past* of wear.

worn-out *adj.* completely used up by wear or work.

worry *n.* anxiety. *v.* **worry** 1. to annoy, to vex. 2. to be anxious. 3. to shake with the teeth, as *a dog worries a rat* (**worries, worrying, worried**).

worse *adj.* (*comparative* of **bad**) bad to a greater extent, as *his cold is worse.* *adv.* **worse** (*comparative* of **badly**) less well, as *he played worse than ever.*

worship *n.* reverence and respect paid to God, or to something greatly admired. *v.* **worship** to show reverence, to adore (**worshipping, worshipped**). *n.* **worshipper** someone paying worship.

his Worship a title of respect.

worshipful honourable.

worst *adj.* (*superlative* of **bad**) bad to the greatest extent, as *this is the worst winter we have had.* *adv.* **worst** (*superlative* of **badly**) least well, as *this is the worst you have done.*

worth *n.* value, good quality. *adj.* **worth** 1. equal in value to. 2. deserving of, as *his courage is worth high praise.* 3. possessing, as *that man is worth a fortune.*

worthless valueless.

worth-while worth time and trouble.

worthy *adj.* 1. valuable. 2. deserving, as *a worthy cause.* *adv.* **worthily.** *n.* **worthiness.**

would *past* of **will.**

wound (1) (*pron.* wownd) *past* of **wind** (2).

wound (2) (*pron.* wō͞ond) *n.* a cut, an injury. *v.* **wound** to injure, to hurt. *adj.* **wounded** injured. *n. pl.* **wounded** men injured in battle.

wove *past* of **weave.**

wrangle *v.* to quarrel and argue (**wrangling, wrangled**).

wrap *v.* to fold round and cover up (**wrapping, wrapped**). *n.* **wrap** a shawl.

wrapped up in absorbed in.

wrapper *n.* a paper cover.

wrapping *n.* a covering.

wrath (*pron.* roth) *n.* rage, fury. *adj.* **wrathful.**

wreath (*pron.* reeth) *n.* a large ring of flowers.

wreathe (*pron.* reeTH) *v.* to decorate with a wreath, to cover (**wreathing, wreathed**).

wreck *n.* 1. the destruction of a ship at sea. 2. anything destroyed, as *the wreck of an aeroplane.* *v.* **wreck** to destroy.

wreckage *n.* the remains of a wreck.

wren *n.* a very small song-bird.

wrench *n.* 1. a sharp twist or pull. 2. (especially in North America) a large spanner. *v.* **wrench** to twist or pull.

wrest *v.* to take by force.

wrestle *v.* 1. to seize someone and try to throw him down. 2. to struggle with something (**wrestling, wrestled**).

wretch *n.* 1. an unlucky, miserable person. 2. a bad person.

wretched *adj.* 1. miserable. 2. poor.

wriggle *v.* to twist and turn (**wriggling, wriggled**).

wring *v.* to twist and squeeze, as *to wring wet clothes* (**wringing, wrung**). *n.* **wringer** a machine for wringing clothes.

wrinkle *n.* a crease in the skin. *v.* **wrinkle** to make wrinkles (**wrinkling, wrinkled**).

wrist *n.* the joint between hand and arm.

wrist-watch a watch worn on the wrist.

write *v.* 1. to put down letters or words with a pen or pencil. 2. to send a letter. 3. to produce a story or article for a magazine or newspaper (**writing, wrote, written**). *n.* **writer** an author.

writhe (*pron.* rīTH) *v.* to twist about in pain (**writhing, writhed**).

written *past* of **write.**

wrong *adj.* 1. not true. 2. not just. 3. not good. *adj.* **wrongful** unjust. *adv.* **wrongly.**

to get out of bed on the wrong side to start the day feeling bad-tempered.

wrote *past* of **write.**

wrung *past* of **wring.**

wry *adj.* twisted, as *a wry smile.*

X

Xmas *n.* a short form for 'Christmas'.
X-rays *n. pl.* rays able to penetrate the flesh and photograph bones.

Y

yacht (*pron.* yot) *n.* 1. a light sailing-ship used for pleasure. 2. a privately owned steamer used for pleasure-cruising.
yak *n.* a kind of shaggy-haired ox used in Tibet.
yam *n.* a kind of potato grown in the tropics.
yap *v.* to bark like a small dog (**yapping, yapped**).
yard (1) *n.* 1. a length equal to 36 inches (91·4 cm). 2. a pole from a ship's mast for supporting a sail.
yard-arm part of a ship's yard.
yard (2) *n.* a small, enclosed space near a building.
yarn *n.* 1. thread for weaving or knitting. 2. a story.
yawn *v.* 1. to open the mouth through sleepiness or boredom. 2. to open wide, as *the pit yawned before them.*
year *n.* the time taken by the earth to move once round the sun, 365 days and nearly 6 hours.
leap-year every fourth year, which has 366 days.
yearly once a year.
yearn *v.* to long for, to wish for.
yeast *n.* a substance used to make bread rise.
yell *v.* to shout very loudly.
yellow *n.* the colour of a lemon or buttercup.
yelp *n.* a sharp bark.
yeoman *n.* a farmer who owns his farm (*pl.* **yeomen**).
yes *adv.* I agree. Opposite of **no**.
yesterday *n.* the day just gone.
yet *adv.* 1. up to now, as *he has not been yet.* 2. still, as *there is yet time.* 3. at some future time, as *he will come yet.* *conj.* **yet** but, as *he went to bed, yet he could not sleep.*
yew *n.* a slow-growing evergreen tree.

yield *v.* 1. to bear, to produce, as *these trees yield fruit.* 2. to surrender.
yodel *v.* to sing like the Swiss with low and very high notes (**yodelling, yodelled**).
yoke *n.* 1. a wooden bar joining oxen working together. 2. slavery, bondage, as *under the yoke of a tyrant.*
yolk *n.* the yellow part of an egg.
yonder *adj.* far-distant, over there.
you *pronoun* the person or persons spoken to.
young *adj.* not fully grown, not old. *n.*
young 1. those not yet old. 2. the offspring of an animal.
youngster *n.* a child, a young boy.
your *adj.* belonging to you. *pronoun*
yours belonging to you. *pronoun*
yourself you (*pl.* **yourselves**).
youth *n.* 1. a young man (*pl.* **youths** *pron.* yōoTHz). 2. the time of being young. 3. young people. *adj.* **youthful**.

Z

zeal *n.* enthusiasm, eagerness.
zealous (*pron.* zel'us) *adj.* eager, full of enthusiasm.
zebra (*pron.* zee'bra *or* zeb'ra) *n.* an African wild animal like a horse with black stripes.
zebra crossing (in Britain) a street-crossing with black and white stripes.
zero *n.* 1. nought, nothing. 2. the lowest point.
zest *n.* eagerness, enthusiasm.
zigzag *n.* a line with repeated sharp turns, left and right.
zinc *n.* a greyish-white metal.
Zion *n.* 1. Jerusalem. 2. heaven.
zip-fastener *n.* a metal clothes-fastener with a sliding tab.
zone *n.* 1. a belt or path. 2. an area or section of the earth's surface. 3. any special region, as *a green zone of country round a city.*
zoo *n.* a zoological garden where wild animals are kept for show.
zoological (*pron.* zōo.o.loj'i.cl) *adj.* concerning the study of animal life.
zoology (*pron.* zōo.o'loj.i) *n.* the study of animal life.

COUNTRIES AND PEOPLES

Afghanistan Afghans
Albania Albanians
Algeria Algerians
Argentina Argentinians
Australia Australians
Austria Austrians

Belgium Belgians
Bolivia Bolivians
Brazil Brazilians
Bulgaria Bulgarians
Burma Burmese

Cameroon Cameroonians
Canada Canadians
Ceylon Sinhalese
Chile Chileans
China Chinese
Colombia Colombians
Congolese Republic Congolese
Cuba Cubans
Cyprus Cypriots
Czechoslovakia Czechoslovakians

Denmark Danes

Ecuador Ecuadoreans
Egypt Egyptians
England English
Ethiopia Ethiopians

Finland Finns
France French

Germany Germans
Ghana Ghanaians
Greece Greeks

Hungary Hungarians

Iceland Icelanders
India Indians
Indonesia Indonesians
Iran (Persia) Iranians (Persians)
Iraq Iraqis
Irish Republic Irish
Israel Israelis
Italy Italians

Jamaica Jamaicans
Japan Japanese

Jordan Jordanians
Kenya Kenyans
Korea Koreans
Malawi Malawians
Malaysia Malaysians
Mexico Mexicans
Morocco Moroccans

Netherlands Dutch
New Zealand New Zealanders
Nigeria Nigerians
Northern Ireland Irish
Norway Norwegians

Pakistan Pakistanis
Paraguay Paraguayans
Peru Peruvians
Philippine Islands Filipinos
Poland Poles
Portugal Portuguese

Rumania Rumanians

Scotland Scots
South Africa South Africans
Spain Spaniards
Sudan Sudanese
Sweden Swedes
Switzerland Swiss
Syria Syrians

Tanzania Tanzanians
Thailand (Siam) Thais (Siamese)
Tunisia Tunisians
Turkey Turks

United Kingdom British
United States of America
        Americans
Uganda Ugandans
Uruguay Uruguayans
U.S.S.R. Russians

Venezuela Venezuelans

Yugoslavia Yugoslavs

Wales Welsh

Zambia Zambians